# The UFO Encyclopedia

## by MARGARET SACHS

## A PERIGEE BOOK

## to Nicholas Vreeland

## Acknowledgments

THE WRITING OF A BOOK of this nature cannot be done without the help of many people. I am deeply grateful to Alex Rebar and Sylvia Hom, who helped me with my research; my photo consultant, Hilde Kron, who was invaluable; Glenn Cowley for his guidance; my editor, Diane Reverand, for her encouragement; Harry Lebelson for reading and commenting on the manuscript; Mark Hurst for his editorial suggestions; and my husband, Bill, for his patience and assistance.

I would also like to extend special thanks to my friend Ernest Jahn, who coauthored my previous book, *Celestial Passengers*.

I also wish to thank J. Richard Allison, Rose Marie Amico, Peter Aubrey-Smith, William Boyes, Al Chop, Trevor James Constable, Leon Davidson, John DeHerrera, Pat Gallagher, Beverly Gray, Gabriel Green, David Haisell, Leslie Hugunin, Philip Klass, Norman Lamb, Alvin Lawson, Bill LeValle, Jim Lorenzen, Giovanni and Piero Mantero, Jim Moseley, Laura Mundo, Francine Newman, Robert Newman, Kevin Olden, M.D., Kathy Parks, Michael Parry, Dennis Pilichis, Art Podell, Jenny Randles, David Rees, Carla Rueckert, Luis Schönherr, Issy Shabtay, Marcia Smith, R. Leo Sprinkle, Maggie Starr, Brad Steiger, Jun-Ichi Takanashi, Colman VonKeviczky, Glen Welker, Lindy Whitehurst, Mr. X and Patricia Zimmerman.

Special acknowledgment is made to the Aerial Phenomena Research Organization, the Association des Amis de Marc Thirouin, the Centro Internazionale Ricerche e Studi sugli UFO, the Comitato Nazionale Independente per lo Studio dei Fenomeni Aerei Anomali, the Interplanetary Space Travel Research Association, the Manchester Aerial Phenomena Investigation Team, the Modern Space Flight Association, *The National Enquirer*, the National Investigations Committee on Aerial Phenomena, the Novosti Press Agency, the Page Research Library, Project SUM, Sun Classic Pictures, the UFO Information Network and the *UFO Space Newsclipping Journal*.

Library of Congress Cataloging in Publication Data

Sachs, Margaret.
  The UFO encyclopedia.
  Bibliography: p.
  1. Unidentified flying objects—Dictionaries.
I. Title.
TL789.S16    001.9′42′03    79-27450
ISBN: 0-399-12365-2
SBN: 399-50454-0 Pbk.

Designed by Bernard Schleifer

PRINTED IN THE UNITED STATES OF AMERICA

Perigee Books
are published by
G.P. Putnam's Sons
200 Madison Avenue
New York, New York 10016

First Perigee Printing, 1980

# contents

# introduction

THE FIRST WRITTEN REPORT of a UFO sighting was that made by the Egyptian Pharaoh Thutmose III in the fifteenth century B.C. Since then, UFOlogy has blossomed into a subject with a literature all its own. Yet there has never been a primary source from which the researcher or interested layman could get an overall look at the international UFO scene from its earliest beginnings to the present. As a researcher, I was frustrated by this fact and decided to attempt to remedy that situation. I initiated a correspondence with writers, researchers and investigators in the United States and around the world and was delighted by the enthusiastic response I received. I began to wonder how many people were aware of the enormous and dedicated cadre of UFOlogists which exists in the world today. One of

the things I hope this book will achieve is to bring their efforts and their fascinating views to the attention of the general public.

For those wishing to keep abreast of the latest events in the world of UFOlogy, the book lists numerous periodicals and several hundred local and national UFO organizations which keep their members informed of new developments in the field.

The cases included in the encyclopedia were selected either because they were considered classics or for the exemplary characteristics they demonstrate.

Since the dividing line between fact and fiction is a difficult one to determine in UFOlogy, I have presented the gamut of UFOlogical history, and leave it to the reader to determine the credible and the incredible.

# chronological list of ufo sightings

(These cases are described in more detail in the A–Z entries of the main body of the encyclopedia where they are listed alphabetically by location.)

| Date | Location | Witnesses | Description |
|---|---|---|---|
| Fifteenth-century B.C. | Egypt | Thutmose III | Fiery disks |
| Sixth century B.C. | Babylonia | Ezekiel | Landing |
| 329 B.C. | Jaxartes River, India | Alexander the Great | Flying shields |
| 322 B.C. | Tyre, Phoenicia | Alexander the Great | Flying shields |
| Ninth century | Lyons, France | Multiple | Occupants |
| 4–14–1561 | Nuremberg, Germany | Various | Cylindrical UFOs, spheres and disks |
| 8–7–1566 | Basel, Switzerland | Various | Fiery globes |
| 8–15–1666 | Robozero, Russia | Multiple | Fiery ball |
| 8–12/13–1883 | Zacatecas, Mexico | José Bonilla and assistant | Cigar-shaped, disk-shaped and spindle-shaped UFO |
| 1897 | Rogers Park, Illinois | Walter McCann | Airship |
| 4–28–1897 | Le Roy, Kansas | Alexander Hamilton and two others | Airship |
| 4–17–1897 | Aurora, Texas | Unknown | Alleged crash |
| 6–30–1908 | Tunguska region, Russia | Multiple | Explosion |
| 2–19–1913 | North America | Multiple | Cyrillids |
| 10–13–1917 | Fátima, Portugal | Multiple | Globe and disk |
| 8–5–1927 | Mongolia | Nikolay Roerich and six others | Oval UFO |
| 8–1–1946 | Florida | Jack E. Puckett and two others | Cylindrical UFO |
| 6–1947 | Maury Island, Washington | Harold Dahl, Fred Crisman and others | Doughnut-shaped UFO |
| 6–24–1947 | Mount Ranier, Washington | Kenneth Arnold | Nine disks |
| 1–7–1948 | Godman Air Force Base, Kentucky | Thomas Mantell and others | Cone-shaped UFO |
| 7–24–1948 | Montgomery, Alabama | Clarence Chiles and John Whitted | |
| 10–1–1948 | Fargo, North Dakota | George T. Gorman | White light |
| 1948/1949 | New Mexico | Multiple | Green fireballs |

| Date | Location | Witnesses | Description |
|------|----------|-----------|-------------|
| 4–24–1949 | White Sands, New Mexico | Charles Moore and others | Ellilptical UFO |
| 8–20–1949 | Las Cruces, New Mexico | Clyde Tombaugh | Luminous rectangles |
| 8–15–1950 | Great Falls, Montana | Nicholas Mariana and secretary | Two disks |
| 3–17–1950 | Farmington, New Mexico | Multiple | Disks |
| 5–11–1950 | McMinnville, Oregon | Mr. and Mrs. Paul Trent | Disk |
| 8/9/10–1951 | Lubbock, Texas | Multiple | Nocturnal lights in formation |
| 1952 | Spitsbergen, Norway | Unknown | Alleged crash |
| 7–2–1952 | Tremonton, Utah | Delbert C. Newhouse and family | Fleet of disks |
| 7–14–1952 | Newport News, Virginia | William Nash and William Fortenberry | Disks in formation |
| 7–16–1952 | Salem, Massachusetts | Shell Alpert | Four egg-shaped UFOs |
| 7–19/20–1952 | Washington, D.C. | Multiple | Nocturnal lights and radar targets |
| 7–26/27–1952 | Washington, D.C. | Multiple | Nocturnal lights and radar targets |
| 9–12–1952 | Flatwoods, West Virginia | Multiple | Monster |
| 9–21–1952 | Morocco | Multiple | Disks |
| 10–17–1952 | Oloron, France | Multiple | Cylindrical UFO and spheres |
| 10–27–1952 | Gaillac, France | Multiple | Cigar-shaped object and disks |
| 1954 | Rouen, France | French military pilot | Disk |
| 7–1–1954 | Walesville, New York | Air Force pilot and radar operator | Disk |
| 9–17–1954 | Rome, Italy | Multiple | UFO and radar targets |
| 10–28–1954 | Rome, Italy | Clare Booth Luce and others | Luminous sphere |

| Date | Location | Witnesses | Description |
|------|----------|-----------|-------------|
| 8–21–1955 | Kelly-Hopkinsville, Kentucky | Sutton family | Siege by possible UFO entities |
| 8–13/14–1956 | Bentwaters and Lakenheath, England | Multiple | Unidentified radar targets and nocturnal lights |
| 7–17–1957 | South-central United States | Six Air Force officers | Nocturnal lights and radar targets |
| 9–10–1957 | Ubatuba, Brazil | Three fishermen | Fragments retrieved from exploded disk |
| 10–5–1957 | Brazil | Antonio Villas-Boas | Abduction |
| 11–2/3–1957 | Levelland, Texas | Multiple | Landings |
| 11–3–1957 | White Sands, New Mexico | Military policemen | Egg-shaped UFO |
| 11–4–1957 | Fort Itaipu, Brazil | Two sentries | Disk |
| 1–16–1958 | Trindade Island, Brazil | Almiro Barauna and others | Disk |
| 6–26–1959 | Boianai, Papua, New Guinea | William Gill and others | Craft with occupants |
| 1960 | Brno, Czechoslovakia | Multiple | Nocturnal light and radar target |
| 8–13–1960 | Red Bluff, California | Police officers and others | Football-shaped UFO |
| 2–1961 | Karelia, Soviet Union | Various | Landing mark |
| 3–16–1961 | Admiralty Bay, Antarctica | Rubens J. Villela and five others | Egg-shaped UFO |
| 4–18–1961 | Eagle River, Wisconsin | Joe Simonton | Occupants |
| 9–19–1961 | New Hampshire | Betty and Barney Hill | Abduction |
| 10–2–1961 | Salt Lake City, Utah | Waldo J. Harris and others | Disk |
| 4–24–1964 | Socorro, New Mexico | Lonnie Zamora | Landing |
| 9–4–1964 | Cisco Grove, California | Donald S. ——— and Vincent A. ——— (last names confidential) | Occupants |

| Date | Location | Witnesses | Description |
|---|---|---|---|
| 12–1964/1–1965 | Washington, D.C. | Multiple | Radar targets, disks and landings |
| 8–3–1965 | Santa Ana, California | Rex Heflin | Hat-shaped UFO |
| 8–8–1965 | Beaver, Pennsylvania | James Lucci and one other | Disk |
| 9–3–1965 | Exeter, New Hampshire | Multiple | Nocturnal lights |
| 10–21–1965 | St. George, Minnesota | Arthur Strauch and four others | Disk |
| 3–20–1966 | Hillsdale, Michigan | Multiple | Glowing, football-shaped UFO |
| 3–21–1966 | Dexter, Michigan | Two policemen and three others | Glowing light |
| 4–16–1966 | Portage County, Ohio | Four police officers | Cone-shaped UFO |
| 1–9–1967 | Mount Clemens, Michigan | Dan and Grant Jaroslaw | Disk |
| 1–25–1967 | South Ashburnham, Massachusetts | Betty Andreasson | Abduction |
| 4–17–1967 | Saigon, Vietnam | Member of U.S. intelligence detachment | Oval UFO |
| 6–1–1967 | San José de Valderas, Spain | Multiple | Disk |
| 7–3–1967 | Calgary, Alberta | Warren Smith and two others | Ellipsoid UFO |
| 10–24–1967 | Moigne Downs, England | Angus Brooks | Flying cross |
| 12–2–1967 | Bucharest, Rumania | Multiple | Conical UFO |
| 8–18–1968 | Cluj, Rumania | Emil Barnea and three others | Disk |
| 10–18–1968 | Sarajevo, Yugoslavia | Multiple | Conical UFO |
| 1–7–1970 | Imjarvi, Finland | Aarno Heinonen and Esko Viljo | Landing |
| 6–26–1972 | Fort Beaufort, South Africa | Bennie Smit and others | Fiery ball |

| Date | Location | Witnesses | Description |
|---|---|---|---|
| 2/3–4–1973 | Piedmont, Missouri | Multiple | Nocturnal lights and landing marks |
| 5–22–1973 | Catanduva, Brazil | Onilson Papero | Landing |
| 10–11–1973 | Pascagoula, Mississippi | Charles Hickson and Calvin Parker | Abduction |
| 10–17–1973 | Falkville, Alabama | Jeff Greenhaw | Occupant |
| 10–18–1973 | Mansfield, Ohio | Lawrence Coyne and others | Cigar-shaped UFO |
| 1–1975 | North Hudson Park, New Jersey | George O'Barski | Landing and occupants |
| 8–13–1975 | Alamagordo, New Mexico | Charles Moody | Abduction |
| 8–20–1975 | Albany, New York | Multiple | Nocturnal lights |
| 10–17–1975 | Akita Airport, Japan | Multiple | Disk |
| 10–27/29/31–1975 | Loring Air Force Base, Maine | Multiple | Nocturnal lights and radar targets |
| 11–5–1975 | Sitgreaves National Forest, Arizona | Travis Walton | Abduction |
| 1–6–1976 | Liberty, Kentucky | Elaine Thomas, Louise Smith and Mona Stafford | Abduction |
| 9–18/19–1976 | Morocco | Multiple | Cylindrical UFO |
| 9–19–1976 | Teheran, Iran | Multiple | Cylindrical UFO and satellite object |
| 9–22–1977 | Petrozavodsk, Soviet Union | Multiple | Jellyfish UFO |
| 5–14–1978 | Ocala, Florida | Multiple | Nocturnal lights |
| 10–21–1978 | Melbourne, Australia | Frederick Valentich | UFO with bright lights |
| 11–10–1978 | Kuwait | Seven technicians | Cylindrical UFO |
| 1978/1979 | New Zealand | Quentin Fogarty and others | Nocturnal lights and radar targets |

**AAAS** *see* **AMERICAN ASSOCIATION FOR THE ADVANCEMENT OF SCIENCE**

**AAMT** *see* **ASSOCIATION DES AMIS DE MARC THIROUIN**

**ABDUCTION,** sometimes referred to as a CLOSE ENCOUNTER OF THE FOURTH KIND (CE–IV), the kidnapping of human beings by UFO occupants. Although abductees are frequently referred to as CONTACTEES, not all contactees are abductees. In alleged contact cases, UFOnauts generally engage in friendly conversation with earthlings during which they impart messages of a spiritual or moralistic nature. The contactee may even be taken on a trip in a flying saucer, sometimes to the aliens' home planet. In abduction cases, on the other hand, humans are taken into spacecraft against their will. There they are subjected to physical examinations before being set free. The most well-known abduction cases are the Betty and Barney Hill case in NEW HAMPSHIRE, the Charles Hickson and Calvin Parker case in PASCAGOULA, MISSISSIPPI and the ANTONIO VILLAS-BOAS case in Brazil.

Many alleged abduction cases have been revealed only through the use of HYPNOSIS, the witnesses having lost all conscious memory of the events. Psychologist R. LEO SPRINKLE has interviewed and hypnotically regressed numerous individuals who apparently were victims of abduction by UFOnauts within amnesic or time loss periods during UFO encounters. However, experiences related during hypnosis cannot be considered unequivocally factual. In experiments conducted at the Anaheim Memorial Hospital in Anaheim, California, in 1977, by clinical hypnotist William C. McCall, technical writer JOHN DeHERRERA and English professor ALVIN LAWSON, imaginary UFO abductions were induced hypnotically in a group of subjects who had never seen UFOs and were uninformed on the subject. The imaginary events described by the control subjects showed no substantive differences from those related by "real" abductees.

Some researchers believe that reports of DISAPPEARANCES of people and objects represent another type of UFO abduction case. Writers have hypothesized that such abductees may be used for food, slavery, experimentation, zoos, museums or some other unknown purpose. The most notorious area where such disappearances are reputed to occur is known as the BERMUDA TRIANGLE.

Bibliography: Lorenzen, Coral and Jim, *Abducted: Close Encounters of a Fourth Kind* (New York: Berkley Publishing Corporation, 1977).

**ABOMINABLE SNOWMAN** *see* **BIGFOOT**

**ABOMINABLE WOODMAN** *see* **BIGFOOT**

**ACOS** *see* **CENTRE FOR UFO STUDIES-AUSTRALIAN CO-ORDINATION SECTION**

**ACOS BULLETIN,** publication of the CENTRE FOR UFO STUDIES—AUSTRALIAN CO-ORDINATION SECTION (ACOS)

**ACUFF, JOHN L.** (address: 5012 Del Ray Avenue, Washington, D.C. 20014; telephone number: 301-654-8091), Chairman of the Board and President of the NATIONAL INVESTIGATIONS COMMITTEE ON AERIAL PHENOMENA (NICAP).

Acuff adheres to no specific theories regarding the identity of UFOs.

Acuff graduated from American University in Washington, D.C., with a B.S. in Biology and minors in Mathematics, Psychology and Chemistry.

From 1963 to 1965, Acuff worked for Technology, Inc., where he held a management position and was primarily responsible for Biomedical Engineering research sales. He was Director of Marketing for Flow Laboratories, Inc., from 1965 to 1967, Executive Director of Photographic Scientists and Engineers from 1967 to 1970, and since 1970 has been President of his own firm, Acuff Associates, Inc., a management services organization. He is also President and Owner of Centennial Corporation, Executive Director and Advisor to the Board of the American Cardiology Technologists Association, Executive Director and Advisor to the Board of the Associated Dental Laboratories, Executive Director and Advisor to the Board of the National Society of Cardiopulmonary Technologists, a charter member and consultant of the Society of Association Managers, a member of the American Society of Association Executives and a member of the International Platform Association.

Acuff has been the Chairman of the Board and President of NICAP since 1970. He has lectured widely on UFOs and other subjects and has been a guest on more than one hundred international television and radio shows.

**ADAMSKI, GEORGE** (b. April 17, 1891; Poland; d. April 23, 1965; near Washington, D.C.), one of the first and most famous CONTACTEES.

Adamski was two years old when his parents moved to Dunkirk, New York, where he grew up. In 1913, he enlisted in the army and served in the 13th Cavalry on the Mexican border. He received an honorable discharge in 1919. He was almost forty when he settled in Laguna Beach, California. A self-styled professor of oriental mystical philosophy, he founded a cult called the Royal Order of Tibet. In 1940, he moved with his followers to the Valley Center, where they set up a small farming project. In 1944, he moved to the southern slope of Mount Palomar, whose peak is the site of a famous observatory. There Adamski worked as a handyman at a hamburger stand.

During the late 1940s, Adamski wrote a novel, entitled *Pioneers of Space,* about an imaginary trip to the moon, Venus and Mars. He listed the book with the Library of Congress for copyright purposes as a work of fiction. In 1953, Adamski co-authored *Flying Saucers Have Landed* (New York: The British Book Centre) with British author Desmond Leslie. The book, which was highly successful, tells of Adamski's first alleged contact with SPACE PEOPLE. According to Adamski's and Leslie's account, on November 20, 1952, Adamski went into the desert accompanied by anthropologist George

Hunt Williamson, his wife Betty Williamson, also an anthropologist and chemist, Mr. and Mrs. Al Bailey, Lucy McGinnis and Alice K. Wells. After spotting a CIGAR-SHAPED UFO, the others waited by the car while Adamski went into a small canyon. There he purportedly met with a Venusian with whom he communicated telepathically and by means of sign language. The Venusian told Adamski he had come to Earth to stop atomic testing because the radiation from fallout was dangerous to the other planets in the solar system. After the spacecraft had left, Adamski noticed that the Venusian had left deep footprints in the sand. Within the outline of the footprints were strange hieroglyphics. The group happened to have brought along some plaster of paris with which George Hunt Williamson was able to make a cast of the footprint.

Adamski's second book, *Inside the Spaceships* (London: Abelard-Schuman, 1955), dealt with his alleged journeys aboard flying saucers. He claimed to have flown behind the moon where he had seen cities, forests, lakes and snow-capped mountains. He had even observed people strolling along the sidewalks. When Russian photographs of the moon's far side revealed a barren surface, Adamski retorted that the Russians had retouched the pictures in order to deceive the United States.

Adamski published several photographs of flying saucers. His best-known picture shows a bell-shaped object with portholes around the upper part and three balls underneath which are supposed to be landing gear. After several years of research, author FRANK EDWARDS came to the conclusion that Adamski's spaceship was in reality the top of a cannister-type vacuum cleaner made in 1937. Astronomer DONALD MENZEL, on the other hand, claimed that the object in Adamski's photograph is clearly identifiable as a well-known type of chicken brooder with three infrared bulbs underneath it. Other researchers have identified the object as

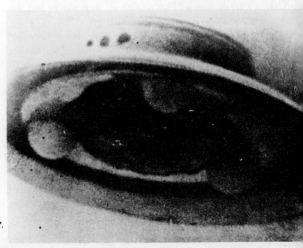

Adamski's famous bell-shaped flying saucer.
*(Courtesy Ground Saucer Watch)*

a tobacco humidor top with a baby nipple on top and three ping-pong balls at the base.

In 1959, Adamski went on a world tour. His self-endowed title of professor and his Palomar address had misled some foreign journalists into thinking he was an astronomer at the observatory. He was received by Queen Juliana of the Netherlands at her palace and was then received in audience at the Vatican by Pope John who presented him with a medallion.

Adamski's third book was published under the title *Flying Saucers Farewell* (London: Abelard-Schuman) in 1961 and under the title *Behind the Flying Saucer Mystery* (New York: Warner Paperback Library) in 1967. He died at the age of seventy-four. At the time of his death, he was offering to teach people how to use self-hypnosis to visit Venus and Mars for a fee of fifty dollars.

His first coauthor, Desmond Leslie, wrote that Adamski, if reborn on another planet, would attempt to visit Earth. Allegedly, the day after his death, an elderly man walking toward Scoriton Down on the edge of Dartmoor in England encountered three flying saucer occupants. One of them, speaking with an American accent, stated that he was "Yamski" from Venus. He referred to "Des Les," which some of Adamski's followers presume to mean "Desmond Leslie."

Several of the witnesses to Adamski's famous first encounter in the desert later recanted their stories. Chemical Engineer LEON DAVIDSON, publisher of *Flying Saucers: An Analysis of the Air Force Project Blue Book Special Report No. 14*, believes that Adamski was the naive and trusting victim of a colossal HOAX perpetrated by government agents. He holds that the spaceships in which Adamski claimed to have traveled were actually man-made structures whose windows were viewing screens showing filmed vistas of space. He points out that Adamski claimed to have been encouraged in his search for flying saucers by four U.S. government scientists. Computer scientist JACQUES VALLEE has suggested that Adamski's experiences were part of a conspiracy to unite the nations of the world by creating a false extraterrestrial threat. He notes that Adamski's major supporter abroad was a former intelligence officer with the British Army, and a Cambridge engineering graduate. Moreover, points out Vallee, according to the host of his Australian tour, Adamski was traveling with a passport bearing special privileges.

Following Adamski's death, Alice K. Wells founded the GEORGE ADAMSKI FOUNDATION. The organization boasts several thousand members worldwide.

## ADAMSKI CORRESPONDENT GROUP, former name of NEW ZEALAND SCIENTIFIC APPROACH TO COSMIC UNDERSTANDING (NZSATCU OR SATCU).

**AD ASTRA,** magazine established in 1978 with a circulation of 15,000. Published six times a year, it is available at newsstands and by subscription. The magazine presents articles on space research and the cosmos as well as science fiction stories and unbiased coverage of mysteries, including UFOs.

Material is written by staff and freelance writers. Articles between 1,000 and 3,000 words in length should be submitted with a self-addressed, stamped envelope, and payment is made upon publication at a rate of ten pounds sterling per 1,000 words. Rights to all features remain with authors. There is usually no payment for photographs. The publishers require that writers be knowledgeable about their subject, and approach it from a serious, objective viewpoint, avoiding technical jargon as far as possible.

James Manning is Editor. *Ad Astra* is published by Rowlot, Ltd., 22 Offerton Road, London S.W.4, England.

## ADEPS *see* ASSOCIATION POUR LA DETECTION ET L'ÉTUDE DES PHÉNOMÈNES SPATIAUX

**ADMIRALTY BAY, ANTARCTICA,** location of a UFO sighting by Brazilian meteorologist Rubens J. Villela and five other witnesses aboard the U.S.S. *Glacier* at about 6:15 on March 16, 1961. Villela was taking part in the United States Navy's Operation Deep Freeze. The sharply-defined, egg-shaped UFO traveled slowly from the northeast to the southwest at about fifty degrees above the horizon on a straight, horizontal trajectory. Villela had the impression that its size was that of a small airplane. Straight, multicolored rays extended backward in a V-formation from the front of the object. The colors changed continually but were predominantly green, red and blue. The object itself was reddish. It left behind it an orange trail which resembled a straight, hollow tube similar to a neon light. Suddenly, the front and rear of the UFO split apart, forming two separate objects, each one identical in every way to the one original object they had been. As the objects changed from red to blue-and-white, they increased in brightness. Abruptly, they vanished.

PHILIP KLASS cites this UFO as a good example of a case which can be explained in terms of PLASMA. The late meteorologist JAMES McDONALD, however, argued that the highly structured nature of the object and the low cloud overcast present at about 1,500 feet were not compatible with Klass's hypothesis.

Bibliography: U.S. Congress, House, Committee on Science and Astronautics, Symposium on Unidentified Flying Objects, Hearings, Ninetieth Congress, Second

Session, July 29, 1968 (Washington, D.C.: U.S. Government Printing Office, 1968).

**ADRUP** *see* **ASSOCIATION DIJONNAISE DE RECHERCHES UFOLOGIQUES ET PARA-PSYCHOLOGIQUES**

**ADVERTISING PLANES,** aircraft, usually Cessnas or helicopters, which carry electronic signs with lights that flash in sequence. Usually airborne between dusk and midnight, they are most frequently observed between 8:00 and 10:00 P.M. Because the advertising plane's message is clear and legible only when the craft is directly above the observer, it is frequently the source of mistaken UFO reports. Many witnesses, seeing the lights flashing from right to left, assume that the lights continue around the craft in a loop. Thus they conclude, falsely, that the craft is disk-shaped and possibly rotating. When the message is completed and the last light goes out, the illusion is created that the entire craft has vanished.

Flight schedules of advertising planes can be checked by telephoning the individual aerial advertising companies listed in the telephone directory. However, in the United States, some advertising planes fly over several states and the witness or investigator may not be able to trace them through local advertising companies.

**AERIAL PHENOMENA GROUP,** formal name given by the UNITED STATES AIR FORCE to the UFO investigative organization whose code name was PROJECT BLUE BOOK.

**AERIAL PHENOMENA INVESTIGATION COMMITTEE (APIC),** presided over by Paul J. Blake, this organization became defunct in 1976.

**AERIAL PHENOMENA INVESTIGATION ORGANIZATION (APIO),** former name of the GREENVILLE UFO STUDY GROUP.

**AERIAL PHENOMENA RESEARCH ORGANIZATION (APRO),** 3910 E. Kleindale Road, Tucson, Arizona 85712; telephone number: 602-323-1825.

The oldest organization in the field, APRO accepts the possibility that UFOs might be extraterrestrial spacecraft from another solar system engaged in a methodical study of Earth. The group's purpose is to gather, study and store UFO reports. APRO originated the field investigator system in 1968 and currently has a network of 500 investigators in the United States and fifty foreign countries. Almost fifty consultants, most of whom possess doctorates, make up advisory panels on biological sciences, medical science, physical sciences and social sciences.

This nonprofit organization is one of the world's major UFO groups. Now possessing a membership of approximately 3,000, APRO was founded in 1952 by CORAL E. LORENZEN and LESLIE JAMES "JIM" LORENZEN, who have authored numerous books on UFOs. The staff consists of International Director Jim Lorenzen, Director of Research JAMES A. HARDER, Public Relations Officer Hal Starr, Secretary-Treasurer Coral Lorenzen, Membership Secretary Madeleine H. Cooper, Staff Librarian Allen Benz and Office Manager Sheila Kudrle. The Board of Directors consists of Jim Lorenzen, Coral Lorenzen, Richard Gerdes, Walter W. Walker and Louis Dougherty. Coral Lorenzen is Editor of the APRO BULLETIN, which was published bimonthly until 1978 and is now published monthly.

APRO has representatives in Argentina, Australia, Belgium, Bolivia, Brazil, Ceylon, Chile, Colombia, Costa Rica, Cuba, Czechoslovakia, Denmark, Dominican Republic, Ecuador, Finland, France, Germany, Greece, Guatemala, Holland, Honduras, Ireland, Italy, Japan, Lebanon, Malta, Mexico, New Guinea, New Zealand, Norway, Peru, Puerto Rico, Philippine Republic, Rumania, Sierra Leone, Singapore, South Africa, Spain, Sweden, Switzerland, Taiwan, Tasmania, Trinidad, Turkey, United Kingdom, Venezuela and Yugoslavia.

**AERIAL PHENOMENON CLIPPING AND INFORMATION CENTER (APCIC),** P.O. Box 9073, Cleveland, Ohio 44137; telephone number: 216-475-1711.

Founded in 1974 by H.R. Cohen, Ron Smotek and Scott MacWilliams, this newsclipping service provides international coverage on a monthly basis of current information on UFO sightings from around the world. The APCIC NEWS BULLETIN consists of a minimum of sixty pages and includes a section on other mysteries, such as BIGFOOT. H.R. Cohen is Editor. Scott MacWilliams is Assistant Editor. Ron Smotek handles photo analysis.

**AESV** *see* **ASSOCIATION D'ÉTUDE SUR LES SOUCOUPES VOLANTES**

**AETHERIUS SOCIETY,** 6202 Afton Place, Hollywood, California 90028; telephone number: 213-465-9652. European headquarters: 757 Fulham Road, London SW6 5UU, England.

Derived from the Greek, Aetherius refers to one who travels through the ether, the upper regions of space, and is the pseudonym given by this international CONTACTEE society to an alleged cosmic master of

Venus. The group believes that UFOs are craft from Venus, Mars and other supposedly Utopian planets in Earth's solar system. Their aim is to promote the teachings of these cosmic intelligences and to prepare Earth's inhabitants for the coming of the next great master. One of their primary missions is Operation Prayer Power, in which spiritual energy created by prayer is supposedly stored in a physical container and released in condensed form to avert or reduce the effects of disasters such as earthquakes, wars and famine.

Members participate in spiritual services and attend classes and lectures. Available for purchase are a large number of books and cassette tapes. Also on sale are rocks from mountains that have been spiritually charged by the cosmic masters.

This nonprofit organization was incorporated in 1956 in the United Kingdom and in 1960 in the United States. GEORGE KING is the President and founder. U.S. Founding Directors are Monique King, Erain Noppe and Charles Abrahamson. The Secretary and Assistant Secretary of European Headquarters are Ray Nielsen and Alan Moseley, respectively. Membership stands at about 1,000. The *Aetherius Society Spiritual Healing Bulletin* and the *Aetherius Society Newsletter* are published bimonthly.

U.S. branches: Edna Sophia Spencer, 16547 Grand River Avenue, Detroit, Michigan 48227; Lillian E. Berndt, Box 212, Beach Lane, Huron Beach, Ocqueoc, Michigan 49763; Virginia Roberts, Canterbury Court Apartments, Apt. 608, 1220 North State Parkway, Chicago, Illinois 60610. Foreign branches: Paul White, 350 Sheffield Road, Birdwell, Barnsley, South Yorkshire S70 5TU, England; Natu Patel, 15 Breedon Hill Road, Derby DE3 6TH, England; Stephen Gibson, 183 Stenley Hill, Amersham, Bucks, England; Jay Greatrex, Witheridge Garden Flat, 8 Oxlea Road, Torquay, Devon T21 2HF, England; Jean Berry, 21 Avon Way, Stoke Bishop, Bristol BS9 1SJ, England; Mr. and Mrs. Stewart Henderson, 1 Antony Road, Warrington, Cheshire WA4 6DD, England; Dorothy Holt, 3 Leith Road, Pennant Hills 2120, New South Wales, Australia; Jochen Peters, P.O. Box 5932, Accra, Ghana, West Africa; S. C. O. Adeyemi, P.O. Box 8420, Lagos, Nigeria.

**AFFA,** alleged extraterrestrial being from the PLANET Uranus who supposedly communicates with Frances Swann of SOUTH BERWICK, MAINE.

**AFO** *see* **ALIEN FLYING OBJECT**

**AFR 80–17** *see* **AIR FORCE REGULATION 80–17**

**AFRICA.** The world's earliest UFO report comes from Egypt where the pharaoh THUTMOSE III observed fiery disks in the fifteenth century B.C. During the MODERN ERA, there have been numerous reports of UFOs in Africa, particularly in Rhodesia and South Africa. There were WAVES of sightings in North Africa in 1950 and 1954, and in Central Africa in 1966. A 1972 wave in South Africa was highlighted by a farmer's encounter with a fiery globe in FORT BEAUFORT. Another wave followed in Rhodesia in 1975. In 1976, a cylindrical UFO was spotted from widely separate locations in Morocco over a one-hour period. In answer to a confidential communique from Ambassador Robert Anderson, Secretary of State Henry Kissinger said, "It is difficult to offer any definitive explanation as to the cause or origin of the UFOs sighted in the Moroccan area. . . ."

There are several UFO and CONTACTEE organizations in Africa. The majority of them are located in South Africa and Rhodesia. Noted personalities in these two countries are UFO investigator CYNTHIA HIND and CONTACTEE ELIZABETH KLARER, who claims to have given birth to an extraterrestrial's child on another PLANET.

**AFR 200–5** *see* **AIR FORCE REGULATION 200–5**

**AFR 200–2** *see* **AIR FORCE REGULATION 200–2**

**AFSCA** *see* **AMALGAMATED FLYING SAUCER CLUBS OF AMERICA**

**AFSCA WORLD REPORT,** newsletter published by the AMALGAMATED FLYING SAUCER CLUBS OF AMERICA (AFSCA) from 1959 to 1961, replacing the semireligious magazine THY KINGDOM COME and in turn replaced by UFO INTERNATIONAL.

**AFTERIMAGE,** visual illusion which occurs when retinal impressions remain after removal of the stimulus. The original image persists momentarily, then is replaced by a negative image in which the color and luminosity of the original are reversed. For example, a dull green object may produce a bright red afterimage. The late astronomer DONALD MENZEL has proposed that afterimages might explain numerous UFO reports, including those made by airline pilots. Since the human eye rarely remains stationary, afterimages moving with the eye give an impression of independently controlled motion. Menzel has cited the sun as one of the most common causes of such an effect, commenting that when the sun is low on the horizon or partly obscured by atmospheric conditions, an observer who has looked at it only briefly may then see one or more dark orbs cavorting about the sky.

Bibliography: von Helmholtz, H.L.F., *Treatise on Physiological Optics* (Ithaca, N.Y.: Optical Society of America, 1924); Menzel, Donald H., and Ernest H. Taves, *The UFO Enigma* (Garden City, N.Y.: Doubleday and Company, 1977).

## AFU *see* ARBETSGRUPPEN FOR UFOLOGI

**AGE DISTRIBUTION OF WITNESSES.** Although no conclusive studies have been made to determine the relevance of the age distribution of UFO witnesses, a 1978 Gallup Poll established that younger people are more likely to have seen UFOs and to believe in their existence. A fairly wide acceptance of the EXTRATERRESTRIAL HYPOTHESIS by younger people is probably due in large part to their exposure at an early age to mankind's own space exploits. However, for the past thirty years, young boys have also been the perpetrators of a large number of UFO HOAXES and trick photographs. Since it is difficult to ascertain the total number of hoaxes committed, it is not possible to compute the percentage of hoaxes carried out by children.

With regard to CONTACTEES, an unofficial study in the 1950s revealed that eighty percent of the proselytes were older, single women, although the leaders of the groups were usually young and middle-aged men. However, since contactees do not often report UFOs, these findings bear little relevance to an overall survey of UFO witnesses.

It has been established that, despite the current preponderance of young witnesses, sightings of anomalous aerial objects are reported by people of all ages all over the world.

## AGGRESSION *see* HOSTILITY

## AGHARTA *see* HOLLOW EARTH HYPOTHESIS

## AGOBARD, ARCHBISHOP OF LYONS, *see* LYONS, FRANCE

**AHO, WAYNE SULO** (b. August 24, 1916, Woodland, Washington; address: 5201 South I Street, Tacoma, Washington 98404; telephone number: 206-569-2594), CONTACTEE, Founder and President of the NEW AGE FOUNDATION (NAF).

Since his first alleged sighting of a flying saucer in the Mojave Desert in 1957, Aho has purportedly seen numerous craft of varying shapes. He believes that UFOs are representations of both advanced and lesser evolved life forms from places and PLANETS in our own solar system and elsewhere who utilize interdimensional means to travel through space and time.

Aho attended business college, the U.S. Officer Candidate School and Shrivenham Army University in England. He joined the Washington Naval Guard in 1937. He served as an officer in the U.S. Army during World War II, achieving the rank of Major. From 1946 to 1956 he served in the U.S. Army Reserve Officers Corps. Since 1957, he has lectured on UFOs and extrasensory perception.

Aho founded Washington Saucer Intelligence in 1957, the New Age Foundation in 1965, and the Cathedral of the Stars, Church of the New Age, in 1975. He is also a founder and member of the Northwest Parapsychology Association, Chinook Captain of the North West Dowsers, and a past commander of the Veterans of Foreign Wars. For his service during World War II, he received a Bronze Star and a Purple Heart Award. He has received several merit awards for lectures from various social clubs.

## AHU STATUES *see* EASTER ISLAND

## AIAA *see* AMERICAN INSTITUTE OF AERONAUTICS AND ASTRONAUTICS

## AIR FORCE *see* UNITED STATES AIR FORCE (USAF)

**AIR FORCE BASES.** The UFO literature is replete with accounts of sightings at Air Force bases and other military installations. This fact has led some supporters of the EXTRATERRESTRIAL HYPOTHESIS (ETH), and in particular the INVASION HYPOTHESIS, to surmise that the objects are extraterrestrial spacecraft engaged in military reconnaissance. Some skeptics argue that the proximity of a UFO to an Air Force base merely suggests the possibility that it is a secret military craft or weapon originating from that base. However, this theory does not seem appropriate in cases where interceptors have been scrambled, as was the case in 1975, when a series of UFO sightings occurred at LORING AIR FORCE BASE, MAINE, and a number of other bases.

Another consideration to be kept in mind is that UFOs seen near military installations may be man-made craft engaged in espionage for the Soviet Union or some other terrestrial nation.

**AIR FORCE REGULATION (AFR) 80–17,** instructions issued by the UNITED STATES AIR FORCE (USAF) on September 19, 1966, replacing AIR FORCE REGULATION 200–5, AIR FORCE REGULATION 200–2 and

AIR FORCE REGULATION 200–2A. AFR 80–17 charged PROJECT BLUE BOOK with two missions: to determine if UFOs presented a possible threat to the United States and to use the scientific or technical data gained from the study of UFO reports.

Two paragraphs, which caused a great deal of controversy, stated the following:

"Air Force activities must reduce the percentage of unidentifieds to the minimum. Analysis thus far has explained all but a few of the sightings reported. These unexplained sightings are carried statistically as unidentifieds. If more immediate, detailed, objective data on the unknowns had been available, probably these, too, could have been explained. However, because of the human factors involved, and the fact that analyses of UFO sightings depend primarily on the personal impressions and interpretations of the observers rather than on accurate scientific data or facts obtained under controlled conditions, the elimination of all unidentifieds is impossible.

". . . Response to Public Interest. The SECRETARY OF THE AIR FORCE, OFFICE OF INFORMATION (SAF-OI) maintains contact with the public and the news media on all aspects of the UFO program and related activities. Private individuals or organizations desiring Air Force interviews, briefings, lectures or private discussions on UFOs will be instructed to direct their requests to SAF-OI. Air Force members not officially connected with UFO investigations will refrain from any action or comment on UFO reports which may mislead or cause the public to construe these opinions as official Air Force findings."

Physicist Edward Condon, Director of the CONDON COMMITTEE's UFO study, maintained that critics were misreading the paragraphs, and that the first did not suggest speculation as to the nature of a sighting but rather that the investigation of a report should be undertaken in a serious and thorough manner. The second paragraph, he maintained, was simply intended to "minimize the circulation of wild stories and premature reports before an investigation is completed."

Bibliography: Condon, Edward U., *Scientific Study of Unidentified Flying Objects* (New York: E. P. Dutton, 1969).

## AIR FORCE REGULATION (AFR) 200–5,

instructions issued by the UNITED STATES AIR FORCE on April 29, 1952, giving PROJECT BLUE BOOK the authority to cut red tape and to contact any Air Force unit in the country without going through channels. It provided for wire transmission of reports to the AIR TECHNICAL INTELLIGENCE CENTER (ATIC), followed with details via air mail. Although AFR 200–5 indicated an increased interest in the phenomenon by authorities and appeared to promise improved communications between local military investigators and personnel at upper levels, little change, if any, was apparent.

AFR 200–5 was modified in 1953 by the release of AFR 200–2.

## AIR FORCE REGULATION (AFR) 200–2.

Before the release of AFR 200–2 on August 26, 1953, many significant UFO reports by active UNITED STATES AIR FORCE (USAF) personnel were made public. The effect of the regulation was to dry up the source of information. AFR 200–2 was issued by the Secretary of the Air Force and classified under "Intelligence Activities." It was a modification of the Air Force position established by AIR FORCE REGULATION 200–5 in 1952. It dealt primarily with procedures for reporting UFOs and restrictions on public discussion. Paragraph nine specified, ". . . information regarding a sighting may be released to the press or the general public by the commander of the Air Force base concerned only if it has been *positively identified as a familiar or known object*." Paragraph eleven stated, "Air Force personnel, other than those of the Office of Information Services, will not contact private individuals on UFO cases nor will they discuss their operations and functions with unauthorized persons unless so directed, and then only on a 'need-to-know' basis." These statements led some civilian investigators to the conclusion that the Air Force was engaged in a COVER-UP of the UFO situation. AFR 200–2A was issued on November 2, 1953, incorporating minor changes. AFR 200–2 was updated again on August 12, 1954. In a February 1958 revision, the Air Force attempted to eliminate those portions of the regulation which might provoke suspicion or misinterpretation by the public. In addition, new procedures were instituted with the aim of countering CONTACTEE claims by giving the FEDERAL BUREAU OF INVESTIGATION (FBI) the names of individuals who were "illegally or deceptively bringing the subject to public attention." AFR 200–2 remained in effect until replaced by AIR FORCE REGULATION 80–17.

Bibliography: Davidson, Leon, *Flying Saucers: An Analysis of the Air Force Project Blue Book Special Report No. 14* (White Plains, New York: Blue-Book Publishers, 1976).

## AIRLINE PILOTS.

Numerous UFO sightings have been reported over the years by airline pilots. In *The UFO Evidence* (Washington, D.C.: National Investigations Committee on Aerial Phenomena, 1964), Richard Hall documents almost fifty such reports involving Aer Lingus—Irish Airlines, Aerolineas Argentinas, Aeropost Airlines, Air France, American Airlines, Braniff Airways, the British Overseas Airways Corporation, California Central Airlines, Capital Airlines, Central Airlines, Chicago and Southern Airlines, Conner Airlines, East African Airways, Mid-Continent Airlines, National Airlines, Pan American Airways, Panagra Airlines, Pioneer Airlines, REAL Airlines, Trans-Canada Airlines, Trans World Airways, United Airlines, Varig Airlines, Vasp Airlines, Venezuelan Airlines and Western Airlines. Two of the most publicized sightings by pilots of major airlines were those witnessed by Eastern Airlines pilots near MONTGOMERY, ALABAMA, in 1948 and by Pan American Airways pilots near NEWPORT NEWS, VIRGINIA, in 1952.

Some UFOlogists claim that many airline pilots who sight UFOs do not report them in order to avoid submitting themselves to hours of questioning and filing written reports.

**AIR QUAKES,** sonic booms emanating from the upper atmosphere. Beginning on December 2, 1977, and continuing into January, 1978, a series of air quakes, also known as skyquakes, shook the Eastern Coast of the United States from Connecticut to South Carolina. In some cases, there were reports of a brilliant yellow flash accompanying the booms. The explosions resulted in broken windows and crockery in some areas. Scientists at the Lamont-Doherty Geological Observatory in Palisades, New York, estimated the power of the blasts to be equal to the energy of one hundred tons of dynamite. Previous readings recorded by Columbia University's Air Pressure Measuring Devices found only nuclear explosions registering a larger reading. The eastern seaboard air quakes occurred approximately fifty miles offshore at an undetermined altitude. Investigator ERNEST JAHN, working in conjunction with the Mitre Corporation, a nonprofit engineering firm of McLean, Virginia, located witnesses in Cornwall, England, who had heard a similar blast on December 21, 1977.

A series of UFO sightings reportedly occurring during the same time period led some UFOLOGISTS to link the two phenomena. Simultaneous malfunction of A.C.-operated smoke detectors and disruption of streetlight service in a New Jersey area affected by the quake seemed to provide further evidence to those who supported the UFO connection. Some hypothesized that the materialization of a UFO from another dimension into our universe would cause a displacement of air with resultant sonic reverberation.

Other theories attributed the quakes to meteorological disturbances, meteors, re-entering satellites, secret military experiments, nuclear testing, undersea quakes, earthquakes and exploding gas from garbage dumped off the coast of New York. Many of these explanations were later ruled out.

The Department of Defense directed the Naval Research Laboratories to investigate the matter. In March 1978, they issued a report in which they stated that the United States Navy and the NATIONAL AERONAUTICS AND SPACE ADMINISTRATION (NASA) had traced all the booms to the activities of military aircraft and the trans-Atlantic flights of the British and French Concorde supersonic transport. They explained that during the unusually cold weather, the booms had bounced off layers of warmer high altitude air, deflecting the sound to areas one hundred to two hundred miles distant from the aircraft. A report issued by the Federation of American Scientists (FAS), pointing out that military craft had been flying in the same areas for many years without causing far-reaching air quakes, concluded that it was probably the Concorde alone which had produced the phenomenon. The FAS report stressed that while the air quakes had occurred in the United States shortly after the Concorde's inaugural flight to New York, they had occurred in Europe in 1976, the first year the Concorde flew there. The Mitre Corporation, after studying six hundred incidents, asserted that only two-thirds of the air quakes could be shown satisfactorily to be the effects of supersonic aircraft activity. Explanations for the remaining incidents remain in the realm of speculation.

Bibliography: Claflin-Chalton, Sandra, and Gordon J. MacDonald, *Sound and Light Phenomena—A Study of Historical and Modern Occurrences* (McLean, Virginia: Mitre Corporation, 1978).

**AIRSHIP WAVE,** UFO sightings occurring over nineteen states from November 1896 to May 1897, with a pause between January and the middle of March. The objects were referred to as airships because their appearance concurred in some respects with popular concepts of anticipated airship design. However, the technology to make airship flight a reality was not developed until several years later.

The sighting which sparked the mystery occurred on November 22, 1896, when a group of streetcar passengers in Oakland, California, saw a winged, CIGAR-SHAPED UFO emitting a stream of brilliant light. As the phenomenon began to spread across the country, the diversity of reports revealed that more than one airship was involved. Descriptions varied considerably from an object eighteen inches in diameter and twelve to thirty feet long, to a seventy-foot long structure with wings and propellers. Sometimes hissing or humming sounds accompanied the craft but generally no sounds were heard. Colored or bright white lights plus red or white searchlights were common features. The objects sailed through the skies, often against the wind, at speeds estimated to range between five and two hundred miles per hour.

This airship (above) seen over Oakland, California, in November 1896, was identical to one seen earlier over Sacramento. *Right:* Winged airship seen in Oakland, California, on November 22, 1896. *(Courtesy ICUFON)*

What differentiated these UFOs from modern day UFOs was that the majority of occupant cases involved flight crews who appeared to be ordinary American citizens and claimed that their invention was about to revolutionize travel and transportation. One series of encounters which perpetuated this claim involved a mysterious man named WILSON. Witnesses often gave or sold water, food and repair equipment to UFO crews. Singing and music was sometimes heard as low-flying UFOs passed overhead. Mysterious rusted iron rods were found on the ground. Attached to them were letters reportedly left by airship crews stating the capabilities of their craft and the impact they would soon have upon the world.

Not all occupant encounters were pleasant. Some witnesses described the appearance of the crews as hideous, while others claimed they jabbered in an unknown language. In LE ROY, KANSAS, Alexander Hamilton reported that his cow had been carried off by an airship. A sensational airship disaster was reported in AURORA, TEXAS, supposedly resulting in the death of its extraterrestrial pilot.

As airship hysteria seized the nation, many HOAXES began to be uncovered. Eager witnesses ascribed fantastic qualities to hot-air balloons constructed of tissue paper, with candles used to supply hot air and light. Journalists wrote tongue-in-cheek tales which sometimes sounded no more absurd than the reports of seemingly sincere and honest citizens. Would-be inventors of the marvelous machines sprung up around the nation. Two photographs taken by Walter McCann in ROGERS PARK, ILLINOIS, were proclaimed genuine by the *Chicago Times-Herald* and the *New York Herald*. The *Chicago Tribune*, however, declared them fakes.

The case of the mystery airships has never been solved. Astronomers from 1896 until the present time have attributed the sightings to misidentifications of STARS, PLANETS, FIREBALLS and PLASMA. Others ascribed the phenomenon to hoaxes, HALLUCINATIONS and alcohol. Among those who believed in the reality of the airships, the prevailing theory was that they were a secret invention. The EXTRATERRESTRIAL HYPOTHESIS (ETH) was considered as a possibility by those who thought Mars was inhabited by normal, air-breathing human beings. Another explanation concerned advertisers who sometimes employed balloons for publicity stunts. Some preposterous theories were developed such as that of the man who claimed he had originated the entire phenomenon by setting loose a pelican with a Japanese lantern tied to its leg.

Present day proponents of the PARALLEL UNIVERSE HYPOTHESIS believe the airship sightings may have been perpetrated by beings from another dimension. Their intention was either a joke to lead people astray, or a hint of future possibilities to spur mankind along the path of technological development. Other UFOLOGISTS suggest that the ETH cannot be ruled out since it is possible that the UFOs were spacecraft inaccurately described in terms of the emerging technology familiar to people of that period.

Bibliography: Jacobs, David Michael, *The UFO Controversy in America* (Bloomington, Indiana: Indiana University Press, 1975); Keel, John A., *UFOs: Operation Trojan Horse* (New York: G.P. Putnam's Sons, 1970).

**AIR TECHNICAL INTELLIGENCE CENTER (ATIC),** UNITED STATES AIR FORCE (USAF) division which was formerly known as the Intelligence Division of the Air Material Command (AMC) at Wright Field, Ohio (now Wright-Patterson Air Force Base), and which was the base for UFO investigations until 1961, when responsibility was transferred to the newly-created FOREIGN TECHNOLOGY DIVISION (FTD).

**AKITA AIRPORT, JAPAN.** In 1975, the Japanese news media reported a UFO sighted near Akita Airport in northern Japan. On the morning of October 17, Masaki Machida, a television reporter for the Akita Broadcasting Company, was at the airport when he caught sight of a disk-shaped object descending from the east. Approximately fifty witnesses, including air traffic controllers and awaiting passengers, watched the bright golden disk, with white lights, shining from its interior, as it hovered at about five thousand feet over the ground, five miles from the airport. Telecommunications officer Kenichi Waga warned all incoming and outgoing pilots to watch out for the UFO. Captain Masarus Saito, a Toa Domestic Airlines pilot with twelve years experience, described the appearance of the object as that of two plates placed together, the top one inverted. After about five minutes, the UFO flew off in the direction of the sea.

**ALAMOGORDO, NEW MEXICO,** location of a UFO encounter involving Air Force Sergeant Charles L. Moody on August 13, 1975. Moody was in the desert observing a meteor shower at about 1:15 A.M. when he saw a glowing, metallic, disk-shaped object falling toward the ground about 300 feet away. The UFO was about fifty feet long and eighteen-to-twenty feet wide. As it descended to an altitude of fifteen-to-twenty feet, it wobbled on its own axis. Then it began moving slowly and steadily toward Moody. He jumped into his car but was unable to start it. The UFO came to a stop about seventy feet away. Moody could hear a high-pitched humming sound. He noticed a rectangular window in the craft through which he could see shadows resembling human forms.

The noise stopped and he felt a numbness crawling over his body. The next thing he remembered was seeing the object rising up into the sky and disappearing into the distance. Moody turned the ignition key and his car started immediately. Terrified, he drove off quickly. When he arrived home, he noticed, to his surprise, that the time was 3:00 A.M. He felt that he had somehow lost about one-and-a-half hours.

The following day Moody experienced a pain in his lower back. Within a few days, a rash broke out over his lower body. Upon the recommendation of a physician, he began to practice self-hypnosis in an effort to recall what had occurred during the lost time period. Over the next few weeks, he was able to piece together an almost complete picture of the events.

According to Moody's subsequent recollection, after being overcome by numbness on August 13, 1975, he had observed two beings approaching his car. About six feet tall, the creatures wore skintight black clothing. After a brief scuffle with them, he was rendered unconscious. He awoke on a slab inside the craft. His limbs felt leaden and immovable. Next to him stood the alien leader. The latter was distinguishable from Moody's two captors by his short stature of about five feet, and the silvery white color of his suit. However, like the others he had a large hairless head, a protruding brow, roundish eyes, small ears and nose, and very thin lips. His skin was whitish-gray. The leader asked Moody telepathically if he was prepared to behave peacefully. When Moody agreed to do so, the leader applied a rodlike device to his back which relieved the paralysis.

Moody was taken to another part of the ship where he was shown the drive unit, a device consisting of a large rod surrounded by three glass-canopied holes. Each hole contained a central crystalline object with one rod on each side of it. One rod had a spherical head, while the other was topped by a T-bar.

As he moved about the craft, Moody noticed a sweet, stifling odor. He was told that the aliens' MOTHER SHIP was situated miles away above Earth. He was promised a future meeting with the occupants but warned that closer contact with Earthmen would not be attempted for another twenty years. The aliens told Moody that he would have no recollection of the incident until about two weeks later. The leader placed his hands on the sides of Moody's head, rendering him unconscious once more. Moody awoke in his car as the UFO was leaving.

The case was investigated by JIM LORENZEN, Director of the AERIAL PHENOMENA RESEARCH ORGANIZATION (APRO), Field Investigator WENDELLE STEVENS and a reporter from THE NATIONAL ENQUIRER. An analysis of Moody's claims by Charles McQuiston, coinventor of the Psychological Stress Evaluator, indicated that he was telling the truth. Lorenzen, however, questions a couple of contradictions in Moody's accounts of the incident. In an early telling, Moody related that the alien mother ship was located 400 miles above Earth. Later, however, he said it was 6,000 miles away. Another point which Lorenzen notes is that Moody at one time referred to his two captors as frail creatures, yet later described them as being six feet tall.

The incident is similar in many details to the Betty and Barney Hill cases which occurred in NEW HAMPSHIRE in 1961.

Bibliography: Lorenzen, Coral and Jim, *Abducted: Close Encounters of a Fourth Kind* (New York: Berkley Publishing Corporation, 1977).

**ALBANY, NEW YORK.** On the evening of August 20, 1975, telephone bells at the police barracks, newspaper offices, radio and television stations in the Albany area began to ring incessantly. Startled citizens were reporting UFOs. State Trooper Michael Morgan was dispatched to the scene of one of the sightings. Upon his arrival, he met a police detective who was already observing a blimp-sized object hovering at five hundred feet over Lake Saratoga. As the reddish, glowing UFO flashed on and off, two smaller objects approached and merged with it. At this point, air traffic controllers at Albany airport were alerted and located the object on a RADAR scanner. After a few minutes, the two smaller objects broke away and left in the direction from which they had come. The first object moved towards the two nervous policemen and, as it passed over them, they were dazzled by a brilliant white light shining out of the center of its base. Silently, the craft turned and began to move away slowly. Suddenly, the UFO disappeared. "It was as if," Morgan remarked, "someone had reached up and turned the lights out." Meanwhile, the Albany tower operators had been following the movements of the UFO. After tracking the target for forty-five minutes, they lost contact with it. However, within a short time they received a call from the pilot of a military airplane flying over the Albany area at eight thousand feet. The pilot warned them that he had just seen a red FIREBALL, one thousand feet above him, headed toward the airport. The controllers located the object just as it entered the fifty-mile range of one of their radarscopes. The anti-clutter device was thrown to ascertain whether or not the blip was an ANGEL. However, the image still came through clearly. The controllers estimated the object's speed to be 3,000 miles per hour. About five

miles outside Albany, the target vanished. The controllers surmised that it had either accelerated to a speed of 5,000 miles per hour or had executed a seemingly impossible vertical maneuver at high speed. They knew that the object could not have been a METEORITE, for at that low altitude a dramatic and audible impact would have occurred.

During the same time frame as the Albany sightings, large disks and bright lights were seen at low altitude less than fifty miles north over the South Glens Falls area and as far north as Lake George.

The case was investigated by ERNEST JAHN, who contacted the SMITHSONIAN INSTITUTION in Cambridge. They were unable to give any explanation for the sightings and a spokesman added that the entry into the atmosphere of a natural body of such immense size would have lit up the whole sky like a Christmas tree.

This is considered one of the best documented UFO cases because it involved civilians, police, the Federal Aviation Administration and military authorities, and was, moreover, confirmed by radar.

Bibliography: Sachs, Margaret, with Ernest Jahn, *Celestial Passengers—UFOs and Space Travel* (New York: Penguin Books, 1977).

**ALBUQUERQUE, NEW MEXICO,** location where PAUL VILLA claimed to have taken a PHOTOGRAPH of a purported flying saucer in 1963. The photograph was identified as a HOAX by GROUND SAUCER WATCH (GSW), as were numerous other photographs taken by Villa of alleged UFOs.

Fake UFO photographed by Paul Villa. *(Courtesy ICUFON)*

Alexander the Great in battle. *(Culver Pictures)*

suddenly appeared from the opposite direction, and approached the first UFO. After a while, the UFOs disappeared. Ali believes that the UFOs carried friendly visitors from another world.

**ALIEN FLYING OBJECT (AFO),** term coined in 1969 by scientist William Hartmann in a paper presented to a symposium on unidentified flying objects sponsored by the AMERICAN ASSOCIATION FOR THE ADVANCEMENT OF SCIENCE (AAAS) to denote a vehicle constructed by alien intelligence. His intention in creating this expression was to reduce the confusion incurred by those who use the term UFO to signify an extraterrestrial spacecraft. However, AFO and alien flying object have not become widely used expressions in UFOLOGICAL terminology.

**ALIENS** *see* **UFONAUTS**

**ALMA** *see* **BIGFOOT**

**ALPERT, SHELL,** *see* **SALEM, MASSACHUSETTS**

**ALPHA,** bimonthly magazine, established in 1979, with a circulation of 32,000. It is available both at newsstands and by subscription. *Alpha* is concerned with all aspects of the paranormal, from extrasensory perception to UFOs, and from meditation to reincarnation. It carries in-depth studies of such subjects and deals with their possible interrelation.

Articles are written by staff and freelance writers. The latter should query first. Self-addressed, stamped envelopes should accompany submissions. Articles should be about 2,000 words in length. Fees are established by mutual agreement. Payment is made upon publication. The publisher pays for photographs. UFOLOGIST and

**ALDRIN, EDWIN "BUZZ,"** *see* **APOLLO 11 and GEMINI 12**

**ALEXANDER THE GREAT,** Macedonian king during whose reign two remarkable UFO incidents were reported.

In 329 B.C., two shining silver shields dived repeatedly on Alexander's army, causing the elephants and horses to panic while they were attempting to cross the Jaxartes River into India.

In 322 B.C., during Alexander's siege of Tyre, a large flying shield, leading a triangular formation of four smaller shields, circled over Tyre while thousands of soldiers on both sides watched in amazement. Suddenly, the largest UFO shot a beam of light at the city's walls. The walls crumbled. More beams were flashed down destroying the remaining walls and towers. As the attackers poured into the city, the flying shields hovered overhead until a victory was accomplished. The objects then took off at high speed, disappearing into the distance.

Bibliography: Drake, W. Raymond, *Gods and Spacemen throughout History* (Chicago: Henry Regnery Company, 1975).

**ALI, MUHAMMAD,** professional boxer and world heavyweight champion who claims to have seen UFOs on at least seven different occasions. On one occasion, while driving along the New Jersey Turnpike, a CIGAR-SHAPED UFO passed in front of his car. The object was surrounded by a row of colored lights. His most publicized UFO encounter occurred while he was jogging in Central Park in Manhattan during the early hours of the morning. Ali was accompanied by several witnesses, including newspaper reporters and his manager, Angelo Dundee. He first caught sight of the object as it traveled slowly and silently over some nearby buildings. Within seconds, the object was positioned directly above him. It descended until it was only a few thousand feet above the ground. Then, a second object

UFO witness Muhammad Ali. *(Columbia Pictures)*

author Ray Stemman is one of the coeditors of the magazine. *Alpha* is published by Pendulum Publishing Company, Limited, 20 Regent Street, Fleet, Hants GU13 9NR, England.

## AMALGAMATED FLYING SAUCER CLUBS OF AMERICA (AFSCA), P.O. Box 39, Yucca Valley, California 92284; telephone number: 714-365-1141.

This CONTACTEE organization holds that flying saucers originate from planets within our own solar system, such as MARS, VENUS and Saturn, as well as from other star systems and galaxies. Surface conditions on these planets, according to AFSCA, are much closer to those of Earth than we are led to believe by scientists. Temperatures, for instance, are supposedly the same or milder than ours. The contradictory information sent to Earth by man-made space probes is said, by the organization, to have been fed into the probes' computer systems by the SPACE PEOPLE themselves. Although the alleged flying saucer occupants have life spans of over several hundred years and vary in height from three to ten feet, they are similar enough to earthlings that many can and do pass among us unnoticed. AFSCA claims that the Space People have repeatedly contacted all heads of major governments. The reported benefits to be received from them include the elimination of disease, poverty and smog, the solving of automation and unemployment problems, a means of financing public works projects and foreign aid without resorting to taxation, an extended life span, greater personal freedom, economic security and interstellar tours. The group maintains that many politicians, church officials and financial institutions reject the Space People's offers of help because any such changes in the status quo would reduce or eliminate their power and control over financial matters. The reason why flying saucers have not landed openly to prove their reality, concludes this organization, is because mankind is not psychologically prepared to receive them in a friendly manner, neither worshipping them as gods nor fearing them as conquerors.

This nonprofit organization was founded in 1959 by GABRIEL GREEN, who has served as its President since that time. AFSCA evolved from Green's organization, the LOS ANGELES INTERPLANETARY STUDY GROUPS, formed in 1957. The group has 5,600 members in twenty-four countries and 138 AFSCA Unit Directors report information to headquarters from their respective locations. Available for purchase are tape recorded messages from alleged Space People, books, photographs, buttons and bumper stickers with slogans such as, "Flying saucers are real, the Air Force doesn't exist." The Los Angeles Interplanetary Study Groups published THY KINGDOM COME from 1957 to 1959. AFSCA published AFSCA WORLD REPORT from 1959 to 1961,

UFO INTERNATIONAL from 1962 to 1965 and FLYING SAUCERS INTERNATIONAL from 1962 to 1969. Back issues are available.

## AMATEURS D'INSOLITE, LES, Boîte Postale 186, 71007 Macon, France.

Investigative organization belonging to the COMITÉ EUROPÉEN DE COORDINATION DE LA RECHERCHE UFOLOGIQUE (CECRU).

## AMERICAN ASSOCIATION FOR THE ADVANCEMENT OF SCIENCE (AAAS), sponsor of a symposium on unidentified flying objects held in Boston, Massachusetts, on December 26 and 27, 1969. The participants were astronomers, physicists, sociologists, psychologists, psychiatrists and a representative of the communications media. Some members of the association were strongly opposed to holding the symposium on the grounds that it might dignify a subject they considered unscientific. The idea was originally proposed by CARL SAGAN and THORNTON PAGE, who subsequently edited a compilation of papers contributed to the symposium by ROBERT M. L. BAKER, FRANK D. DRAKE, Lester Grinspoon, Robert L. Hall, Kenneth R. Hardy, William K. Hartmann, J. ALLEN HYNEK, JAMES E. McDONALD, DONALD H. MENZEL, Philip Morrison, Thornton Page, Alan D. Persky, Douglass R. Price-Williams, Franklin Roach, Carl Sagan and Walter Sullivan.

Bibliography: Sagan, Carl, and Thornton Page (eds.), *UFOs—A Scientific Debate* (Ithaca, N.Y.: Cornell University Press, 1972).

## AMERICAN INSTITUTE OF AERONAUTICS AND ASTRONAUTICS (AIAA), professional society of about 25,000 aerospace scientists and engineers which set up a UFO subcommittee in 1967. The group brought the problem of UFOs to the attention of its membership through articles in its journal, *Astronautics and Aeronautics*. (The latter is no longer published.) In 1970, the institute issued its appraisal of the CONDON REPORT. Although the committee considered the report to be fairly reasonable in its attempt to deal with the matter, they noted that Condon's summary is more his personal view of the situation than a summary of the report. The subcommittee was disbanded in 1974.

## ANCIENT ASTRONAUTS, extraterrestrial space travelers who allegedly visited Earth on one or more occasions in ancient times. Although Swiss author ERICH VON DÄNIKEN is the best known promoter of the ancient astronauts theory, many other authors have dealt with the subject in great detail. These include BRINSLEY LE POER TRENCH, W. Raymond Drake and

Paul Misraki. Much of their supportive evidence is found in the old religions and mythology of various cultures around the world. Von Däniken considers the fact that ancient gods needed vehicles with wheels and wings to travel the skies as indicative of the physical rather than spiritual nature of such beings. Supporters of the ancient astronauts hypothesis contend that space travelers arriving from the sky with seemingly superhuman powers would appear godlike to any primitive culture. The most frequently quoted examples of alleged Biblical accounts of UFO sightings and extraterrestrial visitors are those dealing with ANGELS, the ARK OF THE COVENANT, ELIJAH, ENOCH, EZEKIEL, JACOB, JONAH, MOSES, SAINT PAUL, SODOM AND GOMORRAH and the STAR OF BETHLEHEM.

A great deal of conjecture is based on archaeological curiosities which supposedly could not have been produced by the civilizations which existed at the time of their construction. Such archaeological anomalies include the PYRAMIDS, the Lines of NAZCA, the gigantic statues on EASTER ISLAND, the ZIGGURATS and the stone platforms at BAALBECK, LEBANON. Evidence of advanced knowledge allegedly given to mankind by extraterrestrials is purportedly found in the astronomical records of the MAYA and the ancient civilization of SUMER, the PIRI RE'IS MAP and the primitive Dogon tribe's cognizance of the binary system of SIRIUS. Further evidence of ancient astronauts is allegedly revealed in the TASSILI FRESCOES, the legend of the Central American god QUETZALCOATL and the Epic of GILGAMESH.

Some proponents of the ancient astronauts hypothesis believe that extraterrestrials were actually responsible for the presence of human beings on this planet, either by seeding us here or by interbreeding with Earth animals to create *homo sapiens*. This theory is often referred to as the EARTH COLONIZATION HYPOTHESIS or the seeding hypothesis. Some authors have conjectured that the Biblical story of the Garden of EDEN describes an attempt by ancient astronauts to create a perfect race on Earth.

The study of the ancient astronauts hypothesis is promoted by the ANCIENT ASTRONAUT SOCIETY in Illinois.

Bibliography: Von Däniken, Erich, *Chariots of the Gods?* (New York: G. P. Putnam's Sons, 1970); Drake, W. Raymond, *Gods or Spacemen?* (Amherst, Wisconsin: Amherst Press, 1964); Le Poer Trench, Brinsley, *Temple of the Stars* (New York: Ballantine Books, 1974); Misraki, Paul, *Les Extraterrestres* (Paris: Plon, 1962); Thiering, Barry, and Edgar Castle, (eds.), *Some Trust in Chariots* (New York: Popular Library, 1972); Wilson, Clifford, *Crash Go the Chariots* (New York: Lancer Books, 1972).

**ANCIENT ASTRONAUT SOCIETY,** 1921 St. John's Avenue, Highland Park, Illinois 60068.

This organization is dedicated to the study of the historical, archaeological and mythological evidence which lends support to the ANCIENT ASTRONAUTS hypothesis.

The society was founded in 1973. Gene Phillips serves as Director. There are about 2,000 members. A conference is held annually in Chicago. Members receive the bimonthly magazine, *Ancient Skies*.

**ANDERSON, CARL ARTHUR** (b. November 9, 1912, Wellfleet, Massachusetts; address: 2522 East Pearson Avenue, Fullerton, California 92631).

Anderson's first contact occurred in 1954 when he, his wife, son and daughter were allegedly paralyzed for fifteen minutes by a beam of light from a flying saucer. In 1955, his brother-in-law's burnt hand was reportedly healed by a beam of green light from a hovering saucer. In 1960, Anderson claims to have been taken aboard a huge craft in the Mojave desert where he was given a briefing on the ship's propulsion system by an alien named Kumar. A few months later, on Kumar's instructions, Anderson traveled to Germany where he conveyed this information to rocket pioneer HERMANN OBERTH and a group of German professors. Anderson has been promised a trip to Kumar's home and was selected as an emissary because he lived with Kumar and his people in a previous incarnation.

An electrician by trade, Anderson worked as a Civil Service employee for thirty-six years for the United States Navy Department and is now retired. In 1949, he received a Citizenship Citation for the attempted rescue of a child at San Marino, California. He is an ordained minister of the International Evangelism Crusades and is the author of *Two Nights to Remember* (Los Angeles: New Age Publishing Company, 1956).

**ANDREASSON, BETTY,** see **SOUTH ASHBURNHAM, MASSACHUSETTS**

**ANDROID,** a robot whose outer appearance resembles that of a human being. Although such automatons have not yet been made on Earth, extraterrestrial civilizations may already have utilized them to operate interstellar spacecraft, since they would not be limited by short life spans. In addition, androids would not experience the physical stress which would affect humanoids when executing sharp turns at high speed. Some witnesses, as in the FALKVILLE, ALABAMA, case, have claimed that they were unable to determine whether alleged UFO occupants were natural biological beings or robots. It is possible that UFONAUTS described in such reports were, in fact, androids.

Walter Andrus.

**ANDRUS, WALTER H.,** Jr. (b. December 12, 1920, Des Moines, Iowa; address: 103 Oldtowne Road, Seguin, Texas 78155; telephone number: 512-379-9216), Co-founder and International Director of the MUTUAL UFO NETWORK (MUFON).

Andrus considers the EXTRATERRESTRIAL HYPOTHESIS (ETH) as one of many possible solutions to the UFO mystery. In 1948, he, his wife and their five-year-old son were among a small crowd of people on a downtown street in Phoenix, Arizona, who observed a formation of four round, dull silver objects moving slowly against the wind. At the time, Andrus held a United States Weather Bureau Observer's Certificate and a private pilot's license. Since the sky was clear that day, it was not possible to estimate the altitude of the objects in relation to the height of a particular cloud formation. The apparent size of each of the objects was comparable to that of a shirt button. For a few moments, the objects disappeared as if they were coin-shaped objects which had rolled over, leaving only their extremely thin, imperceptible perimeters facing the witnesses. Three of the objects reappeared, continuing in the same direction until they became too faint to observe. The sighting was not reported to any investigative agency.

Andrus was an electronics technician and instructor for the U.S. Navy from 1943 to 1946 and from 1946 to 1949 was Station Manager for Mid-Continent Airlines (now merged with Braniff International). He is currently the Production Manager of the Automotive Products Division Plant of Motorola, Incorporated, where he has been employed since 1949. In 1969, with Allen Utke and John Schuessler, he founded MUFON, of which he is International Director.

Andrus is a former Chairman of the Quinsippi Section of the American Society for Quality Control and a former President of the Kiwanis Club of Quincy, Illinois. He is presently Chairman of the Board of the Guadalupe Valley Chapter of the National Management Association.

Andrus has edited, singly and jointly, the annual *MUFON UFO Symposium Proceedings* since 1972.

**ANGEL,** a spurious RADAR return, also known as a "GHOST."

**ANGEL,** a spiritual being who, according to the Scriptures, serves as God's messenger. Proponents of the ANCIENT ASTRONAUTS hypothesis conjecture that many of the angels referred to in the Bible were in fact extraterrestrial visitors whose true identity was not understood by human beings. In Genesis 19, two angels, who brought a warning about the destruction of SODOM AND GOMORRAH, ate a meal while staying at Lot's house. This fact has been presented as evidence that the alleged angels were physical beings, not spiritual beings.

Some modern-day Christians believe that UFOs are, in fact, God's angels. Some adherents to this belief also hold that a number of UFO sightings can be attributed to the Devil and his cohorts.

**ANGELS' HAIR,** white, gossamerlike substance which falls from the sky, sometimes in great quantity. Strands range in length from a few inches to more than one hundred feet. In almost half of the cases, it has been seen descending from CIGAR-SHAPED UFOs which have cloudlike formations under or around them. Although these fibers have sometimes been confused with floating spider webs, they can be differentiated by the fact that they dissolve upon contact with the ground. In this respect, angels' hair is similar to DEVILS' JELLY. Examination of several samples has revealed that angels' hair contains boron, silicon, calcium and magnesium. It is similar in composition to borosilicate glass. However, its ephemeral nature renders more specific analysis impossible.

Angels' hair is sometimes compared to ectoplasm, a substance which spiritualists claim to be involved in materialization. This has led UFOLOGISTS who support the PARALLEL UNIVERSE HYPOTHESIS to theorize that angels' hair is the excess materialization energy created when UFOs manifest themselves in our physical world.

Two well-known cases in which angels' hair was observed were the OLORON and GAILLAC sightings in France in 1952.

(See maps on pages 376-377.)

Bibliography: Sachs, Margaret, with Ernest Jahn, *Celestial Passengers—UFOs and Space Travel* (New York: Penguin Books, 1977).

**ANGELUCCI, ORFEO,** CONTACTEE whose alleged encounters with flying saucers and SPACE PEOPLE began in 1955. The propulsion system of extraterrestrial spaceships was explained to him as converted magnetic energy "inherent in all the universe." After taking a trip in a flying saucer, Angelucci began encountering spacemen at unexpected places during the daily routine of life. He lectured, published a newspaper and attended flying saucer conventions. Later on, he claimed to have been spiritually transported to a beautiful planet where he learned that he, himself, had been a spaceman in a previous life. He was warned that unless earthlings change their ways, they will meet calamity in 1986. On another occasion he purportedly met Jesus who informed him that benevolent Space People are everywhere on Earth, living unrecognized among us. They are here to help bring in the NEW AGE.

Angelucci authored two books: *The Secret of the Saucers* (Amherst, Wisconsin: Amherst Press, 1955); and *Son of the Sun* (Los Angeles: DeVorss and Company, 1959).

**ANIMAL MUTILATIONS.** In the 1960s, farmers throughout the United States found the corpses of animals, usually cattle, with vital organs removed, blood completely or partially drained, and sometimes external parts such as eyes or ears surgically removed. The most celebrated case involved a horse called SNIPPY. The phenomenon continued into the 1970s, reportedly spreading to Puerto Rico, Canada, Brazil, Bolivia, Sweden, Australia, Scotland and central Europe. Reports of unmarked helicopters and unidentified lights hovering over the mutilation sites, plus the reported absence of footprints around the remains, led investigators to connect the incidents with the UFO mystery. Some speculated that the livestock are airlifted, muti-

lated and returned to the ground. An earlier incident of animal mutilation occurring in connection with a UFO sighting took place in 1897 in LE ROY, KANSAS.

The Cattle Raisers' Association, the FEDERAL BUREAU OF INVESTIGATION (FBI) and local law enforcement agencies have had little success in solving the problem, although in 1975 the arrest in Colorado of the members of a nomadic satanic cult has led many researchers to conclude that the mutilations were carried out during black magic rituals. However, reports of mutilations continue to come in and one organization, PROJECT STIGMA, exists for the express purpose of investigating this phenomenon. Its records show that many mutilated carcasses do not decompose as rapidly as they should. Moreover, in a large proportion of cases, predators and farmers' dogs, while demonstrating curiosity, do not go within close range of the victims.

TREVOR JAMES CONSTABLE attributes the incidents to biological UFOs which he calls invisible critters, denizens of the atmospheric regions known as ETHERIA.

Bibliography: Smith, Marcia S., *The UFO Enigma* (Washington, D.C.: Library of Congress, Congressional Research Service, 1976).

**ANIMAL REACTIONS.** When UFOs appear in their vicinity, animals usually exhibit signs of extreme fear. Pet owners and farmers have reported cats yowling and fighting, horses whinnying and kicking in their stalls, ducks quacking, cows jumping and temporarily ceasing to give milk. Dogs have whined, barked, pricked up their ears, crawled in abject fear and curled up in tight balls under furniture. Occasionally, their fur stands on end. In some cases, frightened dogs have developed illnesses immediately after the sightings, death following within several weeks. Owners have made a direct correlation between such deaths and the UFO sightings which preceded them although there is no proof to support such a contention.

UFOLOGISTS have conjectured that some UFOs emit a high-pitched sound beyond the range of human hearing which is distressing to animals. Others have hypothesized that UFOs produce a stimulus outside the realm of the human sensory range but detectable by the legendary sixth sense attributed to animals.

Bibliography: Keyhoe, Donald E., and Gordon I. R. Lore (eds.), *Strange Effects from UFOs* (Washington, D.C.: National Investigations Committee on Aerial Phenomena, 1969); Le Poer Trench, Brinsley, *Mysterious Visitors—The UFO Story* (New York: Stein and Day, 1973).

**ANOMALISTIC OBSERVATIONAL PHENOMENA (AOP),** term coined by ROBERT BAKER, who points out that its application is better suited to phe-

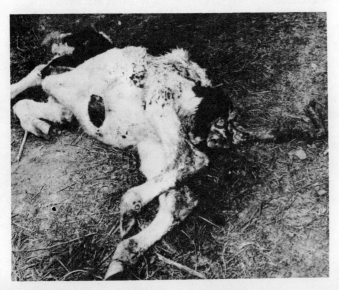

Mutilated calf found in Middleton, Idaho, on October 28, 1975. *(United Press International Photo)*

According to some UFOlogists, the Apollo 11 spacecraft was chased by these two "UFOs" while orbiting the moon. The images have been identified as the spacecraft's light source reflecting on the window panel in front of the camera. *(Courtesy ICUFON/NASA)*

nomena usually referred to as UFOs, which may not always be unidentified, flying or substantive objects.

Bibliography: Baker, Robert, (testimony) in U.S. Congress, House, Committee on Science and Astronautics, Symposium on Unidentified Flying Objects, Hearings, 90th Congress, 2nd Session, July 29, 1968 (Washington, D.C.: U.S. Government Printing Office, 1968).

## ANTIGRAVITY *see* GRAVITATION

**ANTIMATTER,** elementary particles possessing the mass and charge of electrons, protons or neutrons, their counterparts in matter, but for which the charge is reversed. Thus, antiparticles comprise positrons, antiprotons and antineutrons. Antimatter has been produced in laboratories but cannot be collected, since contact between matter and antimatter causes mutual annihilation. The energy released in the meeting of a thimbleful of antimatter with an equal amount of matter would result in a colossal and devastating detonation. Such an explosion may have occurred in 1908 in the TUNGUSKA REGION of the Soviet Union, although some aspects of the incident are not in harmony with this hypothesis.

The existence of an independent antiuniverse composed of antigalaxies, antistars and antiplanets is possible. Nor have scientists ruled out the possibility of the presence of large amounts of antimatter within our universe, although it has been demonstrated that the total relative amount of antimatter within our galaxy

cannot be more than one part in ten million. However, it is not understood how matter and antimatter would have formed and separated within the context of current explanations for the creation of the universe.

Some UFOLOGISTS have hoped that the study of antimatter in relation to matter might provide some clues regarding negative gravity. However, recent experiments indicate that the gravitational reaction between matter and antimatter is identical to that between matter and matter.

## AOP *see* ANOMALISTIC OBSERVATIONAL PHENOMENA

## APCIC *see* AERIAL PHENOMENA CLIPPING AND INFORMATION CENTER

**APCIC NEWS BULLETIN,** publication of the AERIAL PHENOMENA CLIPPING AND INFORMATION CENTER (APCIC).

## APIC *see* AERIAL PHENOMENA INVESTIGATION COMMITTEE

## APIO *see* AERIAL PHENOMENA INVESTIGATION ORGANIZATION

**APOLLO 8,** spacecraft from which ASTRONAUTS Frank Borman and JAMES A. LOVELL reported sighting a UFO. As in the case of all other UFO sightings by astronauts, the NATIONAL AERONAUTICS AND SPACE

ADMINISTRATION (NASA) determined that what had been observed was nothing which could be termed abnormal in the space environment.

**APOLLO 11,** space mission carrying the first men to the moon and during which, according to popular rumor, ASTRONAUTS Neil Armstrong and Edwin "Buzz" Aldrin saw a "space fleet" lined up on the moon's surface. Their report of the sighting was allegedly deleted by officials of the NATIONAL AERONAUTICS AND SPACE ADMINISTRATION (NASA) during the delay between receiving and retransmitting the radio message. Radio hams who supposedly heard the original relay claimed that the astronauts were ordered to photograph the objects. Another rumor purports that the Apollo 11 spacecraft was actually chased by a UFO. NASA has denied these reports.

**APOLLO 12,** space mission which carried the United States' second team of ASTRONAUTS to the MOON. Reportedly, two flashing UFOs accompanied the spacecraft part of the way. Seen through telescopes in European observatories on November 14, 1969, one object appeared to be following the spacecraft while the other traveled ahead of it. On November 15, astronauts Charles "Pete" Conrad, Dick Gordon and Alan Bean observed the objects. As in the case of all other UFO sightings by astronauts, the NATIONAL AERONAUTICS AND SPACE ADMINISTRATION (NASA) later determined that what had been observed was nothing which could be termed abnormal in the space environment.

**APPLEWHITE, MARSHALL HEFF,** *see* **HUMAN INDIVIDUAL METAMORPHOSIS**

**APPROCHE,** joint publication of the SOCIETÉ VAROISE D'ÉTUDE DES PHÉNOMÈNES SPATIAUX (SVEPS) and the SOCIETÉ VAUCLUSIENNE D'ÉTUDE DES PHÉNOMÈNES SPATIAUX (SOVEPS).

**APRO** *see* **AERIAL PHENOMENA RESEARCH ORGANIZATION**

**APRO BULLETIN,** publication of the AERIAL PHENOMENA RESEARCH ORGANIZATION (APRO).

**AQUARIAN DAWN, THE,** publication of the NEW AGE FOUNDATION (NAF).

**ARBETSGRUPPEN FOR UFOLOGI (AFU),** Box 5046, S–151 05 Södertalje 5, Sweden; telephone number: 0755–19 168.

The main objective of this informal group is to form a basis for UFO research by building and maintaining a specialized library and archives. In addition, AFU supporters work in the fields of documentation, bibliographical research, historical research, field investigation and the supplying of information to UFOlogists, organizations, magazines and libraries. The library is open to anyone who pays a small yearly fee or donates materials such as books and magazines. Additionally, names of contributors are placed on the mailing list and receive newsletters.

AFU holds no official view on the identity of UFOs but believes that a large part of the phenomenon is paraphysical in nature.

This nonprofit organization was founded in 1973 by Anders Liljegren, Håkan Blomquist and Kjell Jonsson. Blomquist and Jonsson are librarians. Liljegren is Editor of *Nyhetsblad,* a newsletter published three times a year which covers the latest news on books, organizations and important UFO events.

**ARCANI, GLI,** Italian magazine established in 1972, with a circulation of 25,000. It is available by subscription only. The magazine deals with mysteries, including UFOLOGY. Articles are contributed by freelance writers. It is published by Armenia Editore s.r.l., Viale Ca Granda 2, 20162 Milan, Italy.

**ARCHERS' COURT RESEARCH GROUP** *see* **SOCIETY OF METAPHYSICIANS**

Aristotle. *(Culver Pictures)*

Witnesses claimed that these cloudlike formations hanging over the Argentine Andes were rotating. The photograph was taken on December 7, 1966. *(Courtesy ICUFON/Reyna)*

**ARGENTINA.** After Brazil, Argentina has recorded the second largest number of UFO sightings in Latin America. The country experienced a UFO WAVE in 1962.

There are several UFO organizations in Argentina, including the CENTRO DE ESTUDIOS DE FENÓMENOS AEREOS INUSUALES (CEFAI) and the ORGANIZACION NACIONAL INVESTIGADORA DE FENÓMENOS ESPACIALES (ONIFE).

**ARISTOTLE,** fourth century B.C. Greek philosopher, logician and scientist whose references to "heavenly disks" have been interpreted by some UFOLOGISTS as an indication that he witnessed objects similar to modern UFOs. Aristotle also claimed to have seen a meteorite fall at Aegospotami, rise up in the wind and descend in another place. At the same time, a COMET was glowing in the sky.

Bibliography: Velikovsky, Immanuel, *Worlds in Collision* (Garden City, N.Y.: Doubleday and Company, 1950).

**ARK OF THE COVENANT,** a chest built by Moses, according to the Book of Exodus, following precise instructions given by God. Sacred objects were to be placed in the ark, which was to be carried only by divinely appointed persons. In the Book of Numbers, a warning is given that a person who touched any holy objects would die. The Second Book of Samuel tells of a man named Uzzah who reached out his hand to steady the ark when it was shaken by oxen. He was struck dead upon the spot by God.

ERICH VON DÄNIKEN purports that if the same construction details were followed today, the object produced would function as a radio. He construes that the ark was intended to be a communications device between extraterrestrial ASTRONAUTS and Moses. He claims it was the radio's electrical charge which killed Uzzah.

Writer Clifford Wilson argues that since no two pieces of gold on the chest were separated by an

The Ark of the Covenant.

insulator, there was no possibility of there being one negative and one positive plate. If it had been charged, there would automatically have been a short circuit. In addition, he points out that the Bible contains no reference to von Däniken's claims that the ark was surrounded by flashing sparks and that its bearers were instructed to wear special shoes and clothing. Thus, Uzzah was not killed by electrocution, for had the ark been electrically charged, the bearers, too, holding the chest's gold-covered carrying poles, would have perished. Wilson remarks that God communicated with Moses before the ark was built and therefore had no need for a radio transmitter.

Bibliography: Von Däniken, Erich, *Chariots of the Gods?* (New York: G. P. Putnam's Sons, 1970); Wilson, Clifford, *Crash Go the Chariots* (New York: Lancer Books, 1972).

## ARMSTRONG, NEIL, *see* APOLLO 11

## ARNOLD, KENNETH, *see* MOUNT RAINIER, WASHINGTON

## ARPI *see* ASSOCIATION DE RECHERCHE SUR LES PHÉNOMÈNES INEXPLIQUÉS

## ASHBURNHAM, MASSACHUSETTS, *see* SOUTH ASHBURNHAM, MASSACHUSETTS

**ASHTAR,** entity who is reported to have contacted numerous mediums and UFO CONTACTEES through mental telepathy. Various reports describe him as a high-ranking member of the Intergalactic Federation and the United Council of the Universal Brotherhood. He urges the human beings with whom he communicates to pass on his messages of salvation to the rest of the world. His numerous predictions sometimes come true and sometimes do not.

## ASSOCIATION DE RECHERCHE SUR LES PHÉNOMÈNES INEXPLIQUÉS (ARPI), 13 rue Fortune Jourdan, 13003 Marseille, France; telephone number: 91-644522.

This organization is dedicated to the study of UFOs and paranormal phenomena.

ARPI was founded as a nonprofit organization in 1978 by Michel Langard who serves as President. Gilles Le Neindre is Secretary and Chantal Simonini is Treasurer. The group has thirty members. The group conducts field investigations in the region of Provence, organizes skywatches and studies various methods of electronic detection of UFOs. Members receive a bulletin and may participate in parapsychological experiments.

## ASSOCIATION DES AMIS DE MARC THI-ROUIN (AAMT), 29 rue Berthelot, 26000 Valence, France.

The purpose of this regional organization is to investigate sightings in the Drome and Ardeche regions, to exchange literature and to research ancient and modern sightings. Its goal is to continue the work of Marc Thirouin, Founder of the first private UFO organization in France. The group believes UFOs to be of nonhuman origin, perhaps extraterrestrial or of an unknown nature.

This nonprofit organization was founded in 1973 by former members of the Commission International d'Enquêtes Scientifiques Outanos (CIESO). It is run by President David Duquesnoy, Vice-President Michel Dorier, General Secretary Jean-Pierre Pattard and Assistant Secretary Rolande Dorier. Membership stands at about 100. Michel Dorier is Editor of *UFO Informations,* a quarterly newsletter which deals with all aspects of UFOs and associated phenomena. AAMT serves as a delegation of LUMIÈRES DANS LA NUIT (LDLN), and is a member of the COMITÉ EUROPÉEN DE COORDINATION DE LA RECHERCHE UFOlOGIQUE (CECRU).

## ASSOCIATION D'ÉTUDE SUR LES SOU-COUPES VOLANTES (AESV), 40 rue Mignet, 13100 Aix en Provence, France; telephone number: 16/42-59 4536.

This investigative organization is dedicated to the scientific study of UFOs and extraterrestrial life. AESV holds that UFOs are solid ships piloted by intelligent creatures. It suggests that such beings might be engaging in sociological contact prior to physical contact in order to prepare the human race to face twenty-first century knowledge.

This nonprofit organization was founded in 1974 by Perry Petrakis, who serves as its Director. Michel Hertzog is Vice-President. There are about fifty members. The group has correspondents in fifteen foreign countries. Twenty investigators are located in Aix en Provence (south of France), Orléans (four departments in the north of France), Bordeaux (west of France), Neuchatel (Switzerland), Vevey (Switzerland), Douala (Cameroon, West Central Africa) and in Belgium. Members have access to a reference library, participate in monthly skywatches and attend nationwide conferences at reduced rates. A quarterly journal, *AESV,* contains information from all over the world, sighting reports and information from official organizations such as the UNITED NATIONS and the CENTRE NATIONAL D'ETUDES SPATIALES.

AESV branches: AESV (Centre Loiret), 86 rue Emile Zola, 45000 Orléans, France; AESV Suisse, 2 ruelle du Centre, 1800 CH Vevey, Switzerland; AESV Suisse,

Serge Leuba, Beauregard 3, 20006 Neuchatel, Switzerland; AESV Belgique, Leopold Spruyt, Eikenlaan 4, 2180 Kalmthout, Belgium.

## ASSOCIATION DIJONNAISE DE RECHERCHES UFOLOGIQUES ET PARAPSYCHOLOGIQUES (ADRUP), 11 Le Breuil Orgeux, 21490 Ruffey-les-Echirey, France; telephone numbers: (Patrick Geoffroy) 80-360222, (Pascal Banet) 80-176740 and (Gilles Hammer) 80-723088.

The purpose of this regional investigative organization is to study all those phenomena which are unexplained by conventional science, including all types of UFO encounters, CONTACTEES, lost civilizations, mysterious DISAPPEARANCES, HYPNOSIS, TELEPATHY, psychometry, clairvoyance, clairaudience and aermooptics. Like many French groups, ADRUP believes the UFO phenomenon may represent several different phenomena, such as extraterrestrial spacecraft, parapsychological phenomena, time travelers or the manifestation of an inner Earth civilization. The group supposes that the propulsion system of UFOs involves antigravitation. It also thinks that there is a connection between the development of UFO witnesses' PSI faculties and the state of technological and spiritual advancement of UFO occupants.

This nonprofit organization was founded in 1976 by Patrick Geoffroy who serves as President and who has been an official investigator for the SOCIETÉ VAROISE D'ÉTUDE DES PHÉNOMÈNES SPATIAUX (SVEPS) for several years. Other staff members include Vice-President Gilles Hammer, Treasurer Pascal Banet, Secretary Gilles Alary and Archivist Muriel Fernandez. The group has twelve members. Follow-up investigations of newspaper reports are carried out by the group, which receives collaboration from the police. The group conducts geographical studies of UFO sightings, statistical studies, skywatches and electromagnetic detection. In 1979, it began publication of a review dealing with UFOs, parapsychology, astronomy, astronautics, meteorology, lost civilizations, mysterious disappearances and other unknown phenomena.

ADRUP is a member of the COMITÉ EUROPÉEN DE COORDINATION DE LA RECHERCHE UFOLOGIQUE (CECRU).

## ASSOCIATION FOR THE UNDERSTANDING OF MAN (AUM), P.O. Box 5310, Austin, Texas 78763; telephone number: 512-458-1233.

The purpose of this organization is to promote and finance research into the nature of man and his environment and to educate the public regarding research results and conclusions. Through tax-deductible contributions and sales of literature, the association finances two research divisions, the Center for Parapsychological

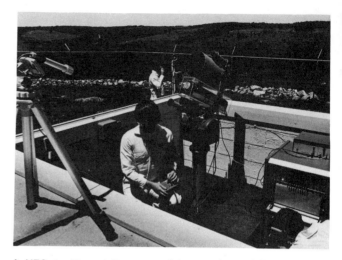

A UFO tracking station manned by members of Project Starlight International, the research division of the Association for the Understanding of Man. *(Courtesy PSI)*

Research and PROJECT STARLIGHT INTERNATIONAL (PSI), involved in the detection and recording of UFO activity. The directors of AUM believe that the scientific solution of the UFO mystery could benefit humanity both materially, in terms of new energy sources and applications, and sociologically, in terms of an expanded world view.

This nonprofit organization was founded in 1971 and has about 1,500 members. Robert P. Dunnam is President. Members receive a periodic newsletter. Other services and benefits available to members include annual membership conferences, lectures and occasional publication of various materials dealing with the physical, mental and spiritual components of humanity.

## ASSOCIATION POUR LA DÉTECTION ET L'ÉTUDE DES PHÉNOMÈNES SPATIAUX (ADEPS), 12 Avenue du Maréchal Joffre, 06160 Juan les Pins, France.

Investigative organization belonging to the COMITÉ EUROPÉEN DE COORDINATION DE LA RECHERCHE UFOLOGIQUE (CECRU).

**ASTRONAUTS.** UFOs were purportedly observed and sometimes photographed during the flights of the MERCURY CAPSULE, MERCURY 7, MERCURY 8, MERCURY 9, the GEMINI CAPSULE, GEMINI 4, GEMINI 7, GEMINI 8, GEMINI 10, GEMINI 11, GEMINI 12, APOLLO 8, APOLLO 11 and APOLLO 12. Astronauts involved in these alleged sightings were Edwin "Buzz" Aldrin, Neil Armstrong, Alan Bean, Frank Borman, Scott Carpenter, Michael Collins, Charles "Pete" Conrad, L. GORDON COOPER, John Glenn, Richard Gordon, JAMES A. LOVELL, James McDivitt, Walter Schirra and John Young. According to officials of the NATIONAL AERO-

NAUTICS AND SPACE ADMINISTRATION (NASA), the agency satisfied itself in every instance that what had been observed was nothing which could be termed abnormal in the space environment. Les Gaver, Chief of the Audio-Visual Branch of the Public Information Division at NASA during the Mercury, Gemini and Apollo programs, states that many of the objects referred to as UFOs were actually reflections, space junk, ice crystals, scratch marks on film, dust on film holders, lights on the ground and other spacecraft and spent boosters. He admits that "there are some frames taken by astronauts that are unexplainable," but he places these in the category of space phenomena such as air glows and AURORAS.

Some astronauts deny reports of their UFO sightings and most assert that they are satisfied by the conventional explanations provided by NASA. It is believed by some UFOlogists that the astronauts have been ordered not to discuss their UFO sightings. One outspoken exception, however, is Gordon Cooper, who believes that extraterrestrial beings visit Earth regularly. He is involved in efforts to end official silence on the matter. Although they were not involved in any UFO sightings, astronauts EUGENE CERNAN, EDGAR MITCHELL and HARRISON SCHMITT have spoken out in support of the possibility that Earth has been visited by extraterrestrials.

Another phenomenon reported by some astronauts was the mysterious flashes seen by Apollo crews. A number of UFOlogists have speculated that these might be signals from aliens in space. While some scientists have attributed them to the stimulating effects of cosmic rays, others have concluded that they were merely optical illusions.

Tapes of the air-to-ground transmissions of all manned space missions are available for review at the Johnson Space Center in Houston, Texas. Some researchers claim, however, that portions referring to UFOs have been removed.

**ASTRONOMERS.** It is a misconception that astronomers do not see UFOs. Old astronomical chronicles contain many reports of unknown objects seen in the heavens. In a 1976 survey of 1356 members of the American Astronomical Society conducted by scientist Peter Sturrock, five percent of the respondents had experienced sightings that they could not explain.

The best known sightings in this category were made by Mexican astronomer José Bonilla in ZACATECAS, MEXICO in 1883, and by the celebrated American astronomer CLYDE TOMBAUGH in 1949.

**ASTRONOMICAL AND METEOROLOGICAL PHENOMENA.** The late astronomer DONALD MEN-

ZEL has been the foremost proponent of the assertion that unusual and little known astronomical and meteorological phenomena play a large role in UFOlogy. The most commonly misidentified phenomena in this category are STARS, PLANETS, METEORS, PARHELIA and PARASELENAE, SUBSUNS and submoons, ICE CRYSTALS, MIRAGES, AURORAS, PLASMA, SAINT ELMO'S FIRE, COMETS and CLOUDS.

**ATIC** *see* **AIR TECHNICAL INTELLIGENCE CENTER**

**ATLANTIS,** legendary island or continent said to have been submerged beneath the waters of the North Atlantic Ocean 12,000 years ago. It was described by the Greek philosopher Plato in two dialogues, the *Timaeus* and the *Critias*. Plato learned of Atlantis from a descendant of the Athenian statesman Solon, who had been told about it by an Egyptian high priest while visiting Egypt. According to this ancient source, the island, which was larger than Libya and Asia put together, lay beyond the Pillars of Hercules, known today as the Straits of Gibraltar. The capital city, Poseidonis, was named after the god of the sea, Poseidon. The symbol of this nation populated by redskinned people was the trident. The highly advanced civilization succumbed to decadence and was destroyed by a tremendous earthquake and devastating tides. The once prosperous continent sank beneath the water. Some writers claim that the time of this alleged cataclysm coincides with that of the great flood reported in the Bible and the religious writings of many other religions.

A host of fables and myths, many of them contradictory, have grown up around the original legend of Atlantis. The BOOK OF DZYAN and purported telepathic communications from a spirit named Phylos the Tibetan profess to give accurate information on the history and culture of the lost continent, including such details as the layout of city streets and a sampling of words from the Atlantean language.

Some writers have placed Atlantis in the Caspian Sea, the North Sea, the Mediterranean and Mongolia. A less exotic theory maintains that Atlantis was an Aegean island whose inhabitants and culture were basically similar to those of its neighboring Greek city-states. However, those who hold that Atlantis was located between America on the one side and Europe and North Africa on the other, cite as evidence the similarities in customs on both sides of the ocean. In particular, they note that the Mayas and the Egyptians both believed their kings were descendants of the sun god. The Mayas and the Incas employed the same art of mummification that was used by the Egyptians and

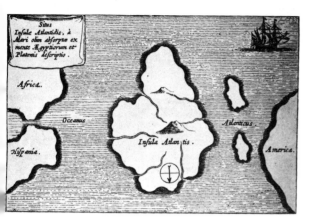

*Below:* Seventeenth century print depicting the lost continent of Atlantis. *(Culver Pictures) Right:* The Bimini Wall. *(Courtesy Peter Tompkins)*

Sumerians. Furthermore, ancient pyramids on both sides of the Atlantic are strikingly similar.

In 1940, Edgar Cayce, the American clairvoyant, predicted that Atlantis would rise in 1968 or 1969 off the coast of Bimini in the Bahamas. Seemingly in accordance with his prediction, gigantic blocks of stone were discovered protruding two feet above the surface of the shifting sand in 1968. These blocks have become known as the Bimini Wall. Further exploration has been carried out by numerous people, including archaeologist J. Manson Valentine, writer Peter Tompkins, archaeologist Robert Brush and Dimitri Rebikoff, Director of the Institute of Marine Technology and President of the Submarine Club of France. Psychics have been employed to locate the sites of possible Atlantean ruins. Lines and mosaic patterns have been found on the ocean floor which seem to indicate the layout of roads, buildings and other structures.

Some researchers today believe that the Atlanteans were technologically superior to our present civilization. They hypothesize that a nuclear explosion sank the continent. Some proponents of the HOLLOW EARTH HYPOTHESIS believe that the survivors escaped in their flying saucers to a subterranean refuge. Others believe that Atlantis still exists today as a flourishing submarine civilization and homeport of flying saucers. A variation on this theory suggests that a submarine Atlantean city serves as a terrestrial base for extraterrestrial ASTRONAUTS.

Bibliography: Chatelain, Maurice, *Our Ancestors Came from Outer Space* (Garden City, N.Y.: Doubleday and Company, 1977); Berlitz, Charles, *The Mystery of Atlantis* (New York: Grosset and Dunlap, 1969); Phylos, *A Dweller on Two Planets* (Alhambra, California: Borden Publishing Company, 1952).

**ATMOSPHERIC ELECTRICITY** *see* **PLASMA**

**ATMOSPHERIC LIFE FORM HYPOTHESIS,** theory that UFOs may be animate creatures indigenous to the atmosphere or to space itself. Such life forms might be amorphous masses of entrapped energy which replenish themselves by feeding on the raw energy abundant in the upper atmosphere in the form of cosmic rays and photons. Because of their great distance from Earth's surface, they would normally be beyond the view of human beings. Additionally, they might exist primarily in a form that is beyond the limited visual range of human eyesight. When descending to lower levels, they might become visible due to the increased friction of a denser atmosphere. Their shapes also might change according to atmospheric density and the speed at which they travel, thus giving us the various shapes associated with UFOs. Their descent to lower levels might be attributed to solar or cosmic cyclic disturbances in the upper atmosphere, invasion of the stratosphere by man-made rockets or the search for free food in industrial areas, where there is a high concentration of power production. If confronted by human beings, these atmospheric life forms could defend themselves with bolts of visible or invisible energy.

A similar concept is supported by writer TREVOR JAMES CONSTABLE, who claims to have photographed "invisible critters" which dwell in a hypothetical invisible world named ETHERIA.

Bibliography: Gaddis, Vincent H., *Mysterious Fires and Lights* (New York: David McKay Company, 1967).

**AUM** *see* **ASSOCIATION FOR THE UNDERSTANDING OF MAN**

**AURORA, TEXAS.** In 1897, the April 19th edition of *The Dallas Morning News* reported that two days previously an airship had flown over Aurora, Texas. Since the celebrated AIRSHIP WAVE had begun five months previously, this fact in itself was not considered particularly unusual. However, on this occasion, the outline of events was somewhat different. Traveling at the slow speed of ten or twelve miles per hour, the craft dropped in altitude until it collided with a windmill belonging to a local judge. A loud explosion scattered debris over several acres and destroyed the windmill, a water tank and the judge's flower garden. The badly disfigured remains of the pilot were picked up. It was evident to the townspeople that he was not of this world. The report claimed that T. J. Weems, a U.S. Army Signal Service officer and an authority on astronomy, identified the pilot as a native of MARS. Papers found on him were written in undecipherable hieroglyphics and were obviously a record of his travels. The fragments of the ship proved to be of an unknown metal, resembling a mixture of aluminum and silver. They were gathered up by the townspeople as souvenirs. The following day the Martian was given a Christian burial.

In 1966, an investigator visited Aurora on behalf of J. ALLEN HYNEK. He discovered that the Masonic Cemetery in Aurora had maintained records showing that every grave was occupied by a human corpse. Moreover, no windmill had been destroyed in the town, for no windmill had ever existed there. T. J. Weems, whose authoritative opinions had been cited, was neither an amateur astronomer nor had he ever been an army officer. He was the town blacksmith. The writer of the original news story, E. E. Haydon, was a part-time reporter for *The Dallas Morning News*. It seems that Haydon had wanted to save Aurora from the decline it was undergoing after being bypassed by a newly built railroad track. He may have hoped that his news report would bring business to the town by attracting tourists.

When interest in his story was revived in 1973 by the INTERNATIONAL UFO BUREAU, tourists did indeed flock to the town. It was claimed that a large rock had been found in the cemetery which indicated the location of the Martian's grave. The rock was engraved with a vague outline of an arrow and three small circles. Unfortunately, when plans were made to analyze the rock to determine the age of the markings, it mysteriously vanished. The International UFO Bureau initiated legal proceedings to exhume the Martian's body, but the Aurora Cemetery Association succeeded in blocking any attempts to start excavating their cemetery.

Enthusiasm for the Aurora case increased when a North Texas State University professor found pieces of metal at the reported crash site. Supposedly, one of the fragments, which consisted mainly of iron, failed to exhibit any magnetic properties. More puzzling was the fact that the metal was said to be shiny and malleable rather than dull and brittle. However, this new piece of evidence proved to be another false lead. Analysis of the fragments by the National Aeronautical Establishment of Canada demonstrated no unusual composition of structural characteristics. The metal was of terrestrial origin.

PHILIP J. KLASS has pointed out that none of the reported fragments of the airship nor the pilot's log have been produced as evidence. Had these items ever existed, they would undoubtedly have been too valuable to destroy or lose. The Aurora case was the first of many unfounded stories about CRASHED FLYING SAUCERS and it was not the last to be exposed as a HOAX.

Bibliography: Klass, Philip J., *UFOs Explained* (New York: Random House, 1974); Hynek, J. Allen, and Jacques Vallee, *The Edge of Reality* (Chicago: Henry Regnery Company, 1975).

## AURORA AUSTRALIS *see* AURORAS

## AURORA BOREALIS *see* AURORAS

**AURORAS,** luminous phenomena of the upper atmosphere. They are caused by the collision of solar particles (guided and accelerated by Earth's magnetic field) with air molecules. The brilliant lights appear in the shapes of curtains, arcs, rays and bands which occasionally flicker and flash. Such displays in the Northern Hemisphere are known as aurora borealis or northern lights. In the Southern Hemisphere, they are called aurora australis or southern lights.

The wide variety of shapes and patterns of auroral displays has led superstitious people in the past to interpret them as both earthly and unearthly images. Descriptions of some auroras are similar to typical modern UFO reports. Authors DONALD MENZEL and

Aurora Borealis observed in Russia on January 21, 1839. *(The Bettman Archive)*

According to witness Laszlo Benedek, he observed this UFO traveling above the water toward the city lights of Perth, Australia, in January 1966. After a few moments, the object reportedly took off vertically at high speed. *(Courtesy ICUFON)*

Ernest Taves have cited as an example a UFO observed throughout England and northern Europe on November 17, 1882. Some witnesses described the light as spindle-shaped, cigar-shaped and discoidal. While a number of observers reported the phenomenon as having no structure, others claimed its outline was clearly-defined. Many described it as glowing. Although the phenomenon caused considerable consternation to many witnesses, astronomers identified it as the aurora borealis.

Bibliography: Menzel, Donald H., and Ernest H. Taves, *The UFO Enigma* (Garden City, N.Y.: Doubleday and Company, 1977).

**AUSTRALIA.** There are several hundred UFO reports per annum in Australia although after investigation eighty-five to ninety percent of these are explained as natural and conventional objects. There are numerous UFO investigative and research organizations in the country and several of them coordinate their activities and file their data with the CENTRE FOR UFO STUDIES—AUSTRALIAN CO-ORDINATION SECTION (ACOS).

One of the most sensational cases which occurred in Australia was that of pilot Frederick Valentich, who in 1978 disappeared in a light plane near MELBOURNE after reporting a UFO.

**AUSTRALIAN CO-ORDINATION SECTION (ACOS)** *see* **CENTRE FOR UFO STUDIES—**

**AUSTRALIAN CO-ORDINATION SECTION (ACOS)**

**AUSTRALIAN FLYING SAUCER REVIEW,** defunct publication of the VICTORIAN UFO RESEARCH SOCIETY (VUFORS), formerly known as the Victorian Flying Saucer Society.

**AUSTRALIAN INTERNATIONAL UFO FLYING SAUCER RESEARCH,** Box 2004, G.P.O., Adelaide, South Australia 5023; telephone number: 08 272 3131.

The purpose of this investigative organization is to correlate, disseminate and tabulate information on unusual UFO sightings as reported by the public. Although the group has a great deal of information on sizes, habits, colors, regions, grid lines and flap periods, it holds no beliefs regarding the identity, origin and purpose of UFOs.

This nonprofit organization, formerly known as the Australian Flying Saucer Research Society, was founded in 1952 by Colin Norris who serves as its Public Relations Officer. Sightings are investigated by qualified personnel, all of whom are university graduates. Branches of the organization are located throughout Australia. Correspondence, magazines and information are exchanged with about seventy-five organizations around the world. A library of 500 books, a tape library and a twelve-inch telescope are available, and public meetings are held monthly. Sixty-four panels of newspaper clippings, collected by Norris and dating back to 1950, are circulated to shopping centers for public display. A quarterly publication, the AUSTRALIAN INTERNATIONAL UFO FLYING SAUCER RESEARCH MAGAZINE, presents analyses of sightings in Australia in addition to other news about UFOs.

## AUSTRALIAN INTERNATIONAL UFO FLYING SAUCER RESEARCH MAGAZINE, publication of AUSTRALIAN INTERNATIONAL UFO FLYING SAUCER RESEARCH.

**AUSTRIA.** Luis Schönherr is the best-known independent researcher in Austria. The MUTUAL UFO NETWORK (MUFON), CENTRALES ERFURSCHUNGS-NETZ AUSSERGEWOHNLICHER PHENOMENE (CENAP) and SKANDINAVISK UFO INFORMATION (SUFOI) have representatives there.

**AUTOKINESIS,** apparent motion of an observed object which can result from uncontrollable, irregular movements of the eyeballs. The movement of UFOs later identified as STARS and PLANETS is often attributed to the autokinetic phenomenon.

Bibliography: Menzel, Donald H., "UFOs—The Modern Myth," in Sagan, Carl, and Thornton Page (eds.), *UFOs—A Scientific Debate* (Ithaca, N.Y.: Cornell University Press, 1972).

Object photographed by Rudolph Nagora in Deutschlandsberg, Austria, on May 23, 1971. *(Courtesy ICUFON/ A. Geigenthaler)*

**AUTOSTASIS,** apparent cessation of motion of an observed traveling object resulting from irregular movements of the eyeballs as they attempt to follow. This phenomenon has led observers of artificial SATELLITES to report them as UFOs which make repeated stops on their flight paths.

Bibliography: Menzel, Donald H., "UFOs—The Modern Myth," in Sagan, Carl, and Thornton Page (eds.), *UFOs—A Scientific Debate* (Ithaca, N.Y.: Cornell University Press, 1972).

**AUTRE MONDE, L',** French magazine, published monthly and available at newsstands. Subjects dealt with include UFOs, the occult and parapsychology. The editorial offices are located at 23 rue Clauzel, Paris 75009, France.

The avro-car on display at the Army Transportation Museum at Fort Eustis, Virginia.

**AVRO-CAR,** saucer-shaped craft built by a Canadian firm, the A.V. Roe Company, for the United States armed forces. Two avro-cars, developed as part of an experimental program in the construction of vertical take-off and landing (VTOL) craft, were built. However, after ten million dollars had been invested in the project it was abandoned as a failure. During tests in 1960, the craft was not able to rise more than four feet above the ground and was difficult to control. The avro-car measures eighteen feet in diameter and weighs 3,600 pounds. It was powered by three gas turbine engines located in the center of the vehicle. This man-made flying saucer is now on display at the Army Transportation Museum at Fort Eustis, Virginia.

**AWARDS** *see* **CUTTY SARK** and **ROBERT LOFTIN MEMORIAL AWARD**

**AWARENESS,** publication of CONTACT INTERNATIONAL.

**BAALBECK, LEBANON,** site of ancient ruins. Huge stone platforms, some weighing as much as a thousand tons, have been speculatively identified as launching pads for the craft of ANCIENT ASTRONAUTS by some researchers. The theory was first proposed by Russian Modest Agrest in an article in Moscow's *Literaturnaya Gazeta* in 1959. Agrest claims that vitrified stones found in the area were probably caused by the fiery exhaust of spaceships. The purpose of the gigantic blocks was to shield the inhabitants of Baalbeck from radiation emitted by the nuclear powered craft.

Bibliography: Bergier, Jacques, *Extraterrestrial Visitations from Prehistoric Times to the Present* (Chicago: Henry Regnery Company, 1973).

**BAKER, ROBERT M. L.,** Jr. (b. September 1, 1930, Los Angeles, California; address: 8123 Tuscany Avenue, Plaza del Rey, California 90291; telephone number: 213-823-4143), scientist and engineer.

Baker was one of six speakers who presented testimony at the HOUSE SCIENCE AND ASTRONAUTICS COMMITTEE HEARINGS on unidentified flying objects in 1968. He described the problems incurred in his examinations and analyses of several UFO movies, including the TREMONTON, UTAH and the GREAT FALLS, MONTANA films. Despite previous explanations of the filmed objects as conventional objects and despite the problems of analysis, Baker stated his conviction that they demonstrated the presence of anomalistic phenomena. Baker made several suggestions on how to achieve more sophisticated analyses of fresh data and, in particular, recommended setting up a task force to obtain hard and soft data supported by a sensor system designed expressly for that purpose, possibly a phased array RADAR, as well as a space-based long-wavelength infrared surveillance sensor system. He also suggested a study be made of the psychiatric and medical problems of determining witnesses' credibility. Baker declares he has no opinion regarding the identity of UFOs because of the continued absence of reliable and conclusive observational data.

Baker received his B.A. in Physics and Mathematics from UCLA in 1954 and was elected to Phi Beta Kappa. In 1956, he was granted an M.A. in Physics and was the recipient of the UCLA Physics Prize. In 1958, he received a Ph.D. in Astronomy and Engineering, the first of its kind to be granted in the nation, with a specialty in orbital mechanics. He was the recipient of the 1976 Dirk Brouwer Award for outstanding contribution to the fields of Astrodynamics and Flight Mechanics.

From 1957 to 1960, Baker was a Senior Scientist at Aeronutronic-Philco-Ford, where he was in charge of the analysis effort for the original Spacetrack System. In 1960, he published the first astrodynamics textbook to be published in the United States. From 1960 and 1961, he was a Project Officer at AFBMD (now SAMSO) where he managed studies in the SAINT follow-on program. From 1961 to 1964, Baker was Head of Lockheed's Astrodynamics Research Center. In 1964, he joined Computer Sciences Corporation and continued research in astrodynamics. He developed the preliminary orbit methods termed the Lagrange-Gauss-Gibbs and Herget's Variation of Geocentric distances utilized by Grumman Aerospace Corporation in their orbit-determination programs. These orbit methods were included in another textbook published by Baker in 1967, *Astrodynamics, Applications and Advanced Topics.*

Baker represented the United States Air Force at the International Astronautical Federation meeting in Stockholm, Sweden, in 1961, represented the United

States at the International Union of Theoretical and Applied Mechanics European Conferences in 1962 and 1965, and was an invitee to the Astronomical Council of the Academy of Sciences of the Soviet Union in Moscow in 1967. From 1961 to 1964, he was the National Chairman of the Astrodynamics Technical Committee of the American Institute of Aeronautics and Astronautics.

Baker has been the Editor of the *Journal of the Astronautical Sciences* since 1963, and he was the joint editor of the *Proceedings* of the 1961 Intern International Astronautical Federation Congress.

Baker was on the faculty of the Department of Astronomy at UCLA from 1959 to 1963. From 1963 to 1971, he was on the faculty of the Department of Engineering at UCLA and associated with the USAF Academy, where he offered courses in astronautics, fluid mechanics and structural mechanics. He is a Trustee of West Coast University and Chairman of their Executive Committee.

# BALLESTER-OLMOS, VICENTE-JUAN (b. December 27, 1948, Valencia, Spain; address: Guardia Civil 9 D–16, Valencia 10, Spain; telephone number: 3613108), manufacturing analyst and writer.

Ballester-Olmos believes that the available data indicates that the UFO phenomenon has a real and objective physical nature. He thinks that the working hypothesis which best fits the phenomenology is the EXTRATERRESTRIAL INTELLIGENCE HYPOTHESIS (ETH).

Ballester-Olmos studied physical sciences for three years at the Faculty of Sciences at the University of Valencia. He received a degree in Technical Engineering from the Polytechnic University of Valencia and a degree in Computer Programming from the Faculty of Philosophy at the University of Valencia.

Vicente-Juan Ballester Olmos.

In 1976, Ballester-Olmos began working as an Analyst in the Manufacturing Cost Analysis Department of Ford of Spain. Since 1978, he has been Senior Analyst for Projects and Reporting in the Financial Analysis Department of Ford of Spain.

Ballester-Olmos is a member of the Editorial Board of UFO PHENOMENA. His articles have been published in numerous UFO magazines. He is author of *A Catalogue of 200 Type-I UFO Events in Spain and Portugal* (Evanston, Illinois: Center for UFO Studies [CUFOS], 1976); and *OVNIS: El Fenomeno Aterrizaje* (Barcelona: Plaza & Janes S.A., 1978).

## BALL LIGHTNING *see* PLASMA

**BALLOONS.** Several hundred balloons are released each day from military and civilian airports, weather stations and research installations around the world. There are several types of balloons, including RADIOSONDE balloons, PIBAL balloons, SKYHOOK BALLOONS, weather balloons and large research balloons which have diameters up to 300 feet. Research balloons are most noticeable around sunrise or sunset when they reflect sunlight and may appear to be self-luminous. Reflected sunlight, moonlight or city lights may cause a balloon's surface to look white, gray, red, amber, silver or metallic. Some balloons carry small lights to alert pilots to their presence. They can assume the shape of a disk, a sphere, a lens, a cone, a teardrop, a pear, a parachute or a sausage. TEMPERATURE INVERSIONS can create a double image of a balloon. Pairs or clusters of balloons may give the impression of an intelligently controlled fleet of UFOs. As balloons change altitude, they are carried along by the prevailing winds. Varying wind streams can cause them to change speed, change direction, trace circles and hover. High altitude jet wind streams can carry balloons along at up to 150 miles per hour. When balloons develop a leak, they may descend rapidly and then level off, giving the impression that they are under intelligent control. The extreme cold of high altitudes may cause balloons to burst and vanish, as though teleported into another dimension.

An observer watching a balloon many thousands of feet overhead cannot accurately determine the object's true height, diameter, distance or speed. This problem is compounded at night when there are fewer visible reference points by which to evaluate the measurements and flight characteristics of the balloon.

To correlate UFO sightings with balloon flights, investigators can check the lists of standard weekly launch times maintained by local U.S. Weather Service stations and Base Weather Service stations at local military air bases.

Four different types of atmospheric research balloons.
*(NCAR Photos)*

In some cases, hot-air balloons have been deliberately sent aloft with candles inside to create a mysterious glow. Nighttime hot-air balloons are usually described as floating orange balls which sometimes burn up, dropping pieces of melted, burning candles. Because of the scarcity of reference points in the sky, these HOAXES have often caused as much confusion as legitimate research and weather balloons.

Bibliography: Menzel, Donald H., and Lyle G. Boyd, *The World of Flying Saucers* (Garden City, N.Y.: Doubleday and Company, 1963); Klass, Philip J., *UFOs Explained* (New York: Random House, 1974).

## BANCHS, ROBERTO ENRIQUE LUIS (b. July 15, 1952, Buenos Aires, Argentina; address: Casilla de Correos No. 9, Suc. 26 (1426), Buenos Aires, Argentina), Cofounder and Director of the CENTRO DE ESTUDIOS DE FENÓMENOS AÉREOS INUSUALES (CEFAI).

Banchs holds that UFOs represent an unknown phenomenon of an apparently intelligent nature. However, he cautions that there is no scientific evidence to support any of the popular theories regarding the identity of UFOs. Banchs has seen disk-shaped UFOs on three occasions in 1967, 1978 and 1979.

Banchs received his Masters degree in Architecture from the University of Belgrano in 1978. He worked for the Compania Argentina de Construcciones Metalicas in 1977 and from 1978 to 1979 was an investigator for the Biology Department of the Centro de Documentación Cientifica. In 1979, he worked as an investigator for the Instituto de Ingenieria Solar. He is a Professor of Educational Audio-Visual Media at the Centro de Ensenanza de Alta Capacitación.

Banchs has been a student of UFOLOGY since 1965 and founded CEFAI in 1972. He conducts field investigations and is a contributor to numerous foreign publications. He is author of *Fenómenos Aéreos Inusuales* (Buenos Aires: CEFAI, 1973); *Las Evidencias del Fenómeno OVNI* (Buenos Aires: Editorial Alonso, 1975); and *La Fenomenología Humanoide en la Argentina* (Buenos Aires: Siu, 1977).

## BARKER, GRAY (b. May 2, 1925, Riffle, West Virginia; address Box 2228, Clarksburg, West Virginia 26301; telephone number: 304-622-4524), publisher.

Barker adheres to no specific theory regarding the identity of UFOs and has never witnessed one himself.

Barker received his B.A. from Glenville State College in 1947. He was a public school teacher from 1948 to 1949, a sales agent for theatrical equipment from 1950 to 1952, and a theatre booker, theatre owner and publisher from 1952 until the present.

As the manager of the SAUCERIAN PRESS, he has been responsible for the publication of a very large number of

Gray Barker.

books about UFOs and flying saucers. He is President of the SAUCERS AND UNEXPLAINED CELESTIAL EVENTS RESEARCH SOCIETY (SAUCERS), and has published several magazines, including THE SAUCERIAN BULLETIN, SAUCER NEWS and *Spacecraft News*. He currently edits and publishes *Gray Barker's Newsletter*, which deals with UFOs.

Barker is a member of the NATIONAL UFO CONGRESS (NUFOC), the National Audio-Visual Association and the Mountaineer Educational Media Association. He was the recipient of a Sales Award from the Technicolor Corporation and the ROBERT LOFTIN MEMORIAL AWARD in 1971.

Barker has written numerous articles and is author of *They Knew Too Much About Flying Saucers* (New York: University Books, 1956); *Gray Barker's Book of Saucers* (Clarksburg, West Virginia: Saucerian Books, 1965); *The Book of Spaceships in Their Relationship with the Earth* (Los Angeles, DeVorss and Company, 1967); *The Silver Bridge* (Clarksburg, West Virginia: Saucerian Books, 1970); and *Gray Barker at Giant Rock* (Clarksburg, West Virginia: Saucerian Books, 1974). He is editor of *The Strange Case of Morris K. Jessup* (Clarksburg, West Virginia: Saucerian Books, 1963); and *Gray Barker's Book of Adamski* (Clarksburg, West Virginia: Saucerian Books, 1967).

## BASEL, SWITZERLAND, location of a UFO sighting on August 7, 1566. At sunrise numerous large, black, red and orange fiery globes appeared in the sky. After dancing about with irregular motions, they faded away rapidly.

Bibliography: Jung, Carl G., *Flying Saucers: A Modern Myth of Things Seen in the Sky* (New York: Harcourt Brace and Company, 1959).

Black, red and orange fiery globes seen over Basel, Switzerland, on August 7, 1566. *(Courtesy ICUFON)*

**BATTELLE MEMORIAL INSTITUTE,** a private research group. In 1952, a boom year for UFO reports, EDWARD RUPPELT, as chief of PROJECT BLUE BOOK, contracted with the Battelle Memorial Institute to carry out a statistical study of UFO characteristics. The purpose of the study was to determine if anything in the air represented technological developments not known to this country, and to build a model of a flying saucer from the data. The report was completed in 1953 and concluded that UFOs did not seem to represent anything unknown or outside the capabilities of human technology. The researchers reported that they could not derive a verified model of a flying saucer from the data that had been gathered to date.

**BEAD LIGHTNING** *see* **CHAIN LIGHTNING**

**BEAN, ALAN,** *see* **APOLLO 12**

**BEAN, ORSON,** television personality whose UFO sighting in September 1968 reportedly changed his life. Bean and his wife, Carolyn, were driving near Patchogue, Long Island, when they saw a golden light hovering over the ocean. It was evening. Although the light had a strange metallic quality, the skeptical Bean decided that it must be a STAR. Suddenly, the "star" moved at an incredible speed that Bean estimated to be about 5,000 miles per hour. The UFO then stopped abruptly. Bean realized that this was neither a star nor a man-made object. As the amazed couple watched, the object suddenly shot upwards at thousands of miles per hour and disappeared. They estimated the object to have been about ten miles away prior to its departure. Bean was convinced that he had seen an extraterrestrial craft of some sort. The couple began to rethink their values and their priorities. They felt a need to open their minds to new experiences. They sold their house

and moved to Australia for fifteen months. When they returned to the United States, they spent the next three years traveling around the country. Bean describes the sighting as an inspiring and liberating experience.

**BEARMAN** *see* **BIGFOOT**

**BEAUMONT, TEXAS,** *see* **WILSON**

**BEAVER, PENNSYLVANIA,** location of an alleged UFO sighting by two teenage boys on August 8, 1965. One of the boys, James Lucci, took two PHOTOGRAPHS of the disk-shaped object as it moved across the sky to the right of the MOON. After duplicating the photograph using a white plate, computer systems analyst ROBERT SHEAFFER concluded that it was a HOAX.

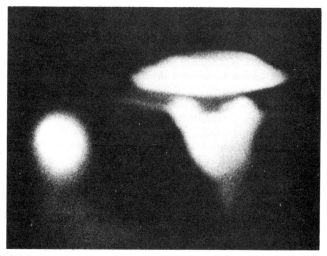

Alleged UFO photographed in Beaver, Pennsylvania, on August 8, 1965. *(Courtesy ICUFON)*

**BECKLEY, TIMOTHY GREEN** (b. July 13, 1947, New Brunswick, New Jersey; address: Suite 1306, 303 Fifth Avenue, New York, N.Y. 10016; telephone number: 212-685-4080), writer, editor and UFOlogist.

Although Beckley has seen several nocturnal lights, he has not seen any UFOs that could be described as spaceships. However, based on his fifteen years of researching the phenomenon, he holds that many of the best UFO-related incidents have been kept from the public because the "powers that be" realize drastic changes will take place in society once we've "linked up" with the cosmos. Once open contact has been established, he claims, civilization as we know it will collapse and there will be a NEW AGE on Earth.

During his career, Beckley has booked rock groups, coproduced a UFO convention, run the School of

Occult Arts and Science for two years and sponsored lectures on psychic phenomena. He has worked as Contributing Editor for FLYING SAUCERS, Managing Editor for *Manhattan Gazette*, Managing Editor for BEYOND REALITY, Managing Editor for SAUCER NEWS, Contributing Editor for SEARCH, Contributing Editor for *Rock*, Movie Review Columnist for *Hustler*, Columnist for UFO REPORT and Editor of UFO REVIEW. He is a stringer for THE NATIONAL ENQUIRER, and President of Global Communications, a worldwide news feature service which supplies materials to 150 publications in more than fifteen countries. He is Founder of the UFO INVESTIGATORS LEAGUE (UFOIL), and runs the UFO NEWS SERVICE, which publishes the bimonthly tabloid UFO REVIEW and UFO books, as well as distributing audio cassette tapes on UFOs. He has appeared on worldwide radio and television shows.

His numerous articles have been published in many newspapers and magazines. He is author of *Inside the Saucers* (New Brunswick, N.J.: Interplanetary News Service, 1962); *The Shaver Mystery and the Inner Earth Mystery* (Clarksburg, West Virginia: Saucerian Press, 1967); *UFOs Around the World* (New York: Global Communications, 1968); *The Boys from Topside* (Clarksburg, West Virginia: Saucerian Press, 1969); *The Book of Space Brothers* (Clarksburg, West Virginia: Science Research Publishing, 1969); *People of the Planet Clarion* (Clarksburg, West Virginia: Saucerian Press, 1970); *Men in Black—the Aliens Among Us* (New York: Global Communications, 1978).

## BEDE THE VENERABLE, SAINT (673–738

A.D.), Anglo-Saxon theologian, historian and chronologist whose *Historia ecclesiastica gentis Anglorum* contains several references to beams of light which stretched between the sky and human corpses. On one occasion, a light from heaven played over the body of a drowned abbot for several nights. These events were interpreted as the passing of the soul into heaven. Modern UFOLOGISTS, however, have considered the possibility that the beams of light were emitted by UFOs. If this were the case, no explanation has been offered for the UFONAUTS' interest in observing dead human beings.

Bibliography: Drake, W. Raymond, *Gods and Spacemen throughout History* (Chicago: Henry Regnery Company, 1975).

## BEHRENDT, KENNETH WALTER (b. May 10, 1951, Elizabeth, New Jersey; address: 274 Second Street, Elizabeth, New Jersey 07206; telephone number: 201-352-6761), Founder and Director of PROJECT TO RESEARCH OBJECTS, THEORIES, EXTRATERRESTRIALS AND UNUSUAL SIGHTINGS (PROTEUS).

Behrendt has studied UFOLOGY since the age of fourteen. He believes UFOs are extraterrestrial spaceships that use bases under the oceans and on the moons of our solar system.

Behrendt received his B.A. in Chemistry from Rutgers University in 1973. He is doing graduate work at the Rutgers University Graduate School of Chemistry. He has held a variety of industrial positions in the electronics and chemical fields in northern New Jersey. His special interests are problems in atomic and molecular structure, electronics and computer systems.

## BELGIUM. Both the English term "UFO" and the French term "OVNI" are used in Belgium. Flying saucers are referred to by the Dutch name "vliegende schotel."

Colonel R. Soufnonguel, Chief of the Operations Branch of the Belgian Air Force, estimates that there are between one and fifty UFO reports each year in Belgium. A number of organizations exist to investigate sightings. Belgium's best-known authority on the subject is JACQUES BONABOT.

## BENDER, ALBERT K., *see* INTERNATIONAL FLYING SAUCER BUREAU (IFSB)

## BENTWATERS AND LAKENHEATH, ENGLAND, Royal Air Force (RAF) stations where a series of radar/visual UFO sightings occurred on the night of August 13–14, 1956.

At approximately 9:30 P.M., a RADAR operator at Bentwaters RAF station observed a strong radar echo moving in a northwesterly direction across his scope at several thousand miles per hour. At about the same time, one of his associates observed twelve to fifteen targets moving together at speeds ranging from 80-to-125 miles per hour. The twelve to fifteen unidentified objects, spread over a distance of six to seven miles, were preceded by three objects in triangular formation at a distance of one thousand feet from each other. The blips were located approximately eight miles southwest of the station. When they had reached a point about fourteen miles northeast of the station, their intensity faded. At a distance of approximately forty miles northeast of the station, the blips merged into a single radar echo whose intensity was described as several times greater than that of a B–36 return under similar conditions. After remaining motionless for ten to fifteen minutes, the single blip resumed its northeasterly motion for another five or six miles. It stopped for three to five minutes, then moved northward until it passed beyond the sixty-mile range of the scope at 9:55 P.M. Five minutes later, another blip was seen moving from east to west at a speed estimated to be more than 12,000 miles per hour.

Two Lockheed T–33 fighters, which searched the area from approximately 9:30 to 9:45 P.M., unaided by airborne radar, were unable to locate any aerial objects which might have accounted for the mysterious radar blips. A small light observed visually for a one-hour period by a control tower sergeant is presumed by most investigators to have been the PLANET MARS. However, another blurred light seen by control tower personnel as it passed overhead at terrific speed was observed concurrently by the pilot of a C–47 aircraft flying at an altitude of 4,000 feet. The pilot described the object as a bright light which streaked westward underneath him.

At 10:55 P.M., the Bentwaters radar station alerted the Lakenheath station about forty miles to the northwest. It was not until ten minutes after midnight that the first unidentified target was seen by Lakenheath radar operators. The blip moved from a position approximately six miles west of the station to a point about twenty miles southwest. There it stopped. Oddly, it remained visible on the scope even while the Moving Target Indicator (MTI) was in operation. Writer PHILIP KLASS has suggested that this was an indication that the MTI was not functioning properly, since only moving targets should have appeared on the radar screen. After about five minutes, the blip accelerated instantaneously to a speed of 400 to 600 miles per hour, traveling northward until it stopped about twenty miles northwest of the Lakenheath station. It continued changing location, always traveling in a straight line at about 600 miles per hour, resting at each spot for three to six minutes. The object's speed was always constant when moving, with no acceleration or deceleration when starting or stopping. The changes in location varied from eight to twenty miles in length.

Finally, a De Havilland Venom was scrambled from an RAF base at Waterbeach, some twenty miles southwest of Lakenheath. The pilot located the target on his radarscope and concurrently observed a bright white light in the sky. When he lost radar and visual contact with the object, the ground controllers directed him toward another target ten miles east of Lakenheath. Again the pilot reported radar contact but, as he approached, the target vanished. The ground controllers advised him that the UFO had moved behind him. The interceptor took evasive action but was unable to shake off the object. Running low on fuel, the pilot headed back to Waterbeach. The UFO followed for a short distance and then stopped. A second Venom was scrambled, but was unable to make contact in the short time before a malfunction forced it to return to base. The last radar unknown was seen at about 3:30 A.M., six hours after the first sighting at Bentwaters.

It was later reported that UNITED STATES AIR FORCE (USAF) ground observers stationed at Lakenheath had seen a luminous object traveling toward the southwest. The UFO had stopped, then moved away toward the east, disappearing in the distance. Sometime afterwards, two moving white lights were seen to merge and take off as one object. The PROJECT BLUE BOOK report does not specify the time of these visual observations.

The Bentwaters-Lakenheath case is considered one of the most significant radar-visual UFO sightings on record. Klass has suggested that the visual sightings may be attributable to the Perseid METEOR shower which was at its peak during that period. He points out that official reports of the incident indicate that the interceptor pilot, alone in the two-seater plane, was performing the difficult task of operating the radar from the pilot's seat. Furthermore, it was evident that he was not familiar with the capabilities of the aircraft's radar system. With regard to ground radar, Klass's investigations have shown that some of the complex equipment was still in the developmental stages and could not be considered totally reliable. British radar specialist E.P. Hall has stated that TEMPERATURE INVERSIONS and flocks of migrating BIRDS are a frequent source of radar ANGELS in the Bentwaters-Lakenheath area. Endorsing Klass's deductions, the late astronomer DONALD MENZEL concluded that the unidentified blip seen following the Venom interceptor was caused by the radar signal bouncing from the plane to some unidentified ground target, then back to the plane. Thus, the two blips represented a direct echo from the plane and a delayed echo from the plane via the ground.

However, since visual sightings by ground observers at Lakenheath seem to confirm the radar sightings of aerial objects performing unconventional maneuvers, many UFOLOGISTS consider this to be one of the best established and most puzzling of UFO cases.

Bibliography: McDonald, James E., "Science in Default: Twenty-two Years of Inadequate UFO Investigations," in Sagan, Carl, and Thornton Page (eds.), UFO's—A Scientific Debate (Ithaca, N.Y.: Cornell University Press, 1972); Klass, Philip J., UFOs Explained (New York: Random House, 1974).

**BERLITZ, CHARLES F.** (b. November 23, 1914, New York, N.Y.), author.

Berlitz is one of the chief proponents of the theory that the disappearances of ships and aircraft in the BERMUDA TRIANGLE might be connected with the UFO phenomenon.

Grandson of the founder of the Berlitz language schools, Berlitz has a working knowledge of about thirty languages. He received his B.A. magna cum laude from Yale in 1936. During World War II, he served as an army officer, achieving the rank of Captain, in the counter-intelligence corps in Europe and Latin America. As Vice-President of the Berlitz Schools of Languages and of Berlitz Publications, he has written and edited more than fifty textbooks, tourist phrase books and pocket dictionaries. His interest in archaeology and scuba diving led him to the study of UFOLOGY and the legends of Atlantis. He is author of *The Mystery of Atlantis* (New York: Grosset and Dunlap, 1969); *Mysteries from Forgotten Worlds* (New York: Dell Publishing Company, 1973); and *The Bermuda Triangle* (Garden City, N.Y.: Doubleday and Company, 1974).

**BERMUDA TRIANGLE,** an area of the Atlantic Ocean where the high number of lost ships and airplanes has been attributed to a mysterious but unknown cause. It is also known as the Devil's Triangle, the Graveyard of the Atlantic, the Hoodoo Sea, Limbo of the Lost, Triangle of Death, Triangle of Tragedy, Pentagon of Death and Port of the Missing. The SARGASSO SEA, within the Bermuda Triangle, is an area in which sometimes only the crew and passengers of ships disappear, leaving their vessels to flounder in the free-floating *Sargassum* seaweed. The DEVIL'S SEA, to the southeast of Japan, has earned a reputation similar to that of the Bermuda Triangle. These areas are two of twelve vile VORTICES established by IVAN SANDERSON.

Authors CHARLES BERLITZ and John Wallace Spencer are the chief proponents of the Bermuda Triangle mystery. According to Berlitz, the Bermuda Triangle extends from Bermuda in the north to southern Florida, and then east to a point through the Bahamas past Puerto Rico to about forty degrees west longitude and then back again to Bermuda. Spencer, who prefers the name Limbo of the Lost, plots the area's boundary from Cape May, New Jersey, straight out to the edge of the continental shelf, following the continental shelf around Florida, through the Florida Straits into the Gulf of Mexico, through the Antilles and north again, including a 440-mile circumference around Bermuda. Other writers claim that the Bermuda Triangle is lozenge-shaped and extends all the way from the Gulf of Mexico to the Azores.

Although ships and airplanes have been known to disappear throughout the world, Berlitz and Spencer claim that such occurrences within the Bermuda Triangle are mysterious because usually no SOS call is sent out and wreckage and bodies are not found. Some pilots and seamen have reported electromagnetic disturbances and a strange effect known as "white water" which blends with a misty sky in such a way that the horizon is indistinguishable.

Reportedly, more than one hundred craft and one thousand people have vanished in the Bermuda Triangle. Writer Lawrence Kusche has pointed out that some of the cases used as evidence occurred hundreds of miles away from the Bermuda Triangle. Since the area is heavily traveled, it is not unfeasible that a fairly large number of craft would be lost, particularly since weather conditions in that part of the world are unpredictable. The local coast guard has attributed reported compass deviations to the fact that the area is one of two places on Earth where a magnetic compass does point towards true north. Normally, it points toward magnetic north. The amount of declination changes by as much as twenty degrees as one circumnavigates the globe and if not compensated for, could dangerously confuse a navigator. Search planes cannot thoroughly comb the area for survivors or wreckage since the area is too vast. Kusche has concluded that the mystery is a manufac-

The U.S.S. Cyclops, lost in the Bermuda Triangle on March 4, 1918. *(Courtesy ICUFON)*

British vessel, also named *Cyclops,* lost during World War II. *(Courtesy ICUFON)*

tured one based on careless research which has been perpetuated by repeated narration until it assumed an aura of truth.

Among those who believe the mystery is not fabricated, the most popular theory about its source concerns UFOs. Reportedly, the incidence of UFO sightings in the Bermuda Triangle is extremely high. In many cases, UFOs are seen entering and leaving the water. It has been suggested that extraterrestrial or submarine civilizations kidnap people and craft for food, slavery, scientific experiments, zoological specimens, museum displays or for some human skill which they do not possess. Some suspect that a space-time warp may exist in the Bermuda Triangle through which ships and airplanes slip into a different dimension. Others suggest that the ruins of ATLANTIS lie on the ocean floor. They hypothesize that an Atlantean power source may still be functioning, switched on and off arbitrarily by ocean currents or some other force. When the device is operating, craft in the area may be sucked down below the water's surface or blasted out of Earth's atmosphere into space. There are a number of variations on these themes in addition to less popular theories.

The account traditionally used as a prime example of the Bermuda Triangle's treachery concerns FLIGHT 19, which vanished in 1945.

Bibliography: Berlitz, Charles, *The Bermuda Triangle* (Garden City, N.Y.: Doubleday and Company, 1974); Spencer, John Wallace, *Limbo of the Lost* (New York: Bantam Books, 1973); Kusche, Lawrence D., *The Bermuda Triangle Mystery—Solved* (New York: Harper and Row, 1975).

**BETHURUM, TRUMAN,** CONTACTEE who allegedly encountered a spacecraft and its occupants in the Nevada desert in 1952. The ship's captain was a beautiful woman named Aura Rhane. The aliens supposedly came from the PLANET Clarion, hidden from Earth by the MOON. Shortly before his death, Bethurum described his contacts with the Clarionites in a book entitled *Aboard a Flying Saucer* (Los Angeles: De Vorss and Company, 1954).

**BETS** *see* **WAGERS**

**BEYOND REALITY MAGAZINE.** This bimonthly magazine was established in 1972, has a circulation of 190,000 and is available at newsstands and by subscription. The range of subjects covered includes UFOs, parapsychology, astronomy, astrology, archaeology, spiritualism and reincarnation.

Articles are written by staff writers and freelance writers. Additional material is obtained from newspaper clippings, United Press International and investigators.

Guidelines for writers are supplied upon receipt of a self-addressed, stamped envelope. Articles between 2,000 and 3,000 words in length should be submitted with a self-addressed, stamped envelope, and payment is made upon publication at a rate of three cents per word for the acquisition of all rights.

Harry Belil is the Editor and Publisher. His publishing company, BRM Publications, Inc., is located at 303 West 42nd Street, New York, N.Y. 10036, and the telephone number is 212-265-1676.

**B–47** *see* **SOUTH CENTRAL UNITED STATES**

**BFSB** *see* **BRITISH FLYING SAUCER BUREAU**

**BIBLICAL UFOs,** aerial phenomena interpreted in the Bible as religious apparitions or visions but which are considered by proponents of the ANCIENT ASTRONAUTS hypothesis as possible evidence of extraterrestrial visitors in ancient times. Biblical passages frequently quoted as examples are those dealing with ANGELS, the ARK OF THE COVENANT, ELIJAH, ENOCH, EZEKIEL, JACOB, JONAH, MOSES, SAINT PAUL, SODOM AND GOMORRAH and the STAR OF BETHLEHEM.

Bibliography: Jessup, Morris K., *The UFO and the Bible* (New York: Citadel Press, 1956); Downing, Barry H., *The Bible and Flying Saucers* (Philadelphia: J. B. Lippincott Company, 1967); Brasington, Virginia F., *Flying Saucers in the Bible* (Clarksburg, West Virginia: Saucerian Press, 1963).

**BIGFOOT,** American name of a legendary anthropoid creature also known as the abominable snowman, the yeti, sasquatch, alma, mono grande, yowie, oh-man, bearman and the abominable woodman. Proponents of the existence of bigfoot hypothesize that the creature

Bigfoot statue at Willowcreek, California. *(Courtesy Donn Davison)*

Alleged bigfoot photographed in 1967 by Roger Patterson at Bluff Creek in northern California.

may be an unknown species of ape or a missing link between ape and man. The large, hairy humanoids, usually between six and nine feet tall and weighing up to 800 pounds, have been reported in the United States, South America, the Himalayas, Russia and Australia.

It is not known whether all the reports refer to an animal of the same breed. However, all the creatures share with man the practice of walking upright. Bigfeet have large feet and hands, their feet measuring about fourteen-to-sixteen inches in length. Their bodies are entirely covered with hair except for their faces, the palms of their hands and the soles of their feet. Their faces resemble human faces rather than those of gorillas, although their black or brown eyes are very large. A strong, unpleasant odor has frequently been associated with bigfeet.

The earliest report of a possible bigfoot sighting involved the eleventh century Nordic explorer, Leif Erikson. Reportedly, during his first landing in the New World, Erikson and his men encountered creatures that were described as "horribly ugly, hairy, swarthy and with great black eyes." During the nineteenth century, numerous newspaper stories told of encounters with large apelike creatures in the American Pacific Northwest. Reports of bigfoot sightings continue today but no conclusive evidence has been found to prove the existence of the shy creature. Plaster casts have been made of gigantic footprints purportedly belonging to bigfeet. The most celebrated photographic evidence is the twenty-eight feet of sixteen-millimeter color movie footage of an alleged female bigfoot, filmed in 1967 by Roger Patterson at Bluff Creek in northern California.

The footage, blurred and unsteady, shows a large, hairy, upright figure walking with an unusual gait from left to right, turning once to look in the direction of the camera and then disappearing into the trees. Whether this film represents a bona fide bigfoot or a man wearing a furry suit is still disputed. Pointing out that the subject in the film has hairy breasts, some skeptics have concluded that the film is a HOAX based on the fact that apes do not have breasts and human breasts are not hairy.

Bigfoot reports are most common in remote, wild areas. However, some reports have come from relatively well populated areas of the United States such as Illinois, Florida and Pennsylvania. An ongoing search for bigfoot in the vast forested region of the American Pacific Northwest is headed by Peter Byrne, Founder of the International Wildlife Conservation Society and a former big game hunter in India and Nepal. He is a full-time bigfoot hunter who hunts with a camera instead of a gun. Byrne and his associates are based at the Dalles, Oregon, where they run the Bigfoot Information Center and the Bigfoot Museum and Exhibition.

Supposedly, UFOs have frequently been observed around bigfoot sighting areas. This has led to the theory that bigfoot may actually be UFOnauts, UFOnauts' pets or participants in experiments being carried out by UFOnauts.

Some writers have suggested that giants referred to in the Bible may be the creatures we call bigfoot today. They quote Genesis 6:4, which states, "There were giants in the earth in those days; and also after that, when the sons of God came in unto the daughters of men, and they bore children to them. . . ." It has been speculated that extraterrestrials mated with bigfeet to produce the human race. As supportive evidence, proponents of this theory point out that in Chapter 25 of Genesis, the Lord told Rebecca that two nations were in her womb. When she gave birth to twins, "the first came out red, all over like an hairy garment."

Bibliography: Byrne, Peter, *The Search for Bigfoot— Monster, Myth or Man?* (Washington, D.C.: Acropolic Books, 1975); Hunter, Don, with René Dahinden, *Sasquatch* (New York: New American Library, 1975).

**BIOLUMINESCENCE,** emission of cold light by living organisms such as insects and fish. It has been suggested that this phenomenon might explain some reports of UFOs and UNIDENTIFIED SUBMARINE OBJECTS (USOs).

**BIRDS.** Some visual UFO reports have been attributed to birds reflecting sunlight during the daytime and city lights at nighttime. In 1951, groups of lights passed regularly over LUBBOCK, TEXAS, causing great bewilderment until it was discovered they were plover reflecting a new type of street lighting from their white breasts. In 1952, a Navy photographer filmed a group of UFOs near TREMONTON, UTAH. The UNITED STATES AIR FORCE (USAF) and the ROBERTSON PANEL concluded that the objects were probably birds, most likely ducks, reflecting the bright desert sunlight, although this explanation is widely disputed by UFOLOGISTS. Astronomer DONALD MENZEL has recounted incidents in which OWLS glowed at night after roosting in dead trees infested with a luminous fungus.

Birds are also responsible for causing RADAR returns. A large bird at close range can create a blip equivalent to that of an aircraft at a somewhat greater distance.

Bibliography: Menzel, Donald H., and Lyle G. Boyd, *The World of Flying Saucers* (Garden City, N.Y.: Doubleday and Company, 1963).

**BLACKOUTS,** the extinguishing of all lights in large areas and entire cities due to power failures. UFOs have frequently been seen hovering near power facilities, sometimes prior to or during blackouts. The highest number of such incidents occurred in the late 1950s and the mid-1960s. The most notorious case was the great northeastern blackout of 1965. During the evening rush hour period of November 9th, thirty million people were plunged into blackness that did not end until the following morning. The area affected covered 80,000 square miles and included parts of eight northeastern U.S. states and most of Canada's Ontario. However, even in New York City where thousands of people were trapped in subway trains and high-rise elevators, panic did not set in.

Utility experts could offer no explanation as to what had touched off the extraordinary failure of the huge Canadian-U.S. Eastern interconnective power grid. In previous years, local blackouts had been prevented from spreading by an extensive safeguard system. Yet on November 9, 1965, a strange surge of electricity had swept unchecked through the grid system, tripping scores of circuit breakers.

During the week following the event, reports of UFO sightings before and during the blackout came in from witnesses in New York City, Greater New York, New Jersey, Pennsylvania and all over New England. Of particular interest was the report that immediately prior to the blackout a pilot had seen a round, glowing object near the Northern Hemisphere's largest power plant at Niagara Falls. Another spherical UFO, seen at the beginning of the blackout, was hovering over the Clay power substation in Syracuse, New York.

Since ELECTROMAGNETIC EFFECTS seem to be an established characteristic of UFOs, some UFOlogists are convinced that the great northeastern blackout was the result of an extremely powerful surge of electromagnetic energy from one or more UFOs, overloading the system so quickly that the safety devices did not have time to operate. Some researchers believe this effect to be accidental. Others have suggested that such blackouts may be tests conducted by alien intelligences in preparation for an invasion. If this be the case, it might be of some relevance that the 1965 blackout occurred in the most heavily populated, most power-dependent region in the Western Hemisphere.

Bibliography: Keyhoe, Donald E., *Aliens from Space* (Garden City, N.Y.: Doubleday and Company, 1973).

**BLANN, TOMMY ROY** (b. January 1, 1947, Marlin, Texas; address: 1002 Edmonds Lane, Lewisville, Texas 75067), Founder and Research Director of the TEXAS SCIENTIFIC RESEARCH CENTER FOR UFO STUDIES and Research Associate of the CENTER FOR UFO STUDIES (CUFOS).

Tommy Roy Blann

Blann began researching and investigating UFOs at the age of nine. He has frequently witnessed anomalous phenomena at the locations of previous UFO sightings. His conclusion is that no one theory can explain the multiplicity of factors encountered in the study of the UFO phenomenon and he describes it as a chameleon in the world of science, art and religion. For the past twelve years, he has also investigated cases of ANIMAL MUTILATIONS.

Upon graduating from high school in 1965, Blann entered the UNITED STATES AIR FORCE (USAF) and served as a radio-intercept analyst. Following his service career, he attended Texas State Technical Institute, where he majored in Chemical and Nuclear Systems Technology. He was then employed as a Process Technician in the Research and Development Laboratory at the CCD Division of Texas Instruments.

Blann is a member of the Authors' Guild, the Authors' League of America and the Smithsonian Institution. He is Project Coordinator of the Pate Museum of Transportation in Fort Worth, Texas.

In addition to his current positions as Research Director of the Texas Scientific Research Center for UFO Studies, and Research Associate for CUFOS, Blann has served as an investigator for the NATIONAL INVESTIGATIONS COMMITTEE ON AERIAL PHENOMENA (NICAP), field investigator for the AERIAL PHENOMENA RESEARCH ORGANIZATION (APRO), State Section Director for the MUTUAL UFO NETWORK (MUFON) and Deputy Director for the INTERNATIONAL UFO BUREAU (IUFOB). He has given lectures throughout the United States, Canada and Mexico, and has made over one thousand radio and television guest appearances on talk shows. His articles have been published in numerous national magazines.

**BLIMP,** a nonrigid or semi-rigid airship dependent on internal gas pressure to maintain its form. In the United States, the Goodyear blimp, with its illuminated advertising sign, has been responsible for numerous UFO reports. The Goodyear Company, located in Akron, Ohio, has a flight schedule which can be checked to correlate the time and place of a UFO sighting.

**BLIP,** a luminous image on a RADARscope, also referred to as a target.

**BLUE BOOK** *see* **PROJECT BLUE BOOK**

**BLUE RIBBON PANEL** *see* **NATIONAL ENQUIRER, THE**

**BLUMRICH, JOSEF F.** (b. March 17, 1913, Steyr, Austria; address: 1139 Novia Street, Laguna Beach, California 92651), space engineer and writer.

Blumrich became interested in the subject of ANCIENT ASTRONAUTS while reading ERICH VON DÄNIKEN's book, *Chariots of the Gods?*. Having spent the greater part of his professional life in the field of design and analysis of aircraft and rockets, he decided to disprove von Däniken's claim that the Biblical prophet EZEKIEL witnessed the landing of extraterrestrial spaceships. The undertaking developed into a book which demonstrates, instead, the validity of the claim. Blumrich's research has carried him on to the study and analysis of Indian traditions in relation to ancient astronauts.

Blumrich earned a B.S. in aeronautical engineering and a B.S. in mechanical engineering. From 1934 to 1944, he worked on design and strength analysis of various aircraft at Gothaer Waggonfabrik A.G. in Gotha, Germany. He was Deputy Chief of the Department of Hydraulic Structures at the United Austrian Iron and Steel Works in Linz, Austria, from 1951 until 1959, when he moved to the United States to join the American space program. He worked at the National Aeronautics and Space Administration's Marshall Space Flight Center on the design research of the Saturn V rocket, various satellites, Skylab and the Shuttle. He was Chief of NASA's Advanced Structural Development Branch when he retired in 1974.

Blumrich is a member of the American Institute of Aeronautics and Astronautics, the American Association for the Advancement of Science and the American Astronautical Society. He was awarded NASA's Exceptional Service Medal in 1974.

Blumrich has written numerous engineering articles and acquired patents in the fields of shell analysis, hydraulic structures and launch vehicle design. He is author of *The Spaceships of Ezekiel* (New York: Bantam Books, 1974).

**BOGEY,** a synonym for UFO sometimes used by military pilots and ASTRONAUTS.

A Goodyear blimp. *(Courtesy the Goodyear Tire and Rubber Company)*

**BOIANAI, PAPUA, NEW GUINEA,** location of a CLOSE ENCOUNTER OF THE THIRD KIND (CE–III) which is considered one of the great classics in UFOLOGY. Its protagonist is Reverend William Booth Gill, an Anglican priest and graduate of Brisbane University. In 1959, he was in charge of the Boianai mission station and had been on the staff of the Anglican mission for thirteen years. During the day of June 26, Gill had written a letter to a friend in which he expressed his opinions regarding UFOs. There had been numerous sightings in recent months in Papua but Gill was still doubtful that UFOs were anything more than electrical phenomena or something brought about by atom bomb explosions. At 6:45 P.M., he came out of the dining hall and glanced up at the sky. He saw VENUS, which was conspicuous at the time. To his surprise, he also saw a sparkling object which began to move toward him. Stephen Gill Moi, a native teacher in the mission, and thirty-six other Papuans joined Gill. As the object descended to an altitude of about five hundred feet, the onlookers could distinguish the forms of four men moving about on top of the craft. The occupants seemed to be working on something and several times left the top deck and reappeared again, individually and together. The UFO was circular, had a large base and smaller upper deck. Two pairs of legs protruded from the base. Occasionally, a thin shaft of blue light shone upward from the center of the deck at an angle of forty-five degrees. The machine and its occupants were surrounded by a glowing halo of light. At 7:20 P.M., the UFO rose through the cloud covering which Gill estimated to be at about 2,000 feet. At 8:28 P.M., the UFO reappeared and descended again. This time it hovered at a slightly lower altitude. Three more UFOs appeared, moving up and down through the clouds. The first object, which Gill called the MOTHER SHIP, remained stationary for a short time before maneuvering through the clouds and across the sea. By 10:50 P.M., the UFOs had all disappeared and were not seen again that night.

The following evening, at approximately 6:00 P.M., a repeat performance of the previous night's sighting occurred. This time the mother ship descended to an altitude of about four hundred feet. Two smaller UFOs remained aloft. Noticing that one of the occupants seemed to be staring down at the onlookers, Gill waved. To everyone's amazement, the figure waved back. A Papuan worker waved two arms. Two figures on the craft each raised both arms in acknowledgment. Delighted, the young mission boys called out, beckoning the visitors to come down to the ground. As darkness fell, Gill used a flashlight to send signals to the UFOnauts. The craft executed a swinging pendulum movement as if in reply. As the waving and flashlight signals continued, the UFO began to move closer but

then stopped. The figures on board went back to their work and soon disappeared below deck. At 6:25 P.M., the occupants reappeared but continued to ignore their audience. At 6:30 P.M., Gill went to dinner. A half-hour later, the smaller UFOs had disappeared. The first craft was still present but had moved further away. All the observers went to the church for evening services. When they were over at 7:45 P.M., the sky had clouded over. There were no UFOs in sight. At 10:40 P.M., a loud explosion was heard which Gill thought might have been due to weather conditions, since a few drops of rain fell twenty-five minutes later.

Gill reported sightings of eight UFOs on the third night, June 28. However, only one object hovered at low altitude and no crew members were seen.

This fantastic series of sightings was brought to public attention by Reverend Normal E. G. Cruttwell, director of the multistation mission in Papua and a UFO investigator for the FLYING SAUCER REVIEW. Twenty-five of the thirty-eight witnesses signed a report attesting to their presence. The late astronomer DONALD MENZEL has implied that the witnesses were not of the highest credibility since all but Gill were Papuans and only seven were adults. He believed that the natives were willing to sign anything to please their holy leader.

The Papua New Guinea case has become one of the most controversial in UFO history. J. ALLEN HYNEK, JACQUES VALLEE, and PHILIP KLASS and Menzel have argued for and against its credibility in a number of books. Each publication has brought to light new details to support the authors' opinions.

Menzel reported that the Royal Australian Air Force (RAAF) analysed the bearing and elevation of the UFOs and concluded that at least three of them were planets. The RAAF noted that light refraction, the changing position of the planets relative to the observers, and the unsettled tropical weather could have created the illusion of increased size and motion. Menzel claims that Venus would have been located in the position where Gill saw the mother ship. At the time, Menzel was not aware that Gill had identified Venus on the first night and that the sighting on the second night had commenced prior to nightfall. Assuming that Gill suffered from myopia and astigmatism in his eye, Menzel himself observed Venus through a lens that would simulate the appropriate visual distortions. He claims that Venus appeared to be saucer-shaped and that his out-of-focus eyelashes gave an impression of projections extending above and below the flattened image. He believed that anyone observing this effect might, with a little imagination, mistake these projections for landing legs and people. The movement of the eye would cause the figures to move around. Hynek points out that this explanation ignores the fact that the UFOs were seen below the cloud cover. Although it was revealed that Gill was indeed myopic, he had been wearing properly corrected glasses at the time of the sighting.

Hynek and Vallee consider the case one of the most convincing on record. They are impressed by the number of witnesses to this event, which was only one of more than sixty sightings in New Guinea during a one-year period. Hynek finds it difficult to believe that a well-educated Anglican priest would invent such a fantastic story involving many witnesses, out of sheer intent to deceive.

Klass, on the other hand, feels this conclusion is outweighed by certain questionable aspects of the case. He finds it relevant that eight months prior to Gill's sighting, Cruttwell had enlisted the aid of his missionaries and the local Papuans in collecting UFO reports. He had a strong interest in the subject and since becoming an official UFO investigator, his files had begun to swell with reports. These cases would soon be analysed and categorized by Cruttwell in a forty-five page report. Klass implies that the filing of UFO reports became an obvious means of entering Cruttwell's good graces. He finds it odd that despite the community's well-established interest in UFOs when Gill reported a sighting by Stephen Gill Moi, he claimed that Moi had never heard of flying saucers. One fact stood out above all others to stimulate Klass's skepticism. On June 26, Gill and his companions watched the first UFO for more than four hours and at one point waited an hour for it to reappear. The following night, when the craft had been visible for only a half-hour and was at its closest, Gill went to dinner and afterwards held church services. Gill reported that by then the crew members were ignoring the observers and were busy with their work. Klass finds it difficult to believe that anyone faced with the imminent possibility of becoming the first human to make contact with extraterrestrial visitors would leave the scene to eat.

Bibliography: Hynek, J. Allen, and Jacques Vallee, *The Edge of Reality* (Chicago: Henry Regnery Company, 1975); Klass, Philip J., *UFOs Explained* (New York: Random House, 1974).

**BOLETIM INFORMATIVO G-PAZ,** publication of the GRUPPO DE PESQUISAS AEROESPACIAIS ZENITH (G-PAZ).

**BOLETIM SBEDV,** publication of the SOCIEDADE BRASILIERA DE ESTUDOS SOBRE DISCOS VOADORES (SBEDV).

**BOLIDE,** term sometimes used to describe a brilliant METEOR, especially one which explodes. Bolides are an occasional source of UFO reports.

Jacques Bonabot.

**BONABOT, JACQUES** (b. October 16, 1939, Brussels, Belgium; address: Leopold I laan, 141. B-8000 Bruges, Belgium), Cofounder and Director of the GROUPMENT POUR L'ÉTUDE DES SCIENCES D'AVANT-GARDE (GESAG).

Bonabot believes there is strong evidence that some UFOs demonstrate intelligent characteristics although he has no firm opinion regarding their identity. At Bruges, on April 15, 1972, he, his wife and his son observed a silvery CIGAR-SHAPED UFO flying from the southeast to the northwest on a straight path at an elevation of approximately forty-five degrees. This incident was confirmation to Bonabot that something mysterious is going on in the lower regions of our atmosphere.

Bonabot has been a Chief Petty Officer in the Belgian Navy since 1957. His interest in UFOs began two years earlier. From 1963 to 1965, he studied the phenomenon with other Belgian researchers. In 1965, together with Jean-Gerard Dohmen and Roger Lorthioir, he founded GESAG, assumed its directorship and became Editor of the *Bulletin du GESAG (UFO INFO)*. Bonabot is an authority on Belgian UFO cases and works in close cooperation with internationally-known UFOlogists.

**BONILLA, JOSÉ,** *see* ZACATECAS, MEXICO

**BOOK OF DZYAN.** Several authors have referred to the *Book of Dzyan* as evidence of extraterrestrial visitation in ancient times. One of the legends it relates is that of a small group of beings who came to Earth thousands of years ago in a metal craft which orbited the PLANET several times before landing. These beings were divided into two factions as a result of disagreements and one group destroyed the other with a weapon similar to an atomic bomb. When the victors saw what they had done, they were ashamed and took off in their vessels, never to return.

The only known record of the *Book of Dzyan* is found in *The Secret Doctrine* written in 1888 by Madame Helena Blavatsky, Cofounder of the Theosophical Society. Blavatsky claimed the *Book of Dzyan* to be a mysterious Oriental source. Scholars, unable to identify that source, believe that Blavatsky's claim is probably fraudulent. Whether this tale originated thousands of years ago or in 1888, the descriptions of the orbiting craft and the lethal weapon are, in any case, ahead of the writer's time.

Bibliography: Condon, Edward U. (ed.), *Scientific Study of Unidentified Flying Objects* (New York: E. P. Dutton, 1969); Edwards, Frank, *Flying Saucers—Serious Business* (New York: Lyle Stuart, 1966); Keyhoe, Donald E., *Aliens from Space* (Garden City, N.Y.: Doubleday and Company, 1973).

## BORDERLAND SCIENCES RESEARCH FOUNDATION (BSRF), P.O. Box 548, Vista, California 92083; telephone number: 714-724-2043.

This international organization serves as a clearing house for information on such subjects as UFOs, ESP, telekinesis, metempsychosis, RADIONICS, RADIESTHESIA, HYPNOSIS, dowsing, psychic surgery, absent healing, underground races, photography of the invisible and a variety of FORTEAN events. These are considered the phenomena of the borderland between the visible and invisible worlds. The foundation supports the EXTRATERRESTRIAL HYPOTHESIS (ETH) on UFOs, believing the UFONAUTS to be an assortment of benevolent missionaries, malevolent colonizers, explorers and tourists. However, they claim that the UNITED STATES AIR FORCE (USAF) and the CENTRAL INTELLIGENCE AGENCY (CIA) have also had flying saucers operational since 1955, possibly capable of lunar missions although not yet capable of interplanetary flight.

The JOURNAL OF BORDERLAND RESEARCH (formerly known as *Round Robin)* publishes the information gathered in the form of reports and newspaper clippings from the five hundred members in the United States, Canada, England, Australia, New Zealand, Brazil, Argentina, France, Spain, Italy, Yugoslavia, Turkey and Hong Kong.

This nonprofit organization was founded in 1945 by the late N. Meade Layne, who handed over the directorship in 1959 to RILEY CRABB.

## BORDERLINE SCIENCE INVESTIGATION GROUP, publishers of LANTERN.

## BORMAN, FRANK, *see* APOLLO 8 and GEMINI 8

**BOYES, IVAN** (b. January 8, 1946, Toronto, Canada; address: 27 Kingsmount Park Road, Toronto, Canada M4L 3L2; telephone number: 416-690-1275), CONTACTEE and Founder of the FLYING SAUCER—HOLLOW EARTH SOCIETY.

Boyes reports that his first contact occurred in 1960, when he saw a bluish white oval disk which shot a beam of light over his body. He claims that telepathic communication occurred and was confirmed by an audible voice. The OCCUPANTS promised to return the following night. Inside were people with metallic bronze skin, wearing bluish suits. Boyes was taken on a tour of the craft, healed of his chronic bronchitis and allergies, and beamed home in the morning with newly developed powers of extrasensory perception. According to Boyes, the aliens were time travelers from the Carboniferous Period. He claims that later contacts occurred with aliens from other places and since 1976 with saucer occupants from Earth's interior. Other contacts, he purports, were made with the occupants of saucers built by German scientists during the Second World War. Boyes became a UFO researcher at the age of fourteen, following his first contact. He claims to have been tortured in 1961 by a "Silent Group" regarding the encounter. In 1962, he founded the *Flying Saucer—Hollow Earth Society* and teamed up with UFO investigator Jeff Mitchel. During the following three years, he reportedly was in constant contact with extraterrestrials and had many UFO sightings at close range. His powers of extrasensory perception continued to develop and he went on to research parapsychology. In 1965, he did field work in British Columbia, where he claims to have had close range flying saucer sightings and DERO encounters. He subsequently returned to Toronto, where he continued his research and alleged contacts with extraterrestrials. From 1967 to 1969, he lectured on ATLANTIS, UFOs and related subjects. In 1969, he went to New Zealand to continue his research. While there, he investigated a rash of UFO landing reports and was interviewed on radio and television. He formed his own group in association with the New Zealand branch of CONTACT INTERNATIONAL, and conducted an investigation of alleged UFO bases in New Zealand. He claims to have been forced to cease the investigations because of a skirmish with the CENTRAL INTELLIGENCE AGENCY (CIA). After completing his research, he returned to Canada and began writing. He has had several articles published in UFO magazines.

**BOYES, WILLIAM WALTER** (b. June 29, 1928, Yonkers, New York; address: 2214 McAuliffe Drive, Rockville, Maryland 20851; telephone number: 301-424-9677), engineer and independent consultant to the

NATIONAL INVESTIGATIONS COMMITTEE ON AERIAL PHENOMENA (NICAP).

Boyes believes UFOs originate from another galaxy.

Boyes received his B.S. from the U.S. Naval Academy in 1951. He attended Norwich University, Brown University and the Georgetown University Law School.

From 1946 to 1955, Boyes was an officer in the United States Navy. From 1956 to 1964, he was a General Engineer at the U.S. Naval Ordnance Laboratory in Silver Spring, Maryland. From 1964 to 1966, he served as an Aerospace Technologist at the NATIONAL AERONAUTICS AND SPACE ADMINISTRATION (NASA) headquarters in Washington, D.C. As a Project Office for Pre-Mission Operations, he was specifically responsible for a varying multitude of tasks associated with the Gemini program. During this time, he was a member of the Gemini Launch Operations Committee and also reviewed annual budgetary and personnel forecasts for NASA, the Office of Management and Budget, and Congress. From 1966 to 1968, Boyes was a Systems Engineer at NASA Headquarters. In 1968, he became Head of the Operations Safety Group for Manned Space Flight. The scope of operational safety included hazardous ground testing, operational launch activities, manned and unmanned hardware testing, test crew and flight crew safety, personnel certification, organization of pad and launch area fire fighting teams, and rescue and emergency egress crews. In 1970, he was promoted to Chief of Ground Operations Safety, a position which he holds at the present time. In addition to his responsibility for the safety of all of NASA's ground operations, he was appointed by the NASA Administrator as the agency interface for all incidents and accidents concerning hazardous materials transportation.

**BRADYTES,** name given by French astronomer Camille Flammarion during the early twentieth century to circular or starlike bodies which resembled METEORS and BOLIDES but moved at exceptionally low speeds. Some witnesses described such objects accelerating and executing right-angle turns. Many reports of objects classified as bradytes resemble modern UFO accounts.

Bibliography: Vallee, Jacques and Janine, *Challenge to Science—The UFO Enigma* (Chicago: Henry Regnery Company, 1966).

**BRAND, ILLO,** *see* **VON LUDWIGER, ILLO BRAND**

**BRAZIL.** UFOs in Brazil are referred to as "OVNI" and flying saucers as "discos voadores." The majority of Latin American UFO reports come from Brazil and many of them deal with landings and OCCUPANTS. Although the Brazilian government takes no official

Disk photographed by Ed Keffel and Joa Martins at Barra da Tijuca on May 7, 1952. *(Courtesy ICUFON/De Sousa)*

stand regarding UFOs, the Brazilian Air Force has a special service to deal with the matter. According to Brazil's Ministry of Aeronautics, UFO sightings were first reported in 1947 and, while at first the average number of reports per annum was between fifty and 100, the number has now grown to somewhere between 100 and 500 per annum. The country experienced UFO WAVES in 1957 and 1962.

The tremendous number of sightings in Brazil has led to a widespread acceptance of the EXTRATERRESTRIAL HYPOTHESIS (ETH) by the general public. Numerous UFO organizations exist. Since the death of OLAVO FONTES in 1968, IRENE GRANCHI has earned the reputation of being Brazil's leading UFOlogist.

Some of the highly sensational cases occurring in Brazil include those at CATANDUVA, FORT ITAIPU, TRINDADE ISLAND and UBATUBA, as well as the alleged ABDUCTION of ANTONIO VILLAS-BOAS.

## BRITISH FLYING SAUCER BUREAU (BFSB),
71 Chedworth Road, Horfield, Bristol B27 9RX, England; telephone number: 696569.

The aims of this investigative organization are: 1. To promote, sustain and stimulate interest in, and to collect and disseminate information concerning unidentified flying objects; 2. To endeavor to determine their nature, origin and purpose; 3. To bring together for free discussion and social contact those interested in these phenomena and related subjects; 4. To assist in dispelling any feelings of anxiety that might result from the possible arrival of visitors from space. The organization holds that UFOs originate from beyond our planetary system and are involved in investigation inspired by a natural urge to explore.

In 1952, the British branch of Albert K. Bender's INTERNATIONAL FLYING SAUCER BUREAU (IFSB) was formed by Denis Plunkett. When national service with the Royal Air Force claimed Plunkett, his father, Captain E. L. Plunkett, took over. When the American headquarters of the IFSB closed down in 1953, its British branch became the British Flying Saucer Bureau. E.L. Plunkett is President, Harold L. Cobley (brother-in-law of Albert K. Bender) is Vice-President, Graham F. N. Knewstub is Honorary Secretary and Clifford Taylor is Honorary Treasurer. Committee Members are M. M. Plunkett, L. G. May, D. Plunkett, N. K. Hillier, J. Mortimore, B. J. Smith, D. Wilson and D. E. Ballam. In the late 1950s, membership was approximately 1,500. However, as a nonprofit, voluntary organization, BFSB was forced to reduce its scope and confine itself to a local bureau. Local cases are investigated and reports are collected from national newspapers. The bureau publishes a newsletter called the UFO NEWS BULLETIN, holds regular meetings,

organizes exhibitions and film slide shows, and provides a library and information service. E. L. Plunkett conducts lectures at the local prison, clubs, elderly citizens' groups, women's institutes, farmers' clubs and church organizations. BFSB is the oldest flying saucer club in the United Kingdom and is a member group of the BRITISH UFO RESEARCH ASSOCIATION (BUFORA).

## BRITISH UFO ASSOCIATION see BRITISH UFO RESEARCH ASSOCIATION

## BRITISH UFO RESEARCH ASSOCIATION (BUFORA), 95 Taunton Road, London SE12 8PA, England; telephone number: 01-852-7653.

The aims of BUFORA, one of Britain's major investigative organizations, are: 1. To encourage, promote and conduct unbiased scientific research into UFO phenomena throughout the United Kingdom; 2. to collect and disseminate evidence and data relating to UFOs; 3. to coordinate UFO research throughout the United Kingdom and to cooperate with others engaged in such research throughout the world. BUFORA holds no corporate views on the identity and origin of UFOs. It considers that there is ample evidence of a UFO enigma but not yet a sufficient amount to pinpoint any one or any combination of identities. Although the organization has found that over ninety percent of reports are misidentifications, examination of the remaining ten percent reveals such variety that BUFORA considers it possible that more than one source is involved.

BUFORA started life in 1959 as the London UFO Research Organization (LUFORO), which issued a monthly duplicated magazine, *LUFORO Bulletin*. Its founders were Paul Teugells, Nigel Stephenson, Susanne Stebbing and Roy Stemman. In 1962, LUFORO, along with seven other British groups, founded the British UFO Association, which was consolidated as BUFORA in 1964. It became legally constituted in 1975 as a nonprofit company. C.A.E. O'Brien is President. Vice-Presidents are the Right Honorable Earl of Clancarty (BRINSLEY LE POER TRENCH), Leonard Cramp, Bryan Winder, Geoffrey G. Doel and Graham F.N. Knewstub. Lionel Beer is Council Chairman and Norman Oliver is Vice-Chairman. Council Members are Larence W. Dale, Stephen Gamble, Anne Harcourt, Robin Lindsay, Charles F. Lockwood, Anthony R. Pace, Stephen Smith, Arnold West and Betty Wood. The group has over 800 members. Approximately 120 field investigators are located throughout the nation. They are supervised by regional coordinators who, in turn, are responsible to the national coordinator. BUFORA organizes monthly lectures and has sponsored a number of UFO conferences, including the First

London International UFO Research Congress in August 1979. Members have access to a library, a tape library and reports, and participate in skywatches. The BUFORA JOURNAL, edited by Norman Oliver, is published bimonthly.

**BRITISH UFO SOCIETY,** 47 Belsize Square, London NW3, England; telephone number: 01-794-3093.

The purpose of this investigative organization is to encourage and promote investigation and research into the UFO phenomenon and to look into the deeper meaning behind the visitations. Although the society believes eighty percent of UFO sightings are explainable in mundane terms, it attributes the remainder to extraterrestrial visitors, time travelers, psychic phenomena or something yet to be determined. It believes the purpose of UFOs may be to raise the consciousness of mankind.

This nonprofit organization was founded in 1965 by Ken Rogers, who serves as Chairman. Red Coombe is in charge of research and evaluation. The society has over 1,500 members. Investigators are located in major cities and towns throughout the United Kingdom. Newspaper reports are received weekly from around the world. These are photocopied and mailed to subscribers. The society's telephone serves as a UFO hotline. Members may phone in reports and receive the latest information twenty-four hours a day. Information is available on research, close encounters, skywatches, festivals, conventions, photos, films, books, authors, organizations, meetings, lectures, T-shirts and badges. Members living in the same area may be put in touch with one another to form local groups. A newsletter is mailed regularly to subscribers.

**BRNO, CZECHOSLOVAKIA,** location of a UFO sighting in 1960 by military men involved in a nocturnal exercise. A strange-colored light appeared in the sky, only to disappear and reappear elsewhere. It continued to move about in this manner for some time until the commanding officer ordered his men to observe it through binoculars and track it on RADAR. Fighter jets were scrambled but, as had occurred in so many similar cases in the United States, radar operators saw the unknown target disappear each time a jet approached. In each instance, the target reappeared in another spot before the interceptors even had time to turn around. After an hour, the UFO disappeared and did not reappear again. The incident was reported in the aeronautical publication *Letectvi a Kosmonautika* in April 1966.

Bibliography: Hobana, Ion, and Julien Weverbergh, *UFOs from Behind the Iron Curtain* (New York: Bantam Books, 1975).

**BRYAN, JOSEPH,** author and former United States Air Colonel who is a member of the Board of Governors of the NATIONAL INVESTIGATIONS COMMITTEE ON AERIAL PHENOMENA (NICAP). Twenty years ago, Bryan asked Lloyds of London what odds they would give him on a one hundred-dollar bet that the existence of UFOs would be proven by 1965, and on another one hundred dollars that we would establish communication with them. Lloyds would not bet. Although 1965 passed without proof of extraterrestrial visitations, his conviction that UFOs are real machines remains unshaken. "One of these days," he says, "a UFO *will* land in full view of responsible, unimpeachable witnesses. I hope I'll be among them."

**BSRF** *see* **BORDERLAND SCIENCES RESEARCH FOUNDATION**

**BUCHAREST, RUMANIA,** location of a multiple-witness UFO sighting involving military personnel on December 2, 1967. A Rumanian lieutenant major was on duty at the Banasea airfield radar station when, at 9:30 P.M., he observed an unusual "craft" hovering about thirty-five degrees over the northern horizon. The conical object shone with a brilliant but vacillating light. Suddenly, the UFO dropped toward the ground then rose rapidly to its original position. It moved a short distance from left to right, paused, then repeated its up and down maneuver once more. The army officer brought the strange phenomenon to the attention of several colleagues, and within a short time dozens of military personnel were watching the UFO. At 11:30 P.M., the object disappeared over the northern horizon. Two days later, another lieutenant major and several other witnesses observed a similar object at the same spot at four o'clock in the morning.

Less than a week later, early in the morning of December 10, a psychologist in Bucharest observed a bluish green UFO with spinelike protrusions traveling slowly through the sky beneath a high-altitude CLOUD layer. The object was clearly visible to the witness for a period of fifteen minutes.

Bibliography: Hobana, Ion, and Julien Weverbergh, *UFOs from Behind the Iron Curtain* (New York: Bantam Books, 1975).

**BUFORA** *see* **BRITISH UFO RESEARCH ASSOCIATION**

**BUFORA JOURNAL,** publication of the BRITISH UFO RESEARCH ASSOCIATION (BUFORA).

**BURNS.** Witnesses and objects have been burned by UFOs both with and without actual physical contact having occurred. In some instances, the generation of HEAT by UFOs seems to have been used as a weapon against human beings. Such was the case on November 4, 1957, in FORT ITAIPU, BRAZIL, where two sentries were reportedly badly burned by a blast of heat emanating from a UFO hovering above them. Some witnesses have reported being burned by beams of light fired at them from a tube held by a UFOnaut or protruding from a UFO. On March 29, 1966, in Hamilton, Ontario, Charles Cozens touched an antenna on one of two UFOs which had landed in a field. As if to keep him away, a flash of light knocked him backwards. His hand was burned, and superficial cuts and scratches appeared along with the burn mark. Some reports have demonstrated that, after observing brilliantly illuminated UFOs which showed no signs of aggression, witnesses have experienced severe sunburn effects.

Glowing and flaming UFOs have been known to burn trees and plants. On February 10, 1975, two boys observed a glowing ball, twenty feet in diameter, hovering over some trees in Annadale, Staten Island, New York. Subsequent examination of the area revealed that several trees had been sheared to a height of about four feet. Some were covered with a black substance which analysis revealed to be carbon based. Although chemists established that it had been produced by a low intensity heat such as the burning of paint thinner or lighter fluid, remnants of neither were found. It was determined that a fire had not been set in the woods but that some heat source had been present over a large area that caused carbonization at bark level only. In contrast, a flaming, spherical UFO in FORT BEAUFORT, SOUTH AFRICA, in 1972, passed through trees and bushes yet left no evidence of burning.

Bibliography: Keyhoe, Donald E., and Gordon I. R. Lore, *Strange Effects from UFOs* (Washington, D.C.: National Investigations Committee on Aerial Phenomena, 1969); Sachs, Margaret, with Ernest Jahn, *Celestial Passengers—UFOs and Space Travel* (New York: Penguin Books, 1977).

**CABASSI, RENZO,** *see* **COMITATO NAZIONALE INDIPENDENTE PER LO STUDIO DEI FENOMENI AEREI ANOMALI**

**CALGARY, ALBERTA.** Two color photographs of a daylight disk were taken by Warren Smith on July 3, 1967, southwest of Calgary. Smith and two companions were returning from a weekend trip when, at about 5:30 P.M., they observed an object traveling toward them from the east gradually losing altitude. Smith shot a picture of the UFO at a distance of about 2,000 feet. It then descended behind some trees. Within seconds, Smith was able to take a second PHOTOGRAPH as the UFO ascended. It hovered momentarily, dropped a small object, then flew off to the south.

Early tests conducted by astronomer J. ALLEN HYNEK and the Defense Photographic Interpretation Center of the Canadian Air Force supposedly established that the two photographs represent an oblate ellipsoid or doughnut-shaped object approximately forty-to-fifty feet in diameter and eleven-and-a-half-to-fourteen feet thick. CLOUD formations in both photographs were declared to be consistent with the ten-to-twenty-second time lapse reported by the photographer. After testing the first of the two photographs, GROUND SAUCER WATCH (GSW) labeled it a bona fide unidentified object. However, when GSW subsequently tested the second of the two photographs, it declared that the film ". . . depicts the crudest attempt at a hoax that we have ever seen."

Bibliography: Hynek, J. Allen, *The UFO Experience: A Scientific Inquiry* (Chicago: Henry Regnery Company, 1972).

Fake UFO photographed near Calgary, Alberta, on July 3, 1967. *(Courtesy Ground Saucer Watch)*

**CAMACHO, VICENTE C.** (b. December 14, 1954, Saipan, Mariana Islands; address: P.O. Box 908, Chalan Piao, Saipan, Mariana Islands CM 96950; telephone number: 6531), Founder and Director of the INDONESIAN UFO REGISTRY.

Camacho reports that during his boyhood he had the strange experience of bumping into a snowy white, cotton-weight man who did not utter a word or make any attempt to communicate. The being, however, tried to block Camacho from moving. Only when Camacho tried to touch it, did the creature let him continue along the dirt road leading to the sparsely populated area where he lived. Camacho was perplexed by the incident until he developed an interest in UFOs. He now believes that there may be some connection between the odd creature and UFOs.

Camacho attended Maui College in Hawaii and Whittier College in California. He also participated in summer sessions at the University of Guam in Guam.

From 1973 to 1974, Camacho worked as an Engineering Aide and Clerk on the Saipan International Airport Project for the Ralph M. Parson Company. From 1974 to 1975, he was a Census Enumerator, Coder/Checker and Post Enumeration Surveyor for the Bureau of Census of the Trust Territory of the Pacific Islands in Saipan. From 1976 to 1977, he was an Editor and Columnist for the Saipan newspaper, *The Munchi Narara*. Since 1977, he has worked concurrently as an Administrative Assistant to three congressmen and Information Researcher for the First Northern Marianas Commonwealth Legislature's Public Information Office. He is a Notary Public.

## CAMBRIDGE UFO RESEARCH GROUP, 362 Kitchener Rod, Cambridge, Ontario, Canada N3H 1A6; telephone number: 519-653-9209.

The aim of this investigative organization is to help resolve the UFO mystery in Canada. The group believes UFOs may be explainable in extraterrestrial and/or extradimensional terms and/or as psychic phenomena. It believes the purpose of UFOs may be to study and analyze Earth.

This nonprofit group was founded in 1976 by Bonnie Wheeler, who serves as President. Jim Tolton is the only Board Member. Lorenzo Massai serves as the group's foreign representative in Italy. The twenty-five members serve as investigators and will travel within a sixty mile radius to cover close encounter cases. The *Cambridge UFO Research Group Newsletter* is published every two months and includes information on cases investigated by the organization. Information and newsletters are exchanged with other UFO groups. The organization is a member of the CANADIAN UFO REPORT EXCHANGE NETWORK (CUFOREN).

**CAMPIONE, MICHAEL J.** (b. August 8, 1912, New York, N.Y.; address: 2202 New Albany Road, Cinnaminson, New Jersey 08077), CONTACTEE.

Campione, who became interested in UFOs in 1948, believes that while some UFOs are man-made craft and others originate from Earth's interior, the majority are from outer space, piloted by advanced civilizations who utilize interdimensional travel. He holds that there are both friendly and unfriendly UFOs. The dangerous ones, he claims, are powered by nuclear devices which can blind, burn or cause cancer to humans who approach within a 200 foot radius. The best defense weapon, recommends Campione, is an ordinary flashlight, whose light beam interferes with the UFO's power system. Friendly UFO OCCUPANTS can be identified, he says, by addressing them telepathically. They will either respond or reveal themselves to the witness. According to Campione, millions of friendly UFO crew members are here, outside our range of vision, ready to evacuate humans prior to drastic changes soon to occur on Earth. An activist in many fields, Campione has urged United States presidents and state governors to publicly recognize the UFO phenomenon and to adopt safety measures to insure national survival. Additionally, he has requested that areas of international airports be apportioned as landing sites for UFOs. Campione asserts that the United States and other nations of the world are controlled by humans who have "negative," insane or criminal minds. The news media, he adds, are tools that brutalize, de-spiritualize and brainwash the public.

Campione, who studied Industrial Management through the International Correspondence School, was employed for forty years as a metalworker, mechanic and machine operator. He has also worked as an inventor, spiritual healer, exorcist and color light therapist. He has lectured widely on UFOs and has appeared on several radio and television shows.

Campione is a member of the International Platform Society, the Dinshsh Health Society, the Humanitarian Society, the Federation of the Blind and the Church of Gospel Ministry.

Campione produces and sells audio cassette tapes on UFOs. He has written many unpublished articles on the subject. He is author and publisher of *Reality of UFOs—Their Danger, Their Hope* (1965), *UFOs—20th Century's Greatest Mystery* (1968), *Cross and Star* (1969), *UFO Manual* (1973) and *Anti-"Black" Magic* (1973).

**CANADA.** Canada is the only country other than the United States to have maintained official records of UFO reports. In 1950, the Department of Transport established Project Magnet, a study group composed of scientists and engineers. Under the leadership of Wilbert H. Smith, the group set up a laboratory in 1953 which was equipped to investigate the electromagnetic and gravitational properties of UFOs. The government withdrew its support of the project in 1954 because of adverse publicity. Smith stated that "The conclusions reached by Project Magnet . . . were based on a rigid statistical analysis of sighting reports and were as follows: There is a ninety-one percent probability that at least some of the sightings were of real objects of unknown origin. There is about a sixty percent probability that these objects were alien vehicles."

Meanwhile, in 1952, the government had established Project Second Story, a study to determine whether or not UFOs warranted a large scale investigative effort. Until 1965, the Air Defense Command (ADC) collected UFO reports but many of their files were later destroyed. Responsibility for UFO investigation was then assumed by the Canadian Forces Headquarters. In 1969, the records were transferred to the National Research Council (NRC) of Canada, which collects and files UFO reports but does not conduct field investigations. The reports are open to public inspection but researchers are required to sign an affidavit that they will not reveal the names and addresses of witnesses.

There are numerous UFO organizations in Canada and several of them have formed a cooperative network known as the CANADIAN UFO REPORT EXCHANGE NETWORK (CUFOREN).

**CANADIAN UFO REPORT,** quarterly magazine, established in 1969, with a circulation of 1,000. It is available by subscription only. The magazine deals mainly with UFO sightings and ABDUCTION cases and carries supplementary information on BIGFOOT sightings.

Articles are written by staff and freelance writers. There is no payment for freelance material. Editor and Publisher JOHN MAGOR is interested in articles in support of UFOs, ranging in length from 500 to 3,000 words. The mailing address is: P.O. Box 758, Duncan, British Columbia, Canada V9L 3Y1.

**CANADIAN UFO REPORT EXCHANGE NETWORK (CUFOREN),** a network in which reports and research data are exchanged mutually between investigators, organizations and researchers across Canada. Each month, all participants prepare copies of their reports listing any sightings they have investigated and showing date, time, duration of sighting, location, description of UFO's appearance, movements, PHYSICAL EFFECTS, data on witnesses and results of investigations. These reports are then mailed to the other participants. CUFOREN was initiated in January 1978 and includes

the CAMBRIDGE UFO RESEARCH GROUP, CANADIAN UFO REPORT, CANADIAN UFO RESEARCH NETWORK (CUFORN), John Musgrave, PROJECT SUM (SOLVING UFO MYSTERIES) UFO RESEARCH, RES BUREAUX, UFO CANADA and U.P. INVESTIGATIONS RESEARCH.

**CANADIAN UFO RESEARCH NETWORK (CUFORN),** P.O. Box 15, Station A, Willowdale, Ontario, Canada M2N 5S7; telephone number: 416-225-5703.

The purpose of this investigative organization is to investigate UFO reports, to gather soil samples for analysis, to keep accurate accounts of all incidents, to carry out research and to inform the public about the UFO phenomenon. The organization holds that some UFOs are craft made of a metallic alloy. It maintains that the propulsion systems of MOTHER SHIPS involve photon rockets and the combination of matter and ANTIMATTER, while smaller UFOs use a system which involves electromagnetic and antigravity fields. The group believes that some UFOs originate from a parallel dimension while others come from other planets, including ZETA RETICULI. It claims that extraterrestrial UFOs have been based underground and underwater on Earth for many years and that some are based underground on the MOON and MARS. The purpose of UFOs, according to CUFORN, is to study the physical and psychological characteristics of humans, to inspect our technology, and to exploit Earth's mineral wealth with underground and underwater mining techniques. CUFORN believes that the creatures seen on board UFOs have no intention of sharing their high technology nor of establishing any permanent friendly relationship with human beings, who are of interest to them only as specimens of primitive creatures.

This nonprofit organization was founded in 1977 by LAWRENCE J. FENWICK, Joseph Muskat and Harry Tokarz, who serve as its Directors. Robert Garrison, Professor of Astronomy at the University of Toronto, serves as a consultant. Membership stands at about fifty and is restricted to those with academic, scientific and other appropriate qualifications. The members serve as field investigators and their fields of expertise currently include anthropology, electronics, photography, journalism, aeronautical engineering, sociology, medicine, astronomy, electrical engineering, aviation, languages, psychology, computer technology, physics, chemistry, parapsychology, philosophy, history, biology, physiology, agronomy and religion. They are located in Ontario, Alberta, Quebec, Newfoundland, England, Brazil, Australia, Illinois, Maryland, Florida, Arizona, Pennsylvania and North Carolina.

CUFORN publicizes its hot line phone number, keeps files of newspaper and magazine articles, participates in open line radio and television shows, makes available consultants for every phase of UFO research, holds meetings, corresponds with other UFO organizations and keeps correspondence files. Members have access at headquarters to a library of 150 books, magazine files, newspaper clipping files, photo files, tapes and close encounter files. Codirector Fenwick prepares monthly reports for members of the CANADIAN UFO REPORT EXCHANGE NETWORK (CUFOREN) of which CUFORN is a member.

**CAROLINA UFO NETWORK,** 315 Cedarwood Lane, Matthews, North Carolina 28105; telephone number: 704-882-1732.

The purpose of this investigative organization is to catalog UFO reports from North Carolina with the aim of correlating and researching the data.

The nonprofit group was founded in 1979 by P. Wayne Laporte, Gayle C. McBride and David M. Oldham, who serve as its Directors. The group works in cooperation with statewide investigators. Information is furnished to other investigators and researchers for the cost of mailing and reproduction expenses. Abstracts of the network's reports are published in the newsletter of the TARHEEL UFO STUDY GROUP.

**CARPENTER, SCOTT,** *see* **MERCURY 7**

**CARR, OTIS T.,** CONTACTEE who raised thousands of dollars to build a flying saucer according to instructions from the SPACE PEOPLE. When his homemade machine failed to fly to the MOON in 1957, he was sued by his investors. Carr was convicted of fraud and received a prison sentence.

**CARSON, CHARLES,** *see* **RED BLUFF, CALIFORNIA**

**CARTER, JIMMY (JAMES EARL),** thirty-ninth president of the United States and first American president to have reported sighting a UFO.

The incident occurred on January 6, 1969. As the local district governor of the Lions Club, Carter was attending a chapter meeting in Leary, Georgia, to make a speech. While waiting outdoors for the meeting to begin at 7:30 P.M., Carter and about ten other Lions Club members observed a sharply outlined light in the sky. Over a ten-to-twelve minute period the light seemed to move toward the observers from a distance, recede slightly, return and finally move away until it had disappeared. During the sighting, the object, which Carter described as larger and brighter than a PLANET, had grown to the apparent size of the MOON. It had also changed from its original bluish color to a reddish color.

Jimmy Carter's UFO report. *(Courtesy NICAP)*

Carter later estimated the light's distance to be perhaps three-hundred-to-one-thousand yards. He did not report the incident publicly until 1973, when he was governor of Georgia. This may be the reason for erroneous accounts indicating that the actual sighting occurred in 1973.

Computer systems analyst ROBERT SHEAFFER reports that attempts to locate ten other corroborating witnesses have been unsuccessful. However, Fred Hart, 1969 President of the Leary Lions Club, recalls seeing the light although it failed to make a great impression on him. Sheaffer believes that Carter's UFO sighting was a misidentification of the planet VENUS. His investigations revealed that in written reports filed more than three years later, Carter incorrectly recalled the date of the sighting as sometime in October 1969. Official records from the Lions Club International headquarters in Oakbrook, Illinois, give the date of Carter's Leary Lions Club speech as January 6 of that year. Carter reported that the UFO appeared from the west about thirty degrees above the horizon. Sheaffer has established that on that night Venus appeared at an altitude of twenty-five degrees in the west-southwest sky as a brilliant evening STAR, nearly one hundred times brighter than a first magnitude star.

While running for president, Carter promised to release to the public all official data on UFOs. However, once elected, he discovered that declassification of the UNITED STATES AIR FORCE'S PROJECT BLUE BOOK files had already been initiated. Carter's science adviser, Dr. Frank Press, charged with answering UFO-related mail, was deluged with letters claiming that additional secret files existed and demanding their release. Government agencies denied having files on UFOs. Overwhelmed by the volume of mail, Press asked Dr. Robert Frosch, Director of the NATIONAL AERONAUTICS AND SPACE ADMINISTRATION (NASA), if his organization would take over the task. In addition, he asked if NASA would consider convening a panel to decide whether or not a new investigation was warranted. After several months, NASA determined that further investigation was not warranted. Frosch, however, offered to make NASA laboratories available for analysis of any physical evidence of UFOs.

In 1978, several newspapers and magazines published a photograph showing a UFO near the helicopter in which the president had just taken off from Fort Clayton, Panama, on June 17 at approximately 1:20 P.M. The object was not sighted visually. Reportedly, the picture was taken by Linda Arosemena to use up the last frame of a roll of film. The thirty-fifth frame, taken five-to-ten seconds previously, showed no evidence of the UFO. According to newspaper accounts, Arosemena, a professional photographer, is the Fort Clayton Visual Information Officer of the Defense Mapping Agency Inter-American Geodetic Survey. She was surprised to see the oval object in the picture and sent a copy to Carter with an explanation of the circumstances.

According to the June 28, 1978, edition of the Panamanian newspaper, *Star and Herald,* some young girls in Fort Amador had a visual sighting of a similar UFO on June 16, one day prior to Carter's departure from Fort Clayton.

Bibliography: Sheaffer, Robert, "President Carter's 'UFO' Is Identified as the Planet Venus," *The Humanist* (Buffalo, N.Y.: American Humanist Association, July/August 1977).

**CASE OF THE ANCIENT ASTRONAUTS, THE,** television documentary (BBC/WGBH/RM Productions, 1977). Executive producer: John Angier; written and produced by Graham Massey; narrator: Don Wescott.

This documentary was presented by public television as part of the NOVA series. It takes a look at some of the theories presented by author ERICH VON DÄNIKEN in his book *Chariots of the Gods?,* in which he proposes that extraterrestrials visited Earth in ancient times. The subjects covered include the EASTER ISLAND statues, the MAYA, the lines of NAZCA, the PIRI RE'IS map, the PYRAMIDS, SIRIUS and the TASSILI FRESCOES. Authorities interviewed include astrophysicist CARL SAGAN, explorer Thor Heyerdahl, science fiction writer Isaac Asimov, author Robert Temple and von Däniken, himself. The documentary concludes with the statement, "Von Däniken's thesis rests on inaccuracies, on unrelated facts and false similarities. It denies man's ingenuity and abilities and it uses phoney evidence in an attempt to prove its case. Von Däniken's theories may be intriguing, even attractive, but there's not a single solid piece of evidence behind them."

**CATANDUVA, BRAZIL,** location of a bizarre UFO encounter reported to the AERIAL PHENOMENA RESEARCH ORGANIZATION (APRO) by Brazilian UFO investigator IRENE GRANCHI.

Forty-one-year-old Onilson Papero, a married man with two children and an organizer of public libraries for the state of San Paulo, was driving home through the rain on May 22, 1973, when his engine and radio began to malfunction. It was 3:00 A.M. He was just outside Catanduva. Suddenly, he noticed a blue circle of light, about eight inches in diameter, inside the car. As it moved about slowly, it passed in front of the dashboard. Papero was puzzled to find that he could see the engine through the circle of light. Then he noticed a beam of blue light shining on him from the top of the hill he was ascending. As the light's source approached, he pulled off the road to avoid a collision. The light kept coming towards him. Overcome by a sensation of HEAT and stuffiness, Papero stepped out of his car but found no relief. He heard a buzzing sound. Looking up at the UFO, he could distinguish a gray structure about twenty-five feet thick and thirty-six feet wide, resembling two soup plates attached rim to rim. A transparent curtain seemed to be moving around the object and when it had completely encircled it, the sensation of heat and airlessness ceased. At this point, a tube stretched out from the UFO's base toward the ground. Panicking, Papero began to run. He got no further than one hundred feet when he felt something holding him back as though a rubber lasso had caught him. His flailing hands could find nothing physical to account for the impediment. Turning, he saw that a rod of blue light from the UFO was moving over his car. The light seemed to make the car transparent, enabling Papero to see all its interior parts. He fainted.

An hour later, two young men drove by. Seeing Papero lying face down in the gushing rainwater, they rushed on to Catanduva, where they reported the matter to the police. Accompanied by an officer, they returned to the scene. A road map lay on the ground in front of the car. Papero's briefcase lay open, the contents strewn about in the car. When the three men turned Papero over to examine him, he regained consciousness. After they had calmed the struggling man who believed them to be kidnappers from the UFO, they listened to his strange tale. The key to his briefcase, which had been locked, was still in his pocket. Nothing had been stolen. The policeman took Papero to a hospital in Catanduva for examination and observation.

The following day, having shown no indications of injury or illness, Papero was released. However, he had begun to feel a slight itchiness on his back and stomach. The next day, irritated patches of skin turned purplish blue. Later, these spots turned yellow and eventually disappeared. Subsequent medical examinations revealed no cause for the discoloration. Dr. Max Berezonski of Sao Paulo found Papero's mental condition to be normal. No other physical abnormalities were found.

Bibliography: Emenegger, Robert, *UFOs, Past, Present and Future* (New York: Ballantine Books, 1974).

**CATHIE, BRUCE LEONARD** (b. February 11, 1930, Auckland, New Zealand; address: 158 Shaw Road, Oratia, Auckland, New Zealand; telephone number: 4291 Glen Eden Auckland), airline pilot and Oceania Representative of the INTERCONTINENTAL GALACTIC SPACECRAFT (UFO) RESEARCH AND ANALYTIC NETWORK (ICUFON).

Cathie, who began investigation and research in 1964 and has seen UFOs himself, claims to have discovered a world energy grid system and mathematical associations with light, mass and gravity. He believes that a large percentage of UFOs are interplanetary machines involved in the surveillance and guidance of our progress, while a small percentage are secret man-made anti-gravity research machines.

Cathie, who holds a School Certificate and a Public Service Certificate, attended Otahuhu Technical College from 1943 to 1947 and took the Royal New Zealand Air Force Wings Course from 1951 to 1953.

Cathie worked as an engineer for New Zealand Forest Producers from 1947 to 1951. He was commissioned in the Royal New Zealand Air Force from 1951 to 1953. Since 1955, he has been an airline captain with New Zealand National Airways and Air New Zealand.

Cathie is a member of the Royal New Zealand Aeronautical Society and the Masonic Lodge.

Cathie is author of *Harmonic 33* (Wellington, New Zealand: A.H. & A.W. Reed, 1968); coauthor, with Peter N. Temm, of *Harmonic 695, The UFO, and Antigravity* (Wellington, New Zealand: A.H. & A.W. Reed, 1971); and author of *Harmonic 288, The Pulse of the Universe* (Wellington, New Zealand: A.H. & A.W. Reed, 1977).

Bruce Cathie.

**CATTLE MUTILATIONS** *see* **ANIMAL MUTILATIONS**

**CAUS** *see* **CITIZENS AGAINST UFO SECRECY**

**CBA** *see* **COSMIC BROTHERHOOD ASSOCIATION**

**CCAP** *see* **CIVIL COMMISSION ON AERIAL PHENOMENA**

**CDRU** *see* **CERCLE DUNKERQUOIS DE RECHERCHES UFOLOGIQUES**

**CEAFI** *see* **CENTRO DE ESTUDIOS ASTRONOMICOS E DE FENÓMENOS INSOLITOS**

**CECRU** *see* **COMITÉ EUROPÉEN DE COORDINATION DE LA RECHERCHE UFOLOGIQUE**

**CEFAI** *see* **CENTRO DE ESTUDIOS DE FENÓMENOS AÉREOS INUSUALES**

**CE–IV** *see* **CLOSE ENCOUNTER OF THE FOURTH KIND**

**CEI** *see* **CENTRO DE ESTUDIOS INTERPLANETARIOS**

**CELEBRITIES.** Actors, politicians and other well-known people alleged to have seen UFOs include MUHAMMAD ALI, ORSON BEAN, JIMMY CARTER, JAMIE FARR, GLENN FORD, JACKIE GLEASON, BUDDY GRECO, DICK GREGORY, CLARE BOOTHE LUCE, SHEILA MACRAE, WARREN OATES, ELVIS PRESLEY, WILLIAM SHATNER, ELKE SOMMER, CLYDE TOMBAUGH, MEL TORME, JOHN TRAVOLTA and RAY WALSTON. In addition, several ASTRONAUTS reported and photographed UFOs during the Mercury, Gemini and Apollo space missions.

**CELESTIAL INTERPRETORS OF NAPPA (CION),** 552 Estate Road, Maple Shade, New Jersey 08052.

The purpose of this religious organization, an outgrowth of the NATIONAL AERIAL AND PSYCHIC PHENOMENA ASSOCIATION (NAPPA), is to foster new dimensions of thought regarding the relationship between God, intelligent beings throughout the universe and the "prophetic" role of UFOs, to teach human beings about universal brotherhood, to awaken them to the realization that our likenesses are more important than our differences and to prepare mankind for the coming of a NEW AGE.

The Church's Director, Frank D'Adamo, promotes exotheology, the theology of outer space. After studying the Bible for more than twenty years, he believes that many of its passages describe spacecraft and that Christ,

Himself, will return to Earth in a spaceship in the year 2011. D'Adamo's mission is to prepare earthlings for that ultimate UFO landing.

**CELESTIO-METATHESIS,** the exchange of matter from one celestial body to another during the passage of one object through space previously occupied by the other. CHARLES FORT has proposed this process as a possible explanation for FAFROTSKIES.

Bibliography: Fort, Charles, *The Book of the Damned* (New York: Boni and Liveright, 1919).

**CELLINI, BENVENUTO,** sixteenth century Florentine goldsmith and sculptor whose notorious autobiography contains a reference to a UFO which appeared in 1537. While traveling to Rome, Cellini and a companion saw a huge beam of fire over Florence, shining brightly and filling the sky with a brilliant light.

Bibliography: *The Autobiography of Benvenuto Cellini* (Harmondsworth, England: Penguin Books, 1956).

**CEMOCPI** *see* **CERCLE D'ÉTUDE DES MYSTÉRIEUX OBJETS CÉLESTES ET DES PHÉNOMÈNES INCONNUS**

**CENAP** *see* **CENTRALES ERFURSCHUNGSNETZ AUSSERGEWOHNLICHER PHENOMENE**

**CENTER FOR UFO STUDIES (CUFOS),** 1609 Sherman Avenue, Evanston, Illinois 66201; telephone number: 312-491-6666.

The center is composed of scientists and other academics concerned about the UFO problem and willing to spend time investigating and examining the issue. The organization's goals are to provide a public source of reliable and authoritative information on UFOs, to provide an international clearing house to which people can report their UFO experiences without fear of ridicule, and to apply the methods of science to the study of the phenomenon. CUFOS takes no official stand on the nature of UFOs.

This nonprofit organization was founded in 1973 by astronomer J. ALLEN HYNEK, who serves as its Director. Researcher Allan Hendry is in charge of coordination and in-depth investigation. David Saunders maintains the computerized catalogue of UFO reports known as UFOCAT. Data is contributed by a number of UFO organizations around the world. The board is assisted by field investigators from the MUTUAL UFO NETWORK (MUFON). Participation is by invitation only. Investigative procedures include soil analysis, spectrographic analysis, studies of UFO movements and luminosity and psychological studies. A toll-free hot-line number is available to law enforcement officials throughout the country to pass on reports of UFO sightings. A monthly newsletter, the INTERNATIONAL UFO REPORTER, is available by subscription to the public. Hynek is Editor-in-Chief.

## CENTRALES ERFORSCHUNGS-NETZ AUSSERGEWOHNLICHER PHENOMENE (CENAP), D–6800 Mannheim-31, Eisenacher Weg 16, West Germany; telephone numbers: 701370 and 707633.

The purpose of this organization is to promote serious investigation of UFOs in Germany and to solve the mystery in a scientific manner. The group holds that UFOs are not under intelligent control but rather are a phenomenon originating in the upper atmosphere or by supernatural processes, possibly explainable in terms of *plasma*.

This nonprofit organization was founded in 1976 by WERNER WALTZER and Hansjürgen Köhler. Walter is Executive Director. Board Members and field investigators are Walter, Köhler, Andreas Gerersdorfer, Christian Pöchhacker and Frank Köther. CENAP has about twenty members worldwide. Field investigators carry out prompt on-the-spot investigations of sightings in West Germany and Austria. Research and comparison studies are conducted on worldwide UFO activity. The *CENAP Report* is published monthly.

Two subcommittees are headed by Andreas Gerersdorfer, located at Wiener Strasse 53, A-3371 Neumarkt, Austria, and by Christian Pöchhacker, located at Feldstrasse 3, A-3373 Kemmelbach, Austria.

## CENTRAL INTELLIGENCE AGENCY (CIA), United States intelligence organization created in 1947 to coordinate the intelligence operations of the government and to advise the president and the National Security Council on security matters. The primary reason why such an agency was established was to ensure that the nation would never again be the unprepared target of a surprise attack as it had been at Pearl Harbor in 1941.

The CIA's official position over the years has been that UFOs are not worth investigating. However, UFO reports, beginning in 1947 with the famous sighting by Kenneth Arnold over MOUNT RAINIER, WASHINGTON, presented the possibility that an unknown enemy might be invading U.S. air space. This potential threat to national security created a situation which clearly fell within the CIA's jurisdiction. UFOLOGIST JIM LORENZEN points out that standard intelligence procedures would require that all information gathered during an investigation be withheld from the general public until definite conclusions could be reached, since

any disclosures might be beneficial to the unknown enemy. If and when firm conclusions were reached, it is possible the information would still remain confidential. There has been a great deal of argument and speculation about what the CIA knows about UFOs and what its involvement has been. In addition, the public's distrust of the clandestine agency has led to a popular belief that the CIA is at the center of an official conspiracy to COVER UP the truth about UFOs.

Author DONALD KEYHOE has been the major proponent of the claim that the CIA is the power behind UFO secrecy. Admiral R.H. Hillenkoetter, Pacific Commander of Intelligence in World War II and Director of the CIA during its first three years of existence, told Keyhoe that the CIA had been keeping a close watch since 1948 on the UFO problem and the UNITED STATES AIR FORCE's investigations.

In 1952, Secretary of the Navy Dan Kimball was one of several witnesses involved in a spectacular UFO encounter. After filing his report with the Air Force, Kimball followed up with a request for further information on the matter. The Air Force refused to discuss it with him. Consequently, Kimball instigated his own investigative operation to handle all UFO reports generated by Navy personnel. A Navy analysis of the UFO film taken by Warrant Officer Delbert C. Newhouse near TREMONTON, UTAH, resulted in the conclusion that the UFOs were "unknown objects under intelligent control." Kimball was asked by the Air Force not to take any action until the Air Force's own analysis was completed. When the November election gave a victory to General Eisenhower, Kimball was replaced by a Republican. According to Keyhoe, although the threat posed by Kimball was over, the CIA knew that more problems could arise with the Navy and that the Air Force could not handle the situation. Keyhoe claims that this led to the CIA's seizing control of the Air Force investigation and its introduction of a ruthless program to put an end to public belief in UFOs.

In January 1953, the CIA arranged a conference at the Pentagon attended by three CIA representatives, Air Force representatives and a group of scientists headed by Dr. H. P. Robertson and henceforth referred to as the ROBERTSON PANEL. According to Keyhoe, the CIA-selected scientists were known skeptics who had little knowledge about UFOs and who considered the subject nonsense. The panel determined that UFO reports, not UFOs, were a threat to national security. Meanwhile, several Air Force officers, including DEWEY FOURNET, ED RUPPELT and ALBERT CHOP, had concocted a plan to give the public the facts about UFOs. In the month following the CIA conference, the Fournet group was ready to hold a press conference when the CIA stepped in. Chop told Keyhoe, "They killed the whole program."

We've been ordered to work up a national debunking campaign, planting articles in magazines and arranging broadcasts to make UFO reports sound like Poppycock." Ruppelt told Keyhoe that they had even been instructed to ridicule witnesses when plausible explanations of UFO sightings were not readily available. According to Keyhoe, the CIA continued to guide and control the Air Force deception of Congress, the news media and the public.

Engineer LEON DAVIDSON believes that the CIA, under its director Allen Dulles, was the creator and operator of UFOs seen in close encounters. Legitimate UFO reports, such as those arising from U.S. military testing, were, according to Davidson, exploited by the CIA as a tool in the cold war. The aim of the entire program was to cause the Soviet Union to waste time and effort in preparing defenses against fictitious craft and weapons. Furthermore, UFOs could be used to capture headlines, diverting attention from unwelcome news coverage. Davidson asserts that Dulles later resorted to using the saucer believers and their clubs as a propaganda vehicle. CONTACTEES carried alleged messages from UFONAUTS urging an end to A-bomb testing. The Russians were overcoming the United States' lead with such speed that any halt in testing would have benefited the United States more than the Soviet Union. However, it was a position which the U.S. government could not take openly. Individual encounters which Davidson specifically attributes to the CIA were those experienced by GEORGE ADAMSKI, DANIEL FRY and police officer Lonnie Zamora in SOCORRO, NEW MEXICO. With regard to RADAR sightings of UFOs, Davidson points out that electronic countermeasure (ECM) equipment, capable of creating phony radar returns, was already being used by the military in 1950. Flying saucers, themselves, remarks Davidson, were notable for their limited flying time of one hour and their inability to travel more than four hundred miles or carry heavy loads. These factors he attributes to the high cost of fuel and small capacity. It is not surprising, Davidson holds, that "midgets" were preferred for crew members.

In 1976, the records of the Air Force's PROJECT BLUE BOOK were made available to the public. Researchers immediately became aware that numerous important cases were missing. Believing that the missing material could be found in CIA files, a number of organizations and individuals, including GROUND SAUCER WATCH (GSW) and CITIZENS AGAINST UFO SECRECY (CAUS), filed suit against the CIA under the provisions of the Freedom of Information Act (FOIA). Documents released by the CIA during 1978 and 1979 revealed that in 1947 the CIA began close monitoring of UFO reports on a worldwide basis. Victor Marchetti, former Executive Assistant to the Deputy Director of the CIA, points out that although the majority of FOIA documents indicate only a routine interest handled largely by non-clandestine units, they also disclose by inference a standing requirement of the Directorate of Science and Technology for gathering UFO data. According to Marchetti, this, in turn, indicates that the Clandestine Services were charged with providing information on the phenomenon from all over the world. Since few such reports were released, Marchetti believes this indicates a cover-up. GSW's Director, WILLIAM SPAULDING, has noted in the documents a strong concern about the psychological effect of UFOs on the public. The CIA has been worried, contends Spaulding, about the possibility of Russia or another foreign nation utilizing the phenomenon as an offensive or defensive weapon. This fear was particularly strong during the cold war of the 1950s. Perhaps of most importance is the CIA's concern over air vulnerability. States Spaulding, "they cannot discern between the real and the phantom."

Meanwhile, efforts continue to obtain more documents from the CIA, particularly any which might refer to CRASHED FLYING SAUCERS. However, numerous documents are being held back, in accordance with the provisions of subsection (b) (1) of the FOIA, which specifically deals with secrecy, on the grounds that to do otherwise might endanger national security.

Bibliography: Keyhoe, Donald E., *Aliens from Space* (Garden City, NY.: Doubleday and Company, 1973); Davidson, Leon, *Flying Saucers: An Analysis of the Air Force Project Blue Book Special Report No. 14* (White Plains, N.Y.: Blue-Book Publishers, 1976); Marchetti, Victor, "How the CIA Views the UFO Phenomenon," *Second Look* (Washington, D.C.: Second Look, Vol. 1, No. 7).

## CENTRAL INVESTIGATIONS NETWORK ON AERIAL PHENOMENA *see* CENTRALES ERFURSCHUNGS-NETZ AUSSERGEWOHNLICHER PHENOMENE (CENAP)

## CENTRE D'ÉTUDES ET DE RECHERCHES DES PHÉNOMÈNES INEXPLIQUÉS (CERPI), 51 rue Saint Pallais, 17100 Saintes, France: telephone number: 46932209 or 46936393.

This investigative group is dedicated to the study of UFOLOGY, parapsychology and mysterious archaeology, and the relationship between them. Additionally, CERPI attempts to inform and arouse the interest of as many people as possible regarding these three subjects. The group has no beliefs regarding the identity and origin of UFOs but considers that several of the popular hypotheses might be valid.

This nonprofit organization was founded in 1975 by

Michel Souris, Robert Souris and Claude Souris. Staff positions change annually. There are 100 members. Ten field investigators are located throughout the Charente and Charente-Maritime regions. Seminars are held annually. The group's journal, *CERPI*, is published bimonthly.

## CENTRE FOR UFO STUDIES—AUSTRALIAN CO-ORDINATION SECTION (ACOS), P.O. Box 546, Gosford, New South Wales 2250, Australia.

Some of the Center's main functions include acting as a clearing house to which all Australian UFO reports are sent by the major UFO organizations and independent investigators throughout Australia, representing the Australian organizations, organizing national conferences and disseminating information to all the organizations within Australia and overseas. ACOS considers the identity, origin and purpose of UFOs as unknown.

This nonprofit organization was founded in 1974 by Harry Griesberg, David Seargent and J. ALLEN HYNEK. Griesberg and Seargent serve as the Center's co-ordinators. Scientific consultants in Sydney include G. Stevens (soil analysis), R. Molnar (anatomy), D. Herbison-Evans (computer analysis), W. Chalker (chemical analysis), A. Chalker (psychology), A. Cole (ACOS computer) and D. Reneke (mechanics). Scientific consultants in Adelaide include F. Gillespie (photographic analysis), P. Delin (psychology), V. Rendall (chemical engineering), R. Clay (physics) and B. J. Perry (hypnotherapy). Participating organizations include UFO RESEARCH (SOUTH AUSTRALIA), UFO RESEARCH (WESTERN AUSTRALIA), UFO RESEARCH (NEW SOUTH WALES), UFO RESEARCH (QUEENSLAND), UFO RESEARCH (FAR NORTH QUEENSLAND), the VICTORIAN UFO RESEARCH SOCIETY, the TASMANIAN UFO INVESTIGATION CENTRE and the UNIDENTIFIED PHENOMENA INVESTIGATION BUREAU.

Reports on unexplained UFO cases are forwarded to ACOS by the participating groups. One copy of these is forwarded to the CENTER FOR UFO STUDIES (CUFOS) in the United States, and one copy is retained by ACOS to form a central Australian library of UFO reports, as well as being coded into an Australian Computer File for research and study purposes. This UFO library is open to all participating organizations and individuals.

ACOS publishes yearly statistics on Australian sightings. The ACOS BULLETIN is published five times a year and is available for public subscription.

## CENTRE INTERNATIONAL D'UFOLOGIE (CIU), 80 rue de la Haie, 1301 Bierge, Belgium.

Investigative organization belonging to the COMITÉ EUROPÉEN DE COORDINATION DE LA RECHERCHE UFOLOGIQUE (CECRU).

## CENTRE NATIONAL D'ÉTUDES SPATIALES (CNES), France's National Center for Spatial Studies which founded and sponsors the UFO research organization GROUPE D'ETUDES DES PHÉNOMÈNES AÉRO-SPATIAUX NON IDENTIFIÉS (GEPAN).

## CENTRO DE ESTUDIO OBJETOS VOLADORES NO IDENTIFICADOS (CEOVNI), Box 1626, San Juan, Puerto Rico 00903.

The purpose of this investigative organization is to carry out field investigations, to conduct comparative analyses of UFO cases, to compile and organize data, and to maintain open cooperation with international organizations. The center holds that UFOs represent a unique phenomenon of an intelligent nature but that insufficient data exists to arrive at conclusions regarding their origin and purpose.

CEOVNI has studied close encounter cases in Puerto Rico and the Dominican Republic, dating back to 1956, in which humanoids have been reported and imprints have been left as evidence. The organization has determined that the behavioral pattern of the phenomenon in the Antilles is the same as in other parts of the world. CEOVNI believes the phenomenon to be beyond human control.

This nonprofit organization was founded in 1972 by Sebastian Robiou, William Santana and Noel Rigau. Robiou, Santana and Freddy Badillo are its Directors. There are twelve members. Representatives are located in the major cities of Puerto Rico. Contact is maintained with the CENTER FOR UFO STUDIES (CUFOS) in the United States. A periodical, *CEOVNI Bulletin*, is published.

## CENTRO DE ESTUDIOS DE FENÓMENOS AÉREOS INUSUALES (CEFAI), Casilla de Correo No. 9, Suc. 26 (1426), Buenos Aires, Argentina.

This organization is dedicated to the scientific investigation of the UFO phenomenon. It holds that UFOs represent a unique and unknown phenomenon of an apparently intelligent nature.

CEFAI was founded in 1972 by Oscar A. Uriondo and ROBERTO E. BANCHS, who serves as Director. Staff members include Ricardo Ruíz, Graciela Ruíz and Roque V. Magno. Field investigations are carried out by a network of collaborators located throughout the country. The group publishes the *CEFAI-Boletin*.

## CENTRO DE ESTUDIOS INTERPLANETARIOS (CEI), Apartado de Correos 282, Barcelona, Spain.

CEI conducts field investigations and carries out scientific research on the UFO phenomenon. It accepts that a high percentage of cases is explainable in natural or conventional terms but that there is a remainder whose explanation escapes our current understanding. The organization has no beliefs as to the identity, origin and purpose of those unexplained UFOs.

This nonprofit organization was founded in 1957 and currently has about 150 members. Pedro Redón-Trabal is General Secretary. Twenty-five investigators, located throughout Spain, cover all the provinces of the country. The *Consejo de Consultores de Stendek* (Consulting Panel of Stendek) was created in 1978. It consists of a group of Spanish scientists seriously dedicated to UFO research and is the sole group of this kind in Spain. Lectures are given monthly and a magazine, *Stendek*, is published quarterly.

## CENTRO DE ESTUDOS ASTRONOMICOS E DE FENÓMENOS INSOLITOS (CEAFI), Rua de Sa da Bandeira 331–30, salas 31 e 32, 4000 Porto, Portugal; telephone number: 380052.

The purpose of this organization is to clarify and disseminate information on the most representative of UFO manifestations and to organize prompt field investigations of UFO sightings on a nationwide basis. The case which this organization considers its most important is that of the discovery of an "unknown organism" found in a sample of ANGELS' HAIR which fell from a fleet of UFOs flying over the city of Evora on November 2, 1959. According to CEAFI, microscopic analysis revealed a "being" measuring approximately four millimeters in length and unknown to earthly biology. The matter was kept secret until October 1978 when it was made public at the First Iberian UFO Congress in Porto, Portugal.

This nonprofit organization was founded in 1972 by Manuel Armando Barrote Dias, José Manuel Ocana Garrido, José Luis Taveira, José Manuel, Maria Rosa Moreira and Mario Rua da Silva Ferreira. The group's coordinating center is made up of Manuel Armando Barrote Dias, Joaquim Fernandes de Conceicaeo, Jaime Germano Ferreira Teixeira, Mario Rocha and Paulo Campos. CEAFI has about 300 active associates and delegate groups located throughout Portugal, Madeira and the Azores. The organization receives cooperation and collaboration from the Portuguese Air Force and the National Republican Guard. Members have access to a library which includes the publications of foreign UFO organizations. Since 1975, CEAFI has published a monthly review called INSOLITO.

## CENTRO DE ESTUDOS UFOLOGICOS (CEU), Caixa Postal 689, CEP 60,000, Fortaleza, Ceara, Brazil; telephone number: 227 74 29.

The purpose of this investigative organization is to collect, research, analyze and disseminate theories and information about UFOs, their crews, their worlds and their physical, psychic, social and biological relationship to Earth. The group holds that UFOs are extraterrestrial vehicles, made of unknown material, which come from other planets and satellites in our own and other solar systems as well as from other galaxies and universes. The purpose of the extraterrestrial travelers, according to CEU, is to explore and study various universes in order to teach and help the inhabitants of other worlds. CEU warns that although UFOs bring us a message of peace and love, sometimes they can burn and hurt humans, therefore people must be careful when they see a UFO.

This nonprofit organization was founded in 1977 by lawyer José Jean Pereira de Alencar, who serves as Director. Accountant Paulo Amerim serves as Secretary, and lawyer Harold Serra serves as Treasurer. The group has approximately seventy members located throughout the twenty-three states of Brazil, in Portugal, Argentina, Spain and Denmark. Almost all of CEU's members serve as field investigators. The group's bulletin, UFONOTAS, is published quarterly.

## CENTRO DE INVESTIGACAO CIVIL DOS OBJECTOS AEREOS NAO IDENTIFICADOS (CICOANI), Caixa Postal 1675, Belo Horizonte, M.G., Brazil.

This investigative organization is dedicated to solving the UFO problem. The group was founded in 1954 by Hulvio Brant Aleixo.

## CENTRO DE INVESTIGACION SOBRE FENÓMENOS DE INTELIGENCIA EXTRATERRESTRE (CIFEX), Casilla de Correo 4046, 1000 Buenos Aires, Republica Argentina.

The purpose of this organization is to investigate and to disclose, in a scientific manner, all information about anomalous phenomena of probable intelligent origin. It believes that UFOs may possibly be extraterrestrial machines, different types of natural phenomena, psychic phenomena or terrestrial machines. CIFEX does not claim to know the origin or purpose of UFOs.

This nonprofit organization was founded in 1974 by Juan Ruben Haleblian, who serves as its Director, and Cristina Teresa d'Addezio, who serves as Public Relations Coordinator. There are twenty-two members. Twenty field investigators are located in the northwestern, western, central, south-central and southern regions of Argentina. The organization publishes the CIFEX BULLETIN.

## CENTRO INTERNAZIONALE RICERCHE E STUDI SUGLI UFO (CIRS UFO), Via G. Ratto

41/9, 16157 Genoa, Italy; telephone number: 010-721528.

The purpose of this investigative organization is to supply accurate information on the UFO phenomenon, to investigate UFO sightings and to conduct experimental research. The group has no official opinion regarding the identity and origin of UFOs. CIRS UFO has investigated ABDUCTION cases and in 1977 its principals carried out OPERATION VERRUGOLI, during which 108 UFOs were sighted.

This nonprofit organization was founded in 1978 by Giovanni and Piero Mantero. The Board of Directors consists of the Mantero brothers, Sergio Martini, Anna Maxena and Rodolfo Bracco. The group has fifty members. Field investigators are located throughout Italy. CIRS UFO is responsible for coordination in Italy of SKY WATCH INTERNATIONAL. The group publishes *Selezione UFO,* a magazine dealing with all aspects of UFOLOGY. The Mantero brothers write a regular column on UFOLOGY for the weekly newspaper *l'Eco di Genova e della Liguria*.

## CENTRO NACIONAL DE ESTUDOS UFO-LOGICOS (CENEU), SQS, 104, Ble., Apt. 305, Brasilia, Brazil; telephone number: 2242157.

This investigative organization supports the EXTRA-TERRESTRIAL HYPOTHESIS (ETH). Its President, AL-FREDO MOACYR DE MENDONCA UCHOA, has been conducting research in the field since 1968 and gives lectures. The group has sponsored conferences and maintains contact with several international organizations.

## CENTRO STUDI E RICERCHE CTA 102, Sky Residence, Corso Francia 222, 10093 Collegno, Italy.

The purpose of this investigative organization is to study and research UFOLOGY, parapsychology and yoga. The group was founded in 1970 by aeronautical engineer Marzio Forgione, who serves as President. There are about 100 members and thirty field investigators are located throughout Italy. The center maintains a library and organizes conferences.

## CENTRO STUDI FRATELLANZA COSMICA, Italian CONTACTEE organization founded by contactee Eugenio Siragusa.

## CENTRO TORINESE RICERCHE UFOLO-GICHE (CTRU), Via Avigliana 38, 10138 Turin, Italy; telephone number: 011-776546.

Convinced that UFO research should not be "defiled by personal persuasions," this investigative organization favors no one particular hypothesis because of lack of supportive evidence. CTRU was founded in 1974 by

Paolo Mercuri, who serves as President, and Gian Paolo Grassino, who serves as Editorial Manager of the group's publication. Staff members include Gianpiero di Candido, Franco dell'Ernia, Gianfranco Cordero and Massimo Lega. The group has fifty field investigators in Italy and others in Europe and other parts of the world. A bimonthly journal, *Notiziario Informativo Interno del Centro Torinese Ricerche UFOlogiche,* contains reports of UFOLOGICAL activities around the world with special emphasis on Italian events and studies.

## CENTRO UFOLOGICO NAZIONALE (CUN), Via Vignola 3, 20136 Milan, Italy.

This nonprofit investigative organization was founded in 1965. It conducts investigations, exchanges information with numerous foreign organizations and maintains a databank which is available to serious researchers in Italy and overseas. Roberto Pinotti is Editor-in-Chief of CUN's monthly magazine *Notiziario UFO*.

## CENTRO UNICO NAZIONALE, former name of the CENTRO UFOLOGICO NAZIONALE (CUN).

## CE-I *see* CLOSE ENCOUNTER OF THE FIRST KIND

## CEOVNI *see* CENTRO DE ESTUDIO OBJETOS VOLADORES NO IDENTIFICADOS

## CERCLE DE RECHERCHE UFOLOGIQUE NIÇOIS (CRUN), 420 Avenue de Pessicart, 06100 Nice, France.

Investigative organization belonging to the COMITÉ EUROPÉEN DE COORDINATION DE LA RECHERCHE UFOLOGIQUE (CECRU).

## CERCLE D'ÉTUDE DES MYSTÉRIEUX OBJETS CÉLESTES ET DES PHÉNOMÈNES INCONNUS (CEMOCPI), 19 rue Massenet, 42270 St. Priest en Jarez, France.

This regional investigative organization is dedicated to the scientific study of UFOs, investigation, detection and release of information to the public. Although the group holds that the phenomenon demonstrates intelligent and selective behavior, it does not consider any of the current hypotheses regarding origin to be valid. CEMOCPI supports the theory argued by JACQUES VALLEE in his book *Passport to Magonia* that modern day UFO accounts can be likened to the myths and legends from all ages and from all over the world which feature supernatural beings such as ANGELS, devils, elves and FAIRIES. The group has investigated several landing cases and has photographed two UFOs, one of which was on the ground. Statistical studies by the group have shown a correlation between UFOs and salt beds, geological faults, thermal springs and pilgrimage centers.

This nonprofit organization was founded in 1969 by Martine Allaguillaume. Staff members include President Patrick Berlier, Vice-President Jean-Pierre Maloriol, Secretary Christine Valentin and Treasurer Patrice Lapierre. There are fifteen members. An investigative team is available to interview UFO witnesses and, in cases of landings, to carry out field investigations with the aid of specialized electronic and photographic equipment. CEMOCPI covers the French departments of the Rhone and the Loire. Members may attend the group's conferences and expositions free of charge.

CEMOCPI is a member of the COMITÉ EUROPÉEN DE COORDINATION DE LA RECHERCHE UFOLOGIQUE (CECRU) and works in cooperation with the investigative network of the magazine LUMIÈRES DANS LA NUIT (LDLN).

## CERCLE DUNKERQUOIS DE RECHERCHES UFOLOGIQUES (CDRU), 57 rue de Normandie Coudekerque, Branche 59 210, France; telephone number: 20-650540.

The purpose of this investigative organization is to collect UFO reports, expose errors and HOAXES and to discover the real nature of the UFO phenomenon. The group hypothesizes that UFOs are perhaps spaceships from other solar systems. Their OCCUPANTS, suggests CDRU, might be here to study or use human beings, or to use our PLANET as a space station. The group holds that accurate UFO observations are very rare and that most people confuse knowledge and belief. The truth about UFOs, concludes CDRU, is not in our hands, nor will it be for a very long time.

This organization was founded in 1969 by Jean-Claude Vannoorenberghe, who still heads it. Mrs. Vannoorenberghe is Treasurer, and Mr. Eeckoudt is Secretary. Board Members are Mr. Moreel, Mr. Livoy and Mrs. Dewees. There are twenty-five members. Eight field investigators cover the northern part of Nord and Pas de Calais. There is a book-lending service for members and meetings are held monthly.

## CERCLE FRANÇAIS DE RECHERCHES UFOLOGIQUES (CFRU), Boîte Postale 1, 57601 Forbach-Cédex, France.

This investigative organization is dedicated to the research of UFOLOGY and related fields such as astronautics, astronomy and parapsychology. The group holds that UFOs are either of extraterrestrial or extradimensional origin.

This nonprofit organization was founded in 1966 by Frances Schaefer, who serves as President. Roland Lienhardt and Michel Turco are Board Members. The group has about 500 members. Field investigators are located in France, Germany, Switzerland, Italy, the United States, Canada, the United Kingdom, Japan, Belgium, Luxembourg and Guadeloupe. CFRU is a representative of the CENTER FOR UFO STUDIES (CUFOS) in the United States. The group publishes a quarterly magazine, UFOLOGIA.

Regional branches: R. Lienhardt/CFRU-Bas-Rhin, 17 rue Voltaire, 67800 Bischheim; Section CFRU du Haut-Rhin, B. P. 2075, 68059 Mulhouse-Cédex; Michel Souris/Section CFRU 17 (Departement de la Charente Maritime), 9 Cité des Buries, 17260 Gemozac; Christian Everaert (Departement du Nord), 18 rue François Mériaux, 59150 Wattrelos; C. Mace (Departement de l'Essonne), Résidence de la Nacelle, 4a rue de la Papéterie, Bt. R 91100 Corbeil-Essonnes; GROUPEMENT NORDISTE D'ÉTUDES DES OVNI (GNEOVNI); and GROUPEMENT PRIVÉ UFOLOGIQUE NANCÉIEN (GPUN)

## CERCLE INTERNATIONAL DES JEUNES UFOLOGUES (CIJU), defunct French organization which published UFOLOGIE BULLETIN.

Astronaut Eugene Cernan. *(Courtesy NASA)*

**CERNAN, EUGENE,** ASTRONAUT who, although he has seen nothing unidentifiable in space, stated on January 4, 1973, at a Los Angeles press conference, "I believe UFOs belong to someone else and they are from some other civilization."

**CERNY, PAUL C.** (b. October 2, 1930, Iowa; address: P.O. Box 1072, Mt. View, California 94042), Western States Director for the MUTUAL UFO NETWORK (MUFON), West Coast Investigator and Special

Representative for the CENTER FOR UFO STUDIES (CUFOS).

An active UFO investigator since 1957, Cerny travels hundreds of miles each week investigating sighting areas and interviewing witnesses. As a result of his work, he firmly believes that UFOs are physical, metallic craft piloted by humanoids from a nearby star system, who are observing our progress and utilizing Earth as a way station for further space exploration. On four different occasions during the past twenty-eight years, Cerny has personally witnessed unusual lights and glowing objects maneuvering and traveling at high speeds.

Paul Cerny.

A mechanical engineer and specialist in electronics and packaging, Cerny has worked in the fields of miniaturization of electronic equipment, design, optics, communications, satellite and space equipment, tracking, microwave and probing systems.

Cerny was Bay Area Chairman of the NATIONAL INVESTIGATIONS COMMITTEE ON AERIAL PHENOMENA (NICAP) from 1961 to 1972. He became the Northern California State Director for MUFON in 1972 and served in this post until 1974, when he was appointed Regional Director for the Western States. In addition to his positions as West Coast Investigator and Special Representative for CUFOS, he is a member of NICAP.

Cerny has been a guest on many local and national radio and television shows. His reports on outstanding UFO sightings, mostly close encounters involving humanoids and physical evidence, have been published in the UFO INVESTIGATOR; *The UFO Evidence* (Hall, Richard [ed.], Washington, D.C.: National Investigations Committee on Aerial Phenomena, 1964); *Strange Effects from UFOs* (Keyhoe, Donald E., and Gordon I.R. Lore [eds.], Washington, D.C.: National Investiga-

tions Committee on Aerial Phenomena, 1969); the MUFON UFO JOURNAL and the INTERNATIONAL UFO REPORTER.

**CERPI** *see* **CENTRE D'ÉTUDES ET DE RECHERCHES DES PHÉNOMÈNES INEXPLIQUÉS**

**CE-III** *see* **CLOSE ENCOUNTER OF THE THIRD KIND**

**CETI,** acronym for COMMUNICATION WITH EXTRATERRESTRIAL INTELLIGENCES.

**CE-II** *see* **CLOSE ENCOUNTER OF THE SECOND KIND**

**CEU** *see* **CENTRO DE ESTUDOS UFOLOGICOS**

**CFRU** *see* **CERCLE FRANÇAIS DE RECHERCHES UFOLOGIQUES**

**CHAIN LIGHTNING,** also known as bead lightning, a line of PLASMAS resembling a chain or string of beads.

Chain lightning. *(Courtesy U.S. Naval Ordnance Laboratory)*

The individual segments may appear as independent objects flying in formation. When traveling against the wind, their movements may give the impression that the objects are moving away from their original straight line formation. Although a rare and little understood phenomenon, chain lightning has been observed on many occasions. Writer PHILIP KLASS has suggested that its unusual appearance might lead an observer to refer to it as a UFO or a formation of UFOs.

Bibliography: Klass, Philip J., *UFO's Identified* (New York: Random House, 1968).

## CHAOS: THE REVIEW OF THE DAMNED,
magazine established in 1978, with a circulation of about forty. It is available by subscription and is published at irregular intervals. Its content is based upon the works of CHARLES FORT and phenomena which are often ignored, overlooked or rejected by the scientific community. UFOLOGICAL reports deal mainly with phantom airships and zeppelins, ball lightning and phantom aerial cities.

Most material is obtained from the files of Mr. X and the RES BUREAUX. However, some original and reprinted articles by freelance writers are published. Submitted articles should range in length from three hundred to 10,000 words or more. Literary reviews, newspaper clippings, translations, quotations, and helpful references are also accepted. Citations and footnotes should be listed on a separate sheet apart from the body of an article. Clippings should bear the name of the source, the date of publication, page number, and the contributor's name on a piece of paper taped to the back of the clipping. First or second world serial rights and reprint rights are purchased and, if first published under the copyright of *CHAOS*, rights other than those purchased are reassigned to the author or agent. Payment ranges from a year's subscription to *CHAOS* to fifteen U.S. dollars for first world rights, and is made upon publication. Freelance writers should query first regarding articles in excess of 1,000 words. Self-addressed, stamped envelopes should accompany submissions. Editor X advises that articles which may be rejected in UFO publications as "not of current interest" may be of interest to readers of *CHAOS*. Writers' guidelines are available upon request and X recommends that they be obtained with the purchase of a sample copy. The magazine is published by Res Bureaux, Box 1598, Kingston, Ontario, Canada K7L 5C8.

## CHARIOTS OF THE GODS?,
documentary (Sun Classic Pictures, 1974). Executive producer: Manfred Barthel; producer: Gunter Eulau; director: Harald Reinl; based on the books *Chariots of the Gods?* and *Gods from Outer Space* by ERICH VON DÄNIKEN.

In this scene from the motion picture *Chariots of the Gods?*, the theory is posed that the sphinx was the handiwork of ancient astronauts. *(Courtesy Sun Classic Pictures)*

This film explores von Däniken's theory that many ancient civilizations developed as a result of advanced knowledge brought to Earth by extraterrestrial visitors. The theory is documented with examples from countries around the world, including such archaeological oddities as the statues on EASTER ISLAND, the PYRAMIDS and cave drawings which allegedly resemble modern-day ASTRONAUTS.

Much of the film's footage was utilized in the 1973 NBC television special, IN SEARCH OF ANCIENT ASTRONAUTS.

## CHARLEMAGNE,
eighth and ninth century Frankish emperor whose subjects subscribed to a belief in the existence of a celestial region called MAGONIA. The inhabitants, sometimes called the tyrants of the air, traveled in aerial ships. The widespread fear that these creatures destroyed crops and kidnapped humans led Charlemagne to issue edicts that not only forbade the perturbing of the air and the provoking of storms, but also imposed penalties on the tyrants of the air. Reportedly, a great number of people had been carried off in aerial ships and shown unheard-of marvels. When these innocents were returned to Earth, many of them were put to death by fire and water. Four people in LYONS, FRANCE, who were seen to alight from an aerial ship,

were saved by Archbishop Agobard from an angry mob intent on lynching them.

Bibliography: Vallee, Jacques, *Passport to Magonia* (Chicago: Henry Regnery Company, 1969).

**CHILES, CLARENCE S.,** *see* **MONTGOMERY, ALABAMA**

**CHINA.** Although the Chinese government does not admit the existence of UFOs and there are no written records of sightings, travelers to China claim to have heard verbal reports of strange objects in the skies. The Chinese terms for UFO and flying saucer are "bu min fei ching ou" and "fay dea," respectively.

**CHINESE DISKS,** granite disks reportedly found in 1938 by Chinese archaeologist Chi Pu Tei in caves in the Payenk Ara Ulaa Mountains near Tibet. Each disk was two-and-one-half feet in diameter and almost an inch thick. Strange symbols were engraved in grooves spiraling out from a central hole to the outer rim. A total of 716 disks was found. They had a high cobalt content and it has been speculated that they were designed to store a vast amount of information by some means similar to magnetic recording. In 1962, Professor Tsum Um Nui of the Peking Academy of Prehistoric Research supposedly succeeded in reconstructing the story behind the disks from partial deciphering of their symbols and from legends originating in the mountainous regions where they were found. He claimed that about 12,000 years ago, a group of strange beings landed in their craft in the area but were soon killed by the local people because of their extreme ugliness. Skeletal remains of small, slender humanoids with large craniums and resilient bones, found in the same caves, are presumed to be the murdered pilots of the alien craft. Further evidence of the possible extraterrestrial origin of the corpses was found on the cave walls where pictures showed the sun, moon and stars linked by tiny dots.

The whereabouts of the stone disks today is unknown to western UFOlogists. One rumor claimed they had been transported to Moscow for analysis. However, because of the combined weight of the objects, if they exist, it seems probable that most of them are still in the caves where they were originally found.

Bibliography: Stoneley, Jack, with A.T. Lawton, *Is Anyone Out There?* (New York: Warner Paperback Library, 1974).

**CHOP, ALBERT M.** (b. January 4, 1916, Calumet, Michigan; address: 73769 Haystack Road, Palm Desert, California 92260), former Press Chief for the UNITED STATES AIR FORCE (USAF), and former Information Officer for the NATIONAL AERONAUTICS AND SPACE ADMINISTRATION (NASA).

As official Air Force spokesman for the UFO project, Chop participated in the radar observations of the celebrated WASHINGTON, D.C., sightings of 1952. He has concluded that UFOs do not originate on Earth and believes that the CONDON REPORT was a deliberate attempt to silence the public, an action he considers poor public relations.

On January 1, 1979, Chop, his wife and their daughter observed a triangular UFO moving slowly eastward over the mountains southeast of Palm Desert, California. The object was about ten times as brilliant as the stars in the background. It appeared to be extremely large but Chop was unable to determine its size since height and distance were not known. The UFO was in sight from approximately 5:00 A.M. until 5:45 A.M., at which time it had become a small, distant light in the eastern sky.

Chop attended the University of Dayton for two years. He was a journalist for the Associated Press and the *Dayton Daily News* from 1937 to 1943. From 1943 to 1944, he worked in public relations for Acme Aluminum Alloys. He was a U.S. Marine Corps combat correspondent from 1944 to 1946. From 1946 to 1950, he was an advertising copywriter for Fuller and Smith and Ross, Incorporated. In 1952, he became U.S. Air Force civilian Press Chief at the Air Materiel Command in Dayton, Ohio. In 1952, he was transferred to the Department of Defense in Washington, D.C., where he worked as a member of the Air Force Press Desk until 1953. From 1953 to 1962, Chop was a Public Relations

Albert Chop at the Mission Control Center in Houston, Texas. *(Courtesy NASA)*

Representative for the Douglas Aircraft Company. He then became Deputy of Public Affairs at NASA from 1962 until 1975. He was Manager of the Atomic Energy Commission's Employee Incentive Program from 1975 until he retired in 1976.

Chop was the recipient of four awards for outstanding performance from the U.S. government.

Chop wrote background material for the 1956 semi-documentary motion picture, UNIDENTIFIED FLYING OBJECTS (U.F.O.), which featured Los Angeles journalist Tom Towers in the starring role as Chop. His report on the Washington, D.C., UFO sightings was published in *Celestial Passengers—UFOs and Space Travel* (New York: Penguin Books, 1977) by Margaret Sachs with Ernest Jahn.

**CHRYSIS,** 48 Britannia Place, Dormanstown, Cleveland, England.

The purpose of this organization is to investigate, catalogue and research UFOs and related phenomena. Although the group has studied various theories, it has not yet committed itself to any one hypothesis on the identity, origin and purpose of UFOs.

This nonprofit organization was founded in 1974 by B. Straight and E. Ollis, and has twenty members. Ten investigators cover the northeastern area of England. Information is also collected from newspapers and from reports mailed in by the public. A newsletter, CHRYSIS 79, is published six times a year.

**CHRYSIS 79,** publication of the organization CHRYSIS.

**CIA** *see* **CENTRAL INTELLIGENCE AGENCY**

Cicero. *(Culver Pictures)*

**CICERO, (MARCUS TULLIUS),** first century Roman statesman and scholar whose writings included references to nine celestial phenomena. Of most interest to UFOLOGISTS is his statement that on one occasion the sun was seen at night accompanied by loud noises in the sky, which seemed to split open, revealing strange spheres.

Bibliography: Kolosimo, Peter, *Not of this World* (London: Souvenir Press, 1970).

**CICOANI** *see* **CENTRO DE INVESTIGACAO CIVIL DOS OBJECTOS AEREOS NAO IDENTIFICADOS**

**CIFEX** *see* **CENTRO DE INVESTIGACION SOBRE FENÓMENOS DE INTELIGENCIA EXTRATERRESTRE**

**CIFEX BULLETIN,** publication of the CENTRO DE INVESTIGACION SOBRE FENÓMENOS DE INTELIGENCIA EXTRATERRESTRE (CIFEX).

**CIGAR-SHAPED UFO,** cylindrical object with blunt or tapered ends. Cigar-shaped UFOs are usually seen at high altitudes and are often associated with an underlying or surrounding CLOUD formation. Their movement may be slow but erratic, with occasional accelerations. They may be horizontal, tilted or vertical. Cigar-shaped UFOs are sometimes referred to as MOTHER SHIPS because of the smaller, disk-shaped objects seen to emerge from them.

Two classic sightings involving cigar-shaped UFOs were those at OLORON and GAILLAC in France in 1952.

**CIJU** *see* **CERCLE INTERNATIONAL DES JEUNES UFOLOGUES**

**CION** *see* **CELESTIAL INTERPRETORS OF NAPPA**

**CIRS UFO** *see* **CENTRO INTERNAZIONALE RICERCHE E STUDI SUGLI UFO**

**CIRU** *see* **CENTRO TORINESE RICERCHE UFOLOGICHE**

**CIRVIS,** acronym for *Communications Instructions for Reporting Vital Intelligence Sightings,* the title of a Joint Chiefs of Staff directive prepared in 1953 and contained in JOINT ARMY-NAVY-AIR FORCE PUBLICATION (JANAP) 146.

**CISCO GROVE, CALIFORNIA,** isolated area in Placer County where a hunter was trapped in a tree overnight by four UFOnauts in 1964. The three men involved in the case have never sought publicity and are usually referred to by their first names and the initial of their last names.

On the evening of September 4, Donald S., Tim T. and Vincent A. went off to hunt after setting up camp. Towards sunset, they separated. Donald S. had lost his way when he observed the approach of a strange flying light, probably attracted by fires he had kindled to signal his location to potential rescuers. Donald climbed a tree, from where he observed the light as it hovered for a while before circling the tree. Suddenly, he saw a flash. A dark object fell to the ground, moved into the underbrush, then reappeared. Donald could discern a dome with a light flashing on it.

Two entities, about five-feet-five-inches tall, approached the tree. They were dressed in silvery white uniforms with hoods or helmets that went straight up from their shoulders. As they looked up at Donald, their large dark eyes were visible. Suddenly, a short, stocky robotlike creature appeared on the scene. Dark gray or black in color, this being also had no discernible neck. Its enormous, glowing, reddish orange eyes illuminated a square, hinged jaw which dropped open to form a rectangular hole in the face. As it did this, white vapor issued forth. Donald gasped for breath, then passed out. When he awakened, he found himself retching. The two humanoids were clumsily attempting to climb the tree. Donald began setting fire to objects in his pockets and pieces of clothing which he then threw at the creatures. This succeeded in making them back away temporarily. Throughout the night, the robot attempted to gas him with the white vapor. Donald passed out repeatedly but always awakened in time to frighten off the aggressors with more burning articles. He shot three arrows at the robot, knocking it back two or three feet. There was a bright flash each time an arrow struck. When Donald threw his canteen at the creatures, one of the humanoids picked it up, appeared to examine it, then threw it away. At dawn, a second robot appeared. Donald lashed himself to the tree with his belt. The two robots stood facing each other at the base of the tree. A series of bright flashes passed between them. Then a large cloud of vapor drifted upward. Donald blacked out.

When he awakened, he found himself hanging by his belt from the tree, exhausted and chilled from the early morning cold. Much of his clothing had been burned during the all-night siege. When Donald finally rejoined his companions, Vincent A. confirmed that he, too, had seen an unusual flying light after nightfall.

Air Force investigators suggested that Donald might have been the victim of a prank perpetrated by teenagers, soldiers on bivouac or Japanese people. It seemed unlikely, however, that teenagers would have carried out such an elaborate HOAX in such a remote area. Donald's inquiry at a nearby Air Force base elicited the reply that no military exercises were being conducted in the area at the time. As for the puzzling suggestion that Japanese people might have been responsible, Donald was convinced his aggressors were not Japanese.

The fact that the witness not only suffered from exposure as a result of burning his clothing, but also avoided publicity regarding the matter, has led some researchers to consider the possibility that this sensational report is authentic. Perhaps of greatest interest to UFOlogists is the apparent aggression demonstrated by the UFOnauts. Some have surmised that the incident reveals an attempt to retrieve an intact biological specimen of the human race.

Bibliography: Keyhoe, Donald E., and Gordon I.R. Lore (eds.), *Strange Effects from UFOs* (Washington, D.C.: National Investigations Committee on Aerial Phenomena, 1969).

**CITE** *see* **CONGRESS FOR INTERPLANETARY TECHNOLOGY AND EDUCATION**

**CITIZENS AGAINST UFO SECRECY (CAUS),** defunct organization founded in 1978 by W. Todd Zechel, Peter A. Gersten and Brad Sparks. Zechel, who served as Director, is a writer who claims to have worked in both overt and covert intelligence roles with the National Security Agency and another agency. A newsletter, JUST CAUSE, was published monthly. Although the organization was short-lived, ceasing its activities in 1979, it was instrumental in releasing numerous government documents relating to UFOs by filing lawsuits against various government agencies under the Freedom of Information Act (FOIA).

**CIU** *see* **CENTRE INTERNATIONAL D'UFOLOGIE**

**CIVIL COMMISSION ON AERIAL PHENOMENA (CCAP),** UFO organization which ceased to operate about 1960.

**CIVILIAN RESEARCH, INTERPLANETARY FLYING OBJECTS (CRIFO),** international UFO research group created by LEONARD H. STRINGFIELD in Ohio in 1953. CRIFO published a monthly newsletter, *Orbit*, which was edited by Stringfield. The organization ceased operating in 1957.

**CIVILIAN SAUCER INTELLIGENCE (CSI),** defunct New York City organization which was once very productive and highly respected by UFOlogists in the United States and overseas. Members and contributors included Isabel Davis, Ted Bloecher and the late Alexander Mebane. Microfilm of the group's newspaper clippings' file was made by the Science and Technology Division of the Library of Congress in 1967.

**CIVILIAN SAUCER INVESTIGATION.** Now defunct, this was the first private UFO research group created in the United States. Founded in 1952 by Ed Sullivan, a technical writer for North American Aviation Corporation, the organization included scientists from the Los Angeles area. Its most prominent member was rocket pioneer Walther Reidel.

**CLANCARTY, EARL OF,** *see* **LE POER TRENCH, BRINSLEY**

**CLEOPATRA,** Egyptian queen whose meeting with Mark Antony in 41 B.C. was reportedly highlighted by the merging of three suns into one. Some UFOlogists have suggested that the historic moment was witnessed by extraterrestrials in three overhead spaceships.

Bibliography: Drake, W. Raymond, *Gods and Spacemen throughout History* (Chicago: Henry Regnery Company, 1975).

**CLEU** *see* **COMMISSION LUXEMBOURGEOISE D'ÉTUDES UFOLOGIQUES**

**CLEVELAND UFOLOGY PROJECT,** 11309 Pleasant Valley, Parma, Ohio 44130; telephone number: 216-843-9978.

This investigative organization is administered by

Earl J. Neff. Public meetings are held monthly. The group is a member of the UFO Oнio network.

**CLEVELAND UFO SOCIETY,** 537 Juneway Drive, Bay Village, Ohio 44140; telephone number: 216-871-2952.

This investigative organization is administered by Lawrence Blazey, holds public meetings and is part of the UFO Oнio network.

**CLIPPING SERVICES** *see* **AERIAL PHENOMENA CLIPPING AND INFORMATION CENTER (APCIC) and UFO NEWSCLIPPING SERVICE (UFONS)**

**CLONING THEORY,** hypothesis proposing that UFO ABDUCTEES might be replaced on Earth by clones who work in such roles as spies, missionaries and agitators on behalf of their extraterrestrial leaders.

**CLOSE ENCOUNTER OF THE FIRST KIND (CE–I),** term coined by astronomer J. ALLEN HYNEK to describe a UFO sighting at close range without tangible physical evidence.

Bibliography: Hynek, J. Allen, *The UFO Experience: A Scientific Inquiry* (Chicago: Henry Regnery Company, 1972).

**CLOSE ENCOUNTER OF THE FOURTH KIND (CE–IV),** term used by some UFOlogists to denote the ABDUCTION of a human being by UFOnauts, and by other UFOlogists to denote a SEXUAL ENCOUNTER with a UFOnaut.

Cleopatra's meeting with Mark Antony. *(Culver Pictures)*

The mother ship hovers over Devil's Tower, Wyoming, in the motion picture *Close Encounters of the Third Kind.* (Columbia Pictures)

## CLOSE ENCOUNTER OF THE SECOND KIND (CE–II),

term coined by astronomer J. ALLEN HYNEK to describe a UFO sighting at close range accompanied by tangible PHYSICAL EVIDENCE.

Bibliography: Hynek, J. Allen, *The UFO Experience: A Scientific Inquiry* (Chicago: Henry Regnery Company, 1972).

## CLOSE ENCOUNTER OF THE THIRD KIND (CE–III),

term coined by astronomer J. ALLEN HYNEK to describe a close range sighting of a UFO and one or more UFONAUTS. This category does not include CONTACTEE encounters.

Bibliography: Hynek, J. Allen, *The UFO Experience: A Scientific Inquiry* (Chicago: Henry Regnery Company, 1972).

## CLOSE ENCOUNTERS OF THE THIRD KIND,

motion picture (Columbia Pictures, 1977). Producers: Julia Phillips and Michael Phillips; associate producer: Clark Paylow; director: Steven Spielberg; screenplay by Steven Spielberg. Cast: Richard Dreyfuss, François Truffaut, Melinda Dillon, Teri Garr and Cary Guffey.

This multimillion-dollar production was highlighted by Douglas Trumbull's special effects. Although it received eight Academy Award nominations, the film won only one Oscar for best cinematography. It was published as a novel by Dell Publishing, Inc.

The story begins when a UFO FLAP occurs in the state of Indiana. Numerous UFO witnesses begin receiving TELEPATHIC visions of a flat-topped mountain. A French scientist and his team receive radio signals from UFOs requesting a meeting at a secret base on top of a truncated mountain called Devil's Tower in Wyoming. Although authorities attempt to evacuate the area, the hero and heroine manage to reach the mountaintop in time to see the arrival of the alien spaceships. Two-way communication is established as the earthlings and the spaceship occupants take turns at playing various series of musical tones. The MOTHER SHIP lands and delivers several earthlings who had disappeared over the years, including the pilots of FLIGHT 19, which was lost in the BERMUDA TRIANGLE in 1945. The aliens step out of the craft. Slender creatures with large heads, they come face-to-face with the observers in a silent but friendly confrontation. The hero is selected to accompany the extraterrestrials on their departure in the mother ship.

Bibliography: Spielberg, Steven, *Close Encounters of the Third Kind* (New York: Dell Publishing, 1977).

Lenticular clouds over Sao Paulo, Brazil. *(Courtesy ICUFON/A. Baguhn)*

**CLOUDBUSTER** *see* **REICH, WILHELM**

**CLOUDS,** visible masses of tiny water droplets or ice crystals suspended in the sky. The three basic shapes of clouds are referred to as cirrus, stratus and cumulus. Cirrocumulus, cirrostratus, altocumulus, altostratus, stratocumulus, nimbostratus and cumulonimbus represent different combinations of the three. In addition, there are some special varieties of clouds. These include smooth, lens-shaped clouds known as lenticular clouds, wave clouds, grindstone clouds, stack of plates clouds, or piles d'assiettes clouds. Lenticular clouds are formed when air is forced to flow over hills or mountains. They usually remain stationary and may occur in a series or piled two or more in a stack. Particularly well-formed lenticular clouds closely resemble flying saucers in shape.

CIGAR-SHAPED UFOs which have cloudlike formations under or around them are sometimes referred to as cloud cigars. Since almost half the reported incidents of falls of ANGELS' HAIR have involved cloud cigars, it has been conjectured that these clouds might actually be composed of the same substance as angels' hair. In other cases, numerous objects, sometimes of varying sizes, have been observed emerging from a large cloud. Consequently, some UFOlogists have hypothesized that UFOs use clouds as camouflage. In cases of alleged DISAPPEARANCES, enormous clouds reportedly descended over the victims prior to their disappearance. This has led some researchers to the conclusion that extraterrestrial spacecraft were hidden inside the clouds.

Those who interpret religious manifestations, described in the Bible, as UFO sightings, point out that clouds are often mentioned in reference to such incidents. For example, according to Chapter 14 of the Book of Exodus, Moses and his people were led through the wilderness by something very similar to a modern-day cloud cigar. Verse 21 states, "And the Lord went before them by day in a pillar of a cloud, to lead them the way; and by night in a pillar of fire, to give them light." Later, in Chapter 19, it is stated, "And the Lord said unto Moses, 'Lo, I come unto thee in a thick cloud.'"

Bibliography: Vallee, Jacques, *Anatomy of a Phenomenon: Unidentified Objects in Space—A Scientific Appraisal* (Chicago: Henry Regnery Company, 1965).

**CLUJ, RUMANIA,** location of a well-publicized UFO sighting on August 18, 1968. Former army officer and technician Emil Barnea, his girlfriend Zamfira Matea and two anonymous companions were picnicking in the Baciu Forest when, at about 1:20 P.M., they observed a round, metallic luminous object moving slowly through the sky. The UFO's brilliance increased and decreased as it moved about, suddenly accelerated and shot upwards and out of sight. It had been visible for approximately two minutes. During that time, Barnea succeeded in taking four PHOTOGRAPHS of the object. One of the photographs was published one month later in several Rumanian newspapers.

Bibliography: Hobana, Ion, and Julien Weverbergh, *UFOs from Behind the Iron Curtain* (New York: Bantam Books, 1975).

**CLYPEUS,** Italian magazine established in 1963 as the official publication of the Centro Studi Clypeologici. The latter was founded in 1959 as an amalgamation of

UFO photographed at Cluj, Rumania, on August 18, 1968. *(Courtesy ICUFON/E. Barnea)*

several small organizations. The magazine has experienced several periods of suspended publication. Since 1977, however, it has been published bimonthly. *Clypeus* deals with UFOs and Fortean phenomena. It has presented articles by many well-known UFOlogists. Its Editor and Publisher is Gianni Settimo, Casella Postale 604, 10100 Turin, Italy.

**CNES,** acronym for the Centre National d'Études Spatiales, France's National Center for Spatial Studies which founded and sponsors the UFO research organization Groupe d'Études des Phénomènes Aéro-spatiaux Non Identifiés (GEPAN).

**CNIFAA** *see* **COMITATO NAZIONALE INDI-PENDENTE PER LO STUDIO DEI FEN-OMENI AEREI ANOMALI**

**COLEMAN, WILLIAM T.,** United States Air Force (USAF) major who was the Pentagon UFO spokesman from April 1961 to January 1962. In 1978, Coleman was Coproducer of the television series Project UFO.

In 1954, prior to his involvement with Project Blue Book, Coleman sighted a UFO while piloting an Air Force attack bomber from Miami, Florida, to Greenville Air Force Base in Mississippi. The object was disk-shaped, about sixty feet in diameter and about ten feet in thickness. The encounter lasted roughly eleven minutes, during which time the Air Force plane chased

the UFO, closing to within an eighth of a mile before losing it. Coleman and his crew found the disk again, then lost it once more. The sighting was reported to Project Blue Book. However, when Coleman joined the project six years later, he was unable to locate any record of the report and was never able to find an explanation as to why it was missing.

**COLLINS, MICHAEL,** *see* **GEMINI 10**

**COLOR.** UFOs observed during daylight are usually described as metallic, silvery, white or like aluminum. Bright colors are rarely associated with daytime sightings.

Nocturnal UFOs, however, have been reported in a variety of shades, primarily white, red, orange, yellow, green, blue and purple. Some have shown more than one color or have changed color during the observation.

Changes in color, and also in luminosity, have been associated with changes in speed. An increase in brightness and a shift toward the red end of the spectrum have accompanied acceleration, while a decrease in luminosity and a shift toward the violet end of the spectrum have accompanied deceleration.

**COLORADO GROUP** *see* **CONDON COMMITTEE**

**COLORADO PROJECT** *see* **CONDON COMMITTEE**

**COLUMBUS, CHRISTOPHER,** acclaimed discoverer of the New World who, in 1492, recorded in his ship's log the sighting of an unidentified moving light in the sky.

Christopher Columbus. *(Culver Pictures)*

Bibliography: Bergier, Jacques (ed.), and the Editors of INFO, *Extraterrestrial Intervention—The Evidence* (Chicago: Henry Regnery Company, 1974).

**COMET,** celestial body which moves around the sun. Some comets move in an elongated elliptical orbit, reappearing periodically. Others move in parabolas or hyperbolas, appearing only once before disappearing into space. A comet consists of a central mass called the nucleus, a surrounding haze called the coma and usually a tail, which is more pronounced when the comet is close to the sun. The nucleus is believed to be composed of meteoric material, ice, frozen methane and ammonia. The coma consists of gases released by the nucleus. The tail is an extension of the coma. Comets lose material each time they pass close to the sun. Eventually, they are reduced to tiny rock cores or break up into fragments. Such fragments are believed to be responsible for the formation of METEOR showers.

Early superstition held that comets were terrible portents. Today, despite the lack of complete understanding of the origin and nature of comets, they are rarely, if ever, misidentified. However, some historical records of aerial phenomena which have been dubbed "UFOs" by UFOlogists may, in fact, refer to comets. In particular, UFOlogists and scientists still debate the cometary explanation for the sighting of a huge fiery sphere at ROBOZERO in the Soviet Union in 1666 and the aerial explosion of a UFO over the TUNGUSKA REGION of the Soviet Union in 1908.

**COMITATO NAZIONALE INDIPENDENTE PER LO STUDIO DEI FENOMENI AEREI**

**ANOMALI (CNIFAA),** Via Rizzoli 4, sc. B, 40125 Bologna, Italy.

The purpose of this independent national committee is to serve as a reference channel for the Italian scientific community, providing it with selected literature in the UFO field, and, in addition, to publish scientific papers in English on the subject. CNIFAA devotes particular attention to the epistemology of UFO studies and is attempting to standardize the methodology and language of UFOLOGY. The group is open-minded regarding the identity of UFOs, holding that research to date has been inadequate to resolve that question.

Instituted in 1973 as a nonprofit organization, the committee is made up of twelve members, most of whom are scientists. They include Renzo Cabassi, Francesco Izzo, Umberto Leotti, Roberto Farabone and Roberto Doretti. A few trained field investigators interview witnesses and collect evidence of UFO sightings. Data is exchanged with colleagues in other countries.

In conjunction with Editecs Publishing House, CNIFAA publishes UFO PHENOMENA, INTERNATIONAL ANNUAL REVIEW (UPIAR), which the committee describes as "the first academic journal in English devoted to the scientific study of UFOs." Other contributions to international literature on the subject include a catalogue of Italian CLOSE ENCOUNTERS OF THE THIRD KIND (CE–III) from 1947 to 1976, prepared by Francesco Izzo, and a volume on the state-of-the-art in UFO studies, entitled *UFOs: Basis Zero* by Renzo Cabassi.

**COMITÉ EUROPÉEN DE COORDINATION DE LA RECHERCHE UFOLOGIQUE (CECRU),** French language network of UFO organiza-

Comet Cunningham photographed on December 21, 1940. *(Hale Observatories)*

tions and individual researchers. Since CECRU consists of totally independent members bound only by a cooperative protocol, it has no office, no president, no finances and no magazine or newsletter. Its sole purpose is to coordinate the work and activities of its members. All members exchange or make available to the others their reports and publications. CECRU convenes two or three times per year. Each member attends at least one session. The host member presides over the meeting, assisted by the hosts of the preceding and following meetings. Members receive a report of the convention's proceedings prepared by the host organization.

Applicants to CECRU must be sponsored by two other members and must provide evidence of their research capabilities. Acceptance or rejection of an applicant is made during the convention following receipt of the application. All members must renew their membership each year during March.

CECRU members include LES AMATEURS D'INSOLITE, ASSOCIATION DES AMIS DE MARC THIROUIN (AAMT), ASSOCIATION DIJONAISE DE RECHERCHES (ADRUP), ASSOCIATION POUR LA DETECTION ET L'ÉTUDE DES PHÉNOMÈNES SPATIAUX (ADEPS) MÉDITERRANÉE, CENTRE INTERNATIONAL D'UFOLOGIE (CIU), CERCLE D'ÉTUDE DES MYSTÉRIEUX OBJETS CÉLESTES ET DES PHÉNOMÈNES INCONNUS (CEMOCPI), CERCLE DE RECHERCHE UFOLOGIQUE NIÇOIS (CRUN), COMITÉ SAVOYARD D'ÉTUDES ET DE RECHERCHES UFOLOGIQUES (CSERU), the COMMISSION LUXEMBOURGEOISE D'ÉTUDES UFOLOGIQUES (CLEU), GROUPE D'ÉTUDES DES OBJETS SPATIAUX (GEOS), GROUPEMENT DE RECHERCHE ET D'ÉTUDE DU PHÉNOMÈNE OVNI (GREPO), GROUPEMENT DE RECHERCHES ET D'ÉTUDES UFOLOGIQUES (GREUFUNO), GROUPEMENT DE RECHERCHES ET D'INFORMATIONS PHOCÉEN SUR LES MYSTÉRIEUX OBJETS CÉLESTES (GRIPHOM), GROUPEMENT D'ÉTUDE RÉGIONAL DES OVNI (GERO), GROUPEMENT LANGEADOIS DE RECHERCHES UFOLOGIQUES (GLRU), GROUPEMENT NORDISTE D'ÉTUDES DES OVNI (GNEOVNI), GROUPEMENT PRIVÉ UFOLOGIQUE NANCEIEN (GPUN), GROUPE PALMOS, GROUPE TROYEN DE RECHERCHES SUR LES OVNI (GTR-OVNI), SOCIÉTÉ PARISIENNE D'ÉTUDES DES PHÉNOMÈNES SPATIAUX ET ETRANGES (SPEPSE), SOCIÉTÉ VAROISE D'ÉTUDES DE PHÉNOMÈNES SPATIAUX (SVEPS) and VÉRIFICATION ET ÉTUDES DES RAPPORTS SUR LES OVNI POUR NIMES ET LA CONTRÉE AVOISINANTE (VERONICA).

## COMITÉ SAVOYARD D'ÉTUDES ET DE RECHERCHES UFOLOGIQUES (CSERU), 266 Quai Charles Ravet, 73000 Chambery, France; telephone number: 79-334385.

The purpose of this regional organization is to inves-

tigate UFOs, study the evidence, inform the public and publish the results of its work. The group supports the EXTRATERRESTRIAL HYPOTHESIS (ETH).

This nonprofit organization was founded in 1976 by historian Nicolas Greslou, who serves as President. Jacques Roulet and Jacques Bosso are Vice-Presidents. Marc Derive is Secretary. There are sixty-five members. CSERU has an archivist, field investigators and electronics technicians. Investigations cover the Savoie and Haute Savoie areas. Members have access to a library, and may attend conferences. A thirty-six-page review, Le Phénomène OVNI, is published quarterly.

CSERU is a member of the COMITÉ EUROPÉEN DE COORDINATION DE LA RECHERCHE UFOLOGIQUE (CECRU).

## COMMISSION LUXEMBOURGEOISE D'ÉTUDES UFOLOGIQUES (CLEU), Boîte Postale 9, Belvaux, Luxembourg.

This investigative organization, dedicated to the study of UFOs, has no beliefs regarding the identity and origin of UFOs. It was founded in 1974 by Christian Petit, who serves as President. Other staff members include Secretary Monique Sassel, Treasurer Monique Linden, Sylvere Fedeli and Alain Baltenweg. About twenty field investigators are located throughout Luxembourg, France and Belgium. Les Chroniques de la CLEU is published quarterly.

CLEU is a member of the COMITÉ EUROPÉEN DE COORDINATION DE LA RECHERCHE UFOLOGIQUE (CECRU).

## COMMITTEE FOR THE SCIENTIFIC INVESTIGATION OF CLAIMS OF THE PARANORMAL (CSICP)—UFO SUBCOMMITTEE, c/o Philip J. Klass, 560 "N" Street S.W., Washington, D.C. 20024; telephone number: 202-554-5901.

The purpose of the UFO Subcommittee is to investigate significant UFO cases that have been characterized as unexplainable by other investigators. First-hand investigation is carried out where possible. The committee believes that all UFO reports have prosaic, terrestrial explanations. It has concluded that some leaders of the UFO movement are prepared to go to any lengths, including the use of falsehoods, to promote public belief in UFOs.

The parent committee was founded in 1976 under the sponsorship of the American Humanist Association. It is composed of forty-three scientists, science journalists, educators and magicians, including astronomer CARL SAGAN, psychologist B.F. Skinner, author Isaac Asimov and magician James ("The Amazing") Randi. The UFO Subcommittee was instituted in 1977. PHILIP J. KLASS serves as Chairman. Vice-Chairmen are ROBERT

SHEAFFER and JAMES OBERG. Membership in this nonprofit organization is by invitation only. The subcommittee currently has ten members. Reports of activities are included in the parent committee's quarterly publication, *The Skeptical Inquirer* (formerly *Zetetic*).

## COMMUNICATION WITH EXTRATERRESTRIAL INTELLIGENCES (CETI), name given to the efforts to establish contact with extraterrestrial civilizations through the use of RADIO ASTRONOMY. The program is currently referred to as the SEARCH FOR EXTRATERRESTRIAL INTELLIGENCE (SETI).

## CONDON COMMITTEE, team of scientific investigators and researchers at the University of Colorado who participated in an eighteen-month Air Force/taxpayer-sponsored investigation and evaluation of UFOs.

Following the recommendations of the O'BRIEN REPORT that the UFO program be strengthened, the Air Force entered into a formal agreement in October 1966 with the University of Colorado, having been turned down by the Massachusetts Institute of Technology, Harvard University, the University of North Carolina and the University of California. The project was to be directed by Edward U. Condon, a highly respected physicist. Although the Air Force's alleged goal had been to institute an impartial investigation, Condon soon made his attitude clear when he stated, "It is my inclination right now to recommend that the government get out of this business. My attitude right now is that there's nothing to it . . . but I'm not supposed to reach a conclusion for another year. . . ."

The situation was further aggravated when two of the project members, David Saunders and Norman E. Levine, discovered a memorandum which had been written by Project Coordinator ROBERT LOW almost three months before the start of the project. In it, Low stated, "Our study would be conducted almost exclusively by nonbelievers who, although they couldn't possibly *prove* a negative result, could and probably would add an impressive body of evidence that there is no reality to the observations. The trick would be, I think, to describe the project so that to the public, it would appear a totally objective study, but, to the scientific community, would present the image of a group of nonbelievers trying their best to be objective, but having an almost zero expectation of finding a saucer. One way to do this would be to stress investigation, not of the physical phenomena, but rather of the people who do the observing—the psychology and sociology of persons and groups who report seeing UFOs. If the emphasis were put here, rather than on

examination of the old question of the physical reality of the saucer, I think the scientific community would quickly get the message. . . .

"It is premature to have much of an opinion, but I'm inclined to feel at this early stage that, if we set up the thing right and take pains to get the proper people involved and have success in presenting the image we want to present to the scientific community, we could carry the job off to our benefit. . . ."

Saunders and Levine sent a copy of the memorandum to DONALD KEYHOE, who in turn sent a copy to JAMES MCDONALD. When the matter came to Condon's attention in February, 1968, he immediately fired Saunders and Levine for insubordination. Two weeks later, Low's Administrative Assistant, Mary Louise Armstrong, resigned, stating that the project members had no confidence in Low's leadership and had arrived at radically different conclusions from those reached by Low, who had spent very little time reviewing the relevant data. The NATIONAL INVESTIGATIONS COMMITTEE ON AERIAL PHENOMENA (NICAP) and the AERIAL PHENOMENA RESEARCH ORGANIZATION (APRO), who had been cooperating with the Condon Committee, withdrew their support.

As a result of the dissension within the group, the study had lost some prestige by the time it was completed in June 1968. In an apparent attempt to counteract any credibility gap, Condon sent the report to the NATIONAL ACADEMY OF SCIENCES (NAS) for review. After receiving their stamp of approval, the CONDON REPORT was released to the public on January 1969.

Bibliography: Condon, Edward U., *Scientific Study of Unidentified Flying Objects* (New York: E.P. Dutton, 1969); Saunders, David, and R. Roger Harkins, *UFOs? Yes!* (New York: World Publishing Company, 1968).

## CONDON REPORT, published results of the eighteen-month Air Force/taxpayer-sponsored study of UFOs carried out by the CONDON COMMITTEE at the University of Colorado. The report was issued in January 1969 with the seal of approval of the NATIONAL ACADEMY OF SCIENCES (NAS).

The main conclusion of the Condon Report, as stated by Condon in his summary, was that "nothing has come from the study of UFOs in the past twenty-one years that has added to scientific knowledge. Careful consideration of the record as it is available to us leads us to conclude that further extensive study of UFOs probably cannot be justified in the expectation that science will be advanced thereby." Condon avoided mentioning that more than twenty-five percent of the cases examined had remained unsolved. He ignored many of the conclusions reached by other contributors to the report and his appraisal of the UFO phenomenon reflected, for the most part, his personal views. However, the general public accepted his opinion that further study of UFOs was of no value. Consequently, the UNITED STATES AIR FORCE (USAF) canceled PROJECT BLUE BOOK in December 1969.

Bibliography: Condon, Edward U., *Scientific Study of Unidentified Flying Objects* (New York: E.P. Dutton, 1969); Saunders, David, and R. Roger Harkins, *UFOs? Yes!* (New York: World Publishing Company, 1968).

**CONGRESS** *see* **UNITED STATES CONGRESS**

**CONGRESS FOR INTERPLANETARY TECHNOLOGY AND EDUCATION (CITE),** Suite 6B, 17901 E. Chapman Avenue, Orange, California 92669; telephone number: 714-538-8537.

The purpose of this CONTACTEE organization is to promote and finance NEW AGE technology. CITE was founded in 1978 by BRIAN SCOTT, in conjunction with James Frazier. Scott's initial projects, allegedly assigned to him by the SPACE PEOPLE, are as follows: to write the Space People's history; to design solar-powered PYRAMIDS to be built in Bolivia, Egypt, England and the United States; to create a technology by which machines respond to mental commands; to bury time capsules; and to create a technology of "quantum displacement physics" for space travel.

**CONGRESS OF SCIENTIFIC UFOLOGISTS,** former name of the NATIONAL UFO CONFERENCE (NUFOC).

**CONRAD, CHARLES "PETE,"** *see* **APOLLO 12 and GEMINI 11**

**CONSPIRACY HYPOTHESIS** *see* **CENTRAL INTELLIGENCE AGENCY (CIA) and MIND CONTROL**

**CONSTABLE, TREVOR JAMES** (b. September 17, 1925, Wellington, New Zealand), writer and CONTACTEE.

Constable supports the theories of the late WILHELM REICH. He contends that UFOs comprise two main categories of objects, both of which exist in ETHERIA, or the invisible world. Living creatures, which Constable calls invisible "critters," live in the atmosphere as fish live in the ocean. Human witnesses often confuse them with actual craft piloted by ETHEREAN intelligences. Throughout the 1950s and 1960s, with his partner James Woods, Constable claims to have captured both types of UFOs on infrared film.

Constable began his career in the National Broadcast-

Trevor James Constable. *(Gloria Scott)*

ing Service of New Zealand. In 1944, he joined the New Zealand Merchant Navy as a radio officer until 1946, when he joined the British Merchant Navy. In 1952, he moved to the United States and resided in California until 1978. He was involved in a variety of business activities until his return to sea duty with the United States Merchant Marine during the Vietnam war. He is currently the Radio-Electronics Officer of the S.S. *Maui* and recently assumed the presidency of Merlin Weather Engineering, Incorporated, in Las Vegas, Nevada.

Constable is a member of the BORDERLAND SCIENCES RESEARCH FOUNDATION (BSRF), the American Federation of Labor and Congress of Industrial Organizations, and the American Radio Association. In 1977, he won the Book of the Year Award from Aviation and Aerospace Writers of America for *Fighter Aces of the Luftwaffe,* coauthored with Raymond Toliver.

His first book, *They Live in the Sky* (Los Angeles: New Age Publishing Company, 1958), was written under the pen name Trevor James. In 1965, he formed a literary partnership with Raymond Toliver, and they wrote the following aviation histories: *Fighter Aces* (New York: Macmillan Publishing Company, 1966); *Horrido!* (New York: Macmillan Publishing Company, 1968); *The Blond Knight of Germany* (New York: Doubleday and Company, 1970); *Hidden Heroes* (London: Arthur Barker, 1972); *Fighter Aces of the Luftwaffe* (Fallbrook, California: Aero Publishers, 1977). Constable is also the author of *The Cosmic Pulse of Life* (New York: Steinerbooks, 1975) and *Sky Creatures—Living UFOs* (New York: Pocket Book Library, 1978).

**CONTACTEE,** a person who claims repeated contacts with OCCUPANTS of flying saucers. A contactee is distinguishable from a UFO ABDUCTION victim, who usually claims only one encounter with UFONAUTS.

Contactees hold that UFOs are extraterrestrial spacecraft piloted by benign beings from PLANETS within and beyond our solar system. Some contactees actually claim to have visited the homes of the friendly SPACE PEOPLE. Contact is usually TELEPATHIC, often without the physical presence of the saucer occupants. Some of the Space People allegedly live unrecognized among human beings. Communications are usually of a religious nature and warn against such evils as war, atomic energy and pollution. Reincarnation plays a dominant role in the belief systems of the contactees and Jesus is considered to have been an incarnation of an extraterrestrial spaceman.

Although contactees do not usually file UFO reports or attempt to prove their claim, UFOLOGISTS blame them for bringing ridicule to the subject.

Some psychologists attribute the contactee phenomenon to hallucinations, postwar fear of atomic destruction and a need for religious fulfillment in a modern context. The voices heard by contactees have been compared to the disembodied voices attributed to God and saints in former centuries. Some contactees receive messages from their alleged space contacts through voice channeling. This process is similar to the Christian phenomenon known as "speaking in tongues" and is believed by some psychologists to originate entirely in the individual's own mind.

Author JACQUES VALLEE has speculated that contactees might be the victims of MIND CONTROL brought about through the use of PSYCHOTRONIC TECHNOLOGY. The perpetrators might be a group of human beings on Earth attempting to confuse and discredit the UFO issue in order to prevent close scrutiny by scientists. Their long-term goal could be to avert World War III by creating a belief in an extraterrestrial threat and thus uniting the nations of the world.

Engineer LEON DAVIDSON believes that the CENTRAL INTELLIGENCE AGENCY (CIA) is responsible for staging UFO contacts in order to confuse the Russians about American technological capabilities and to divert attention from specific Soviet space achievements by capturing news headlines with flying saucer reports.

Contactees worldwide number in the thousands. The most famous was the late GEORGE ADAMSKI. Others include ORFEO ANGELUCCI, TRUMAN BETHURIUM, DANIEL FRY, GABRIEL GREEN, HOWARD MENGER, RHEINHOLD SCHMIDT and GEORGE VAN TASSELL.

**CONTACT INTERNATIONAL,** 5/15 Kew Gardens Road, Richmond, Surrey, England.

The purpose of this worldwide organization is to investigate all aspects of the UFO phenomenon and to exchange information with other reputable UFO organizations. Although individual members have their own opinions regarding the identity of UFOs, the group's policy is open-mindedness and constant flexibility, a healthy curiosity, progressive thought and properly placed speculation. Contact International has concluded that UFO activity is cyclic and that the cycles appear to coincide consistently with known solar flare activity, at least as far back as 1700 A.D.

This nonprofit organization was founded in 1967 by BRINSLEY LE POER TRENCH (now Earl of Clancarty, following the death of his older brother), who serves as President. Staff members include President Ruth Rees, Vice-President Ivar Mackay, Secretary J. B. Delair, Treasurer Neil Pike and Philip Burden. There are approximately 11,000 members. Branches in thirty-four different countries are administered independently. Regular liaison and exchange of material occurs between all member countries and with other leading UFO investigative bodies in other parts of the world. Contact (UK) has over 100 field investigators located throughout the British Isles. Distribution of investigators overseas varies according to the needs of each specific country. The Data Research Centre, run by Bernard Delair, is located in Oxford and serves as the research headquarters for the entire organization. Through direct investigation, liaison with other organizations and use of newsclipping services, Contact International keeps itself fully informed of all major developments in the UFO field. The group holds an annual general meeting and sponsors lectures and exhibitions of UFO material. Contact (UK) publishes the quarterly magazine AWARENESS, which features special UFO investigations, news, views, reports, articles, letters, book reviews, and information generally relating to Contact (UK); and an annual journal, *The UFO Register,* which features tabulated statistics, data graphs, maps, charts, landing patterns, UFO behavioral and performance trends, activity graphs, catalogues of UFO shapes, lists of early and historical sightings and so forth. Many member countries publish their own publications.

**CONTACTOS EXTRATERRESTRES,** monthly magazine which deals with UFOs, ANCIENT ASTRONAUTS and the SEARCH FOR EXTRATERRESTRIAL INTELLIGENCE (SETI). The magazine's Editor-in-Chief is Ariel Rosales. It is published by Editorial Posada, José Maria Rico No. 204, Mexico 12, D.F., Mexico.

**CONTACTO SIDERAL,** publication of the FRATERNIDAD UNIVERSAL VIAJEROS DEL ESPACIO (FUVE).

**COOPER, L. GORDON,** ASTRONAUT who observed a UFO while orbiting Earth in the MERCURY 9 spacecraft on May 16, 1963. Cooper, now Vice-President of Engineering at Walt Disney Enterprises, has

become an outspoken supporter of the EXTRATERRES-
TRIAL HYPOTHESIS (ETH). He claims that while an Air
Force pilot in Germany during the early 1950s, he was
one of several witnesses to a series of high-altitude flying saucer flights over a two-day period. Cooper has
stated, "Intelligent beings from other planets regularly
visit our world in an effort to enter into contact with
us. . . . NASA and the American government know this
and possess a great deal of evidence. Nevertheless, they
remain silent in order not to alarm people. . . . I am
dedicated to forcing the authorities to end their silence."

## CORONA DISCHARGE *see* PLASMA

## COSMIC BROTHERHOOD ASSOCIATION
(CBA), Japanese CONTACTEE organization whose name
and that of its leader, Yusuke Matsumura, are known
internationally although not always identified or recognized as a contactee group.

The CBA movement was at a peak in 1959 and 1960
when it conducted an extensive campaign promoting
predictions that the world was about to end. The group
contended that the event would be caused by a drastic
shift in Earth's axis. The date was pinpointed as March
21, 1960, then changed successively to June 21, 1960,
and November 22, 1960, when the prediction was not
realized. Members were promised that when the date
approached they would receive coded cables stating,
"Send Apple, C," the "C" standing for "catastrophe."
Members and their families were to gather on the
shores of Japan's largest body of water, Lake Biwa. Two
hundred flying saucers would arrive to transport the
privileged CBA members to safety on another PLANET.
Following the failure of this prediction, several of CBA's
financial contributors filed lawsuits against the group.
CBA is now an underground organization with no fixed
address.

## COSMOLOGY NEWSLINK, monthly magazine es-
tablished in 1972, with a circulation of 1,000. Single
copies are available from the publisher. The range of
subjects covered includes metaphysics, cosmology,
geology, UFOLOGY, philosophy, space, science and
technology.

Material is obtained from staff writers, freelance
writers and newspaper clippings. Freelance writers
should query first. Submissions should be accompanied
by self-addressed, stamped envelopes. There is no
payment for articles although the publishers occasionally pay for photographs. The publication provides a
platform for new writers to make themselves known and
to publicize their work. Edward Harris is Editor, and
David Prockter serves as Coeditor on a part-time basis.

The magazine is published by CNK Press, 37 The
Close, Dunmow, Essex CM6 1EW, England.

**COVER-UP.** THE UNITED STATES AIR FORCE'S policy
of secrecy and its debunking program led many people
to believe that it was covering up the truth about UFOs
during the twenty-one years of its official investigation.
During that period, former Marine Corps Major
DONALD KEYHOE and the NATIONAL INVESTIGATIONS
COMMITTEE ON AERIAL PHENOMENA (NICAP) were
involved in an aggressive campaign to make the Air
Force admit that UFOs represented an unknown phenomenon, possibly an extraterrestrial threat.

After the PROJECT BLUE BOOK files had been made
available to the public at the NATIONAL ARCHIVES in
1976, it was discovered that numerous reports were
missing. Believing the missing information to be in the
files of the CENTRAL INTELLIGENCE AGENCY (CIA),
individuals and groups such as GROUND SAUCER WATCH
(GSW) and CITIZENS AGAINST UFO SECRECY (CAUS)
filed suit against the CIA under the provisions of the
Freedom of Information Act (FOIA). Numerous documents were released during 1978 and 1979 but many
were withheld on the basis that their release might
endanger national security. Meanwhile, UFOLOGISTS

A grounded UFO allegedly witnessed by a former private, first
class, at Fort Riley, Kansas, in November 1964. *(Drawn by
Larry Blazey for* UFO Ohio—*Courtesy the UFO Information
Network)*

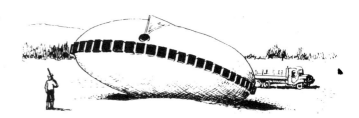

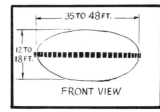

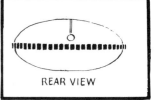

are pursuing the matter in the hope that they will eventually secure documents proving that the Air Force has one or more CRASHED FLYING SAUCERS hidden at an Air Force base somewhere in the United States.

There has been a great deal of speculation as to why the Air Force and other government agencies would adopt a secrecy policy. During the late 1940s, when the fear existed that UFOs might be secret enemy weapons, normal intelligence procedures dictated such a policy. After the EXTRATERRESTRIAL HYPOTHESIS (ETH) had become popular, some people assumed that the United States was in a race with the Soviet Union to uncover the secret to the advanced technology involved in UFO propulsion. If such were the case, the release of any evidence might have served only to help the Russians to solve the mystery first. During the 1950s, a number of people supported the SECRET WEAPONS HYPOTHESIS, believing that UFOs were experimental craft being tested by our own government. However, this theory becomes more untenable as the years pass since the government continues to sponsor the development of craft and weapons whose capabilities are primitive in comparison to the alleged capabilities of UFOs. Engineer LEON DAVIDSON is the chief proponent of a theory that the UFO phenomenon was created and utilized by the CIA to cause the Russians to waste their time and effort designing defenses against non-existent objects.

Some UFOlogists believe that government secrecy is merely a face-saving policy to conceal the Air Force's lack of control over its own air space. If the Air Force were to admit that it does not know what UFOs are and cannot intercept or outmaneuver them, the public would lose confidence in its capability as a defensive force. Additionally, the government might fear that the public's loss of confidence might deteriorate into panic. Even if the government knew that UFOs represented an alien force of some kind, it is possible that they would consider it unnecessary or unwise to inform the public of the truth. Authors JACQUES and Janine VALLEE have pointed out that throughout history, special interest groups have considered the introduction of new knowledge to be a threat to their financial status, their power and their ability to manipulate the masses.

On the other hand, J. ALLEN HYNEK, astronomer and former consultant to the Air Force, has suggested that the Air Force's apparent bungling of certain aspects of its UFO investigation was not intended to cover up the facts. Instead, it was merely the result of a poorly organized, inefficient program.

Some UFOlogists claim that the Air Force and other agencies are still involved in the investigation and cover-up of UFO data. According to NICAP's JACK ACUFF, government agencies are regularly receiving reports on UFO sightings from all over the world and information also comes through on domestic cases to the National Security Agency. Many of the documents obtained from the CIA through the FOIA have confirmed an ongoing interest by that agency.

**COYNE, LAWRENCE,** *see* **MANSFIELD, OHIO**

**CRABB, RILEY HANSARD** (b. April 2, 1912, Minneapolis, Minnesota; address: P.O. Box 548, Vista, California 92083; telephone number: 714-724-2043), Director of the BORDERLAND SCIENCES RESEARCH FOUNDATION (BSRF).

Crabb believes UFOs are the patrol vehicles of an advanced race, operating both from bases on the MOON and from MOTHER SHIPS orbiting Earth. He compares the threat to our civilization with that faced by the Aztecs in 1513 when they were invaded by the Spaniards. He holds that a vast adjustment in our thinking has to be made, if we are to survive.

Crabb became interested in the occult sciences in 1934 when he began to read the large collection of metaphysical literature at the library of the Theosophical Society in Minneapolis, Minnesota. At that time, he also began psychic research. During World War II, military service took Crabb to Hawaii where he returned in 1946. He remained there for thirteen years and during this time studied pagan magic. Soon after his move to California in 1957, Crabb was employed as a Visual Information Specialist for the United States Navy's Pacific Missile Range at Point Magu. In 1959, he became Director of BSRF at the invitation of N. Meade Layne, Founder and first Director.

Crabb is a Doctor of Metaphysics in the Society of St. Luke the Physician and received his Doctorate of Divinity from Williams College, Berkeley, California.

He has lectured widely on the subject of unusual phenomena, and among his lectures published by BSRF are thirteen discourses on flying saucers.

**CRASHED FLYING SAUCERS.** The two best-documented but inconclusive cases of crashed unidentified flying objects occurred in the TUNGUSKA REGION of the U.S.S.R. in 1908, and in UBATUBA, BRAZIL, in 1957. The former incident may have an astronomical explanation. The latter incident may be a HOAX. If it actually occurred as described by the witnesses, it is one of the most positive indications of alien visitation.

The earliest recorded report of a flying saucer fatality occurred in 1897 in AURORA, TEXAS. Half a century later, a series of such reports began. In the summer of 1947, news wires ran stories of several Swedish GHOST ROCKET crashes. Many of these UFOs fell into lakes.

The alleged victim of a rough flying saucer landing near Mexico City.

Claims that fragments were retrieved by the military have been denied by officials.

The most notorious episode was narrated by a former *Variety* columnist, Frank Scully, in his 1950 book, *Behind the Flying Saucers*. Scully reported that in 1948 the Air Force had captured three flying saucers in New Mexico and Arizona. Sixteen corpses were removed from each craft and medically examined. Apart from their approximately three-and-a-half-foot stature and flawless teeth, the aliens resembled normal human beings. Scully had learned of this incident at a lecture given by Silas Newton at the University of Denver. Newton, professing to be a millionaire from Texas, alleged that his associate, "Dr. Gee," had personally participated in the autopsies performed on the aliens. In reality, "Dr. Gee" was a confidence trickster named GeBauer. He and Newton were arrested two years later for trying to sell worthless war surplus equipment as oil detection devices. Although it became obvious almost immediately that the content of Scully's book was a hoax, the rumors continued to spread and became lavishly embellished in the process. Scully's book became a bestseller. Despite devastating exposés and the professional discredit suffered by Scully, subsequent claims of flying saucer crashes have paralleled his account in almost every detail.

During the 1950s a Cologne newspaper published a PHOTOGRAPH depicting the alleged victim of a rough spaceship landing near Mexico City. Two men in trenchcoats hold the arms of the twenty-eight-inch Martian corpse while two women look on. The origin of the photograph remains a mystery. Some researchers have concluded that the creature is either a wax mannequin or a shaved monkey. Two versions of the photograph are in circulation, one showing the diminutive being wearing boots and a loincloth, and one showing him without these garments.

In 1952, European news services carried the story of a UFO crash in SPITSBERGEN, NORWAY. Reportedly, British and American military experts were called in to assist in the investigation. The story remains controversial to this day.

The most dramatic foreign report dealt with the injured survivor of a crash in Poland in 1959. The alien was taken to a hospital where doctors struggled to take off his metal suit. When they removed an unusual armband, the patient died. Before his body was sent to Russia for examination, it was observed that he had an unusual number of digits and that his blood and organs were different from those of human beings.

Numerous accounts of saucer crashes continue to appear in print today. In each case, it is reported that the craft and small bodies were retrieved and hidden by the Air Force. All purported witnesses state that the incidents occurred some time during the 1950s. The rumors were perpetuated in 1974 by a wave of television and radio reports in which it was declared that the craft and frozen alien corpses were being held at Wright-Patterson Air Force Base in Dayton, Ohio. Claims that President GERALD FORD would shortly make a public announcement disclosing these facts

Crashed flying saucer allegedly seen in a five-minute film shown to several military radar specialists in 1953. The film also showed the small corpses of the purported occupants. *(Drawn by Larry Blazey—Courtesy the UFO Information Network)*

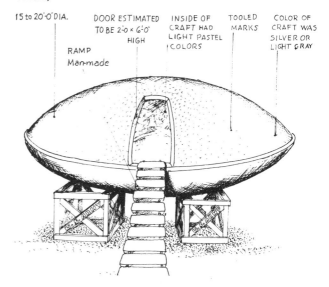

15 to 20'-0" DIA.

DOOR ESTIMATED TO BE 2'-0" x 6'-0" HIGH

INSIDE OF CRAFT HAD LIGHT PASTEL COLORS

TOOLED MARKS

COLOR OF CRAFT WAS SILVER OR LIGHT GRAY

RAMP Man-made

never materialized. In 1978, UFOlogist LEONARD STRINGFIELD announced that he had reports from twenty-four unimpeachable sources that spaceships and frozen alien corpses are being held at Wright-Patterson Air Force Base. In 1979, in international newspaper, radio and television interviews, WILLIAM SPAULDING of GROUND SAUCER WATCH (GSW) stated that his organization possessed signed affidavits from retired colonels in military intelligence attesting to the fact that a crashed disk and a thumbless entity had been retrieved and transported to a military base, possibly Langley Field.

Ancient preserved corpses have occasionally been proffered to the general public as victims of unspecified flying saucer wrecks. In 1932, a mummified body was found in the Rocky Mountains. The six-and-a-half-inch tall creature was put on display at Casper, Wyoming. Paleontologists have identified the mummy as *Hesperopithecus,* an anthropoid inhabitant of Earth during the Pliocene period. A similar creature, purportedly discovered in Arizona, has also been cited as the corpse of a LITTLE GREEN MAN from another world.

Bibliography: Stringfield, Leonard H., *Situation Red: The UFO Siege* (Garden City, N.Y.: Doubleday and Company, 1977). Jacobs, David Michael, *The UFO Controversy in America* (Bloomington, Indiana: Indiana University Press, 1975); Hobana, Ion, and Julien Weverbergh, *UFOs from Behind the Iron Curtain* (New York: Bantam Books, 1972).

**CRIFO** *see* **CIVILIAN RESEARCH, INTERPLANETARY FLYING OBJECTS**

**CROSSES** *see* **FLYING CROSSES**

**CRUN** *see* **CERCLE DE RECHERCHE UFOLOGIQUE NIÇOIS**

**CSI** *see* **CIVILIAN SAUCER INTELLIGENCE**

**CSICP** *see* **COMMITTEE FOR THE SCIENTIFIC INVESTIGATION OF CLAIMS OF THE PARANORMAL**

**CUARTA DIMENSION,** monthly magazine, established in 1973, with a circulation of 25,000. It is available both at newsstands and by subscription. It is published by the ORGANIZACION NACIONAL INVESTIGADORA DE FENÓMENOS ESPACIALES (ONIFE).

**CUFOREN** *see* **CANADIAN UFO REPORT EXCHANGE NETWORK**

**CUFORN** *see* **CANADIAN UFO RESEARCH NETWORK**

**CUFOS** *see* **CENTER FOR UFO STUDIES**

**CUMMINGS, JERRY,** UNITED STATES AIR FORCE (USAF) lieutenant who headed PROJECT GRUDGE from March 1951 to September 1951.

**CUN** *see* **CENTRO UFOLOGICO NAZIONALE**

**CUR, THE,** derogatory acronym for the *Colorado University Report* issued by the CONDON COMMITTEE.

**CUTTY SARK,** Scotch whisky company located at 42 Albemarle Street, Mayfair, London W1X 3FE, England, which sponsored UFO competitions during 1978 and 1979. The company offered a prize of one million pounds for a device which could be proven to have been activated to arrive on Earth from beyond our solar system. The rules stated that the device, which had to be delivered to the sponsors by June 30, 1979, had to be either a craft capable of interstellar travel which had transported extraterrestrial beings to Earth or an unmanned reconnaissance vehicle or a missile or an artifact. A second competition, which closed on June 30, 1979, offered a prize of one thousand pounds for a scientific paper judged to contribute most to understanding and knowledge of the UFO phenomenon.

Nobody entered the first competition. The second was won by computer specialist JAMES OBERG for his essay, entitled "The Failure of the 'Science' of UFOLOGY," subsequently published in *New Scientist* (London: New Scientist, October 11, 1979).

**CYBORG,** acronym for *cyb*ernetic *org*anism, denoting a hypothetical biological being, modified by the substitution of artificial organs and other body parts. Such a being could be specifically designed to endure long journeys through space and to function in an atmosphere different from that of its home PLANET. The alleged rigidity of movement of some UFOnauts, as well as their apparent imperviousness to bullets, has led to speculation that they may, in fact, be cyborgs.

**CYRILLIDS.** On February 9, 1913, hundreds of witnesses from Central Canada, right across the United States to Cape Sao Roque in Brazil, were thrilled by a spectacular display of fiery red and orange lights that traveled in formation, slowly and majestically, on a horizontal path across the evening sky. Because it occurred on the feast day of St. Cyril of Alexandria, the event was classified under the name Cyrillids. Though often referred to as a METEOR shower, the low altitude,

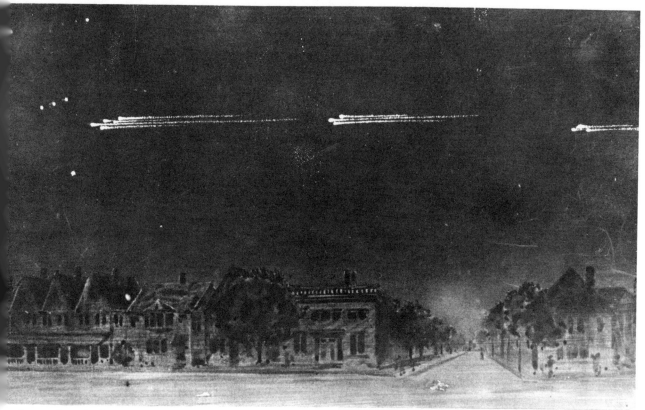

An eyewitness's oil painting of the Cryillids. *(Courtesy ICUFON)/Dunlap Observatory)*

low speed, horizontal trajectory, extended duration of visibility and prolonged course contradict all established characteristics of meteor showers. Moreover, meteor showers very rarely arrive in February and no fragments were ever found. Many explanations have been advanced for this celestial parade of lights, but the most widely accepted theory is that the UFOs were a group of natural objects in space that, upon approaching Earth, were captured by it. As temporary SATELLITES of this PLANET, moving in an orbit of low eccentricity, they were slowly consumed by atmospheric friction.

On February 10, 1913, witnesses in Toronto saw several unidentified objects maneuvering over Lake Ontario. Some UFOLOGISTS speculate that these may have been the same objects as those seen the night before. They reject the astronomical explanation and conclude that the Cyrillids were extraterrestrial space-craft performing a reconnaissance mission as a follow-up to an expedition that ended disastrously in the TUNGUSKA REGION of Russia in 1908.

Bibliography: Sachs, Margaret, with Ernest Jahn, *Celestial Passengers—UFOs and Space Travel* (New York: Penguin Books, 1977); Bergier, Jacques, *Extraterrestrial Visitations from Prehistoric Times to the Present* (Chicago: Henry Regnery Company, 1973).

**CZECHOSLOVAKIA.** Flying saucers are referred to as "letajici talir" in Czechoslovakia. The AERIAL PHENOMENA RESEARCH ORGANIZATION (APRO) has a representative there.

One of the country's best known cases involved the sighting of a nocturnal light by military personnel at BRNO in 1960.

**D'ADAMO, FRANK,** *see* **CELESTIAL INTER-PRETORS OF NAPPA (CION) and NATIONAL AERIAL AND PSYCHIC PHENOMENA ASSOCIATION (NAPPA)**

**DÄNIKEN, ERICH VON,** *see* **VON DÄNIKEN, ERICH**

**DÄNIKENITIS,** name given by the Australian news media to the enthusiasm engendered by and for author ERICH VON DÄNIKEN's theories concerning ANCIENT ASTRONAUTS.

**DANSK UFO CENTER,** P.O. Box 7938, DK–9210 Aalborg SØ, Denmark.

The center is a one-man organization run by Director Willy Wegner. However, several individuals occasionally participate in specific research projects. Wegner, an author and bibliographer, has been involved with UFOLOGY since 1964, and his special field of interest is its literature. He also has an interest in the historical development of UFOLORE. It is Wegner's opinion that the UFO enigma will never be solved.

This nonprofit organization was founded in 1969 by Wegner, Steen Holmgren, Steen Landsy, Jens Anker Petersen and Sejer Sejersen. There are no members. The center publishes a magazine, *UFOralia—tidsskrift for UFO-litteratur*, three to six times a year. Wegner is Editor and the five staff writers are Per Borgaard, Frank Pedersen, Torsten Dam-Jensen, Kristian Kristiansen and Erik Schou. The magazine publishes book and magazine reviews, bibliographic research, interviews with authors, editors and publishers, reviews of UFO meetings and conventions, articles concerning the development in the field of UFOlore and UFOlogy, and analysis of the contents of UFO magazines. *UFOralia*

has a circulation of about three hundred, consisting mainly of editors of Scandinavian UFO magazines, publishers, journalists and librarians. Wegner describes it as a magazine which is not loved by UFO buffs because of its critical attitude to the subject and the sparsity of stories about sightings and UFOnauts.

Some of the center's research projects have been published. These include: Wegner, Willy, *Dansk UFO-Litteratur 1946–1970* (Copenhagen: Institute of Folklore, University of Copenhagen, 1972)—a bibliography of UFO literature in Denmark; Wegner, Willy, *UFO-Landinger i Danmark* (Copenhagen: Frit UFO Studium [FUFOS], 1975)—a catalogue of Danish UFO sightings between 1951 and 1972; Wegner, Willy, *Skandinavisk UFO-Litteratur* (Copenhagen, Dansk UFO Center, 1976)—a bibliography of UFO literature published in Scandinavia between 1950 and 1975; Wegner, Willy, *Däniken i søgelyset* (Copenhagen: Frit UFO Studium (FUJOS), 1977)—a critical analysis of some of the theories set forth by ERICH VON DÄNIKEN; Wegner, Willy, and Ib Jensen, *Astro-Arkaeologisk Litteratur 1968–1977* (Copenhagen: Dansk UFO Center, 1978)—a bibliography of literature dealing with astro-archaeology.

**DAVIDSON, LEON** (b. October 18, 1922, New York, N.Y.; address: 64 Prospect Street, White Plains, N.Y. 10606), chemical engineer.

Davidson is the chief proponent of the theory that the CENTRAL INTELLIGENCE AGENCY (CIA) created the UFO situation as a front to confuse the Russians about the United States' technological capabilities. According to Davidson, the CIA took over the public image of "flying saucers" which were reported after secret flights of U.S. aircraft and artificial meteor research during 1947 and 1948. By 1950, he claims, the CIA had initiated a program of encouraging public belief in interplanetary travel by guiding the release of planted information and secretly sponsoring CONTACTEE clubs and UFO organizations such as the NATIONAL INVESTIGATIONS COMMITTEE ON AERIAL PHENOMENA (NICAP). Moreover, he states, contact experiences, such as those reported by GEORGE ADAMSKI and DANIEL FRY, were actually HOAXES perpetrated by the CIA. The UNITED STATES AIR FORCE (USAF), contends Davidson, was delegated by the CIA to act as the official investigative body to stave off public inquiry.

Davidson received his Ph.D. in Chemical Engineering from Columbia University in 1951. He was a junior scientist at Columbia's S.A.M. Laboratories from 1943 to 1944. He was employed as a chemical engineer at the Thermal Diffusion Plant in Oak Ridge from 1944 to 1945, as a senior technical engineer at the Gaseous Diffusion Plant from 1945 to 1946, and as associate engineer at the Brookhaven National Laboratory in 1947. While a member of the staff of the Los Alamos Scientific Laboratory from 1949 to 1952, he worked with the semi-official project looking for GREEN FIREBALLS in association with the Laboratory security organization. Subsequently, he worked as an operations analyst for the U.S. Atomic Energy Commission from 1952 to 1953, senior engineer at Nuclear Development Associations, Incorporated, from 1953 to 1958, manager of Datatron Operations from 1958 to 1959, associate head of the laboratory programming section at General Precision, Incorporated, from 1959 to 1960, senior programmer at Teleregister Corporation from 1960 to 1961, and manager of the programming section from 1961 to 1962. He worked in advanced applications development and the advanced systems development division for the International Business Machines Corporation from 1962 to 1963. He worked on a metroprocessing project from 1963 to 1968, and was technical director of the Metroprocessing Association in 1968. In 1968, he started his own company, the Metroprocessing Corporation of America. The latter was dissolved in 1969 and replaced by Blue-Book Publishers, of which Davidson is President. The company publishes leaflets and reprints of government documents. During his career, Davidson worked for classified government projects and held high U.S. security clearance for over fifteen years.

Davidson is author of *Flying Saucers: An Analysis of the Air Force Project Blue Book Special Report No. 14* (White Plains, N.Y.: Blue-Book Publishers, 1976).

## DAYLIGHT DISK (DD), term coined by J. ALLEN HYNEK to denote an oval, metallic-looking UFO observed in the daytime. Reports of daylight disks are less frequent than those of UFOs observed at night, which are known as NOCTURNAL LIGHTS (NL).

Bibliography: Hynek, J. Allen, *The UFO Experience: A Scientific Inquiry* (Chicago: Henry Regnery Company, 1972).

## DAY THE EARTH STOOD STILL, THE, motion picture (Twentieth Century-Fox, 1951). Producer: Julian Blaustein; director: Robert Wise; screenplay by Edmund H. North, based on the story "Farewell to the Master" by Harry Bates. Cast: Michael Rennie, Patricia Neal, Hugh Marlowe, Sam Jaffe, Billy Gray, Frances Bavier, Lock Martin and Drew Pearson (as himself).

An alien and a robot land in Washington, D.C., in a giant glowing flying saucer. The humanoid alien informs the world that if atomic tests do not cease, Earth will be destroyed by other PLANETS in the galaxy. After the world's leaders have decided that the alien is a HOAX, he is shot while returning to his flying saucer. He is retrieved by the robot and subsequently comes back to life. Before returning to his home planet, he gives the world a warning and a demonstration of his power. He makes the Earth stand still.

## DD *see* DAYLIGHT DISK

## DEBRIS. Apart from unsubstantiated reports of hidden remnants of CRASHED FLYING SAUCERS, the instances in which physical pieces of UFOs have been found are very few. The best known case is that of the metallic disk which exploded over the sea by UBATUBA, BRAZIL, scattering some small fragments onto the beach where they were picked up by fishermen.

Falls of hardware from the sky have occurred, however, without prior or subsequent UFO sightings. On June 12 in 1960, a sonic boom accompanied the fall of a fiery object from the sky over the St. Lawrence

A piece of the unidentified object which fell from the sky in 1975 in Carlisle, New York. *(Courtesy Ernest Jahn)*

River. The object split into two pieces, both of which plunged into the water about twenty miles upriver from Quebec City. The pieces were retrieved and analyzed. It was found that while there was nickel present, it was insufficient for the metallic objects to be of meteoric origin. Yet further experiments resulted in a number of unusual reactions not consistent with the normal characteristics of terrestrial metal.

In a similar episode in 1975, Leonard Tillapaugh, a farmer in Carlisle, New York, was almost killed when a small flying object struck his tractor, missing him by inches. ERNEST JAHN investigated the case and submitted the object for analysis to Northwestern University and subsequently to the Los Alamos Scientific Laboratory in New Mexico. An absence of nickel ruled out the possibility of meteoric origin. The chemical composition was found to be consistent with known compositions of common cast iron, establishing the fragment as a manufactured object. However, it was of such poor grade that the cost of producing such a substance would have been greater than its value. The Los Alamos scientists were unable to identify its origin.

Other debris that has been found on the ground, sometimes following UFO sightings, includes ANGELS' HAIR and DEVILS' JELLY. Many unusual items which have fallen from the sky and which may be associated with UFOs, are known as FAFROTSKIES.

Bibliography: Sachs, Margaret, with Ernest Jahn, *Celestial Passengers—UFOs and Space Travel* (New York: Penguin Books, 1977).

**DEBUNKING,** colloquial term to denote the exposing of false or exaggerated claims. In UFOLOGY, it refers to the discrediting of UFO reports and sometimes UFO witnesses themselves. Many UFOLOGISTS believe that the UNITED STATES AIR FORCE (USAF) carried out an intentionally indiscriminate debunking program during the course of its official investigations. Many witnesses were ridiculed and their reports given conventional explanations that, in many cases, were unsubstantiated. This led to the belief that the Air Force knew something disconcerting about the UFO phenomenon and was involved in a COVER-UP. Some UFOlogists have speculated that the Air Force believed, and still believes, the public needed to be protected from the truth. Others have conjectured that the Air Force attempted to debunk UFO stories rather than admit their own ignorance regarding the true nature of the phenomenon. Whatever the reason for debunking UFO reports, the subsequent embarrassment experienced by some witnesses discouraged many others from reporting their sightings.

**DECATUR UFO GROUP,** founded in 1957 and now defunct. This group ascribed to the theory that the governments of several nations have obtained evidence of the identity and origin of UFOs and are concealing this information from the public. Members concurred that the policy of secrecy is not improper and that to prevent panic such information should be presented gradually in an organized educational program.

**DeHERRERA, JOHN ANDREW** (b. November 29, 1939; Alamosa, Colorado; address: 417 N. Orange, Fullerton, California 92633; telephone number: 714-879-7525), technical writer and investigator of phenomena such as UFOs, visions and poltergeists.

DeHerrera believes there is an intelligence behind the UFO phenomenon. In 1957, he was traveling in a pick-up truck east on Highway 160 in Alamosa, Colorado, when an oval metallic aircraft approached on the left side from the opposite direction. It was traveling at approximately fifty miles per hour, ten feet above the ground. The UFO was approximately the size of an automobile. There were no air foils, canopy or windows. A long, colorful flame shot out of the back as it crossed the highway directly over the pick-up truck and vanished at tremendous speed. The object had been at a distance of no more than 100 feet when at its closest. Several other people traveling on the highway reported the incident to the *Pueblo Chieftain* newspaper.

After researching the subject for many years, DeHerrera became interested in the hypnotic regression of alleged UFO ABDUCTION victims. Aware that a hypnotized person can be very creative, he decided to find out if someone, who has never seen a UFO and is uninformed on the subject, can be encouraged to fabricate a story involving a UFO and its OCCUPANTS while under HYPNOSIS. In cooperation with English professor ALVIN LAWSON and clinical hypnotist William C. McCall, experiments were carried out which showed control subjects' responses to be similar to those provided by "real" abductees.

After receiving his Associate of Arts degree in Metallurgy in 1972, DeHerrera continued his education in chemistry, physics, psychology, computers, electronics, instrumentation and technical writing at Fullerton College, California.

From 1959 to 1966, DeHerrera worked for an autobody and paint business. From 1966 to 1968, he was a sheet-metal worker, and from 1968 to 1970, he was a metallurgical laboratory technician. From 1970 to 1974, he worked as a test engineer. Since 1974, he has worked as a technical writer in the field of microelectronics and clinical/industrial instrumentation.

DeHerrera is a member of the ASM Metallurgical Society, Toastmasters, the Medical Instruments Society, and the AERIAL PHENOMENA RESEARCH ORGANI-

ZATION (APRO). He has been the recipient of several metallurgical and speech contest awards. He is author of *Etherean Invasion* (Los Alamitos, California: Hwong Publishing Company, 1978).

## DEIMOS *see* MARTIAN MOONS

## DELAIR, J. B., *see* CONTACT INTERNATIONAL

**DELTA,** publication of the GRUPO PELOTENSE DE ESTUDIOS E PESQUISAS DE PARAPSICOLOGIA, PSICOTRONICA E OBJECTOS AEREOS NAO IDENTIFICADOS (PPOANI).

**DEL VAL UFO,** 948 Almshouse Road, Ivyland, Pennsylvania 18974.

This CONTACTEE organization holds that UFOs are spaceships of both a physical and ethereal nature from PLANETS in and beyond our solar system and from PARALLEL UNIVERSES. Their purpose, according to this group, is to aid in the spiritual transformation of man by introducing new dimensions of being.

The stated principles and purpose of the organization are as follows: "to reach those who seek the truth that much inspiration and guidance can be gained from an understanding of the UFO phenomena and UFO OCCUPANTS; to foster new dimensions of thought in relationship to the oneness of the infinite, the heavenly father and his children of the universe; to reach across the vastness of space with universal love as the true light of cosmic consciousness, with the desire to commune with the SPACE BROTHERS and Sisters on all levels of existence; to teach universal brotherhood, and awaken man to the realization that our samenesses are infinitely more important than our differences; and to prepare mankind for the coming of the dawn of a NEW AGE. The stated goals of the group are as follows: "to establish communications with other groups of similar interests and to develop an exchange of information and ideas; to supplement the existing membership; to enlighten the group about the more positive aspects of UFOs; to prepare the board members as public speakers, in order to reach a greater number of people through lectures, interviews and the news media; to form a library offering the best available books on the subject of spacecraft and space visitors; and to make a documentary film presenting the truth about the visitations of the Space Brothers and Sisters and the reason for their presence."

This nonprofit organization was founded in 1972 by MICHAEL CAMPIONE. The staff includes President Anthony Volpe, Vice President Lynn Volpe, Treasurer Andy Serbin and Secretary Lyda Spaeter. Del Val UFO

has 500 members. The *Del Val UFO Newsletter* is published monthly.

**DENVER EXTRATERRESTRIAL RESEARCH GROUP (DERG),** 330 East 10th Avenue, Apartment 902, Denver, Colorado 80203; telephone number: 303-832-6951.

The purpose of this organization is to investigate UFO sightings and to study the correlation between precognitive dreams and UFO encounters. The group claims that through the interpretation and study of UFO dreams and visions it has had excellent results in predicting actual sightings. DERG believes it is premature to determine the identity, origin and purpose of UFOs. However, it is also dedicated to the study of highly developed alien civilizations in an attempt to discover their purpose and the effects they might have on mankind now and in the future.

This nonprofit group was founded in 1977 by Petrillio "Pat" J. Richardson, who serves as President, and Rick L. White, who serves as Vice-President. Donna Pommer is Treasurer, and Beverly K. Cross is Secretary. The organization has fifteen local members and ten out-of-state members, some of whom are UFO witnesses and allegedly possess psychic abilities. Two field investigators cover the state of Colorado and nearby locations. Information is also gathered from newspapers and other reliable sources. Follow-up research is carried out to verify the authenticity of newspaper reports. Contacts in Canada and Sweden supply the group with information on foreign sightings. *Cause and Effect Newsletter* is published quarterly. Its contents include information on UFO-related paranormal phenomena. T-shirts and bumper stickers are also available.

**DETECTOR,** device designed to alert its owner to the presence of a UFO by sounding an alarm when its system experiences ELECTROMAGNETIC interference. Several models are sold commercially. In the United States, they are manufactured by the following companies: Force Field Instruments, Department A, 3711 Michiana Drive, Michigan City, Indiana 46360; and Shields Enterprises, 1004 Indian Falls Road, Emmaus,

UFO detectors. *(Courtesy Malcolm Jay)*

Pennsylvania 18049. In continental Europe, they are produced by Impressions Plastiques, Box 31, Chatelaine 1211, Switzerland. Both a standard model and a pocket size model are manufactured by Skywatch UFO Detectors (SKUFOD), 102 Nelson Road, Chingford E4 9AS, England.

For those wishing to build their own detectors, a variety of designs are available from the following companies: Raschick, 19216 Junipero Serra, Sonoma, California 95476; and UFO Alert, Box 1741, Owensboro, Kentucky 42301.

**DERO,** acronym for *de*trimental *ro*bots, evil characters described in a series of stories by RICHARD SHARPE SHAVER and published as factual stories in the science fiction magazine *Amazing Stories*. The savage creatures were said to be descendants of extraterrestrials who, after colonizing ATLANTIS and LEMURIA, moved into underground cities to escape solar radiation. While their counterparts, the *in*tegrative *ro*bots (tero), tried to assist earthmen, the dero are blamed for the unexplained accidents and misfortunes that befall human beings.

Bibliography: "I Remember Lemuria," *Amazing Stories,* Vol. XIX, No. 1 (March, 1945).

**DETECTOR SIDIP (SOCIÉTÉ INTERNATIONALE DE DÉVELOPPEMENT DES IDÉES POUR LE PROGRÈS),** Résidence Amboise, Domaine de Mont St. Alban, Boulevard Emile Bockstael 431, 1020 Brussels, Belgium.

Although this investigative organization holds no official position regarding the identity of UFOs, it considers the EXTRATERRESTRIAL HYPOTHESIS (ETH) and the PARALLEL UNIVERSE HYPOTHESIS as possible explanations for the phenomenon.

Although this group began functioning in 1970, it was officially founded in 1975 by M. M. Sossah, Charles Raveydts, Francis Windey and Guy O. Vanackeren. Sossah, Vanackeren and Windey serve as Directors. The Administrative Council consists of Claude Castremanne, Daniel Ritiere, Jean-Luc Jorion, Chantal Heylenbosh and Christine Carliez. There are 180 active members. The group has about 100 field investigators located in Belgium, France, the Canary Islands, Peru, Germany and the West African nation of Togo. The group also organizes numerous research expeditions to all parts of the world. It also gives courses in UFOLOGY and sponsors conferences. Its newsletter, *Vigilance,* is published bimonthly.

**DETROIT UFO RESEARCH GROUP,** nonprofit investigative group which published *The Visitor* and disbanded in 1965.

**DEUTSCHE UFO/IFO-STUDIENGESELL- SCHAFT (DUIST),** Postfach 130 185, 6200 Wiesbaden 13, West Germany; telephone number: 25604.

This organization holds that UFOs are interplanetary spacecraft. Its research covers every area of UFOLOGY, including sightings, CONTACTEES, astronautics, EXOBIOLOGY, ANCIENT ASTRONAUTS and paranormal events.

DUIST was founded in 1956 by UFOLOGIST and lecturer Karl L. Veit, who serves as President. German rocket scientist Hermann Oberth is the Honorable Chairman. Staff members and consultants include Anny F. Veit (Editor and Correspondence Supervisor), Cläre Müller (translator), COLMAN VONKEVICZKY (New York Representative), Rho Sigma (energy field and propulsion systems specialist), Willi Laun (physics/astronomy/ meteorology specialist), Jürgen Blunck (planetary cartography/history specialist), Research Director Karl Maler (flight and radar/paleolithic studies specialist), Heinrich Ragaz (UFOlogy specialist), Wolfram Fragner (physicist and mathematician), Engineer Geigenthaler (Scientific Co-ordinator) and W. Losensky-Philet (Space physics and hermetic studies specialist).The organization is the European representative of the INTERCONTINENTAL GALACTIC SPACECRAFT (UFO) RESEARCH AND ANALYTIC NETWORK (ICUFON). It also represents itself as a member of the Hermann Oberth Society, the AMERICAN INSTITUTE OF AERONAUTICS (AIAA) and the NATIONAL INVESTIGATIONS COMMITTEE ON AERIAL PHENOMENA (NICAP). DUIST cooperates and exchanges publications with about eighty international organizations. It organizes monthly conventions attended by UFOlogists from all over Germany and also sponsors international UFO conventions in Germany. The Ventla publishing company, owned by Veit, publishes German language editions of UFO and contactee books from around the world. The bimonthly newspaper *UFO-Nachrichten,* the official organ of DUIST, is distributed to eighty-eight nations. Veit is Editor-in-Chief.

**DEVILS' JELLY,** green slime or mysterious gelatinous objects which fall from the sky and are occasionally found at UFO landing sites. Usually in a globular or irregular form, the jelly shrinks and vanishes a short time after landing. In this respect it is similar to ANGELS' HAIR. A detailed report of the substance was given by police detective Faustin Gallegos in Miami, Florida, in 1958. He described a pulsating object that fell into his backyard as being transparent like glass. The surface glittered and it seemed to be composed of thousands of tiny cells. The odorless blob spread out over the lawn and dissolved. Although the detective had managed to scoop some of the material into a jar, when he delivered it to the nearby police station, the sample had dissipated, leaving no trace.

The green slime that fell on a large area of Foggy Bottom in Washington, D.C., in 1978, was discovered to have been the result of a malfunction in a vacuum system that removes soot from a heating plant in nearby Georgetown. However, the green slime in this case was not identical to devils' jelly since it did not dissipate. Instead it left a thick film on buildings, vehicles and foliage which caused plants to wilt and die, and poisoned animals that ate the coated grass. To date, devils' jelly has never demonstrated any harmful properties.

Bibliography: Gaddis, Vincent H., *Mysterious Fires and Lights* (New York: David McKay Company, 1967); "Green Slime Invades Washington," *Believe It* (Kensington, Maryland: Maryland Center for Investigation of Unconventional Phenomena, November, 1978, Vol. 1, No. 1).

**DEVIL'S SEA,** an area to the southeast of Japan sharing the reputation of the BERMUDA TRIANGLE as a mysterious danger zone for ships and aircraft, and constituting one of twelve vile VORTICES designated by IVAN SANDERSON. The Devil's Sea stretches between Iwo Jima and Marcus Island. Superstitious fishermen once believed that devils and monsters frequented the area, seizing the ships of the unwary. Modern losses of ships and their crews share some of the characteristics attributed to losses in the Bermuda Triangle. Extensive searches fail to locate wreckage or oil slicks. In the middle of the Devil's Sea, a compass needle will point to true north as it does within the Bermuda Triangle. Normally, it points toward magnetic north.

Reportedly, a team of scientists went out in 1955 aboard the *Kaijo Maru No. 5* on a government sponsored investigation. The ship vanished and was never seen again. The Devil's Sea has now been officially proclaimed a danger zone by Japanese authorities.

Bibliography: Berlitz, Charles, *The Bermuda Triangle* (Garden City, N.Y.: Doubleday and Company, 1974).

## DEVIL'S TRIANGLE *see* BERMUDA TRIANGLE

**DEVIL'S TRIANGLE, THE,** documentary (UFO/ Cinema National, 1974). Producer/director: Richard Winer; associate producer: Larry Kelsey; screenplay by Richard Winter; narrator: Vincent Price.

The film presents evidence of disappearances in the BERMUDA TRIANGLE from 1880 to 1967. Various experts are interviewed about the possible causes. The theories discussed range from kidnappings by extraterrestrials to

a change in dimension caused by ELECTROMAGNETIC fields.

**DEXTER, MICHIGAN,** location of one of two historically significant UFO sightings during the 1966 Michigan WAVE. On March 21, two police officers and three other witnesses saw a large, glowing object rise from a swampy area on a farm in Dexter. The object hovered for a few minutes at about 1,000 feet, then left the area.

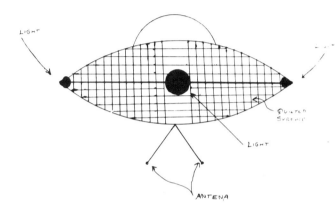

Witness's drawing of the UFO seen at Dexter, Michigan, on March 21, 1966. *(United Press International Photo)*

Since a UFO had been sighted the previous evening in HILLSDALE, MICHIGAN, newspaper reporters picked up the story and pressured the Air Force to investigate. The marshy locations of both sightings led J. ALLEN HYNEK to proffer the notorious and much-abused SWAMP GAS explanation.

Bibliography: Jacobs, David Michael, *The UFO Controversy in America* (Bloomington, Indiana: Indiana University Press, 1975).

**DIGAP** *see* **DIRECT INVESTIGATION GROUP ON AERIAL PHENOMENA**

**DIRECT INVESTIGATION GROUP ON AERIAL PHENOMENA (DIGAP),** 24 Bent Fold Drive, Unsworth, Bury BL9 8NG, England; telephone number: 061-766-4560.

This small organization has twenty members and eight field investigators in the South Lancashire area of England. Its aims are to promote scientific investigation of the UFO phenomena, to collect and disseminate evidence and to cooperate with other researchers. The organization has a library of UFO literature and meetings are held monthly. The group's belief regarding

UFOs is that they are exactly what their name implied—unidentified.

Reports of local phenomena are disseminated through DIGAP's newsletter, NUFON (NORTHERN UFO NEWS).

The organization is presided over by G. Cliffe, supported by Secretary A. Tomlinson and Treasurer W. Skelton.

**DISAPPEARANCES.** Many witnesses have claimed that UFOs have vanished instantaneously in midair. Some UFOLOGISTS hypothesize that this impresssion is created when a UFO accelerates to a SPEED that takes it beyond the observer's range of vision faster than the eye can follow. Supporters of the PARALLEL UNIVERSE HYPOTHESIS believe that the moment of disappearance is the moment that the UFO returns to its original dimension.

PHILIP KLASS has proposed that UFOs which disappear in this mysterious manner are merely glowing PLASMAS that dissipate their energy and merge with the surrounding air. The late DONALD MENZEL proposed other natural phenomena, such as SUBSUNS, as the explanation for disappearing UFOs. These natural phenomena create images which cease to exist when the causative conditions cease to exist.

In some cases, witnesses have described objects that have faded away gradually. Although the natural phenomena cited by Klass and Menzel could account for some of these cases, they would not apply to cases involving craftlike objects which leave physical evidence of a solid structure.

Indirectly related to UFOLOGY are the countless reports of the disappearance of terrestrial objects and human beings from all parts of the globe. The greatest concentration of loss of ships and airplanes is reported to occur in the BERMUDA TRIANGLE and the DEVIL'S SEA. Submarines, riverboats and cars have also been the alleged victims of this mysterious phenomenon. In 1942, observers aboard two patrol boats in the San Francisco harbor watched in amazement as an overhead Navy blimp, the L-8, suddenly soared upwards into a cloud. Hours later, the blimp crashed in the streets of San Francisco. There was no one aboard. The Navy had no explanation for the disappearance of the two-man crew.

In many cases, CLOUDS are reported to have enveloped objects and people prior to their disappearance. UFOlogists have associated these clouds with the clouds that sometimes surround CIGAR-SHAPED UFOs.

The most distressing stories are, of course, those involving the disappearance of human beings. CHARLES FORT has catalogued a great number of missing person reports. Other researchers have pointed out the connec-

The wreckage of the L-8 Blimp after its two-man crew had mysteriously disappeared. *(Courtesy Donn Davison)*

tion between the high proportion of children who have disappeared over the centuries and the widespread cultural beliefs in FAIRIES, leprechauns and other mischievous little people reputed to kidnap children. Traditionally, humans raised by fairies return centuries later, having aged only a few days. This has led UFOlogists to speculate that fairies might be extraterrestrial astronauts who take their captives on interstellar voyages during which, according to the theory of relativity, less time would pass for the travelers than for the people remaining on the home planet. Since many of these reports do not describe when and where the children disappear, it seems probable that the majority of missing youngsters are either runaways or the victims of crimes.

Reports such as that of farmer David Lang, who supposedly vanished in full view of witnesses, are less easily explained. Lang was walking in a field near Gallatin, Tennessee, on September 23, 1880, when his wife, children, a judge and one other guest saw him disappear into thin air. An investigation turned up no clues and found no discrepancies in the witnesses' stories. The credibility of a popular tale about a young boy who disappeared in Wales, however, is suspect when compared to an almost identical story set in the United States. In both versions, an eleven-year-old boy named Oliver was sent outside to fetch some water. Within moments, a shout was heard. The adults ran outside, where they heard his voice above them crying, "Help! They're taking me away." Then there was silence. Footprints in the snow, leading away from the well, stopped abruptly. The pail lay a few feet beyond them. Oliver was never seen again. The American version of the story took place in 1889. The boy's last name was Larch. The Welsh version occurred ten years later and in this instance the boy's last name was Thomas.

The most sensational cases involve the alleged disappearance of entire armies. During the Spanish War of Succession at the beginning of the eighteenth century, four thousand soldiers were reported to have disappeared, together with their equipment and horses. In 1885, about six hundred members of the French colonial forces were on the march, fifteen miles from Saigon. They were not under attack from the enemy yet every man vanished leaving no trace. During heavy fighting on August 21, 1915, twenty-two men of the New Zealand Army Corps' First Field Company claimed to have seen the One-Fourth Norfolk Regiment engulfed by a brown cloud which rose up and flew away. The British regiment was never seen again. Once more, in 1939, 2,988 Chinese troops were reported to have vanished from their camp, south of Nanking. Equipment, guns and cooking fires were found at the camp, which appeared orderly and undisturbed.

The anecdotal nature of these accounts makes their verification difficult. The possibility that extraterrestrials might gather human beings and their property for zoos and museums or other purposes is a theme often encountered in science fiction stories. If this is the explanation, collecting armies in deserted areas would be an excellent way of obtaining a large number of specimens in one quick swoop. In a limited number of cases, victims have reappeared elsewhere on Earth within an extremely short period of time. The science fiction term TELEPORTATION is used to describe this experience.

Bibliography: Bergier, Jacques, *Extraterrestrial Visitations from Prehistoric Times to the Present* (Chicago: Henry Regnery, 1973); Edwards, Frank, *Stranger than Science* (New York: Lyle Stuart, 1959).

The Discojet. Seated inside are motion picture producer Donn Davison *(left)* and Discojet President Paul Moller *(right)*. *(Courtesy Donn Davison)*

**DISCOJET CORPORATION,** 920 Third Street, Davis California 95616. This company has many ongoing research and development projects related to aerodynamics, noise suppression and transportation. It holds patents on a number of mechanical designs, including a vertical take-off and landing (VTOL) aircraft called "Discojet," which resembles a small flying saucer. It has been designed to combine the most attractive features of the helicopter and the light airplane. Discojet President Paul Moller hopes that the Discojet will one day replace or supplement the automobile as a convenient means of transport for the private individual.

**DOR,** acronym for *deadly orgone radiation*, toxic exhaust purportedly emitted by extraterrestrial spacecraft. The ORGONE ENERGY theory, formed by the late WILHELM REICH, has been promoted by TREVOR JAMES CONSTABLE and JEROME EDEN.

Bibliography: Eden, Jerome, *Planet in Trouble—The UFO Assault on Earth* (Hicksville, N.Y.: Exposition Press, 1973).

**DPRG UFO PHOTO ARCHIEVES (DUPA)** *see* **PARASEARCH**

**DRAKE, FRANK D.** (b. May 28, 1930, Chicago, Illinois; address: National Astronomy and Ionosphere Center, 404 Space Sciences Building, Cornell University, Ithaca, New York 14853; telephone number: 607-256-3734), professor and radio astronomer.

Drake believes UFOs can be explained as natural phenomena, misperceptions, HALLUCINATIONS and HOAXES. As a participant in the 1969 symposium on unidentified flying objects sponsored by the AMERICAN ASSOCIATION FOR THE ADVANCEMENT OF SCIENCE (AAAS), he described his own direct dealings with eyewitnesses of several unusual incidents. Approaching the subject of UFOs as an agnostic, his investigations led to two observations regarding witnesses. First, he found that there is a psychological need to carry out frauds and hoaxes. Second, he concluded that because the human mind does not always have perfect sensors, it is an imperfect computer in dealing with the stimuli it receives.

Well known, however, for his beliefs that life exists elsewhere in the universe, Drake is a leading authority on methods for the detection of extraterrestrial intelligent radio signals. His pioneering efforts began with PROJECT OZMA in 1960. Among the first to show how interstellar messages could be constructed for easy radio transmission, he pioneered the development of binary coded messages from which a "picture" could be obtained from proper decryption of the codes. Drake constructed the Arecibo Message of November 1974, the first interstellar message ever transmitted by radio waves from our planet for the benefit of any extraterrestrial civilizations. Subsequent messages utilizing his techniques and methods were sent on the PIONEERS 10 AND 11 and Voyager spacecraft. In 1961, Drake devised the GREEN BANK FORMULA to assess the probable number of communicative extraterrestrial civilizations we might find in our galaxy. He is currently conducting his own SEARCH FOR EXTRATERRESTRIAL INTELLIGENCE (SETI) program at the Arecibo Observatory in Puerto Rico.

Drake received his Bachelor of Engineering Physics degree from Cornell University in 1956. In 1958, he received his Ph.D. in Astronomy, also from Harvard University.

From 1592 to 1955, Drake was an electronics officer in the U.S. Navy. At Harvard, he was associated with the Agassiz Station Radio Astronomy Project from 1955 to 1958. From 1958 to 1963, he was Head of the Telescope Operations and Scientific Services Division at the National Radio Astronomy Observatory at Green Bank, West Virginia. In 1963, he became Chief of the Lunar and Planetary Sciences Section of the Jet Propulsion Laboratory of the California Institute of Technology. He became Associate Professor of Astronomy at Cornell University in 1964, and full Professor in 1966. From 1964 to 1965, he served as Associate Director of the Center for Radiophysics and Space Research at Cornell University, and from 1966 to 1968 was the Director of the Arecibo Observatory. From 1969 to 1971, he was Chairman of the Astronomy Department at Cornell University. He assumed his current positions as Director of the National Astronomy and Ionosphere Center in 1971, and the Goldwin Smith Professor of Astronomy at Cornell University in 1976.

Drake is a member of the NATIONAL ACADEMY OF SCIENCES (NAS), the International Astronomical Union, the American Association for the Advancement of Science (AAAS), the U.S. Commission of the International Scientific Radio Union, the Explorers' Club and the Society of Sigma Xi. He is a counselor of the American Astronomical Society, and a member of its Committee on Corporate Membership. He is a Fellow of the American Academy of Arts and Sciences.

Drake is a member of the Board of Directors of the Northeast Radio Astronomy Corporation, and the New York Astronomical Corporation. He serves on the Advisory Committee for the Very Large Array of the National Radio Astronomy Observatory. Drake has served as chairman and member of numerous committees and panels. He was a member of the Physical Sciences Committee of the NATIONAL AERONAUTICS AND SPACE ADMINISTRATION (NASA), and is a member of the Workshop on Interstellar Communication, and the Workshop on the Detection of Extrasolar Planetary Systems, both of the Ames Research Center of NASA. He is also a member of the Workshop on the Utilization of Existing Radio Antennas to Search for Extraterrestrial Intelligent Civilizations at the Jet Propulsion Laboratory.

Drake is the author of over one hundred papers and articles, has lectured widely and appeared on national and international television documentaries. He has been a contributing author to numerous books and encyclopedias and is author of *Intelligent Life in Space* (New York: Macmillan Publishing Company, 1962) and coauthor with CARL SAGAN, Ann Druyan, Timothy Ferris, Jon Lombers and Linda S. Sagan of *The Murmurs of Earth—The Story of the Voyager Record* (New York: Random House, 1979).

**DUIST** *see* **DEUTSCHE UFO/IFO-STUDIEN-GESELLSCHAFT**

**DUPA** *see* **PARASEARCH**

**DUPLANTIER, GENE** (b. Toronto, Canada; address: 17 Shetland Street, Willowdale, Ontario, Canada M2M 1X5), editor, publisher and commercial artist.

Duplantier has sighted UFOs on six occasions but thinks there is not enough evidence to establish their identity. Although he admits that, "Once you become involved with UFOLOGY, it's very hard to ever leave," he nevertheless smiles at those who are dedicated to solving the mystery. "What will they do then, if successful," he asks, "take up butterfly collecting?" He concludes that since the mystery remains unfathomed despite the accumulation of thousands of reports, the solution will be revealed if and when the intelligences behind UFOs decide to do so, and not until then.

Duplantier has worked in the advertising and editorial departments of several Toronto companies. His illustrations and cartoons have appeared in various UFO publications and from 1959 to 1973 he published and edited his own UFO magazine, *Saucer Space and Science*. He has given lectures and has been a guest on television and radio shows. His company, S. S. & S. PUBLICATIONS, publishes booklets and serves as a mail order house for UFO books, pamphlets, audio cassette tapes and records. Duplantier is editor and publisher of *UFOLK* (Toronto: S. S. & S. Publications, 1978).

**DZYAN** *see* **BOOK OF DZYAN**

**EAGLE RIVER, WISCONSIN.** In 1961, Joe Simonton, a sixty-year-old chicken farmer, was a lone witness in one of the most preposterous UFO cases on record. Despite the controversial nature of the case, UNITED STATES AIR FORCE (USAF) investigators and the local sheriff agreed that Simonton was not perpetrating a HOAX. He obviously believed in the reality of his story.

Simonton lived alone in a shack on the outskirts of Eagle River. At about 11:00 A.M. on April 18, he was eating breakfast when he heard a sound similar to "knobby tires on a wet pavement." Looking out the window, he saw a silvery object descending into his yard. The craft resembled two enormous bowls attached rim to rim. Exhaust pipes, about six or seven inches in diameter, ran along the edge of the vehicle. As the object settled a few inches off the ground, Simonton approached it. A hatch opened, revealing three dark-skinned, clean-shaven men with black hair. They were about five feet tall and reminded Simonton of Italians. One of the men handed him a silvery, two-handled jug and indicated that he wanted something to drink. Simonton went into the house, filled the jug with water and returned. After handing the jug back to the first man, Simonton saw that another man was apparently frying some food on a flameless grill. When he expressed an interest in the food, one of the men handed him three greasy pancakes perforated with small, round holes. Then the man nearest to the doorway picked up a strap which he attached to a hook on his clothing. The hatch closed leaving a barely perceptible outline on the surface of the craft. The object rose about twenty feet into the air before taking off in a southerly direction. Some nearby pine trees were buffeted by air turbulence as the craft passed overhead. The entire incident had taken place within a five-minute period.

Simonton contacted a friend of his in Eagle River, a county judge and a member of the NATIONAL INVESTIGATIONS COMMITTEE ON AERIAL PHENOMENA (NICAP). The judge sent one of the pancakes to NICAP headquarters with the request that it be analyzed. At the time, NICAP was busy trying to promote a Congressional hearing on UFOs and had little time to pursue what it considered a rather absurd story. However, the pancake was submitted to a couple of laboratories and it was a number of weeks before any preliminary results were obtained. In the meantime, the Eagle River judge mailed another pancake to the Air Force. The analyses revealed that the pancakes consisted of hydrogenated oil shortening, starch, buckwheat hulls, soybean hulls and wheat bran. Although Simonton, who had tasted one of the pancakes, said it tasted like cardboard, the Food and Drug Laboratory of the United States Department of Health, Education and Welfare concluded that the substance was an ordinary pancake of terrestrial origin.

The case was investigated by Air Force representatives Major ROBERT FRIEND, J. ALLEN HYNEK and an officer from Sawyer Air Force Base. Their conclusion was that Simonton had been having pancakes for breakfast when he had experienced a waking dream which he had been unable to distinguish from his conscious activities.

Author JACQUES VALLEE questions this hypothesis and considers the similarities between this tale and traditional folklore. Irish FAIRIES were reputed to live on pancakes and to utilize the exchange of food as a means of making contact. Vallee notes that salt, a substance which fairies eschew, was not found in the Wisconsin pancakes. Moreover, he points out that buckwheat was a popular grain in the legends of Brittany. Although he finds no explanation for the incident in these analogous details, he believes they lend support to the possibility that Joe Simonton's story is real and not a dream. He reminds us of the Biblical injunction: "Be not forgetful to entertain strangers, for thereby some have entertained ANGELS unaware."

Bibliography: Menzel, Donald H., and Lyle G. Boyd, *The World of Flying Saucers* (Garden City, N.Y.: Doubleday and Company, 1963); Vallee, Jacques, *Passport to Magonia* (Chicago: Henry Regnery Company, 1969).

**EARTH COLONIZATION HYPOTHESIS,** also known as the seeding hypothesis, theory that the human race was seeded on Earth by extraterrestrials or was created by the crossbreeding of extraterrestrials and earthly animals. It has been conjectured that the Biblical story of the Garden of EDEN is, in fact, an account of seeding by extraterrestrials. Supporters of this hypothesis believe that the extraterrestrial beings continue to visit Earth in flying saucers to monitor and manipulate our development.

The EARTH COLONIZATION RESEARCH ASSOCIATION (ECRA) in New Zealand devotes itself to the study of this theory.

Bibliography: Sendy, Jean, *Those Gods Who Made Heaven and Earth* (New York: Berkley Publishing Corporation, 1972).

**EARTH COLONIZATION REPORT,** publication of EARTH COLONIZATION RESEARCH ASSOCIATION (ECRA).

**EARTH COLONIZATION RESEARCH ASSOCIATION (ECRA),** 39 Callender Terrace, Paraparaumu, New Zealand; telephone number: 58-84245.

The main purposes of this investigative organization are to study the EARTH COLONIZATION HYPOTHESIS and to investigate UFO sightings. While the group remains undecided about the identity of UFOs, it has concluded that on the basis of the evidence accumulated to date, extraterrestrial ASTRONAUTS did visit this PLANET in ancient times and that there is a strong possibility they were responsible for man's presence on Earth.

ECRA carries out on the spot investigations throughout New Zealand through its investigation division, known as the NEW ZEALAND UFO STUDIES CENTRE (NUSC). Research on ANCIENT ASTRONAUTS is undertaken by members and authors in New Zealand and overseas. All information is disseminated through the monthly newsletter, *Earth Colonization Report,* and at annual seminars.

This nonprofit association was founded in 1976 by D. R. P. (Rocky) Wood, Juanita A. Wood and David K. Sim. Rocky Wood is President, and Juanita Wood is

Secretary. Jan F. de Bock is Director of UFO investigations. Paul L. Talley and D. A. Blennerhassett serve as field investigators. ECRA has approximately 250 members in New Zealand, the United States of America, England, Switzerland, France, Spain and West Germany. The organization is represented in Spain by Professor Francisco Villascusa, Miguel Gold 4-1°A, Yecla, Murcia, Spain; and in the United Kingdom by Dana J. Parry, 132 Ramnoth Road, Wisbech, Cambridgeshire PE13 2JD, England.

**EARTHLINK,** publication of the ESSEX UFO STUDY GROUP (EUFOSG).

**EASTER ISLAND,** an island located in the South Pacific, 2,300 miles west of Chile. The island is famous for its enormous stone statues, of which there are more than six hundred. Author ERICH VON DÄNIKEN, a major proponent of the ANCIENT ASTRONAUTS hypothesis, has suggested that these mammoth figures were constructed by extraterrestrial visitors or with the aid of extraterrestrials. He believes the volcanic rock of which the statues are made is too hard to have been cut with primitive tools within any reasonable period of time. He argues that the enormous weight of the statues prevented the possibility of their being transported and erected by the local people. According to von Däniken, there was no wood on the island to build wooden rollers. Additionally, he claims, the population could not have been large enough to supply the manpower to carve over 600 statues using primitive implements. As evidence of the presence of extraterrestrials on the island, he points out that the unwritten legends of the natives tell of flying men who once landed on the island.

Norwegian explorer Thor Heyerdahl disputes von Däniken's suggestions. In 1955, on a visit to the island, Heyerdahl watched the natives carve, transport and erect a statue. The carving was done with crude stone picks, thousands of which are scattered about the old quarries. Although the work began slowly, water was splashed over the rock at intervals to soften it and once the rock's hard outer surface had been penetrated, the work became much easier. Within three days, the outline of a statue was clearly visible. Heyerdahl estimated that even the largest statue could be completed in less than a year. Using rope, 180 men were able to drag a statue over the ground. Although most of Easter Island's trees have been either destroyed by fire or cleared for agriculture, they were once abundant on the island. Using three wooden logs as levers, and rocks as supports, twelve men were able to erect a twenty-five-ton statue within an eighteen-day period. Heyerdahl maintains that since the tradition of building statues endured for more than a thousand years and the island

A scene from the motion picture *Chariots of the Gods?* showing the gigantic statues on Easter Island. *(Courtesy Sun Classic Pictures)*

was capable of supporting a population of twenty thousand, it cannot be argued that there were insufficient resources, time and manpower to build the famous Easter Island statues.

Bibliography: Von Däniken, Erich, *Chariots of the Gods?* (New York, G. P. Putnam's Sons, 1970); Heyerdahl, Thor, *Aku-Aku—The Secret of Easter Island* (London, George Allen and Unwin, 1958).

**EASTERN AIRLINES** *see* **MONTGOMERY, ALABAMA**

**ECRA** *see* **EARTH COLONIZATION RESEARCH ASSOCIATION**

**EDEN,** Biblical garden suggested by some UFOLOGISTS to have been a biological laboratory in which ANCIENT ASTRONAUTS attempted to create a perfect race. By giving human beings everything they needed, it was hoped that greed and the desire to create would be repressed, thus eliminating the development of self-destructive technology, such as atomic bombs and germ warfare. It has been conjectured that the serpent was a piece of communications equipment such as a cable attached to a speaker through which extraterrestrials who opposed this genetic tampering instructed Eve to avail herself of the tree of knowledge, an apparatus from which she acquired the learning of her creators. Once the exterrestrial scientists knew that their experimental subjects had slipped from their

control, they threw them out of the laboratory. The flaming sword which protected the tree of knowledge thereafter, has been interpreted as an electronic device which guarded the scientific apparatus from further encroachment by human beings. Exponents of this theory point out that in Genesis 6 in the New English Bible it is stated that, "When mankind began to increase and to spread all over the earth and daughters were born to them, the *Sons of the Gods* saw that the daughters of men were beautiful so they took for themselves such women as they chose." These sons of gods are presumed to have been the sons of the extraterrestrial scientists who had originally set up the colony on Earth. Exponents of this theory cite Genesis 6:3, in which it is stated that the Lord is made of flesh like man, as evidence that the Lord referred to in the first book of the Bible is not God in the traditional sense.

Bibliography: Friedrich, George, *UFO or God?* (New York: Carlton Press, 1975).

**EDEN, JEROME** (b. August 23, 1925, New York, N.Y.; address: Box 34, Careywood, Idaho 83809), writer, editor and publisher.

Eden has observed UFOs on many occasions and in 1971 suffered severe conjunctivitis and a high fever after being struck by a beam of light from a UFO. A twenty-five year study of UFOs has led him to the conclusion that they are extraterrestrial spacecraft which present the gravest problem facing humanity. Eden holds that the drought conditions caused by the toxic exhaust from these vehicles must be counteracted by a global effort to

Jerome Eden.

utilize the discoveries and inventions of the late WILHELM REICH. Eden, himself, is registered with the State of Idaho's Department of Agriculture as a weather modification operator. For the past few years, he has been experimenting with a weather modification machine used by Reich to break droughts and with which Reich purportedly disabled several alien spaceships.

Eden received his B.A. from New York University and his M.A. from Columbia University. He served in World War II and the Korean War as a member of the United States Naval Hospital Corps. Subsequently, he was the Managing Editor of the *American Water Works Association Journal,* City and Military Editor of the *Idaho Falls Post Register* and First Director of the Eastern Idaho Special Services Agency. He is currently Publisher and Editor of the EDEN BULLETIN. He is a member of the Order of St. John of Jerusalem.

Eden has written extensively on the subject of ORGONE ENERGY. His published works are: *Suffer the Children* (Mt. Vernon, N.Y.: Eden Press, 1959); *Orgone Energy—The Answer to Atomic Suicide* (Hicksville, N.Y.: Exposition Press, 1972); *Planet in Trouble—The UFO Assault on Earth* (Hicksville, N.Y.: Exposition Press, 1973); *Animal Magnetism and the Life Energy* (Hicksville, N.Y.: Exposition Press, 1974); *View from Eden—Talks to Students of Orgonomy* (Hicksville, N.Y.: Exposition Press, 1976).

**EDEN BULLETIN,** quarterly publication established in 1974 to promote the theories of the late WILHELM REICH on ORGONE ENERGY, specifically with respect to the dangers posed by alleged extraterrestrial spacecraft employing orgone energy in their propulsion systems. Editor JEROME EDEN holds that the resultant toxic exhaust, called DOR or deadly orgone radiation, lacks oxygen and water, and is therefore the principal agent involved in drought and the formation of desert areas on this PLANET. Other subjects covered are ANIMAL MUTILATIONS, weather modification and the results of experiments using Reich's inventions.

This magazine is available by subscription only and is published by Eden Press, Box 34, Careywood, Idaho 83809.

**EDITECS PUBLISHING HOUSE** *see* **COMITATO NAZIONALE INDIPENDENTE PER LO STUDIO DEI FENOMENI AEREI ANOMALI (CNIFAA)**

**EDMONTON UFO SOCIETY,** 8008 129A Avenue, Edmonton, Alberta T5C 1XZ.

This investigative group is dedicated to the scientific study of the UFO phenomena. Although individual members hold different opinions, some in violent opposition to others, the society itself holds no beliefs regarding the identity of UFOs.

This nonprofit organization was founded in 1967. Its staff consists of President John Brent Musgrave, Vice-President Ashley Pachel, Investigations Chairman Bill Holt and Corresponding Secretary Ann Pachel. Field investigations are carried out locally. Membership stands at approximately thirty. The society sponsors a special award at an annual science fair and maintains a lending library for members. A newsletter is published monthly. Meetings are held once a month between September and June.

**EDWARDS, FRANK ALLYN** (b. August 4, 1908, Mattoon, Illinois; d. June 23, 1967, Indianapolis, Indiana), journalist and radio commentator.

Edwards, who first became interested in flying saucers in the 1940s, was an adherent of the EXTRATERRESTRIAL HYPOTHESIS (ETH). However, he rejected the authenticity of contact claims. In addition to UFOs, his interest spanned the entire field of unknown phenomena and mysteries.

Edwards was a sometime golf professional and a technical adviser in a shipyard in Evansville, Indiana. He began his radio career in 1924 with KDKA in Pittsburgh, Pennsylvania. Subsequently, he was employed by WHAS and WLAP in Louisville, Kentucky, from 1925 to 1934. He worked as a news analyst for the Mutual Broadcasting System from 1942 to 1954, and again from 1959 to 1961. He was a White House correspondent from 1949 to 1954. He served as a commentator in Indianapolis for WTTV from 1955 to 1959 and again from 1961 to 1962, for WXLW from 1964 onward, and for WLWI-TV from 1965 onward. From 1963 to 1964, he was a lecturer on Broadcast Journalism at Butler University.

Edwards was a member of the Board of Governors of the NATIONAL INVESTIGATIONS COMMITTEE ON AERIAL PHENOMENA (NICAP) from 1957 until the time of his death. He was a member of the Radio-TV Correspondents Association, the Indianapolis Press Club, the Elks and the Indianapolis Columbia Club. He was cited with Edward R. Murrow and Lowell Thomas as one of the nation's top three broadcasters in the *Radio Daily* poll in 1953.

Edwards wrote a column which was syndicated in more than 400 newspapers from 1950 to 1954. His column, "Strange to Relate," was syndicated internationally to about 300 newspapers by Central Newsfeatures of London in 1966. He was a contributing editor to FATE magazine from 1957 until his death. He was author of: *My First Ten Million Sponsors* (New York: Ballantine Books, 1956); *Strangest of All* (Secaucus. N.J.: Citadel Press, 1956); *Stranger Than Science* (New

York: Lyle Stuart, 1959); *Strange People* (New York: Lyle Stuart, 1962); *Strange World* (New York: Lyle Stuart, 1964); *Flying Saucers—Serious Business* (New York: Lyle Stuart, 1966); and *Flying Saucers Here and Now* (New York: Lyle Stuart, 1967).

**EFO** *see* **EXTRAORDINARY FLYING OBJECT**

**ELECTROMAGNETIC EFFECTS,** frequently reported disruption of electrical circuits occurring in association with UFO sightings. In many cases, these malfunctions are reported independently of the UFO witnesses who themselves may not have observed any electromagnetic interference. The most commonly reported effects are stalling and near-stalling of automobile motors; dimming, flickering and extinguishing of car headlights and house lights; static, fading and loss of radio reception; distortion and loss of television picture; stopping of wristwatches and clocks; malfunctioning of compasses; odd noises over telephone lines; and city-wide power failures resulting in BLACKOUTS. Oddly, upon the departure of the UFO, the affected systems reportedly begin to function again of their own accord.

Authors DONALD MENZEL and Lyle Boyd have pointed out that radio and television interference may be the result of a number of conventional and natural causes, including passing airplanes and bright meteors. However, no electrical field can interrupt the functioning of an automobile motor, its lights or a dashboard clock. Moreover, they stress, it could not stop a person's watch without seriously injuring the wearer.

Some UFOLOGISTS believe that reported electromagnetic effects are a side effect of controlled use of electromagnetic waves by UFO occupants.

Bibliography: *Electromagnetic Effects Associated with Unidentified Flying Objects* (Washington, D.C.: National Investigations Committee on Aerial Phenomena, 1960); Menzel, Donald H., and Lyle G. Boyd, *The World of Flying Saucers* (Garden City, N.Y.: Doubleday and Company, 1963).

**ELECTROMAGNETISM,** phenomenon resulting from the mutual interaction of electricity and magnetism. Numerous ELECTROMAGNETIC EFFECTS attributed to UFOs have led some researchers to suppose that electromagnetism may play an important role in the propulsion systems of UFOs.

**ELEMENTAL,** hypothetical being who inhabits another space-time continuum. While occultists have used the term to describe a variety of spirits, ANGELS, devils and FAIRIES, UFOLOGISTS who support the PARALLEL UNIVERSE HYPOTHESIS believe elementals may represent the intelligent forces behind UFOs. Author JOHN KEEL states that elementals are able to manipulate the electrical circuits of the human mind to produce images of UFOs and to create parapsychological events.

Bibliography: Keel, John A., *UFOs: Operation Trojan Horse* (New York: G. P. Putnam's Sons, 1970); Spence, Lewis, *An Encyclopedia of Occultism* (New Hyde Park, N.Y.: University Books, 1960).

**ELIJAH,** Hebrew prophet who, according to some proponents of the ANCIENT ASTRONAUTS hypothesis, was taken on a ride in a spaceship. The source of this claim is Chapter two of the Second Book of Kings, where it is stated: "And it came to pass, as they still went on and talked, that, behold, there appeared a chariot of fire, and horses of fire, and parted them both asunder; and Elijah went up by a whirlwind into heaven."

Bibliography: Le Poer Trench, Brinsley, *Mysterious Visitors—The UFO Story* (New York: Stein and Day, 1973).

**ELKINS, DONALD T.** (b. February 27, 1930, Louisville, Kentucky; address: P.O. Box 5195, Louisville, Kentucky 40205), CONTACTEE.

Elkins is a partner of L/L RESEARCH, has observed several UFOs and has experimented in contact with extraterrestrial entities since 1962.

He was an engineering and physics professor at the University of Louisville and the University of Alaska until assuming his current employment as a corporate and commercial airline pilot.

Elkins is a member of New Science Advocates and is coauthor, with CARLA RUECKERT, of *Secrets of the UFO* (Louisville, Kentucky: L/L Company, 1977).

**EM,** acronym for ELECTROMAGNETISM.

**EME,** acronym for ELECTROMAGNETIC EFFECTS.

**ENCOUNTERS,** publication of UFOCENTRE ALPHA TORQUAY.

**ENERGY HOTLINE,** monthly newsletter, established in 1979, with a circulation of 450. This publication replaces the quarterly magazine *Energy Unlimited,* which was established in 1978. It is available by subscription only. The range of subjects covered includes UFO propulsion systems, astrosonics and pyramid power, the inventions of Nikola Tesla, space geometry, PSYCHOTRONICS, rejuvenation therapy, weather control, transmutation of elements, wireless power transmission, superconductivity through alignment, ancient Atlantean technology, optic power generators, RADIONICS, pollution-free environment and power manipulation concepts.

Articles are written by staff and freelance writers. Payment is made in the form of a year's free subscription to the newsletter. The Editors are Kathleen Joyce and Walter P. Baumgartner. The newsletter is published by Energy Unlimited, 3562 Moore Street, Los Angeles, California 90066.

**ENERGY UNLIMITED,** quarterly magazine which was replaced in 1979 by a monthly newsletter, ENERGY HOTLINE.

**ENOCH,** seventh patriarch in the Book of Genesis and the subject of abundant apocryphal literature. In the Second Book of Enoch, the patriarch is visited by two unusual-looking men of very great height. Enoch is taken on a tour of the seven tiers of heaven and becomes the recipient of secret knowledge from God. Some proponents of the ANCIENT ASTRONAUTS hypothesis believe that Enoch was visited by extraterrestrial beings who took him on a tour of seven different PLANETS. They stress Enoch's claim that while the trip lasted only a few days for him, centuries had passed on Earth when he returned. According to the theory of relativity, very little time would elapse for ASTRONAUTS traveling just below the SPEED OF LIGHT, while a comparatively long period of time would elapse on Earth between their departure and return.

Bibliography: Bergier, Jacques, *Extraterrestrial Visitations from Prehistoric Times to the Present* (Chicago: Henry Regnery Company, 1973).

**EPIC OF GILGAMESH** *see* **GILGAMESH**

**E.P.I. GROUPE 03100 SECTION FRANÇAISE DE QUEZACOLOGIE,** 13 rue Beaumarchais, 03100 Montlucon, France.

The purpose of this CONTACTEE group is to study the UFO phenomena and its interaction with the individual and collective human consciousness. In addition, the organization wishes to expose what it believes to be a manipulation of mankind by a nonhuman psychic force. The group has investigated numerous contact and ABDUCTION cases, some of which it claims are unknown to the public.

This organization was founded in 1943. Research, investigations and other activities are carried out as a joint effort by all members, coordinated by Jean Giraud. Investigative operations include field investigations, interviews with witnesses, complete analysis of evidence, and psychological and neurophysiological studies. The group covers all of France, as well as a number of foreign countries. A review, *INFO OVNI*, is published three times a year and distributed gratis to all of the group's researchers.

**ESSEX UFO STUDY GROUP (EUFOSG),** 16 Raydons Road, Dagenham, Essex, England.

The purpose of this group is to investigate UFO reports and inform the public about the subject. The organization holds that UFOs probably originate from different sources, some from other dimensions. It conjectures that most UFOs are here because we are at a dangerous point in Earth's history, possibly on the verge of local self-destruction. The purpose of some UFOs, the group suggests, is to show mankind that there is life in other dimensions which can be contacted. EUFOSG has investigated CONTACTEE and psychic contactee cases as well as humanoid sightings. Overall investigative efforts have revealed a prevalence of sightings near or over rivers. The group has concluded that to understand and communicate with UFOs, it is necessary to learn more about psychic, esoteric and spiritual matters.

This nonprofit organization was founded in 1970 and has a membership of approximately 100. Its staff is composed of Public Relations Officer John Saville, Group Secretary Gloria Saville, Journal Editor Daniel Goring and Group Executive C. W. Eden. Approximately twenty investigators cover the Essex and North and East London areas. The organization conducts meetings and skywatches. *Earthlink,* published quarterly, is edited by Daniel Goring and contains reports on the UFO phenomena both at home and abroad, as well as exploring related subjects.

**ESTIMATE OF THE SITUATION,** military term applied to an intelligence report on any vital problem. In UFOlogy, it refers to a specific report on the UFO phenomenon made by the AIR TECHNICAL INTELLIGENCE CENTER (ATIC) shortly after the 1948 Eastern Airlines sighting near MONTGOMERY, ALABAMA. Classified Top Secret, the report concluded that UFOs were extraterrestrial spacecraft. The estimate received considerable attention until it reached Chief of Staff General Hoyt S. Vandenberg, who rejected it on the ground that it lacked proof. Some months later, the report was declassified and incinerated. Its rejection led to a change in policy at PROJECT SIGN, and those who believed UFOs were conventional objects took charge.

Bibliography: Ruppelt, Edward J., *Report on Unidentified Flying Objects* (Garden City, N.Y.: Doubleday and Company, 1956).

**ET,** acronym for *extra*terrestrial.

**ETH,** acronym for EXTRATERRESTRIAL HYPOTHESIS.

**ETHEREANS,** hypothetical, invisible creatures who inhabit ETHERIA.

Bibliography: Constable, Trevor James, *The Cosmic Pulse of Life* (Santa Ana, California: Merlin Press, 1976).

**ETHERIA,** name given to a hypothetical invisible world composed of ether, an invisible substance that has been postulated by physicists as pervading space and functioning as the medium for the transmission of radiant energy. UFOLOGISTS who support the etheric hypothesis, claim that UFOs are both inanimate craft and living aeroforms, propelled and sustained by ORGONE ENERGY, that exist in the etheric realms. Inhabitants of Etheria are known as Ethereans.

Bibliography: Constable, Trevor James, *The Cosmic Pulse of Life* (Santa Ana, California: Merlin Press, 1976).

**ET HYPOTHESIS** *see* **EXTRATERRESTRIAL HYPOTHESIS**

**ETI,** acronym for *extraterrestrial intelligence.*

**ETI HYPOTHESIS** *see* **EXTRATERRESTRIAL INTELLIGENCE HYPOTHESIS**

**EUFOSG** *see* **ESSEX UFO STUDY GROUP**

**EVRENDE ZEKI HAYAT,** publication of the SPACE PHENOMENA RESEARCH GROUP.

**EXETER, NEW HAMPSHIRE,** location of a series of UFO sightings which occurred during the fall of 1965. The sightings were studied and documented by several investigators, including journalist John G. Fuller. His preliminary account of the investigation was published in *Look* magazine on February 22, 1966. He assembled his final results into a book, *Incident at Exeter*.

The sighting which received the most publicity occurred on September 3, 1965. At about 1:30 A.M., Patrolman Eugene Bertrand of Exeter found a parked car on the side of a road. The driver told him that a huge, silent, airborne object had followed her for a distance of about twelve miles. The object had brilliant, flashing red lights and kept within a few feet of her car. It had suddenly taken off at tremendous speed and disappeared among the stars. Disbelieving, Bertrand did not take the woman's name. When he checked into the police station shortly afterwards, he found that a frightened young man, named Norman Muscarello, had just come into the station to report an encounter with a similar object. Bertrand accompanied Muscarello back to the scene at about 3:00 A.M. The two men walked into the field where Muscarello had seen the UFO. Although there was no sign of anything unusual at first, horses on a nearby farm and dogs in nearby houses began making a great deal of noise. Suddenly, Mus-

carello yelled, "I see it! I see it!" Bertrand turned and saw the brilliant, roundish object as it rose silently from behind some trees. The object moved toward them like a leaf fluttering from a tree. Its brilliant red lights bathed the entire area in light. It approached within about 100 feet of the two men, hovering with a rocking motion. Bertrand reached for his gun, then, changing his mind, pushed it back into its holster. He grabbed Muscarello and headed to the car to take cover. As they watched the UFO, its lights seemed to be dimming or pulsating from left to right and then from right to left, covering about two seconds for each cycle. It was difficult to make out the shape of the object because of the brilliance of the lights. After several minutes, it began to move eastward, performing maneuvers that defied conventional aerodynamic patterns as it darted, turned rapidly and slowed down. Patrolman David Hunt, who had heard the radio conversation between Bertrand and the police station, arrived at the scene in time to witness the UFO for several minutes before it disappeared. A B–47 aircraft flew over shortly afterward, providing an extreme contrast to the strange object which they had observed in the clear, moonless sky. Moments later, Patrolman Reginald Toland, the desk officer on duty, received a call from an Exeter telephone operator. She had just received a call from an hysterical man in a phone booth who told her that a flying saucer had come right at him. Suddenly, the anonymous caller was cut off. He was never located.

During his investigation, Fuller tracked down about sixty different people who had witnessed similar objects, usually near power lines, over a period of several weeks during the autumn. So impressed was Muscarello by the sighting that he and his mother waited on a mountainside almost every evening for three weeks following the incident. On one of those evenings, they sighted a UFO again. Other people in the area kept vigil in parked cars by power lines, often being rewarded by the appearance of glowing UFOs. In some cases, military aircraft were seen, apparently chasing the objects. During one such skywatch, Fuller, himself, observed a high-altitude reddish-orange disk being pursued by a jet.

The Air Force made inquiries about the incident and for some time after it had happened, Air Force officers patrolled the roads at night. Almost two months later, on October 27, 1965, the Pentagon issued a press release which stated that the UFO sightings in Exeter on September 3 were the result both of misidentified aircraft participating in a high-altitude Strategic Air Command exercise out of Westover, Massachusetts, and of the atmospheric distortion of STARS and PLANETS. During the third week of November, officers Bertrand and Hunt received a letter from Major HECTOR QUIN-

TANILLA, Chief of PROJECT BLUE BOOK. Contradicting the Pentagon news release, the letter stated that a final evaluation of the case had not yet been made but that the objects observed might have been aircraft involved in a military air operation, "Big Blast." However, the high-altitude exercises had taken place between midnight and 2:00 A.M. The police officers had observed the UFO at approximately 3:00 A.M. Embarrassed by the Pentagon evaluation, Bertrand and Hunt wrote to Quintanilla twice but never received an answer. On February 9, 1966, after the case had earned a great deal of publicity, they finally received a conciliatory letter from the Pentagon, stating that the Air Force had been unable to identify the object observed on the night of September 3.

DONALD MENZEL concluded that suggestion or MASS HYSTERIA were factors in some of the sightings, leading to exaggerated or confused reports. Fuller and other investigators hypothesized that the proximity of many of the UFOs to high-tension lines might signify that the objects were either utilizing some kind of electromagnetic force or were attracted to the power that flowed through the lines. PHILIP KLASS, however, holds that the phenomenon witnessed was corona discharge, luminous ionized air containing electrified particles, which can form along power lines. This rare occurrence happens most often when a scarcity of rainfall allows the lines to be contaminated by dust, salt deposits or swarms of insects. Klass established that the area around Exeter had received barely half its usual rainfall during the period immediately preceding the sightings. He further pointed out that the predominant colors of the UFOs matched statistically those of ball lightning.

Bibliography: Fuller, John G., *Incident at Exeter* (New York: G. P. Putnam's Sons, 1966); Klass, Philip J., *UFOs Identified* (New York: Random House, 1968).

**EXOBIOLOGY,** the branch of space biology which deals with the study of EXTRATERRESTRIAL LIFE.

**EXOTHEOLOGY,** the theology of outer space, a religious formulation adhered to by some supporters of the ANCIENT ASTRONAUTS theory as an alternative to traditional religions. Such a theology accepts not only the existence of extraterrestrial intelligences but also the possibility of active extraterrestrial intervention in our own evolution on Earth. Exotheologists hold that explanations as to how things occur should be left in the hands of science and that religion should be looked at in terms of values on a cosmic level.

Bibliography: Jennings, Reverend Jack A., "Ancient Astronauts—Religion's Third Great Challenge," *Ancient Skies* (Highland Park, Illinois: Ancient Astronaut Society, September–October 1978, Volume 5, Number 4).

**EXPLORING OTHER DIMENSIONS,** quarterly magazine, established in 1965 as *Infinity Newsletter* and published under that name for approximately ten years. Available by subscription only, its circulation varies between 500 and 2,000. The range of subjects covered includes UFOs, FORTEAN events, paranormal activity, ancient and contemporary world religions, science, philosophy and reincarnation.

Editor David D. Graham obtains his material from direct contacts, newspaper clippings and information accumulated during thirty years of personal research.

The magazine is published by David Graham Associates, Box 401, Decorah, Iowa 52101.

**EXTRADIMENSIONAL HYPOTHESIS** *see* **PARALLEL UNIVERSE HYPOTHESIS**

**EXTRAORDINARY FLYING OBJECT (EFO),** term coined by scientist William Hartmann to denote a UFO that remains unidentified after investigation and which therefore may be considered as something beyond the bounds of recognized natural phenomena.

Bibliography: Sagan, Carl, and Thornton Page (eds.), *UFOs—A Scientific Debate* (Ithaca, N.Y.: Cornell University Press, 1972).

**EXTRATERRESTRIAL HYPOTHESIS (ETH),** theory that UFOs are vehicles piloted by beings from one or more extraterrestrial civilizations. Since the term technically refers to any extraterrestrial phenomenon such as a METEOR, it is more correctly though less frequently referred to as the extraterrestrial intelligence (ETI) hypothesis.

Since the beginning of the MODERN ERA in 1947, the ETH has been the most popular of the various exotic theories applied to UFOs. This may be, in part, because of the burgeoning popularity during the 1950s of science fiction in comic books, motion pictures, television and art. The theory's popularity may also be attributable to the twentieth century's space age interpretations of poorly understood phenomena and the human need to believe in a higher power. Hence, UFOs have been compared to the FAIRIES, Olympian gods and Valkyries of former times. Despite the fact that the ETH is still the most widely accepted explanation for UFOs among those who believe them to be manifestations of an erotic phenomenon, the ETH began losing ground during the 1970s to other HYPOTHESES, particularly the PARALLEL UNIVERSE HYPOTHESIS.

The weakest aspect of the ETH involves the logistics of interstellar travel. It is generally accepted (except by CONTACTEES) that intelligent life does not exist on any of the other PLANETS in our solar system. Therefore, extraterrestrial visitors must originate from other solar systems. A vehicle moving at the speed of light would require four years to reach Alpha Centauri, our closest stellar neighbor. Compared to the lengthy ocean voyages of the fifteenth- and sixteenth-century explorers, this is not an excessive period of time. However, the fastest vehicle man has launched to date travels at only seven miles per second, a tiny fraction of the speed of light. At this speed, it would take a spacecraft eighty thousand years to reach the nearest star.

Astronomer CARL SAGAN, although not opposed to the possibility of extraterrestrial visitation, contends the high number of UFO reports invalidates the ETH. Although there are at least several UFO reports per day, he starts with the premise that only one such report per year represents a true extraterrestrial visitation. Based on a reasonable estimate of the number of extant civilizations in the galaxy and a conservative estimate of the number of planets worth visiting, he calculates that each civilization would have to launch 10,000 interstellar spacecraft per year. Other skeptics have further argued that the building materials and energy required for such trips renders the hypothesis unfeasible.

Some supporters of the ETH conjecture that extraterrestrial travelers might be able to circumvent the limitations of time and space by utilizing some unknown concept, such as the hypothetical area called HYPERSPACE. By this means, travel between solar systems might be instantaneous.

If UFOs are the ships of interstellar travelers who have not transcended the physical limitations of velocity as we know them, it is conceivable that they might have developed a method of modifying their life spans. This could be achieved through artificial hibernation or cryogenic preservation. On the other hand, the occupants of such craft might be automatons sent out by planetbound beings or independent, intelligent robots who have evolved into the successors of their humanoid creators. With unlimited life spans, the astronomical distances of interstellar travel would be no barrier to them.

Another theory involves giant, immobile brains with separate mobile sensory organs. The concept is outlined by Arthur C. Clarke in his book *Profiles of the Future* (New York: Harper and Row, 1963). The immortal brains, sustained by pumps and chemical plants, would be fixed in one place. Their sensory organs, however, need not be part of the same main structure attached by the communications links of the nervous system. Instead, they could be connected by means of mobile radio links, free to roam hundreds, thousands or millions of miles in any direction. With its center of awareness stored in a safe place, such an entity could enjoy numerous experiences which might otherwise be too dangerous. Thus, it has been suggested that UFOs might be the sensory devices of giant brains living in another part of the universe.

There has been considerable speculation as to why extraterrestrials might travel to our planet. Such visitors might be benign, indifferent or hostile. Their presence here could be unintentional: the result of having lost their way, having come across our planet by chance, being forced to land because of mechanical problems or needing to seek asylum. If intentional, their visits could be for scientific, military, political, commercial, educational or recreational purposes.

If such visitors showed little interest in contacting the human race, it might be because they feared an aggressive reaction. Although more advanced, they would not necessarily be impervious to Earth's weapons, just as twentieth-century man is not impervious to the spears and knives of primitive jungle tribes. In any case, advanced extraterrestrial entities might have as much interest in contacting earthlings as the average human being has in communicating with ants.

In general, UFOLOGISTS today believe that emphasis on the ETH confuses the issue. Astronomer J. ALLEN HYNEK holds that the primary question is not the validity of the ETH, but rather whether or not the UFO phenomenon, regardless of any beliefs concerning its origin, is a legitimate subject for scientific study.

Bibliography: Sachs, Margaret, with Ernest Jahn, *Celestial Passengers—UFOs and Space Travel* (New York: Penguin Books, 1977); Sagan, Carl, "UFOs: The Extraterrestrial and Other Hypotheses," in Sagan, Carl, and Thornton Page (eds.), *UFOs—A Scientific Debate* (Ithaca, N.Y.: Cornell University Press, 1972).

**EXTRATERRESTRIAL INTELLIGENCE HYPOTHESIS,** theory more commonly referred to as the EXTRATERRESTRIAL HYPOTHESIS (ETH).

**EXTRATERRESTRIAL LIFE.** Although mankind has not yet found any evidence of the existence of extraterrestrial intelligence, extraterrestrial life has been discovered in the form of organic compounds found in meteorites. In 1970, the NATIONAL AERONAUTICS AND SPACE ADMINISTRATION (NASA) announced that for the first time man possessed definitive proof of extraterrestrial life. A research team headed by Cyril Ponnamperuma, a geochemist at the University of Maryland, had identified amino acids and hydrocarbons (the constituents of complex organic cells) in a meteorite which landed on September 28, 1969, at Murchison in Australia.

To date more than fifty molecular or molecule-like compounds have been detected in interstellar dust. This has led British cosmologist Fred Hoyle and his Sri

Lankan colleague N. Chandra Wickramasinghe at University College in Cardiff, Wales, to develop the theory that living organisms have arisen in outer space itself.

Although the 1976 Viking mission to MARS failed to establish the existence of life on that PLANET, scientists have not ruled out the possibility that microbial life forms exist on or below the Martian surface. Similarly, the failure of the 1979 Voyager mission to detect life on Jupiter has not discouraged scientists from speculating that organic compounds probably exist within the Jovian atmosphere.

Although life forms may exist on our neighboring planets or their moons, there is little likelihood of intelligent life having evolved in our solar system except on Earth. Most UFOLOGISTS reject the claims of CONTACTEES that benevolent beings inhabit Mars, VENUS and other nearby planets. However, some UFOlogists concede that UFO bases may have been established on these planets.

The 1961 GREEN BANK FORMULA, an equation devised by members of the NATIONAL ACADEMY OF SCIENCES (NAS), demonstrated a possibility of there being a minimum of forty and a maximum of fifty thousand planets in our galaxy which support advanced civilizations capable of radio communication with Earth. Recent estimates by a number of prominent scientists have suggested a probability of at least one million advanced civilizations in the Milky Way. Since our galaxy is believed to be about ten billion years old, and Earth is roughly five billion years old, there must be many STARS in the galaxy that are billions of years older than our sun. When we reflect on what science has achieved on Earth in this century alone, we realize that the advances that could occur in a civilization a billion years older than ours are far beyond the limits of our imagination. Likewise, there must be many worlds that straggle far behind us on the path of technological achievement. In assessing which solar systems in particular might be the dwelling places of other humanoid species, we can eliminate those whose suns are larger than ours, for they burn out too quickly to provide the necessary time for the evolution of complex beings. Solar systems whose suns are smaller than ours would be suitable if they have planets close enough to achieve comfortable temperatures. Stars the same size as our sun, with one or more planets at approximately the same distance from them as Earth is from our sun, would of course make ideal locations. The ten closest stars to Earth known or suspected to have planets or unseen companions within reasonable zones of habitability are listed as follows in order of proximity with their respective distances in light years from our sun in parentheses: Alpha Centauri A and B (4.3), Barnard's Star (5.9), Epsilon Eridani (10.7), 61 Cygni A (11.2),

Epsilon Indi (11.2), Tau Ceti (11.9), 70 Ophiuchi A and B (16.7) and BD + 43°4305 (16.9).

The question of whether UFOs are vehicles from these or other star systems is disputed by many scientists on the grounds that the vast distances involved render interstellar travel unfeasible. According to the laws of physics, matter cannot travel faster than the speed of light, which in a vacuum is 186,000 miles per second. Merely to reach our closest stellar neighbor, a spacecraft moving at that velocity would require four years. Although this is not an unreasonable period of time, opponents of the EXTRATERRESTRIAL HYPOTHESIS (ETH) point out that the fastest vehicle man has ever launched travels at only seven miles per second, a tiny fraction of the speed of light. At seven miles per second, it would take a spacecraft eighty thousand years to reach the nearest star. Supporters of the ETH argue that interstellar travelers might have overcome this problem by modifying their life spans through artificial hibernation or cryogenic preservation. Alternatively, they point out, interstellar travelers might be ANDROIDS or robots whose life spans are unlimited. Another theory promoted by some supporters of the ETH is that extraterrestrial intelligences have circumvented the limitations of the speed of light barrier by utilizing interdimensional travel or the hypothetical area known as HYPERSPACE.

Despite the scientific establishment's skepticism regarding extraterrestrial visitation, both Russian and American scientists are conducting efforts to establish contact with extraterrestrial civilizations through the use of RADIO ASTRONOMY. The various programs are referred to as the SEARCH FOR EXTRATERRESTRIAL INTELLIGENCE (SETI)

Bibliography: Sagan, Carl, *The Cosmic Connection* (Garden City, N.Y.: Anchor Press, 1973); Shklovskii, I.S., and Carl Sagan, *Intelligent Life in the Universe* (San Francisco: Holden-Day, 1966).

**EZEKIEL,** Biblical prophet believed by some proponents of the ANCIENT ASTRONAUTS hypothesis to have observed an extraterrestrial spacecraft on four different occasions more than 2,500 years ago. Without the appropriate vocabulary and mechanical knowledge, Ezekiel would have been forced to describe such encounters in terms familiar to him. In the first chapter of the Book of Ezekiel, he states, ". . . a stormy wind came out of the north, and a great CLOUD, with brightness round about it, and fire flashing forth continually, and in the midst of the fire, as it were gleaming bronze. And from the midst of it came the likeness of four living creatures. And this was their appearance: they had the form of men, but each had four faces, and each of them had four wings. Their legs were straight, and the soles of their feet were round; and they sparkled like burnished bronze. . . . In the midst of the living creatures there was something that looked like burning coals of fire, like torches moving to and fro among the living creatures; and the fire was bright, and out of the fire went forth lightning. . . . Now as I looked at the living creatures, I saw a wheel upon the earth beside the living creatures, one for each of the four of them. . . . The four wheels had rims; and their rims were full of eyes round about. . . . Over the heads of the living creatures there was the likeness of a firmament, shining like rock crystal, spread out above their heads. . . . And when they went, I heard the sound of their wings like the sound of many waters, like the thunder of the Almighty, a sound of tumult like the sound of a host; when they stood still, they let down their wings. . . . And above the firmament over their heads there was the likeness of a throne, in appearance like sapphire; and seated above the likeness of a throne was a likeness as the appearance of a man upon it above."

From these and other descriptions in the Book of Ezekiel, JOSEF F. BLUMRICH, former Chief of the Advanced Structural Development Branch of the NATIONAL AERONAUTICS AND SPACE ADMINISTRATION (NASA), has reconstructed the design of a spacecraft consisting of a capsule on a main body supported by four helicopter units with telescopic legs, retractable wheels and mechanical arms. Blumrich interprets the "wings" as rotary blades which made a loud noise while moving, and which folded like wings when not in use. He believes the robotlike appearance of the helicopter units may have led Ezekiel to describe them as having the form of men and the likeness of living creatures. Later, Ezekiel refers to them as cherubim. Blumrich concludes that this was because he had realized they were not men.

Author Clifford Wilson criticizes this theory, pointing out that Ezekiel specifically stated that he was describing visions. He supports the religious interpretation of Ezekiel's experiences. Writer R. L. Dione agrees that Ezekiel had visions, but argues that they were induced HALLUCINATIONS caused by UFOs. On the other hand, DONALD MENZEL believed the incidents had a natural explanation. He proposed that Ezekiel's visions were inspired by rare, fully developed PARHELIA.

Bibliography: Blumrich, Josef F., *The Spaceships of Ezekiel* (New York: Bantam Books, 1974); Dione, R. L., *God Drives a Flying Saucer* (New York: Exposition Press, 1969); Menzel, Donald H., and Ernest H. Taves, *The UFO Enigma* (Garden City, N.Y.: Doubleday and Company, 1977).

**FAFROTSKIES,** acronym for unusual objects that have *fallen from the skies*. This term, coined by IVAN SANDERSON, refers to a variety of organic and inorganic items. Most commonly reported are frogs, fish, eels, blood, flesh, enormous chunks of ice, hardware, coal, bricks, wool, milk, ANGELS' HAIR and DEVIL'S JELLY. The earliest records of fafrotskies are to be found in Pliny's *Historia Naturalis* and Julius Obsequens's *Libro de Prodigiis*. After a rain of flesh that occurred in 416 B.C., Pliny claims that none of the flesh left unplundered by BIRDS of prey went bad. CHARLES FORT accumulated a large number of reports on such falls, and noted that many of them occurred after tornados or hurricanes. However, some objects have fallen out of clear, blue skies. In recent years, metal DEBRIS has fallen to Earth that remains unidentifiable despite extensive analysis. In April of 1978, two blocks of green ice fell in Tennessee and in France, weighing twenty-five and fifty pounds respectively. Investigators speculate that they may have been the frozen, disinfected waste of airplane toilets although no airplanes were visible at the time.

While the explanation for some of these incidents may be a natural one, it is the origin of such items as hardware, flesh and blood that forms the greater part of the mystery. Some researchers have suggested that the falls of flesh and blood are all that remain of humans and animals abducted by UFOs and that the chunks of hardware are fragments of the UFOs themselves.

Bibliography: Fort, Charles, *The Book of the Damned* (New York: Boni and Liveright, 1919); Sanderson, Ivan T., *Investigating the Unexplained* (Englewood Cliffs, N.J.: Prentice-Hall, 1972); Sachs, Margaret, with Ernest Jahn, *Celestial Passengers—UFOs and Space Travel* (New York: Penguin Books, 1977).

**FAIRIES,** also known as the little people, elves, leprechauns, goblins, gremlins, banshees, brownies and pixies; mythical beings, skilled in magic, who resembled small human beings and were capable of appearing or disappearing at will. Prominent in medieval European folklore, fairies have lost their popularity in the human belief system.

Author JACQUES VALLEE has pointed out the similarities between myths relating to fairies and modern accounts of UFOs and their OCCUPANTS. A classic example is the case of Joe Simonton in EAGLE RIVER, WISCONSIN. Simonton encountered a UFO whose small occupants asked him for water and gave him some pancakes in return. Fairies supposedly drank only pure water. Irish fairies were reputed to live on pancakes and to utilize the exchange of food as a means of making contact. Analysis of the Wisconsin pancakes revealed that they contained buckwheat, a popular grain in the folklore of Brittany. Furthermore, there was a complete absence of salt, a substance which fairies eschewed.

Visitors to fairyland sometimes found on their return that many years had passed. This has led to speculation that such travelers might have unknowingly been on interstellar journeys. According to Einstein's theory of relativity, ASTRONAUTS traveling just under the SPEED OF LIGHT would age very little between departure and return, while many years would pass on their home PLANET.

Fairy legends and UFO reports also share many features common to religious myths, such as those of the Olympian gods, Nordic Valkyries and American Indian kachinas. Hence, it has been postulated by proponents of the PARALLEL UNIVERSE HYPOTHESIS that all these entities are the physical manifestations of extradimensional intelligences. The form they assume is intentionally compatible with the cultural beliefs and technological development of the existing human civilization. These entities, whose alleged meddling in human affairs can be both harmful and beneficial, could possibly be dependent on human beings in some unknown way. It may also be that they utilize telepathy to cause the visual perception of apparent three-dimensional images, rather than manifesting themselves physically.

An alternative explanation is that fairies and UFOs might be some kind of self-generated psychic projection which fulfills the psychological needs of the observer.

Bibliography: Vallee, Jacques, *Passport to Magonia* (Chicago: Henry Regnery Company, 1969).

**FAIRY RINGS,** fungus growths which form expanding rings in lawns and grassland. Fairy rings can be confused with circular UFO LANDING MARKS but, aside from their shape, do not share any other characteristics. UFO landing marks can be distinguished by evidence of heating or burning, the rearrangement of vegetation by air turbulence, the flattening of vegetation by pressure from a solid object, and the absence of any fungus growth.

**FALKVILLE, ALABAMA,** location of an encounter with an alleged UFONAUT on October 17, 1973. During the evening, Police Chief Jeff Greenhaw received a telephone call that a UFO with flashing lights had landed in a field near the town. When Greenhaw arrived at the scene, he saw a creature resembling a man wrapped in aluminum foil. The entity had an antenna on its head. Its gait was stiff and mechanical. As it approached, Greenhaw snapped four PHOTOGRAPHS with his Polaroid camera. When he turned on his patrol car spotlight, the creature turned and ran down the dirt road. Greenhaw pursued it in his patrol car but was unable to keep up with it. "He was running faster than any human I ever saw," he said.

The following day, the police chief received several calls from local residents who had observed UFOs at the time of Greenhaw's encounter. The sighting was widely-publicized and resulted in personal and professional problems for Greenhaw. Within one month of the incident, he was divorced from his wife and resigned from his job at the request of the local mayor.

Bibliography: Blum, Ralph, with Judy Blum, *Beyond Earth—Man's Contact with UFOs* (New York: Bantam Books, 1974).

Robotlike creature photographed by Police Chief Jeff Greenhaw in Falkville, Alabama, on October 17, 1973. *(Courtesy ICUFON/Greenhaw)*

**FALLING OBJECTS** *see* ANGELS' HAIR, DEBRIS, DEVILS' JELLY AND FAFROTSKIES

**FARGO, NORTH DAKOTA,** location over which a second lieutenant of the North Dakota National Guard, George T. Gorman, engaged in a dogfight with a UFO on October 1, 1948.

At approximately 9:00 P.M., Gorman was circling over Fargo in an F–51 fighter when he noticed a blinking light which he presumed, at first, to be the rear navigation light of an aircraft. The object appeared to be making a circle around the city at approximately 1,000 feet, traveling at the same rate of speed as the F–51. Gorman estimated the size of the sharply-defined, spherical white light to be from six-to-eight inches in diameter. After checking with the control tower, Gorman took off in pursuit of the light. As he attempted to turn with the object, he blacked out temporarily from the excessive speed. Unable to catch up with it, he proceeded to cut it off as it turned. His speed varying

between 300 and 400 miles per hour, Gorman cut to the right toward the UFO as it circled to the left. Just as collision seemed inevitable, the object veered and passed about 500 feet over the F–51. Gorman reports that the object then made a 180-degree turn and initiated a pass at him. It was now a steady white light, no longer blinking on and off. As the object pulled up just prior to reaching the F–51, Gorman, too, pulled up in an attempt to ram the UFO. At 14,000 feet, the F–51 stalled. The UFO was 2,000 feet above, circling to the left. Gorman circled with it twice before the object pulled away and then commenced another head-on pass. This time, however, it did not complete its approach, breaking away toward the northwest. Gorman gave chase. Twenty-five miles southeast of Fargo, he again tried to catch the object in a diving turn. The UFO turned around and made another head-on pass. When the object pulled up, Gorman pulled up also, watching the UFO as it traveled straight upward until it disappeared from view. The confrontation had lasted for twenty-seven minutes. Gorman returned to the field at Fargo and landed.

Gorman's efforts had been observed by the traffic controller, the assistant traffic controller and two witnesses aboard a Piper Cub. All had seen the unidentified light but did not observe it performing the complicated maneuvers described by Gorman.

Air Force investigators arrived at Fargo within twenty-four hours. When the F–51 was tested, it was found to have the slightly increased amount of radioactivity shown by all planes after flight. The following night, a weather balloon was dispatched and a Navy pilot purportedly succeeded in duplicating the event. The officials of PROJECT SIGN finally concluded that Gorman had done battle with a lighted weather BALLOON which had been released from the weather station at Fargo ten minutes before Gorman had first sighted the UFO.

Donald Menzel has proposed that the Air Force's explanation was applicable to the first part of the sighting only. He has suggested that when Gorman relocated the steady white light after losing sight of the blinking light, he actually located a mirage of the planet Jupiter instead of the weather balloon. TEMPERATURE INVERSIONS near the ground and at higher altitudes supplied the ideal conditions to produce a planetary mirage which could have been increased in size by the defocusing action of Earth's atmosphere. Under these conditions, the size and brightness of the light would have fluctuated. When they diminished, the light would have seemed to race toward him. As a result of SPATIAL DISORIENTATION, other apparent movements would have been related to the movement of the observer's plane. The geographical elevation to the southwest of

Fargo would have concealed the setting planet from the ground observers. As Gorman maneuvered, high buttes would have repeatedly cut off the planet from his view, creating the impression that the image was racing in and out and performing evasive movements. Menzel has pointed out that on October 1, 1948, the image of Jupiter sank below the horizon between 9:27 and 9:28 P.M., the same time that Gorman saw the light climb up into the sky and disappear.

Bibliography: Steiger, Brad (ed.), *Project Blue Book* (New York: Ballantine Books, 1976); Menzel, Donald H., and Lyle G. Boyd, *The World of Flying Saucers* (Garden City, N.Y.: Doubleday and Company, 1963); Flammonde, Paris, *UFO Exist!* (New York: G. P. Putnam's Sons, 1976).

**FARISH, LUCIUS** (b. April 27, 1937, Plumerville, Arkansas; address: Box 220, Route 1, Plumerville, Arkansas 72127; telephone number: 501-354-2558), writer and Editor of the UFO NEWSCLIPPING SERVICE (UFONS).

Despite several sightings since 1956 of unusual objects and nocturnal lights in Arkansas, Farish has no firm opinions regarding the identity of UFOs, although he thinks there is currently too much speculation on the PARALLEL UNIVERSE HYPOTHESIS and other such theories that have evolved as a result of the diminishing popularity of the EXTRATERRESTRIAL HYPOTHESIS (ETH). He believes the purportedly paraphysical qualities of UFOs can probably be attributed to a highly advanced technology.

Farish is a member of the AERIAL PHENOMENA RESEARCH ORGANIZATION (APRO), the INTERNATIONAL FORTEAN ORGANIZATION (INFO), the SOCIETY FOR THE INVESTIGATION OF THE UNEXPLAINED (SITU), the

Lucius Farish.

ANCIENT ASTRONAUT SOCIETY and the Forgotten Ages Research Society.

Farish has been researching unexplained phenomena since 1957, and began freelance writing in the early 1960s. His articles have been published in numerous UFO magazines and he has been a contributor to several anthologies on UFOs. He has been the Editor of UFONS since 1977.

## FARMINGTON, NEW MEXICO,

location of the sighting of multiple UFOs by hundreds of observers during a period of approximately one hour during the morning of March 17, 1950. Witnesses' estimates of the number of objects ranged from 500 to several thousand. Authors EDWARD RUPPELT, DONALD MENZEL and Lyle Boyd have explained the case as a misidentification of the fragments of a shattered SKYHOOK BALLOON launched that morning from Holloman Air Force Base.

The late meteorologist JAMES MCDONALD contended, however, that witnesses' descriptions of fast-moving disk-shaped objects do not support the Skyhook explanation. McDonald contacted Holloman Air Force Base and the Office of Naval Research. Their records showed that no Skyhooks or other experimental balloons had been released from the Holloman area or any other part of the country on or near the date of this incident.

Bibliography: Menzel, Donald H., and Lyle G. Boyd, *The World of Flying Saucers* (Garden City, N.Y.: Doubleday and Company, 1963); U.S. Congress, House, Committee on Science and Astronautics. Symposium on Unidentified Flying Objects. Hearings, 90th Congress, 2nd Session, July 29, 1968 (Washington, D.C.: U.S. Government Printing Office, 1968).

## FARR, JAMIE,

actor and Emmy nominee for supporting role in the television series *M*A*S*H*, who

UFO witness Jamie Farr.

observed a UFO near Yuma, Arizona, in the early 1960s. Farr and his wife-to-be, Joy, were driving down a deserted road at about midnight when they caught sight of a light zigzagging across the sky at an incredible speed. It stopped in mid-air, hovered for a while, then took off again at high speed. The UFO approached within one hundred yards of the car, then paced it as Farr maintained a speed of sixty miles per hour. The couple could distinguish a domed apparatus with a light swinging around its base. The desert sand swirled around underneath it. Joy, who had read many books about UFOs, suggested that they should pull over to the side of the road and attempt to make contact. Farr was frightened and kept driving. Suddenly, the UFO took off at phenomenal speed and vanished in the distance. Farr, who did not believe in UFOs prior to the incident, now believes they are spaceships from another PLANET, possibly from another galaxy.

## FATE,

monthly magazine, established in 1948, with a circulation of 150,000. It is available at newsstands and by subscription. The range of subjects covered includes UFOs, ESP, TELEPATHY, ghosts, reincarnation, altered states of consciousness, sorcery, divination, possession, FORTEAN phenomena, monsters, and biographies and autobiographies of personalities in psychic or occult fields. Every aspect of the UFO mystery is considered, particular emphasis being given to detailed examination of individual cases rather than brief summaries of numerous sightings. Documented exposés of fraudulent reports are also published.

Articles are written by staff writers and freelance writers. Editor Mary Margaret Fuller recommends that prospective contributors send one-paragraph outlines on the subject matter of proposed submissions. Articles between 300 and 3,500 words in length should be submitted with a self-addressed, stamped envelope. Payment is made after editing at a minimum rate of three cents per word for the acquisition of all rights. There is a payment of up to five dollars for fillers of any length up to three hundred words. Additional payment is made for PHOTOGRAPHS supplied with manuscripts.

*Fate* is published by Clark Publishing Company, located at 500 Hyacinth Place, Highland Park, Illinois 60035.

## FÁTIMA, PORTUGAL,

village where ten-year-old Lucia dos Santos and her two cousins saw aerial phenomena and a white-robed lady on May 13, 1917, and each subsequent month until October. Following the first incident, crowds attended each sighting in progressively growing numbers. The manifestations were usually preceded by a flash of light and a decrease in the sun's warmth and luminosity. A glowing globe which

Traditional rendering of the apparition at Fátima, Portugal. *(Religious News Service)*

stopped over a tree sometimes emitted a faint buzzing sound. Occasionally, a white CLOUD formed about the light. On two occasions, a substance resembling ANGELS' HAIR floated earthward. Although the thousands of witnesses observed the aerial phenomena, none but Lucia and her cousins observed and heard the small woman who appeared at the center of the globe. An explosive sound was sometimes heard just before the globe flew away.

On October 13, a crowd of 70,000 gathered to see a predicted miracle. After the customary arrival and departure of the apparition, the rain which had been pouring down heavily suddenly ceased. The clouds parted, revealing a brilliant pearly disk rotating on its own axis and emitting rays of colored lights in all direction. When the disk stopped spinning and began to plunge toward the ground with a falling leaf motion, the crowd, believing it to be the sun, fell to their knees in horror. Finally, the disk retreated and disappeared into the sun. The overjoyed crowd noticed that their wet clothes and the rain soaked ground had completely dried out.

Although the miracle at Fátima has been traditionally interpreted as a religious experience, many UFOlogists have pointed out the similarity of the observations to UFO incidents. Some believe that TELEPATHY might explain the inability of the crowds to hear the words spoken to Lucia by the white-robed

entity. Two witnesses, who observed the sharply-defined, rotating disk through binoculars, reported seeing a ladder and two beings.

Many of the predictions made to Lucia proved valid within the following years. An envelope containing a secret prophecy entrusted to the pope was opened by John XXIII in 1960, but its contents have never been made public. Lucia's cousins both died within three years of the miraculous event. Lucia became a Carmelite nun in 1948. At the request of the white-robed lady who had identified herself as the Lady of the Rosary, a shrine was built at Fátima.

Bibliography: Vallee, Jacques, *The Invisible College* (New York: E. P. Dutton, 1975).

**FAWCETT, GEORGE D.** (b. July 21, 1929, Mount Airy, North Carolina; address: 602 Battleground Road, Lincolnton, North Carolina 28092; telephone number: 704-735-5725), UFO investigator, lecturer and writer.

Fawcett believes that some UFOs are intelligently controlled machines from beyond our solar system while others are of ultraterrestrial origin. In 1951, he was the lone witness of a large, bright orange object which had the shape of a bisected globe. Fawcett was able to observe the sharply-defined object for about four-and-a-half minutes until it bounced up and down five times and then silently departed.

Fawcett graduated from Lee McRae College, North Carolina, in 1950, graduated from Lynchburg College, Virginia, in 1952 with a B.A. in Psychology and Education, and received his Professional Y.M.C.A. Certification from George Williams College, Wisconsin, in 1954. From 1955 to 1956, he served with the United States Army in the Panama Canal Zone. Between 1952 and 1972, he served as a Professional Y.M.C.A. Executive

George Fawcett.

Director in six states. After a one-year stint as a traveling salesman, he became a newspaper reporter and, since 1975, has served as the General Manager and Advertising Salesman for North Carolina's *Maiden Times*.

Fawcett is a member of the Professional Y.M.C.A. Directors' Association, the Professional Carolinas Newspapers Association, the Maiden Lions Club in Maiden, North Carolina, and was a 1962 Man of the Year nominee for the Jaycees in Woburn, Massachusetts.

Fawcett has researched and investigated UFOs since 1944. He is the State Director of North Carolina for the MUTUAL UFO NETWORK (MUFON), and is a member of the NATIONAL INVESTIGATIONS COMMITTEE ON AERIAL PHENOMENA (NICAP), the AERIAL PHENOMENA RESEARCH ORGANIZATION (APRO) and the CENTER FOR UFO STUDIES (CUFOS). He was founder of the NEW ENGLAND UFO STUDY GROUP, the PENNSYLVANIA AND NEW JERSEY TWO-STATE UFO STUDY GROUP, the FLORIDA UFO STUDY GROUP and the TARHEEL UFO STUDY GROUP. He has lectured widely on UFOs, and has been a guest on several radio and television programs. Fawcett has written more than one hundred articles which have been published in various UFO magazines, and he is the author of *Quarter Century Studies of UFOs in Florida, North Carolina and Tennessee* (Mount Airy, North Carolina: Pioneer Printing Company, 1975).

## FBI *see* FEDERAL BUREAU OF INVESTIGATION

## FEDERACION PANAMERICANA DE ESTUDIOS CIENTIFICO-FILOSOFICO DE VIDA EXTRATERRESTRE, Juncal 2061-1-13, Buenos Aires, Argentina.

This flying saucer organization is dedicated to the study of extraterrestrial life. Its staff consists of President Juan A. Aliandri, Vice-President JOSÉ CARLOS PAZ GARCÍA, C. and Secretary Ariel Ciro Rietti.

## FEDERAL BUREAU OF INVESTIGATION (FBI), the investigative arm of the U.S. Department of Justice, headquartered in Washington, D.C. The bureau has several thousand pages of documents on UFOs, many of which are available to the public through the Freedom of Information Act. The documents deal with UFO activity between 1947 and 1964.

The FBI's official involvement began on July 30, 1947, as the result of a request by Army Air Force Intelligence officer General G. F. Schulgen that the FBI interview UFO witnesses to determine whether or not any of the reports had been generated by subversive individuals for the purpose of creating mass hysteria.

Bureau Director J. Edgar Hoover agreed to the request on the condition that the FBI would have full access to any crashed disks which were recovered. Agents were instructed to conduct intensive investigations of UFO reports and the Washington office began to accumulate a mass of data. However, in September of that year, an FBI agent obtained a copy of a restricted letter addressed to several Commanding Generals of the Army Air Forces from Intelligence officer Colonel R. H. Smith, Assistant Chief of Staff at Air Defense Command headquarters. The letter implied that the FBI was being used to investigate only those cases which were considered unimportant or even ridiculous. In a letter to Major General George C. McDonald, Assistant Chief Air Staff-2 at the Pentagon, Hoover stated the following:

"I have been advised . . . that the Air Forces would interview responsible observers while the FBI would investigate incidents of disks found on the ground, thereby relieving the Air Forces of running down incidents which in many cases turn out to be 'ash can covers, toilet seats and whatnot!'

"In view of the apparent understanding by the Air Forces of the position of the Federal Bureau of Investigation in this matter, I cannot permit the personnel and time of this organization to be dissipated in this matter.

"I am advising the Field Divisions of the Federal Bureau of Investigation to discontinue all investigative activity regarding the reported sightings of flying disks, and am instructing them to refer all complaints received to the appropriate Air Force representative in their area."

Accordingly, only two months after the FBI's official involvement had begun, a directive was issued instructing Bureau agents to refer all reports connected with flying disks to the Air Forces. However, the FBI continued to be unofficially involved with UFOs for another sixteen years. Agents continued to file brief reports and interviewed Air Force personnel on several occasions. In addition, unsolicited copies of Air Force, Office of Naval Intelligence and Army Intelligence documents and UFO reports continued to come in to FBI headquarters.

In 1948, mysterious GREEN FIREBALLS began to make frequent appearances over highly-restricted areas in the southwestern United States. The FBI was brought back into the picture because of their obligation to protect vital installations. In January, 1949, the Bureau received a confidential statement from the Air Material Command (AMC) Resident Engineer who was the principal army technician at the Nuclear Energy for the Propulsion of Aircraft Research Center at Oak Ridge, Tennessee. He expressed his personal opinions about UFOs based on review of the known facts and theoretical conjectures made by himself and other scientists. The following month, the Bureau received from the Air Force a memorandum which contained a prototype sighting form. Copies of the memorandum were sent to Special Agents in Charge accompanied by a letter from Hoover, referring to the information supplied to the Bureau by the AMC engineer. In the letter, Hoover stated the following:

"For your confidential information, a reliable and confidential source has advised the Bureau that flying disks are believed to be man-made missiles rather than natural phenomenon. It has also been determined that for approximately the past four years the USSR has been engaged in experimentation on an unknown type of flying disk. The Department of the Air Force has furnished to the Bureau the attached memorandum classified 'restricted' dated February 15, 1949, entitled 'Unconventional Aircraft.' This memorandum is being furnished to you in order that all agents assigned to your office can be informed of the type of information desired by the Air Force in this matter."

Artist's rendering of a photograph of an alleged Martian in the custody of U.S. Military Policemen. The photograph was found in FBI files, accompanied by the notation that it was received on May 24, 1950, from an Intelligence and Security officer at the New Orleans Port of Embarkation. The FBI does not endorse the photograph's authenticity. *(Drawn by Larry Blazey—Courtesy the UFO Information Network)*

"As set forth in Bureau Bulletin #47 . . . no investigation should be conducted by your office relative to flying disks, however, the attached memorandum should be referred to in securing data from persons who desire to voluntarily furnish information to your office relating to flying disks."

In March 1950, Hoover asked the Air Force for its official opinion regarding UFOs and received the usual evasive answer. He was told that most reports could be explained and that the Air Force was no longer investigating them. However, during the 1952 WAVE, the FBI was informed by the Air Force that "the Air Force has failed to arrive at any satisfactory conclusion in its research regarding numerous reports of flying saucers and flying disks sighted throughout the United States. . . . It is not entirely impossible that the objects sighted may possibly be ships from another PLANET, such as MARS."

The most recent documents available from the *FBI Law Enforcement Bulletin* contained a five-page article by J. ALLEN HYNEK summarizing the UFO situation and advising law enforcement agencies to pass on UFO reports to the CENTER FOR UFO STUDIES (CUFOS) via its toll-free hotline.

Bibliography: Maccabee, Bruce S., "UFO-Related Information from the FBI File," Supplement to the *GSW Bulletin* (Phoenix, Arizona: Ground Saucer Watch, December 1977); serialized in the following publications: the UFO INVESTIGATOR (starting November, 1977), the APRO BULLETIN (starting October, 1977) and the MUFON UFO JOURNAL (starting November, 1977).

## FEDERATION UFO RESEARCH (FUFOR), 2 Acer Avenue, Crewe, Cheshire, England.

The purpose of this group is to investigate UFO incidents in an objective and unbiased manner. FUFOR believes that knowledge gained by investigation is contrary to public ideas about the phenomenon, which are the product of sensationalistic press and television reports. The organization holds that the majority of investigations are carried out in a poorly-organized and unobjective manner. One of its prime objectives, therefore, is to constantly improve its own methods and capabilities through the standardization of investigative equipment, familiarization with natural and man-made phenomena and other appropriate procedures. The group, as a whole, takes no stand on the identity and origin of UFOs.

This nonprofit organization was founded in 1977 by Stephen Cleaver, who serves as Chairman, and Nigel Brown. Mark A. Tyrrell serves as Secretary. FUFOR has six members, all of whom are field investigators and conduct investigations at their own expense. Investigative activity covers the South Cheshire area, bordering Staffordshire and Shropshire, as well as North Wales. The organization considers newspaper reports to be unreliable. *UFO Insight* is published four or five times a year. Its contents include articles on astronomical phenomena, comments on investigative techniques and a few sightings reports. Mark Tyrell is Editor.

**FENWICK, LAWRENCE JOEL** (b. April 18, 1936, Hamilton, Ontario), journalist, lecturer and Co-director of the CANADIAN UFO RESEARCH NETWORK (CUFORN).

Fenwick believes that some UFOs are machines from other PLANETS, some are machines from another dimension and a few are living creatures from a PARALLEL UNIVERSE. He holds that some UFOs have bases on Earth and underground bases on the MOON and MARS. They visit Earth, according to Fenwick, for exploration, food, fuel and scientific experiments.

Fenwick received his Bachelor of Applied Arts degree in Journalism from Ryerson Polytechnical Institute in Toronto. He studied History and Psychology for two years at McMaster University in Hamilton, Ontario. He received a Certificate from the Dale Carnegie Institute.

From 1958 to 1962, and again from 1964 to 1966, Fenwick held multiple responsibilities at his family's company, Judy Lawrence Dolls' Wear Limited. From 1969 to 1972, he was Editor of the monthly tabloid supplement of the *Daily Commercial News and Building Record* in Toronto. From 1973 to 1974, he was Editor of *Electrical Business* and Associate Editor of *Cable TV & Communications Business*, published by Kerrwil Publications in Toronto. From 1974 to 1977, he was Editor of *United Florists News* published by United Flowers-by-Wire, Limited, in Toronto. From 1977 to 1978, he was Assistant Editor of *Canadian Travel Press*, published by Baxter Publishing Company in Toronto. In 1977, he was a contributing writer and subsequently Associate Editor of *The UFO Pulse Analyzer*.

In addition to being a Codirector of CUFORN, Fenwick is a member of the AERIAL PHENOMENA RESEARCH ORGANIZATION (APRO), the CENTER FOR UFO STUDIES (CUFOS), the MUTUAL UFO NETWORK (MUFON), the CANADIAN UFO RESEARCH EXCHANGE NETWORK (CUFOREN), GROUND SAUCER WATCH (GSW), CITIZENS AGAINST UFO SECRECY (CAUS) and the METEMPIRICAL UFO BULLETIN (MUFOB). He is a former investigator for the First Private Canadian UFO Club, which is no longer in existence.

While at university, Fenwick received a Special Bursary for Journalism, and was awarded honors in Media Writing, English Novels and English Poetry.

Fenwick's articles have been published in several UFO magazines. He has also lectured on UFOs.

Aerial phenomena photographed at a Swiss airport in the summer of 1966. Philip Klass identified the objects as fireballs. *(Courtesy ICUFON/E. Baguhn)*

**FERGUSON, DONALD FREDERICK** (b. February 12, 1949, Harvey, West Australia; address: P.O. Box 261, Bunbury, West Australia 6230), Cofounder of PHENOMENA RESEARCH (WEST AUSTRALIA).

Ferguson's fifteen-year interest in UFOs stems from curiosity and from knowing people who have sighted strange animals and other unusual phenomena. He, himself, has had several sightings of NOCTURNAL LIGHTS.

Ferguson is employed as a postman. He joined the UNEXPLAINED PHENOMENA INVESTIGATION BUREAU (UPIB) in 1976 and, together with his wife, Jeannette Ferguson, organized meetings, carried out some research and published a newsletter for the organization. Dissatisfied with UPIB's lack of research and investigative activity, the Fergusons left the group. In 1969, they formed Phenomena Research (West Australia).

Ferguson has a large private collection of UFO books and magazines.

**FIREBALL,** a brilliant METEOR. In several well-known cases, UFOs have been explained by some investigators as fireballs. These include the Chiles/Whitted sighting near MONTGOMERY ALABAMA, the Coyne sighting over MANSFIELD, OHIO, and the GREEN FIREBALLS seen over New Mexico in 1948 and 1949.

**FIREBALL FIGHTERS** *see* **FOO FIGHTERS**

**FIREFLY,** also known as a lightning bug or a glow-worm, a flying insect which emits short, rhythmic flashes of cold light. It has been suggested that fireflies may account for some UFO reports.

**FIRST PRIVATE CANADIAN UFO CLUB,** defunct organization which was located in Ontario. Principals included Dennis Prophet, Nich Proach, Joe Muskat and Harry Tokarz.

**FISH, MARJORIE,** see **ZETA RETICULI**

**FISHER, JOHN MORRIS** (b. April 20, 1922, Fairhaven, Ohio; Pleasant Hill, Boston, Virginia 22713; telephone number: 703-825-8336), Member of the Board of Governors of the NATIONAL INVESTIGATIONS COMMITTEE ON AERIAL PHENOMENA (NICAP).

Although he has no opinion regarding the identity of UFOs, Fisher believes more research should be conducted in order to find the answer to the mystery.

Fisher received his B.A. from Miami University in Oxford, Ohio, in 1947. He attended Brooklyn Law School from 1950 to 1951, and Northwestern University from 1954 to 1955. He received an honorary L.L.D. from Nasson College in 1972.

Fisher was employed by Belden Manufacturing Company in Richmond, Indiana, in 1941. From 1943 to 1945, he served in the United States Army Air Force, achieving the rank of First Lieutenant. He worked as a special agent for the FEDERAL BUREAU OF INVESTIGATION (FBI) from 1947 to 1953. During 1953, he was an executive trainee at Sears Roebuck and Company in Chicago. From 1953 to 1957, he was their Executive Staff Assistant to the Vice-President of Personnel and Employee Relations, and Chairman of the Security Committee from 1957 to 1961. From 1956 to 1957, he was organizer and President of Fidelifax, Incorporated. From 1956 to 1957, he was also the Operating Director of the American Security Council, and has been its President and Chief Executive Officer since 1957. From 1959 to 1960, he was Chairman of the Merchandising Division of the National Safety Council and Chairman of the Chicago Retail Safety Conference. Since 1961, he has been President of the American Research Foundation and First Vice-Chairman of the Trades and Services Section of the National Safety Council. From 1962 to 1965, he served as Consultant to the Chairman of the Committee on Cold War Education at the National Governors' Conference, and since 1962 he has been President of the Education Foundation of the American Security Council. From 1963 to 1964, he was a special advisor to the Illinois Superintendent of Public Instruction. From 1964 to 1965, he served on the Board of the Visitors Freedom Foundation. From 1965 to 1968, he was a Board Member of the State Civil Defense Advisory Council. Since 1968, he has been an Executive Member of the National Captive Nations Committee. From 1971 to 1972, he was President of the American Council for World Freedom. He served as Director of the Center for International Security Studies, and has

been President of the Communications Corporation of America since 1972. He has served on the Board of Directors of the American Foreign Policy Institute since 1975, and has been a member of the Board of Governors of the James Madison Library since 1977. He has been a member of the Board of Governors of NICAP since 1978.

Fisher is a member of the American Society of Industrial Security, the Masons, the Army Navy Club, the Democratic Club and the Capitol Hill Club.

Fisher was decorated with an Air Medal with clusters. He was a recipient of the 10th Anniversary medal and scroll from the Assembly of Captive European Nations, and received the Order of Lafayette Freedom Award in 1973.

**FLAP,** term describing a highly-publicized concentration of UFO sightings within a small geographical area or a short time period. It is distinguished from a WAVE, which denotes a period of several months during which multiple nationwide or worldwide sightings occur and which may or may not be publicized. There is some speculation as to whether or not flaps are in fact generated by heightened news media attention during periods when there is little competitive news.

**FLATWOODS, WEST VIRGINIA,** village where the famous Flatwoods Monster was seen on September 12, 1952.

At about 7:15 P.M., Neal Nunley, Ronald Shaver and Theodore Neal were playing on the Flatwoods football field when they saw a glowing bright red, roundish object traveling through the sky. It hovered momentarily above a nearby hill, then dropped behind the crest. A bright orange light flared up, then faded to a dull red glow. As the boys ran toward the hill, the light continued to brighten and dim repeatedly. On the way, they were joined by Kathleen May, her sons Edward and Theodore, seventeen-year-old National Guardsman Eugene Lemon and young Thomas Hyer. Lemon's dog ran ahead of them. No sooner had he rounded the last bend in the path than he reappeared, streaking homeward in terror. The two adults and six children began to notice an unusual mist spreading over the ground. A strange, sickly odor caused their eyes to water and their noses to smart. As they rounded the final bend, they caught sight of two eyes glowing in a tree to their left. One of the boys turned a flashlight toward the tree, revealing a huge creature, about ten feet tall, whose only distinctive feature was its head. The body had the bulk of a large man but no arms or protrusions were visible. Some writers have described the creature's face as blood-red with glowing greenish-orange eyes. Author IVAN SANDERSON, who personally investigated the case, reported the head as being shaped like an ace of spades with a large circular window through which shone two fixed beams of pale blue light. To the right of the astonished witnesses lay a black object, about twenty feet in diameter and shaped like an ace of spades, its point directed upward. It pulsated from a dull cherry-red glow to an orange brilliance. The monster seemed to be floating over the ground. Lemon passed out. As the creature began to float toward them, there was panic. Lemon was pulled to his feet and everyone took off down the hill, bruising and scratching themselves as they ran in blind terror.

A team headed by the local sheriff searched the area that same evening but found only a sickly, irritating odor. The following day a fifteen-foot circular area of flattened grass and depressed soil was found at the UFO's alleged landing site.

According to several other witnesses, five other low-flying objects were sighted at exactly the same time as the Flatwoods UFO. They were spaced about five miles apart, except for one which was thirty-five miles from its nearest companion. Two were seen to crash or land, and a third disintegrated in mid-air. One object reportedly changed direction in mid-flight.

Air Force investigators concluded that the witnesses had seen a meteor which was observed by thousands of people in Virginia and West Virginia that night. They presumed the Flatwoods Monster to have been a normal woodland animal whose glowing eyes had frightened the group into believing something mysterious was happening.

Ivan Sanderson concluded that a fleet of intelligently controlled objects flew over the area that night. Something went wrong, causing one or two to land, one or two to crash and one to explode in the air. Both craft and occupants dissolved either because of incompatibility with the temperature or through contact with hostile chemical substances.

Bibliography: Sanderson, Ivan T., *Uninvited Visitors: A Biologist Looks at UFOs* (New York: Cowles Education Corporation, 1957).

## FLICKER FLASHES *see* ASTRONAUTS

**FLIGHT 19**, a naval training flight which disappeared over the BERMUDA TRIANGLE, an area considered mysterious because of the high number of ships and airplanes lost within its boundaries. The account of Flight 19 is traditionally used as a prime example of the Bermuda Triangle's enigmatic nature.

On December 5, 1945, five Navy Grumman TBM–3 Avenger torpedo bombers left Fort Lauderdale Naval Air Station on a routine training flight, designated Flight 19. Although three men had been assigned to

Five TBM Avengers similar to those of Flight 19. *(Courtesy U.S. Navy)*

each airplane, one fortunate man had not reported for duty. The fourteen crew members took off around 2:05 P.M. for a scheduled flight of two hours' duration. At about 3:15 P.M. the instructor in command, Lieutenant Charles Taylor, reported to the Naval Air Station that they were lost. The station radio operator instructed Taylor to fly west. Fifteen minutes later, the senior flight instructor at Fort Lauderdale contacted Taylor and learned that his compasses were not functioning. Since Taylor believed he was over the Florida Keys, he was advised to fly north using the sun to get a bearing. Shortly thereafter, Flight 19 passed over a small isolated island, indicating that they were not over the Keys after all. Since radio interference was increasing, Taylor was asked to switch to a less-used frequency. Apparently out of fear that he would lose communication with the other four planes, Taylor ignored this suggestion. Contact was lost with the Naval Air Station, although the tower was able to hear transmissions between the airplanes. Discernibly confused as to which direction would take them back to Florida, the pilots flew east and west in an attempt to locate land. They made one excursion north to find out if they were over the Gulf of Mexico. The last communication heard from Flight 19 came at 7:04 P.M. Their fuel supply was sufficient to keep them aloft until 8:00 P.M. They were never heard from or seen again.

Meanwhile, several rescue planes had been scrambled, among them a Martin Mariner PBM flying boat. To compound the confusion and horror of that day, the Martin Mariner and its crew of thirteen were never seen again.

Writer Lawrence Kusche demonstrates that the records of the Navy Inquiry Board, convened to investigate the incident, contradict claims made by proponents of the theory that a mysterious force causes ships and airplanes to disappear in the Bermuda Triangle. In particular, much of the dialogue attributed to the Flight 19 crew does not appear in the Navy's transcripts of the transmission. Disk jockey Art Ford revealed in 1974 that a ham operator had heard Taylor say, "Don't come after me . . . they look like they are from outer space." Navy records indicate that Taylor did say, "Don't come after me," but in a different context. When the senior flight instructor had told Taylor to fly north while he flew south to meet him, Taylor had responded, "I know where I am now. I'm at 2,300 feet. Don't come after me." In addition, Kusche contends that many other details, including weather conditions and the time of day given for some events, are totally inaccurate. For example, Charles Berlitz writes that the Martin Mariner took off at 4:25 P.M. In reality, it did not leave until 7:27 P.M. and thus its flight path would have brought it in twenty-three minutes to the exact location where an explosion was reported at 7:50 P.M. Nicknamed "flying gas tanks" because of the prevalence of fumes, a Mariner could be ignited by one wayward spark, reports Kusche. He concludes, based on the findings of the Navy Board, that the loss was the result of several factors, of which the most crucial was the failure of Taylor's compasses. Recently transferred to Fort Lauderdale, Taylor was unable to determine his location visually by geographical references. Out of contact with his base and out of fuel, the disoriented instructor and four student pilots were forced to ditch at sea on a dark, stormy night.

Navy investigators reportedly stated that they "were not able to make even a good guess as to what happened." This statement has been denied by several Navy officers. However, the Navy subsequently produced its own documentary film, *The Ocean Desert*, reconstructing the frightening events of December 5, 1945, and showing a team of scientists testing the Sargassum seaweed unique to the area. Although the results were negative, their efforts to determine whether or not there could be any connection between the odd, floating seaweed and the disappearance of craft in the area implied that there was at least some doubt about the validity of the official explanation for the loss of Flight 19.

Arthur Ford claims that the mother of one of the lost men, after attending hearings on the case in Washington, confided to him that she believed her son was still alive somewhere, perhaps in space. Perpetuating the extraterrestrial connection, the Flight 19 story was woven into the plot of the motion picture CLOSE ENCOUNTERS OF THE THIRD KIND. At the beginning of the film, the five Avengers are found abandoned and undamaged in the desert. At the climax of the film, an extraterrestrial spacecraft lands. The aliens release a number of human captives. The men of Flight 19 are among them.

Bibliography: Berlitz, Charles, *The Bermuda Tri-angle* (Garden City, N.Y.: Doubleday and Company, 1974); Kusche, Lawrence D., *The Bermuda Triangle Mystery—Solved* (New York: Harper and Row, 1975).

**FLORIDA,** location of a UFO sighting by Captain Jack E. Puckett, Assistant Chief of Flying Safety for the Tactical Air Command, on August 1, 1946. Puckett was flying a C–47 airplane from Langley Field, Virginia, to MacDill Field in Tampa, Florida. While traveling at an altitude of 4,000 feet, just northeast of Tampa, Puckett, his copilot and the flight engineer observed what they at first thought to be a METEOR on a collision course with their aircraft. At a distance of about 1,000 yards, the object turned sideways, crossing the C–47's path. The three men observed that it was about twice the size of a B–29 bomber and cylindrical in shape with luminous portholes. A stream of fire trailed behind it. The object was in view for about three minutes.

Skeptics have speculated that the UFO was, in fact, a meteor and that the windows were an optical illusion.

Bibliography: Hall, Richard H. (ed.), *The UFO Evidence* (Washington, D.C.: National Investigations Committee on Aerial Phenomena, 1964).

**FLORIDA UFO STUDY GROUP,** organization founded in 1968 by GEORGE D. FAWCETT. It ceased operation in 1972.

**FLYING CROSSES.** Many historical references to aerial crosses can be attributed to a solar phenomenon known as PARHELIA. In 1967, however, an unusual cross-shaped UFO was observed at MOIGNE DOWNS, ENGLAND, which, according to the witness, demonstrated the characteristics of a controlled flying vehicle.

**FLYING FLAPJACK** *see* **FLYING PANCAKE**

Flying Pancake. *(Courtesy U.S. Navy)*

**FLYING PANCAKE,** also known as the flying flap-jack, experimental vertical take-off and landing (VTOL) aircraft with a flat disk-like shape. The craft differed from the traditional flying saucer, however, for it had two large propellors and small wings. The flying pan-cake was born before World War II in the mind of Charles H. Zimmerman, who devoted more than a dozen years to designing and overseeing the con-struction of the two prototypes by the Vought Corpora-tion. One version, the V–173, was full-scale but lightly built, weighing 2,258 pounds, with two eighty-horse-power engines. Boone T. Guyton flew it for the first time on November 23, 1942. Company and Navy pilots, as well as Charles A. Lindbergh, flew the yellow and silver V–173 more than 200 times in 131 flight hours. A heavier version, the XF5U–1, weighing 14,550 pounds, was completed with two Pratt and Whitney R–2000–7 engines of 1,600-horsepower each. With still more powerful engines projected, it was hoped the airplane could take off and land almost vertically like a helicopter and still be capable of flying 500 miles per hour. The XF5U–1 never passed beyond its taxi tests. The Navy canceled the multimillion dollar contract in 1947 in favor of jet manufacturing. The XF5U–1 was destroyed, and the V–173 went to the Smithsonian Institution's storage building.

**FLYING SAUCER,** aerial object, usually disk-shaped, which is assumed by the observer to be a spacecraft of extraterrestrial origin. It is to be dis-tinguished from a UFO, which is accepted as an unknown object of unknown origin.

**FLYING SAUCER BOOKSTORE,** 359 West 45th Street, New York, N.Y. 10036; telephone number: 212-582-6380.

This bookstore, run by James S. Rigberg, was opened in 1953 and carries an enormous selection of occult and UFO books. Rigberg also runs the FLYING SAUCER NEWS CLUB OF AMERICA (FSNCA) and those on his mailing list receive copies of the biannual newsletter, FLYING SAUCER NEWS, and book catalogues.

**FLYING SAUCER BULLETIN,** defunct publica-tion which was published and edited by BONITA ROMAN.

**FLYING SAUCER—HOLLOW EARTH SO-CIETY,** 27 Kingsmount Park Road, Toronto, Ontario, Canada M4L 3L2; telephone number: 416-690-1275.

This CONTACTEE organization, which supports the HOLLOW EARTH HYPOTHESIS, holds that UFOs are craft, three-quarters of them from Earth, and the remainder from other PLANETS and other eras. It claims that their purpose is to watch and guide our civilization and to prevent us from destroying Earth. The group believes that the Earth's flying saucers originate from both the surface and the interior of the planet. It asserts that some of these craft were constructed by German scien-tists during the Second World War, some by American physicist Nikola Tesla, and others by scientists in Brazil who had allegedly worked under Italian physicist Guglielmo Marconi. The organization also believes that groups of people from our own civilization left this planet in the past to form new civilizations in space. Additionally, other people from our past, including the Atlanteans, are supposedly now awakening and return-ing to the world after remaining in a state of suspended animation for several thousand years. The society's purpose is to contact and establish links with extrater-restrials, to select people to help build a new civilization and research the unknown, to conduct expeditions to the inner Earth and to research parapsychology.

This nonprofit organization was founded in 1962 by IVAN BOYES. Its Director is Tawani W. Shoush, who is located in Missouri, where he runs the sister organiza-tion INTERNATIONAL SOCIETY FOR A COMPLETE EARTH (HOLLOW EARTH SOCIETY). Boyes runs the Canadian branch, in association with Field Representative Jeff Mitchel. Members, who are elected, are given assign-ments. Other information regarding membership, field investigators and overseas representatives is classified. The organization has no newsletter. For sale are copies of a special publication purporting to be part of Rear Admiral Richard E. Byrd's "missing" diary relating to his alleged discovery of the polar ingress to Earth's interior.

**FLYING SAUCER INFORMATION CENTER,** 7803 Ruanne Court, Pasadena, Maryland 21122; tele-phone number: 301-437-3753.

The purpose of this CONTACTEE organization is to serve as a public information bureau on UFOs. The group holds that UFOs are the spaceships of highly-advanced SPACE PEOPLE coming from PLANETS within and beyond our solar system. It believes that energy from accelerating sunspots is making our atmosphere and weather increasingly more unbearable, causing human minds to go on to negative extremes. The Space People, according to the organization, are coming to Earth in insulated spaceships in the hope of removing to safety as many Earth people as possible. The group contends that the Space People cannot come to us openly because it is in our nature to shoot first and ask questions afterwards. The group also believes that there are a great many Space People living quietly among us, pretending to be Earth people.

This nonprofit organization was founded in 1954 by LAURA MUNDO, who serves as Codirector with Carmella

Falzone, Florence Steller and Jim Wales. Information is accumulated from newspapers, UFO newsclipping services and international correspondence. There is no membership. An international readership of about 300 persons receives free copies of the monthly publication, *The Mundo Monitor*, which includes information on saucer sightings, landings, contacts, book reviews and research data on sunspots.

**FLYING SAUCER INVESTIGATING COMMITTEE,** 748 Alameda Avenue. Cuyahoga Falls, Ohio 44221; telephone number: 216-794-1842.

This investigative organization is administered by Larry Moyers. Public meetings are held monthly and a newsletter is published. The group is a member of the UFO OHIO network.

**FLYING SAUCER NEWS,** biannual newsletter, established in 1953 as the official publication of the FLYING SAUCER NEWS CLUB OF AMERICA (FNSCA). It is published and edited by James S. Rigberg, proprietor of the FLYING SAUCER BOOKSTORE, 359 West 45th Street, New York, N.Y. 10036.

**FLYING SAUCER NEWS CLUB OF AMERICA (FSNCA),** 359 West 45th Street, New York, N.Y. 10036; telephone number: 212-582-6380.

The club was founded in 1953 by James S. Rigberg, proprietor of the FLYING SAUCER BOOKSTORE, who mails book catalogues and a biannual newsletter, FLYING SAUCER NEWS, to those on his mailing list.

**FLYING SAUCER REVIEW (FSR),** bimonthly magazine established in 1955 with a circulation of approximately 5,000. It is available by subscription only and is distributed in sixty-five countries. FSR is popular with UFOLOGISTS around the world and serves as an international platform for debate, discussion and news dissemination. Reports and investigative articles are presented on major world UFO events.

All material is solicited from freelance writers. No staff writers are employed, although there are several regular contributors and subeditors, including Gordon Creighton and JENNY RANDLES. Although no minimum and maximum length is specified, articles containing over 5,000 words are rarely published. The customary length of articles is between 1,000 and 2,500 words. Since FSR is not primarily a commercial venture, there is no payment for articles. Contributing writers are usually those who are concerned with informing a wide audience of informed and experienced UFOLOGISTS of events and results that they consider important. Charles Bowen is Editor. The magazine is published by FSR

Publications, Limited, West Malling, Maidstone, Kent, England.

**FLYING SAUCERS,** magazine published by the late RAY PALMER and now incorporated in the quarterly publication, SEARCH.

**FLYING SAUCERS: FRIEND, FOE OR FANTASY?,** television documentary presented by the CBS News Department in 1966. The show was narrated by Walter Cronkite. Its theme was that UFO reports are attributable to MISIDENTIFICATIONS, HOAXES, social stress and the desire to believe in extraterrestrial visitation.

UFOLOGISTS criticized the documentary because it inaccurately reported that UFOs are not tracked on RADAR or by SATELLITE-tracking cameras. Moreover, a great deal of time was devoted to the unscientific opinions of several CONTACTEES.

**FLYING SAUCERS INTERNATIONAL,** newsletter published by the AMALGAMATED FLYING SAUCER CLUBS OF AMERICA (AFSCA). It replaced UFO INTERNATIONAL in 1966. Publication was discontinued in 1969, but back issues are still available from AFSCA.

**FLYING SAUCERS INTERNATIONAL (FSI).** This defunct organization published the well-known magazine, *Saucers*, from 1953 to 1959, with Max Miller as Editor.

**FONTES, OLAVO** (b. June 9, 1924, Bahia, Brazil; d. May 9, 1968), physician and Brazilian representative of the AERIAL PHENOMENA RESEARCH ORGANIZATION (APRO).

Fontes believed UFOs to be extraterrestrial craft whose occupants are perhaps hostile or, at best, coldly indifferent to mankind.

Fontes graduated Brazil's National School of Medicine in 1947. He became Professor of Medicine at the school and was Chief of the Gastroenterological Section at the time of his death.

As an APRO representative, he became noted as an authority on UFOs in South America. Among the well-known cases he handled were the ANTONIO VILLAS-BOAS incident and the sighting at UBATUBA, BRAZIL. Fontes was author of many medical papers, as well as numerous UFO articles published in the APRO BULLETIN and the FLYING SAUCER REVIEW.

**FOO FIGHTERS,** UFOs, also known as foo balls, kraut fireballs or fireball fighters, observed by bomber pilots during World War II and sporadically during the Korean and Vietnam wars. Foo fighters were first reported by Allied bombers flying over Europe during the winter of 1944/1945. The glowing spheres and disks, ranging in size from one-to-five-feet in diameter, sometimes exhibited changes in color, usually from orange to red to white and back to orange. Rare daylight sightings revealed globes with a metallic finish. Foo fighters were not detected on RADAR and, when they demonstrated no signs of aggression, pilots assumed them to be psychological weapons sent up by the enemy. Attempts to outmaneuver and lose the objects were usually unsuccessful. Sometimes flying in formation, they always played uninvited escort to single, isolated aircraft. These UFOs were named foo fighters after the popular comic strip *Smokey Stover* had made a pun of the French word "feu" (for fire) in the phrase, "Where there's foo, there's fire."

In 1945, foo fighters were reported by Allied bomber pilots flying over Japan. After the war, it was discovered that the Germans and the Japanese had also been perplexed by the same phenomenon. Originally, American military officials had surmised that fatigued pilots had been the victims of HALLUCINATIONS. Intelligence officers investigating the Japanese sightings, however, ascribed the sightings over the Pacific to misidentification of the PLANET VENUS, since the objects were always seen in the east at a time when Venus was particularly brilliant.

Reportedly, foo fighters observed over Korea and Vietnam were sometimes tracked on radar. A scientific investigative team sent to Korea by the Air Force was able to spot only one foo fighter during their mission. The object was identified as the MOON.

Most UFOlogists concur that at least some foo fighters may have been attributable to ball lightning, CHAIN LIGHTNING and SAINT ELMO'S FIRE. Astronomer DONALD MENZEL has pointed out that foo fighters appeared during the last stages of World War II, when many of the airplanes were considerably damaged. He contended that the aerodynamic imperfections produced by repair patches could have resulted in eddies of air which in turn could have created highly reflective clusters of ice crystals. The resultant glows might have given the impression of independent objects pacing the airplanes. This explanation, however, does not explain those cases in which foo fighters approached an airplane at high speed from a distance, circled or paced it for a short time and then departed from the area.

There is no unanimous agreement on the identity of foo fighters. Some UFOlogists, who believe they were intelligently controlled objects, suspect their mission was to monitor Earth's military activities.

Bibliography: Lore, Gordon I.R., and Harold H. Deneault, *Mysteries of the Skies* (Englewood Cliffs, New Jersey: Prentice-Hall, 1968); Chamberlin, Jo, "The

Foo fighter photographed over Austria in May 1944. *(Courtesy ICUFON/DUIST)*

Foo Fighter Mystery," *American Legion Magazine* (Washington, D.C.: American Legion, December 1945).

**FORCE BEYOND, THE,** also known as *Secrets of the Gods,* documentary (Film Ventures International, 1975). Producer: Donn Davison; director: William Sachs; written by Donn Davison and William Sachs.

This film deals with UFOs, BIGFOOT, the BERMUDA TRIANGLE and ATLANTIS, and the possible connection between all four. In addition to extensive footage of UFOs, the film includes interviews with noted authorities in the field, UFO witnesses and police officials, a visit to the headquarters of the AERIAL PHENOMENA RESEARCH ORGANIZATION (APRO) and a look at a UFO convention in Fort Smith, Arkansas.

**FORD, GERALD R.,** 38th President of the United States who, as House Republican minority leader in 1966, formally requested Congressional hearings on UFOs as a result of his constituents' concern over sightings in Michigan. The state's residents were par-

In the documentary film *The Force Beyond,* this artist's rendering shows a truck driver's encounter with UFO occupants. *(Courtesy Donn Davison)*

ticularly angry about the suggestion by astronomer and UNITED STATES AIR FORCE (USAF) consultant J. ALLEN HYNEK that sightings in DEXTER, MICHIGAN, and HILLSDALE, MICHIGAN, might be attributable to SWAMP GAS.

On March 28th Ford wrote to L. Mendel Rivers, Chairman of the House Armed Services Committee. Referring to various explanations which had been given for recent sightings, Ford said, "I do not agree that all of these reports can be or should be so easily explained away. . . . Because I think there may be substance in some of these reports and because I believe the American people are entitled to a more thorough explanation than has been given them by the Air Force to date, I am proposing that either the Science and Astronautics Committee or the Armed Services Committee of the House schedule hearings on the subject of UFOs and invite testimony from both the executive branch of the government and some of the persons who claim to have seen UFOs." Ford enclosed several newspaper articles and quotes from various individuals criticizing the Air Force investigation of sightings in Michigan and New Hampshire. He concluded his letter by stating, "I think we owe it to the people to establish credibility regarding UFOs and to produce the greatest possible enlightenment on this subject."

This request resulted in the HOUSE ARMED SERVICES COMMITTEE HEARINGS, which were held on April 5, 1966.

**FORD, GLENN,** actor who in 1974 purportedly saw a UFO over the Pacific Ocean while staying at his beach house in Trancas, California. Ford first saw the blue-green, metallic object at about ten o'clock in the evening. It was shaped like two disks "pressed inward toward each other." The rotating rim had what appeared to be windows illuminated by blue, green and fluorescent gray lights. The object was about 500 feet in diameter and made no sound. As Ford watched, the UFO cavorted about the sky. Sometimes it hovered, wobbling as it did so. After about eleven minutes, the object shot up into the sky, then sped off at an abrupt ninety-degree angle, disappearing into the distance. Prior to this sighting, Ford, who had tracked UFOs on radar while in the Navy during World War II, believed that UFOs could be explained as weather BALLOONS or other conventional objects. His 1974 sighting changed his mind. He is convinced that what he saw was an extraterrestrial spacecraft.

**FOREIGN TECHNOLOGY DIVISION (FTD),** Air Force Systems Command agency which took over responsibility for PROJECT BLUE BOOK from the AIR TECHNICAL INTELLIGENCE CENTER (ATIC) in 1961.

**FORESIGHT,** bimonthly magazine, established in 1970, with a circulation of approximately 800 to 1,000. The range of subjects covered includes psychic phenomena, mysticism, occultism, spiritualism and world news in relation to NEW AGE developments. All aspects of UFOLOGY are covered, including the HOLLOW EARTH HYPOTHESIS, the EXTRATERRESTRIAL HYPOTHESIS, (ETH), the SECRET WEAPON HYPOTHESIS and psychic manifestations. The magazine is concerned with the establishment of peace and a new world order.

Articles are written by Editors John W. B. Barkham and Mrs. J. Barkham, as well as freelance writers. The Editors prefer that writers query prior to submitting manuscripts. Self-addressed, stamped envelopes should be sent with submissions. Articles should range between approximately 500 and 2,500 words in length. Poems should not contain more than four verses of four lines each. There is no payment for articles and photographs contributed, except for a free copy of the edition in which the article appears.

The magazine is published by the Foresight Organization, 29 Beaufort Avenue, Hodge Hill, Birmingham B34 6AD, England.

**FORT BEAUFORT, SOUTH AFRICA,** location of a four-hour sighting of a spherical UFO on June 26, 1972.

At 9:00 A.M., Bennie Smit of Braeside farm, nine miles outside Fort Beaufort, was alerted by a laborer to the presence of a fiery ball hovering over some trees. The red ball, about two-and-a-half feet in diameter, was shooting out flames. The laborer let out a shout and the UFO, leaving a grayish-white smoke trail, moved sideways about three hundred yards until it was hidden by a large bush. After a while, the ball reappeared but now it was green. Suddenly, it changed to a yellowish-white. Smit rushed to his house, called the police and returned with a rifle. He fired several shots, which seemed to have no effect on the object. However, Smit thought he heard a thud after his eighth shot. The ball then moved up and down and again disappeared behind the trees.

An hour after the UFO's first appearance, Warrant officer P. R. van Rensburg, the Fort Beaufort station commander, arrived with Sergeant P. Kitching. After Smit and Kitching had fired a few more shots toward the trees, a shiny black sphere emerged. It gradually disappeared from sight and then reappeared. It seemed undisturbed by the shots fired at it, yet dodged behind bushes and trees when anyone approached. Smit managed to sneak up within about twenty yards of the object, which by then had turned grayish-white. As he fired twice, the UFO darted away over the treetops, whirring loudly. The foliage parted for the ball as it rushed along but Smit was convinced that there was no air blast to cause this effect.

The July 5th edition of the *Pretoria News* reported that Mr. C. S. Kingsley, a lecturer in the Department of Geology at Fort Hare University, had examined imprints found on Smit's farm. Kingsley stated that the clearly-defined marks were made by a heavy, hard, spherical object with various narrow indentations on its surface. Further examination of the area revealed no evidence of burned branches or foliage, despite the flaming UFO's proximity to trees and bushes.

The highly-publicized Fort Beaufort case was one of many sightings during a 1972 FLAP in South Africa.

**FORT, CHARLES HOY** (b. August 6, 1874, Albany, N.Y.; d. May 3, 1932, Bronx, N.Y.), researcher and writer.

Fort is renowned for his extensive research and cataloguing of unexplained data about archaeological anomalies, rains of frogs, balls of fire, showers of blood, appearances and DISAPPEARANCES, spontaneous combustion and other oddities. His work is colored with his personal theories about the phenomena he reports. He was the first researcher to draw attention to UFOs, before they were known by that name, and the first to speculate about the ANCIENT ASTRONAUTS hypothesis. In 1919, in *The Book of the Damned*, he stated:

> "I think we're property.
> I should say we belong to something:
> That once upon a time, this earth was No-man's Land, that other worlds explored and colonized here, and fought among themselves for possession, but that now it's owned by something:
> That something owns this earth—all others warned off."

Fort spent his early adulthood earning a living from journalism and embalming butterflies. At the age of forty-two, he came into a small inheritance which permitted him to devote the rest of his life to collecting unexplained data. He found his material in old scientific journals, popular magazines and back issues of newspapers at the New York Public Library and at the British Museum in London, where he spent several years during the 1920s.

The term FORTEAN is derived from his name, and refers to any phenomena that cannot be explained by contemporary scientific theories. The Fortean Society was founded in 1931, and was succeeded by the INTERNATIONAL FORTEAN ORGANIZATION (INFO).

In addition to a novel entitled *The Outcast Manufacturers* (New York: Rickey, 1909), Fort was author of *The Book of the Damned* (New York: Boni and Liveright, 1919); *New Lands* (New York: Boni and Liveright, 1923); *Lo!* (New York: Claude H. Kendall, 1931); and *Wild Talents* (New York: Claude H. Kendall, 1932).

**FORTEAN,** adjective used to describe any event or occurrence which does not have a rational, scientific explanation. The word derives from the name of CHARLES FORT, the early twentieth-century journalist and compiler of strange and unusual phenomena.

**FORTEANA,** matters and events of the type collected and catalogued by CHARLES FORT.

**FORTEAN TIMES,** quarterly journal established in 1973, with a circulation of 1,000. It is available by subscription. In addition to all FORTEAN phenomena, various different aspects of UFOLOGY are covered. These include all paraphysical and parapsychological aspects of UFOs; UFOs in antiquity; HYPOTHESES; so-called anomalous artifacts and sophisticated ancient technology; UFOs in conjunction with natural catastrophes, such as earthquakes; critical investigation of historical cases; and UFO-like natural phenomena, such as ball lightning.

Articles are written by staff and freelance writers. Publisher and Editor R. J. M. Rickard is planning to improve the magazine, expand its distribution and initiate a payment system for freelance materials used. The publication's address is: c/o. FT-DTWAGE, 9–12 St. Annes Court, London W1, England.

**FORTENBERRY, WILLIAM,** *see* **NEWPORT NEWS, VIRGINIA**

**FORT ITAIPU, BRAZIL,** location of an apparent attack by a UFO on November 4, 1957. At 2:00 A.M., two sentries observed a brilliant light above them, which they assumed to be a STAR. However, they soon realized that the object was hurtling towards them at high speed. About a thousand feet above them, it abruptly reduced speed and continued its silent descent. Surrounded by an orange glow, the UFO was circular, measuring about 100 feet in diameter. At about 150 feet above the fort, the object stopped. Spotlighted by an orange glow, the sentries were too frightened to move. They could hear a steady hum emanating from the object. Suddenly, a blast of searing HEAT engulfed the men. One sentry fell to the ground. The other ran for shelter, screaming in agony. The garrison troops, awakened by his cries, began to jump out of their beds. Suddenly, the lights went out. The interior of the fort seemed strangely hot. Panic set in. A minute later, the heat ended and, within moments, the lights came on again. As some of the soldiers came running to their battle stations, they saw the glowing UFO as it sped away. The two sentries, who had been severely burned, were placed under medical care.

United States Army and Air Force officers assisting

the Brazilian Air Force investigators were baffled by the case and were unable to offer any explanation for the unprovoked attack.

Bibliography: Keyhoe, Donald E., *Aliens from Space* (Garden City, N.Y.: Doubleday and Company, 1973).

## FOUÉRÉ, RENÉ see GROUPEMENT D'É-TUDE DE PHÉNOMÈNES AERIENS (GEPA)

**FOURNET, DEWEY J.** (b. November 29, 1921, St. Martinville, Louisiana), aeronautical engineer and member of the Board of Governors of the NATIONAL INVESTIGATIONS COMMITTEE ON AERIAL PHENOMENA (NICAP).

As a UNITED STATES AIR FORCE (USAF) major assigned to Air Technical Intelligence in the Pentagon, Fournet worked as liaison with PROJECT BLUE BOOK for Air Force Headquarters during 1952, one of the most dramatic years in UFO history. Before his association with the project, he had looked on the subject of UFOs with considerable skepticism. However, after examining the Blue Book files, his attitude changed. Five years after his release from the Air Force, he agreed to serve on the Board of Governors of NICAP, having concluded that the Air Force project was increasingly assuming the appearance of a travesty.

Fournet received his B.S. in Mechanical Engineering from Louisiana State University in 1941. He was also a graduate of advanced Reserved Officers Training Corps in 1941. He was employed by the Lockheed Aircraft Corporation in Burbank, California, from 1941 until 1942, when he began his military service. He achieved the rank of captain during his first year in the South West Pacific Area in the Corps of Engineers. He spent the next one-and-a-half years as a Technical Air Intelligence Officer before returning to the United States as Head of Performance Section at the AIR TECHNICAL INTELLIGENCE CENTER (ATIC) at the Anacostia Naval Air Station in the District of Columbia. At the end of World War II, Fournet resumed his civilian employment with the Lockheed Aircraft Corporation as a Weight Engineer and Aerodynamicist during 1946. He subsequently joined the faculty of Louisiana State University, where he taught engineering and did graduate work in business administration. He began his second tour of military duty during the Korean War in 1951. He was promoted to major, and spent his first three months at the Air Command and Staff School. For the balance of his tour, he was assigned to Air Technical Intelligence in the Pentagon, during which time he monitored the Air Force UFO project. Upon release from duty in 1952, he resigned his commission. Fournet returned to Louisiana, where he assumed his current position as an executive with the Ethyl Corporation.

**FOWLER, PATROLMAN A. J.,** *see* **LEVELLAND, TEXAS**

**FOWLER, RAYMOND E.** (b. November 11, 1934, Salem, Massachusetts; address: 13 Friend Court, Wenham, Massachusetts 01984; telephone number: 617-468-4815), Administrative Supervisor, Director of Investigations for the MUTUAL UFO NETWORK (MUFON), Scientific Associate for the CENTER FOR UFO STUDIES (CUFOS) and Consultant to the NATIONAL INVESTIGATIONS COMMITTEE ON AERIAL PHENOMENA (NICAP).

Fowler believes that UFOs are extraterrestrial and/or extradimensional craft controlled by superintelligent beings with paranormal abilities and/or technology. He has observed UFOs on four different occasions. He sighted a white object resembling a parachute canopy during the daytime in 1947; an unconventionally lit object during the nighttime in 1966; a white disk-shaped object during the daytime in 1969; and two white, glowing oval objects during the daytime over the Atlantic Ocean, while he was flying between London and Boston, Massachusetts, in 1969. None of these objects was seen close at hand or for more than a minute. Although there was insufficient data for evaluation, Fowler did have the impression that he was viewing something extraordinary in each case.

Fowler received his B.A. in 1960 from the Gordon College of Liberal Arts. He graduated Magna Cum Laude and was elected to the Phi Alpha Chi Honors Society and the Lambda Iota Tau National Literary Honors Society.

Fowler served in the United States Air Force from 1952 to 1956. He received training for Radio Intercept Operations and served overseas for thirty-two months in the USAF Security Service under the auspices of the

Raymond Fowler.

National Security Agency. Since 1960, he has been employed by GTE Sylvania, where he is currently a Project Administrative Supervisor.

In addition to the positions he holds with MUFON, CUFOS and NICAP, Fowler is also a member of the AERIAL PHENOMENA RESEARCH ORGANIZATION (APRO).

Fowler has written numerous articles on UFOs. He is author of *UFOs—Interplanetary Visitors* (New York: Exposition Press, 1974) and *The Andreasson Affair* (Englewood Cliffs, N.J.: Prentice Hall, 1979).

## FOXFIRE *see* SWAMP GAS

## FRANCE.
The French word for UFO is "OVNI," which stands for "objet volant non identifié" (unidentified flying object). Flying saucers are referred to as "soucoupes volantes."

France has two highly respected UFO magazines— LUMIÈRES DANS LA NUIT (LDLN) and PHÉNOMÈNES SPATIAUX. There are an enormous number of UFO organizations, many of which are united by networks, such as the COMITÉ EUROPÉEN DE COORDINATION DE LA RECHERCHE UFOLOGIQUE (CECRU) and LDLN. In 1977, a scientific research group called GROUPE D'ÉTUDES DES PHÉNOMÈNES AÉROSPATIAUX NON IDENTIFIÉS (GEPAN) was founded by France's CENTRE NATIONAL D'ÉTUDES SPATIALES (CNES), a governmental agency similar to the NATIONAL AERONAUTICS AND SPACE ADMINISTRATION (NASA) in the United States.

During the ninth century, there were many reports in France of aerial beings who traveled through the sky in ships. One report told of the landing of one of these ships in LYONS and the disembarkation of its passengers. Two of the most sensational sightings of the MODERN ERA were those at OLORON and GAILLAC in 1952. The country experienced a heavy WAVE of sightings during 1954, and it was during this year that a military pilot took a photograph near ROUEN which closely resembled the famous UFO photographs taken in MCMINNVILLE, OREGON.

## FRATERNIDAD UNIVERSAL VIAJEROS DEL ESPACIO (FUVE),
Apartado Aereo 4485, Cali, Colombia; telephone number: 751428.

This organization is concerned with UFO investigation, extraterrestrial studies and cosmic science. It is run by Director Domingo Spatare and Coordinator J. Ricardo Nunez, who also edits the bimonthly review, *Contacto Sideral*.

## FREEMASONS *see* SECRET SOCIETIES

## FREUDIAN HYPOTHESIS,
theory proposing that UFO witnesses and UFOlogists are victims of the classic Freudian breast/penis syndrome, thus accounting for the cigar shapes and saucer shapes of UFOs. The hypothesis was suggested in 1969 by psychiatrists Lester Grinspoon and Alan Persky at a symposium on UFOs sponsored by the AMERICAN ASSOCIATION FOR THE ADVANCEMENT OF SCIENCE (AAAS).

Bibliography: Sagan, Carl, and Thornton Page (eds.), *UFOs—A Scientific Debate* (Ithaca, N.Y.: Cornell University Press, 1972).

## FRIEDMAN, STANTON TERRY
(b. July 29, 1934, Elizabeth, New Jersey; address: 31628 Trevor Avenue, Hayward, California 94544; telephone number: 415-471-0160), nuclear physicist, lecturer on UFOs, Founder and Director of the UFO RESEARCH INSTITUTE (UFORI).

Friedman is the only space scientist in North America known to be devoting full time to UFOs. After twenty

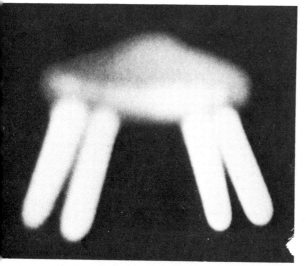

UFO photographed by a medical doctor in Barjols, France, on March 23, 1974. *(Courtesy ICUFON/A. Baguhn)*

Stanton Friedman.

years of study and investigation, he is convinced that the evidence is overwhelming that Earth is being visited by intelligently controlled extraterrestrial spacecraft. He believes there is every indication that the United States government and other governments have engaged in a cover-up of many of the best cases involving data obtained by military personnel, RADAR and instrumentation not submitted to PROJECT BLUE BOOK. Having spent fourteen years as a nuclear physicist on advanced nuclear and space development programs, many of which were highly classified, Friedman feels confident in stating that the government can keep secrets.

Friedman received a B.S. in Physics from the University of Chicago in 1955, and an M.S. in Physics from the University of Chicago in 1956.

From 1956 to 1959, Friedman worked on the experimental and analytical development of advanced radiation shielding systems for nuclear aircraft in the General Electric Air Craft Nuclear Propulsion Department. From 1959 to 1963, he was employed by Aerojet General Nucleonics in San Ramon, California, where he worked on the development of high performance nuclear systems for space applications, including fusion space propulsion systems. From 1963 to 1966, he worked at the Allison Division of General Motors in Indianapolis, Indiana, where he was involved in the development of compact mobile nuclear reactors, nuclear breeders, etc., and was in charge of all aspects of radiation shielding for the Military Compact Reactor program. From 1966 to 1968, he worked at the Westinghouse Astronuclear Laboratory in Pittsburgh, Pennsylvania, where he worked on the analysis, experimentation, development and testing of the radiation-shielding aspects of the nuclear rocket program. He also worked on the review of nuclear aircraft design. From 1969 to 1970, he was employed by TRW Systems in Redondo Beach, California, where he worked on nuclear power supply radiation levels for the PIONEER spacecraft. Since 1970, Friedman has earned his living by presenting an illustrated lecture, *Flying Saucers ARE Real*, at more than 400 colleges and to dozens of professional groups in forty-seven states and four Canadian provinces.

Friedman is a member of the AMERICAN ASSOCIATION FOR THE ADVANCEMENT OF SCIENCE (AAAS), the American Nuclear Society, the American Physical Society, the AMERICAN INSTITUTE OF AERONAUTICS AND ASTRONAUTICS (AIAA), MENSA, the World Future Society, the NATIONAL INVESTIGATIONS COMMITTEE ON AERIAL PHENOMENA (NICAP), the AERIAL PHENOMENA RESEARCH ORGANIZATION (APRO), the MUTUAL UFO NETWORK (MUFON), CITIZENS AGAINST UFO SECRECY (CAUS), the American Federation of Television and Radio Artists and the International Program Association. He is a Fellow of the British Interplanetary Society and an Associate Member of the National Entertainment and Campus Activities Association.

Friedman provided testimony to the U.S. HOUSE SCIENCE AND ASTRONAUTICS COMMITTEE HEARINGS in 1968, and to the United Nations in November, 1978. He has appeared on hundreds of radio and television programs throughout North America, was the technical adviser to Universal Studios on THE UFO INCIDENT and has appeared in several documentaries on UFOs. Friedman has written numerous classified and unclassified reports, and has published articles on UFOs, as well as on radiation shielding. He was a contributing author to *Worlds Beyond* (Berkeley, California: And/Or Press, 1978).

**FRIEND, ROBERT,** UNITED STATES AIR FORCE (USAF) lieutenant colonel who headed PROJECT BLUE BOOK from October 1958 to August 1963, and who was involved in the controversial Swann case in SOUTH BERWICK, MAINE.

**FRIT UFO STUDIUM (FUFOS),** Haraldsgade 41, DK 2200 Copenhagen N, Denmark; telephone number: 01-83 87 33.

The purpose of this nationwide investigative organization is to collect UFO reports, investigate claims of psychic phenomena, study the science of cosmology and to inform the public about all these subjects. Composed of members with widely divergent opinions, FUFOS takes no public stands on the identity of UFOs. Some of the theories considered are that UFOs might be spaceships, time travelers, psychic phenomena or natural phenomena.

This nonprofit UFO organization, the largest in Denmark, was founded in 1968, and has 3,400 members. Steen Landsy is Chairman and Vagn Kamp Justesen is Vice-Chairman. Henning B. Frederiksen is Treasurer, and John La Fontaine is Public Relations Officer. Ten district coordinators are situated throughout Denmark. Each coordinator carries out investigations and has four or five assistants. Contact and exchange of information with international organizations is coordinated by representative Hans Lauritzen, headquartered at Vollsmose Alle 416, 13, 5240 Odense NØ, Denmark. Meetings are held in each district six times a year and in Copenhagen every two weeks.

*UFO-Aspekt*, the organization's thirty-two-page magazine with illustrations, is published six times a year. Vagn Kamp Justesen is Editor. Subjects covered include Danish UFO reports and worldwide news on UFO contacts, sightings, theories, astronomy, space travel, psychic phenomena and spiritual science.

## FROGSTEIN'S FLYING SAUCER MUSEUM,
2140 North Pennsylvania Street, Indianapolis, Indiana 46202.

The museum consists of a private collection of exhibits, paintings and research projects at the home of artist and science fiction buff John Bigelow. The chief attractions are a sixteen-foot flying saucer, which Bigelow is constructing in his living room, and an upstairs laboratory, where he conducts experiments in ball lightning. His main research goal is to develop a free energy device based on an electromagnetic propulsion system. Bigelow gives a course in flying saucer construction at the Free University of Indianapolis. His quarterly *Frogstein Papers* are available by subscription with the warning that anyone who can understand them will receive "an honorary degree from the Institute of Intergalactic Metaphysics."

## FRONT UFOLOGIE NOUVELLE (FUNO),
Boîte Postale 41, 94202 Ivry Principal, Cédex, France; telephone number: 31-1-672-37 04.

The purpose of this organization is to develop and carry out UFO research projects in collaboration with individual members and participating authors according to specific guidelines set out by the parties involved. FUNO also aims to disseminate to as large an audience as possible up-to-date information about the current thinking on the UFO phenomenon. The group holds that it is not yet possible to form a definitive opinion about the identity and origin of UFOs.

FUNO was founded in 1978 by Jean Marc Bonay after the dissolution of his former organization, Groupement de Recherches et d'Études UFOlogiques (GREU). The group consists of Bonay, who serves as Honorary President; Francis Sélaries, who serves as President; Dominique Bromanjey, in charge of International Relations, and twenty active members, including Dominique Séguineau, Claudio Falardi, Bruno Mouchet and Philippe Gaubert. Honorary President Bonay is a correspondent of COLMAN VONKEVICZKY'S INTERCONTINENTAL GALACTIC SPACECRAFT (UFO) RESEARCH AND ANALYTIC NETWORK (ICUFON) in the United States. FUNO is a member of the COMITÉ EUROPÉEN DE COORDINATION DE LA RECHERCHE UFOLOGIQUE (CECRU).

Aquitaine Representative: Bruno Mouchet, MO 05/106 MTO, Base Aérienne 106, 33707 Merignac-Air-France.

## FRY, DANIEL WILLIAM (b. July 19, 1908, Verdun, Minnesota; address: 1606 Mountain View Drive, Alamogordo, New Mexico 88310; telephone number: 505-434-2832), CONTACTEE, Founder and President Emeritus of UNDERSTANDING.

Daniel Fry.

Fry believes UFOs are the craft of beings of superior intelligence who have been dwelling in space for many eons. In a book published in 1954, Fry claimed that he had seen a landed spacecraft in 1950 near the White Sands Proving Grounds in New Mexico, where he was working at the time. As he walked up to the saucer, Fry heard a voice say, "Better not touch the hull, pal, it's still hot." The voice, which later identified itself as "A-lan," belonged to an extraterrestrial being in a MOTHER SHIP that was hovering about 900 miles above Earth. The landed saucer was a crewless, remotely-controlled cargo carrier. The extraterrestrials, Fry was told, were descendants of earthmen who had migrated to space in ancient times. Fry was invited aboard the saucer, where the ship's power system was explained to him. He was then whisked off on a test ride to New York and back in about thirty minutes. Fry was charged with preaching to mankind the extraterrestrials' message that understanding is the key to peace and happiness.

UFO photographed by Daniel Fry. *(Courtesy Ground Saucer Watch)*

Fry studied at UCLA for three years, conducted a personal pursuit of knowledge at libraries at night after work and acquired honorary degrees in Ministry, Cosmology and Law.

Prior to his full-time lecturing and administration of Understanding, Fry was employed by Aero-Jet at White Sands, New Mexico, and was Vice-President of Crescent Engineering Company in El Monte, California.

Fry is author of *The White Sands Incident* (Louisville, Kentucky: Best Books, 1966), which is a combination of two earlier books, *The White Sands Incident* (Los Angeles: New Age Publishing Company, 1954) and *A-lan's Message to Men of Earth* (Los Angeles: New Age Publishing Company, 1955). His other books include *Atoms, Galaxies and Understanding* (El Monte, California: C.S.A. Publishing Company, 1960) and *The Curve of Development* (Lakemont, California: C.S.A. Publishing Company, 1965).

In *UFOs Explained*, PHILIP KLASS questions Fry's reliability by pointing out several discrepancies in Fry's books. According to *The White Sands Incident*, the date of Fry's first saucer encounter was July 4, 1950. Yet more than ten years after the book's first publication, Fry stated that he had made a mistake and that the incident had occurred in 1949. Fry is described in the book as an internationally known scientist, researcher and electronics engineer, recognized by many as the world's best informed scientist on space and space travel. Klass's investigations showed Fry to have been merely a skilled instrument-maker who had designed and built several small devices used in missile-control systems. Klass also discovered that Fry's Ph.D. from "St. Andrews College of London, England" was a degree awarded by a small religious organization in exchange for the submission of a ten-thousand word thesis and a modest fee of under one hundred dollars.

LEON DAVIDSON, who sees a link between *A-lan* of the spaceship and then director of the CENTRAL INTELLIGENCE AGENCY (CIA), *Allen* Dulles, believes the incident was a HOAX played upon Fry. He considers the incident to be part of a campaign to create public belief in flying saucers and thus mislead Russia into wasting effort on defenses against objects having the extreme capabilities attributed to UFOs.

**FSI** *see* **FLYING SAUCERS INTERNATIONAL**

**FSNCA** *see* **FLYING SAUCER NEWS CLUB OF AMERICA**

**FSR** *see* **FLYING SAUCER REVIEW**

**FTD** *see* **FOREIGN TECHNOLOGY DIVISION**

**FUFOR** *see* **FEDERATION UFO RESEARCH**

**FUFOS** *see* **FRIT UFO STUDIUM**

**FUNO** *see* **FRONT UFOLOGIE NOUVELLE**

**FUTURE FANTASY,** bimonthly magazine which suspended publication in 1978. It was edited by TIMOTHY GREEN BECKLEY and published by Cousins Publications. Subjects covered include science fiction movies, books and art, speculation about the future and UFOs.

**FUVE** *see* **FRATERNIDAD UNIVERSAL VIAJEROS DEL ESPACIO**

**GAILLAC, FRANCE,** location of a classic UFO sighting which occurred toward the end of the 1952 European WAVE. On October 27th, about one hundred witnesses observed a long CIGAR-SHAPED UFO tilted at a forty-five-degree angle and moving slowly toward the southwest. A plume of smoke emerged from the upper end. About ten pairs of disks accompanied the cylinder, flying in zigzag motions. The procession hovered over the town for ten minutes while large quantities of ANGELS' HAIR fell earthward. The substance settled on trees and houses, only to dissolve within a short time. This event was a replay of a sighting which had occurred in OLORON, FRANCE, only ten days previously.

A few minutes after the Gaillac sighting, a single disk and a cylindrical UFO were sighted more than 125 miles to the northeast at a Brives-Charensac meteorological station.

Bibliography: Michel, Aimé, *The Truth about Flying Saucers* (New York: Criterion Books, 1956).

**GAIRY, ERIC,** former Prime Minister and Minister for Foreign Affairs of GRENADA, who has seen UFOs over the Caribbean on two occasions, and in 1977 urged the UNITED NATIONS to establish a UFO agency. Gairy is convinced there are "other men, other forms, dwelling elsewhere in the universe, and that the world is surrounded by superior forces." His efforts to establish an agency ended when he was ousted from his position as prime minister in 1979.

**GALLUP POLLS** *see* **POLLS**

**GAP** *see* **GRUPO AGARTHA DE PESQUISAS**

**GARCÍA, C. (JOSÉ) CARLOS PAZ** (b. March 10, 1924, Lima, Peru; address: Jr. Anibal Maurtua 402,

Sir Eric Gairy addressing the United Nations General Assembly on UFOs on October 12, 1978. *(United Nations/Photo by Saw Lwin)*

Barranco, Lima 4, Peru; telephone number: 670681), CONTACTEE and Founder and President of the INSTITUTO PERUANO DE RELACIONES INTERPLANETARIAS (IPRI).

García claims to have observed UFOs and communicated with their OCCUPANTS during monthly skywatches organized by IPRI in Chilca. He believes that an interplanetary airport exists under the sea near the beach at Chilca. García holds that UFOs are spacecraft from our own and other solar systems. They are here, he purports, to help mankind achieve peace.

García attended Pacific University from 1957 to 1960 and received a Master's degree in Human Relations. He attended the Highest Military Studies Center from 1963 to 1964. In 1968 he studied parapsychology in Uruguay. Since 1955 he has served as President of IPRI.

García is Vice-President of the FEDERACION PAN-AMERICANA DE ESTUDIOS CIENTIFICO-FILOSOFICO DE VIDA EXTRATERRESTRE, South American representative of the INTERCONTINENTAL GALACTIC SPACECRAFT (UFO) RESEARCH AND ANALYTIC NETWORK (ICUFON) and a representative of the Fratellanza Cosmica of Italy and the IRMAN DADE COSMICA CRUZ DO SUL—GRUPO DE PESQUISA E DIVULGACAO SOBRE NAVEXOLOGIA of Brazil.

**GARUDA,** giant bird of Indian mythology on whose back the gods Vishnu and Krishna purportedly traveled the heavens. Today the name is also given to giant creatures resembling prehistoric BIRDS which have been reported in various parts of the United States. Occasionally, such creatures have allegedly attempted to carry away children and animals in their claws. The creature has been compared to MOTHMAN, a legendary humanoid monster with huge bat-like wings.

Reports of giant birds have been explained by scientists as MISIDENTIFICATIONS of turkey vultures, California condors and eagles.

Bibliography: Keel, John A., *The Mothman Prophecies* (New York: New American Library, 1976).

Garuda. *(The Bettmann Archive)*

**GELLER, URI** (b. December 20, 1946, Tel Aviv, Israel; address: Kadima Productions, Inc., P.O. Box 1807, F.D.R. Station, New York, N.Y. 10022; telephone number: 212-751-8866), lecturer, demonstrator of paranormal phenomena and CONTACTEE.

Geller has observed three UFOs, two of which he photographed. He believes there are "extaterrestrial civilizations visiting our planet from different dimensions in the universe." In his book *Uri* (Garden City, N.Y.: Doubleday and Company, 1974), physician Andrija Puharich revealed that Geller had been the recipient of messages from an alleged cosmic intelligence since 1949. In *The Invisible College* (New York: E.P. Dutton, 1975), JACQUES VALLEE, who thinks highly of Geller's talent, points out that some of the communications erroneously refer to light years as units of time, an error which Geller himself made in an interview. Vallee surmises, therefore, that a phenomenon is involved which uses or emanates from Geller's brain. Geller and Puharich have received predictions similar to those reported by other contactees, specifically regarding mass landings of UFOs.

Geller's psychic abilities were reportedly apparent throughout his childhood. In 1969, having served three years as a paratrooper in the Israeli army, he began holding stage shows in which he demonstrated his psychokinetic and TELEPATHIC powers. These powers, he claims, derive from a source beyond his control. As his fame for psychically bending keys and repairing watches spread, he traveled overseas to perform in universities, lecture halls and on television. In 1970, he came to the United States. His powers have been tested and studied at many universities, research institutes and government laboratories, including Kent State University in Ohio, Stanford Research Institute in California, Kings College at the University of London and the Telemetery Laboratory at the Foch Hospital in Suresnes, France.

Geller is author of *Uri Geller: My Story* (New York: Praeger, 1975).

**GEMINI 4,** space mission during which ASTRONAUT James McDivitt sighted and attempted to photograph a UFO shaped like a white cylinder with a long, white, thin cylinder protruding from it. The NATIONAL AERONAUTICS AND SPACE ADMINISTRATION (NASA) subsequently released PHOTOGRAPHS of sun flares reflecting on the multiple-paned windows of the space capsule and claimed that McDivitt had misidentified the sun flare. He, however, claims that these were not the photographs he took. "I went back," he says, "and looked through all the frames of all the photographs that were taken on the flight and there wasn't anything in there that looked like what I'd taken." However, he did not

Photograph of a sun flare released by NASA as the UFO photograph taken by James McDivitt during the Gemini 4 mission. McDivitt claims, however, that the image in the photograph is not the UFO he was attempting to photograph. *(Courtesy NASA)*

take the photographs under ideal conditions. There was no time to set the camera for the right speed or distance. McDivitt just snapped the pictures, then the sun came across the window. By the time he had flown the spacecraft back to a position where the sun was no longer on the window, the UFO was out of view. Since many of the photographs taken during the mission came out blank, overexposed and underexposed, McDivitt believes it is possible that his camera never captured the image he was observing.

Although the UFO was tentatively identified as the satellite Pegasus B, the CONDON COMMITTEE rejected this explanation and listed the case as a "puzzler." Science writer JAMES OBERG believes that the UFO observed by McDivitt was his own Titan booster stage. Oberg points out that McDivitt had seen the booster earlier at the point in the Gemini orbit where the UFO appeared, he had failed to recognize the booster on another occasion, and, at the time of the UFO sighting, was suffering an eye irritation due to an accidental urine spill which had contaminated the cabin's atmosphere. McDivitt, who is openminded on the subject of UFOs, asserts that he has no idea what it was he saw.

Bibliography: Sachs, Margaret, with Ernest Jahn, *Celestial Passengers—UFOs and Space Travel* (New York: Penguin Books, 1977); Oberg, James E., *Official UFO* (New York: Myron Fass, October 1976).

**GEMINI 7,** space mission during which a PHOTOGRAPH was allegedly taken of two hexagonal glowing UFOs. However, the photograph purporting to show the UFOs is a HOAX. The original picture showing the sun's glare on two rocket thrusters was doctored to make the thrusters appear as separate detached objects.

Bibliography: Oberg, James E., *Official UFO* (New York: Myron Fass, October 1976).

**GEMINI 8,** space mission during which ASTRONAUTS Frank Borman and JAMES LOVELL allegedly photographed two oval UFOs with glowing bases on December 4, 1965. As in the case of all other UFO sightings by astronauts, the NATIONAL AERONAUTICS AND SPACE ADMINISTRATION (NASA) claimed that nothing had been observed or photographed which could be termed abnormal in the space environment. Lovell denies having seen or photographed UFOs.

**GEMINI 10,** space mission during which ASTRONAUTS Michael Collins and John Young saw a cylindrical UFO accompanied by two bright SATELLITE OBJECTS moving in polar orbit on July 18, 1966. Young, who photographed the UFOs, says, "Odds are that UFOs exist." As in the case of all other UFO sightings by astronauts, the NATIONAL AERONAUTICS AND SPACE ADMINISTRATION (NASA) claimed that nothing had been observed or photographed which could be termed abnormal in the space environment.

**GEMINI 11,** space mission during which ASTRONAUTS Charles "Pete" Conrad and Richard Gordon observed and photographed a UFO or a cluster of UFOs during their sixteenth revolution on September 13, 1966. A transcript of a taped report of the sighting reads, "We had a wingman flying wing on us going into sunset here off to my left. A large object that was tumbling at about 1 rps, and we flew. . . . We had him in sight, I say fairly close to us, I don't know, it could depend on how big he is, and I guess he could have been anything from our ELSS [extravehicular life support system] to something else. We took pictures of it."

Of the three PHOTOGRAPHS taken, the second and third showed four distinct white blobs surrounded by a red-orange corona. The blobs are in a different arrangement in each picture, suggesting either individual motion of separate objects or some sort of rotation of a single large object in the intervals between the taking of the pictures. The CONDON REPORT concluded that the photographs recorded multiple pieces of the Russian space launch vehicle, Proton 3. But the North American Radar Defense (NORAD) report on the Proton 3 lists only two pieces, satellite and booster. In an article in *Science and Mechanics* (New York: Science and Mechanics Publishing Company, June, 1969), Lloyd Mallan established that since the astronauts were facing southeast toward the sunset and away from the direction of Proton 3, which was actually about 250 miles behind them, it would have been impossible for them to have seen the Proton 3 through the tiny windows of the space capsule, which permitted only a narrow forward view. Moreover, he pointed out that Gordon had stated that when the object was first seen through their left window "it flew out in front of us and then we lost it when it sort of dropped down in front of us." Therefore, concluded Mallan, the direction of the object or objects was opposite that of Proton 3. Mallan's information on the position of Proton 3 was obtained from NORAD's computer. However, science writer JAMES OBERG reports that at the time of the sighting, Proton 3 was already in a decaying orbit, well ahead of the schedule which had been programmed into NORAD's computer.

In a paper presented at a meeting of the American Physics Society in 1975, physicist BRUCE MACCABEE calculated that if the blobs were to be explained as Proton 3, the image sizes on the photographs are much larger than they should be, the image brightness much greater and the relative motions of the individual blobs much greater than could be expected for relative motions between the satellite and its booster during the period (a minute or less) between pictures. Maccabee considers the possibility of the object or objects being trash, but asserts that it could not have been trash from Gemini 11, since it was in a different orbit. He submits that the likelihood of a close encounter with trash in another orbit is statistically miniscule but not impossible. The sighting is listed as "unidentified" by the NATIONAL AERONAUTICS AND SPACE ADMINISTRATION (NASA).

**GEMINI 12,** space mission during which ASTRONAUTS Edwin "Buzz" Aldrin and JAMES LOVELL allegedly saw a row of four linked UFOs on November 11, 1966. As in the case of all other UFO sightings by astronauts, the NATIONAL AERONAUTICS AND SPACE ADMINISTRATION (NASA) claimed that nothing had been observed which could be termed abnormal in the space environment. Lovell denies having seen UFOs.

**GEMINI CAPSULE,** U.S. spacecraft launched from Cape Kennedy in 1964 and allegedly accompanied by four UFOs during an entire orbit around Earth. The UFOs, which reportedly were tracked on RADAR, gave the impression that they were examining the Gemini capsule.

**GENPI** see **GROUP D'ÉTUDES NORMAND DES PHÉNOMÈNES INCONNUS**

**GEORGE ADAMSKI FOUNDATION,** 314 Lado de Loma Drive, Vista, California 92083.

The purpose of this CONTACTEE organization is to distribute the literature of GEORGE ADAMSKI and the information that has allegedly been given to the group by people from other PLANETS without changing or distorting the information. In addition, the foundation serves as a source of original information to the public concerning Adamski and his work. The organization holds that UFOs are extraterrestrial craft from our solar system, and in some cases from other solar systems, whose OCCUPANTS are here to observe our planet and the affairs of its people.

This nonprofit organization was founded in 1965 by Alice K. Wells. It is run by a team of coordinators, consisting of Wells, Fred Steckling and Steve Whiting. The foundation estimates the number of worldwide members to be several thousand. The group has representatives in many foreign countries including England, Belgium, France, Denmark, Mexico, Yugoslavia, Argentina and Japan. Information is exchanged through lectures, magazine articles and international correspondence. *Cosmic Bulletin*, published quarterly, releases new information as it is obtained from the SPACE PEOPLE, as well as from the group's own scientific circles. Articles on cosmic philosophy are also included.

**GEOS** see **GROUPE D'ÉTUDES DES OBJETS SPATIAUX**

**GEPA** see **GROUPEMENT D'ÉTUDE DE PHÉNOMÈNES AERIENS**

**GEPAN** see **GROUP D'ÉTUDES DES PHÉNOMÈNES AÉROSPATIAUX NON IDENTIFIÉS**

**GEPO** see **GROUPE D'ÉTUDES DU PHÉNOMÈNE OVNI**

**GEPU** see **GRUPO DE ESTUDOS E PESQUISAS ULTRATERRENOS "MARCUS DE ORION"**

Alleged UFO photographed near Hamburg, Germany, on March 7, 1977, by Walter Schilling. *(Courtesy ICUFON/DUIST)*

**GERMANY.** Flying saucers are referred to as "fliegende untertassen" in Germany.

Reportedly, experimental flying disk-shaped craft were produced in Germany during World War II. Some UFOLOGISTS claim that the scientists involved continued their work for the Russians and Americans after the war.

Rocket pioneers Hermann Oberth and Walter Riedel have frequently been quoted as supporters of the EXTRATERRESTRIAL HYPOTHESIS (ETH) and have been involved in UFO research. Germany has several UFO organizations, of which the DEUTSCHE UFO/IFO-STUDIENGESELLSCHAFT (DUIST) is best-known overseas.

One of the oldest cases on record occurred in NUREMBERG, GERMANY, in 1561.

**GERO** *see* **GROUPEMENT D'ÉTUDE RÉGIONAL DES OVNI**

**GERSTEN, PETER A.,** *see* **CITIZENS AGAINST UFO SECRECY (CAUS)**

**GESAG** *see* **GROUPEMENT POUR L'ÉTUDE DES SCIENCES D'AVANT-GARDE**

**GHOST,** a spurious RADAR return, also known as an ANGEL.

**GHOST ROCKETS,** UFOs observed in Scandinavia, Western Europe, Turkey and North Africa between 1946 and 1948. A concentration of sightings occurred in Sweden during the summer and autumn of 1946. Mysterious FIREBALLS and CIGAR-SHAPED UFOs constituted the majority of the reports. The objects usually traveled at altitudes between about one thousand and three thousand feet. They were variously described as traveling slower than airplanes or crossing the sky in seconds at fantastic speeds. The objects generally appeared from the south or southeast but were known to travel in all directions and to execute turns and circular maneuvers. Aerial explosions were frequently reported in association with ghost rockets but seemed to provide no DEBRIS. Reports of UFOs falling into lakes led to rumors that Swedish military investigators had recovered metallic fragments which were being examined. These stories were never confirmed.

During this postwar period, it was commonly believed that the ghost rockets were secret weapons developed by the Russians who had taken over the German rocket program at Peenemünde. Retired U.S. Air Force Lieutenant General James H. Doolittle visited Sweden purportedly on business for the Shell Oil Company. However, the press announced that he was assisting the Swedish authorities in their investigation.

In October 1946, the Swedish defense ministry issued a communiqué stating that eighty percent of the one thousand reports of ghost rockets could be attributed to natural phenomena but that radar had detected about two hundred objects "which cannot be the phenomena of nature or products of imagination, nor can they be referred to as Swedish airplanes."

Bibliography: Flammonde, Paris, *UFO Exist!* (New York: G. P. Putnam's Sons, 1976).

**GIANT ROCK CONVENTION,** annual convention organized by CONTACTEE GEORGE VAN TASSELL from 1954 until 1977, just prior to his death. Van Tassell claimed that the Giant Rock area in California is a "natural core of receptivity for flying saucers."

**GILGAMESH,** ancient Mesopotamian king whose exploits are recounted in the *Epic of Gilgamesh*. The most complete text in existence was found on twelve clay tablets in the library of the ancient Assyrian king, Ashurbanipal, at Ninevah. Some of the gaps in this version have been partially filled by fragments found elsewhere. Scholars believe that Gilgamesh probably lived during the first half of the third millenium B.C. There is, however, no historical evidence to confirm the details of his exploits.

Author ERICH VON DÄNIKEN has suggested that Gilgamesh, who was alleged to be part divine and part human, was the result of interbreeding between an extraterrestrial and a human being. Von Däniken proposes that Enkidu, a major character in the epic, was taken for a ride in a spaceship. The third tablet of the epic describes a CLOUD of dust which approached from a distance. With a loud roaring sound, the "Sun God" arrived, picking up Enkidu in its claws. As he was carried through the air, Enkidu's body felt as heavy as a boulder. Von Däniken attributes this sensation to the effect of acceleration, an effect which he believes must have been unknown to the ancient chroniclers. On a later high-altitude flight in the claws of an eagle, Enkidu describes the land and sea as porridge and a water trough. Von Däniken contends that only someone who had observed the globe from above could have described the appearance of the land and sea in this way. He also points out that in the seventh tablet a door was alleged to have spoken like a human being. Von Däniken identifies the phenomenon as a loudspeaker.

Bibliography: Von Däniken, Erich, *Chariots of the Gods?* (New York: G. P. Putnam's Sons, 1970); Wilson, Clifford, *Crash Go the Chariots* (New York: Lancer Books, 1972).

**GILL, WILLIAM BOOTH,** *see* **BOIANAI, PAPUA NEW GUINEA**

**GIORNALE DEI MISTERI,** monthly magazine, established in 1971, with a circulation of 100,000. It is available both at newsstands and by subscription. The range of subjects covered includes UFOLOGY, parapsychology, astronomy, esoteric doctrines and astrology. Articles on UFOLogy deal with the major Italian cases, news from the United States and around the world, ancient sightings, the involvement of secret services and the relationships between UFOs and ESP.

Articles are written by Italian and foreign contributors as well as by Italian and foreign research organizations. Giulio Brunner is Editor.

The magazine is published by Corrado Tedeschi Editore, Via Massaia 98, 50134 Florence, Italy.

**GIRVIN, CALVIN C.** (b. October 10, 1926, Lancaster, Pennsylvania; address: 6711 Yucca Street, Hollywood, California 90028; telephone number: 213-465-1217), artist, art restorer, machinist and CONTACTEE.

Girvin claims to have had his first close sighting of an interplanetary spacecraft in 1948. He reports that in a subsequent encounter he was invited aboard a spacecraft. Inside was a machine resembling a television which showed 360 degrees of space, giving the OCCUPANTS a visual range of hundreds of miles. Girvin maintains that subsequently, while working in Washington, D.C., as secretary of the Airmen's Open Mess, he had access to government files and read many reports about interplanetary spacecraft visiting Earth. He asserts that, just before his military service ended, he was taken aboard another ship which accommodated 2,500 men and women. On that occasion he was asked by a highly advanced gentleman from VENUS to go out and tell the world of the SPACE PEOPLE's way of life and its beauty.

Calvin Girvin.

Girvin holds that Christ's words, "In my Father's house, there are many mansions," refer to the many civilizations in space. He believes the human form is universal, differing only in such aspects as size, color and degree of development. He claims that the history of our distant past lies hidden among distorted and perverted fables, legends and religious writings. His study into the historical records of our past is supposedly being aided through inspirational writings and mental contact with a higher intelligentsia. According to Girvin, the people who are now sending flying saucers to us are the former colonizers of Earth, who are monitoring our progress. A previous civilization, he says, destroyed itself in the Garden of EDEN by experimenting with thermonuclear devices. Only through the peaceful use of our natural forces, says Girvin, shall we once again be able to progress without killing and destruction, and then be welcomed by our other planetary friends in free exchange.

A high school graduate, Girvin served four years in the U.S. Army and four years in the U.S. Air Force, during which time he was a paratrooper in the Airborne Division in the Philippine Islands and Japan, Secretary of the Airmen's Open Mess in Washington, D.C., and Chief Clerk in the Food Service Office in the Hawaiian Islands. He was employed by Con Air in Glendale, California, where he was foreman of the night shift, in charge of the Honing and Lap Department, and involved in hiring, training and supervising. He then worked at Los Angeles Gauge in California, where he was a metrologist in the Lapping Laboratory. Subsequently, he was employed by Solrac, Incorporated, in North Hollywood, California, where he was a Supervisor, Foreman and Company Representative. During his twenty-five years as an artist specializing in landscapes and still life, Girvin's original paintings have won various awards throughout Southern California. He has lectured on flying saucers and appeared on local and national radio and television programs.

Girvin is author of *The Great Accident* (Los Angeles: the author, 1957); *The Night has a Thousand Saucers* (El Monte, California: Understanding Publishing Company, 1958); and *A Vital Message* (Los Angeles: the author, 1958).

**GLEASON, JACKIE,** comedian and actor who has allegedly seen UFOs on two separate occasions. The first sighting occurred while Gleason was staying at the Grosvenor Hotel in London in 1965. Looking out of his window at two o'clock one morning, he saw a very brilliant light maneuvering in the sky at high speed. The object made abrupt directional changes, sometimes coming closer, sometimes receding. Finally it disappeared. Gleason's second sighting took place near his

Florida home. While walking his dog one night, he watched another bright light traveling in various directions at high speed and gyrating. After a couple of minutes, the UFO disappeared. Gleason claimed that, in 1948, he was told privately by a government official that UFOs exist. He personally believes that mankind is being studied by beings from other PLANETS.

**GLENN, JOHN,** *see* **MERCURY CAPSULE**

**GLI ARCANI,** *see* **ARCANI, GLI**

**GLOBAL COMMUNICATIONS,** Suite 1306, 303 Fifth Avenue, New York, N.Y. 10016; telephone number: 212-685-4080. This worldwide news feature service, which supplies materials to 150 publications in more than fifteen countries, also publishes and sells UFO books through the mail. UFOlogist TIMOTHY GREEN BECKLEY is President of the company.

**GLOBE LIGHTNING** *see* **PLASMA**

**GLRU** *see* **GROUPEMENT LANGEADOIS DE RECHERCHES UFOLOGIQUES**

**GNEOVNI** *see* **GROUPEMENT NORDISTE D'ÉTUDES DES OVNI**

**GOC** *see* **GROUND OBSERVER CORPS**

**GODMAN AIR FORCE BASE, KENTUCKY,** location of the famous Mantell incident in which an Air National Guard pilot was killed while chasing a UFO.

Shortly after noon on January 7, 1948, the Kentucky State Police received a large number of calls from the towns of Maysville, Owensboro and Irvington, reporting a high-flying UFO moving west at high speed. The police relayed the information to the control tower of Godman Air Force Base, near Fort Knox. When the tower operators had spotted the UFO, they were joined by the base commander and a number of other witnesses. Several observers watched the object through binoculars. It was described variously as a silvery white, ice cream cone shape tipped with red; conical or teardrop-shaped changing fluidly to round; and umbrella-shaped. An incoming flight of four P–51 planes was asked to identify the object. One P–51, low on fuel, landed, while the other three took off after the UFO, led by Captain Thomas Mantell. The three planes had no oxygen aboard because they had been on a low-flying ferrying flight. They began to climb toward the UFO. Mantell advised the tower that he had the object in sight. "It appears to be a metallic object or possibly the reflection of sun from a metallic object," he said, "and it

An artist's rendering of the attempted intercept at Godman Air Force Base, Kentucky, on January 7, 1948. *(Courtesy ICU-FON)*

is of tremendous size." He continued to climb but the other two pilots, who hadn't seen the object, refused to fly any higher without oxygen. Mantell radioed the tower again to report that he was at an altitude of 22,000 feet and still climbing. He announced that he was going to close in for a better look. It was the last transmission received from him. About an hour later, his body was found in the wreckage of his plane. Investigators concluded that he had blacked out from lack of oxygen. His plane had gone into a spiral dive, crashing into the ground.

The incident launched speculation and rumors that Mantell had been shot down by an extraterrestrial spacecraft. The original UNITED STATES AIR FORCE (USAF) explanation was that Mantell had been chasing VENUS. However, in the early 1950s, the Navy released information that they had been testing SKYHOOK BALLOONS in the area at the time. The experimental balloons, which were used for high-altitude photographic reconnaissance, were part of a classified project. The Air Force then attributed the UFO sighting to a Skyhook balloon released from Clinton County in Southern Ohio. However, no Skyhook balloons were released from Clinton County on January 7, 1948.

Nevertheless, witnesses' descriptions of the object closely matched the appearance of Skyhook balloons. Authors David Saunders and R. Roger Harkins suggest that Mantell did pursue a Skyhook balloon, but that it was one that had been launched from Camp Ripley, Minnesota, early on the morning that Mantell was killed.

Bibliography: Saunders, David, and R. Roger Harkins, *UFOs? Yes!* (New York: World Publishing Company, 1968); Flammonde, Paris, *UFO Exist!* (New York: G.P. Putnam's Sons, 1976).

**GOLDWATER, BARRY M.** United States Senator and former Republican presidential candidate who is a member of the Board of Governors of the NATIONAL INVESTIGATIONS COMMITTEE ON AERIAL PHENOMENA (NICAP). Goldwater considers the EXTRATERRESTRIAL HYPOTHESIS (ETH) to be a possible explanation for the UFO phenomenon.

**GONDWANALAND,** hypothetical continent in the Southern Hemisphere which included South America, Africa, Southern India, Australia and Antarctica. Geological evidence lends support to the theory that this enormous land mass may have existed until sometime between 225,000,000 and 65,000,000 years ago, when it began to separate into the land masses we know today. Geologists consider the possible existence of Gondwanaland as a natural stage of prehistoric continental drift.

Some proponents of the existence of lost continents, such as ATLANTIS and HYPERBOREA, believe that Gondwanaland was an inhabited land which divided into two parts, forming LEMURIA and MU, both of which were ultimately destroyed by earthquakes.

Bibliography: Hutin, Serge, *Alien Races and Fantastic Civilizations* (New York: Berkley Publishing Corporation, 1975).

**GONTOVNICK, HOWARD** (b. April 10, 1959, Montreal, Canada; telephone number: 514-688-6473), Founder and Codirector of UFO CANADA.

Gontovnick holds no opinion regarding the identity of UFOs. He believes that the study of the phenomenon has advanced a great deal since the days when people began to take a serious interest in the subject. However, he thinks that a large portion of the population remains incorrectly informed concerning recent happenings in the field.

Gontovnick, a student of psychology, published *The UFO Researchers' Newsletter* from 1976 to 1977. In 1977, he founded UFO Canada, and since that time has published its journal, UFO CANADA, in association with ROBERT SAPIENZA. He has written articles on UFOs for various newspapers and magazines.

**GOODYEAR BLIMP** *see* **BLIMP**

**GORDON, RICHARD,** *see* **APOLLO 12 and GEMINI 11**

**GORMAN, GEORGE T.,** *see* **FARGO, NORTH DAKOTA**

**GOSSAMER** *see* **ANGELS' HAIR**

**G-PAZ** *see* **GRUPO DE PESQUISAS AEROSPACIAIS ZENITH**

**GPUN** *see* **GROUPE PRIVÉ UFOLOGIQUE NANCÉIEN**

**GRANCHI, IRENE** (b. November 26, 1913; address: Caixa Postal 12058, ECT Copacabana, 20.000 Rio de Janeiro, Brazil), leading Brazilian UFOLOGIST.

Granchi's interest in UFOs was spurred by a daytime sighting in 1947 of a bright, metallic disk, about one foot in diameter, oscillating at treetop level above and along some nearby railroad tracks. She believes that UFO research and investigation is a highly sensitive mission of future historical impact which justifies the endless and often seemingly fruitless efforts of those involved.

Granchi was born a British subject and raised in Italy. Her native languages are English and Italian, although she also speaks French, German and Portuguese. She graduated from the Scuola Femminile A. Manzoni in Milan and subsequently attended the École des Interpretes in Geneva, Switzerland. She began her career as an artist but gave up painting when her children were

Irene Granchi.

born. She also worked as an interpreter at various international congresses. For the past twenty years, she has taught English professionally.

Granchi began investigating UFO sightings in 1967. She joined the AERIAL PHENOMENA RESEARCH ORGANIZATION (APRO) in 1962, and became an APRO field investigator in 1970. She has also been a field investigator for the CENTER FOR UFO STUDIES (CUFOS) since 1975. She is Vice-President and Rio de Janeiro representative of the Associacao de Pesquisa Exologica (APEX), and Editor of OVNI DOCUMENTO. Granchi has participated in numerous UFO symposia and has organized UFO skywatches, lectures and conferences.

## GRAND RAPIDS FLYING SAUCER CLUB,
organization created in 1951 and later disbanded when members disagreed over CONTACTEE claims. It published a periodical called *UFOrum,* and organized lectures with attendances as high as 750.

## GRASSINO, GIAN PAOLO, see CENTRO TORINESE RICHERCHE UFOLOGICHE (CTRU)

## GRAVEYARD OF THE ATLANTIC see BERMUDA TRIANGLE

## GRAVITATION, force by which every object possessing mass attracts every other object possessing mass. As mass increases, the intensity of the gravitational field increases. Terrestrial gravitation or gravity is the gravitational force that draws all bodies in Earth's sphere toward the center of the PLANET.

Gravitation is one of two fields, the other being ELECTROMAGNETISM, which falls off in intensity as the square of the distance. The gravitational field is the weaker of the two and seems not to produce a force of repulsion. In contrast, the electromagnetic field produces forces of both attraction and repulsion.

The strength of the downward force humans usually feel on Earth is described as one G. A pilot flying on a horizontal trajectory feels the same effect. However, if he executes a sudden steep climb, according to the laws of inertia, the tendency of his body to keep moving in the same direction will cause him to feel several G's. If UFOs are intelligently piloted craft utilizing conventional propulsion systems, the rapid acceleration and instantaneous directional changes attributed to them should cause their passengers to be crushed against the walls of the machines, which themselves would burn up because of excessive friction with the atmosphere. Many UFOLOGISTS have proposed that the ability to control gravity would provide a means of circumventing the laws of inertia. They hypothesize that if a craft had its own gravitational field, the surrounding air would be held against it and would travel with it. This effect is compared to the manner in which the atmosphere is held around Earth by gravity, despite the planet's motion in space. The cushion of air, it is suggested, would prevent friction between the craft and the atmosphere.

Hypothetical antigravity or negative gravity would provide a valuable means of propulsion. By neutralizing weight, it would be possible to hover in mid-air. By increasing the gravitational force of repulsion an object could move away from a planet with steadily increasing speed. Some witnesses have reported observing humanoids floating between UFOs and the ground, as in the 1970 case of IMJARVI, FINLAND. Although LEVITATION, the ability of an individual to independently defy gravity, has also been attributed to famous religious personages, scientists have never detected negative gravity. The expectancy that the study of ANTIMATTER might provide evidence to support the existence of negative gravity has not born fruit so far. Recent experiments indicate that the gravitational force between matter and antimatter is identical to that between matter and matter.

Bibliography: Clarke, Arthur C., *Profiles of the Future* (New York: Harper and Row, 1963); Keyhoe, Donald E., *Aliens from Space* (Garden City, N.Y.: Doubleday and Company, 1973).

## GRAVITY see GRAVITATION

## GREAT BRITAIN see UNITED KINGDOM

## GREAT FALLS, MONTANA. At approximately 11:25 A.M. on August 15, 1950, Nicholas Mariana, General Manager of the Great Falls baseball team, saw two silvery flying disks while working at the Great Falls ball park. Mariana reported that he ran to his car to get his movie camera, which had a telephoto lens. As he did so, he called his secretary, who ran outside to observe the UFOs. Mariana filmed the objects as they traveled southeast and finally disappeared about fifteen-to-twenty-five seconds from when they had first appeared. The developed film showing two bright circular points of light became one of the most disputed pieces of evidence in the UFO controversy.

In October, 1950, the film was turned over to the Air Force whose initial response was that it was too dark to distinguish any recognizable objects. When it was returned to him, Mariana asserted that about thirty-five frames of the film were missing. These frames, according to Mariana and numerous witnesses who had seen them prior to the Air Force examination, had shown the disks at their clearest when their spinning motion was apparent.

UFOs filmed at Great Falls, Montana, on August 15, 1950. *(Courtesy Ground Saucer Watch)*

In November *Cosmopolitan* published an article by Bob Considine, whose information regarding Mariana's film had been obtained directly from the Air Force. Considine reported that two bright disks had been visible on the film but were identifiable as sun reflections on the ball park's water tower. The moving objects Mariana and his secretary had observed were Air Force jets which had landed at a nearby field at 11:30 A.M. and 11:33 A.M. The thrust of the article was to demonstrate the invalidity of UFO reports, with the claim that their investigation had cost millions of dollars and some lives. Mariana sued Considine and the publishers for libel, claiming that the article implied that he was a liar who had intentionally caused the Air Force to waste time and money. The litigation dragged on for four years, Mariana unable, in the end, to win his case because Considine's article had specified that some UFO cases could be attributed to honest mistakes.

In the meantime, increased activity and interest in the UFO field in 1952 led the Air Force to request a second look at Mariana's film. Written reports of additional Air Force interviews with Mariana in 1953 contained enough misleading information to cause considerable confusion in the CONDON COMMITTEE'S investigation of the case. Eventually, however, they concurred with the NATIONAL INVESTIGATIONS COMMITTEE ON AERIAL PHENOMENA (NICAP) in labeling the case as unexplained. In 1968, scientist ROBERT BAKER, who had conducted an analysis of the film in 1955 and 1956, restated his earlier cautious conclusion by saying that the images could not be explained by any natural phenomenon known at that time. Although he had originally considered the possibility that the lights were reflections from F–94 jets, he later conducted tests which indicated the photographic equipment used by

Mariana would have resolved an F–94 into a noncircular image at a distance of up to ten miles. His calculations demonstrated that if the objects had indeed been F–94 jets, they would not have been further away than six-and-one-half miles. Writer PHILIP KLASS has argued that a PHOTOGRAPH taken by Baker of a one-hundred-foot-long airliner at a distance of approximately twelve miles, showing a round spot of light, is evidence that a forty-foot-long F–94 could produce the same image at a distance of approximately five miles. In the late 1970s, GROUND SAUCER WATCH (GSW) subjected the film to computer image enhancement testing. Their analysis indicated that the images in the Great Falls, Montana, film represent two bona fide UFOs.

Bibliography: Saunders, David, and R. Roger Harkins, *UFOs: Yes!* (New York: World Publishing Company, 1968); Klass, Philip J., *UFOs Explained* (New York: Random House, 1974); Spaulding, William H., "Modern Image Processing Revisits the Great Falls, Montana, and Tremonton, Utah, Movies," *1977 MUFON UFO Symposium Proceedings* (Seguin, Texas: Mutual UFO Network, 1977).

**GREAT SHAVER MYSTERY** *see* **SHAVER, RICHARD SHARPE**

**GRECO, BUDDY,** singer who allegedly observed a UFO in 1962 while driving with his wife through the desert between Los Angeles and Las Vegas. At about 3:00 A.M. on a clear night, he saw a metallic dome spinning on the ground. Brilliant white lights flashed around its rim. Suddenly, the object rose vertically and shot up into the sky at an incredible speed. Terrified, Greco accelerated and sped off.

**GREEN, GABRIEL** (b. November 11, 1924, Whittier, California; address: P.O. Box 39, Yucca Valley, California 92284; telephone number: 714-365-1141), CONTACTEE, Founder and President of the AMALGAMATED FLYING SAUCER CLUBS OF AMERICA (AFSCA).

Green, who claims to have had over one hundred sightings of flying saucers, was reportedly asked by a visitor from a planet of Alpha Centauri to run for the presidency of the United States in 1960. He campaigned as an independent nonpartisan candidate on an economic reform platform, but withdrew to support President Kennedy. In 1962, he ran for the United States Senate from California and received 171,000 votes in the Democratic primaries. In 1972, he was the presidential candidate of the Universal Party, an outgrowth of an organization formed by DANIEL FRY, Green's vice-presidential running mate. The party offered the people of the United States the opportunity to become aware of the solutions recommended by extraterrestrial beings to national and international problems. Green is a proponent of Universal Economics, a non-money system of economics supposedly used on other advanced PLANETS.

Formerly a professional photographer for the Los Angeles Board of Education, Green has devoted full time to flying saucers since 1959. In 1956, he formed the Los Angeles Interplanetary Study Groups, which evolved in 1959 to AFSCA. He has been its Director since that time and edits the organization's newsletter, FLYING SAUCERS INTERNATIONAL. He lectures on flying saucers and past life regression, and is coauthor with Warren Smith of *Let's Face the Facts About Flying Saucers* (New York: Popular Library, 1967).

**GREENAWALD, WALTER HARRY** (b. June 2, 1928, Bethlehem, Pennsylvania; address: 20709 Collins Street, Woodland Hills, California 91367; telephone number: 213-887-6632), aerospace engineer and independent UFO researcher.

After observing a white cylindcrical UFO during a daytime flight aboard a commercial airliner in 1969, Greenawald's curiosity about the UFO mystery was aroused. He read avidly on the subject for several years before becoming actively involved. During the 1973 WAVE, he observed another UFO in North Huntsville, Alabama, at 8:50 P.M. on December 2. For two or three minutes, he watched through binoculars as an object at least 100 feet in length, with two very bright headlights in the front and at least one red light in the rear, traveled silently at a speed of approximately ninety miles per hour. The UFO was tilted, nose up, at an angle of fifteen to twenty degrees with respect to the horizon. Greenawald estimated it to be one-quarter-to-one-half-mile away at its closest approach. Its altitude was between 300 and 500 feet. The object executed a wide turn before disappearing from view behind a hill. Greenawald has concluded that some UFOs are spaceships from distant planetary systems.

Greenawald received a B.S. in mechanical engineering from Pennsylvania State University in 1952, and has worked in the aerospace industry since graduation. During most of his professional career he has been involved in the development of jet and liquid rocket engines. He is currently the Project Engineer of the Lance program at the Rocketdyne Division of Rockwell International.

Greenawald is an erstwhile member of the NATIONAL

Gabriel Green.

Walter Greenawald.

INVESTIGATIONS COMMITTEE ON AERIAL PHENOMENA (NICAP), the AERIAL PHENOMENA RESEARCH ORGANIZATION (APRO), the MUTUAL UFO NETWORK (MUFON) and the CENTER FOR UFO STUDIES (CUFOS). He participated in the formation of the Pacific Research Organization—UFOs (PRO-UFO), now inactive. As an independent researcher, he has investigated and documented numerous UFO sightings in the Huntsville, Alabama, and Los Angeles areas. He has delivered several lecture series on UFOs at universities and clubs, in addition to speaking on the subject on radio and television. Greenawald has conducted surveys on newspaper reporting of UFOs, airline pilots and UFOs, and UFO researchers. His papers on the results of these surveys have been published in the MUFON UFO JOURNAL.

**GREEN BANK FORMULA,** equation devised by FRANK DRAKE in November 1961 at a National Academy of Sciences meeting in Green Bank, West Virginia, to assess the probable number of extant technical civilizations on PLANETS within our galaxy. Headed by Otto Struve, the meeting was also attended by Dana W. Atchley, Jr.; Melvin Calvin; Giuseppe Cocconi; Su-shu Huang; John C. Lilly; Philip Morrison; Bernard M. Oliver; J. P. T. Pearman and CARL SAGAN. Their calculations demonstrated a possibility of there being a minimum of forty and a maximum of fifty thousand planets in the Milky Way which support advanced civilizations capable of radio communication with Earth.

Bibliography: Shklovskii, I. S., and Carl Sagan, *Intelligent Life in the Universe* (San Francisco: Holden-Day, 1966).

**GREEN CHILDREN,** a boy and a girl with green skin, wearing clothes of unusual color and material, who reportedly wandered out of a cave in England during the twelfth century. The story is recounted by William de Newburgh in *Historia Rerum Anglicarum*. Over a period of several months, the children's skin faded to a normal color. When they had learned to speak some English, they explained that they had come from a land of twilight which was not warmed by the beams of the sun. The boy, the younger of the two, soon died. The girl died a few years later.

Another version of the same story is set in Spain in the late nineteenth century. At that time, it was considered possible that the children might have come from MARS. Supporters of the HOLLOW EARTH HYPOTHESIS believe the children may have wandered from Earth's interior through a series of subterranean passages leading to a cave on the surface.

Bibliography: Wilkins, Harold T., *Strange Mysteries of Time and Space* (New York: Citadel Press, 1959);

Bergier, Jacques, *Extraterrestrial Visitations from Prehistoric Times to the Present* (Chicago: Henry Regnery Company, 1973).

**GREEN FIREBALLS,** large, brilliant objects which appeared frequently in the skies over New Mexico during 1948 and 1949. They resembled METEORS except for their bright green color, horizontal trajectories and slow speed. Although many of the FIREBALLS exploded in brilliant flashes of green light, no fragments were ever found. The large number of sightings alarmed the UNITED STATES AIR FORCE (USAF) for New Mexico was a sensitive area where numerous military bases and research installations carried out vital work in ballistics, guided missiles, atomic energy and space science. Faced with the possibility that the fireballs might represent experimental guided missiles from the Soviet Union, the Air Force consulted Dr. Lincoln La Paz, head of the University of New Mexico's Institute of Meteoritics and a world-renowned authority on astronomy. La Paz announced that the green fireballs differed from meteors in their trajectory, speed, size, brilliance, color and apparent lack of fragments. He concluded that they were not natural phenomena.

In February 1949, the Air Force organized a conference at Los Alamos to discuss the problem. It was attended by military officers, intelligence officers, physicists and astronomers. After two days of studying the evidence, the majority of the conferees concluded that the green fireballs were unusual meteors and therefore not a threat to national security. As a precaution, the matter was turned over to the Air Force's Cambridge Research Laboratory for further study. The Research Laboratory instituted PROJECT TWINKLE in an attempt to determine the precise identity of the objects but the effort failed. Sightings ceased as soon as the project's observation posts became operational. Project Twinkle was terminated.

Green fireballs were sighted sporadically in various parts of the United States during the following five years. Author DONALD KEYHOE claims that the mysterious wreckage of a Transocean DC–6 in 1953 may have been attributable to green fireballs which had been reported in the area at the time. Astronomer DONALD MENZEL was one of several thousand witnesses who observed an enormous green fireball which passed slowly over New Mexico and Colorado on September 18, 1954. The object interfered with radio and television transmission as it passed over Albuquerque, and it lit up the entire night sky over Denver. La Paz was interviewed by the news media and pronounced the phenomenon to be no ordinary meteor but something unusual. The public began once more to speculate that New Mexico was being revisited by extraterrestrial spaceships. Having witnessed the object himself, Menzel concluded that it was nothing more than an unusual meteor.

Bibliography: Menzel, Donald H., and Lyle G. Boyd, *The World of Flying Saucers* (Garden City, N.Y.: Doubleday and Company, 1963); Keyhoe, Donald E., *Aliens from Space* (Garden City, N.Y.: Doubleday and Company, 1973).

**GREENHAW, JEFF,** *see* **FALKVILLE, ALABAMA**

**GREENVILLE UFO STUDY GROUP,** 506 Central Avenue, Mauldin, South Carolina 29662; telephone number: 803-963-8300.

This local investigative group, formerly known as the AERIAL PHENOMENA INVESTIGATION ORGANIZATION (APIO), is an affiliate of the MUTUAL UFO NETWORK (MUFON). Its purpose is to collect, investigate and evaluate UFO reports and to serve as a sounding board for UFO witnesses. While the majority of its members support the EXTRATERRESTRIAL HYPOTHESIS (ETH), many remain undecided on the identity and origin of UFOs. The group has concluded that most people accurately report what they see. It cites as an example the release of a barium CLOUD which resulted in reports that were consistent with the facts.

This nonprofit organization was founded by Margaret Pine in 1973. Pine, who serves as President, is also a State Section Director for MUFON and State Director for the INTERNATIONAL UFO BUREAU (IUFOB). Ron Voyles is Vice-President. Approximately eight field investigators, located in Greenville County, cover cases referred to them by the police, radio stations and newspapers. About forty of MUFON's consultants also serve the Greenville UFO Study Group.

Membership fluctuates and currently stands at about thirty. Members receive a nonscheduled newsletter, may attend monthly meetings and gain free admission to lectures sponsored by the organization.

**GREGORY, DICK,** comedian, author and political activist who purportedly observed three UFOs on October 12, 1967, at Big Sur just south of San Francisco. Gregory was at a party with friends when the three lights appeared in the clear night sky. One was fiery red, while the other two were bright green. The objects were larger than stars and darted about the sky sideways, backward, in circles, in jagged lines and in formation as though they were performing an aerial display. The objects were extremely bright and very high, making it difficult to distinguish their shape. When Gregory's writer, Jim Saunders, signaled with a flashlight, the objects seemed to respond by moving in the same direction as the beam. The partygoers watched the lights for about forty minutes. Gregory took two Polaroid PHOTOGRAPHS, which show a red object at the top of each picture and two green ones at the bottom.

**GREGORY, GEORGE T.,** UNITED STATES AIR FORCE (USAF) captain who headed PROJECT BLUE BOOK from April 1956 to October 1958.

**GRENADA,** small island nation in the Caribbean which, in 1978, under its then-Prime Minister, SIR ERIC GAIRY, was responsible for submitting a draft resolution to the UNITED NATIONS which would have the Secretary General appoint a group of experts, under the aegis of the Committee on the Peaceful Uses of Outer Space, to define guidelines for a United Nations study of "the nature and origin of unidentified flying objects and related phenomena." Grenada's political activities in the UFO field ended when Gairy was ousted from his position as Prime Minister in a *coup d'etat*.

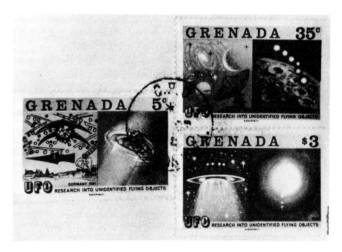

Commemorative stamps issued by Grenada in 1977 and 1978. *(Courtesy ICUFON)*

**GREPO** *see* **GROUPEMENT DE RECHERCHE ET D'ÉTUDE DU PHÉNOMÈNE OVNI**

**GREU** *see* **FRONT UFOLOGIE NOUVELLE (FUNO)**

**GRINDSTONE CLOUDS** *see* **CLOUDS**

**GRIPHOM** *see* **GROUPEMENT DE RECHERCHES ET D'INFORMATIONS PHOCÉEN SUR LES MYSTÉRIEUX OBJETS CÉLESTES**

**GROUND OBSERVER CORPS (GOC),** an organization of civilians who watched the skies for enemy planes that might have broken through the U.S. RADAR network. The GOC was created in January 1950, and inactivated on January 31, 1959, when the improvement of electronic detection equipment reduced the need to supplement the air detection network of the Air Defense Command (ADC).

ADC made the GOC available to PROJECT BLUE BOOK and told its members to report any UFOs to ADC, which would then forward the reports to the AIR TECHNICAL INTELLIGENCE CENTER (ATIC). During the period of its operation, the GOC logged hundreds of sightings of unexplainable aerial phenomena.

Bibliography: Hall, Richard H. (ed.), *The UFO Evidence* (Washington, D.C.: National Investigations Committee on Aerial Phenomena, 1964).

**GROUND SAUCER WATCH (GSW),** 13238 N. 7th Drive, Phoenix, Arizona 85029; telephone number: 602-942-7216.

This national investigative organization has concluded that UFOs are physical craft of extraterrestrial origin involved in the surveillance of this planet and its military activities. GSW's work is directed toward discovery of the exact purpose and sources of the phenomenon through the investigation of UFO sightings, the technical analysis of evidence, the procurement of government documentation of UFOs through the Freedom of Information Act, and the disclosure of HOAXES. Full efforts are concentrated on encounters involving ground markings, radiation, RADAR-visual observations, ELECTROMAGNETIC EFFECTS and OCCUPANT reports. Computers are employed to detect patterns regarding colors, speed, shapes, geographical concentration and other aspects of the phenomenon. Laboratories are utilized for experimental research on UFO-related anomalies, such as electromagnetic effects. Among other resources available to GSW are a nondestructive testing laboratory for hardware evaluation, and chemical and metallurgical testing facilities for soil and foliage evaluation.

GSW's most publicized contribution to UFOLOGY is its application of the NATIONAL AERONAUTICS AND SPACE ADMINISTRATION's computer enhancement techniques in the analysis of PHOTOGRAPHS. Computerized enhancement of UFO photographs on a video screen can establish fine detail, size, cross-sectional shape, density, distance, surface reflectivity and, in some cases, the speed at which an object was moving. Using this process, retouched emulsion, supporting wires and threads, manufacturers' logos on lens caps, rare CLOUDS and other natural and man-made objects have been identified. By 1979 GSW had analyzed a backlog of almost seven hundred photographs and movies, of which thirty-eight proved to depict bona fide UFOs. These include photographs and movies taken at GREAT FALLS, MONTANA; MCMINNVILLE, OREGON; ROUEN, FRANCE; TREMONTON, UTAH and TRINIDADE ISLAND, BRAZIL.

This nonprofit organization was founded in 1957 by Ted Starrett. WILLIAM H. SPAULDING is the Western Division Director. James A. Spaulding, based in Cleveland, Ohio, is Eastern Division Director. Directors of the Board are Robert Howard and Daniel Johnson. Approximately five hundred members in thirty states actively participate as consultants, researchers and investigators. Many are related to the aerospace industry or are associated with universities. Trained and certified field investigators, with complete field operational equipment, are ready to investigate any valid UFO report within several hours' notice.

The *GSW Bulletin,* published three to four times a year, provides updated information on the organization's activities. Research and investigation are conducted in cooperation with the CENTER FOR UFO STUDIES (CUFOS), the MUTUAL UFO NETWORK (MUFON) and CITIZENS AGAINST UFO SECRECY (CAUS), headed by GSW's Director of Research, Todd Zechel. GSW has representatives in Mexico, Australia and the United Kingdom.

**GROUPE D'ÉTUDES DES OBJETS SPATIAUX (GEOS),** St. Denis-les-Rebais, 77510 Rebais, France; telephone number: 4045505.

This nonprofit investigative organization was founded in 1969 and has a membership of 1,500. Gerard Lebat is President. *Les Extraterrestres,* a magazine with numerous PHOTOGRAPHS, is published quarterly. Other services available to members include a library, photographic slides and conferences.

**GROUPE D'ÉTUDES DES PHÉNOMÈNES AÉROSPATIAUX NON IDENTIFIÉS (GEPAN),** Centre Spatial de Toulouse, 18 Avenue Edouard Belin, 31055 Toulouse, France.

This scientific research group was founded in 1977 by engineer Claude Poher under the auspices of the CENTRE NATIONAL D'ÉTUDES SPATIALES (CNES). The latter, which also funds GEPAN, is an agency similar to the NATIONAL AERONAUTICS AND SPACE ADMINISTRATION (NASA) in the United States. Poher headed GEPAN until 1978, when he went on a two-year sabbatical. Scientist Alain Esterle took over as Chief of the organization, which consists of about ten scientists.

In an analysis of eleven cases studied in 1978, the group concluded that in nine of the cases a physical phenomenon was involved whose description compared to a flying machine whose origin and propulsion and/or sustenance systems are beyond human knowledge.

## GROUPE D'ÉTUDES DU PHÉNOMÈNE OVNI (GEPO), Ecole Publique, rue des Ecoles, 42470 Saint Symphorien de Lay, France.

The purpose of this investigative organization is to collect and disseminate information.

This nonprofit group was founded under its former name, GEPI, in 1976 by Dominique Delille, who runs GEPO with Thierry Rocher. There are fourteen members. The group has investigators in Ardèche, Aude, Finistère, Loire, Essone, Paris, Var, Meurthe and Moselle. A South American investigator is located in Guatemala. GEPO serves as official investigator for LUMIÈRES DANS LA NUIT (LDLN), official correspondent for the COMMISSION LUXEMBOURGEOISE D'ÉTUDES UFOLOGIQUES (CLEU) in Luxembourg, regional delegate of the CENTRE D'ÉTUDES ET DE RECHERCHE DES PHÉNOMÈNES INEXPLIQUÉS (CERPI) in Belgium, and correspondent for the GROUPE PRIVÉ UFOLOGIQUE NANCÉIEN (GPUN) and the Centre National de Recherches sur l'Etrange (CNRE). GEPO conducts field investigations, carries out statistical and cartographic studies, maintains archives and produces regional and worldwide catalogues. *GEPO Informations,* formerly *Siècle Inconnu,* is published quarterly.

## GROUPE D'ÉTUDES NORMAND DES PHÉNOMÈNES INCONNUS (GENPI), 18 rue Vauquelin, 14300 Caen, France; telephone number: 854173.

This regional investigative organization is dedicated to the study of UFO sightings and to research regarding experiences of mental or psychic induction of the UFO phenomenon. According to the group, its investigations confirm that UFO manifestations have been brought about by witnesses' spontaneous efforts to make UFOs appear by using mental concentration. GENPI hopes that by improving and exploiting the mental induction process it can provoke the appearance of a UFO at a preselected time and place in order to attempt direct contact with the phenomenon. The organization does not believe that UFOs represent physical machines but rather that they probably emanate from a plasmatic type of energy medium.

This nonprofit organization was founded in 1971 by Guillaume Chevallier, who serves as President. Christian Valeix is General Secretary, and Rodolphe Chevallier is Treasurer. There are nineteen members. About ten investigators are available to conduct field investigations throughout the French department of Calvados. The group also conducts skywatches, research of newspaper archives and psychic experiments. Reports are published in national UFO magazines in France and overseas. Members have access to all records and documentation of the group's work.

## GROUPE 5255, 20 rue de la Maladière, 52000 Chaumont, France.

The purpose of this investigative organization is to collect and disseminate all local information about the UFO phenomenon. The group remains uncommitted regarding the identity and origin of UFOs.

This nonprofit organization was founded in 1977 by Roger Thome, who serves as President; Christine Zwygart, who serves as Secretary; Lionel Danizel, who serves as Treasurer; and Patrick Koenig, who serves as Assistant Secretary. René Thome is Assistant Treasurer. The group has about thirty members. About ten field investigators cover the areas of Haute-Marne and Meuse in the northeast of France. The group conducts skywatches and organizes conferences. A newsletter is published semiannually.

Groupe 5255 is a regional delegate of LUMIÈRES DANS LA NUIT (LDLN).

## GROUPEMENT DE RECHERCHE ET D'ÉTUDE DU PHÉNOMÈNE OVNI (GREPO), Maison de Jeunes et d'Education Permanente, avenue Pablo Picasso, 84700 Sorgues, France; telephone number: 90-312617.

This investigative organization is dedicated to the study of the UFO phenomenon and related phenomena. The group holds that UFOs are physical objects of artificial construction which demonstrate intelligent behavior. A certain percentage, however, are socio-psychological, according to GREPO. While the majority of members lean toward the EXTRATERRESTRIAL HYPOTHESIS (ETH), and others consider the possibilities that UFOs are time travelers or visitors from a PARALLEL UNIVERSE, the organization itself adheres to no specific hypothesis.

This nonprofit organization was founded in 1975 by Pierre Monnet. Camille Ferrier is the Honorary President. Staff members include President René Faudrin, Vice-President Jean-Pierre Troadec and General Secretary Lilyane Troadec. The group has fifty members, all of whom serve as investigators. Members have access to a library and participate in conferences and skywatches. *Vaucluse UFOlogie* is published quarterly.

GREPO is a member of the COMITÉ EUROPÉEN DE COORDINATION DE LA RECHERCHE UFOLOGIQUE (CECRU).

## GROUPEMENT DE RECHERCHES ET D'ÉTUDES UFOLOGIQUES (GREU) *see* FRONT UFOLOGIE NOUVELLE (FUNO)

## GROUPEMENT DE RECHERCHES ET D'INFORMATIONS PHOCÉEN SUR LES MYSTÉRIEUX OBJETS CÉLESTES (GRIPHOM), Boîte Postale 74, 13368 Marseille Cédex 4, France.

Investigative organization belonging to the COMITÉ EUROPÉEN DE COORDINATION DE LA RECHERCHE UFOLOGIQUE (CECRU).

## GROUPEMENT D'ÉTUDE DE PHÉNOMÈNES AÉRIENS (GEPA), 69 rue de la Tombe-Issoire, 75014 Paris, France; telephone number: 3275624.

The principal objective of this investigative organization is to try to establish in a cautious, precise manner the real, technically anomalous nature of the UFO phenomenon. In this way, the group hopes to awaken the interest of the international scientific establishment and thus to obtain governmental authority to upgrade investigative standards and to organize a UFO detection system on a worldwide scale. The latter would be accomplished by alerting professional observers and by utilizing the most powerful equipment available today. GEPA holds that if all RADAR operators around the world had adequate information and proper instructions, there would be an instant and valuable improvement in the level of research. The group warns that preconceived opinions and beliefs regarding the identity of UFOs mislead and hinder research, particularly since the nature of the phenomenon may be beyond our conceptual ability and beyond our view of the world, which is that of one species and one epoch. While GEPA does not dogmatically support the EXTRATERRESTRIAL HYPOTHESIS (ETH), at the same time it believes that such a theory should not be ignored. The organization is primarily interested in good, detailed sighting reports and believes that each one should be studied independently and carefully, rather than statistically. GEPA also believes that lay persons should be involved in the study of the phenomenon, not only because a nontechnician may sometimes have a valuable idea which may not occur to the qualified investigator or researcher, but also because the phenomenon, which seems endowed with some kind of intelligence or instinct, could have a significance affecting the life or thinking of all human beings.

This nonprofit organization was founded in 1962 at the instigation of Engineer and Scientist René Hardy, a former consultant to the AERIAL PHENOMENA RESEARCH ORGANIZATION (APRO) and delegate for the NATIONAL INVESTIGATIONS COMMITTEE ON AERIAL PHENOMENA (NICAP). Its first official President was industrialist Claude Daquillon, who was succeeded by Louis Frager, an engineer. French Air Force General Lionel Max Chassin served as President from 1964 until his death in 1970. During his presidency, the group's administrative and editorial activities were run by René Fouéré, an engineer, serving as General Secretary, and his wife Francine Fouéré, serving as Treasurer. Following Chassin's death, GEPA's presidency was assumed in turn by polytechnician Edmond Campagnac, René Fouéré and Francine Fouéré, who is president at the present time. René Fouéré is Honorary President. Other staff members include Vice-Presidents Patrick Lebail and Paul Misraki, General Secretary Jean-François Ulysse, Assistant Secretaries Lina Cristi, Régine Robin and Michel Troublé and Secretary-Treasurer Renée Corriol. Public meetings are held about three times a year. One of GEPA's chief activities is the publication of *Phénomènes Spatiaux*, an internationally renowned magazine which was originally called *Bulletin du GEPA*. Its name was changed in 1964. During 1978, a slowdown of activities led to a temporary reduction in the number of annual issues published. *Phénomènes Spatiaux* is now published once a year instead of quarterly. René Fouéré is Editor.

## GROUPEMENT D'ÉTUDE RÉGIONAL DES OVNI (GERO), Boîte Postale 1263, 25005 Besancon Cédex, France.

This investigative organization is dedicated to UFO research. It holds that UFOs are of extraterrestrial origin. GERO was founded by Pierre Cailletau. It is a nine-member group run by President R. Froidevaux, Vice-President M. Gautier and Treasurer F. Legrigny. Two field investigators cover the area of Franche Comte. The bimonthly review, *Limites,* is edited by Marc Marinello.

## GROUPEMENT LANGEADOIS DE RECHERCHES UFOLOGIQUES (GLRU), c/o Gilbert Peyret, Résidence le Poitou, Bât. F., Vals près le Puy, 43000 Le Puy, France.

The purpose of this investigative organization is to research and study local UFO sightings, to keep the public informed and to establish a citizen-band network in the Puy-de-Dôme and in the Haute-Loire areas. The group has no collective opinion regarding the nature and origin of the UFO phenomenon, each member having his or her own ideas about the phenomenon.

This nonprofit organization was founded in 1977 by Gilbert Peyret, who serves as President. Other staff members include Vice-President Pierre Peyrot, Secretary Jean Achard and Treasurer François Mouilhade. There are forty members. Ten field investigators cover the departments of Haute-Loire and Puy-de-Dôme. Members may attend conferences and expositions free of charge. The group's journal, *OVNI 43*, has a distribution of about 500 and contains articles on UFOs, astronomy, the conquest of space, science fiction, citizen-band information, humor and games.

GLRU is a member of the COMITÉ EUROPÉEN DE COORDINATION DE LA RECHERCHE UFOLOGIQUE (CECRU).

## GROUPEMENT NORDISTE D'ÉTUDES DES OVNI (GNEOVNI), Route de Béthune, 62136, Lestrem, France; telephone number: 21-261773.

The goal of this investigative organization is to understand the UFO phenomenon. The group has no collective beliefs about the identity and origin of UFOs.

This nonprofit organization was founded in 1965 by Messrs. Villette, Francesini and D'Hondt. Jean Pierre D'Hondt serves as General Secretary. There are fifty members. Five field investigators cover UFO sightings in the north of France. The group maintains archives and a library. The results of its regional investigations are published in GNEOVNI's quarterly newsletter, *Recherches UFOlogiques*.

GNEOVNI represents the CERCLE FRANÇAIS DE RECHERCHES UFOLOGIQUES (CFRU) in the Pas-de-Calais department and is a member of the COMITÉ EUROPÉEN DE COORDINATION DE LA RECHERCHE UFOLOGIQUE (CECRU).

## GROUPEMENT POUR L'ÉTUDE DES SCIENCES D'AVANT-GARDE (GESAG), Leopold I laan 141, B–800 Bruges, Belgium; telephone number: 050-310344.

One of the main purposes of this investigative organization is to inform national and international organizations and scientists about UFO incidents in Belgium. As part of this activity, GESAG is involved in the codification of Belgian cases for UFOCAT. Many of these cases have shown a high degree of credibility and strangeness. The organization has concluded that although there is no definite explanation for the phenomenon, intelligent characteristics are evident.

GESAG was founded as a nonprofit organization in 1965 by JACQUES BONABOT, Jean-Gerard Dohmen and Roger Lorthioir. Bonabot is Director and Editor of the quarterly newsletter, *Bulletin du GESAG—UFO INFO*. The organization has approximately 220 members. The Belgian territory is covered by about thirty investigators who are divided into a French network (GESAG) and a Dutch network (SPW). Cedric Heyndrickx heads the Dutch investigative network. Rudy de Groote is Director and Editor of the Dutch publication, *UFO INFO—SPW*.

Belgian associates include researcher and author Christine Piems; consultant in psychology Jos Hermans; and consultant in astronomy Claude Martin. Foreign associates include Jean-Marie Bigrone of the French

organization LUMIÈRES DANS LA NUIT, Jean Bastide, French author and researcher; Ignacio Darnaude, Spanish correspondent; Alain Gamard, specialist in humanoids cases; John Musgrave, Canadian researcher; Jean-Claude Proust, UFO researcher; and Peter Rogerson, British specialist in close encounter cases.

## GROUPEMENT UFOLOGIQUE BULLOIS (GUB), La Casa, 1635 La Tour-de-Treme, Switzerland; telephone number: 029-25083.

The purpose of this investigative organization is to research UFOs and inform the inhabitants of the Canton of Fribourg of its findings. The group believes that UFOs are unknown natural phenomena and extraterrestrial spaceships engaged in the exploration of Earth.

This nonprofit organization was founded in 1977 by Jean-Claude Bussard, Pierre-Alain Dupasquier, Claude Schafer, Christian Morand and Michel Ruffieux, who run GUB, together with Philippe Ruffieux and Jean-Luc Bertschy. The group has twelve active members and 150 regular members. Information is collected from newspapers and sightings are covered by field investigators. GUB has representatives in Ireland and Spain, and maintains contact with many French and English organizations. Benefits available to members include a book-lending service and free admission to GUB's conferences. The GUB BULLETIN, published three times a year, includes articles on Swiss cases, sightings in the Canton of Fribourg, UFO sightings during the past centuries in Switzerland, investigations and research results.

## GROUPE PALMOS, 1 rue Parlier, 34000 Montpellier, France; telephone number: 67-660088 or 67-660061.

This nonprofit, investigative organization is dedicated to the research and study of the UFO phenomenon. It was founded in 1977 by Jean-Pierre Charton and Bernard Dupi, who serves as President. Other staff members include L. Noiret, J. P. Roger, M. Solbes and G. Noiret. The group has fifty members. Field investigations are carried out in the Herault Department. *OVNI-INFO 34* is published bimonthly.

Groupe Palmos is a member of the COMITÉ EUROPÉEN DE COORDINATION DE LA RECHERCHE UFOLOGIQUE (CECRU).

## GROUPE PHOBOS, 64 Bd. St. Michel, 91150 Etampes, France; telephone number: 4948094.

This organization was founded in 1973 by Frederique Sagnes who runs it. There are seven members. The group is involved in investigation, research and experimentation in the fields of UFOLOGY and parapsychology.

## GROUPE PRIVÉ UFOLOGIQUE NANCÉIEN (GPUN), 15 rue Guilbert de Pixérécourt, 54000 Nancy, France.

This investigative organization holds that UFOs are spaceships from another PLANET or unidentified energy from another dimension. Its goal is to establish scientific proof of the existence of UFOs.

GPUN was founded in 1975 by Martial Robé who serves as President. Raoul Robé serves as Secretary. The group has thirty members. One hundred field investigators are distributed throughout the Lorraine area. It conducts skywatches and publishes a quarterly magazine, *Réalité ou Fiction*.

GPUN is a member of the COMITÉ EUROPÉEN DE COORDINATION DE LA RECHERCHE UFOLOGIQUE (CECRU).

## GROUPE TROYEN DE RECHERCHE SUR LES OVNI (GTR/OVNI), 2 rue Louis Ulbach, 10000 Troyes, France.

The purpose of this local investigative organization is to study and research the UFO phenomenon. The group adheres to no specific theory regarding the identity of UFOs, preferring to approach its research without preconceived ideas.

This nonprofit organization was officially founded in 1978 by the GROUPE D'ÉTUDES DES OBJETS SPATIAUX (GEOS) and Guy Capet, who serves as General Secretary. Other staff members include President Jean-Michel Pissier, Vice-President Paul Charpentier, Assistant Secretary Patrick Koenig, Treasurer Jean-Luc Medard and Scientific Consultant Bernard Duranton. The organization has eighty supporters, of whom about twenty are active members. Investigations are carried out in association with local organizations and investigators throughout the department of the Aube and part of the Champagne region. The bulletin *Entre Nous* is published bimonthly.

GTR/OVNI is a member of the COMITÉ EUROPÉEN DE COORDINATION DE LA RECHERCHE UFOLOGIQUE (CECRU).

## GRUPO A. A. OVNI, % Martin F. Villaran, 5-bajo C, Portugalete (Vizcaya), Spain.

The purpose of this organization is to investigate and study UFO sightings, primarily from the psycho-sociological and anthropological point of view. The group holds that while many UFO reports are the result of misinterpretations of known phenomena, or are due to mystification, there nevertheless exist unexplainable cases. However, the group systematically refuses to adopt any position on the origin of UFOs and deplores the use and abuse of the EXTRATERRESTRIAL HYPOTHESIS (ETH). Its objective is not to attempt to identify UFOs but to discover the mythical and social roots of belief in UFOs.

This nonprofit organization was founded in 1968 by José M. Cano, Natxo Pereira and Jésus Maria Sanchez, who serves as Director-Coordinator. The group's investigations commission is made up of six people. There are about 100 active members. About fifty field investigators are located primarily in the Pais Vasco area. The organization covers almost the entire Iberian Peninsula and the Canary Islands. Contact is maintained with about fifty organizations and publications overseas, primarily in Europe and America. *Noticias OVNI* is published quarterly.

## GRUPO AGARTHA DE PESQUISAS (GAP), Caixa Postal No. 8414, Curitiba Paraná, C.E.P. 80.000, Brazil; telephone number: 321060 and 237042.

This CONTACTEE organization holds that UFOs originate from the center of Earth, from other galaxies and from other dimensions.

GAP was founded in 1977 by Thomé Sabbag and Mercilio Cesar Casagrande. It has twenty-eight members. The group conducts field investigations and publishes a monthly bulletin.

## GRUPO DE ESTUDOS E PESQUISAS ULTRA-TERRENOS "MARCUS DE ORION" (GEPU), Caixa Postal No. 83, 83.100 Sao José do Rio Preto, S.P., Brazil; telephone number: 214852.

This CONTACTEE organization believes UFOs are spaceships from other PLANETS in our solar system whose OCCUPANTS are engaged in teaching Christian ethics to earthlings.

GEPU was founded by attorney Décio Estrella, who edits its journal, *Saturno*.

## GRUPO DE PESQUISAS AEROESPACIAIS ZENITH (G-PAZ), Caixa Postal No. 4108, Agencia Alameda, 40.000 Salvador, Bahia, Brazil; telephone number: 247-6599.

This investigative organization holds that the reality of the UFO phenomenon has been proven by the evidence of physical and physiological effects. It notes that Latin American countries, particularly Brazil and Argentina, seem to experience a higher concentration of sightings and landings than other parts of the world.

G-PAZ was founded in 1972 by Alberto Romero, who serves as President. Other staff members include Vice-President Helbio C. Palmeira, Secretary Irene San Martin and Director of Operations Emanoel Paranhos Correa. There are twenty members. The group has ten field investigators and a number of correspondents located throughout the state of Bahia. Information is exchanged with several foreign organizations. The group collects information, conducts comparative analyses of such data, maintains a bibliography, offers courses and organizes lectures. The BOLETIM INFORMATIVO G-PAZ is published annually.

## GRUPO PELOTENSE DE ESTUDOS E PESQUISAS DE PARAPSICOLOGIA, PSICOTRONICA E OBJECTOS AEREOS NAO IDENTIFICADOS (PPOANI),
Rua Benjamin Constant 1548, Caixa Postal 289, Pelotas—RS. 96.100, Brazil; telephone number: 251670.

The purpose of this CONTACTEE organization is to inform the people of Earth of the truth about UFOs and extraterrestrial beings, and to maintain friendly contact with extraterrestrial civilizations. The group holds that UFO OCCUPANTS are highly-spiritual beings sent by God on peace missions from other PLANETS and other solar systems. Some UFOs, according to PPOANI, come from VENUS, MARS, Jupiter and Saturn.

This organization was founded in 1978 by Luiz Mar Soria, who serves as President; Jacira Bidigaray Soria, who serves as Vice-President; and Anita C. Bidigaray, who serves as Director. Other staff members include Joao Antonio de Souza Loureiro, Elson Bidigaray, Yara Maria and Eraldo Mendes Fonseca. The group has approximately fifty members and collaborators. PPOANI publishes a monthly journal called *Delta*.

Portuguese investigator: Joao Antonio de Souza Loureiro, Estrada da Circunvalacao T.C.D., 1800 Lisboa, Portugal.

## GSW *see* GROUND SAUCER WATCH

## GTR/OVNI *see* GROUPE TROYEN DE RECHERCHE SUR LES OVNI

## GUARDIA, FERNANDO JORGE CERDA (b.
June 28, 1956, Barcelona, Spain; address: % Santurce 1, 1°-A, Madrid [17], Spain), UFO investigator.

Guardia has seen UFOs on several occasions. His primary areas of interest in UFO research are the MEN IN BLACK (MIB), apparitions of the Virgin Mary and the NAZI HYPOTHESIS. He thinks that the EXTRATERRESTRIAL HYPOTHESIS (ETH) is the least likely explanation for the phenomenon.

Guardia founded the UNION NACIONAL DE ESTUDIOS E INVESTIGACIONES CIENTIFICO COSMOLOGICAS (UNEICC) in 1971. He is a correspondent for more than twenty-five foreign UFO organizations and translates articles into Spanish from their publications.

## GUB *see* GROUPMENT UFOLOGIQUE BULLOIS

## GUB BULLETIN,
publication of the GROUPEMENT UFOLOGIQUE BULLOIS (GUB).

## GUERNSEY UFO RESEARCH GROUP,
organization whose aims are to provide an information source for those interested in the subject, to investigate local reports and to further UFO research wherever possible in collaboration with the BRITISH UFO RESEARCH ASSOCIATION (BUFORA) and other groups. The group holds that evidence of both physical and non-physical aspects of UFO reports suggest the possible existence of a parallel reality or of travel from extraterrestrial sources by non-physical means.

This nonprofit organization, formerly known as the Guernsey UFO Club, was founded in 1973 by G. Torode. Staff members include Secretary R. Huddle, Treasurer Jean Dutton, Librarian D. Brehaut and Geoffrey Falla, who is in charge of historical research. The group has ten members. It maintains a library and publishes the quarterly *Guernsey UFO Research Group News Circular*.

**HAISELL, DAVID A.** (b. October 24, 1939, London, England; address: P.O. Box 455, Streetsville, Mississauga, Ontario, Canada L5M 2B9; telephone number: 416-826-6073), Cofounder and Codirector of U.P. INVESTIGATIONS RESEARCH.

Haisell believes that the UFO mystery probably incorporates a number of different unknown phenomena. The major focus of his investigations has been a case involving a man, pseudonymously referred to as Gerry Armstrong, who has had several UFO encounters and psychic experiences. During Armstrong's childhood, there had been a seven-hour period for which he could not account and which he later believed to be connected with his subsequent UFO encounters. In 1978, Haisell arranged for Armstrong to undergo regressive HYPNOSIS. After two sessions, Haisell was able to piece together an account of Armstrong's ABDUCTION by UFO OCCUPANTS during the missing seven hours. Many of the details match those of other classic abduction cases such as the NEW HAMPSHIRE and ALAMOGORDO, NEW MEXICO, incidents.

Haisell received his B.Sc. from the University of Toronto in 1962. He was subsequently engaged in cancer research and then agricultural research at the University of Guelph, Ontario. He became a Professional Agrologist in 1965. Since 1969, he has been Professor of Computer Studies at the Humber College of Applied Arts and Technology in Rexdale, Ontario.

Haisell is a member of the Agricultural Institute of Canada, the Ontario Institute of Professional Agrologists and the Association for Systems Management. He is a field investigator for the MUTUAL UFO NETWORK (MUFON) and a Foreign Correspondent for *The UFO Examiner,* published by PRIVATE UFO INVESTIGATIONS (PUFOI). He founded U.P. Investigation Research with

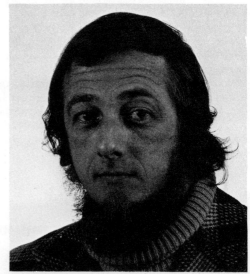

David Haisell.

his wife, Paula Haisell, in 1977, and is Editor of its publication, *Journal UFO (JUFO)*.

Haisell is author of *The Missing Seven Hours* (Markham, Ontario: PaperJacks, 1978).

**HALDANE, JOHN BURDON SANDERSON** (1892–1964), noted British geneticist and biometrician who conjectured that perhaps human beings unknowingly possess capabilities which do not manifest themselves in our own environment but which might be of interest or service to an extraterrestrial culture. He compared this hypothetical situation to that of the trained seal which balances a ball on its nose for the entertainment of human beings. The activity is one which has no meaning for the seal and serves it no purpose. Haldane considered the possibility that human beings might be the victims of kidnapping by extraterrestrials because of some such capability.

## HALL, RICHARD H. (address: 4418 39th Street, Brentwood, Maryland 20722), editor and writer.

Hall thinks that UFOs probably represent extraterrestrial manifestations. He holds that UFO cases that contain measurable detail and that defy explanation after careful investigation constitute a scientific problem badly in need of high-level study. They number in the thousands, he asserts, but unfortunately, the best qualified scientists not only lack the funds and motivation to become involved, but also face a barrier of "scientific ridicule" from their often unscientific colleagues. Crackpotism and amateurism, says Hall, no matter how well-intentioned, also cloud the issues. Thorough investigation and objective evaluation of physical evidence, RADAR and film cases should, according to Hall, be undertaken by competent scientists on an international scale.

Hall received his B.A. in Philosophy from Tulane University in 1958. Since that time, he has been employed by various associations and firms in the Washington, D.C., area. From 1958 to 1967, he was Assistant Director and Acting Director of the NATIONAL INVESTIGATIONS COMMITTEE ON AERIAL PHENOMENA (NICAP). He was a consultant to the CONDON COMMITTEE from 1966 to 1967.

Hall has been a Board Member of the MUTUAL UFO NETWORK (MUFON) since 1976, and is a member of the CENTER FOR UFO STUDIES (CUFOS).

Hall was Editor of *The UFO Evidence* (Washington, D.C.: National Investigations Committee on Aerial Phenomena, 1964), and has been Editor of the MUFON UFO JOURNAL since 1976.

Richard Hall.

**HALLUCINATION,** the perception of objects that are not actually present or the experiencing of sensations despite the absence of the usual cause. Hallucinations occur in certain mental disorders such as schizophrenia and can be induced by physical or emotional deprivation. Although few UFO reports were considered attributable to hallucinations in the early years of the MODERN ERA, the increasing popularity of hallucinogenic drugs has increased the likelihood that a UFO sighting may in fact be an hallucination. However, since hallucination is a subjective experience, it is improbable that it could be the cause of multiple witness cases.

A number of UFOLOGISTS have hypothesized that some UFOs might be hallucinations accidentally or intentionally induced by some unknown force or some unknown intelligence. This might be achieved through the use of drugs, gases, or, possibly, electromagnetic waves directed at the brain.

## HALOS *see* PARHELIA

## HALSEY, TARNA L. (b. October 26, 1925, Tipton, Indiana; address: P.O. Box 24, Logan, Utah 84321), CONTACTEE.

Halsey claims that since her childhood she has encountered hundreds of extraterrestrial spacecraft all over the United States piloted by beautiful, spiritual beings. The outer space people, she holds, have been visiting Earth since before the time of Christ and were involved in the building of both visible and concealed PYRAMIDS all over the PLANET. Although there are both good and bad SPACE PEOPLE, according to Halsey, she has never seen the "ugly monster type creatures." Her alleged contacts have been with loving SPACE BROTHERS, who offer mankind such benefits as free energy.

Halsey received a DDLLD from the Christ Brotherhood in 1958. She was ordained a minister of the International Evangelism Crusades in 1960, and received a Bachelor of Divinity Degree from the Faith Bible College and Theological Seminary in Florida in 1966.

A former singer and ballet dancer with some television and radio experience, Halsey traveled all over the country with her husband, Wallace C. Halsey, Founder and President of the Christ Brotherhood, teaching and lecturing about the Bible, healing, space visitors, pyramids, TELEPORTATION, extrasensory perception and other NEW AGE philosophies and paranormal phenomena. Upon the death of her husband in a plane crash in 1963, Halsey took over the presidency of the Christ Brotherhood, continuing the work alone.

In 1964, Halsey received a citation from President Lyndon B. Johnson in memory of her late husband and in recognition of his service to the country in the Armed Forces of the United States.

## HAMILTON, ALEXANDER, see LE ROY, KANSAS

**HARDER, JAMES A.**, Professor of Civil Engineering and Director of Research of the AERIAL PHENOMENA RESEARCH ORGANIZATION (APRO).

**HARDIN, CHARLES A.**, UNITED STATES AIR FORCE (USAF) captain who headed PROJECT BLUE BOOK from March 1954 to April 1956.

**HARRIS, JAMES R.** (b. April 30, 1960, Mt. Carmel, Illinois; address: Route 4, Lisa Lane, Mt. Carmel, Illinois 62863; telephone number: 618-262-5581), Founder and Director of Research of UFOCUS RESEARCH.

Although not committed to any one theory on the identity of UFOs, Harris suggests that although UFOs are probably capable of space flight, they are perhaps not spaceships in the normal sense of the word. They are probably extradimensional in nature, he theorizes, and do not fly, but simply float. They move, he conjectures, not by repelling gravity or by any method of propulsion, but rather by ignoring gravity, which is probably nonexistent in their reality.

Harris is a student at Wabash Valley College, majoring in Business Administration and Accountancy. In addition to his position as Director of Research for UFOCUS Research, he is Editor of its newsletter.

Harris is a member of the National UFO CONFERENCE (NUFOC), the SOCIETY FOR THE INVESTIGATION OF THE UNEXPLAINED (SITU) and the INTERNATIONAL FORTEAN ORGANIZATION (INFO).

## HARRIS, WALDO, J., see SALT LAKE CITY, UTAH

**HART, CARL R.**, UNITED STATES AIR FORCE (USAF) major who was the Pentagon UFO spokesman from February 1962 until the summer of 1963.

## HARTLEY, BRYAN, see NORTHERN UFO NETWORK (NUFON) AND UFO INVESTIGATORS NETWORK (UFOIN)

**HARTMAN, TERRY A.** (b. February 25, 1948, Waukegan, Illinois; address: P.O. Box 40213, Portland, Oregon 97240; telephone number: 503-667-4613), CONTACTEE and HYPNOSIS consultant.

Hartman has frequently observed NOCTURNAL LIGHTS (NL) displaying unusual flight behavior. He believes

that UFOs are the physical manifestations, to which we can relate, of life forms and substances that exist outside our system.

Hartman received his B.F.A. degree from the Art Center College of Design in Los Angeles. He is also a graduate of the Modern Hypnosis Instruction Center in Phoenix, Arizona.

As a hypnotechnician, Hartman specializes in regressing amnesia victims of UFO ABDUCTIONS and contacts. He allegedly develops trace channel communications with extraterrestrial beings and searches past life influences for present Karmic ties. He is conducting an evaluation of case histories of ordinary men and women whose lives have purportedly been dramatically changed for the better by space contacts. He also practices more traditional hypnotherapy for calming nerves, increasing self-confidence, heightening creativity and improving recall of amnesic victims in police investigations. He lectures on hypnosis, parapsychology, UFOs and reincarnation.

Hartman is the Oregon State Director and Research Specialist in Hypnosis for the MUTUAL UFO NETWORK (MUFON); hypnosis investigator for the CENTER FOR UFO STUDIES (CUFOS); Hypnosis Consultant to GROUND SAUCER WATCH (GSW); an Associate Member of the Smithsonian Institution and the Association to Advance Ethical Hypnosis (AAEH); an Ordained minister of the Church of Essential Science; a listed member of the International Psychic Register; and a member of the Editorial Board of UFO PHENOMENA, INTERNATIONAL REVIEW (UPIAR).

**HARTRANFT, JOSEPH B.**, member of the Board of Governors of the NATIONAL INVESTIGATIONS COMMITTEE ON AERIAL PHENOMENA (NICAP). Hartranft is President of the Aircraft Owners and Pilots Association, and was the founder of the National Intercollegiate Flying Club. He is also involved in other aviation groups, including the Bates Foundation for Aeronautical Education, and was instrumental in founding of the Civil Air Patrol. Through the years, he has had frequent reports from civilian pilots "in which various experiences have been related concerning objects in the sky which they have often described in detail. These reports have come from many parts of the country—and some foreign—from people unknown one to the other and yet some of the descriptions have remarkable similarity." However, Hartranft remains open-minded about the identity of UFOs.

**HAUCK, DENNIS WILLIAM** (b. April 8, 1945, Hammond, Indiana), mathematician and Indiana State Director of the MUTUAL UFO NETWORK (MUFON).

Hauck believes that UFOs originate from a complex

interplay of human mental energy and an everpresent cosmic force. His interest in the subject was sparked in Austria when he and two skiing companions saw a gray, spinning UFO hovering over a large rock as they came over a rise. As they approached, it disappeared. He later interpreted the image as an optical effect created by the dark stone giving off heat reflections in the cold atmosphere.

Hauck received a B.S. in Mathematics from Indiana University in 1968 and a Ph.D. in Mathematics from the University of Vienna in Austria in 1972.

Hauck joined the INTERNATIONAL UFO REGISTRY (IUFOR) in 1972, and became its North American Director in 1973. In 1974, he became a member of the AERIAL PHENOMENA RESEARCH ORGANIZATION (APRO), the NATIONAL INVESTIGATIONS COMMITTEE ON AERIAL PHENOMENA (NICAP) and the MUTUAL UFO NETWORK (MUFON), and became a Mathematics Consultant to GROUND SAUCER WATCH (GSW). In 1975, he became Indiana State Director of MUFON, and Editor of UFOLOGY magazine. From 1976 to 1977, he was Editor of OFFICIAL UFO and the MUFON UFO JOURNAL. He is currently a member of the CENTER OF UFO STUDIES (CUFOS) and a number of foreign organizations. He is an honorary member of the ANCIENT ASTRONAUTS SOCIETY and a member of the American Parapsychological Association.

Hauck has written numerous magazine articles and is author of *Some Technical Considerations on Biofeedback Research* (Los Angeles: Alpha Publishing Company, 1975); and *The UFO Manual* (Munster, Indiana: International UFO Registry, 1976).

**HAUSER, KASPAR,** German youth of unknown identity whose sudden appearance in Nuremberg on May 26, 1828, initiated one of the nineteenth century's most celebrated mysteries. The seventeen-year-old Hauser, who walked with difficulty, could speak only two sentences in the German language. As if reciting meaningless phrases, the boy would repeat, "I want to be a soldier like my father was," and, "I don't know." He held two letters. One purported to be from his mother. Dated sixteen years before, it asked the finder to send her son to Nuremberg, when he became seventeen years old, to enlist in the Sixth Cavalry Regiment, of which his father had been a member. The other letter purported to be from someone who had found the boy and cared for him but who could no longer support him. It was soon found that both letters had been written with the same ink on the same kind of paper. The youth, who was able to write only the name Kaspar Hauser, seemed to be completely unfamiliar with the commonplace objects and experiences of the everyday affairs of human beings. He showed the

surprise and amazement of a tiny child and even tried to seize the flame of a candle with his hand.

Hauser was placed in the care of Georg Friedrich Daumer, an educationist, and was later looked after by an English nobleman, the Fourth Earl of Stanhope. Hauser's portrait was posted throughout Germany in an attempt to find someone who could provide information about him. His story spread, drawing curious sightseers to the boy's home from all over Europe. Hauser quickly learned the German language but always spoke it with a foreign accent. His ability to learn was so remarkable that many writers presumed him to be an imposter who had already had a fair education.

In 1829, Hauser wrote his own story, claiming that he lived on bread and water in a dark cell until the age of sixteen or seventeen. He had known only one man who had treated him kindly, although he had struck him on one occasion for being noisy.

On October 17, 1829, Hauser was found in Daumer's cellar, bleeding from a cut in his forehead. He claimed that a masked man had stabbed him. Two policemen were assigned to guard him but, again, in May 1831, one of his guards found him with a pistol wound in his forehead. This time, Hauser claimed that he had accidentally discharged a gun. On December 14, 1833, Hauser ran from a park with a deep stab wound in his side. He claimed to have been attacked by a stranger. No footprints, other than Hauser's, were found in the fresh snow, nor was any weapon discovered. Hauser was taken to his home where he died on December 17, 1833.

The mystery of Kaspar Hauser's identity, origin and mysterious death has never been solved. Many contradictory versions of his story have been told. Plays, novels, poems and a motion picture were inspired by him. Some claim he was an imposter. Others believe him to have been the son of a nobleman. Some believe he was murdered, while others claim he committed suicide. Some UFOLOGISTS, who think Hauser may in some way have been connected with the UFO phenomenon, quote German jurist and writer von Feuerbach, a contemporary of Hauser, who stated, ". . . one might feel oneself driven to the alternative of believing him to be a citizen of another PLANET, transferred by some miracle to our own."

Bibliography: Fort, Charles, *Lo!* (New York: Claude H. Kendall, 1931).

**HEALTH RESEARCH,** P.O. Box 70, Mokelumne Hill, California 95245. This mail-order house sells books on a number of subjects, including UFOs. Out-of-print books are located for a small fee. The company also reprints its own editions of some unusual and out-of-print titles.

**HEAT.** UFOs have occasionally generated a blast of heat, presumably as a weapon. With respect to the WALESVILLE, NEW YORK, incident in 1954, it has been suggested that the tremendous heat which engulfed an F–49 Starfire was intended to prevent the interceptor from closing in on the UFO. If this was the case, the tactic was successful, for the pilots were forced to eject, leaving their unmanned aircraft to crash into the town, killing four people. At FORT ITAIPU, BRAZIL, in 1957, two sentries watched as a UFO plummeted towards them. The object stopped 150 feet overhead, emitting a steady hum. The sentries, who had been paralyzed with fear, were suddenly struck by an invisible, blistering heat which knocked one man to the ground and sent the other running for shelter. The garrison troops, awakened by the screams, could feel the heat within the fort, although to a lesser degree. After a minute, the heat ceased and the UFO took off at high speed. The two sentries were placed under medical care for severe BURNS.

Another example of heat in connection with a UFO occurred in CATANDUVA, BRAZIL, in 1973. Onilson Papero experienced relatively mild discomfort which forced him to get out of his car in a vain attempt to escape a sensation of heat and stuffiness. Papero apparently was not burned, although he later felt itchiness on areas of his skin which subsequently showed temporary discoloration similar to bruising.

**HEFLEY PSYCHIC REPORT, THE,** bimonthly magazine, established in 1976, with a circulation of approximately 200,000. It is available both at newsstands and by subscription. The range of subjects covered includes articles on psychic happenings, paranormal research and development, ghosts, UFOs, strange occurrences, personal sightings of BIGFOOT, monsters and apparitions, ESP, NEW AGE discoveries, and interviews with recognized authorities on UFOs, psychic phenomena and the occult.

Material is written by staff and freelance writers. Articles should range between 600 and 800 words, and should be accompanied by one or more clean, sharp PHOTOGRAPHS in black-and-white or color. Manuscripts or other materials not accompanied by self-addressed, stamped envelopes will not be returned. First rights only are acquired unless otherwise stated. Payment is made upon publication. Although the Report will go as high as 500 dollars for special exclusive articles on spectacular subject matters, the average payment range is between thirty-five and 100 dollars, depending on subject, effort and quality of photographs. Editor Carl D. Hefley recommends that all submissions be factual, informative, clear in purpose and subject, concise, human and enjoyable to read.

The magazine is published by U.S. Research, Incorporated, P.O. Box 7242, Burbank, California 91505.

**HEFLIN, REX,** *see* SANTA ANA, CALIFORNIA

**HEINONEN, AARNO,** *see* IMJARVI, FINLAND

**HEWES, HAYDEN COOPER** (b. December 29, 1943, Cape Girardeau, Missouri; address: P.O. Box 441, Edmond, Oklahoma 73034; telephone number: 405-348-4225), writer, lecturer, Founder and Director of the INTERNATIONAL UFO BUREAU (IUFOB).

Interested in UFOs since the age of fourteen, Hewes believes humans may have been created by entities from another space-time continuum. He theorizes that UFOs may be the craft from which these beings conduct genetic experiments and monitor our development. Together with six Oklahoma Highway Patrol troopers, Hewes saw a multicolored UFO at the Oklahoma Highway Patrol communications Tower in Edmond on August 2, 1965. A color PHOTOGRAPH of the object was analyzed by Air Force and civilian investigators. The results indicated that the UFO was a mile away and fifty feet in diameter. Hewes considered this incident as a sign that he should continue his research.

Hewes majored in aeronautical space engineering at Oklahoma University and in psychology at Oklahoma City University. He founded the International UFO Bureau in 1957, and has served as its Director since that time. He is also Director of the International Association for the Investigation of the Unexplained. He is Vice-President of the New Age Center Corporation, the Institute of PSI, and Sasquatch Investigations of Mid-America. He is a member of the Authors Guild. In 1959, he was honored by the Oklahoma City Geological Society as Junior Scientist for solar energy research.

Hewes has lectured widely and has appeared on over

Hayden Hewes.

six hundred television and radio programs. His numerous articles on UFOs have been published on a regular basis in newspapers and magazines since 1965. He is author of *The Truth about Flying Saucers* (Edmond, Oklahoma: International UFO Bureau Press, 1966); *The Aliens* (Edmond, Oklahoma: International UFO Bureau Press, 1970); *The Intruders* (Edmond, Oklahoma: International UFO Bureau Press, 1970); *Earthprobe* (Edmond, Oklahoma: International UFO Bureau Press, 1973); and coauthor, with Brad Steiger, of *UFO Missionaries Extraordinary* (New York: Pocket Books, 1976).

**HEYERDAHL, THOR,** *see* **EASTER ISLAND AND KON-TIKI**

**HICKS, DIANE MARIE** (b. September 3, 1954, Rochester, New York), Assistant Director of PROJECT TO RESEARCH OBJECTS, THEORIES, EXTRATERRESTRIALS AND UNUSUAL SIGHTINGS (PROTEUS).

Hicks is interested in exploring the religious and sociological implications of the worldwide UFO phenomenon.

After graduating from high school in 1972, Hicks attended the Barley School of Music in Fairport, New York. She has been employed in the restaurant business, and is currently involved in marketing for a large supermarket chain in New Jersey. She plans to attend Caldwell College and to major in the area of business administration.

**HICKSON, CHARLES,** *see* **PASCAGOULA, MISSISSIPPI**

**HILBERG, RICK,** *see* **NORTHERN OHIO UFO GROUP**

**HILL, BETTY AND BARNEY,** *see* **NEW HAMPSHIRE**

**HILLSDALE, MICHIGAN,** location of one of two historically-significant UFO sightings during the 1966 Michigan WAVE.

On the evening of March 20, 1966, a civil defense director, an assistant dean and eighty-seven female students at Hillsdale College watched for four hours as a glowing, football-shaped object maneuvered erratically over a swampy area a few hundred yards from the women's dormitory. At one point, the object approached the dormitory, stopped and then retreated to the marsh. Reportedly, the object also made a sweep around an airport beacon light. The witnesses related that the UFO's luminosity diminished when police arrived in their cars to investigate the incident. After the officers' departure, the light brightened again. Civil

Defense Director William Van Horn, who observed the object through binoculars, declared that it was definitely some kind of craft. It eventually disappeared over the nearby swamps.

When a UFO was sighted the following day in DEXTER, MICHIGAN, newspaper reporters picked up the story and pressured the UNITED STATES AIR FORCE (USAF) to investigate. The marshy locations of both sightings led Air Force Consultant J. ALLEN HYNEK to proffer the notorious and much-abused SWAMP-GAS explanation.

Bibliography: Flammonde, Paris, *UFO Exist!* (New York: G. P. Putnam's Sons, 1976).

**HIM** *see* **HUMAN INDIVIDUAL METAMORPHOSIS**

**HIND, CYNTHIA RHONA** (b. June 10, 1923, Cape Town, South Africa; address: P.O. Box 768, Salisbury, Rhodesia, and P.O. Box 781131, Sandton 2146, Transvaal, South Africa; telephone number: Salisbury 701515), company director, writer and Field Investigator for the MUTUAL UFO NETWORK (MUFON).

Hind is almost certain that UFOs are not of terrestrial origin but that their concept is something far beyond the range of our current knowledge of physics.

Hind matriculated from Good Hope Seminary in Cape Town and received her B.A. from Cape Town University. She served for three years with the South African Air Force during the Second World War. After her marriage, she lived in England for eleven years, returning to Africa in 1957. She joined a manufacturing firm and eventually became a director of the company. She resigned in 1978.

Hind is President of Soroptimist International of Salisbury, an Executive Member of the Salisbury Writers' Club, a member of SF Alpha of Rhodesia and a Field Investigator for MUFON.

Hind has worked as a freelance writer for over twenty-five years. She is the author of magazine articles, serials and short stories, several of which have appeared in anthologies. She has also written for radio. Her numerous articles on UFOs have been published in magazines in the United States, South Africa and Rhodesia.

**HISTORY.** UFOLOGISTS contend that UFOs in past eras were interpreted according to the belief systems and level of technology of the observers. Thus many aerial phenomena were regarded as manifestations of supernatural forces.

Earliest evidence of such phenomena are allegedly to be found in prehistoric cave drawings, such as the TASSILI FRESCOES. The earliest written record dates

An old Chinese drawing and an old Persian miniature provide evidence of an ancient belief in the existence of flying machines. *(Culver Pictures)*

A broadsheet commemorating the appearance of strange astral bodies, interpreted as omens of hard times by superstitious observers. *(The Bettmann Archive)*

back to circa 1504–1450 B.C. and describes a sighting by Egyptian Pharaoh THUTMOSE III. The ancient Greek and Roman scholars such as ARISTOTLE, LIVY and CICERO catalogued a number of sightings of flying disks, shields and other strange objects. Biblical sightings of aerial phenomena, which were interpreted by the ancient Hebrews in a religious context, are considered by some UFOlogists to be UFOs. Religious legends from other parts of the world also contain references to flying craft and allegedly extraterrestrial beings, such as the Indian VIMANAS and the Central American god, QUETZALCOATL.

There are few records of aerial phenomena between the time of Christ and the ninth century. However, a belief in aerial beings became prevalent among French peasants during the ninth-century reign of Emperor CHARLEMAGNE. During the following century, reports of aerial phenomena included sightings of fiery armies in the skies.

After the twelfth century, documentation of such events became more widespread, particularly in religious chronicles. Drawings made in the sixteenth century show unusual aerial objects observed over NUREMBERG, GERMANY, and BASEL, SWITZERLAND.

Many references to aerial phenomena sighted between the year 1600 and the nineteenth century can be found in old astronomical chronicles and the works of CHARLES FORT.

After the year 1800, UFO reports were published in numerous scientific journals. The century culminated in the sensational AIRSHIP WAVE of 1896 and 1897.

The twentieth century's first UFO wave involved the FOO FIGHTERS observed by military pilots during World War II. This was followed by a series of sightings of GHOST ROCKETS in Scandinavia from 1946 to 1948. The period known as the MODERN ERA began in 1947 when pilot Kenneth Arnold observed nine disk-shaped objects flying over MOUNT RAINIER, WASHINGTON. UFOLOGY was born as a subject to be investigated, documented and debated.

Bibliography: Drake, W. Raymond, *Gods and Spacemen throughout History* (Chicago: Henry Regnery Company, 1975); and Vallee, Jacques, *Anatomy of a Phenomenon: Unidentified Objects in Space—A Scientific Appraisal* (Chicago: Henry Regnery Company, 1965).

## HITLER, ADOLF, *see* NAZI HYPOTHESIS

**HOAXES.** Only 1.66 percent of all cases studied by the UNITED STATES AIR FORCE'S PROJECT BLUE BOOK were identified as hoaxes. As a result of the publicity generated by Kenneth Arnold's historic UFO sighting over MOUNT RAINIER, WASHINGTON, in 1947, prank-

sters began tossing disk-shaped objects from the tops of high buildings. Since people were anxious to see flying saucers, these hoaxes succeeded in causing considerable excitement and hysteria. However, the objects were quickly identified. One of the most popular hoaxes carried out by teenagers during the following years was the launching of hot-air BALLOONS illuminated by candles to create a mysterious glow.

In April 1971, an experiment in mass psychology was conducted by several high school students in the sociology class of the West Central Community School in Westgate, Iowa. Three members of the class burned a circular area in a field. They added four smaller circles to suggest the marks of landing legs. The following day, one of the students called the local radio station to report that he had seen a UFO the previous evening and that he had just found its landing site. Within twenty-four hours, news of the landing was gaining nationwide attention. Referring to a PHOTOGRAPH of the burned area of the field, one newspaper stated "the boys have pictures to *prove* some sort of 'unidentified flying object' *really did* touch down in Fayette County Tuesday evening." A number of people in eastern Iowa reported sighting a UFO on the night of the alleged landing. One man claimed that he had observed the object repeatedly over a two-week period and could tell from its actions "that it was going to land." Members of the sociology class conducted a poll in which ninety percent of those questioned stated that they believed the story. Feeling that the situation was getting out of control, the students' teacher publicly announced that

These helium-filled bags with aluminum foil attached were a source of UFO reports in Baton Rouge, Louisiana, on October 19, 1973. The "UFO" was captured after a 90-minute chase. *(United Press International Photo)*

the incident had been part of an experiment. In a subsequent poll, those who had originally admitted to believing the story now said that they had had doubts all along and did not believe in UFOs.

The students reached several conclusions regarding mass psychology and its implications for the UFO situation. Not only can the news media be misled, it can also mislead. The students noted that reporters embellished the original version of the story. Yet many people were convinced that the story was true merely because it was covered by the news media. About five hundred people had visited the alleged landing site. This demonstrated to the experimenters how excited people were by a new experience which relieved the monotony of life's daily routine. Of particular interest was the fact that normally skeptical people were caught up in the group reaction. Allowing their emotions to cloud their reasoning had resulted in the temporary suspension of their ability to think critically.

The most popular form of hoax seems to be the photograph. The majority of UFO photographs have been exposed as frauds. Well-known examples include the numerous photographs taken by GEORGE ADAMSKI and PAUL VILLA, and a photograph of two aerial objects taken at TAORMINA, SICILY. Another well-known photograph whose authenticity is much debated is that taken near TRINDADE ISLAND, BRAZIL, in 1958. Astronomer DONALD MENZEL has pointed out that the photographer was actually a professional photographer who specialized in trick photography.

In one case, an admission of guilt by the perpetrator failed to convince some UFOlogists that his photograph is a hoax. In April 1976, the staff of Canada's PROJECT SUM (SOLVING UFO MYSTERIES) UFO RESEARCH found a UFO photograph on display at a science fair in a shopping center. They interviewed the photographer, Paul Knight, who claimed to have photographed the disk-shaped object the previous month in St. Catharines, Ontario. Examination by several investigators of Project SUM revealed that the original negative had not been tampered with. In May, Malcolm Williams, a freelance photographer and UFO investigator, made enlargements of the negative. According to Williams, an enlargement of the photograph to 4,000 times its original size revealed what appeared to be an OCCUPANT sitting in a depression in the center of the disk. The being's eyes, nose and mouth were almost discernible. On May 24th, before arranging publicity in local papers, Project SUM's Director, Kenneth Kroeker, and his associates asked Knight to confirm the photograph's authenticity. Suddenly, Knight announced that the picture was a hoax. He claimed the object was a gas-driven, remotely controlled model. When Williams was informed of Knight's confession, he expressed puzzlement about the fact that an occupant was visible in the photograph. Kroeker and an assistant visited the location of the alleged sighting. They discovered that a tree in the photograph was only about thirty-five feet high, suggesting that the object in the photograph must have been only a few feet in diameter. However, on July 6, Knight told Kroeker and his associates that he had told them the UFO photograph was a hoax only to get them "off his back for a while." His claim that he was becoming too involved in the case

Alleged UFO photographed by Paul Knight in St. Catherines, Ontario, in March 1976. Enlargement of Paul Knight's photograph. (Courtesy Project SUM)

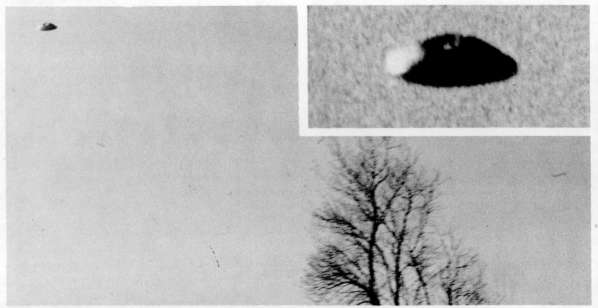

seemed reasonable to the Project SUM staff. They had Knight sign several documents testifying that the photograph was not a fake. In September, articles about the case were sent by Project SUM to several magazines. George Potts, the photoanalyst of CANADIAN UFO REPORT, wrote to Kroeker, pointing out that, based on the photographic data accompanying the photograph, the trees in the distance should be in focus, whereas they are actually further out of focus than the closer group. The UFO is clearly in focus and Potts's calculations put it within fifty feet of the camera. When these facts were presented to Knight, he admitted that, after all, the whole story had been a hoax from beginning to end. The UFO was a Volkswagen hubcap with a dent on top.

With regard to the apparent "occupant" seen in the enlargement of the photograph, Kroeker concluded that the whitish portions represent sunlight reflecting off the dent made in the middle of the hubcap, while the apparent eyes, nose and mouth are the result of random grain patterns of the films used when the progressive enlargements were made. On October 14, 1976, Project SUM officially labeled the photograph a hoax and informed researchers in Toronto and elsewhere of this fact. Some researchers stated that they would believe it a hoax only if it were proven as such. Since Knight could not find a successful way to prove it a hoax, the photograph was still considered genuine by some Canadian UFOlogists.

On April 8, 1977, however, Knight had the opportunity to remedy the situation. CJRN Radio of Niagara Falls broadcast a three-hour call-in show during which numerous listeners telephoned the station to discuss Knight's photograph. When Knight learned the program was in progress, he called the station and, to approximately 300,000 listeners, admitted that he had faked the photograph by using a hubcap tossed into the air. He wanted to see, he said, how far an organization would go in the investigation of such a case.

Bibliography: Menzel, Donald H., and Ernest H. Taves, *The UFO Enigma* (Garden City, N.Y.: Doubleday and Company, 1977); Klass, Philip J., *UFOs Explained* (New York: Random House, 1974).

**HOLLOW EARTH HYPOTHESIS.** Adherents to the theory that our PLANET is a hollow sphere inhabited by eight million beatific giants, base their beliefs on an amalgamation of ancient and modern myths. Asian legends of the subterranean kingdom of Agharta have been blended with a variety of tales of the polar Shangri-La supposedly discovered by Rear Admiral Richard E. Byrd and subsequent explorers. Recent evidence to support these stories is said to be found in photographs taken by ESSA–3, ESSA–7 and ATS–1

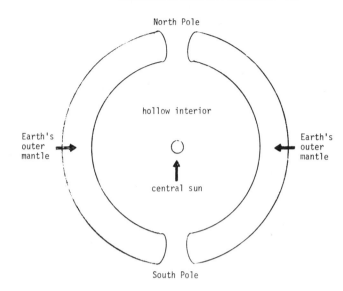

Diagram showing Earth as a hollow sphere with holes at the North and South Poles.

SATELLITES, which reveal an enormous circular hole in Earth's crust at the North Pole.

According to numerous texts on this subject, inside the 800-mile thick mantle on which we live is a hollow region 6,400 miles in diameter. A small, central sun provides a subtropical climate and, of course, perpetual daylight. Within this world live the survivors of ATLANTIS, who fled the doomed continent in their flying saucers. Their life span ranges from four hundred to eight hundred years, and this highly evolved civilization communicates telepathically. Ruler of this land of gigantic people, animals and plant life is the King or Master of the World, whose ancient symbol is the swastika.

There is much disagreement on the whereabouts of entrances to the interior of our planet. The most favored locations are the North and South Poles, secret tunnels under the PYRAMIDS, a portal between the paws of the sphinx at Gizeh, Mont Saint-Michel, the Forest of Broceliande and the legendary city of Shamballah in Tibet. Some researchers, however, assert that Shamballah is not in Tibet but is, in fact, the subterranean capital of Agharta. The polar ingresses enjoy popularity as a result of misinterpreted references by Admiral Byrd to "that land beyond the pole." The ultimate development of this thesis is a document, presented by the FLYING SAUCER—HOLLOW EARTH SOCIETY of Canada, which purports to be Byrd's secret diary. The text describes Byrd's visit to a city beneath the pole where he received profound revelations from the Master of the World. Lieutenant Commander David Bunger is another explorer reputed to have observed an ice-free

Antarctic land speckled with large, warm, multicolored lakes.

To further sustain the hollow Earth hypothesis are claims that the further one travels north within the Arctic Circle, the warmer the temperature becomes. Birds, insects and vegetation flourish and the sea is not frozen. Presumably, some barrier prevents the sea from spilling over into the polar cavity. In 1893, footprints on an iceberg led to the corpses of five unidentified men who, it is concluded, must have been subterraneans. One of the reasons why few people have the benefit of seeing the enormous hole is because compasses do not function correctly in that region of the world. Hence, it is suggested, tourist flights cautiously fly to one side of the pole, while the claims by other explorers to have reached the pole cannot be considered valid. Hollow Earth theorists also interpret the AURORA BOREALIS as the rays of the central sun shining through the polar aperture.

The few UFOLOGISTS who give credence to the hollow Earth hypothesis believe that the former Atlanteans have been forced into making excursions to the outer world as a result of the explosions of nuclear bombs which endanger their survival as well as ours. Hence, UFOs are not extraterrestrial but intraterrestrial craft.

Bibliography: Bernard, Raymond, *The Hollow Earth* (Mokelumne Hill, California: Health Research, 1963); Bernard, Raymond, *Flying Saucers from the Earth's Interior* (Joinville, Brazil: Raymond Bernard, 1966); Emerson, Willis George, *The Smoky God* (New York: Fieldcrest Publishing Company, 1964).

**HOLLOW EARTH SOCIETY** *see* **FLYING SAUCER—HOLLOW EARTH SOCIETY and INTERNATIONAL SOCIETY FOR A COMPLETE EARTH (HOLLOW EARTH SOCIETY)**

**HOLOGRAM HYPOTHESIS,** theory proposing that UFOs are three-dimensional projections of an image. UFO-holograms might be beamed to Earth by extraterrestrials from their home PLANETS or from devices located in outer space. Since some UFOs seem to leave PHYSICAL EVIDENCE, it has been suggested that an alien race might have developed holograms with mass. Another variation on the theory proposes that UFO-holograms might be projections from the future, perhaps from our own planet.

If the hologram hypothesis were valid, the purpose of projecting such images might be an attempt to convey some message to mankind or an effort to guide our progress. However, the theory is given little credence by most UFOLOGISTS.

Bibliography: Briazack, Norman J., and Simon Mennick, *The UFO Guidebook* (Secaucus, New Jersey: Citadel Press, 1978); Vallee, Jacques, *Passport to Magonia* (Chicago: Henry Regnery Company, 1969).

**HOODOO SEA** *see* **BERMUDA TRIANGLE**

**HOSTILITY.** The lack of evidence of hostility in the UFO phenomenon was partially responsible for the UNITED STATES AIR FORCE's conclusion that UFOs posed no threat to national security. However, potential hazards have been recorded in a number of cases. The late physicist and UFOLOGIST JAMES McDONALD, rejecting "hostility" as a general characteristic of the UFO phenomenon, noted that one may accidentally kick an anthill, killing many ants and destroying the ants' entrance, without any prior "hostility" toward the ants. Similarly, to walk accidentally into a whirling airplane propellor is fatal, yet the aircraft holds no "hostility" toward the unfortunate victim.

The most common adverse physiological effects reported by UFO witnesses are BURNS and near-suffocation due to unusual HEAT. In the WALESVILLE, NEW YORK, case, extreme heat was apparently used by a UFO as a defense weapon to prevent the close approach of an Air Force jet. The death of pilot Charles Mantell, while pursuing a UFO over GODMAN AIR FORCE BASE in Kentucky, led some members of the public to fear that UFOs were dangerous. The case of the young man who was trapped in a tree by four UFONAUTS at CISCO GROVE, CALIFORNIA, in 1964, seemed to demonstrate some form of hostility. However, the creatures did not harm the young man and may have been attempting to capture him without damaging him. An entire family was held siege in KELLY-HOPKINSVILLE, KENTUCKY, in 1955, by strange little creatures associated with a UFO. In this case, it was the human beings who demonstrated aggression by firing shots at the entities.

Human hostility toward UFOs seems more apparent than UFO aggression toward people. A typical example is the 1972 FORT BEAUFORT, SOUTH AFRICA, case. Farmer Bennie Smit fired numerous shots at a spherical UFO which had shown no signs of hostility.

Although the Air Force's policy was that intercept pilots should attempt to capture UFOs during the period of its official involvement, the 1952 WAVE led to a temporary change in procedure. Fearing an attack, the Air Defense Command ordered pilots to fire on UFOs. According to writer DONALD KEYHOE, top H.Q. officers soon realized the firing order was a mistake. It was canceled and the capture attempts were resumed.

**HOT-AIR BALLOONS** *see* **BALLOONS**

**HOUSE ARMED SERVICES COMMITTEE**

**HEARINGS,** congressional hearings on the UNITED STATES AIR FORCE's involvement in UFOs held on April 5, 1966, following the suggestion of GERALD R. FORD, who was then House Republican minority leader. Under the chairmanship of L. Mendel Rivers, the committee invited only three people to testify: Secretary of the Air Force Harold D. Brown, PROJECT BLUE BOOK Director HECTOR QUINTANILLA and astronomer J. ALLEN HYNEK, consultant to PROJECT BLUE BOOK.

First to testify was Brown, who reported that of 10,147 cases studied from 1947 to 1965, 9,501 had been identified. He noted that the Air Force had not found any threat to national security or any evidence that UFOs were extraterrestrial spacecraft. He stated, "I know of no one of scientific standing or executive standing or with a detailed knowledge of this, in our organization who believes that they come from extraterrestrial sources." However, he assured the committee that the Air Force would continue to investigate reports with an open mind.

In response to the charge that he was an Air Force "puppet," Hynek read a statement which, he said, "has certainly not been dictated by the Air Force." He asserted that UFOs deserved the scientific community's attention and called for the appointment of a civilian panel of scientists to examine the program and to determine whether or not a major problem existed.

In general, the committee members expressed disbelief in the EXTRATERRESTRIAL HYPOTHESIS (ETH) and confidence in the Air Force's handling of the subject. However, its approval of the recommendations of the O'BRIEN REPORT was conducive to their implementation.

Bibliography: U.S. Congress, House, Committee on Armed Services, Unidentified Flying Objects, Hearings, 89th Congress, 2nd Session, April 5, 1966 (Washington, D.C.: U.S. Government Printing Office, 1966).

**HOUSE OF LORDS,** British Parliamentary body which conducted a UFO debate on January 18, 1979. The Earl of Clancarty (BRINSLEY LE POER TRENCH) initiated the debate by proposing a motion that a governmental study of UFOs be established. Clancarty summarized the history of UFOs and the positions taken by foreign governments.

The second speaker was Lord Trefargne, who opposed the motion on the grounds that many UFOs can be explained by "logical scientific theory" and that belief in extraterrestrial beings is not compatible with Christian faith.

The Earl of Kimberly supported the motion, declaring that, "UFOs defy worldly logic." The Viscount of Oxfuird expressed a desire to know where UFOs come from. Lord Davies of Leek also supported the motion,

stating that, "If one human being out of the tens of thousands who allege to have seen these phenomena is telling the truth, then there is a dire need for us to look into the matter."

The Lord Bishop of Norwich, while in favor of the motion, expressed his concern that, "The mystery surrounding UFOs today . . . is in danger of producing a twentieth century superstition in our modern and scientific days which is not unlike the superstition of past years." He cautioned against "the danger of the religious aspect of the UFO situation leading to the obscuring of basic Christian truths."

Lord Gladwyn opposed the motion and pointed out that "the more over-populated our PLANET becomes, the greater the violence and the more appalling the wars, the more, unconsciously perhaps, we want to leave it if we can or trust in other worldly intervention; and the more intense therefore the longing, the greater the temptation to believe that there actually is somewhere else to which we can physically go or to which we can somehow make an appeal." He concluded, "If the UFOs contain sentient beings, we can only leave it to

Cover page of the Official Report of the House of Lords Parliamentary Debates on January 18, 1979. *(Courtesy ICUFON/Earl of Clancarty)*

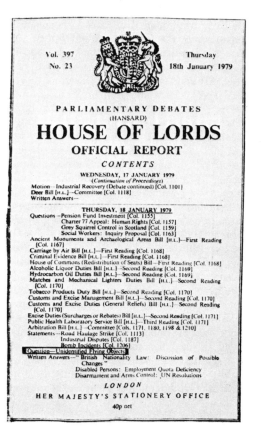

such beings to get in touch with us when, and if, they will. Up to now, if they exist, they have done no harm of any kind. Apparently, they have done no harm for the last two or three thousand years. So there seems to be no great need to set up intragovernmental machinery to investigate the whole phenomena. The mystery may suitably remain a mystery, and so far as I can see nobody will be in any way the worse off if it does."

Lord Kings Norton, while expressing skepticism, supported the motion. Lord Rankeillour, on the other hand, stated that, "I suspect that the British Government do (sic) have a Department studying UFO sightings, for why else should they (sic) bother to go to such trouble to publicly debunk reported ones if they are of no interest to them? (sic) Quite apart from the fact that the Government have (sic) not admitted to the existence of UFOs, these machines are potentially dangerous. They give off blinding light, crippling rays and sometimes beams that immobilize humans; they start forest fires, eradicate crops and cause great distress to animals."

The Earl of Halsbury discussed some natural explanations for UFOs, and was followed by Lord Hewlett who pointed out that, "Over the United Kingdom, Jodrell Bank's radio telescope, the first and still one of the most powerful in the world, has observed thousands of possible subjects for identification as UFOs, but not a single one has proved other than natural phenomena." He was answered by the Earl of Cork and Orrery, who argued that "the fact that the Jodrell Bank telescope has not seen something not only does not prove, but is not even particularly good evidence, that it was not there."

The final speaker was the Earl of Strabolgi, who asked, "Why have they never tried to communicate with us? Why has there been no evidence on radio of attempts at communication? And would not such a large number of movements be picked up by our defense radar system? Why has not a single artifact been found? Assuming that each visit does not represent a journey from a distant star, where are these alien space craft supposed to be hiding? Now that the idea of such bases on the MOON or on another planet in our solar system is barely tenable, UFOLOGISTS have had to claim that the aliens are based in the depths of the sea or in a great hole in the earth, or even that they come from invisible universes and other space-time continuua. Anyone who accepts the hypothesis of large numbers of alien visitations seems forced towards explanations that are ever more fantastic, and incapable of either proof or disproof." He closed the debate by saying, "Her Majesty's Government do (sic) not consider that there is any justification for the expenditure of public money on such a study. . . . As for telling the public the truth about UFOs, the truth is simple. There really are many

strange phenomena in the sky, and these are invariably reported by rational people. But there is a wide range of natural explanations to account for such phenomena. There is nothing to suggest to Her Majesty's Government that such phenomena are alien space craft."

## HOUSE OF REPRESENTATIVES SUBCOMMITTEE ON ATMOSPHERIC PHENOMENA,
subcommittee of the Select Committee on Astronautics and Space Exploration (later the Science and Astronautics Committee). The subcommittee was chaired by Congressman John McCormack and, on August 8, 1958, held an informal hearing on UFOs. Briefings were given by Air Force chief science advisor Francis Arcier, PROJECT BLUE BOOK chief George Gregory, Majors Best and Byrne of Air Force Intelligence, and Majors Brower and Tacker of the Office of Public Information. By the end of the day, McCormack declared that he was satisfied with the Air Force's handling of the matter and no formal hearings would be necessary.

Bibliography: Smith, Marcia S., *The UFO Enigma* (Washington, D.C.: Congressional Research Service, Library of Congress, 1976).

## HOUSE SCIENCE AND ASTRONAUTICS COMMITTEE HEARINGS,
congressional symposium on UFOs held on July 29, 1968. The hearings were held because of the continuing controversy over UFOs despite the reassurances which had followed the SMART COMMITTEE hearings of 1960 and the HOUSE ARMED SERVICES COMMITTEE HEARINGS in 1966. On this occasion, no UNITED STATES AIR FORCE (USAF) representatives were invited to testify, and the speakers were not allowed to make judgments on PROJECT BLUE BOOK.

The committee was chaired by Congressman J. Edward Roush. Testimony was presented by astronomer and consultant to the Air Force J. ALLEN HYNEK, meteorologist JAMES E. McDONALD, astronomer CARL SAGAN, sociologist Robert L. Hall, engineer JAMES A. HARDER and astronautical engineer ROBERT M. L. BAKER. In addition, written statements were prepared for the record by astronomer DONALD MENZEL, psychologist R. LEO SPRINKLE, geophysicist Garry C. Henderson, nuclear physicist STANTON FRIEDMAN, psychologist Roger N. Shepard and exobiologist FRANK B. SALISBURY.

Hynek related that at the beginning of his official involvement with UFOs he had considered the subject to be nonsense but he had since realized that there were UFO reports which had potential scientific value. "By what right," he asked, "can we summarily ignore [witnesses'] testimony and imply that they are deluded or just plain liars? Would we so treat these same people if they were testifying in court, under oath, on more mundane matters?" He pointed out that several misconceptions about UFOs were that only UFO buffs report sightings, that they are never reported by scientifically trained people, they are never seen at close range, they have never been detected by radar and they have never been recorded by scientific cameras. Concluding that "signals continue to point to a mystery that needs to be solved," he recommended that Congress establish a UFO Scientific Board of Inquiry for an in-depth investigation of the UFO phenomenon and that the United States seek the cooperation of the UNITED NATIONS to set up means for international exchange of information on UFOs.

McDonald outlined his experiences in the field of interviewing UFO witnesses, and concluded that, "UFOs are entirely real and we do not know what they are. . . . The possibility that these are extraterrestrial devices, that we are dealing with SURVEILLANCE from some advanced technology, is a possibility I take very seriously."

Sagan, who was asked to testify on the possibility of extraterrestrial life, stated that there is nothing in physics to prevent interstellar travel, but he would have to have "extremely convincing evidence of an advanced technology in a UFO" before he could accept it. He felt that stronger evidence was required to justify an investigation on the order of that suggested by Hynek. He recommended that if Congress was truly interested in studying extraterrestrial life, it should support the Mariner and Voyager programs of the NATIONAL AERONAUTICS AND SPACE ADMINISTRATION (NASA), and the radio astronomy programs of the National Science Foundation, rather than UFOs.

Dealing with UFOs from a purely socio-psychological standpoint, Hall presented his belief that some cases definitely result from HYSTERICAL CONTAGION. He concluded, however, that in the hard-core cases, hysterical contagion was highly improbable.

Harder was called as a witness to discuss propulsion systems necessary for interstellar travel and the types of maneuvers described in UFO reports. Harder declared his opinion that "on the basis of the data and ordinary rules of evidence, as would be applied in civil or criminal courts, the physical reality of UFOs has been proved beyond a reasonable doubt." He described a case in which a witness viewing a UFO through polarized glasses had seen a series of rings around the object and concluded that this was due to atmospheric disturbance from a magnetic field type of propulsion system. He suggested that UFOs might use gravitational fields in some way of which we are not aware. He concluded that the study of UFOs might prove valuable for our civilization because, "In the UFO phenomena, we have

demonstrations of scientific secrets we do not know ourselves." He suggested a program for obtaining more scientific data on UFOs, which involved the establishment of an early warning network, the putting together of instrument packages that could be shipped to a UFO site on short notice, and cooperation with the Air Force for logistics and high speed transportation of these packages.

Baker, who had analyzed the TREMONTON, UTAH, and GREAT FALLS, MONTANA, films, was convinced that the objects photographed were not natural phenomena. However, he was not willing to say they were extraterrestrial, either. He made several suggestions on how to achieve more sophisticated analyses of fresh data and recommended setting up a task force to obtain hard and soft data supported by a sensor system designed expressly for that purpose, possibly a phased array radar, as well as a space-based long-wavelength infrared surveillance sensor system. He also suggested that a study be made of the psychiatric and medical problems of determining witnesses' credibility.

Menzel's paper dealt with his theories that UFOs are natural phenomena such as MIRAGES, reflections and TEMPERATURE INVERSIONS. His paper was accompanied by a letter, addressed to Roush, stating, "Am amazed, however, that you could plan so unbalanced a symposium, weighted by persons known to favor Government support of a continuing, expensive and pointless investigation of UFOs without inviting me, the leading exponent of opposing views and author of two major books on the subject."

Sprinkle's paper declared his acceptance of "the hypothesis that the Earth is being surveyed by spacecraft which are controlled by representatives of an alien civilization or civilizations. I believe the 'spacecraft hypothesis' is the best hypothesis to account for the wide range of evidence of UFO phenomena." He suggested that a national research center be established for continuous, formal investigation of the physical, biological, psycho-social and spiritual implications of UFO phenomena."

Henderson criticized the Air Force's handling of the UFO situation. "The public has been led to believe," he said, "that everything has been done to either prove or disprove the existence of UFOs—rubbish!" With regard to the Air Force's tendency to dismiss UFOs on the grounds that they did not pose a threat to national security, he pointed out that, "The discovery of Noah's Ark in Times Square would not necessarily pose a threat to national security either, but it would certainly be a find worthy of the most intensive investigation whether certain individuals accepted its existence or not." Henderson recommended an improved system for collecting, collating and analyzing UFO data.

Friedman's paper presented a critical analysis of the positions of UFO debunkers. He claimed that they "made strong attempts to make the data fit their HYPOTHESES rather than trying to do the much more difficult job of creating hypotheses which fit the data." Friedman concluded that "the Earth is being visited by intelligently-controlled vehicles, whose origin is extraterrestrial."

Shepard's statement dealt with the problems of finding patterns and order in the mass of UFO data. He stated his conviction that very few cases could be explained as psychological aberrations, such as illusions, HALLUCINATIONS, delusions and AFTERIMAGES. He concluded that "the claims that the UFOs reported even by seemingly responsible citizens represent lapses of a basically psycho-pathological character have generally come from people who have neglected to study closely either into the literature on psychopathology, or into that on UFOs, or (in many cases, I fear) both."

Salisbury countered the arguments of UFO debunkers and warned that it is unscientific to attribute human motivation to nonhuman intelligence. He concluded his paper with reviews of several major UFO case histories.

Since the purpose of the hearings was to serve as a forum, not to resolve the UFO situation, the symposium did not lead to the establishment of any new programs or any change in Air Force policy.

Bibliography: U.S. Congress, House, Committee on Science and Astronautics, Symposium on Unidentified Flying Objects, Hearings, 90th Congress, 2nd Session, July 29, 1968 (Washington, D.C.: U.S. Government Printing Office, 1968).

## HUMAN INDIVIDUAL METAMORPHOSIS (HIM), religious UFO cult which made the headlines in October 1975, when it was announced that a score of people from Weldport, Oregon, had disappeared, abandoning family and property, after telling friends that they were leaving Earth on a one-way trip in a UFO.

The story began in 1972, when divorcé Marshall Herff Applewhite met nurse Bonnie Lu Trusdale Nettles at the Houston hospital where she worked. They immediately struck up a friendship based on their mutual interest in astrology and their belief that they had known each other in previous lives. The son of a Presbyterian minister, the charismatic Applewhite earned his Master's degree in Music from the University of Colorado. During his career, he had held positions as choir director of several churches, opera singer at the Houston Grand Opera, Assistant Professor of Music at St. Thomas University, Musical Director for the Houston Music Theatre Studio Seven and Music Director for St. Mark's Episcopal Church, a post he was holding at the time of his first meeting with Nettles.

A growing awareness of their higher destiny led Applewhite and Nettles to open a Christian Arts Center in Houston, an organization specializing in various

Marshall Herff Applewhite and Bonnie Lu Trusdale Nettles. *(United Press International Photo)*

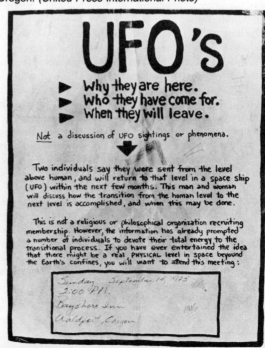

Bo and Peep's announcement of their meeting at Waldport, Oregon. *(United Press International Photo)*

occult disciplines. When Nettles's claims to be in contact with a long-dead nineteenth-century monk were publicized, Applewhite was fired from his job at St. Mark's Episcopal Church. The couple set out on a tour of the country and, during this period, formulated their UFO religion. They based their beliefs in their mission and their identity on a passage from the Book of Revelation in which it is stated that two messengers from a heavenly kingdom will prophesy "a thousand-two-hundred-and-threescore days, clothed in sack-cloth." These two messengers would be assassinated and their bodies left in the street for three-and-a-half days. They would then return to life and ascend to heaven in a cloud, interpreted by Applewhite and Nettles as a UFO. Choosing the pseudonyms Bo and Peep to represent their image as space-age shepherds, the couple began recruiting followers at private meetings. In exchange for renouncing all private possessions and family ties, converts were promised they would accompany Bo and Peep, also known as the Two, on their post-resurrection flight to a higher level of consciousness. The UFO voyage was predicted to occur within six months. Eager to set out on this short road to salvation, few proselytes questioned their leaders' claims to be extraterrestrial beings, millions of years old, incarnated in human bodies. None were aware that in 1974 Applewhite and Nettles had been arrested and jailed in Texas—Applewhite on a charge of auto theft and Nettles for possession of stolen credit cards.

When Bo and Peep appeared at the famous Waldport, Oregon, meeting, they already had a flock of more than two dozen followers from Los Angeles. From Waldport, they moved across the country recruiting disciples from Oregon, California, Arizona, Washington, Colorado, Texas, Wisconsin, New York, New Jersey and Florida. When the six-month deadline passed and the predicted assassination had not occurred, the Two extended their remaining terrestrial life span to ten years. Disillusioned, large numbers of followers defected.

Two sociologists who infiltrated the nomadic group found that the majority of followers were long time truth seekers who had been disappointed by previous excursions into astrology, yoga, transcendental meditation, scientology and other forms of spiritual enlightenment. Since many members had actually deserted problems and unsatisfactory relationships, rather than wealth and love, to join the group, the mass defections did not prevent the group from growing to an estimated membership of more than one thousand men and women. By 1979, however, membership had shrunk to about fifty. The Two and their flock were reported to be living in Wyoming during the summer and in Texas during the winter.

Bibliography: Steiger, Brad, and Hayden Hewes,

*UFO Missionaries Extraordinary* (New York: Pocket Books, 1976).

**HUMANIST, THE,** publication of the American Humanist Association, sponsor of the COMMITTEE FOR THE SCIENTIFIC INVESTIGATION OF THE PARANORMAL (CSICP).

**HUNEEUS, ANTONIO** (b. September 23, 1950, Rockville Center, New York; address: 336 East 6th Street, New York, N.Y. 10003), writer.

Huneeus believes that the explanation for UFOs may combine both the EXTRATERRESTRIAL HYPOTHESIS (ETH) and aspects of physical reality still unknown to contemporary science. He holds that due to increasing ecological destruction of Earth and the permanent danger of annihilation posed by military technology, it is important for humanity to solve the UFO mystery and thus, perhaps, trigger unity among the nations of the world.

Huneeus studied French Language and Civilization at the Sorbonne University, Paris, in 1970; Journalism at the University of Chile, Santiago, from 1972 to 1973; and Theory of Mass Communication at the Catholic University of Chile, Santiago, in 1974.

As a reporter, Huneeus has attended numerous symposia and conferences. He is the author of more than 250 articles published in newspapers and magazines in Chile, Colombia and the United States. The subjects he has dealt with include ecology, space, UFOs, scientific research, energy, psychic phenomena, drugs, Latin American news and book reviews.

Huneeus is a founding member of the Ecology Institute of Chile, for which he served as secretary, librarian and public relations officer from 1974 to 1975. He is a staff member of the INTERCONTINENTAL GALACTIC SPACECRAFT (UFO) RESEARCH AND ANALYTIC NETWORK (ICUFON).

**HUSTON, POLICE OFFICER WAYNE,** *see* **PORTAGE COUNTY, OHIO**

**HYNEK, J. ALLEN** (b. May 1, 1910, Chicago, Illinois; address: 1609 Sherman Avenue, Evanston, Illinois 66201), astronomer, Founder and Director of the CENTER FOR UFO STUDIES (CUFOS).

Hynek is considered by many to be the leading authority in the field. His involvement began in 1948 when he became the astronomical consultant to the UNITED STATES AIR FORCE (USAF) on their UFO project. Initially, he was skeptical about UFO reports. In 1966, he issued the famous SWAMP GAS explanation for two of several sightings in Michigan. The news media misrepresented his statement as a blanket explanation for all the sightings and Hynek became a target of public criticism. Shortly thereafter, he became more open-minded about the EXTRATERRESTRIAL HYPOTHESIS (ETH), adopted the opinion that there might be extremely valuable paydirt in the UFO phenomenon and "that therefore a scientific effort on a much larger scale than any heretofore should be mounted for a frontal attack on this problem." After PROJECT BLUE BOOK was terminated, he became critical of the Air Force's investigative methods. In 1973, he established CUFOS and, since 1975, has been a full-time UFOlogist. Although he ascribes to no particular theory regarding the nature of UFOs, he projects that the solution to the mystery will provide a mighty and totally unexpected quantum jump in human understanding.

Hynek attended the University of Chicago, where he received his B.S. in 1931 and his Ph.D. in astrophysics in 1935. He was an Assistant Professor at the University of Chicago Yerkes Observatory in 1934; Instructor in Physics and Astronomy at Ohio State University from 1935 to 1941; Astronomer at Ohio State's Perkins Observatory from 1935 to 1956; Assistant Professor of Physics and Astronomy at Ohio State University from 1941 to 1945; Supervisor of Technical Reports at the Applied Physical Laboratory of the Johns Hopkins University from 1942 to 1946; Associate Professor of Physics and Astronomy at Ohio State University from 1946 to 1950; and Professor of Astronomy from 1950 to 1956; Assistant Dean of the Graduate School from 1950 to 1953; Visiting Lecturer at Harvard University from 1956 to 1960; Chief of the Section of Upper Atmosphere Studies and Satellite Tracking and Associate Director of the Smithsonian Astrophysical Observatory from 1956 to 1960; and Chairman of the Department of Astronomy and Director of Dearborn Observatory at Northwestern University from 1960 to 1975.

Hynek served as astronomical consultant to the USAF on UFOs from 1948 to 1968. He was the first speaker to present testimony at the 1968 HOUSE SCIENCE AND ASTRONAUTICS COMMITTEE HEARINGS. He was techni-

cal advisor on the motion picture CLOSE ENCOUNTERS OF THE THIRD KIND. In 1978, he was a speaker at a United Nations meeting on the proposed establishment of an agency or a department to conduct and coordinate research into UFOs and related phenomena. In addition to his role as Director of CUFOS, he is Editor-in-Chief of the Center's newsletter, THE INTERNATIONAL UFO REPORTER.

Hynek is a Fellow of the Royal Astronomical Society and a member of the American Astronomical Society, the International Astronomical Union and the AMERICAN ASSOCIATION FOR THE ADVANCEMENT OF SCIENCE (AAAS).

Hynek is the author of numerous technical papers in astrophysics and the author of several textbooks. He is the author of *The UFO Experience: A Scientific Inquiry* (Chicago: Henry Regnery Company 1972); coauthor, with Jacques Vallee of *The Edge of Reality* (Chicago: Henry Regnery Company, 1975); and author of *The Hynek UFO Report* (New York: Dell Publishing Company, 1977).

**HYPERBOREA,** mythical polar region of sunshine and everlasting spring beyond the mountains of the north wind. Ancient legend described it as an earthly paradise whose inhabitants enjoyed life spans of 1,000 years. Modern legends compare Hyperborea to ATLANTIS, GONDWANALAND, LEMURIA and MU, claiming it was eventually submerged during an abrupt change in climate caused by a displacement of Earth's axis, which altered the position of the poles. Proponents of this theory believe Siberia, Alaska, Greenland, SPITSBERGEN, Jan Mayen Island and Iceland are vestiges of the lost continent.

Others believe Hyperborea to be an indestructable earthly paradise which is inaccessible to ordinary human beings. Some writers claim that the polar paradise was sighted from an airplane by Rear Admiral Richard E. Byrd. This claim, however, is also held up by proponents of the HOLLOW EARTH HYPOTHESIS as evidence that Byrd discovered the polar entrances to the interior of our planet.

Bibliography: Hutin, Serge, *Alien Races and Fantastic Civilizations* (New York: Berkley Publishing Corporation, 1975).

**HYPERSPACE,** hypothetical area, also known as superspace, used in science fiction to circumvent the limitations of traveling below the SPEED OF LIGHT. The concept is based on a theory that a fourth dimension exists through which one can take short cuts that are inaccessible in a three-dimensional universe. According to this hypothesis, holes exist within our space-time continuum through which matter can enter into or exit

J. Allen Hynek. *(Courtesy ICUFON)*

from hyperspace. Travelers entering this unknown area would transcend the limits of time and space. Thus travel could be accomplished in a very short time or even instantaneously. To translate this concept into three-dimensional terms, biochemist and author Isaac Asimov uses the analogy of a large, flat piece of paper on which a snail must travel from one end to the other. Since a snail travels slowly, it will take him a long time to reach the other end of the two-dimensional sheet of paper. If, however, the paper is bent into a circle, bringing the two ends close to each other, the snail need only cross the small air gap that now separates him from his destination.

If hyperspace exists, it would validate, though not prove, the EXTRATERRESTRIAL HYPOTHESIS (ETH) and the PARALLEL UNIVERSE HYPOTHESIS. With regard to the former it would, of course, eliminate the time problem of interstellar travel which has been one of the major factors in diminishing the feasibility of ETH. With regard to the parallel universe hypothesis, hyperspace could, of course, be inhabited by intelligent creatures who are able to move in and out of our universe at will. However, hyperspace remains a useful tool for the science fiction writer and its existence at present is no more than a mathematical abstraction.

Bibliography: Berry, Adrian, *The Next Ten Thousand Years* (New York: New American Library, 1975); Asimov, Isaac, *Please Explain* (New York: Dell Publishing Company, 1973).

## HYPNAGOGIC *see* HYPNOPOMPIC

**HYPNOPOMPIC,** drowsy state following awakening during which images can be self-generated within the human mind, regardless of whether the eyes are open or closed. A similar state, just before falling asleep, is referred to as hypnagogic. According to surveys, hypnopompic and hypnagogic imagery have been found to occur in fifty-one to seventy-seven percent of the population. Although the sensations experienced are generally visual or auditory, they may also involve heat, cold, odor and touch. Lasting from a few seconds to a few minutes, the imagery may be of such extreme clarity and vividness that it is almost indistinguishable from reality. The unusual quality of color and lighting and the bizarre nature of some hypnopompic and hypnagogic imagery has led many people to attribute it to supernatural causes. This mechanism has been cited by some psychologists as an explanation for UFO sightings which have occurred immediately prior to or following sleep.

Bibliography: Basterfield, Keith, "Hypnagogic and Hypnopompic Imagery," *UFO Canada* (Chomeday, Quebec: *UFO Canada*, Vol. 3, No. 2, February, 1979).

**HYPNOSIS,** physically induced sleeplike state in which facilitated access to the subconscious mind is attained. Thus information is more easily retrieved from the memory and, at the same time, suggestions are more readily received. Since the subconscious mind does not distinguish between the fantasies it produces and the reality it registers, events recalled during a hypnotic trance cannot be considered unequivocally factual.

Hypnotic regression has been used to enable witnesses to relive their UFO encounters in order to elicit details of the experience that they may not have remembered during the waking state. During sessions with twenty-five out of fifty witnesses interviewed, Dr. LEO SPRINKLE of the University of Wyoming has found an amnesic or loss of time period during the UFO experience. During a dream state, meditation or hypnosis, a witness recalls that he or she was taken aboard a landed craft, subjected to a physical examination by aliens and released after being told that he or she would remember nothing of the experience. An incident of this kind, which received worldwide publicity, involved Betty and Barney Hill, who sighted a UFO in NEW HAMPSHIRE in 1961. The implication is that UFOnauts themselves use posthypnotic suggestions to erase such encounters from the conscious minds of the human beings with whom they make contact. However, because of the limitations of the subconscious mind, hypnotic procedures do not provide conclusive evidence that the experiences related actually occurred.

Clinical hypnotist William C. McCall, technical writer JOHN DEHERRERA and English professor ALVIN LAWSON have conducted experiments in which imaginary UFO ABDUCTIONS were induced hypnotically in a group of subjects with no significant knowledge about UFOs. Eight situational questions relating to the major components of a "real" abduction were asked of each subject. Their responses indicated a wide range of imaginative invention. Significantly, the imaginary experiences related under hypnosis by the test subjects showed no substantive differences from those related by "real" abductees. Further studies by the three men established extensive and complex parallels among a series of phenomena which seem analogous to the UFO abduction experience. These include out-of-body experiences, HALLUCINATIONS, life after death experiences, religious conversions, shamans' trances and encounters with "little people." These parallels involve a bright light and a tunnel-tube image through which the witnesses pass to a door leading to a "big room." In the room are entities who give the witness an "examination" (moral or physical), occasionally including body dismemberment. There is a message exchanged, then the witness is returned. There is often some kind of aftermath in which the witness experiences personality changes. One tentative conclusion is that the imagery in all these experiences is very suggestive of birth trauma, indicating that psychological processes may be at the base of everything from UFOs to encounters with "little people."

An example of another type of hypnotic experiment was described by J. ALLEN HYNEK in 1971 at the Eastern UFO Symposium sponsored by the AERIAL PHENOMENA RESEARCH ORGANIZATION (APRO). A subject was given the post-hypnotic suggestion that he would see an unusual object appear in the sky from a specific direction. Although the subject was hostile to the idea of UFOs, he alerted his companions at the specified time to an unidentified object in the sky. None of the other witnesses could see the object, which was described by the subject as a black football with small objects behind it. Hynek has suggested that some UFO sightings may result from self-hypnosis but that this probably cannot account for cases in which UFOs are seen by multiple witnesses.

Bibliography: Sprinkle, R. Leo, "Hypnotic Time Regression Procedures in the Investigation of UFO Experiences," in Lorenzen, Coral E. and Jim, *Abducted!* (New York: Berkley Publishing Corporation, 1977); Lawson, Alvin, "Hypnosis of Imaginary UFO 'Abductees,'" *UPIAR—UFO Phenomena International Annual Review* (Published by Editecs in conjunction with the Comitato Nazionale Indipendente per lo Studio dei Fenomeni Aerei Anomali in Bologna, Italy; 1979, Vol. III.); Hynek, J. Allen, "UFO Research—A Progress Report," in Lorenzen, Coral E. (ed.), *Proceedings of the Eastern UFO Symposium* (Tucson, Arizona: Aerial Phenomena Research Organization, 1971).

**HYPOTHESES.** Since the beginning of the MODERN ERA in 1947, the EXTRATERRESTRIAL HYPOTHESIS (ETH) has been the most popular theory pertaining to the origin of UFOs. It was strongly endorsed by the late meteorologist JAMES MCDONALD and author DONALD KEYHOE. During the 1970s, however, the ETH lost some ground to other hypotheses. Predominant among these is the PARALLEL UNIVERSE HYPOTHESIS, expounded on by several writers such as JOHN KEEL and JACQUES VALLEE. Other theories include the SECRET WEAPON HYPOTHESIS, the HOLLOW EARTH HYPOTHESIS, the TIME TRAVEL HYPOTHESIS, the ATMOSPHERIC LIFE FORM HYPOTHESIS, the SUBMARINE HYPOTHESIS, the HOLOGRAM HYPOTHESIS, the INDUCED DREAM HYPOTHESIS, the THOUGHT FORM HYPOTHESIS and the INNER SPACE HYPOTHESIS. One school of thought is that UFOs are the instruments of a conspiratorial group utilizing MIND CONTROL, probably through the use of

PSYCHOTRONIC TECHNOLOGY. Other theories hold that UFOs are connected with SECRET SOCIETIES, FAIRIES, ELEMENTALS, ETHERIANS, ANGELS, an unknown organization similar to WINGS OVER THE WORLD (WOW) or the survivors of ATLANTIS.

Most UFOLOGISTS agree that the majority of UFO reports can be explained in natural or conventional terms. They contend, however, that there is a residue which can be accounted for by one or more of the above mentioned hypotheses or by an explanation which is as yet unthought of and possibly beyond human conception.

**HYSTERICAL CONTAGION,** psychological condition in which a group of people can be led to share a false belief that some event is taking place. The appropriate situation arises when a high level of anxiety or tension is combined with some kind of ambiguous circumstance which is interpreted as posing a threat. The ambiguous circumstance is psychologically transformed into an unambiguous event which apparently serves as justification for the diffuse anxiety or tension which preceded it. Documented cases of hysterical contagion usually last a few days or, at most, a few weeks.

The most often-quoted example of hysterical contagion in UFOLOGICAL circles is that of the "June Bug" epidemic in North Carolina in 1962. Workers from one section of a textile factory reported a disease, symptomized by nausea, fainting spells and skin rash, caused by the bites of a tiny insect. In fact, there was no insect. The symptoms had manifested themselves as an outgrowth of frustration and anxiety shared by the workers who were in close and constant contact.

Some skeptics have blamed UFO FLAPS on this psychological phenomenon. However, social psychologist Robert Hall believes that although hysterical contagion might account for some UFO reports, it in no way explains the hardcore, well-documented cases. He points out that, contrary to the psychological processes of hysterical contagion, the majority of UFO witnesses first try to assimilate their observations into something understood and familiar. They usually do not interpret a UFO as a threat but rather as something puzzling. Moreover, Hall points out, the continuation of worldwide UFO reports over more than three decades would constitute an unprecedented case of hysterical contagion.

Bibliography: Kerckhoff, A. C., and K. Back, *The June Bug: A Study of Hysterical Contagion* (New York: Appleton-Century-Crofts, 1968); Hall, Robert L., "Sociological Perspectives on UFO Reports," in Sagan, Carl, and Thornton Page (eds.), *UFOs—A Scientific Debate* (Ithaca, N.Y.: Cornell University Press, 1972).

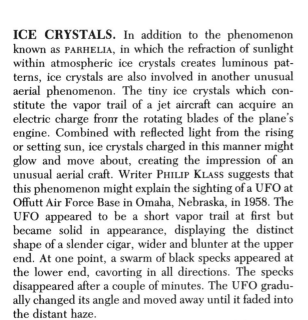

**ICE CRYSTALS.** In addition to the phenomenon known as PARHELIA, in which the refraction of sunlight within atmospheric ice crystals creates luminous patterns, ice crystals are also involved in another unusual aerial phenomenon. The tiny ice crystals which constitute the vapor trail of a jet aircraft can acquire an electric charge from the rotating blades of the plane's engine. Combined with reflected light from the rising or setting sun, ice crystals charged in this manner might glow and move about, creating the impression of an unusual aerial craft. Writer PHILIP KLASS suggests that this phenomenon might explain the sighting of a UFO at Offutt Air Force Base in Omaha, Nebraska, in 1958. The UFO appeared to be a short vapor trail at first but became solid in appearance, displaying the distinct shape of a slender cigar, wider and blunter at the upper end. At one point, a swarm of black specks appeared at the lower end, cavorting in all directions. The specks disappeared after a couple of minutes. The UFO gradually changed its angle and moved away until it faded into the distant haze.

A UFO captured on film and observed by Major Robert M. White while piloting an X–15 aircraft in 1962 was tentatively identified by officials of the NATIONAL AERONAUTICS AND SPACE ADMINISTRATION (NASA) as ice crystals flaking off the frosty surface of the research aircraft.

Bibliography: Klass, Philip J., *UFOs Identified* (New York: Random House, 1968); Sachs, Margaret, with Ernest Jahn, *Celestial Passengers—UFOs and Space Travel* (New York: Penguin Books, 1977).

**ICUFON** *see* **INTERCONTINENTAL GALACTIC SPACECRAFT (UFO) RESEARCH AND ANALYTIC NETWORK**

**ICUFON ARCHIVES,** collection of UFO photographs belonging to the INTERCONTINENTAL GALACTIC SPACECRAFT (UFO) RESEARCH AND ANALYTIC NETWORK (ICUFON).

**IDEAL'S UFO MAGAZINE,** quarterly magazine, established in 1977, with a circulation of 60,000. The four yearly issues are supplemented by an annual. The magazine is available both at newsstands and by subscription. It deals with every aspect of UFOLOGY and paranormal events related to UFOs, especially recent encounters of an unusual nature.

All articles are written by freelance writers. Writers should query first about subject matter and length of articles. Self-addressed, stamped envelopes should accompany submissions. All rights are purchased. Payment varies according to the length of the article and is made upon acceptance. Photographs are paid for only when used on covers. D.C. Thorpe is Editor. The magazine is published by Ideal Publishing Corporation, 2 Park Avenue, New York, New York 10016.

**IDENTIFIED FLYING OBJECT (IFO),** an object which, originally labeled as unidentified, has been recognized as a conventional object or a natural phenomenon. Approximately eighty-to-ninety percent of all UFOs reported are eventually classified as IFOs.

CONTACTEES sometimes refer to UFOs as IFOs because they believe them to be extraterrestrial spacecraft and therefore not "unidentified."

**IDEOPLASTY,** the act of creating real physical phenomena by the conscious or subconscious use of the psychic powers of the observer. It has been suggested that this hypothetical process might explain some UFO sightings.

**IFSB** *see* **INTERNATIONAL FLYING SAUCER BUREAU**

**IFO** *see* **IDENTIFIED FLYING OBJECT**

**ILLUSION** *see* **OPTICAL ILLUSION**

**IMJARVI, FINLAND,** location of a CLOSE ENCOUNTER OF THE THIRD KIND (CE–III) on January 7, 1970. Aarno Heinonen and Esko Viljo were skiing just outside Imjarvi when, at about 4:45 P.M., they stopped to rest. Suddenly, they heard a buzzing sound and saw a glowing red-gray CLOUD descending from the sky. When the cloud was about fifty feet off the ground, the two men could discern within it a round metallic object with a flat base. Then the buzzing sound became louder and the object continued its descent. The cloud was gradually dispersing. The object came to a stop about ten feet off the ground and the buzzing ceased. Suddenly, a beam of bright light was emitted from a short tube underneath the object. It moved over the snow, then formed a brightly illuminated circle about three feet in diameter. A red-gray mist settled over the area.

The skiers suddenly noticed a three-foot tall, thin-limbed creature who had appeared on the ground in the center of the circle of light. The strange entity was holding a black box. He aimed the opening in the box toward Heinonen. A blinding light shone from it. A thick mist came down from the craft, enveloping the area. Red, green and purple sparks were scattered over the spot where the skiers stood. Suddenly, the light beam was retracted, taking the UFONAUT with it. The mist evaporated and the object left.

Following the sighting, the two men reportedly suffered severe internal complaints which the local doctor was unable to diagnose fully.

Bibliography: Le Poer Trench, Brinsley, *Mysterious Visitors—The UFO Story* (New York: Stein and Day, 1973).

**IMSA** *see* **INSTITUT MONDIAL DES SCIENCES AVANCÉES**

**INDONESIAN UFO REGISTRY,** P.O. Box 908, Chalan Piao, Saipan, Mariana Islands CM 96950; telephone number: 6531.

The purpose of this investigative organization is to foster an interest in and promote belief in the existence of the UFO phenomena as well as to be prepared for sightings and contacts. The group holds that UFOs come from far beyond the galaxies, and that their OCCUPANTS are not planetary people as is widely speculated in many books. It believes that they are here to study the universal galactic system and to assist other civilizations through good will, peace and universal understanding. The organization finds it difficult to reach conclusions regarding local sightings because of conflict with local customs and superstition. One of its major cases involved the mysterious death of a person who allegedly shot at a "cattle-like cat" in an abandoned airfield on the island of Tinian. The island is equipped with runways from which the planes that dropped atomic bombs on the Japanese cities of Hiroshima and Nagasaki in 1945 were launched. Today, the airfield is the site of numerous UFO sightings.

This nonprofit organization was founded in 1976 by VICENTE C. CAMACHO, who serves as Director. The group has about twenty-five members who participate in field investigations, skywatches, collection of information and group discussions.

**INDUCED DREAM HYPOTHESIS,** theory that UFOs seen at very close range interfere with the normal functioning of the brain by acting on the cerebral structure known as the Locus Coeruleus. HALLUCINATIONS might be produced in which the witness would perceive a mixture of the real world and his or her inner unconscious world. Thus a witness might subconsciously embellish a UFO experience with preconditioned ideas about spaceships and extraterrestrial beings. When the effect ceases, he or she would remember the event without being able to distinguish between the reality and the dream.

Bibliography: Rifat, Claude, "Is the Locus Coeruleus, an Important Anatomical Center of the Brain, Involved in the Most Bizarre Aspects of UFO Reports? The Induced Dream Hypothesis." *UPIAR—UFO Phenomena International Annual Review* (Published by Editecs in conjunction with the Comitato Nazionale Indipendente per lo Studio dei Fenomeni Aerei Anomali in Bologna, Italy; 1977, Vol. II, No. 1).

**INFINITY NEWSLETTER,** former name of EXPLORING OTHER DIMENSIONS.

**INFO** *see* **INTERNATIONAL FORTEAN ORGANIZATION**

**INFORESPACE,** publication of SOCIETÉ BELGE D'ÉTUDE DES PHÉNOMÈES SPATIAUX (SOBEPS).

**INFORME OVNI,** Brazilian CONTACTEE newsletter also called OVNI.

**INNER EARTH HYPOTHESIS** *see* **HOLLOW EARTH HYPOTHESIS**

**INNER SPACE HYPOTHESIS,** theory that UFOs are some unknown manifestation of psychic energy.

**IN SEARCH OF ANCIENT ASTRONAUTS,** television special (NBC Television, 1973). Alan Landsburg Productions produced this adaptation of the motion picture CHARIOTS OF THE GODS? Rod Serling was narrator.

**INSECTS.** A theory presented in 1966, proposing that some UFOs are created by swarms of insects, was studied and tested in 1978 by entomologist Philip S. Callahan and physicist R. W. Mankin of the U.S. Agricultural Research Service Laboratory in Gainesville, Florida. They demonstrated that insects, which have been known to fly in swarms up to sixty-four miles long and sixteen miles wide, can trigger electrical discharges when flying beneath a storm front. Their exoskeletons serving as dielectics and their body fluids serving as electrolytes, bugs confined within laboratory-generated electric fields displayed brightly colored flares from exposed pointed surfaces such as antennae and leg joints. This fluorescent glowing phenomenon, similar to SAINT ELMO'S FIRE, can occur in a natural electric field generated by appropriate weather conditions. The predominant color would be blue because nitrogen is one of the gases involved. Bright red and green glows would appear also. A large swarm consisting of millions of glowing points would resemble a humming flying saucer which would seem to disappear as the insects escaped the electric field. Typical UFO-associated ELECTROMAGNETIC EFFECTS, such as radio and television static, could be explained in some cases by the swarms of insects moving over power lines. Callahan and Mankin have suggested that multiple sightings of UFOs near Roosevelt, Utah, between 1965 and 1968 may be attributable to an infestation of spruce budworms recorded by the U.S. Forest Service.

Bibliography: Callahan, Philip S., and R. W. Mankin, "Insects as Unidentified Flying Objects," *Applied Optics* (Washington, D.C.: Optical Society of America, November 1, 1978, Vol. 17, No. 21).

**INSOLITO,** publication of the Portuguese CENTRO DE ESTUDOS ASTRONOMICOS E DE FENÓMENOS INSOLITOS.

**INSTANT TRANSFERENCE** *see* **TELEPORTATION**

**INSTITUT MONDIAL DES SCIENCES AVANCÉES (IMSA),** Imp. Les Platanes No. 04, La Beaucaire, 83200 Toulon, France.

This organization is devoted to the investigation and research of UFOLOGY, futurology, esotericism, neo-hermeneutics of traditions and religions, archaeology, occult trends in history, radiesthesia, lost civilizations and mysterious creatures, such as BIGFOOT.

IMSA was founded by Jimmy Guieu, Christine Dequerlor, Guy Tarade, Jean H. Casgha, Eric Guerrier, Roger-Luc Mary and Alain Le Kern. The institute serves as a meeting place for individual researchers and member groups involved in multidisciplinary research. It organizes expeditions and field trips to such areas as the BERMUDA TRIANGLE, Mexico and Peru. It conducts seminars and publishes a bimonthly bulletin.

**INSTITUTO PERUANO DE RELACIONES INTERPLANETARIAS (IPRI),** Jr. Junin 402. Barranco, Lima 4, Peru; telephone number: 670681.

The purpose of this CONTACTEE organization is to investigate UFOs, to study life on other worlds, to attempt contact with extraterrestrial beings and to exchange knowledge with other investigators. The group claims to have discovered two UFO bases, an abandoned one in Cuzco and another underwater base currently in use in the Pacific Ocean near Lobos de Afuera Island.

This nonprofit organization was founded in 1955 by C. (JOSÉ) CARLOS PAZ GARCÍA, who serves as President, Gustavo Villar, Augusto Vásquez, Manuel Olórtegui and Victor Pool. Its staff consists of Vice-President Manuel Garrido, Director Félix Acosta, Secretary Sara C. de Cabanillas, Treasurer Alfredo Salinas, Librarian Raúl Flores and Spokesman Percy Cabanillas. The group has about 425 members and several field inves-

Dorsal view of a predatory stink bug giving off electrical discharges. *(Courtesy P.S. Callahan)*

tigators located throughout Peru. Investigators are separated into three teams—a UFO Committee, a Parapsychology Committee and a Science Committee. Members attend two meetings a week, during which conferences are held and lectures are given about EXTRATERRESTRIAL LIFE and UFOs. The group also organizes field trips during which skywatches are conducted and attempts are made to establish telepathic and physical contact with UFO occupants. The organization publishes a bimonthly magazine, *Mas Alla*.

**INTEGRATON,** four-story high, dome-shaped machine built by CONTACTEE GEORGE VAN TASSELL according to instructions allegedly given to him by the SPACE PEOPLE. The Integraton's purpose was to rejuvenate the elderly and prevent the aging of the young. After Van Tassell's death in 1978, the unfinished machine was purchased by the Christology Church, P.O. Box 4648, San Diego, California 92104.

**INTELLIGENTS' REPORT, THE,** publication of the NEW AGE FOUNDATION (NAF).

**INTERCONTINENTAL GALACTIC SPACECRAFT (UFO) RESEARCH AND ANALYTIC NETWORK (ICUFON),** Apartment 4G, 35–40 75th Street, Jackson Heights, New York 11372; telephone number: 212-672-7948.

This organization believes that UFOs have been identified as galactic spacecraft by the military forces of the United States and other nations. It holds that they originate from the outer solar systems of the galaxy and use our neighboring celestial bodies, such as the MOON, VENUS and MARS, as transit bases. Their earthbound operations, according to the group, have been verified by astronomers' sightings during the past one hundred years. ICUFON describes the activities of UFOs as military strategic reconnaisance and scientific exploration. The organization's goals are: 1. to establish within the United Nations an international UFO authority to assure global security and to conduct scientific research; 2. to seek contact and communication with extraterrestrial exploring forces, using military intelligence as a liaison between Earth's nations and the galactic powers. ICUFON holds that it is vital to solve the UFO problem through the full cooperation of the national defense forces, the scientific community and the civilian UFO organizations.

This nonprofit organization was founded in 1966 by COLMAN VONKEVICZKY, who serves as Director. The staff includes Walter Zabawski, Clarence W. Stackhouse, Peter Robbins, Edwin Slade, Attila VonKeviczky and Brian Levens. Continental Representatives include Karl L. Veit and Hans C. Petersen in Europe, PETER

TOMIKAWA in Asia, ELIZABETH KLARER in Africa, Earl J. Neff in North America, Francisco Han and C. (JOSÉ) CARLOS PAZ GARCÍA, in South America, and BRUCE L. CATHIE in Oceania. ICUFON is affiliated with DEUTSCHE UFO/IFO STUDIENGESELLSCHAFT (DUIST) in West Germany and with the International Get Acquainted Program in Europe (IGAPE). ICUFON is not a membership organization.

**INTERNATIONAL FLYING SAUCER BUREAU (IFSB),** formed in 1952 by Albert K. Bender, this group closed down in 1953 following alleged harrassment by the MEN IN BLACK (MIB).

**INTERNATIONAL FORTEAN ORGANIZATION (INFO),** 7317 Baltimore Avenue, College Park, Maryland 20740; telephone number: 301-779-1873.

The purpose of this organization is to continue the late CHARLES FORT'S work of collecting and cataloguing reports of all manner of strange events. FORTEANS criticize the scientific establishment because, contrary to its own philosophy, it often excludes that which it cannot accommodate within its current framework of theory. However, INFO and its members declare themselves skeptics rather than true believers in the peculiar matters in which they are interested. Their goal is to support an attitude both open-minded and critical.

This nonprofit organization was founded in 1965 by Ron and Paul Willis and is the successor to the original Fortean Society, founded in 1931. Astronomer John Carlson is President. International membership stands at 500. Information is collected from members and the worldwide press. Services available to members include a library and an annual convention known as Fortfest. The *INFO Journal* is published bimonthly and contains information on such Fortean subjects as UFOs, appearances and DISAPPEARANCES of people and objects, FAFROTSKIES, archaeological anomalies, LEVITATION, spontaneous human combustion, lake monsters, sea monsters, BIGFOOT, poltergeists, lost continents, unusual darknesses during the day and brightnesses at night, ball lightning and parapsychology. RICHARD HALL is Editor.

**INTERNATIONAL PARANORMAL BULLETIN,** former publicaton of NEDERLANDS STUDIEKRING VOOR UFOLOGIE.

**INTERNATIONAL SOCIETY FOR A COMPLETE EARTH (HOLLOW EARTH SOCIETY),** % Tawani W. Shoush, RR 1, Box 63, Houston, Missouri 65483.

This organization is run by Tawani W. Shoush, Director of its sister organization, the FLYING SAUCER—

HOLLOW EARTH SOCIETY, in Canada. The society's main mission is to launch an expedition by zeppelin to the alleged aperture at either the north or south pole and to enter the alleged inner world of the hollow Earth which is supposedly populated by a blond, blue-eyed, super race. The group claims that this expedition will confirm that Rear Admiral Richard E. Byrd did, in 1947, accidentally enter the hollow Earth. It also claims that since that time, great and powerful forces have attempted to suppress the truth from mankind. There will be world peace, according to this society, only when we are finally joined with the super race of the inner Earth.

Members and supporters of the group may purchase badges of the old Thule Society of Deutschland. Also for sale is a booklet, entitled "A Flight to the Land Beyond the North Pole," which purports to be Byrd's missing secret diary.

## INTERNATIONAL UFO BUREAU (IUFOB),
P.O. Box 441, Edmond, Oklahoma 73034; telephone number: 405-348-4225.

This investigative association has determined that ninety percent of all UFOs reported can be identified. They conclude that the remaining ten percent indicate the presence of a very advanced civilization studying Earth and its people.

The nonprofit organization was founded in 1957 by HAYDEN C. HEWES, who has served as its Director since that time. The staff includes Vice-President Dean Sterling, Deputy Director James Maney, Public Relations Officer DeWayne Critchfield, Historian and Artist Hal Crawford and Secretary Troi Lynn. Representatives are located in all fifty states of the Union and in thirty-five foreign countries. Worldwide membership stands at 2,000.

The International UFO Bureau offers no regular publication at the present time. Its erstwhile newsletter was originally published under the name *Interplanetary Intelligence Report*, renamed the *UFO Analysis Report*, and later renamed *The UFO Reporter*. Information on cases investigated by the bureau is released to the general public in articles written by Hewes and in books published by the International UFO Bureau Press.

## INTERNATIONAL UFO REGISTRY (IUFOR),
P.O. Box 3073, Munster, Indiana 46321.

In addition to its Munster office, this organization has branches in Innsbruck, Austria, and Yokohama, Japan. DENNIS HAUCK is the group's North American Director.

## INTERNATIONAL UFO REPORTER, publication of the CENTER FOR UFO STUDIES (CUFOS).

## INTERNATIONAL URD FOUNDATION, Box

454, S–101, 26 Stockholm Sweden; telephone number: 08–7673314.

The purpose of this investigative group is to identify UFOs. It believes the identity and origin of UFOs to be unsolved to date.

This nonprofit group was founded in 1975 by Sten Lindgren, who serves as President. The staff consists of Vice-President Bjarne Håkansson, Secretary Karl-Erik Fälldin, and Treasurer Haral Thuresson. Board Members are Sven-Olof Frediksson and Rabbe Fogelholm. There are thirty-one members. Foreign representatives are located in Finland, Norway and Denmark. Information is collected from a surveillance group and trained field investigators. The data is codified and put into a computer system. In 1978, the organization published *Project URD Report No. 1—Characteristics of a UFO Report File*.

## INTERPLANETARY NEWS, monthly magazine
established in 1957. Information on its circulation is classified. It is available by subscription only. The magazine deals with all spatial subjects including astronomy, science fiction, astronautics and UFOs, as well as news about books, films, radio and television programs, music and conventions.

Articles are written by staff and freelance writers. The latter should query prior to submitting manuscripts. Self-addressed, stamped envelopes should be sent with submissions. Articles should range in length from 250 to 1,000 words. Payment of one pound per 100 words for the purchase of all rights is made within three weeks of publications. The publishers pay for PHOTOGRAPHS.

The magazine is edited by Michael Parry and published by the INTERPLANETARY SPACE TRAVEL RESEARCH ASSOCIATION—UNITED KINGDOM (ISTRA), 21 Hargwyne Street, Stockwell, London SW9 9RQ, England.

## INTERPLANETARY SPACE TRAVEL RESEARCH ASSOCIATION (ISTRA)—UNITED KINGDOM, 21 Hargwyne Street, Stockwell, London SW9 9RQ; telephone number: 01-733-4814.

The purpose of this organization is to promote interest in all spatial matters at the amateur level and to consolidate worldwide organizations engaged in similar activities. The group's main areas of interest are astronomy, space research, UFOLOGY and science fiction. ISTRA holds that UFOs are exactly what their name implies but that if they should prove to be vehicles, they might originate from outside our solar system, another time zone or a PARALLEL UNIVERSE. The group has concluded that the press reacts to weird and sensational UFO reports but ignores serious study and investigation of the phenomenon.

This nonprofit association was founded in 1957 by Edward Harris, and reorganized under its current title in 1968 by MICHAEL PARRY, who serves as Honorary President. The staff consists of Vice-President Michael Roberts, Honorary Secretary Tina Woolgar, Honorary Assistant Secretary John Murphy, Honorary Treasurer Ralph Stonehouse, Honorary Research Officer Thomas O'Neill and Honorary Publicity Officer Derek Neil Mounsey. Seventy-two Branch Chairmen are located throughout the United Kingdom. Information regarding membership is classified by the organization. Members may purchase a kit consisting of a membership certificate, a handbook, an enamel badge, notepaper, envelopes, a wallet, business cards and membership identity card. Other services available include a library, meetings, lectures and film shows. Organizations from any part of the world wishing to cooperate with other groups demonstrate that desire by adding the words "Member of the ISTRA (International)" to their stationery and publications. Their letterheads are sent to the promoting organization which passes them on to the other member organizations. Small organizations benefit from combined advertising and several member groups offer various kinds of assistance such as printing, loan of equipment and help with publications. In addition to a monthly newsletter, ISTRA publishes INTERPLANETARY NEWS, ISTRA JOURNAL, an annual review named SPACE DIGEST, specialist newsletters on space, astronomy, science fiction and UFOLOGY, "Space Enthusiast" booklets on each subject and databank information on each subject.

Foreign branches: Jan Borrefelt, ISTRA-Denmark, Aagaarden 6 IMF, DK–2635-Ishoej, Denmark; Anthony Lee, ISTRA-Hong Kong, G.P.O. Box 682, Hong Kong; James Stringham 322, ISTRA-Canada, Ashland Avenue 1, Winnipeg, Manitoba, Canada R36 1L7; George Strich, ISTRA-U.S.A., 16 Burbank Avenue, Stratford, Connecticut 06497, U.S.A.; José L. Garcia Barreiro, ISTRA-Spain, Puerto de Galapagar 5, 60 Madrid 31, Spain; Michael Hervey, ISTRA-Australia, 12/12 Wolsley Street, Drummoyne, New South Wales 2047, Australia.

**INTERPLANETARY THINK-IN,** Suite D. 257 Van Buren, Monterey, California 93940; telephone number: 408-372-3437.

The purpose of this organization is to reach beings who might exist in outer space by "ESP power." The first experiment was conducted in 1978. A prepared message was sent to participants who were asked to think the text and concentrate on projecting their thoughts into outer space. Participants were located in Alaska, Hawaii, Washington, Utah, Idaho, California, Oregon, New York, New Jersey, Pennsylvania, British Columbia and Saudi Arabia.

Gene Buck, a public relations and advertising consultant, is the originator and Director of the project. He believes it is possible for millions of persons to transfer their thought waves in unison more effectively than radio waves. The first experiment elicited no reply. Buck hopes that greater news media participation will increase the impact of the "ESP power."

**INTERSTELLAR RESEARCH GROUP,** 3 Cottage Place, 420 Rifle Range Road, Towerby, 2190 Johannesburg, Republic of South Africa; telephone number: 683-2144.

This group represents CONTACT INTERNATIONAL in South Africa. It is administered by Chairperson ELIZABETH KLARER, Technical Adviser Sigfried Kiesel, Public Relations Officer Aubrey Fielding and Secretary P. F. Warther.

**INVASION HYPOTHESIS,** theory that UFOs are the reconnaissance forces of an extraterrestrial army which plans to invade Earth. One of the leading proponents of this hypothesis is retired Hungarian army major COLMAN VONKEVICZKY, Director of the INTERCONTINENTAL GALACTIC SPACECRAFT (UFO) RESEARCH AND ANALYTICAL NETWORK (ICUFON). VonKeviczky contends that the strategic military locations of many UFO sightings provide an indication of the hostile intentions of UFOs. (See map on page 378.)

**INVASION OF THE BODY SNATCHERS,** motion picture (Allied Artists, 1956). Producer: Walter Wanger; director: Don Siegel; screenplay by Daniel Mainwaring, based on the novel by Jack Finney. Cast: Kevin McCarthy, Dana Wynter, Larry Gates, Carolyn Jones, King Donovan, Ralph Dumke, Jean Willes, Virginia Christine, Tom Fadden, Beatrice Maude, Bobby Clark, Sam Peckinpah, Richard Deacon and Whit Bissell.

Pods from outer space take on the form of human beings and assimilate their human counterparts while they sleep. The hero loses his friends one by one to the extraterrestrial takeover, but finally escapes to report his story to the authorities.

**INVASION OF THE BODY SNATCHERS,** motion picture (United Artists, 1978). Producer: Robert H. Solo; director: Phil Kausman; screenplay by W. D. Richter, based on the novel by Jack Finney. Cast: Donald Sutherland, Brooke Adams, Leonard Nimoy, Veronica Cartwright and Jeff Goldblum.

This film is a remake of the 1956 Allied Artists' motion picture of the same title, and was notable for its special effects.

**INVISIBLE COLLEGE,** term used by J. ALLEN HYNEK to describe the growing number of scientists who provide discreet support to the CENTER FOR UFO STUDIES (CUFOS) and to UFO research in general.

The term originated in the seventeenth century when famous scientists in England held private meetings to exchange views and to discuss the results of their experiments. The incorporation of the Royal Society in 1662 gave them legitimate international recognition.

**INVISIBLE CRITTERS** *see* **CONSTABLE, TREVOR JAMES**

**IPRI** *see* **INSTITUTO PERUANO DE RELACIONES INTERPLANETARIAS**

**IRISH UFO NEWS,** publication of IRISH UFO RESEARCH CENTRE (IUFORC).

**IRISH UFO RESEARCH CENTRE (IUFORC),** 205 Dunluce Avenue, Belfast BT9 7AX, Northern Ireland; telephone number: 662386.

The purpose of this organization is to coordinate investigative work and to provide services to its members. The group has no collective belief regarding the identity and origin of UFOs.

This nonprofit organization was founded in 1974 by Miles Johnston and John Hind. Johnston serves as Chairman, and David Patterson is in charge of Public Relations. The remainder of the staff includes Hind, Ken Patterson, Gary Laird and Seamus McConnell. The group has sixty-eight members and a ten-person investigative team, based in Belfast. Associated teams are located in Derry and Dublin. A hotline service is available to the public. Benefits available to members include meetings, publications and an extensive research library. IRISH UFO NEWS is published quarterly and deals with UFOLOGY and related subjects. The latter includes articles of a scientific nature on Psi phenomena, space flight, COMMUNICATION WITH EXTRATERRESTRIAL INTELLIGENCE (CETI) and mythology, as well as articles of a nonscientific nature on speculation, philosophy, fiction and so forth.

**IRMANDADE COSMICA CRUZ DO SUL— GRUPO DE PESQUISA E DIVULGACAO SOBRE NAVEXOLOGIA,** Caixa Postal 72, 94.000 Gravatay, Rio Grande do Sul, Brazil.

This organization holds that UFOs are spaceships from other PLANETS within our solar system and from other solar systems both within our universe and from other universes. It believes that extraterrestrials utilize subterranean and submarine bases here on Earth. The group has created the word *navex* to represent *nave*

*extraterrestre* (extraterrestrial spaceship) and the term *navexologia* (navexology) to denote the study of spaceships and extraterrestrial civilizations.

The organization was founded in 1972 by J. Victor Soares, who serves as President. It publishes the *Boletim Informativo*.

**ISAKOWER PHENOMENON,** syndrome representing an unusual variation of the HYPNAGOGIC state. Documented in 1938 by Otto Isakower, the phenomenon involves the visual perception, usually just prior to sleep, of an amorphous or round mass which swells to enormous size as it approaches the subject, then shrinks to nothing as it recedes. This experience, which has been compared to UFO experiences, was defined by Isakower as an early memory of the approaching and receding mother's breast.

Bibliography: Grinspoon, Lester, and Alan D. Persky, "Psychiatry and UFO Reports," in Sagan, Carl, and Thornton Page (eds.), *UFOs—A Scientific Debate* (Ithaca, N.Y.: Cornell University Press, 1972).

**ISTRA** *see* **INTERPLANETARY SPACE TRAVEL RESEARCH ASSOCIATION—UNITED KINGDOM**

**ISTRA JOURNAL,** quarterly publication established in 1968. Information on its circulation is classified by the publishers. It is available by subscription only. The magazine deals with all spatial subjects including astronomy, space travel, UFOs and science fiction, as well as reports on the activities of the INTERPLANETARY SPACE TRAVEL RESEARCH ASSOCIATION (ISTRA).

Articles by freelance writers are used occasionally. Submissions should be accompanied by a self-addressed, stamped envelope. Articles should range in length from 500 to 1,000 words, and should deal with general news on the subjects covered. Payment of one pound per 100 words for all rights is made upon acceptance. The publishers pay for photographs.

The journal is edited by Michael Roberts, and published by ISTRA, 21 Hargwyne Street, Stockwell, London SW9 9RQ, England.

**ITALY.** UFOs are referred to in Italy by the English term UFO (pronounced "oo-foe") and less frequently by the Spanish and French name OVNI, which in Italian stands for "oggetto volante non identificato." Flying saucers are referred to as "dischi volanti."

UFO research in Italy has been somewhat hampered by the constant merging, disbanding and reforming of the various organizations. However, one group which has endured throughout the years is the CENTRO

The famous Monguzzi photograph allegedly taken in the Italian Alps and exposed by the Centro Ufologico Nazionale as a hoax. The flying saucer and its "occupant" were miniature models. *(Courtesy ICUFON/A. Baguhn)*

UFOLOGICO NAZIONALE (CUN), formerly known as the Centro UFOlogico Unico.

Several magazines exist in Italy which deal with UFOs and related phenomena. The major ones are GLI ARCANI, CLYPEUS, GIORNALE DEI MISTERI and a new but scholarly publication called UFO PHENOMENA, INTERNATIONAL ANNUAL REVIEW (UPIAR).

Italy's capital, ROME, was the location of a well-known multiple witness sighting in 1954. In late 1978, a UFO WAVE occurred in Italy. Witnesses throughout the country observed cigar-shaped objects and spheres and in some cases took PHOTOGRAPHS of the UFOs.

**ITF,** acronym for *Instant transference*, also referred to as TELEPORTATION.

**IUFOB** *see* **INTERNATIONAL UFO BUREAU**

**IUFOR** *see* **INTERNATIONAL UFO REGISTRY**

**IUFORC** *see* **IRISH UFO RESEARCH CENTRE**

**IZZO, FRANCESCO,** *see* **COMITATO NAZIONALE INDIPENDENTE PER LO STUDIO DEI FENOMENI AEREI ANOMALI (CNIFAA)**

## JACK O' LANTERN *see* SWAMP GAS

**JACKS, MASTON,** UNITED STATES AIR FORCE (USAF) major who served as the Pentagon UFO spokesman from the summer of 1963 until December 17, 1969.

**JACOB,** Biblical character who had a vision of ANGELS ascending and descending a ladder set up between Earth and heaven. Some UFOLOGISTS believe Jacob may have observed UFONAUTS climbing up and down the boarding ladder of a large flying saucer.

DONALD MENZEL has suggested that a full-scale display of the AURORA BOREALIS may have given the impression of looking through a large, hollow cylinder resembling a ladder. The rapid movement of the light pattern might have created the illusion of entities moving up and down.

Bibliography: Menzel, Donald H., "UFOs—The Modern Myth," in Sagan, Carl, and Thornton Page (eds.), *UFOs—A Scientific Debate* (Ithaca, N.Y.: Cornell University Press, 1972).

**JAHN, ERNEST THOMAS** (b. April 13, 1936, Staten Island, New York), communications specialist and field investigator for the NATIONAL INVESTIGATIONS COMMITTEE ON AERIAL PHENOMENA (NICAP).

Jahn's interest in UFOs began when he joined the UNITED STATES AIR FORCE (USAF) in 1955. He worked in the radar and communications center, where he encountered first-hand hard evidence of UFOs on the RADAR screen. During his four years' service, he was involved in a dozen cases that were considered unexplainable. Official forms were completed and sent to a base at Colorado Springs. However, the official reports that followed did not seem to bear out the initial accounts by the original witnesses, all of whom were well-trained, intelligent individuals, not likely to jeopardize their military careers by making false and unfounded allegations. Jahn is frustrated that he has never had a visual sighting of a UFO. What keeps him involved and interested are the facts that there are so many sound cases with reliable witnesses, that interest in the phenomenon continues to grow, and that, as in any other scientific venture, simply because one cannot find the answers immediately is no reason to give up on the whole project.

Jahn attended the Staten Island Community College and the University of Maryland Air Force Education Program.

Jahn served in the Air Force from 1955 to 1959 as a radar and radio specialist. He trained and worked in electronic counter-measure techniques (the jamming of radar and radio equipment) and Sage Equipment (semi-automatic ground environmental radar), which was used in testing the Bomarc Guided Missile System. While overseas, he worked as part of a three-man intelligence team. From 1961 to 1966, Jahn was a New York City police officer. Since 1966, he has worked as a communications specialist in the Technical Services Division of the New York Telephone Company.

Jahn is a member of the National Space Institute (NSI), the Smithsonian Institution (Scientific Event Alert Network) and the Communications Workers of America. He served as a Technical Advisor on the motion picture THE FORCE BEYOND. He received a NICAP Certificate of appreciation in 1976, and a Citation of Merit from the Muscular Dystrophy Association of America in 1978.

Jahn is coauthor, with Margaret Sachs, of *Celestial Passengers—UFOs and Space Travel* (New York: Penguin Books, 1977).

April 3, 1974: A disk-shaped craft over the Kenmon Bridge, between Moji and Shimonosheki in Japan, photographed by a high school sophomore. *(ICUFON/P. Tomikawa)*

**JAMES, TREVOR,** *see* **CONSTABLE, TREVOR JAMES**

**JANAP-146** *see* **JOINT ARMY-NAVY-AIR FORCE PUBLICATION 146**

**JAPAN.** UFO reports are frequent in Japan and are investigated and documented by a number of organizations, of which the best-known are the MODERN SPACE FLIGHT ASSOCIATION (MSFA), the JAPAN FLYING SAUCER ASSOCIATION (JFSA), the JAPAN SPACE PHENOMENA SOCIETY (JSPS), the JAPAN SPACE UNIDENTIFIED FLYING OBJECT SOCIETY and the JAPAN UFO RESEARCH ASSOCIATION (JUFORA).

Author JUN-ICHI TAKANASHI, Founder and Chairman of MSFA, represents the AERIAL PHENOMENA RESEARCH ORGANIZATION (APRO) and the MUTUAL UFO NETWORK (MUFON) in Japan and exchanges information with several foreign groups.

A UFO case which received international publicity was the multiple witness sighting of a disk-shaped object at AKITA AIRPORT in 1975.

**JAPAN FLYING SAUCER ASSOCIATION (JFSA),** 2–19–18 Higashi-Gotanda, Shinagawa-ku, Tokyo, Japan.

Founded in 1955, JFSA was an active research group until 1960, when it became a one-man organization run by Kin-ichi Arai. The society's main purpose is to disseminate information to the news media and the public. Public lectures are held and exhibition materials are available. Arai's public relations activities are largely responsible for widespread knowledge about UFOs in Japan.

Thirty-two issues of the magazine *Uchiki* (Spacecraft) were published during the society's more active days.

**JAPAN SPACE PHENOMENA SOCIETY (JSPS),** 5–2 Kamiyama-cho, Shibuya-ku, Tokyo, Japan.

JSPS, founded in 1971, is presided over by Shinichiro Namiki. It represents a conglomeration of several small groups consisting largely of university students and specialists in various research fields. The organization is dedicated to the scientific investigation of UFOs. Its regular publications are *Unidentified Flying Objects—Information and Studies* and *JSPS's UFO Information*.

## JAPAN SPACE UNIDENTIFIED FLYING OBJECT SOCIETY, Kaguchi-ura, Takanabe-cho, Koyu-gun, Miyazaki Prefecture, Japan.

This research society was found in 1974 by Yukio Nami. It is dedicated to the scientific investigation of UFOs and related subjects, including psychic phenomena. It publishes a newsletter, entitled *UFO*.

## JAPAN UFO RESEARCH ASSOCIATION (JUFORA), 142–161 Ioroi Kande-cho, Tarumi-ku, Kobe, Japan.

Established in 1965 as a commercial enterprise by Tomezo Hirata, this organization pursues a policy of scientific investigation of the UFO phenomenon. The group publishes a newsletter, entitled *JUFORA*.

## JEFFERS, JOAN L. (address: 112 Maplewood Avenue, Bradford, Pennsylvania 16701; telephone number: 814-368-8558), UFO researcher.

Jeffers has had an interest in the UFO phenomenon since 1943 when, at the age of 11, she sighted a strange flying object. The reality of UFOs was confirmed to her after a close encounter in 1967. She tries to keep an open mind about the various theories applied to UFOLOGY since she believes this produces greater objectivity in investigation. However, she would like to think that UFONAUTS are anthropologists from the future, doing their field-work via time machines, traveling into the past to do their research. This she considers an optimistic view, since it would mean the world survives and earthlings continue to make progress.

Jeffers graduated from the Millard Fillmore School of Nursing in Buffalo, New York, in 1953. After twenty years of experience in the nursing field, during which her last position was that of a Coronary Care nurse, she returned to college. She graduated *magna cum laude* from the University of Pittsburgh in 1976, with a B.S. in Psychology. She received a second major with departmental honors in Anthropology. From 1976 to 1978, she was Director of the Pennsylvania Center for UFO Research. Still affiliated with the Center, she works as an independent researcher. Although she has an investigative interest in all aspects of the phenomenon, her research has been mainly concerned with cases involving a psychic component.

**JELLYFISH UFO,** term denoting a UFO which has or temporarily assumes the shape of a jellyfish. A classic case involving a jellyfish UFO occurred in Petrozavodsk, Russia, in 1977. The story was released by TASS, the official Soviet news agency, and was subsequently picked up by news services around the world. Although news reports quoted the date of the incident as September 22, science writer JAMES OBERG gives the date as September 20. The sighting occurred at about 4:00 A.M. A huge "STAR" suddenly appeared in the night sky over Petrozavodsk about 130 miles from the Finnish border. It moved slowly over the city then spread out in the sky like an enormous jellyfish. It hovered for about twelve minutes, emitting numerous thin light rays. The

Jellyfish UFO seen at Petrozavodsk in the Soviet Union on September 22, 1977. *(Courtesy ICUFON/A. Baguhn)*

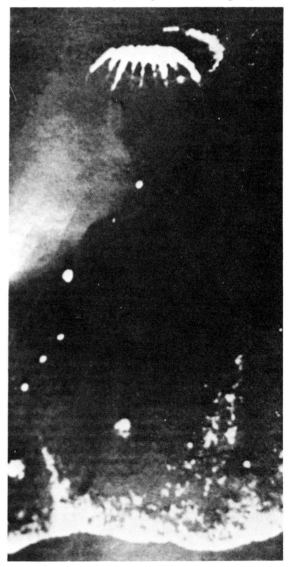

mass of light then turned into a bright semi-circle and resumed its journey toward Lake Onega. Once above the horizon, it appeared as a red semi-circular light glowing within a gray cloud mass. The UFO was observed across the border in Finland and as far away as Helsinki.

Local meteorologists and astronomers who witnessed the phenomenon were unable to explain it. Soviet authorities claimed that there were no technical experiments being conducted at the time. The possibility of its being a MIRAGE was dismissed because of the high number of people who saw and described the light in the same way.

Oberg has attributed the sighting to a secret spy SATELLITE launched at 3:58 A.M. on September 20, 1977, from a space satellite launch center situated near the Russian town of Plesetsk. The existence of this supposedly secret launch center is well-known to space experts in the West and it is the origin of half the world's space launches. Oberg conjectures that the story was released because news censors failed to recognize the initial accounts as descriptions of a satellite launching. Subsequently, Soviet authorities issued two different statements in an attempt to conceal the true nature of the incident. At first, they explained the sighting as a satellite falling from orbit and burning up in the atmosphere. Later, in an article in the journal *Aviatsiya I Kosmonavtika,* scientist M. Dimitriyev attributed the phenomenon to glowing smog.

Bibliography: Oberg, James, "Flight of the Jellyfish UFO," *True Flying Saucers and UFOs Quarterly* (New York: Histrionics Publishing Company No. 10, Summer 1978).

**JFSA** *see* **JAPAN FLYING SAUCER ASSOCIATION**

**JOINT ARMY-NAVY-AIR FORCE PUBLICATION (JANAP) 146,** a Joint Chiefs of Staff directive, entitled Communications Instructions for Reporting Vital Intelligence Sightings (CIRVIS). Established in December 1953, CIRVIS details the procedures to be followed in the filing of reports from pilots and crews of military aircraft and surface vessels regarding information of vital importance to the security of the United States. Paragraph 201 of JANAP-146 includes unidentified flying objects under information to be reported. Such reports require immediate transmission to the Aerospace Defense Command, the Secretary of Defense and the nearest military command. The directive applies also to civilian pilots who report UFOs through official channels.

Paragraph 210 of JANAP-146 prohibits the unauthorized transmission or revelation of the contents of CIRVIS reports. Violation of this restriction is a crime punishable under the laws of the Espionage Act. Since these restrictions apply to all persons aware of the contents or existence of a CIRVIS report, military pilots, as well as commercial airline pilots who have filed CIRVIS reports, are subject to long jail sentences and/or heavy fines if they discuss their UFO sightings publicly.

Bibliography: Tacker, Lawrence, J., *Flying Saucers and the U.S. Air Force* (Princeton, N.J.: D. Van Nostrand Company, 1960).

**JONAH,** Biblical character reportedly swallowed by a great whale and disgorged three days later, alive and well, on a beach. Some UFOLOGISTS have hypothesized that Jonah was taken aboard a cigar-shaped UNIDENTIFIED SUBMARINE OBJECT which was either the amphibious flying craft of extraterrestrial visitors or the vessel of a submarine civilization.

Bibliography: Friedrich, George, *UFO or God?* (New York: Carlton Press, 1975).

**JORNAL SATURNO,** former name of *Saturno,* publication of the GRUPO DE ESTUDOS A PESQUISAS ULTRATERRENOS "MARCUS DE ORION" (GEPU).

**JOURNAL OF BORDERLAND RESEARCH,** newsletter of the BORDERLAND SCIENCES RESEARCH FOUNDATION.

**JSPS** *see* **JAPAN SPACE PHENOMENA SOCIETY**

**JUFORA** *see* **JAPAN UFO RESEARCH ASSOCIATION**

**JUNE BUG EPIDEMIC** *see* **HYSTERICAL CONTAGION**

**JUNG, CARL GUSTAV** (1875–1961), Swiss psychologist and psychiatrist. Jung wrote a book entitled *Flying Saucers: A Modern Myth of Things Seen in the Sky* (New York: Harcourt, Brace and Company, 1958) in which he speculated that UFOs are psychic projections resulting from mankind's need to believe in the existence of a higher power in a world pervaded by anxiety and the threat of nuclear annihilation. A member of the NATIONAL INVESTIGATIONS COMMITTEE ON AERIAL PHENOMENA (NICAP), Jung wrote to the organization just before his death in 1961 stating that he had reached the conclusion that UFOs did appear to be spaceships.

**JUST CAUSE,** former newsletter of CITIZENS AGAINST UFO SECRECY (CAUS).

**KANON, GERGORY M.** (b. July 2, 1949, Hastings, Nebraska), Field Investigator for the AERIAL PHENOMENA RESEARCH ORGANIZATION (APRO).

Kanon believes UFOs might be spaceships from another world, or conveyances for time travelers, or simply an unknown atmospheric phenomenon. He thinks there is little chance the mystery will be solved by man but rather that the solution will reveal itself when the time is right.

Kanon received his B.A. in Political Science from the University of Arizona. Since 1975, he has been author of a weekly syndicated column, "The Unknown," which appears in newspapers in the United States and Canada. He is currently News Editor of *The Southwest Star* in Stafford, Texas.

Kanon is a former Provincial Director in Nova Scotia, Canada, for the MUTUAL UFO NETWORK (MUFON), and is currently a Field Investigator for APRO and a member of the SOCIETY FOR THE INVESTIGATION OF THE UNEXPLAINED (SITU).

**KARELIA, SOVIET UNION,** location where the apparent LANDING MARK of a UFO was discovered in February 1961. Forester Vasili Bradski found the mysterious crater on the bank of a frozen lake. He knew that it had not been there two days previously. The hole was about 100 feet long, fifty feet wide and ten feet deep. The base was remarkably smooth and narrower than the top. Around the edge were lumps of grass and soil. However, there was no trace of the soil which had been excavated from the trench.

Six investigators arrived the following day from Leningrad. On the bank of the lake, they found mysterious, crumbling black pellets which resembled buckwheat grains. The ice covering the lake had been broken near the crater. Loose pieces of broken ice were hauled to the bank. Their submerged bases were found to be green. Divers discovered a 330-foot strip where the soil had been displaced across the floor of the lake. Another 330-foot gully was found in the center of the lake. It appeared as if something had landed near the lake, sliding across the ground and down under the water, ploughing up the soil as it did so. Yet, the object which had left these apparent skid marks was nowhere to be found. Whatever it was had apparently resumed its flight. The investigators rejected the possibility that the trenches had been caused by ball lightning because there was no evidence of scorching. The case was studied at Leningrad University under Professor Vsevolod Charmov. Samples of ice, water and soil revealed nothing unusual, although the green coloration of parts of the ice could not be explained. The black pellets which had been found on the bank of the lake were submitted to microscopic examination. They were found to have a metallic sheen which supposedly does not occur in any known organic material. When the pellets would not dissolve in acid, chemists concluded they were an inorganic substance, probably not of natural origin. The case has never been solved. Some UFOLOGISTS have presumed that an intelligently-controlled craft, experiencing some mechanical difficulty, crashed by the lake but managed to take off again after being submerged.

Bibliography: Hobana, Ion, and Julien Weverbergh, *UFOs from Behind the Iron Curtain* (New York: Bantam Books, 1972).

**KARSLEIGH, ZELRUN WALLACE** (b. February 26, 1891, Kansas City, Missouri; address: 3620 S.E. 84th Avenue, Portland, Oregon 97266; telephone number: 503-775-2140), CONTACTEE, Cofounder and Secretary-Treasurer of the UNIVERSARIUN FOUNDATION.

Karsleigh believes UFOs come from other PLANETS in our solar system and beyond, and also from the inner Earth. He himself has had many sightings and one close encounter at a GIANT ROCK CONVENTION. He says that although he has never been taken for a ride in a flying saucer, he welcomes the OCCUPANTS' interest in our affairs and will welcome the day when they will evacuate "us" from this rat race.

Karsleigh studied Electrical Engineering for three years at the University of Kansas. He took an electronics course at Marquette University and holds several diplomas from radio and electronics schools. He received a Doctorate of Sacred Philosophy from the World University.

Karsleigh worked as an Instructor at the Central Radio School in Kansas City, Missouri, and subsequently as a Radio and Electronics Instructor at Multnomah College in Portland, Oregon. He is a retired member of the International Brotherhood of Electrical Workers Local 48 in Portland.

Karsleigh is a Trustee of the World University Roundtable in Tucson, Arizona. In addition to being Cofounder and Secretary-Treasurer of the Universarium Foundation, he is considered by the organization to be its "primary channel." Karsleigh is also Editor of the group's magazine, *The Voice of Universarius*.

## KEEL, JOHN (b. March 25, 1930), author and lecturer who has been writing about UFOs since 1945.

He holds that UFOs are the manifestation of intelligences which intentionally deceive mankind and interfere in human affairs. The entities, which he refers to as ultraterrestrials (UTs), or ELEMENTALS, supposedly manifest themselves in whatever form is appropriate for the level of culture or technology achieved by the human race. Hence, they appeared as FAIRIES in the Middle Ages, and now appear as extraterrestrial spacecraft.

Keel is author of numerous magazine articles and several books, including: *Why UFOs?* (New York: Manor Books, 1970); *Strange Creatures from Time and Space* (New York: Fawcett Books, 1970); *UFOs: Operation Trojan Horse* (New York: G. P. Putnam's Sons, 1970); *Our Haunted Planet* (New York: Fawcett Books, 1971); *Jadoo* (New York: Pyramid Publications, 1972), and *The Mothman Prophecies* (New York: New American Library, 1976).

## KELLY-HOPKINSVILLE, KENTUCKY, location of a classic CLOSE ENCOUNTER OF THE THIRD KIND (CE–III).

At about 7:00 P.M. on August 21, 1955, teenager Billy Ray Sutton went outside the family farmhouse to get a drink from the well. When he returned, he announced

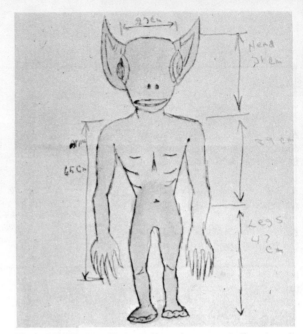

The Kelly-Hopkinsville creature drawn according to witnesses' descriptions. *(Courtesy Donn Davison)*

that he had seen a large bright object land about a city block away. Little attention was given to his statement until almost an hour later when a barking dog alerted the family to the approach of a glowing creature, less than four feet tall with long arms raised over its round head. When it was about twenty feet from them, two of the men fired at it. The little man somersaulted and hurried away into the darkness. When a second creature appeared at the window, a shot was fired at it right through the screen. The entity seemed to have been hit and disappeared. As one of the men led the way through the door to see if the creature was dead, a clawlike hand reached down at him from the roof. Another entity was seen on a tree branch. The men fired at both creatures. The bullets seemed to ricochet off them as if they were covered in nickel-plated armor. The creature in the tree floated to the ground, then scuttled away. Soon the eight adults and three children had locked themselves inside the house. From time to time, the entities appeared at the windows. They were impervious to bullets. However, their glowing round yellow eyes seemed sensitive to the house lights and the Suttons concluded that this was what prevented the creatures from coming toward the doors. Since no more than two entities were ever seen at one time, it was not clear exactly how many there were.

At about 11:00 P.M., the frightened family abandoned the house and drove in panic to the Hopkinsville police station. State, county and city police drove to the farmhouse. On the way, one of the officers saw what he later described as a strange shower of METEORS coming from the direction of the Sutton homestead. As he looked out of the car, two passed overhead with a loud swishing sound. At the farmhouse, the police could find no sign of the humanoids or a landed craft, although it was evident that a shootout had occurred.

The incident was investigated by the UNITED STATES AIR FORCE (USAF), local authorities, journalists and civilian UFO investigators. It was classified as unidentified by PROJECT BLUE BOOK.

Bibliography: Hynek, J. Allen, *The UFO Experience: A Scientific Inquiry* (Chicago: Henry Regnery Company, 1972).

**KENT UFO NEWS BULLETIN,** former name of the UNEXPLAINED PHENOMENA NEWS BULLETIN.

**KEYHOE, DONALD E.** (b. June 20, 1897, Ottumwa, Iowa), author and former Director of the NATIONAL INVESTIGATIONS COMMITTEE ON AERIAL PHENOMENA (NICAP).

A pioneer in the field, Keyhoe became interested in UFOLOGY in 1949. One of the leading proponents of the EXTRATERRESTRIAL HYPOTHESIS (ETH), the retired Marine Corps Major is noted for his attacks against the UNITED STATES AIR FORCE (USAF) and other government agencies for their alleged COVER-UP and debunking of UFO information.

Keyhoe is a graduate of the U.S. Naval Academy, the Marine Corps Officers School and the Naval Aviation Training Station in Pensacola, Florida. After serving as a Marine aircraft and BALLOON pilot, he was injured in a night flight at Guam. Subsequently, he served as Chief of Information for the Department of Commerce. He was Manager of the Admiral Byrd North Pole plane tour of the United States and Aide to Charles Lindbergh on his flying tour of the United States. During World War II, he served with the Naval Aviation Training Division.

Keyhoe served as NICAP's director from 1957 to 1969. He has been a guest on several hundred television and radio programs.

Keyhoe is the author of numerous magazine articles and two books dealing with aviation and espionage. He is the author of six UFO books: *The Flying Saucers Are Real* (New York: Fawcett Publications, 1950); *Flying Saucers from Outer Space* (New York: Henry Holt, 1953); *The Flying Saucer Conspiracy* (New York: Henry Holt, 1955); *Flying Saucers: Top Secret* (New York: G. P. Putnam's Sons, 1960); and *Aliens from Space* (Garden City, N.Y.: Doubleday and Company, 1973). He is editor, with Gordon I. R. Lore, of *Strange Effects from UFOs* (Washington, D.C.: National Investigations Committee on Aerial Phenomena, 1969).

**KING, GEORGE** (b. January 23, 1919, Wellington, England; address: 6202 Afton Place, Hollywood, California 90028 or 757 Fulham Road, London SW6 5UU, England), CONTACTEE, Founder and President of the AETHERIUS SOCIETY.

In 1954, after ten years of studying yoga and spiritual philosophy, George King claims to have heard a voice commanding him, "Prepare yourself! You are to become the voice of Interplanetary Parliament." Eight days later, an Indian yogi taught him how to achieve TELEPATHIC contact with a being from VENUS, who was given the pseudonym Aetherius. King received many communications, which he published in a newsletter. His following grew and, in 1956, he founded the Aetherius Society.

King has been interviewed on radio and television in several countries. He received his Doctorate of Divinity from the International Evangelism Crusades, and a Doctorate in Philosophy from Tennessee Christian University in 1978. He was named "Outstanding Educator of the Year for 1977" by the Children's Education Society of Claremont College, California, for his work in

Donald Keyhoe. *(United Press International Photo)*

George King.

the field of spiritual healing. He is a governor and member of the Royal National Lifeboat Institution of Great Britain.

His twenty-nine works, published by the Aetherius Society, include *The Nine Freedoms, You Are Responsible, The Twelve Blessings, Contact Your Higher Self Through Yoga* and *You, Too, Can Heal*.

**KITES.** Made in a variety of shapes and capable of attaining great altitude, kites have frequently been reported as UFOs. HOAXES have been perpetrated by attaching small flashlights and flares to kites. Checking weather bureau records for wind direction can be of help in determining whether or not a UFO may be explained as a kite.

**KLARER, ELIZABETH MARGERY** (b. July 1, 1910, Mooi River, Natal, South Africa; address: 3 Cottage Place, 420 Rifle Range Road, Towerby, Johannesburg 2190, Republic of South Africa; telephone number: 683-2144), CONTACTEE.

Klarer says that although she grew up on Earth, she feels herself to be an alien. She claims to have encountered a spaceship and its two-man crew numerous times between 1954 and 1963. She allegedly accompanied them on a trip to their home PLANET in the solar system of Proxima Centauri. During her four-month stay there, she supposedly gave birth to a son, whose father was an extraterrestrial.

In 1924, Klarer studied at the Trinity College of Music and the Royal Drawing Society in London. From 1925 to 1927, she studied art and music in Florence, Italy. From 1928 to 1932, she attended Cambridge University and received a diploma in Meteorology. She studied and taught pianoforte from 1934 to 1936. From 1937 to 1939, she was engaged in weather research and the interpretation of METEOROLOGICAL PHENOMENA. During this period, she also piloted light aircraft at the DeHavilland Experimental Aircraft Establishment in Hertfordshire, England. From 1940 to 1945, she served in the South African Air Force, assigned to Royal Air Force Intelligence. Since 1946, she reportedly has been engaged in research into the effects of propulsion systems in the atmosphere and the reporting of UFO sightings to the South African Air Force.

Klarer has received numerous awards in the fields of music, art, flying and equestrian performance.

Klarer is National Chairman of the South African branch of the INTERSTELLAR RESEARCH GROUP and is the South African representative of the INTERCONTINENTAL GALACTIC SPACECRAFT (UFO) RESEARCH AND ANALYTIC NETWORK (ICUFON). She was a guest speaker at the 1975 Eleventh International UFO Congress in Wiesbaden, Germany. She is author of *Jenseits der Lichtmauer* (Wiesbaden, Germany: Ventla-Verlag, 1977).

**KLASS, PHILIP J.** (b. November 8, 1919, Des Moines, Iowa; address: 560 "N" Street Southwest, Washington, D.C. 20024; telephone number: 202-554-5901), Technical Journalist and Chairman of the UFO Subcommittee of the COMMITTEE FOR THE SCIENTIFIC INVESTIGATION OF CLAIMS OF THE PARANORMAL (CSICP).

As the nation's leading UFO skeptic, Klass has been called the "Sherlock Holmes of UFOLOGY." After more than twelve years of investigating famous UFO reports, he has yet to find one that he considers to be even weakly suggestive of extraterrestrial visitors. He believes that all UFO reports have prosaic/terrestrial explanations. Klass has challenged UFO believers "to put their money where their mouths are" with what has come to be known as his "ten-thousand-dollar offer." Parties who wish to enter into a signed agreement with Klass must pay him $100 each year up to a maximum of $1,000 or until adequate evidence is supplied proving that extraterrestrial visitation has occurred during this century. Within thirty days of the provisions of such proof, Klass will pay $10,000 to each signatory of the agreement. He will accept as proof any crashed spacecraft or other evidence which the U.S. NATIONAL ACADEMY OF SCIENCES (NAS) announces to be affirmation of visitations by extraterrestrial intelligences, or the appearance before the National Assembly of the UNITED NATIONS or on a national television program of an extraterrestrial visitor born on another PLANET. Klass's obligations to pay $10,000 remain in force until the death of either one of the two parties to the agreement. Fewer than a dozen UFOLOGISTS have signed such an

UFO photographed by Elizabeth Klarer in 1956. *(Courtesy ICUFON/E. Klarer)*

Philip Klass.

agreement, and only one has kept up his annual payments. In addition, Klass has offered to buy back all copies of his book, *UFOs Explained,* if any evidence of extraterrestrial visitors is found that meets the conditions specified in his ten-thousand-dollar offer.

Klass received his B.S. in Electrical Engineering from Iowa State University in 1941. He worked as an Engineer for General Electric from 1941 to 1952. Since 1952, he has served as the Senior Avionics Editor for *Aviation Week & Space Technology* magazine.

In 1973, Klass was named a Fellow of the Institute of Electrical and Electronics Engineers in recognition of his technical writing. He also is a member of the Aviation/Space Writer's Association, the National Press Club, and the AMERICAN ASSOCIATION FOR THE ADVANCEMENT OF SCIENCE (AAAS). He is a Founding Fellow of the Committee for the Scientific Investigation of Claims of the Paranormal, and Chairman of its UFO Subcommittee. He received the Aviation/Space Writers award for the best book on space (*UFOs Explained*) in 1974.

Klass is author of *UFOs Identified* (New York: Random House, 1968); *Secret Sentries in Space* (New York: Random House, 1971); and *UFOs Explained* (New York: Random House, 1974).

**KONTAKT-BERICHTE,** nonprofit German CONTACTEE magazine which is published ten times a year. It originally contained communications allegedly received by a German contactee from UFONAUTS from the PLANET Korendor. It now contains reports found in newspapers and magazines and information from various contactees. Publisher and Editor Ursula Jahnke claims that all stories published in the magazine are previously examined by Rosicrucians, members of The Bridge to Freedom or members of parapsychological associations.

The magazine's mailing address is: Postfach 200 432, D-40000 Düsseldorf 1, West Germany.

**KON-TIKI,** raft in which Norwegian biologist Thor Heyerdahl and five companions sailed across the Pacific Ocean in 1947 to demonstrate the possibility that ancient people from America could have colonized Polynesia. During the journey, Heyerdahl observed balls of light three feet and more in diameter in the ocean, flashing at irregular intervals like electric lights turned on for a moment. Some UFOLOGISTS have placed these lights in the category of UNIDENTIFIED SUBMARINE OBJECTS.

Bibliography: Heyerdahl, Thor, *Kon-Tiki* (Chicago: Rand McNally & Company, 1950).

**KRAUT FIREBALLS** *see* **FOO FIGHTERS**

**KROEKER, KENNETH J.,** *see* **PROJECT SUM (SOLVING UFO MYSTERIES) UFO RESEARCH**

**KRUPTOS,** French magazine established in 1975. It is available by subscription only. The range of subjects covered includes UFOLOGY and CONTACTEES, UFOs and symbolism, the astronautic gods of prehistory, ancient gods and contactees, ancient monuments and UFOs, time travel and parapsychology.

Hervé Laronde is Editor. The magazine is published by Laronde and a group called S.E.I.P.P. The mailing address is Boîte Postale No 114, 69643 Caluire Cedex, France.

**KUGELBLITZ** *see* **PLASMA**

**KULKULCAN** *see* **QUETZALCOATL**

**KUNINGAS, TAPANI,** *see* **SUOMEN UFOTUTKIJAT RY**

**KUWAIT.** The first UFO FLAP in Kuwait took place in November 1978. Until that time, the small oil-rich Arab emirate had not produced a single UFO report, according to Security Chief Brigadier Muhammad Al-Hamad. The highlight of the month's aerial activity occurred at Umm Al-Aish in northern Kuwait on November 10. Seven technicians, including an American, employed at the local oil pumping station, saw a cylindrical object larger than a Boeing 747 jumbo jet, with a dome and flashing red lights. As the UFO landed silently, the oil pumps stopped working. The technicians, frozen with horror, did not dare approach. After seven minutes, the UFO took off silently, without leaving any traces. The pumps resumed their activities. It was later revealed that telecommunications between Kuwait and the outside world had been interrupted for the duration of the sighting. Within two weeks of the Umm Al-Aish encounter, Minister of State Abdul Aziz Hussein announced the formation of a government-appointed UFO investigative committee made up of scientists, civil aviation officials and Interior Ministry representatives.

LABORATORY OF INSTRUMENTED UFO RESEARCH *see* PROJECT STARLIGHT INTERNATIONAL (PSI)

LADY OF FÁTIMA *see* FÁTIMA, PORTUGAL

LAKENHEATH, ENGLAND, *see* BENTWATERS AND LAKENHEATH, ENGLAND

LAKE ST. CLAIR *see* MOUNT CLEMENS, MICHIGAN

A 90-foot burned-out circle found in a soybean field in Goldfield, Iowa, in June 1972. *(Courtesy ICUFON/J. Eden)*

LANDING MARKS, areas of burned ground or depressed vegetation, usually circular in shape, where UFOs are purported to have landed. Hundreds of such marks have been reported both in the United States and abroad. Some of these, however, have been attributed to a fungus which grows in a pattern known as a FAIRY RING. Areas of swirled, swampy vegetation which have been found primarily in Australia are known as UFO NESTS.

Some circular landing marks contain three or four depressions allegedly made by landing pads. In some

cases, only the alleged landing pad marks are present, as in the SOCORRO, NEW MEXICO, landing.

**LANTERN,** quarterly magazine, established in 1972, with a circulation of 200. It is available by subscription only. The range of subjects covered includes UFOs, psychic research, folklore, legends and geomancy.

Material is supplied by staff writers and freelance writers. Ivan A. W. Bunn is Editor. *Lantern* is published by the Borderline Science Investigation Group, 3 Dunwich Way, Oulton Board, Lowestoft, Suffolk NR32 4R2, England.

**LAPUTA,** name of a fictitious flying island. In JONATHAN SWIFT's *Gulliver's Travels,* Gulliver one day looks up to see a vast, opaque object flying toward him across the ocean. As it approaches, Gulliver observes that it is a circular island, four-and-a-half miles in diameter, floating two miles above the sea. A chain is lowered and Gulliver is hauled up to the hovering island. There he learns the language of the inhabitants who converse in mathematical and musical terms. The island can be propelled upwards, downwards and in any direction by an enormous magnet fixed in the center of Laputa. The story has caught the attention of UFOLOGISTS because of its use of the theory that the attracting and repelling forces of magnetism could be utilized as an aerial propulsion system. Magnetism has frequently been suggested as an explanation for unusual maneuvers performed by some UFOs.

**LATIN AMERICA** *see* **SOUTH AMERICA**

**L'AUTRE MONDE** *see* **AUTRE MONDE, L'**

**LAWSON, ALVIN HUSTON** (b. October 11, 1929, Fort Bragg, California; address: English Department, California State University, Long Beach, California 90840; telephone number: 714-897-4836), Professor of English and UFO researcher.

Lawson describes himself as an ETH skeptic, and believes that the origin of UFOs is more likely to be inner space than outer space. His experiments with regressive HYPNOSIS have revealed that when imaginary UFO ABDUCTIONS are induced hypnotically in control subjects with no significant knowledge about UFOs, their responses show no substantive differences from those provided by "real" abductees. Lawson is persuaded by his experience that however "real" UFO experiences may be, the entire sensibility of witnesses is probably involved in their UFO encounters. This means, he states, that to assess adequately a witness's UFO report, we need to know a good deal more about his or her psychological and physiological makeup than we ever learn in current investigative procedures. In the continuing absence of unambiguous physical evidence, he concludes, the only likely source of additional reliable information about the UFO phenomenon may be in-depth analyses of witnesses themselves.

Lawson received his B.A. from the University of California, Berkeley, in 1952; his M.A. from Stanford in

Alleged pad prints found outside a farmhouse after a UFO sighting near Alingsas, Sweden, on August 30, 1970. *(Courtesy ICUFON/GICOFF)*

1958; and his Ph.D., also from Stanford, in 1967.

Lawson has been a member of the California State University, Long Beach, faculty since 1962 and is professor of English. His teaching specializations include Nathaniel Hawthorne and writing for children. Since 1974, he has taught a class in the rhetorical analysis of the UFO controversy, "UFO Literature: The Rhetoric of the Unknown." Since 1975, he has operated the UFO REPORT CENTER OF ORANGE COUNTY, a twenty-four-hour hotline service. He is a member of the MUTUAL UFO NETWORK (MUFON) and the CENTER FOR UFO STUDIES (CUFOS).

Lawson's papers have appeared in several publications. He is author of a class text, *UFO Workbook* (1975), and two class casebooks, *Classic UFO Cases No. 1: Boianai, New Guinea* and *Classic UFO Cases No. 2: Socorro, New Mexico,* all of which were privately printed.

## LAYNE, N. MEADE, *see* BORDERLAND SCIENCES RESEARCH FOUNDATION (BSRF)

## LEBELSON, HARRY (b. March 25, 1937, Bronx, N.Y.: address: 400 68th Street, Guttenberg, N.J. 07093), writer.

As an investigator and writer, Lebelson hopes to prove the extraterrestrial nature of UFOs through careful documentation and the utilization of scientific methods of analysis.

Lebelson attended Cooper Union from 1956 to 1958, and the School of Visual Arts in New York from 1960 to 1962. He worked as a freelance photo journalist from the late 1950s to the mid-1960s. Since then, he has worked as a freelance writer. He is an Assistant Editor at *OMNI* magazine and contributes periodically to its "UFO Update" column.

Lebelson is a Field Investigator for the AERIAL PHENOMENA RESEARCH ORGANIZATION (APRO).

## LEMURIA, legendary continent said to have existed in the Indian Ocean in prehistoric times. It purportedly predated ATLANTIS and was similarly destroyed by a cataclysm. The Lemurians reportedly developed an advanced civilization in which magic played a dominant role. The continent has shared many of the legends attributed to the lost civilizations of Atlantis, MU, and HYPERBOREA, including the suggestion that UFOs may originate from an underwater Lemurian base which survived the cataclysm.

The large island off Madagascar off the southeast coast of Africa is considered by some researchers to be a major geographical vestige of Lemuria, whose name is derived from the lemur, a primitive primate indigenous to Madagascar and neighboring islands. Some writers, however, place Lemuria in the Pacific, using the name interchangeably with Mu. Others maintain that Lemuria and Mu were two independent land masses existing concurrently and deriving from one original land mass known as GONDWANALAND.

Bibliography: Hutin, Serge, *Alien Races and Fantastic Civilizations* (New York: Berkley Publishing Corporation, 1975).

## LENTICULAR CLOUDS *see* CLOUDS

## LE POER TRENCH, (WILLIAM FRANCIS) BRINSLEY, EARL OF CLANCARTY (b. September 18, 1911, London, England; address: 6 Lyall Street, London SW1X 8LJ, England), author.

A world-renowned UFO author and a leading UFO authority in Britain, Clancarty believes that UFOs are alien spacecraft from the twelfth PLANET Marduk, the Great Bear, the Little Bear and Sirius areas. He considers it possible that some may be based underground on Earth. He holds that OCCUPANTS either seeded us here or caused animal man to be mutated into *Homo sapiens*. They come back periodically, he states, to see how their protegés are progressing or to arrest their decline.

Clancarty attended the Nautical College at Pangbourne, England, from 1926 to 1929. From 1930 to 1939, he was employed by the Standard Bank of South Africa. From 1939 to 1946, he served in the Royal Artillery in the Middle East, achieving the rank of captain. From 1947 to 1972, he worked for various magazines in the advertising field and became Advertisement Manager of *RAF Flying Review* and *Practical Gardening*.

From 1956 to 1959, Clancarty was Editor of FLYING SAUCER REVIEW (FSR). In 1967, he founded the worldwide UFO organization, CONTACT INTERNATIONAL, of which he is President. He is Vice-President of the BRITISH UFO RESEARCH ASSOCIATION (BUFORA), and is an Honorary Life Member of the ANCIENT ASTRONAUT SOCIETY. He is a regular contributor to CANADIAN UFO REPORT. Following the death of his older brother, he assumed the title of Earl of Clancarty. In 1979, he introduced a three-hour debate on UFOs in the HOUSE OF LORDS, as a result of which the subject is being kept permanently in front of Parliament and a House of Lords All-Party UFO Study Group has been formed.

Clancarty is author of *The Flying Saucer Review's World Round-up of UFO Sightings* (New York: Citadel Press, 1958); *Men Among Mankind* (London: Neville Spearman, 1962; and published as *Temple of the Stars* by Ballantine Books, New York, 1974); *Forgotten Heritage* (London: Neville Spearman, 1964), *The Flying Saucer Story* (London: Neville Spearman, 1966); *Op-*

*eration Earth* (London: Neville Spearman, 1969); *The Eternal Subject* (London, Souvenir Press, 1972; and published as *Mysterious Visitors: The UFO Story* by Stein & Day, New York, 1973); and *Secret of the Ages* (London, Souvenir Press, 1974).

## LE ROY, KANSAS,

**LE ROY, KANSAS,** location of one of the most famous UFO sightings during the AIRSHIP WAVE of the nineteenth century and a forerunner of the mysterious ANIMAL MUTILATIONS episodes of the twentieth century.

On April 28, 1897, Alexander Hamilton was awakened by a commotion among his cattle at around 10:30 P.M. He went outside, where he found an airship descending by his barn. He roused his son and a tenant, and the three men returned to the corral armed with axes. They stood within fifty yards of the craft, which was thirty feet above the ground. In the illuminated carriage, made mostly of glass, they could see six hideous people, who jabbered unintelligibly. When the craft's huge spotlight revealed the three men to the OCCUPANTS, an enormous propellor was switched on, raising the airship to an altitude of about three hundred feet. At that point the three onlookers saw that a red cable hanging from the craft was attached to a two-year-old heifer which had become tangled in a wire fence. Unable to release the animal from the fence, the men cut the wire. To their amazement, heifer and airship rose up and moved off to the northwest. The following day, a neighbor found the legs, hide and head in his field. Ten local citizens, including the sheriff, postmaster, justice of the peace, a banker and an attorney, signed a sworn affidavit testifying to Hamilton's reputation for "truth and veracity."

Bibliography: Vallee, Jacques, *Anatomy of a Phenomenon: Unidentified Objects in Space* (Chicago: Henry Regnery Company, 1965).

## LES AMATEURS D'INSOLITE see AMATEURS D'INSOLITE, LES

## LES CHRONIQUES DE LA CLEU,

**LES CHRONIQUES DE LA CLEU,** publication of the COMMISSION LUXEMBOURGEOISE D'ÉTUDES UFO-LOGIQUES (CLEU).

## LEVELLAND, TEXAS,

**LEVELLAND, TEXAS,** location of a series of independent sightings of a UFO on the night of November 2/3, 1957.

Just before 11:00 P.M., Patrolman A. J. Fowler, the duty officer in Levelland, received a telephone call from a farmhand named Pedro Saucedo. The frightened Saucedo had just encountered a brilliantly illuminated UFO while driving with a companion, Joe Salaz (also referred to as Salav, Salvos, Palav and Palaz) about four miles east of the town. The two men had first noticed

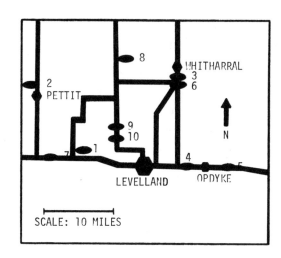

Street map of Levelland, Texas, and environs showing location of UFO sightings by Pedro Saucedo (1), grain combine drivers (2), José Alvarez (3), Jim Wheeler (4), Newell Wright (5), Frank Williams (6), Ronald Martin (7), Fire Marshal Ray Jones (8), James Long (9) and Sheriff Weir Clem (10).

the object as a flash of light in a nearby field. "We didn't think much about it," Saucedo said, "but then it rose up out of the field and started toward us, picking up speed." The UFO became distinguishable as a yellow-and-white torpedo-shaped object, about 200 feet long. "When it got nearer," said Saucedo, "the lights of my truck went out and the motor died. I jumped out and hit the deck as the thing passed over the truck with a great sound and a rush of wind. It sounded like thunder, and my truck rocked from the blast. I felt a lot of HEAT." The men watched the object disappear in the distance and, as it did so, the truck lights came on again.

Thinking that Saucedo was under the influence of alcohol, Fowler paid little attention to the call. About an hour later, however, Fowler received a second call, this time from Jim Wheeler. Driving along a highway about four miles east of the town, Wheeler had encountered a 200-foot egg-shaped object resting in the center of the road. As he approached the brilliantly-illuminated UFO, his car's engine and lights failed. Wheeler started to get out of his car. As he did so, the UFO rose into the air. At an altitude of about 200 feet, its lights went off. Simultaneously, the car lights came on again.

Wheeler's call was followed by another from José Alvarez, who related an almost identical encounter on a road eleven miles north of Levelland in Whitharral.

At 12:05 A.M., Newell Wright (who did not report the experience until the following day) encountered an elliptical object on the road about five miles east of the spot where Wheeler had seen it. His car lights out, his engine stalled, he sat watching the UFO for several minutes before it rose up in the air and disappeared northward.

At 12:15 A.M., the duty officer received another

phone call from Frank Williams, who had encountered the UFO on the road close to where Alvarez had seen it in Whitharral. The UFO's lights had been pulsating on and off. Each time the lights came on, Williams's car lights went off. Finally, the glowing object rose into the air with a loud roar. At an altitude of about 300 feet, its lights went out and it was lost from view.

Reports continued to come in to Fowler. At 12:45 A.M. Ronald Martin was driving a truck a few miles west of the spot where Saucedo had encountered the object almost two hours previously. A glowing, reddish UFO landed on the road just ahead of him, turning bluish-green as it did so. The truck stalled and its lights went out. A minute later, the object rose vertically, changing back to its original reddish color. A half hour later, James Long underwent the same experience on a road about five miles north of the town.

In the meantime, Sheriff Weir Clem and some of his officers had begun patrolling the roads in search of the mysterious craft. At about 1:30 A.M., close to the spot where Long had encountered the UFO fifteen minutes previously, Sheriff Clem and Deputy Pat McCulloch saw brilliant red oval lights streak across the highway about 300 yards ahead of them. Driving along a few miles behind them, Patrolman Lee Hargrove and Floyd Gavin saw what appeared to them as "a strange looking flash" close to the ground about a mile in front of them.

Later reports revealed that earlier in the evening two grain combines at Pettit, about fifteen miles northwest of Levelland, had stalled as a UFO passed across the sky. Later, sometime after 1:00 A.M., Fire Marshal Ray Jones had seen the UFO about ten miles north of Levelland. During this encounter, his car lights dimmed and the engine almost died, but started up again.

Subsequent investigation revealed that a UFO had been sighted in the Texan towns of Amarillo, Canadian and Midland, and at Clovis, New Mexico. In Canadian, witnesses had observed a figure standing by a landed "submarine-shaped" object. The following day, UFO landings were reported by an Air Force sergeant at Abilene and by an army patrol at White Sands, New Mexico. An unidentified object was observed flying over Deming, New Mexico.

Within a radius of twenty miles around Levelland, ten very similar UFO encounters had occurred in less than three hours. A few days later, a UNITED STATES AIR FORCE (USAF) investigator visited the town. He stayed for about seven hours and interviewed only six of the fifteen witnesses. The Air Force report stated that only three people had seen the "big lights." It was explained as a "weather phenomenon of electrical nature, generally classified as ball lightning or SAINT ELMO'S FIRE, caused by stormy conditions in the area,

including mist, rain, thunderstorms and lightning." The car engine and light failures were attributed to "wet electrical circuits." Authors DONALD MENZEL and Lyle Boyd have pointed out that at the beginning of November 1957, the region was experiencing an unusual number of electrical storms and the month proved to be the wettest on record in West Texas. They contend that it is an overwhelming probability that the UFO was ball lightning. However, since all the witnesses reported overcast, mist or light rain but *no storms or lightning*, UFOLOGISTS have given little credence to this explanation.

Because the Levelland sightings occurred on the same night that Sputnik 2 was launched, engineer LEON DAVIDSON has conjectured that the encounters were engineered by the CENTRAL INTELLIGENCE AGENCY (CIA) as part of a conspiracy to preempt news coverage of the Russians' achievements in space. The Levelland sightings did, in fact, make headlines around the country. They are remembered as the highlight of a UFO WAVE which lasted throughout 1957.

Bibliography: Hynek, J. Allen, *The UFO Experience: A Scientific Inquiry* (Chicago: Henry Regnery Company, 1972); Hall, Richard H. (ed.), *The UFO Evidence* (Washington, D.C.: National Investigations Committee on Aerial Phenomena, 1964).

**LEVINE, NORMAN,** *see* **CONDON COMMITTEE**

**LEVITATION,** the rising and floating of a human body in the air without any means of physical support. This ability has been attributed to many saints and spiritualist mediums. Jesus' walking on the water is an example of levitation. DONALD MENZEL has suggested that this event might have been the result of a MIRAGE. An incident in the nineteenth century involving British spiritualist Daniel D. Home has often been cited as proof of levitation. Reportedly, numerous witnesses, including some respected names in London society, claimed to have seen Home float out of a third story window and into another. Close examination of the records, however, reveals that the witnesses observed the activity from a room centered between the room Home left and the room he entered. Thus observers only saw Home as he passed their window, a feat that could be engineered by natural means.

Modern claims of levitation frequently involve UFOnauts who apparently float in and out of their hovering craft, as in the PASCAGOULA, MISSISSIPPI, case. Sometimes the UFOnauts levitate within a beam of light attached to the UFO, as in the 1970 case in IMJARVI, FINLAND. Witnesses to such events have sometimes described a feeling of WEIGHTLESSNESS.

Since levitation defies the laws of GRAVITATION as perceived by mankind today, it is not understood how such a feat could be accomplished.

Bibliography: Le Poer Trench, Brinsley, *Mysterious Visitors—The UFO Story* (New York: Stein and Day, 1973).

**LEY HUNTER, THE—THE MAGAZINE OF EARTH MYSTERIES,** bi-monthly magazine, established in 1969, with a circulation of over 2,000. It is available at specialized bookstores and by subscription. The range of subjects covered includes LEYS, the recovery of lost ancient knowledge and science, research into little-known Earth forces and strange phenomena, including UFOs, near ancient sites and along ley lines.

The magazine contains articles by freelance writers and editorial material. There is no payment for freelance articles. *The Ley Hunter* is edited and published by Paul Devereux, P.O. Box 152, London N.10, England.

**LEYS,** the straight alignments which appear to link ancient monuments and holy places across distances of many miles. The ancient trails were first noticed in England in the early 1920s by merchant Alfred Watkins. He also noted that certain words reappeared frequently within the names of sites falling along the lines. These included red, white, black, cole, cold, dod, merry and ley. He named the lines after the latter.

Some researchers have speculated that leys represent artificially created lines of magnetic current and that they may be utilized by the propulsion systems of UFOs. Ley lines are closely associated with the phenomenon of ORTHOTENY. Research on the subject is dealt with in the British magazine THE LEY HUNTER.

Bibliography: Watkins, Alfred, *The Old Straight Track* (London: Methuen and Company, 1925).

**LGM,** acronym for LITTLE GREEN MEN. LGM was used as a nickname for PULSARS when they were first discovered because of the fleeting suspicion that they might be signals from distant extraterrestrial civilizations.

**LIBERTY, KENTUCKY,** home of Elaine Thomas, Louise Smith and Mona Stafford, victims of a reported ABDUCTION by UFO OCCUPANTS on January 6, 1976.

The three women were driving home at night when they saw a domed disk plunging toward them. The massive object stopped short and paced the car, which soon became filled with a blue light and a suffocating HEAT. The car, accelerating of its own accord, headed towards a gateway in a stone wall. Suddenly, the women found themselves approaching the nearby town of Hustonville. When they reached home, they discovered a period of one hour and twenty-five minutes had elapsed for which they could not account. Strange red marks were found on their necks and back, and cold water burned their skin. The following day they found that small areas of paint had bubbled up on the car.

The case was investigated by the AERIAL PHENOMENA RESEARCH ORGANIZATION (APRO), the MUTUAL UFO NETWORK (MUFON), the OHIO UFO INVESTIGATORS' LEAGUE (OUFOIL) and THE NATIONAL ENQUIRER. During hypnotic regressions conducted by R. LEO SPRINKLE, the women described being taken aboard the UFO and subjected to painful physical examinations. Events during and after the encounter described by the women, some of them difficult to connect with the UFO experience, have a nightmarish quality. This incident is similar to the classic Betty and Barney Hill encounter in NEW HAMPSHIRE.

Bibliography: Stringfield, Leonard H., *Situation Red: The UFO Siege* (Garden City, N.Y.: Doubleday and Company, 1977).

**LIMBO OF THE LOST** *see* **BERMUDA TRIANGLE**

**LIMITES,** publication of the GROUPEMENT D'ÉTUDE RÉGIONAL DES OVNI (GERO).

**LINK,** publication of the MANCHESTER UFO RESEARCH ASSOCIATION (MUFORA).

**LITTLE BLUE BOYS,** nickname applied to the staff of PROJECT BLUE BOOK, also referred to as the little boy blues.

**LITTLE GREEN MEN (LGM),** humorous but inaccurate term used to describe UFO OCCUPANTS. The origin of the word "green" in connection with saucer-occupants is unknown and may derive from green extraterrestrial beings described in science fiction stories of the 1950s.

**LITTLE PEOPLE** *see* **FAIRIES**

**LIVY,** first century B.C. Roman historian who recorded thirty celestial phenomena, some of which are reminiscent of modern UFO sightings. He reported that, in 218 B.C., phantom ships gleamed in the sky, while in the district of Amiternum men in shining clothes were seen at a distance. Another passage from Livy's writings describes an altar surrounded by men in white clothes which was seen in the sky at Hadria in 214 B.C.

Bibliography: Drake, W. Raymond, *Gods and Space-*

*men throughout History* (Chicago: Henry Regnery Company, 1975).

**L/L RESEARCH,** P.O. Box 5195, Louisville, Kentucky 40205.

This organization has no membership but is a partnership between DONALD ELKINS and CARLA RUECKERT. Although they occasionally carry out field investigations of cases involving lost time, their primary function is to research the CONTACTEE phenomenon. Since 1962, Elkins and Rueckert have organized weekly experiments with a study group. During these sessions they reportedly have conversed with beings who channel their responses through the vocal apparatus of the members of the study group. The sources of these communications are supposedly members of a Confederation of Planets, who exist as astral rather than physical bodies but are capable of manifesting themselves within our physical reality. Research has concentrated less on the identity of these beings and more on their purpose in contacting people on Earth. Elkins and Rueckert claim that their studies reveal a marked similarity in communications received by thousands of contactees around the world and this aspect is the theme of their book, *Secrets of the UFO* (Louisville, Kentucky: L/L Company, 1977).

L/L Research was founded by Elkins and Rueckert in 1970.

**LOMBARD, CHARLES FRANCIS** (b. June 2, 1930, La Tronche, France), Senate Aide and Member of the Board of Governors of the NATIONAL INVESTIGATIONS COMMITTEE ON AERIAL PHENOMENA (NICAP).

Lombard believes UFOs may represent an extraterrestrial or fourth-dimensional phenomenon which is as yet unexplained.

Lombard received his B.S. from Georgetown University in 1952, and his M.A. from the Fletcher School of Law and Diplomacy in 1956.

From 1952 to 1955, Lombard served in the United States Army in Korea. Subsequently, he was vice-president of a company engaged in real estate and commercial development. Since 1968, he has been a member of the U.S. Senate Staff in various capacities, including Minority Counsel of the Aeronautical and Space Sciences Committee. He is currently Special Assistant to Senator BARRY GOLDWATER for Commerce, Science and Transportation.

Lombard joined the NICAP Board of Governors in 1978.

**LONDON UFO RESEARCH ORGANIZATION (LUFORO)** *see* **BRITISH UFO RESEARCH ASSOCIATION (BUFORA)**

Coral Lorenzen.

**LORENZEN, CORAL E.** (b. April 2, 1925, Hillsdale, Wisconsin; address: 3910 E. Kleindale Road, Tucson, Arizona 85712; telephone number: 602-793-1825), writer, Cofounder of the AERIAL PHENOMENA RESEARCH ORGANIZATION (APRO), and Editor of the APRO BULLETIN.

Coral Lorenzen thinks that UFOs are probably extraterrestrial craft from another solar system. She observed her first UFO at the age of nine. In 1947, while in Arizona, she sighted a glowing sphere which ascended vertically, disappearing into the sky. She saw a third UFO at Sturgeon Bay in Wisconsin. The huge object, traveling southwest to northeast, was observed by about three hundred other witnesses on the Door Peninsula.

Coral Lorenzen graduated from high school in 1941 and subsequently held a number of different positions as a proofreader, feature writer and reporter for newspapers; a lathe machinist and shipfitter during World War II; and a Project Mission Reporter at Holloman Air Force Base in New Mexico.

In 1952, together with husband LESLIE JAMES "JIM" LORENZEN, she founded APRO and has become one of the most prominent researchers and writers in the field. She has been Editor of the *APRO Bulletin* since its inception in 1952.

Coral Lorenzen is author of *The Great Flying Saucer Hoax* (New York: William Fredericks Press, 1962); *Flying Saucers—The Startling Evidence of the Invasion from Outer Space* (New York: New American Library, 1966); and *Shadow of the Unknown* (New York: New American Library, 1970). She is coauthor, with Jim Lorenzen, of *Flying Saucer Occupants* (New York: New American Library, 1967); *UFOs over the Americas* (New York: New American Library, 1968); *UFOs—The Whole Story* (New York: New American Library, 1969); *En-*

Jim Lorenzen.

counters with UFO Occupants (New York: Berkley Publishing Corporation, 1976) and Abducted: Close Encounters of a Fourth Kind (New York: Berkley Publishing Corporation, 1977).

## LORENZEN, LESLIE JAMES "JIM"

**LORENZEN, LESLIE JAMES "JIM"** (b. January 2, 1922, Grand Meadow, Minnesota; address: 3910 E. Kleindale Road, Tucson, Arizona 85712; telephone number: 602-793-1825), electronics technician, Cofounder and International Director of the AERIAL PHENOMENA RESEARCH ORGANIZATION (APRO).

Jim Lorenzen shares the opinion of his wife, CORAL E. LORENZEN, Cofounder of APRO and Editor of the APRO BULLETIN, that some UFOs are probably of extraterrestrial origin. As Director of the world's oldest UFO organization, he has become one of the most prominent investigators in the field.

Jim Lorenzen graduated high school in 1938 and Army Air Corps Radio School in 1942. He attended the Electronic Technical Institute in Los Angeles from 1950 to 1951.

From 1942 to 1945, Jim Lorenzen served as a radio operator in the United States Army Air Corps. He worked as a professional musician from 1945 until 1951. From 1951 to 1954, he was a radio station engineer. He worked as an electronics technician at the Holloman Air Force Base Data Reduction Facility from 1954 to 1960, and from 1960 to 1967 was a Technical Associate at the Kitt Peak National Observatory. Since 1967, he has been owner of Lorenzen Music Enterprises in Tucson, Arizona.

Jim Lorenzen was awarded an Air Medal with cluster, a Distinguished Flying Cross with cluster, and a Presidential Citation.

He is coauthor, with Coral Lorenzen, of Flying Saucer Occupants (New York: New American Library, 1967); UFOs over the Americas (New York: New American Library, 1968); UFOs—The Whole Story (New York: New American Library, 1969); Encounters with UFO Occupants (New York: Berkley Publishing Corporation, 1976); and Abducted: Close Encounters of a Fourth Kind (New York: Berkley Publishing Corporation, 1977).

## LORING AIR FORCE BASE, MAINE

**LORING AIR FORCE BASE, MAINE,** location of several UFO sightings on October 27, 29 and 31, 1975, which marked the beginning of a series of sightings at military bases and defense installations. The first sighting began at about 8:00 P.M. The white strobe and reddish orange lights of an unidentified object were seen descending to within 300 yards of a weapons dump containing nuclear bombs. A whirring sound could be heard. RADAR controllers located the target on their radarscopes and tracked it as it flew over and around the base. At about 9:30 P.M., the UFO departed.

Two nights later, radar controllers detected an unknown target headed toward the weapons storage area again. A helicopter was directed to within 1,000 feet of the UFO but failed to make visual contact.

The third incident occurred on October 31. Once more, an unidentified craft was observed three times but a pursuing helicopter, carrying members of the UNITED STATES AIR FORCE (USAF) Office of Special Investigations, was unable to intercept it.

Meanwhile, UFOs were observed flying in formation over a weapons storage area at Wurtsmith Air Force Base, Michigan, on October 30 and 31. A tanker was sent up but failed to catch up with the craft.

One week later, another series of sightings occurred at Malmstrom Air Force Base and several Intercontinental Ballistic Missile launch control sites in Montana, as well as at Minot Air Force Base in North Dakota. Over four consecutive nights bright lights moved about in the sky. On November 8, seven objects traveling at altitudes between 9,500 and 15,500 feet were pursued by F-106 interceptors. The UFOs accelerated from a speed of approximately eight miles per hour to about 170 miles per hour and then slowed down again to three-and-a-half miles per hour. A confidential communiqué issued by the Combat Operations Center of the NORTH AMERICAN AIR DEFENSE COMMAND (NORAD) on November 11, 1975, reported that ". . . as the interceptors approached the lights went out. After the interceptors had passed the lights came on again. One hour after the F–106s returned to base, missile site personnel reported the object increased to a high speed, raised in altitude, and could not be discerned from the stars." The document also described a sighting which occurred on November 11 at NORAD's Falconbridge radar station near Sudbury, Ontario. The report stated, "Falconbridge reported search and height finder radar paints on an object twenty-five to thirty nautical miles south of the site ranging in altitude from 26,000 feet to 72,000 feet. The site commander and other personnel say the object appeared as a bright star but much closer. With binoculars, the object appeared as a 100-foot diameter sphere and appeared to have craters around the outside."

The document concluded, "To date, efforts by Air Guard helicopters, SAC helicopters and NORAD F–106s have failed to produce positive I.D."

## LOS ANGELES INTERPLANETARY STUDY GROUPS, CONTACTEE organization founded by GABRIEL GREEN in 1956. In 1959, it evolved into the AMALGAMATED FLYING SAUCER CLUBS OF AMERICA (AFSCA).

## LOT see SODOM AND GOMORRAH

Astronaut James Lovell. (Courtesy NASA)

## LOVELL, JAMES A., JR., ASTRONAUT who reportedly observed UFOs during his space flights aboard GEMINI 8, GEMINI 12 and APOLLO 8. Some reports claim that he actually photographed two oval UFOs during the Gemini 8 flight. Lovell, however, denies having observed or photographed UFOs. He states, "During my four space flights, I saw nothing that could not be explained or was not the result of a natural phenomenon."

## LOW, ROBERT, Project Coordinator of the UFO study conducted by the CONDON COMMITTEE at the University of Colorado.

## LUBBOCK LIGHTS, formations of unidentified lights seen passing over Lubbock, Texas, on several nights during August, September and October of 1951.

At about 9:00 P.M. on August 25, an employee of the Sandia Corporation, a subsidiary of the Atomic Energy Commission, and his wife saw what appeared to be a huge, silent craft passing rapidly and at low altitude over ALBUQUERQUE, NEW MEXICO. The two observers described the object as resembling a V-shaped wing with dark stripes running along it. There were six-to-eight soft, glowing, bluish lights on the afteredge.

Twenty minutes later, in Lubbock, four Texas Technical College professors noticed a semi-circular formation of twenty-to-thirty lights passing across the sky from north to south at high speed. Just over an hour later, a second formation of lights appeared and was followed by a third just before midnight. While some reports state that the objects were blue-green, others state that the men could not agree on the color except that it was yellowish-to-white, with a soft glow. All the groups of lights appeared suddenly, not gradually, at about the same position in the sky and disappeared as suddenly as they appeared.

The following morning, a nearby Air Defense Command radar station reported that two sets of equipment had registered an unknown target traveling 900 miles per hour at 13,000 feet. The target had remained on the RADAR screens for six minutes before an F–86 was scrambled. By the time the airplane was airborne, the UFO had disappeared.

The story of the professors' sightings appeared in the local newspaper, Evening Avalanche, on the following Sunday. Five days later, on Friday, August 31, Carl Hart, an amateur photographer and college freshman, arrived at the newspaper office with five photographs of a V-formation of lights which he claimed to have photographed the previous night.

During the rest of August, September and October, the four college professors, sometimes accompanied by another professor and a graduate student, watched the skies and were rewarded by seeing the lights on twelve more occasions. Although the first two groups had been in semi-circular formations, subsequent sightings involved random patterns of lights. The objects always moved from north to south. However, when the team tried watching from two different locations, the observers situated in the country location were never able to see the lights.

The UNITED STATES AIR FORCE (USAF) did not arrive on the scene until two months after the initial sightings. Their investigators found a rancher in Brownsville, Texas, about thirty miles from Lubbock, who, together with his wife, had also observed the three groups of lights passing overhead on August 25. However, as the

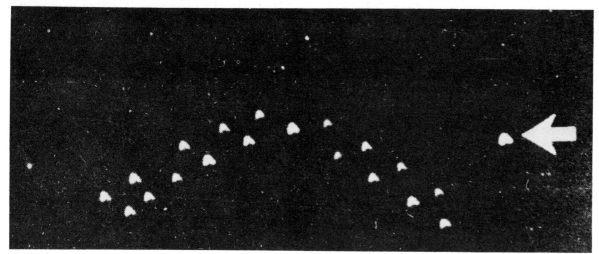

The Lubbock Lights. *(Courtesy Ground Saucer Watch)*

third group passed, he had distinguished the forms of BIRDS and heard the familiar cry of the plover. It was established that the oily white breasts of the plovers had reflected ground lights, an effect that was exaggerated by a new type of street lighting which had recently been installed in Lubbock.

Oddly, PROJECT BLUE BOOK investigator EDWARD RUPPELT continued to regard the Lubbock Lights as a mystery and labeled the case "unknown." Some years afterward, he wrote that an anonymous scientist had discovered a natural explanation for the incident but that he, Ruppelt, had promised not to reveal the answer. In a reprint of his first book, he added the unsubstantiated explanation that the lights had been moths reflecting street lights.

An investigation of PHOTOGRAPHS taken by Carl Hart revealed that the photographed objects did not resemble the lights seen by the professors. While the visual observations were of softly glowing lights, the objects in the photographs were sharply outlined and intensely bright. Writers DONALD MENZEL and Lyle Boyd have pointed out that the V-formation never reversed its position in the photographs as it should have done if the photographer panned with the lights' movement as he claimed to have done. Moreover, although the lights show evidence of slight motion during the exposure, the amount of blurring is less than it should be. Many UFOlogists suspect that the Lubbock Lights photographs were a HOAX, although this has never been proven.

Bibliography: Ruppelt, Edward J., *The Report on Unidentified Flying Objects* (Garden City, N.Y.: Doubleday and Company, 1956); Menzel, Donald H. and Lyle G. Boyd, *The World of Flying Saucers* (Garden City, N.Y.: Doubleday and Company, 1963).

**LUCE, CLARE BOOTHE,** playwright and former U.S. Congresswoman who was among dozens of witnesses who sighted a UFO in Rome in 1954. Luce was serving as U.S. Ambassador to Italy when the sighting occurred on October 28. A luminous sphere sped across the sky, followed by a trail of ANGELS' HAIR. Luce stated, "I saw something, but I don't know what it was."

**LUFORO** *see* **BRITISH UFO RESEARCH ORGANIZATION (BUFORA)**

**LUFORO BULLETIN** *see* **BRITISH UFO RESEARCH ASSOCIATION (BUFORA)**

**LUMIÈRES DANS LA NUIT (LDLN),** French magazine, established in 1958 and published ten times per year. It is available both at newsstands and by subscription. The magazine is dedicated to the study of all aspects of the UFO phenomenon. LDLN is served by a nationwide network of investigators, regional delegates and UFO organizations.

The magazine is edited and published by R. Veillith. The Editorial Committee consists of Veillith, Ch. Gueudelot, F. Lagarde and M. Monnerie. AIMÉ MICHEL is Technical Consultant. The editorial offices are located at "Les Pins," 43400 Le Chambon sur Lignon, France.

**LUNATIC FRINGE,** term sometimes used to describe psychically unbalanced individuals, religious fanatics and visionaries who, as a means of furthering their own cosmic and religious beliefs, promote the theory that UFOs are visitors from outer space. Conservative UFOlogists place CONTACTEES in this category. Astronomer J. ALLEN HYNEK points out that, although the lunatic fringe has impeded the acceptance of the UFO phenomenon as a subject worthy of scientific study, rarely do UFO reports come from this section of society.

Members of the lunatic fringe are usually incapable of composing articulate reports and, in any case, are uninterested in providing factual support for their beliefs.

**LYONS, FRANCE.** In the writings of Agobard, Archbishop of Lyons, is the strange tale of three men and a woman who were seen alighting from an aerial ship during the ninth century. An angry mob gathered around the four strangers. Their emperor, CHAR-LEMAGNE, had issued edicts which imposed penalties on aerial travelers. These four visitors were thought to be magicians sent by Charlemagne's enemy, Grimaldus, Duke of Beneventum, to destroy the French harvests. In vain, the four strangers protested that they were compatriots and had been carried off by miraculous men who had shown them unheard-of marvels. As the people were about to throw their captors into the fire, they were interrupted by Agobard, their well-respected Archbishop. He pronounced both groups' stories to be untrue. He declared that since it was impossible for people to fall out of the sky, it could not have happened. The citizens of Lyons, respecting the authority of their Archbishop, rejected the evidence witnessed by their own eyes and liberated the four strangers.

Bibliography: Vallee, Jacques, *Passport to Magonia* (Chicago: Henry Regnery Company, 1969); Emenegger, Robert, *UFOs, Past, Present and Future* (New York: Ballantine Books, 1974).

Aerial ships seen in the sky in France. *(Courtesy The New York Public Library Picture Collection)*

**MACCABEE, BRUCE SARGENT** (b. May 6, 1942, Rutland, Vermont), physicist and Maryland State Director of the Mutual UFO Network (MUFON).

Maccabee's research on the UFO phenomenon has led him to the conclusion that something strange is happening which could be attributable to any of a number of possibilities. He believes, however, that there is not yet enough information for positive identification.

Maccabee received a B.S. in Physics from the Worcester Polytechnic Institute in 1964. He received a M.S. and Ph.D. in Physics from the American University in 1967 and 1970, respectively.

Maccabee's general areas of interest are physics, biophysics, astronomy and electronics. He has conducted research on the biophysics of electric fish, critical point phenomena, gravity and electronics, and holds three patents. He has had teaching experience in basic quantum mechanics, electronics and laboratory instruction. His numerous articles on these subjects have been published in various scientific publications.

From 1970 to 1973, Maccabee was an Electronics Consultant to the Compackager Corporation. He served as Laser Physics Consultant to Tracor, Incorporated, from 1970 to 1971, and to Science Applications, Incorporated, from 1973 to 1974. In 1971, he was a Research Physicist for Sparcom, Incorporated. In 1972, he assumed his current position as a Research Physicist at the Naval Surface Weapons Center in Silver Spring, Maryland.

Maccabee is a member of the American Association for the Advancement of Science (AAAS), the American Physical Society, the Federation of American Scientists, the Optical Society of America and the Cousteau Society.

In addition to his position as Maryland State Director of MUFON, he is Physics Consultant to the National Investigations Committee on Aerial Phenomena (NICAP), consultant to Ground Saucer Watch (GSW), a member of the Scientific Board of the Center for UFO Studies (CUFOS), a member of the editorial board of UFO Phenomena International Annual Review (UPIAR) and a member of the International Fortean Organization (INFO). He is author of numerous articles on the subject of UFOs.

**MACKAY, IVAR,** *see* **CONTACT INTERNATIONAL**

**Mac Rae, Sheila,** actress and nightclub performer who has seen UFOs on two separate occasions. Her first sighting occurred in 1965 near Las Vegas. She saw two cigar-shaped UFOs which silently hovered and darted back and forth over Lake Meade in broad daylight. In December 1973, while driving through a snowstorm in St. Louis, Missouri, a silver UFO with flashing lights hovered over her car.

**MAGONIA,** legendary celestial region. French villagers in the ninth century referred to the purported inhabitants of Magonia as the tyrants of the air. These entities supposedly traveled in aerial ships. Because of the widespread fear that they destroyed crops and kidnapped humans, Emperor Charlemagne issued edicts that not only forbade the perturbing of the air and the provoking of storms, but also imposed penalties on the tyrants of the air. One notable case in which four human beings were allegedly abducted by these creatures occurred in Lyons, France. The incident is recorded in the writings of Agobard, Archbishop of Lyons.

Bibliography: Vallee, Jacques, *Passport to Magonia* (Chicago: Henry Regnery Company, 1969).

**MAGOR, JOHN FERGUSON** (b. March 2, 1915, Passaic, New Jersey; address: RR 5, Duncan, British Columbia, Canada V9L 4T6), Publisher and Editor of CANADIAN UFO REPORT.

Twice during 1973, Magor observed unusual lights maneuvering soundlessly just above treetop level. They appeared to be under intelligent control but were not like normal aircraft, since one moved erratically in a zigzag manner and the other shot sparks from its tail. Magor was impressed by the apparent reality of the UFO phenomenon before he began his magazine in 1969. Since then, he has interviewed approximately 500 witnesses whose sightings impressed him as authentic. Now he is entirely convinced we are being visited by intelligent creatures from space. He believes distance between the stars is not necessarily a problem since our visitors may long ago have established bases in our solar system.

Magor received his B.A. from Columbia College, New York, in 1936, and his M.S. from the Columbia University School of Journalism in 1937. At the outbreak of the Second World War, he was a Parliamentary Correspondent for the British United Press in Ottawa. He then became a pilot for the Royal Canadian Air Force. After the war, he became Publisher of the *Prince Rupert Daily News* and the *Cowichan Leader,* both in British Columbia. In 1969, he started the *Canadian UFO Report,* of which he is currently Publisher and Editor.

In 1963, Magor received an Alumnus Award for Publishing from the Columbia School of Journalism.

Magor is author of *Our UFO Visitors* (Victoria, British Columbia: Hancock House, 1977).

**MAINBRACE** *see* **OPERATION MAINBRACE**

**MALDEK,** hypothetical PLANET, also known as Clarion and Phaeton, which was supposedly destroyed by a nuclear holocaust. Located between MARS and Jupiter, the alleged remnants of the planet now constitute the asteroid belt. Survivors reportedly landed on Earth. Some proponents of this theory claim that the survivors were the colonizers of LEMURIA and ATLANTIS, while others claim they became the early gods and kings of our own civilization. Some people have speculated that a scarcity of oxygen on Maldek might have given a bluish tinge to its inhabitants. This, supposedly, explains the blue blood associated with royalty today.

Maldek, Clarion or Phaeton is occasionally confused with VULCAN, a hypothetical planet suggested to exist between Mercury and the sun.

Bibliography: Drake, W. Raymond, *Gods and Spacemen throughout History* (Chicago: Henry Regnery Company, 1975).

**MANCHESTER AERIAL PHENOMENA INVESTIGATION TEAM (MAPIT),** 92 Hillcrest Road, Offerton, Stockport, Cheshire SK2 5SE, England; telephone number: 061-483-4210.

The purpose of this organization is to investigate and research UFOs and related phenomena. Additionally, the group aims to help the public to understand the UFO phenomenon. MAPIT is open-minded regarding the identity and origin of UFOs, although it has concluded that UFOLOGY is related to other subjects such as BIGFOOT and ghosts.

This nonprofit organization was founded in 1973 by JENNY RANDLES and DAVID REES, who serves as Secretary. The group has sixty members. Ten field investigators cover a fifty-mile area. Foreign representatives are V. I. Sanarov in the Soviet Union, Omiros Karajas in Greece, Marek S. Iwaniec in Poland and Lorenzo Massai in Italy. Information is collected from newspapers and other organizations. Services available include a reference library, an information service, meetings and up-to-date news on UFO lectures around the country. A bimonthly magazine, SKYWATCH, is edited by Rees and is distributed in twenty-three countries.

**MANCHESTER UFO RESEARCH ASSOCIATION (MUFORA),** 597 Mauldeth Road West, Chorton, Manchester M21 2SH, England.

This is an investigative organization whose research activities are currently leaning toward a "think tank" concept with a view to the "brainstorming" hypothesis. The group has reached the conclusion that very few people involved in UFO research are sufficiently objective.

This nonprofit organization was founded in the early 1960s. Peter Warrington serves as Chairman. There are fewer than twenty-five members. The group's investigators work alongside those of other organizations in the region. MUFORA covers an area of approximately thirty miles' radius, and is part of the NORTHERN UFO NETWORK (NUFON). The organization has published infrequent issues of LINK, which has served as a medium to express conceptual observations and comments on the UFO phenomenon.

**MAN-MADE FLYING SAUCERS.** In *German Weapons and Secret Weapons of World War II and Their Development* (New York: Philosophical Library, 1959), author Rudolph Lusar reports on the development of several types of disk-shaped aircraft in Germany between 1941 and the end of World War II. German scientists Schriever and Habermohl allegedly designed a craft consisting of a stable dome-shaped cabin surrounded by a flat, rotating rim. In a test flight at Prague on February 14, 1945, it reportedly reached a speed of almost 1,250 miles per hour and achieved an altitude of 40,000 feet within three minutes of take-off. Toward the end of the war, all the models and prototypes were supposedly destroyed before they could be found by the Allies. According to a popular rumor, however, the Russian army succeeded in capturing one prototype.

After the war, Miethe, another German scientist involved in the design of flying disks, came to work for the United States and Canada. Habermohl was allegedly taken to the Soviet Union. Some proponents of the SECRET WEAPON HYPOTHESIS hold that the Nazis' work on flying saucers was continued in the United States and/or the Soviet Union. Opponents of this theory argue that if any world government had succeeded in producing craft with the alleged capabilities of UFOs, they would not be wasting funds on the research and production of our relatively primitive modern-day aircraft. Moreover, they express doubt that the existence of such devices could be kept secret for over thirty years.

Some supporters of the HOLLOW EARTH HYPOTHESIS contend that, after World War II, German flying saucer builders escaped to the North Pole, where they joined the inhabitants of the inner Earth and continued production of their disklike craft.

Engineer LEON DAVIDSON is among those who believe that UFOs are man-made machines. He holds that they are used by the CENTRAL INTELLIGENCE AGENCY (CIA) as part of a conspiracy to confuse the Russians about the United States' technological capabilities.

One disklike craft, whose existence was not kept secret, was the FLYING PANCAKE (also known as the Flying Flapjack), which was built by the United States Navy during World War II. Its production was canceled in 1947 in favor of jet manufacturing. The AVRO-CAR, a flying saucer built by a Canadian firm for the United States armed forces, was tested in 1960 and subsequently abandoned as a failure. It is now on display at the Army Transportation Museum at Fort Eustis, Virginia.

The United States Government has issued numerous PATENTS for craft resembling flying saucers. One such invention, patented by PAUL S. MOLLER, has been under development for several years at the DISCOJET CORPORATION in Davis, California.

## MANSFIELD, OHIO.

During the height of the 1973 UFO FLAP in Ohio and only three days after the state's governor, John Gilligan, had seen a UFO near ANN ARBOR, MICHIGAN, a four-man Army Reserve helicopter crew encountered a UFO which seemed to exert control over their craft.

Just after 11:00 P.M. on October 18, the Bell Helicop-

238,938
AIRCRAFT
Paul S. Moller, Dixon, Calif., assignor to
Discojet Corporation, Davis, Calif.
Filed Mar. 24, 1975, Ser. No. 561,234
Term of patent 14 years
Int. Cl. D12—07
U.S. Cl. D12—79

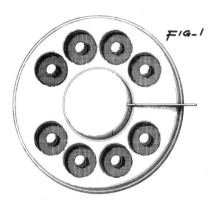

FIG-1

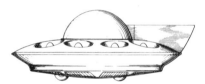

Patent design for a flying saucer under development at the Discojet Corporation.

ter Corporation UH–1H was traveling over the Mansfield area. Sergeant Robert Yanacsek alerted Captain Lawrence Coyne to a red light on the eastern horizon. Initially, the light seemed to be pacing them but within a short time it began to close on the helicopter. To avoid a collision, Coyne put the craft into a twenty-degree dive at 2,000 feet per minute. As they reached 1,700 feet, the object was still heading straight for them. The crew braced themselves for impact. Just as the collision seemed imminent, the object stopped about 500 feet above the aircraft. Looking up through a stream of green light which flooded the bubble canopy of the helicopter, they saw a sixty-foot long object resembling a streamlined fat cigar. The front end of the UFO was a red light. At the rear was a green spotlight which had swung around to illuminate the helicopter. Between the lighted ends was a gray metallic hull which reflected the red and green lights. A dome protruded at the center. Copilot Arrigo Jezzi tried to make radio contact with an airport but, although the equipment was functioning, he did not succeed in transmitting or receiving. After

UFO witness Lawrence Coyne addressing the Special Political Committee at the United Nations on November 27, 1978. He was part of the delegation attempting to establish a U.N. study of UFOs. *(United Nations/Photo by Y. Nagata)*

only a brief moment, they felt a bounce and the UFO took off toward the west. As it changed its course to northwest, the green light turned to white. Then the object made a climbing turn and disappeared. Meanwhile, Coyne had caught sight of his altimeter. Surprisingly, the needle was rising. All controls were set for a twenty-degree dive, yet they had climbed from 1,700 to 3,500 feet with no power and were still climbing at 1,000 feet per minute. The four men had felt no G-forces or other noticeable strains. Within six or seven minutes, radio contact was established.

PHILIP KLASS has concluded that the Mansfield UFO was a large FIREBALL of the Orionid METEOR shower. The bright red leading edge is characteristic of the hot ionized air produced by an object entering the atmosphere at high speed. The usual color of Orionid meteors is blue-green and this, combined with the fact that the overhead portion of the helicopter's transparent canopy was green-tinted to reduce glare, could explain the green light which flooded the cockpit. Klass suggests that as the long, luminous tail of the fireball passed over the helicopter it gave the impression of hovering. Since that area of Ohio is 1,300 feet over sea level, the 1,700-foot altitude reported by Coyne translates into their being only 400 feet above the ground. Klass assumes that Coyne or his copilot instinctively pulled back on the controls to pull the craft out of its dive because he knew they would crash. Klass also points out that when he asked Coyne what he had done to terminate the ascent, Coyne replied that he had pulled

the collective pitch up and put the cyclic pitch back to neutral. Klass asserts that, under the circumstances, such action would have increased the helicopter's lift and rate-of-climb rather than have reduced them. He believes there is nothing unusual in the failure to make radio contact. Jezzi had changed frequencies rapidly and may not have stopped at any one long enough to establish contact. Moreover, only one tower was within close range and Klass points out that there are numerous instances when a pilot's call fails to elicit a reply.

Those who reject Klass's claim that Coyne and his three-man crew misinterpreted a natural object believe that the UFO, or some intelligence connected with it, deliberately saved the helicopter and its crew from almost certain destruction.

Bibliography: Klass, Philip J., *UFOs Explained* (New York: Random House, 1974).

**MANTELL, THOMAS,** *see* **GOODMAN AIR FORCE BASE, KENTUCKY**

**MANTERO, GIOVANNI AND PIERO,** *see* **CENTRO INTERNAZIONALE RICERCHE E STUDI SUGLI UFO (CIRS UFO)**

**MAPIT** *see* **MANCHESTER AERIAL PHENOMENA INVESTIGATION TEAM**

**MARCEN** *see* **MARYLAND CENTER FOR IN-VESTIGATION OF UNCONVENTIONAL PHENOMENA**

**MARIANA, NICHOLAS,** *see* **GREAT FALLS, MONTANA**

**MARIANA ISLANDS.** UFO activity in this island chain, located in the west Pacific Ocean, is monitored by the INDONESIAN UFO REGISTRY, headed by VICENTE C. CAMACHO.

**MARIE CELESTE,** American brigantine discovered sailing erratically without a crew in 1872. Although the story of the *Marie Celeste* has often been set in the SARGASSO SEA, she was actually found between the Azores and Lisbon by the crew of the British ship, *Dei Gratia*. Her sails were set, all was in order, and there were sufficient food supplies aboard. Numerous versions of the story supply many different details, some of them contradictory. In one report, a strange groove was found on the side of the ship. In another account, the last words in the captain's log were, "Something strange is happening. . . ." While most writers agree that there were no indications of foul play, some claim that the main cabin had been boarded up. An upright phial of oil supposedly found on the sewing machine used by the captain's wife is considered as evidence that there had been no rough weather.

In addition to the theory that the captain, his wife and the crew were carried off by extraterrestrial ASTRONAUTS, there are numerous HYPOTHESES involving piracy, mutiny, disease and madness. Lloyds of London, who paid the insurance, conjectured that the alcohol cargo may have ignited transitorily, frightening the crew off the ship. Another hypothesis concerns the possibility that the vessel was taken by persons already known to the ship's company. Having disposed of the crew, the brigands could have claimed to have discovered the ship empty, thus permitting them to claim it as a prize. In this respect, it is interesting to note that the *Dei Gratia* was moored alongside the *Marie Celeste* for over a week in New York and set sail shortly after the ill-fated ship's departure.

Bibliography: Fort, Charles, *Lo!* (New York: Claude H. Kendall, 1931); Wilkins, Harold, *Strange Mysteries of Time and Space* (New York: Citadel Press, 1959).

**MARK-AGE,** 327 N.E. 20 Terrace, Miami, Florida 33137; telephone number: 305-573-3967.

The stated purpose of this CONTACTEE organization is to educate spiritual workers about the second coming of Sanada (known in his last Earth incarnation as Jesus Christ of Nazareth) as part of a program conducted by the spiritual government of the solar system. The group describes the Mark-Age period as the forty-year period between 1960 and the year 2000, during which man must cleanse himself and the Earth sufficiently to permit his entry into the fourth dimension, a new mental and physical dimension of spiritual life. The organization states that during man's many millions of years on Earth, he has been guided and aided by our fellowmen from higher planes. It holds that UFOs represent our brothers and sisters from other planes and PLANETS, mostly of this solar system, who are helping prepare us for the NEW AGE. According to this theory, UFOs are one part of the widespread program to alert people on Earth to life in other realms and to assist us in rising to the fourth-dimensional vibration.

This nonprofit organization was founded in 1960 by Charles B. Gentzel and Pauline Sharpe. Sharpe is also known as Nada-Yolanda, and is allegedly the primary channel of information from the spiritual government of the solar system. Services provided by Mark-Age are weekly meditation tapes, books, home study courses, public meetings and lectures, counseling and training in the field of New Age spiritual work and leadership. *Main* magazine is published ten times yearly. The organization has published several books, including *Visitors from Other Planets* (Miami: Mark-Age, 1974), which purports to be information channeled through Nada-Yolanda explaining the identity and purpose of UFOs and how they are helping man into a new cycle of evolution.

**MARS,** the fourth PLANET from the sun. In 1898, H. G. Wells's science fiction novel, THE WAR OF THE WORLDS, popularized the idea that our nearest neighbors in space might be located on Mars. When Orson Welles's realistic radio adaption of the story was broadcast in 1938, many people were frightened into believing that a Martian invasion was actually taking place. The publicity given to UFO reports after Kenneth Arnold's historic 1947 sighting over MOUNT RAINIER, WASHINGTON, placed Mars in the forefront as the possible origin of interplanetary visitors. Some researchers attempted to find a correlation between UFO sightings and the periods when Mars is at its nearest to Earth. Although there seemed to be some coincidence in peaks of UFO sightings and Mars' opposition, authors DONALD MENZEL and Lyle G. Boyd have pointed out the fallacy of the theory that this would indicate visitation by Martians. Since both planets are moving in elliptical orbits of different sizes and at different speeds, an Earthbound traveler from Mars would have to achieve an elliptical orbit that would eventually intersect Earth's path. To do this, the traveler would have to leave Mars a considerable amount of time before the

The Martian landscape photographed by a camera aboard the Viking 1 lander. *(Courtesy NASA)*

planet was in opposition to Earth. Accordingly, the traveler would reach Earth a considerable amount of time after two planets had achieved their greatest proximity to each other. Menzel and Boyd suggest that any increase in the number of UFO reports when Mars is in opposition should be attributed to the planet's extreme brilliance at the time. Atmospheric refraction and dispersion can cause a planet or STAR to appear to have unusual shapes, flash brilliantly with red, green and blue colors, and seem to move up and down, sideways, and back and forth.

Several CONTACTEES, including RUTH NORMAN, claim to have visited busy metropolises and underground cities on Mars. However, preliminary exploration by U.S. and Soviet space probes has failed to find any indications of intelligent life. In 1976, Viking 1 and Viking 2 made their historic landings on Mars. One of the Viking mission's main objectives was the search for microbial life forms. Since the Viking findings were inconclusive, scientists have not excluded the possibility that life exists on Mars. However, such life would almost certainly be microbial and incapable of interplanetary travel.

Bibliography: Sachs, Margaret, and Ernest Jahn, *Celestial Passengers—UFOs and Space Travel* (New York: Penguin Books, 1977); Menzel, Donald H., and Lyle G. Boyd, *The World of Flying Saucers* (Garden City, N.Y.: Doubleday and Company, 1963).

## MARSH GAS *see* SWAMP GAS

**MARTIAN MOONS.** More than two-and-a-half centuries ago, JONATHAN SWIFT wrote about the two SATELLITES that orbit MARS. One-and-a-half centuries later, the two satellites were discovered by Asaph Hall. They were named Phobos and Deimos, the Greek words for "fear" and "terror." An acceleration in the motion of Phobos led Russian astrophysicist Iosif S. Shklovskii to propose in 1959 that Phobos and perhaps Deimos might be hollow, artificial satellites. His theory

was supported by a number of respectable scientists, including President Eisenhower's Special Space Adviser, S. Fred Singer. This encouraged some flying saucer enthusiasts in their belief that Swift had had access to ancient manuscripts passed down along a secret line of adepts, from an advanced civilization of the past. These documents supposedly revealed that the Martian moons were artificial satellites created by a lost civilization. However, Swift's mysterious knowledge of the satellites may have been based on Johannes Kepler's prediction in 1610 of the existence of the two small Martian moons.

In 1971, Mariner 9 sent back its first photographs of Phobos and Deimos. Craters revealed the natural origin of the moons. The irregularity in their shapes and sizes has explained their unusual orbits. There is no further speculation that they are of artificial origin.

Bibliography: Briazack, Norman J., and Simon Mennick, *The UFO Guidebook* (Secaucus, N.J.: Citadel Press, 1978).

## MARYLAND CENTER FOR INVESTIGATION OF UNCONVENTIONAL PHENOMENA (MARCEN), Box 218, Kensington, Maryland 20795; telephone number: 301-384-0816.

The purpose of this organization is to investigate and report in a scientific and scholarly manner all unconventional phenomena traditionally ignored by the scientific establishment and to help precipitate more scientific studies of such phenomena. The group holds that UFOs are extraterrestrial spacecraft from another STAR system involved in the surveillance of Earth. It believes that the ancestors of present-day UFO OCCUPANTS may possibly have colonized Earth.

This nonprofit organization was founded in 1978 by Williard F. McIntyre, who serves as Director, and Arthur F. Rosen, who serves as Assistant Director. The Board of Governors consists of McIntyre, Rosen and Luckett V. Davis. The group has 1,550 members. Six hundred Participating Members, all of whom have advanced degrees or training in the physical or sociological sciences, serve as field investigators and are located in forty-nine states, Puerto Rico, Canada and six other foreign countries. Services available to members include a library, research information, bibliographies, a speakers' bureau and a publishing outlet. The center's journal, *Believe It*, is published monthly.

**MAS ALLA,** publication of the INSTITUTO PERUANO DE RELACIONES INTERPLANETARIAS (IPRI).

**MASS HYSTERIA,** wild, uncontrolled excitement or panic experienced collectively by a large number of people. Some skeptics have blamed mass hysteria and HYSTERICAL CONTAGION for UFO FLAPS. However, documented cases of mass hysteria have not involved phenomena that were simultaneously observed through different media such as direct visual contact and RADAR contact, witnesses reluctant to report their experiences, independent witnesses who participated in calm, prolonged observations, and worldwide reports persisting for decades.

The danger of mass hysteria resulting from belief in an invasion by extraterrestrials was demonstrated in 1938, when Orson Welles's radio adaption of H. G. Wells's WAR OF THE WORLDS sent frightened listeners running for the hills.

Bibliography: U.S. Congress, House, Committee on Science and Astronautics, Symposium on Unidentified Flying Objects, Hearings, 90th Congress, 2nd Session, July 29, 1968 (Washington, D.C.: U.S. Government Printing Office, 1968).

**MATSUMURA, YUSUKE,** *see* **COSMIC BROTHERHOOD ASSOCIATION (CBA)**

**MAURY ISLAND, WASHINGTON,** location of an alleged sighting of six flying saucers in June 1947. The principals in the case were Harold A. Dahl and Fred. L. Crisman, who described themselves as harbor patrolmen but were later identified as salvagers of floating lumber. Reportedly, Dahl was boating just off Maury Island near Tacoma with his fifteen-year-old son, two crewmen and the boy's dog when a group of doughnut-shaped UFOs appeared above them. Dahl shot several feet of film with a movie camera he happened to have with him. One of the craft, which seemed to be experiencing some kind of mechanical difficulty, showered some light-colored metallic flakes and hot slaglike material over the boat. The dog was killed and the young boy's arm was injured. The UFOs left.

Dahl reported the incident to Crisman, whom he described as his superior officer. The following day, Crisman went to the scene, where he found the materials described by Dahl strewn along the shoreline of Maury Island. Then he, too, saw a doughnut-shaped UFO flying by.

Crisman mailed some of the slag and an account of the incident to magazine publisher RAY PALMER. Kenneth Arnold, who lived not far from Tacoma and who had become famous for his much-publicized sighting of a fleet of UFOs over MOUNT RAINIER, WASHINGTON, was asked by Palmer to investigate. Arnold found himself lost in a web of mystery. He called in the help of Air Force Intelligence. Two officers, Captain William Davidson and Lieutenant Frank M. Brown, arrived from Hamilton Air Force Base, California. They found that Dahl's boat showed no evidence of having been bombarded from above, and that the slaglike material was, in fact, slag from a local smelting plant. Dahl was unable to produce the film he claimed to have taken of the UFOs. Deciding that the whole affair was a HOAX, the officers boarded their B-25 aircraft for the return flight to Hamilton Air Force Base. On board was a box containing samples of the slaglike material which Crisman had given the officers. About fifteen or twenty minutes after take-off, the plane's left engine burst into flame. Two enlisted men on board parachuted to safety. Davidson and Brown stayed with the aircraft. About ten minutes later, the plane plunged to the ground, carrying them to their deaths.

This tragedy led to rumors that a conspiracy was involved. Although the Air Force attributed the disaster to a mechanical defect, some people suggested that the plane had been sabotaged by extraterrestrials. Later, however, Crisman and Dahl confessed that they had invented the entire story about the UFO encounter in order to sell it to a magazine. The hoax had gotten out of hand. The government considered prosecuting the men but, since they obviously could not have foreseen the resultant tragedy, the idea was abandoned.

Today some UFOLOGISTS still believe that the Maury Island mystery was a conspiracy involving either U.S. or Soviet intelligence agencies. Palmer claimed that samples of the slag were stolen from his office. Dahl allegedly disappeared after the incident. Crisman, reportedly, was recalled into the service and transferred first to Alaska, then to Greenland. Twenty years later, Crisman's name cropped up again in connection with another conspiracy. District Attorney James Garrison of New Orleans subpoenaed Crisman to testify before the Grand Jury listening to Garrison's evidence against Clay Shaw. The latter was accused of having conspired to murder John F. Kennedy but was found innocent and freed. Because of his alleged involvement in the Kennedy assassination, it was rumored that Crisman was either a member of the CENTRAL INTELLIGENCE AGENCY (CIA) or had been engaged in undercover activity in the field of industrial warfare.

Bibliography: Arnold, Kenneth, and Ray Palmer, *The Coming of the Saucers* (Amherst, Wisconsin: Amherst Press, 1952); Menzel, Donald H., and Lyle G. Boyd, *The World of Flying Saucers* (Garden City, N.Y.: Doubleday and Company, 1963); Keel, John A., *Our Haunted Planet* (New York: Fawcett Publications, 1971).

**MAYA,** Central American Indians who, prior to the Spanish Conquest, possessed one of the greatest civilizations of the western hemisphere. Much information about their culture has been lost because the early Spanish conquerors destroyed the records of this advanced civilization as the instruments of paganism. Those writings which survived the religious purge are in the form of hieroglyphs which remain largely undeciphered today.

The Maya knew that the world is a sphere. They knew the number of days in the Venusian year and calculated the duration of a terrestrial year to the closest figure reached by any calendar outside of our contemporary one. Some proponents of the ANCIENT ASTRONAUTS hypothesis suggest that the Maya received their advanced astronomical and mathematical knowledge from extraterrestrial visitors. Evidence to support this claim is allegedly found in a carving on a sarcophagus lid excavated from the ruins of Palenqué in the Yucatán. The stone relief shows a man sitting in a complex apparatus resembling a rocket ship. Exhaust flames seem to be issuing from its base. The man's knees are drawn up to his chest and his hands appear to be manipulating levers or control switches. A strange tubelike device is attached to his nose. Author ERICH VON DÄNIKEN has concluded that the carving represents an extraterrestrial astronaut.

In a television documentary entitled THE CASE OF THE ANCIENT ASTRONAUTS, written and produced by Graham Massey for the British Broadcasting Corporation's NOVA series, Ian Graham, an expert on Mayan symbols, repudiates von Däniken's claims. He points out that the carving shows a man whose sloping forehead is characteristic of the Maya. His clothing is typically ornamental. The tubelike device attached to the figure's nose is, according to Graham, a nose plug. The man's hands are in delicate positions typical of Mayan manual gestures. Graham interprets the "exhaust flames" as the stylized representation of two serpents joined at the middle, whose beards resemble flames.

Other authors have suggested that the Maya were the survivors of the lost continent of ATLANTIS. They were reputed to have escaped from a mysterious land which sank into the Atlantic Ocean. Author Serge Hutin points out that the Mayan civilization appeared at the time of

A drawing of the Palenque sarcophagus lid.
*(Courtesy ICUFON)*

the alleged submergence of the legendary continent. Furthermore, there is a striking similarity between the Mayan pyramids and those of Egypt, suggesting that they are perhaps the cultural remnants of a civilization which was once located between the American and African continents. However, it has also been conjectured that continental drift might account for the similarity between the two cultures. Africa and South America might originally have been a single continent which split down the middle, after which the two halves drifted apart. Hutin contends that this theory does not eliminate the possibility that Atlantis emerged subsequently, and then sank after the continental drift.

Bibliography: Von Däniken, Erich, *Chariots of the Gods?* (New York: G. P. Putnam's Sons, 1970); Hutin, Serge, *Alien Races and Fantastic Civilizations* (New York: Berkley Publishing Corporation, 1975); Thiering,

Barry, and Edgar Castle (eds.), *Some Trust in Chariots* (New York: Popular Library, 1972).

James McCampbell.

**McCAMPBELL, JAMES M.** (b. May 10, 1924, Nashville, Tennessee; address: 12 Bryce Court, Belmont, California 94002; telephone number: 415-593-8848), consultant, author, and Director of Research for the MUTUAL UFO NETWORK (MUFON).

McCampbell believes UFOs are metallic machines exhibiting flight technology exceeding Earth-based knowledge.

McCampbell received a B.A. in 1949, and a B.S. in Engineering and Physics in 1950 from the University of California at Berkeley. He did extensive graduate studies in physics and mathematics.

McCampbell did research on the effects of nuclear weapons from 1950 to 1955, and on nuclear reactor design from 1955 to 1959. He was involved in technical studies and engineering management from 1959 until 1971. Since that time he has been a consultant on the planning and managing of large-scale, technical projects, such as Environmental Protection for the Alaskan Pipeline, the Solar Energy Research Institute and the Technical Integration of LMFBR Large Plant Study.

McCampbell is a member of the AMERICAN ASSOCIATION FOR THE ADVANCEMENT OF SCIENCE (AAAS), the AMERICAN INSTITUTE OF AERONAUTICS AND ASTRONAUTICS (AIAA) and the American Nuclear Society.

McCampbell is author of *UFOlogy: New Insights from Science and Common Sense* (Millbrae, California: Celestial Arts, 1976).

**McCANN, WALTER,** *see* **ROGERS PARK, ILLINOIS**

**McDIVITT, JAMES,** *see* **GEMINI 4**

**McDONALD, JAMES EDWARD** (b. May 7, 1920, Duluth, Minnesota; d. June, 1971), meteorologist.

McDonald's interest in UFOs began in the mid-

1950s. Over the years, he investigated numerous sightings and interviewed hundreds of witnesses. By 1966, he had become the best-known authority on the subject. In an effort to educate the public and the scientific establishment about the serious nature of the phenomenon, he lectured nationwide and wrote thousands of letters to scientists, military personnel and private citizens. In 1968, he was the second speaker to present testimony at the HOUSE SCIENCE AND ASTRONAUTICS COMMITTEE HEARINGS on UFOs.

In 1971, as a representative of a NATIONAL ACADEMY OF SCIENCES (NAS) panel, McDonald testified once more before Congress. This time the subject was the supersonic transport (SST). McDonald contended that the SST would reduce the protective layer of ozone in the atmosphere, creating the risk of an additional 10,000 cases of skin cancer annually in the United States. Supporters of the SST cited McDonald's involvement in the UFO controversy in an attempt to discredit his testimony. Disparaging remarks about "these flying saucers" and "LITTLE GREEN MEN" brought derisive laughter from some spectators and congressmen. It was the first time that McDonald's professional credibility had been ridiculed because of his beliefs about UFOs. Suffering from depression and a broken marriage, McDonald committed suicide in June of that year at the age of fifty-one.

Although McDonald favored the EXTRATERRESTRIAL HYPOTHESIS (ETH), his opinion was "that if the UFOs are not of extramundane origin, then I suspect that they will prove to be something very much more bizarre, something of perhaps even greater scientific interest than extraterrestrial devices."

McDonald received his B.A. in Chemistry from the University of Omaha in 1942; his M.S. in Meteorology from the Massachusetts Institute of Technology in 1945; and his Ph.D. in Physics from Iowa State University in 1951.

McDonald served in the U.S. Navy in Intelligence and Aerology from 1942 to 1945. He was an Instructor at the Department of Physics of Iowa State University from 1950 to 1953, and research physicist at the University of Chicago from 1953 to 1954. In 1954, he joined the faculty of the University of Arizona, where he was Associate Professor of the Department of Physics from 1954 to 1956; Professor of the Department of Physics from 1956 to 1957; and Professor of the Department of Meteorology and Senior Physicist at the Institute of Atmospheric Physics from 1958 until 1971.

McDonald was a member of the AMERICAN ASSOCIATION FOR THE ADVANCEMENT OF SCIENCE (AAAS), the American Meteorological Society, Sigma Xi, the American Geophysical Union, the Royal Meteorological Society, the Arizona Academy of Science and the

American Association of University Professors. He served on several scientific panels.

McDonald published the texts of several of his speeches on the subject of UFOs.

## McINTYRE, WILLIARD F., see MARYLAND CENTER FOR INVESTIGATION OF UNCONVENTIONAL PHENOMENA (MARCEN)

## McKAY, HENRY H. (b. March 23, 1927, Toronto, Canada; address: P.O. Box 54 Agincourt, Ontario, Canada M1S 3B4), electrician, researcher and Regional Director of the MUTUAL UFO NETWORK (MUFON).

McKay believes the UFO phenomenon is a reality. His priorities are to direct a major international UFO symposium to cover all disciplines in seminars, lectures and public participation, and to see established a non-governmental center for the advancement of scientific and social research and study regarding the phenomenon.

McKay served in the Royal Canadian Air Force. He studied Electro-Technology, Commerce and Construction at M.I.T. in Winnipeg and at the R.C.E.M.E. School in Barryfield, Ontario. He is an electrician by profession.

McKay was an active member of the Canadian Aerial Phenomena Investigation Committee (CAPIC) and the Canadian Aerial Phenomena Research Organization (CAPRO), both now defunct. He contributed data to the CONDON COMMITTEE. He was Founder of the UFO Research Center in Ontario. He also served as its Chairman until 1979. He is currently the Canadian and Ontario Regional Director for MUFON.

McKay has initiated courses entitled "UFOs: A Canadian Approach" at the Centennial College in Toronto and at schools in Scarborough. He has participated in UFO conferences and has written papers on the subject.

## McMINNVILLE, OREGON, location at which two famous UFO PHOTOGRAPHS were taken on May 11, 1950. According to the witnesses, Mr. and Mrs. Paul Trent, they saw the UFO silently approaching their house at about 7:45 P.M. The object was very bright, almost silvery. Mrs. Trent ran indoors to fetch a camera. Mr. Trent was able to take two photographs before the object zoomed away to the northwest. When the photographs were developed, they showed a disk-shaped object with a lower and upper structure and a small turretlike protrusion on top.

The photographs were studied by commercial photographers for *Life* magazine and by the UNITED STATES AIR FORCE (USAF). Subsequently, an analysis was conducted by astronomer William Hartmann for the CONDON COMMITTEE. Hartmann concluded that "This is one of the few UFO reports in which all factors investigated, geometric, psychological and physical, appear to be consistent with the assertion that an extraordinary flying object, silvery, metallic, disk-shaped, tens of meters in diameter, and evidently artificial, flew within sight of two witnesses. It cannot be said that the evidence positively rules out a fabrication, although there are some physical factors, such as the accuracy of certain photometric measures of the original negatives, which argue against a fabrication."

Writer PHILIP KLASS arranged to have the photographs analyzed by computer systems analyst ROBERT SHEAFFER. Klass was skeptical about certain facets of the Trents' story. In the first newspaper account of the incident, Mrs. Trent was quoted as saying, "Both of us saw the object at the same time." However, in a subsequent radio interview, Mrs. Trent related that she had been outside *alone* when she saw the object. She had called out to her husband, she stated, and when he failed to respond, she ran inside to get him. Klass also points out that the Trents were REPEATERS, who claimed to have seen numerous UFOs both before and after May 11, 1950. Prior to this incident, Mrs. Trent had complained that no one would believe that she had seen UFOs. Hartmann points out, however, that the area was one where UFO sightings occurred frequently. Klass finds it suspicious that the Trents did not have the

UFO photographed by Paul Trent at McMinnville, Oregon, on May 11, 1950. *(Courtesy ICUFON)*

photographs developed immediately. Instead, they waited until they had used up the three remaining frames on the roll of film. Even after the pictures had been developed, the Trents showed them only to friends. However, two local bankers convinced them to offer the photographs to a local newspaper, which published them almost a month after they had been taken. When a reporter went to the Trents' home to obtain the negatives, they were found under a piece of furniture where the Trents' children had been playing with them. Klass considers this a curious way to treat allegedly authentic photographs of an extraterrestrial spaceship.

Sheaffer's analysis of the photographs revealed the most damaging piece of evidence against the Trents' claims. Shadows caused by the eaves on the east wall of the Trents' garage indicated that the photographs had been taken at about 7:30 in the *morning,* not at 7:45 in the *evening* as reported. A check of local weather records for that day showed that while the sky had been perfectly clear in the evening, it had been smoky in the morning, just as it was in the photographs. Moreover, Sheaffer's analysis indicated that the pictures had been taken in the reverse order to that reported and that they had been taken a few minutes apart rather than a few seconds apart as reported. After conducting some photographic experiments using a streetlight hanging from a pole, Sheaffer concluded that the Trent UFO appeared bright because a smudged lens had diffused the bright sky surrounding the object. Utilizing the same methods Hartmann had used to determine distance, Sheaffer was able to "prove" that the top of the street-light pole was further away from the camera than the base of the same pole, even though both were, in fact, at the same distance. Sheaffer conjectured that the McMinnville UFO was a model hanging from a power line. Hartmann rejected his own analysis and the Condon Committee concurred with Sheaffer's conclusion.

Other analyses have been more favorable to the Trents. Physicist BRUCE MACCABEE made densitometric scans of the photograph, which led him to the conclusion that the object could be a large, structured disk, fifty feet or more in diameter. Computer analysis of the photographs was conducted by GROUND SAUCER WATCH (GSW). The organization confirmed that the pictures had been taken between 7:30 and 8:00 in the morning rather than in the evening as reported by the Trents. However, in every other respect, their analysis confirmed the Trents' claim that the UFO was a large, solid, three-dimensional disk-shaped object flying at a great distance from the observers. By measuring the resolution of the pixel data on the edges of the object and comparing the results with other features in the photographs whose distances were known, it was deter-

mined that the object was approximately sixty-five-to-one-hundred feet in diameter. Digital densitometry revealed a brighter gray value for the UFO than for the shadows on the garage wall, indicating that the UFO was at a great distance from the camera. In addition, the sharpness of the foreground images in comparison to that of the UFO is also indicative of the latter's great distance from the camera. An electron microscopic examination of the original negatives revealed no evidence of any form of support attaching the UFO to the overhead power line. A digital density evaluation comparing the two photographs showed only a slight differential in a measurement of selected shadows. This, together with the size and position of the shadows, indicated that the pictures were taken within five minutes or less of each other.

Researchers continue to disagree about the authenticity of the McMinnville photographs. Further credence was given to the case, however, in 1954 when a French military pilot photographed an almost identical UFO near ROUEN, FRANCE. In July, 1957, the French photograph was published by *RAF Flying Review,* which described it as "one of the few [photographs] which seem authentic."

Bibliography: Klass, Philip J., *UFOs Explained* (New York: Random House, 1974); Spaulding, W. H., "UFOlogy and the Digital Computer," *Quality* (Wheaton, Illinois-Hitchcock Publishing Company, January 1978).

**MEKIS, KARL,** a former member of Adolf Hitler's S.S. guard who, together with confidence trickster Frank Weber-Richter, perpetrated a six-year CONTACTEE swindle which garnered him a fortune of over three hundred thousand dollars. From headquarters in Santiago, Chile, the two men sent out advertisements to European science fiction magazines, claiming that an army from VENUS was about to take over the world. As Venus Security Commissar on Earth, Mekis offered jobs, security and Venusian passports in exchange for cash. Earthwomen who wished to participate in the creation of a new master race could pay in advance for Venusian husbands. When the Chilean police became curious about their activities, Mekis and Weber-Richter moved to Rome. The invasion date was postponed but money continued to pour in as terrified people attempted to buy their future security. Mekis was arrested during a visit to Austria. He was convicted on seventeen counts of fraud and swindling and sentenced to five years in jail. Weber-Richter, who had remained in Italy, escaped arrest.

Bibliography: Hynek, J. Allen, and Jacques Vallee, *The Edge of Reality* (Chicago: Henry Regnery Company, 1975).

**MELBOURNE, AUSTRALIA.** In 1978, the disappearance of a pilot shortly after reporting a UFO made worldwide headlines. On October 21, twenty-year-old Frederick Valentich was flying a rented, single-engine Cessna 182 from Moorabbin Airport to King Island across the Bass Strait, which separates Tasmania from mainland Australia. He had been flying for eighteen months and was accumulating hours in order to obtain a commercial pilot's license. At 7:06 P.M., he radioed Melbourne Flight Service Control to report a large aircraft flying at about 4,500 feet. Ground controllers responded that there were no aircraft in the area below 5,000 feet. Valentich said, "It has four bright lights . . . appear to be landing lights. Aircraft has just passed over me, about 1,000 feet above." "Can you identify the aircraft?" asked the controllers. "It isn't an aircraft," said Valentich, "it's. . . ." Then there was silence. Two minutes later, Valentich's voice was heard again, saying, "Melbourne, it's approaching from due east toward me. . . . It seems to be playing some sort of game . . . flying at a speed I cannot estimate. . . . It is flying past. . . . It is a long shape . . . cannot identify more than that . . . coming for me right now. . . . It seems to be stationary . . . I'm orbiting and the thing is orbiting on top of me also. . . . It has a green light and sort of metallic light on the outside." Suddenly, Valentich reported that his engine was choking. His voice was replaced by a metallic scratching sound. Then there was silence. It was 7:12 P.M.

When Valentich's Cessna did not arrive at King Island on schedule, an air search was carried out. Royal Australian Air Force planes discovered an oil slick about eighteen miles north of King Island. Transportation officials, however, claimed that it was not made by a light aircraft. A week-long search by eight airplanes and an Air Force maritime reconnaissance plane, covering a 10,000 square-mile area, found no wreckage and no indication that the Cessna had plunged into the sea.

Controversy over the case increased when *The Australia*, a national newspaper, reported that the Department of Transportation was withholding part of the transcript of the tape-recorded conversation between Valentich and the air traffic controllers. The missing piece allegedly contained a detailed description of the UFO. According to the newspaper, it had obtained this information from a Department of Transportation source. However, Ken Williams, a spokesman for the Department of Transportation in Melbourne, denied the charge. He said that all the information from the tapes between 7:06 P.M. and 7:12 P.M. relating to the pilot's UFO sighting had been made public and that the rest of the tape contained jargon.

Many investigators were surprised by the reaction of the pilot's father, Guido Valentich, who said that he believed his son was alive and being held by someone from another world. He reported that his son had been interested in UFOs for many years and had sighted one about ten months previously. When it was discovered that Frederick Valentich had filed a one-way flight plan, indicating that he perhaps did not expect to return from the island, many investigators became suspicious that a HOAX was involved.

An Air Transport official, speculating that the inexperienced pilot had become disoriented, suggested that his airplane had turned upside down and that the pilot had seen reflections of the King Island and Cape Otway lighthouses on the clouds. The Cessna's engine would have failed if it were flown upside down, causing it to plunge into the sea.

The Australian Civil Aviation Department file on the DISAPPEARANCE of Frederick Valentich remains open.

**MENGER, HOWARD,** CONTACTEE whose first encounter allegedly took place during his childhood when he met a beautiful spacewoman in the woods. She told him the SPACE PEOPLE would always watch over him. According to Menger, in the mid-1950s a rash of UFO sightings around his New Jersey home was followed by regular social visits from the Space People. He performed favors for his alien friends and even acted as their barber, cutting their long blond hair in order that they could pass unnoticed among earthlings. Menger was rewarded with a trip to the MOON, where he breathed easily in a surface atmosphere similar to Earth's. He brought back some lunar potatoes which reportedly contained five times the protein found in terrestrial potatoes. Their nutritive value could not be proved, however, because Menger had supposedly handed them over to the U.S. government, which was keeping them a secret.

Menger related his experiences in a book entitled *From Outer Space to You* (Clarksberg, West Virginia: Saucerian Press, 1959). He narrates his story and performs music allegedly taught him by the Space People on a record, entitled *Music from Another Planet,* which is available through mail order advertisements.

**MEN IN BLACK,** also known as MIB or MIBs, mysterious characters who reportedly question, threaten and sometimes harass UFO witnesses and researchers. They have been active on the American UFO scene since 1947 but rarely appear in foreign countries. Dressed in black suits and wrap-around sunglasses, MIBs are slender, dark-complexioned men whose facial features have sometimes been described as Oriental. They generally travel in groups of three in large, black automobiles, usually Cadillacs. They pose as FBI and CIA agents, military personnel, insurance brokers and telephone inspectors. Researchers who accept the existence of MIBs conclude that they are either secret government agents or extraterrestrials living on Earth. The most famous case involving MIBs was that of investigator and author Albert K. Bender, who was reportedly silenced by three men in black in 1953.

Bibliography: Barker, Gray, *They Knew Too Much About Flying Saucers* (New York: University Books, 1956).

**MENZEL, DONALD HOWARD** (b. April 11, 1901, Florence, Colorado; d. December 14, 1976), astronomer and astrophysicist.

From the early 1950s until his death, Menzel was the leading opponent of the EXTRATERRESTRIAL HYPOTHESIS (ETH) and was sometimes referred to as the archdemon of saucerdom. He believed that all UFOs could be explained in natural or conventional terms such as MIRAGES, astronomical and atmospheric phenomena and HOAXES. He, himself, observed what appeared to be a UFO while flying in the Arctic zone near Bering Strait in 1955. A bright light shot toward his aircraft from the southwestern horizon. Flashing green and red lights, it stopped abruptly at an apparent distance of 300 feet from the plane. The UFO then seemed to execute evasive action. It disappeared over the horizon, then reappeared. Menzel suddenly recognized the light as the out-of-focus image of the star SIRIUS. Its sudden disappearance, he realized, had been due to a distant mountain, which had momentarily cut off the STAR from view.

Menzel received his B.A. in 1920 and his M.A. in 1921 from the University of Denver. He received an M.A. in 1923 and his Ph.D. in 1924 from Princeton University.

Menzel held the following positions during his career: instructor in astronomy at the University of Iowa from 1924 to 1925; assistant professor of astronomy at Ohio State University from 1925 to 1926; assistant astronomer from 1926 to 1932 at Lick Observatory; assistant professor of astronomy from 1932 to 1935; associate professor of astrophysics from 1935 to 1938; professor of astrophysics from 1938 to 1971; Paine Professor of Practical Astronomy from 1956 to 1971; Director of Harvard Observatory from 1954 to 1966; Smithsonian Astrophysical Observatory research scientist from 1966 to 1971, at Harvard University; chief scientist at the Geophysics Corporation of America from 1959 to 1969; vice-president and member of the board of directors of Colorado Instruments, Incorporated, and Silver Bell Mines; member and director of solar eclipse expeditions in France, Italy, Peru, Canada, Mexico, Greece, West Africa and Russia; State Department specialist for Latin America, lecturing there in 1965.

Menzel was a member of the International Astronomical Union (IAU), the American Astronomical Society (AAS), the American Philosophical Society (APS), the NATIONAL ACADEMY OF SCIENCES (NAS), the American Mathematical Society, the American Physical Society, the American Geophysical Union, the American Association of Variable Star Observers, the Royal Astronomical Society, the American Academy of Arts and Sciences, Phi Beta Kappa and Sigma Xi. He was President of the IAU's commission on solar eclipses from 1948 to 1955, the IAU's commission 17-the moon from 1964 to 1967; and the AAS from 1954 to 1956. He was director-at-large of the AAS as of 1959. He was Vice-President of the APS from 1965 to 1968, and the NAS from 1935 to 1938. He was the recipient of the A. Cressy Morrison Prize of the New York Academy of Sciences in 1926, 1928 and 1947, an M.A. from Harvard University in 1942, a D.Sc. from the University of Denver in 1954, the James H. Rand scholarship in astrophysical computation in 1955, the Thomas Alva Edison Foundation Award in 1957 and the John Evans Award from the University of Denver in 1965. In honor of his contribution to astrophysics, the Minor Planet Center of the International Astronomical Union named an asteroid for him.

Menzel lectured extensively on UFOs around the world, including South America and Mexico. He was the author of numerous scientific papers and articles, as well as some science fiction stories. He authored, coauthored, revised and edited numerous books, including: *Mathematical Physics* (Englewood Cliffs, N.J.: Prentice-Hall, 1947); *Elementary Manual of Radio Propagation* (Englewood Cliffs, N.J.: Prentice-Hall, 1948); *Flying Saucers* (Cambridge, Massachusetts: Harvard University Press, 1953); (with Lyle G. Boyd) *The World of Flying Saucers: A Scientific Examination of a Major Myth of the Space Age* (Garden City, N.Y.: Doubleday and Company, 1963); *Astronomy* (New York: Random House, 1970); *Survey of the Universe* (Englewood Cliffs, N.J.: Prentice-Hall, 1971); and (with Ernest H. Taves) *The UFO Enigma* (Garden City, N.Y.: Doubleday and Company, 1977).

**MERCURI, PAOLO,** *see* **CENTRO TORINESE RICERCHE UFOLOGICHE (CTRU)**

**MERCURY 7,** spacecraft in which ASTRONAUT Scott Carpenter observed several UFOs and photographed one with a hand camera on May 24, 1962. Carpenter believed the objects to be ice crystals which had broken off the outside of the spacecraft.

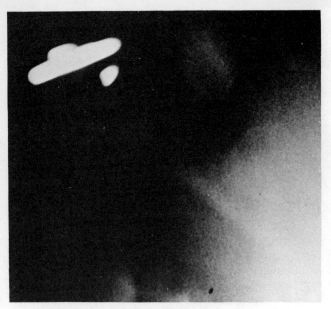

UFO photographed by astronaut Scott Carpenter and tentatively identified as ice crystals. *(Courtesy NASA)*

**MERCURY 8,** spacecraft from which ASTRONAUT Walter Schirra reported observing large glowing masses over the Indian Ocean on October 3, 1963. As in the case of all other UFO sightings by astronauts, the NATIONAL AERONAUTICS AND SPACE ADMINISTRATION (NASA) determined that what had been observed was nothing which could be termed abnormal in the space environment.

**MERCURY 9,** spacecraft from which ASTRONAUT L. GORDON COOPER observed the approach of a glowing green UFO with a red tail while passing over Australia on May 16, 1963, during his fifteenth orbit around Earth. The object was also observed by personnel at ground tracking stations. As in the case of all other UFO sightings by astronauts, the NATIONAL AERONAUTICS AND SPACE ADMINISTRATION (NASA) determined that what had been observed was nothing which could be termed abnormal in the space environment.

**MERCURY CAPSULE,** spacecraft in which ASTRONAUT John Glenn made the first U.S. orbital space flight on February 20, 1962. Reportedly, Glenn observed three UFOs during the flight which followed him and then passed his capsule at varying speeds. As in the case of all other UFO sightings by astronauts, the NATIONAL AERONAUTICS AND SPACE ADMINISTRATION (NASA) determined that what had been observed was nothing which could be termed abnormal in the space environment.

**METAPHYSICAL DIGEST,** publication of the SOCIETY OF METAPHYSICIANS.

**METEMPIRICAL UFO BULLETIN (MUFOB),** British magazine established in 1968 and published quarterly. MUFOB serves as a medium for exchange of views, opinions and data, and for publication of original research. Investigations are occasionally conducted by the editorial staff on an ad hoc basis.

The Editorial Panel consists of Editor John Rimmer, John Harney, Peter Rogerson and Roger Sandell. The editorial offices are located at 11 Beverly Road, New Malden, Surrey KT3 4AW, England.

**METEOR,** term which originally referred to any unusual atmospheric phenomenon and which now refers specifically to a small piece of solid material which enters Earth's atmosphere from outer space and burns up in the upper part of it. The term also refers to the bright streak formed by the incandescence produced as the object is heated by its swift passage through the atmosphere. A meteor leaves a fiery trail and often scatters what appear to be sparks. Bright meteors are known as BOLIDES or FIREBALLS. Faint meteors are popularly known as shooting stars, although they are, of course, not STARS. Extremely faint meteors are actually particles no larger than a grain of sand. Shooting stars are very common and can be seen at frequent intervals on a clear, moonless night.

The entry into Earth's atmosphere of a group of meteors at the same time and place is known as a meteor shower. The latter is thought to result from the breaking up of a COMET. Some showers return annually, others at greater intervals, irregular intervals, or not at all.

According to authors JACQUES VALLEE and Janine Vallee, studies of the time distribution of the most significant UFO sightings have shown no correlation whatsoever with the periods of activity of the major showers. However, several UFO sightings have been attributed to witnesses' MISIDENTIFICATION of a bright meteor, as in the case of the Chiles/Whitted sighting near MONTGOMERY, ALABAMA, the Coyne sighting over MANSFIELD, OHIO, and the GREEN FIREBALLS seen over New Mexico in 1948 and 1949.

**METEORITE,** a piece of stone, iron, or a mixture of the two, which reaches Earth's surface from outer space. UFOLOGISTS often compare the history of scientific recognition of meteorites to that of UFOs. Ancient people accepted the fact that lumps of metal and stone sometimes fell out of the sky. Sometimes they preserved and worshipped these objects. However, in the eighteenth century, reports of stones falling from the skies were dismissed as nonsense by the scientific establishment because such an occurrence was considered impossible. The French Academy of Sciences explained one bona fide meteorite, whose fall had been witnessed, as an ordinary stone that had been struck by lightning. It was not until a shower of over 2,000 stones fell at L'Aigle, France, that the reality of falls of stones from outer space was finally established in 1804.

Some UFOlogists have speculated that an unknown object which exploded over the TUNGUSKA REGION in the Soviet Union in 1908 was an extraterrestrial spacecraft. However, it was originally classified as the Tunguska meteorite. Some scientists today still believe that the object was a meteorite, although others have suggested alternative natural explanations for the explosion.

**METEOROLOGICAL PHENOMENA.** Strongly advocated by astronomer DONALD MENZEL as the explanation for most UFO reports, meteorological phenomena include PARHELIA and PARASELENAE, TEMPERATURE INVERSION, MIRAGES, CLOUDS, SUBSUNS and submoons, ICE CRYSTALS, PLASMA and AURORAS.

**MEXICO.** UFO WAVES occurred in 1949/50 and 1965 in Mexico. A very famous case occurred in ZACATECAS in 1883 involving astronomer José Bonilla, who observed and photographed hundreds of UFOs passing in front of the sun.

In the 1950s, a photograph appeared in German newspapers of an alleged UFO crash victim. The incident was supposed to have occurred just outside Mexico City, but is believed to have been a HOAX. No one has succeeded in tracing the original source of the story or the source of the photograph.

In 1978, another bizarre tale emerged from Mexico. A spaceship OCCUPANT allegedly appeared at a doctor's office requesting an examination. The physician, known as Dr. Diaz, reportedly had impeccable credentials and supposedly became the subject of a secret investigation

Alleged UFO photographed in Cocoyoc, Mexico, on November 3, 1973. *(Courtesy ICUFON/R. Smotek)*

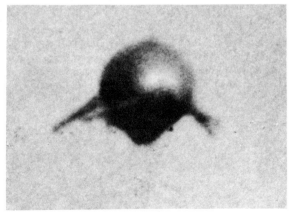

at the UNITED NATIONS. It was later discovered that the doctor was the husband of the director of a UFO organization and had participated in the stunt at the urging of his wife.

Both the AERIAL PHENOMENA RESEARCH ORGANIZATION (APRO) and SKANDINAVISK UFO INFORMATION (SUFOI) have representatives in Mexico.

**MIB** *see* **MEN IN BLACK**

**MICHEL, AIMÉ** (b. May 12, 1919, St. Vincent les Forts, France), field investigator and writer.

A leading figure in the study of paranormal phenomena in France, and one of the best known UFO-LOGISTS in the world, Michel introduced the term and concept ORTHOTENY to UFOLOGY. He has stated that, "In UFOlogy, the rule is to think of everything and to believe nothing." He suggests that UFOs are involved in a control system of history and calculates that open contact could occur within the next half century.

Michel attended the Universities of Aix-en-Provence, Grenoble and Marseilles and received his Licence de Philosophie in 1939 and his License de Lettres in 1944. He studied Accoustical Engineering in Paris in 1944.

From 1944 to 1974, Michel was a Research Fellow at the state-owned Service de la Recherche de l'Office de Radio Television Française. During this period, he spent some years at the Short Wave Service and three months as a technical adviser in Tunisia in 1958.

From 1958 to 1974, Michel worked as a UFO field investigator. During this time, he wrote many articles which were published in the FLYING SAUCER REVIEW (FSR) and other specialized reviews. His writings also dealt with philosophical speculation on astrophysical matters. Michel is author of *Lueurs sur les Soucoupes Volantes* (Paris: Mame, 1954) and *Mystérieux Objets Célestes* (Paris: Arthaud, 1958). They were published in the United States as *The Truth About Flying Saucers* (New York: Criterion Books, 1956) and *Flying Saucers and the Straight Line Mystery* (New York: Criterion Books, 1958).

**MIDWESTERN UFO NETWORK** *see* **MUTUAL UFO NETWORK**

**MIGRATION HYPOTHESIS,** theory that UFOs are extraterrestrial spacecraft carrying intelligent beings from a dying PLANET who are looking for a new world in which to settle their people. Such beings might be surveying Earth to determine whether it is a suitable place to live, whether to invade or attempt peaceful integration, and whether or not earthlings might use nuclear weapons against them.

In such a situation, the human race faces danger even

if a small-scale migration occurred by mutual agreement. Although we might share the benefits of advanced technological knowledge, we would face the risk that the aliens' superior capabilities would eventually be used to dominate us.

**MIND CONTROL,** manipulation of a person's mind by another person. UFOlogist JACQUES VALLEE has proposed that the UFO phenomenon may be the creation of a secret form of PSYCHOTRONIC TECHNOLOGY. CONTACTEES and ABDUCTION victims, he suggests, are victims of this deception and pawns in a conspiracy to bring about radical social change on our PLANET. Author Robert Temple has conjectured that such a plan could be executed through the use of sophisticated hypnotic procedures. Highly suggestible subjects could be located in advance of the experience, hypnotized, and given the posthypnotic suggestion that a UFO contact will occur upon a specific occasion or upon hearing a code-word or phrase. When the reaction is triggered, the subject would be overwhelmed by a flood of recollections of his or her preprogrammed encounter which would appear to be happening at that very moment. The preprogramming might actually have involved a charade acted out by people dressed as extraterrestrials while the subject was in a trance. However, verbal suggestion alone would be sufficient for highly suggestible subjects who could be instructed to experience both auditory and visual hallucinations in trance. According to a report in the July, 1975, issue of the *American Journal of Clinical Hypnosis,* hypnotic induction by video tape is as effective as induction by a live person. Temple conjectures that "using video machines one hypnotist could actually induce HYPNOSIS in every single contactee in America over television without moving from his desk."

Temple also points out that specific responses could be elicited from an alleged UFO abduction victim by a skilled hypnotist whose phrasing and intonation subtly conveys to the hypnotized subject what the hypnotist wishes to hear. He suggests that UFO investigators should look more closely into the backgrounds and methods used by hypnotists specializing in the use of hypnosis in contact cases.

Vallee has speculated that a UFO conspiracy based on mind control might be the work of a hypothetical, highly secret international group which has been simulating an extraterrestrial threat since World War II in order to unite mankind and prevent World War III.

Bibliography: Vallee, Jacques, *Messengers of Deception* (Berkeley, California: And/Or Press, 1979); Temple, Robert K. G., "Taking Us To Their Leader," *Second Look* (Washington, D.C.: *Second Look,* Vol. 1, No. 7, May 1979).

**MINISTRY OF UNIVERSAL WISDOM,** CONTACTEE organization based in Yucca Valley, California, whose Founder and Director was the late GEORGE VAN TASSELL. The organization published *Proceedings,* which was edited by Van Tassell.

**MIRAGE,** an optical illusion in which the distortion and/or displacement of a distant object is caused by the bending of light rays as they pass through layers of air of different densities and temperatures. Since the light rays bend in a curved path, an object below the horizon may be visible to an observer as an image floating above the horizon. Mirages of setting PLANETS may appear to maneuver at high speed when changing atmospheric conditions cause them to change size and shape. Astronomer DONALD MENZEL, who has attributed numerous UFO sightings to mirages, proposed that such an effect created the UFO seen at FARGO, NORTH DAKOTA, in 1948. Other objects which might appear as mirages above the horizon, and which might not be immediately recognizable, are towers, beacons, automobile and train headlights and ships' lights.

Menzel also points out that hot air over a road will produce a mirage resembling a wet spot on the surface. Sometimes this spot will assume a cigar shape and have a metallic sheen. He suggests that a motorist watching the mirage recede as he or she approaches might mistake it for a UFO pacing the automobile.

Bibliography: Menzel, Donald H., and Ernest H. Taves, *The UFO Enigma* (Garden City, N.Y.: Doubleday and Company, 1977).

**MISIDENTIFICATIONS.** Investigation has revealed that a very high proportion of UFO reports can be explained as misidentifications of ASTRONOMICAL AND METEOROLOGICAL PHENOMENA, natural effects such as BIOLUMINESCENCE and SWAMP GAS, flying creatures such as BIRDS and INSECTS, and man-made objects such as conventional aircraft, ADVERTISING PLANES, BLIMPS, BALLOONS, KITES, artificial SATELLITES, missiles, flares, reflections of searchlights on cloud surfaces, and CLOUDS of sodium or barium gases released for research purposes.

In some cases, the misperception of an object or its movements is due to effects such as TEMPERATURE INVERSION or OPTICAL ILLUSION. Another factor which contributes to the confusion in identifying conventional and natural objects is the human being's inability to perceive accurately such details as distance, size and speed.

In many cases, misidentification is the result of the brain's *interpretation* of the visual image which may be based on an unconscious wish to believe in the presence of extraterrestrial spacecraft. Thus an observer seeing

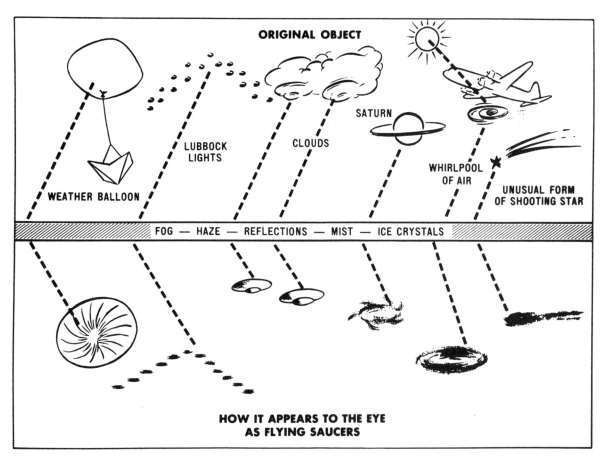

ORIGINAL OBJECT

WEATHER BALLOON — LUBBOCK LIGHTS — CLOUDS — SATURN — WHIRLPOOL OF AIR — UNUSUAL FORM OF SHOOTING STAR

FOG — HAZE — REFLECTIONS — MIST — ICE CRYSTALS

**HOW IT APPEARS TO THE EYE AS FLYING SAUCERS**

Various objects which may be misidentified because of atmospheric distortion. *(United Press International Photo)*

Astronaut Edgar Mitchell. *(Courtesy NASA)*

the flashing lights moving from right to left on the electronic sign of an advertising plane might assume that the lights continue around the other side of the craft in a loop. Based on this assumption, he or she deduces that the craft is round and probably rotating. The witness then becomes adamant in the belief that he or she has seen a bona fide flying saucer.

Bibliography: Hendry, Allan, *The UFO Handbook* (Garden City, N.Y.: Doubleday and Company, 1979).

**MITCHELL, EDGAR,** ASTRONAUT who feels that the evidence is very strong that UFOs do exist, but that if their explanation is extraterrestrial visitation, then their creators have learned something about the laws of nature that we do not know yet. If this is the case, he projects that studies in the realm of mental phenomena and the unified or multiple field area will in due course give us the answer. Mitchell thinks it very likely that UFOs come from another dimension. "I am sure," he says, "there is intelligent control somewhere behind them."

**MOCK MOONS** *see* **PARASELENAE**

## MOCK SUNS *see* PARHELIA

**MODERN ERA,** in UFOLOGY, the period dating from Kenneth Arnold's famous sighting over MOUNT RAINIER, WASHINGTON, in 1947 until the present time. Arnold's sighting did not represent the first major UFO activity of the twentieth century. It was preceded by the sightings of FOO FIGHTERS by military pilots during World War II and a series of sightings of GHOST ROCKETS in Scandinavia in 1946. However, the publicity generated by the Mount Rainier incident encouraged hundreds of people to report their own UFO sightings and set the stage for widespread public interest, controversy and government involvement. Arnold's description of disk-shaped objects which flew like saucers skipping over water led newspaper headline writers to coin the term "flying saucer." The designation "unidentified flying object" and its acronym, "UFO," were not created until 1951 when the UNITED STATES AIR FORCE (USAF) decided to replace the term "flying saucer" which they considered too frivolous.

Although at the beginning of the Modern Era many people suspected that UFOs might be secret Russian weapons or phenomena resulting from atomic testing, the EXTRATERRESTRIAL HYPOTHESIS (ETH) soon became the most popular theory among those who believed UFOs were not natural phenomena or conventional objects. Science fiction movies of the 1950s reinforced the idea that extraterrestrials might be visiting Earth. Some individuals, who later became known as "CONTACTEES," claimed to have communicated and traveled to other PLANETS with extraterrestrial beings. Rumors spread that the Air Force had actually captured a CRASHED FLYING SAUCER.

Jun-Ichi Takanashi with members of the Operating and Investigation Committees at the Modern Space Flight Association office.

Meanwhile, UFO reports continued to come in over the years from reputable people in all walks of life, including military pilots, airline pilots, scientists, businessmen, ministers and public officials. Dissatisfied with the Air Force program (which was initiated in 1947 and terminated in 1969), many civilian researchers formed private organizations to conduct their own investigations of UFO cases.

In the 1960s, a new pattern began cropping up in some UFO reports. Witnesses claimed to have been abducted aboard flying saucers where they were subjected to physical examinations by the alien OCCUPANTS.

In the early 1970s, a new dimension was added to the UFO mystery. Author ERICH VON DÄNIKEN popularized the theory that Earth was visited in ancient times by extraterrestrial ASTRONAUTS. The excitement over this possibility was soon followed by a wave of interest in the BERMUDA TRIANGLE, an area where ships and airplanes supposedly disappear in a mysterious manner. Some writers speculated that the DISAPPEARANCES were caused by UFOs.

Hundreds of books about UFOs have been written since 1947. Witnesses have continued to file reports, sometimes sporadically, sometimes in WAVES. The numerous UFO organizations have maintained records and statistical analyses of the data. Since the late 1970s, UFOLOGISTS and the public have begun to lean away from the ETH toward the PARALLEL UNIVERSE HYPOTHESIS. As the 1980s bring the Modern Era into its fifth decade, there is still no irrefutable proof that convinces the scientific or political establishment that UFOs represent an intelligence beyond or outside that of mankind. Public opinion POLLS, however, have shown a constantly increasing tendency among the general public to believe that UFOs are not conventional objects or natural phenomena.

## MODERN SPACE FLIGHT ASSOCIATION (MSFA), C.P.O. Box 910, Osaka, Japan; telephone number: 06-761-3017.

The purpose of this organization is to investigate all UFO-related phenomena and to disseminate the relevant data and conclusions. The group holds that UFOs are extraterrestrial ships from other solar systems engaged in exploration. MSFA has investigated major UFO sightings in Japan, including the 1973 incident in which a huge, spherical UFO sucked up water from a bay in Hokkaido.

This nonprofit organization was founded in 1956 by Jun-Ichi Takanashi, who serves as Chairman. The Operating Committee consists of Tusutaka Kawase, Takashi Morino, Motoshige Akai, Kazuo Hayashi, Hiroshi Yabushita and Masaji Kashiko. The Investigation Committee consists of Tasutaka Kawase, Kazuo Hayashi,

Motoshige Akai, Hideo Suzuki, Kunio Narazaki, Hiroshi Yabushita and Yashuhiro Ujihara. There are about 2,500 members. Field investigators are located in different areas of the country. The organization has several foreign correspondents and is willing to cooperate with any UFO research organization in the world to investigate sightings and to compare data and opinions. MSFA sponsors meetings, discussion panels, lectures, exhibitions, the lending and supplying of materials for exhibition purposes and the distribution of domestic and foreign materials, such as books, magazines and photographs. The organization publishes *Soratobu Enban Kenkyu* in Japanese and *MSFA UFO Report* in English. Both magazines are edited by Jun-Ichi Takanashi and are published at irregular intervals.

## MOIGNE DOWNS, ENGLAND.

On the night of October 24, 1967, two policemen in Devon chased an enormous, illuminated FLYING CROSS for a distance of twelve miles. The UFO disappeared but was later reported in other areas of the country. A Ministry of Defense spokesman announced that the witnesses had observed American airplanes refuelling. Reportedly, the American Air Command issued a prompt denial of this explanation.

Two days later, Angus Brooks, a retired flight administrative officer for the British Overseas Airways Corporation and a former RAF photographic interpretor, was taking his usual morning walk on Moigne Downs in Dorset with his two dogs, a German shepherd and a Dalmatian. He lay down in a hollow to shelter from the strong wind while his dogs ran off to look for game. Almost immediately, he saw a contrail in the sky which disappeared revealing an object hurtling down toward the ground. The UFO stopped at an altitude of about two-hundred-to-three-hundred feet. It was made up of a central disk, about twenty-five feet in diameter and twelve feet thick, from which protruded four fuselages estimated to be about seventy-five feet long, seven feet high and eight feet wide. As the object approached, three of the fuselages were lined up next to each other behind the central chamber while the remaining fuselage pointed forward. On deceleration, the two outer fuselages at the rear swung forward ninety degrees so that all four fuselages formed a cross with the disk at the center. As soon as it had stopped its descent, the entire object rotated ninety degrees clockwise. It then hovered silently, unaffected by the very strong wind. Made of a translucent material, the craft assumed the color of the sky above it, changing as CLOUDS passed overhead. Nose cones and groove fins were visible under the fuselages. Dark shadows spotted the bottom surfaces of the disk and the fuselages. The German shepherd dog, obviously distraught, pestered Brooks in

an attempt to make him leave the area. Brooks, however, did not move. After twenty-two minutes, the front and rear fuselages moved around to line up with one of the lateral fuselages. The object took off to the east northeast, the single fuselage in front and the three parallel fuselages in the rear.

On subsequent visits to the area, the German shepherd showed signs of nervousness. She died of acute cystitis within six weeks of the sighting.

An investigator from the Ministry of Defence concluded that Brooks, who had undergone a corneal transplant some years previously, had observed a piece of loose matter floating in the vitreous fluid of his eyeball. He suggested that this effect and the prior UFO publicity might have triggered a dream state while Brooks was resting. Brooks argued that a vitreous floater would have followed the upward and downward movements of the eye muscle. Instead, the object entered his field of vision at thirty degrees, remained completely still for twenty-two minutes, then left his field of vision at 320 degrees. Brooks remained firm in his opinion that he had observed a controlled flying vehicle of unique design and performance.

Bibliography: Keyhoe, Donald E., and Gordon I. R. Lore (eds.), *Strange Effects from UFOs* (Washington, D.C.: National Investigations Committee on Aerial Phenomena, 1969).

## MOLLER, PAUL S.,

former associate professor of the University of California at Davis who, as President of the DISCOJET CORPORATION, has since 1969 been designing and building experimental flying saucers.

## MONGOLIA see ROERICH, NIKOLAY

## MONGUZZI see ITALY

## MONO GRANDE see BIGFOOT

## MONTANA MOVIES see GREAT FALLS, MONTANA

## MONTGOMERY, ALABAMA,

location over which a UFO was sighted by two airline pilots in 1948. Although various authors have given the date of the incident variously as July 20, 23 and 25, the majority place the event on July 24. Captain Clarence S. Chiles and John B. Whitted were flying an Eastern Airlines DC–3 from Houston to Atlanta when, at about 2:45 A.M., they saw a large red light headed toward them from the east. As the aircraft veered to the left in an attempt to avoid collision, the UFO seemed to execute an intelligently controlled maneuver, passing to the right of the DC–3, pulling up with a burst of flame from its rear and zooming up into the CLOUDS. There is uncertainty in the record and in the recollection of the pilots as to whether or not the aircraft was rocked in the wake of the UFO.

Chiles and Whitted described the object as cigar-shaped, approximately one hundred feet in length and about thirty feet in diameter. On the nose of the UFO was a pointed protrusion resembling a radar antenna. Two rows of rectangular windows glowed brilliantly like burning magnesium. The object's underside glowed a phosphorescent blue. An orange-red flame extended about fifty feet from its rear.

Only one passenger was awake at the time of the sighting. He observed a bright object flashing by the aircraft but was unable to discern any details. That same night, a cigar-shaped object shooting flames from the rear was observed independently by another pilot in the vicinity and by observers at Robbins Air Force Base in Georgia.

UFOLOGISTS have noted the similarity of the object's appearance to that of a UFO seen a few days before, on July 21, over The Hague in Holland. Dutch observers reported a CIGAR-SHAPED UFO with two parallel rows of windows.

The July 24th sighting was classified as a METEOR by the Air Force's astronomical consultant J. ALLEN HYNEK. He conjectured that the impression of windows was supplied by the witnesses' imagination. Writers DONALD MENZEL and PHILIP KLASS concurred in this assessment. Menzel pointed out that amateur astronomers had observed many exceptionally bright meteors that night from the Delta Aquarid METEOR shower. Atmospheric physicist JAMES MCDONALD contested this explanation, pointing out that a meteor could not have performed the maneuvers described by the pilots. Chiles and Whitted, themselves, rejected the possibility that the UFO might have been a meteor.

Bibliography: Ruppelt, Edward J., *The Report on Unidentified Flying Objects* (Garden City, N.Y.: Doubleday and Company, 1956); U.S. Congress, House, Committee on Science and Astronautics, Symposium on Unidentified Flying Objects, Hearings, 90th Congress, 2nd Session, July 29, 1968 (Washington, D.C.: U.S. Government Printing Office, 1968); Menzel, Donald H., and Lyle G. Boyd, *The World of Flying Saucers* (Garden City, N.Y.: Doubleday and Company, 1963).

**MOODY, CHARLES L.,** *see* **ALAMOGORDO, NEW MEXICO**

**MOON,** some UFOLOGISTS claim that pilots of extraterrestrial spacecraft maintain bases on the moon hidden under dark-colored domes. Supposedly, amateur astronomers have been observing the appearance and disappearance of these domes on various parts of the moon's surface since the 1920s.

In 1953 John J. O'Neill, a science writer for the New York *Herald-Tribune,* observed through his telescope

Spires on the lunar surface allegedly photographed by Orbiter 2. *(Courtesy ICUFON/NASA)*

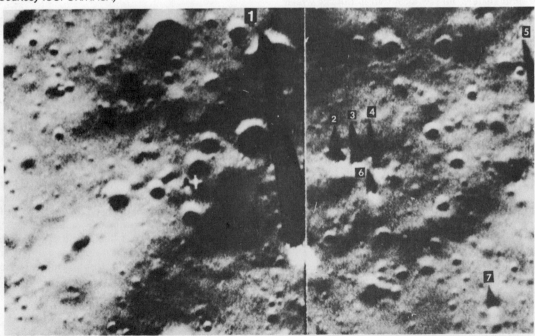

what appeared to be a bridge twelve-to-twenty miles long over the *Mare Crisium*. The feature had never been seen before. A few weeks later, British amateur astronomer H. P. Wilkins confirmed the presence of the "moon bridge." Astronomer DONALD MENZEL concluded that the object, which subsequently disappeared, was a high plateau illuminated by the setting sun while the rest of the crater wall was already in darkness.

In November 1966, the United States' Orbiter 2 spacecraft photographed the moon's surface from a distance of twenty-three miles. One of these photographs, which circulates among UFO researchers, shows the alleged shadows of eight megalithic spires. The largest is estimated to be between fifty and seventy feet in height.

Another rumor purports that Apollo 11 ASTRONAUTS observed and filmed two UFOs that landed near the lunar module. The film has supposedly been put under tight security wraps by the NATIONAL AERONAUTICS AND SPACE ADMINISTRATION (NASA). The agency denies that any such sighting ever occurred.

Bibliography: Wilkins, Harold T., *Flying Saucers on the Moon* (London: Peter Owen, 1954); Leonard, George H., *Somebody Else Is on the Moon* (New York: David McKay Company, 1978).

## MOONDOGS *see* PARASELENAE

## MOROCCO.

Peak periods of UFO activity in Morocco occurred in September during the worldwide WAVE of 1952 and again in September of 1976. On September 21, 1952, reports of flying disks poured in across the country. In Casablanca, a UFO was seen by five thousand people attending a boxing match.

On September 24, 1976, American Ambassador to Morocco, Robert Anderson, sent a confidential communiqué to Secretary of State Henry Kissinger requesting information on unidentified flying objects. He reported that, the previous day, a Moroccan official had visited him to discuss UFO sightings on the night of September 18–19. Reports had come in from Agadir, Kalaa-Sraghna, Essaouira, Casablanca, Rabat, Kenitra, Meknes and the Fez region. The object was sighted from 1:00 A.M. to 2:00 A.M., traveling slowly on a south to north course generally parallel to the Moroccan Atlantic coast. The silent object was estimated to be at an altitude of approximately 3,300 feet. While some witnesses described it as a silvery luminous disk, others described it as a large, luminous tube-shaped object. A Moroccan official clarified this discrepancy when he explained that he himself had seen the UFO which appeared circular until it came close, at which time he saw it as a cylindrical object. Intermittent trails of bright

sparks and fragments were given off by the UFO. Ambassador Anderson, intrigued by the similarity of descriptions from widely separate locations, requested a prompt response from the State Department. Kissinger replied by describing past efforts to study the phenomenon, concluding that the object might have been a spectacular METEOR or, on account of the burning fragments, slow velocity and absence of noise, a decaying SATELLITE. Since the sightings occurred from 1:00 A.M. to 2:00 A.M., it is difficult to attribute this event to a meteor, which would not have been visible for a one-hour period within such a small area. With regard to decaying satellite parts, there was no re-entry record to account for an object seen on that date. Considering the weaknesses of these two HYPOTHESES, it is not inappropriate that Kissinger stated, "It is difficult to offer any definitive explanation as to the cause or origin of the UFOs sighted in the Moroccan area . . . September 19, 1976."

Bibliography: Declassified communiqués between the United States Embassy in Morocco and the U.S. Secretary of State on September 24 and October 1, 1976, available from the Freedom of Information Office, Department of State, Washington, D.C.

## MOSELEY, JAMES W.

(b. August 4, 1931, New York, N.Y.; address: P.O. Box 163, Fort Lee, N.J. 07024), author, lecturer, Publisher and Editor of SAUCER "XYZ."

While interviewing two witnesses to a previous UFO sighting in 1953, Moseley observed a white glowing light with a pulsating orange light surrounding it, traveling at high speed across the night sky. Although the UFO's approximately straight trajectory resembled that of a SATELLITE, there was no satellite which could have accounted for the sighting. Moseley believes that UFOs may possibly originate from a fourth dimension.

After studying for two years at Princeton University, Moseley pursued a life of adventure and travel. He participated in a number of major expeditions to Africa. He went treasure hunting among Inca burial grounds in Peru and for several years exported pre-Colombian artifacts to the United States. Moseley describes his career history as sketchy. He is currently an investment manager.

In 1954 Moseley founded the SAUCER AND UNEXPLAINED CELESTIAL EVENTS RESEARCH SOCIETY (SAUCERS), now defunct. He was Editor of its publication, *Saucer News*. In addition to publishing and editing his own newsletter, *Saucer "XYZ,"* Moseley is Chairman of the NATIONAL UFO CONFERENCE (NUFOC).

Moseley has appeared on countless radio and television programs across the country, and was a regular guest on the former Long John Nebel program in New

York. He has lectured to groups of engineers, scientists and educators nationwide. His articles on flying saucers have been published in numerous UFO magazines. He is author of *Jim Moseley's Book of Saucer News* (Clarksburg, West Virginia: Saucerian Press, 1967), and *The Wright Field Story* (Clarksburg, West Virginia: Saucerian Press, 1971).

**MOSES,** Hebrew prophet who delivered his people from Egyptian slavery and founded the religious community known as Israel. Proponents of the ANCIENT ASTRONAUTS theory claim that the Hebrews were aided in their flight from Egypt by an extraterrestrial spaceship. Verse 21 of Chapter 13 of Exodus is often quoted as evidence of the presence of a typical CIGAR-SHAPED UFO: "And the Lord went before them by day in a pillar of a CLOUD, to lead them the way; and by night in a pillar of fire, to give them light; to go by day and night." Author Barry H. Downing speculates that the cigar-shaped UFO also caused the parting of the Red Sea and undertook defensive measures against the pursuing Egyptian army. He quotes verses 24 and 25 of Chapter 14 of Exodus: "And it came to pass that in the morning watch the Lord looked unto the host of the Egyptians through the pillar of fire and of the cloud, and troubled the host of the Egyptians, And took off their chariot wheels, that they drave them heavily: so that the Egyptians said, Let us flee from the face of Israel; for the Lord fighteth for them against the Egyptians."

"And the Lord went before them by day in a pillar of cloud. . . ." *(The Bettmann Archive)*

Supporters of this hypothesis claim that the extraterrestrial astronauts continued to assist the wandering people by dropping sustenance in the form of manna. Later, according to the Book of Exodus, God instructed Moses to build the ARK OF THE COVENANT. Author ERICH VON DÄNIKEN has speculated that the ark served as a radio.

Bibliography: Downing, Barry H., *The Bible and Flying Saucers* (Philadelphia: J. B. Lippincott Company, 1967).

**MOTHER SHIP,** enormous cylindrical or CIGAR-SHAPED UFO which apparently serves as a carrier for small disk-shaped UFOs. Exponents of the EXTRA-TERRESTRIAL HYPOTHESIS (ETH) suggest that mother ships are interstellar craft, while the small disks they contain are designed for flight within the planetary atmosphere.

Writer Barry Downing suggests that mother ships are actually misidentified holes in the space-time continuum through which UFOs travel to and from a PARALLEL UNIVERSE. When the holes close, they give the impression of a craft departing at an extremely high speed.

Bibliography: Downing, Barry H., *The Bible and Flying Saucers* (Philadelphia: J. B. Lippincott Company, 1967).

**MOTHMAN,** a strange humanoid monster with huge batlike wings allegedly seen by more than one hundred people in West Virginia during 1966 and 1967. The name was given to the creature by an anonymous copy editor and derives from the Batman comic character who was the subject of a popular television series at the time of the sightings. Most witnesses described Mothman as gray, featherless and larger than a man, with a wingspan of about ten feet. He took off vertically and did not flap his wings in flight. Although no one could remember the creature's face, many witnesses described his eyes as round, glowing and red.

Mothman was reported to chase motorists, to have a penchant for scaring women who were menstruating, and to cause conjunctivitis in some witnesses. Some researchers have speculated that Mothman originates from UFOs.

Sightings of giant creatures resembling prehistoric birds have been reported in other parts of the United States. They are known as GARUDAS, named after the giant birds described in the mythology of India. A Garuda differs from Mothman in that its body is not humanoid.

Writer JACQUES VALLEE has compared Mothman to the mysterious nineteenth century character known as SPRINGHEEL JACK.

Bibliography: Keel, John A., *The Mothman Prophecies* (New York: New American Library, 1976).

## MOUNT CLEMENS, MICHIGAN,

location where two brothers, Dan and Grant Jaroslaw, allegedly saw a UFO over Lake St. Clair on January 9, 1967. The two boys took four PHOTOGRAPHS of the object which were subsequently reproduced in numerous UFO magazines.

Hoax UFO from Mount Clemens, Michigan. *(Courtesy ICU-FON)*

Nine years later, the Jaroslaw brothers wrote a letter to astronomer J. ALLEN HYNEK confessing that the incident was a HOAX and that the object in the photograph was a model hanging on a thread.

Bibliography: Hendry, Allan, *The UFO Handbook* (Garden City, N.Y.: Doubleday and Company, 1979).

## MOUNT RAINIER, WASHINGTON,

location of the first reported UFO sighting of the MODERN ERA. Kenneth Arnold, the witness, was a member of the Idaho Search and Rescue Mercy Flyers, flying deputy for the Ada County Aerial Posse, acting deputy federal United States marshal, aerial salesman and originator of the Great Western Fire Control System. An experienced pilot with over 4,000 hours of flying experience over mountains, he was flying his private plane from Chehalis to Yakima, Washington, on June 24, 1947, when he decided to look for a plane that had been missing for several days in that area. At about 3:00 P.M., Arnold was approaching Mount Rainier from the west when a tremendously bright flash lit up the surface of his plane. He could not see the source of the flash. Suddenly the light struck again. He looked around and saw nine objects rapidly approaching the mountain on a southern heading. As they neared, he saw that they were flat, disk-shaped objects arranged in a "diagonally stepped-down echelon formation" stretched out over about five miles. Using the peaks of Mount Rainier and Mount Adams as reference points, he clocked their speed at 1,700 miles per hour. Allowing for some degree of error, he subtracted 500 miles per hour, giving a speed that was still well above 1,000 miles per hour. In 1947, the only man-made object that could travel that fast was a rocket.

Upon landing at Yakima, Arnold related his experience to Central Aircraft General Manager Al Baxter. Word quickly spread around the airport. By the time Arnold had reached the next stop on his route, Pendleton, Oregon, interested but skeptical news reporters were waiting for him. Arnold's standing as a reputable citizen changed their attitude and the incident was reported as a serious news item. When he described the objects as flying "like a saucer would if you skipped it across the water," newspaper headline writers coined the term *flying saucer*.

The official UNITED STATES AIR FORCE (USAF explanation for the sighting was that Arnold had seen a MIRAGE in which the tips of the mountain peaks appeared to float above the mountain chain due to a layer of warm air. Astronomer J. ALLEN HYNEK, however, in his official capacity as consultant to the Air Force, concluded that the sighting could probably be explained as a fleet of airplanes. He found irreconcilable differences in the data which brought Arnold's calculations into doubt. Arnold had stated that the objects were twenty-to-twenty-five miles away and their size about forty-five-to-fifty feet long. Hynek noted that an object of that size cannot be resolved by the human eye at that distance. Therefore, Arnold's estimation of distance was incorrect. Hynek assumed that the objects were probably closer to the pilot and therefore traveling at subsonic speeds which were within the capability of 1947 aircraft. UFO investigator Ted Bloecher counters Hynek's argument by saying that Arnold had used fixed reference

Kenneth Arnold. *(Courtesy ICUFON)*

points to determine the distance of the objects and that it was therefore the size estimate which was wrong. This presents the possibility that the objects were of much greater size than Arnold realized. However, Bloecher also points out that Arnold originally misidentified the mountain peaks, further confusing the accuracy of the distance estimate.

Another explanation for the sighting offered by astronomer DONALD H. MENZEL is that Arnold was observing raindrops on the window of his plane which were picking up light from the distant sky and which created an illusion of craft in formation while his eyes were focused on the distant mountains. Menzel and writer Lyle G. Boyd question Arnold's reliability as a witness by pointing out that when he later decided to sell his story to science fiction writer, editor and publisher RAY PALMER, some of the details were considerably changed and embellished.

Despite the investigation and controversy launched by the Arnold sighting, it has not been definitely resolved to this day.

Bibliography: Arnold, Kenneth, and Ray Palmer, *The Coming of the Saucers* (Amherst, Wisconsin: Amherst Press, 1952); Menzel, Donald H., and Lyle G. Boyd, *The World of Flying Saucers* (Garden City, N.Y.: Doubleday and Company, 1963).

**MSFA** *see* **MODERN SPACE FLIGHT ASSOCIATION**

**MSFA UFO REPORT,** publication of **Modern Space Flight Association (MSFA).**

**M2–F3,** wingless aircraft developed by the NATIONAL AERONAUTICS AND SPACE ADMINISTRATION (NASA) to demonstrate that such a craft could operate throughout a wide range of airspeeds and make safe, unpowered approaches and landings. These are areas of concern to engineers involved in the design and construction of the space shuttle. The craft is of some interest to UFOlogists because of its unconventional shape and its ability to land unaccompanied by traditional engine sounds.

**MU,** legendary continent said to have been submerged beneath the waters of the Pacific Ocean some time between 12,000 and over 50,000 years ago. Although usually placed in the Indian Ocean, the lost continent of LEMURIA is believed to be the same as Mu by some writers who use the two names interchangeably. Others maintain that Mu and Lemuria were two independent land masses existing concurrently and deriving from one original land mass, known as GONDWANALAND. Mu shares many of the legends attributed to ATLANTIS, Lemuria and HYPERBOREA, and its advanced civilization was allegedly destroyed by a series of cataclysmic earthquakes. Some researchers believe it to have been the Garden of EDEN, home of Earth's first civilization. EASTER ISLAND is said to have served as a factory where giant stone statues were manufactured for export to other parts of Mu.

The popularity of the legend of Mu is due chiefly to author and British army officer James Churchward, who reportedly learned Mu's history at the beginning of this century from arcane documents in the possession of a Burmese Buddhist priest. In his writings on the subject, Churchward has reconstructed the Mu alphabet and produced precise maps of the legendary land.

One theory, supported by very few UFOlogists, proposes that survivors of Mu's destruction built an underwater civilization from which UFOs originate.

Bibliography: Churchward, James, *The Lost Continent of Mu* (New York: Ives Washburn, 1931).

The M2-F3 flanked by two other experimental aircraft. *(Courtesy NASA)*

**MUFOB** *see* **METEMPIRICAL UFO BULLE-TIN**

**MUFON** *see* **MUTUAL UFO NETWORK**

**MUFON UFO JOURNAL,** newsletter of the MUTUAL UFO NETWORK.

**MUFORA** *see* **MANCHESTER UFO RE-SEARCH ASSOCIATION**

**MUHAMMAD ALI** *see* **ALI, MUHAMMAD**

**MULTIPLE WITNESS CASE,** any case involving two or more witnesses. Some investigators give a low PROBABILITY RATING to any case involving only one witness. However, as has been demonstrated in several instances, the presence of multiple witnesses at a sighting does not eliminate the possibility of a HOAX or the MISIDENTIFICATION of a conventional object or natural phenomenon. Writer PHILIP KLASS cites the ZOND IV case as a demonstration of this point. Some psychologists have speculated that false UFO reports made by multiple witnesses may be attributable to HYSTERICAL CONTAGION or MASS HYSTERIA.

Some of the well-known cases involving multiple witnesses are those which occurred at ALBANY, NEW YORK; BOIANAI, PAPUA, NEW GUINEA; FARMINGTON, NEW MEXICO; FLATWOODS, WEST VIRGINIA; GAILLAC, FRANCE; KELLY-HOPKINSVILLE, KENTUCKY; LEVELLAND, TEXAS; OLORON, FRANCE; PIEDMONT, MISSOURI; SAN JOSÉ DE VALDERAS, SPAIN; TEHERAN, IRAN; TRINDADE ISLAND, BRAZIL and WHITE SANDS, NEW MEXICO.

**MUNDO, LAURA** (b. March 6, 1913, Boston, Massachusetts), CONTACTEE, Founder and Codirector of the FLYING SAUCER INFORMATION CENTER.

Mundo claims to have observed a bell-type saucer and remotely controlled disk over her Dearborn, Michigan, home in 1955. The bell-type saucer was similar to the one shown in photographs taken by the late GEORGE ADAMSKI. Mundo claims also to have received radio messages from the SPACE PEOPLE. In contrast to the less-evolved Space People, those who are more advanced, according to Mundo, do not use TELEPATHY since it is based on the same scientific principle as that of radio and television and therefore is subject to distortion of the atmosphere by the accelerated activity of sunspots. She has become aware, she asserts, of the Space People living incognito amongst us. She claims to have met Orthon, a spaceman supposedly encountered previously by Adamski. Mundo believes the Space People are here to help mankind through the extreme planetary changes which are about to take place on Earth.

Mundo describes herself as self-educated beyond high school. She has worked in radio and television on women's shows and, for a time, ran a children's theater. Her activities in the UFO field include writing, research and lecturing. For six months, she wrote a column on UFOs in a Michigan publication, *North Broadsider*. She is author of *Flying Saucer and the Father's Plan* (Clarksburg, West Virginia: Saucerian Press, 1956); *Pied Piper from Outer Space* (Los Angeles: Planetary Space Center Working Committee, 1964); and several booklets published by the Flying Saucer Information Center.

Laura Mundo.

**MUNDO DESCONOCIDO,** monthly magazine dealing with UFOsand other mysteries and studies of the paranormal. The magazine's Editor is Andreas Faber-Kaiser. Its mailing address is Pje. José Llovera 5, Barcelona 21, Spain.

**MUSEUMS** *see* **FROGSTEIN'S FLYING SAUCER MUSEUM AND UFO IDENTIFICATION BUREAU AND SCIENCE MUSEUM**

**MUSKAT, JOSEPH,** *see* **CANADIAN UFO RESEARCH NETWORK (CUFORN)**

**MUTE,** abbreviation denoting "mutilation" or "mutilated," sometimes used in reference to mysterious ANIMAL MUTILATIONS.

**MUTUAL UFO NETWORK (MUFON),** 103 Oldtowne Road, Seguin, Texas 78155; telephone number: 512-379-9216.

This vast, international investigative network, originally known as the Midwestern UFO Network, is one of the world's major UFO organizations. Its purpose is to answer the following four questions: 1. Are UFOs some form of spacecraft controlled by an advanced intelligence conducting a SURVEILLANCE of our Earth, or do they constitute some unknown physical or psychological manifestation associated with the PLANET Earth that is not understood by present-day science? 2. If UFOs are found to be extraterrestrial craft controlled by intelligent beings, what is their method of propulsion and means of achieving unbelievable maneuverability and speed? 3. Postulating that they may be controlled by an extraterrestrial intelligence, where do they originate—our Earth, our solar system, in our galaxy, or in some distant galaxy in the universe? 4. Assuming that some of the craft are piloted by beings (humanoids), what can we learn from their apparently advanced science and civilization through study or possibly through direct communications with the OCCUPANTS of these vehicles?

More than 1,000 of MUFON's 1,100 members participate as investigators. State Directors, in almost every state of the Union, head teams of State Section Directors, who correlate the activities of the Field Investigators in each section. Three amateur radio networks, operating weekly in the forty and seventy-five meter amateur radio bands, are utilized to receive and disseminate UFO sighting reports and current UFO information. All reports are passed on to the CENTER FOR UFO STUDIES (CUFOS) for compilation and analysis. Seventy consultants, most of whom possess doctorates, make up MUFON's Advisory Board.

This nonprofit organization was founded in 1969 by WALTER H. ANDRUS, JR., John Schuessler and Allen R. Utke. At the annual MUFON UFO Symposium, scientists, engineers and authors lecture on their particular specialization or contributions to resolving what MUFON considers the greatest mystery of our time. The organization publishes the MUFON UFO JOURNAL (formerly known as SKYLOOK) as well as the annual *MUFON UFO Symposium Proceedings*. The MUFON Board of Directors consists of: Walter H. Andrus, Jr., International Director; John F. Schuessler, Deputy Director, Administration; Thomas H. Nicholl, Deputy Director, Business Management; Sam Gross, Corporate Secretary; John Donegan, Treasurer; Michael Sinclair, International Coordinator; RICHARD H. HALL, Editor, the *MUFON UFO Journal;* JAMES M. MCCAMPBELL, Director of Research; RAYMOND E. FOWLER, Director of Investigations; Ted Phillips, Specialization Coordinator; LEONARD H. STRINGFIELD, Director of Public Relations; Joseph Santangelo, Regional Director, Eastern U.S.A.; Charles L. Tucker, Regional Director, Central U.S.A.; PAUL C. CERNY, Regional Director, Western U.S.A.; HENRY H. MCKAY, Regional Director, Canada. MUFON is also represented in Africa, Argentina, Australia, Austria, Belgium, Brazil, Canada, Central America, Finland, France, Germany, Holland, Italy, Japan, New Zealand, Norway, Romania, South America, Spain, Sweden, United Kingdom and Yugoslavia.

**MUTILATIONS** *see* **ANIMAL MUTILATIONS**

NADA-YOLANDA *see* MARK-AGE

NAF *see* NEW AGE FOUNDATION

NAPPA *see* NATIONAL AERIAL AND PSYCHIC PHENOMENA ASSOCIATION

NAS *see* NATIONAL ACADEMY OF SCIENCES

NASA *see* NATIONAL AERONAUTICS AND SPACE ADMINISTRATION

NASCA *see* NAZCA

NASH, WILLIAM B., *see* NEWPORT NEWS, VIRGINIA

NATIONAL ACADEMY OF SCIENCES (NAS). Following controversial publicity regarding the UFO study carried out by the CONDON COMMITTEE, Edward Condon sent the completed CONDON REPORT to the NAS for review prior to publication. An NAS panel, chaired by G. M. Clemence of Yale and comprised of eleven scientists without previous experience in the UFO field, gave its stamp of approval to the report. It found that the study's scope was adequate, the methodology well-chosen and the conclusions justified. The panel concluded by stating, "We are unanimous in the opinion that this has been a very creditable effort to apply objectively the relevant techniques of science to the solution of the UFO problem. . . . While further study of particular aspects of the topic (e.g., atmospheric phenomena) may be useful, a study of UFOs in general is not a promising way to expand scientific understanding of phenomena. On the basis of present knowledge, the least likely explanation of UFOs is the hypothesis of extraterrestrial visitations by intelligent beings."

Bibliography: Condon, Edward U., *Scientific Study of Unidentified Flying Objects* (New York: E. P. Dutton, 1969).

NATIONAL AERIAL AND PSYCHIC PHENOMENA ASSOCIATION (NAPPA), 552 Estate Road, Maple Shade, New Jersey 08052.

NAPPA's President Frank D'Adamo and Research Analyst Joseph Seigeldorf have carried out photographic analyses of UFO photographs and lectured on UFOs and ANCIENT ASTRONAUTS to high school audiences. D'Adamo reorganized this investigative organization as the Church of the CELESTIAL INTERPRETORS OF NAPPA (CION).

NATIONAL AERONAUTICS AND SPACE ADMINISTRATION (NASA), the U.S. Agency responsible for planning and conducting the nation's program of space exploration. During several space missions, NASA ASTRONAUTS reported phenomena not immediately explainable. However, according to NASA officials, the agency satisfied itself in every instance that what had been observed was nothing which could be termed abnormal in the space environment. The air-to-ground tapes of all manned missions are available for review at the Johnson Space Center in Houston, Texas.

In July of 1977, Dr. Frank Press, Director of Science and Technology Policy, Executive Office of the President, wrote to Dr. Robert A. Frosch, the NASA Administrator, suggesting NASA should answer all UFO-related mail and also to consider whether NASA should conduct an active research program on UFOs. In a letter dated December 21, 1977, Frosch agreed that NASA would continue to respond to UFO-related mail as it has in the past. He went on to say, ". . . If some new element of hard evidence is brought to our attention in the future, it would be entirely appropriate for a NASA laboratory to analyze and report upon an otherwise unexplained organic or inorganic sample; we stand ready to respond to any bona fide physical evidence from credible sources. We intend to leave the door open for such a possibility.

"We have given considerable thought to the question of what else the United States might and should do in the area of UFO research. There is an absence of tangible or physical evidence available for thorough laboratory analysis. And, because of the absence of such evidence, we have not been able to devise a sound scientific procedure for investigating these phenomena. To proceed on a research task without a sound disciplinary framework and an exploratory technique in mind would be wasteful and probably unproductive.

"I do not feel that we could mount a research effort without a better starting point than we have been able to identify thus far. I would therefore propose that NASA take no steps to establish research in this area or to convene a symposium on this subject.

"I wish in no way to indicate that NASA has come to any conclusion about these phenomena as such; institutionally, we retain an open mind, a keen sense of scientific curiosity and a willingness to analyze technical problems within our competence."

In 1978, NASA released Information Sheet Number 78–1, which stated that NASA is the focal point for answering public inquiries to the White House relating to UFOs. The Information Sheet also asserted that NASA is not engaged in a research program involving these phenomena, nor is any other government agency.

With regard to future space travel, Shuttle crews will be briefed to alert them to possible unscheduled experiments which could be of value if an unanticipated incident, such as a UFO sighting, should occur. The Shuttle equipment would be able to probe the light density and the radiation fields of a UFO and the high-powered cameras would be able to take photographs of greater clarity than those taken by earthbound photographers. Scientific equipment utilized on some of the more advanced Shuttle missions may even be able to identify the materials of which a UFO are made. It is hoped that later Shuttle missions will carry computer equipment capable of communicating with or receiving messages from other forms of life.

**NATIONAL ARCHIVES,** the repository for U.S. national records since 1774. In 1975, the UNITED STATES AIR FORCE (USAF) offered the records of PROJECT BLUE BOOK to the National Archives. To protect witnesses' anonymity, restrictions on the release of material included the deletion of names of witnesses and all other identifying data, investigators' conclusions, confidential sources of information and investigative techniques. Since the enormous budget and manpower required for such a task rendered it impractical, the records remained inaccessible for some time. It was only after dozens of requests were filed under the provisions of the Freedom of Information Act that a private company was commissioned to complete the task. On July 12, 1976, the records were finally made available to the public, but the deletion of so much pertinent data had diminished their value to the researcher. Researchers immediately became aware that numerous important cases were missing from the records. The Air Force responded that any missing cases might be those which had generated CIRVIS (Communication Instructions for Reporting Vital Intelligence Sightings) reports. The release of such cases would be dependent upon review on an individual basis. Believing that the missing material could be found in the files of the CENTRAL INTELLIGENCE AGENCY (CIA), a number of organizations and individuals, including GROUND SAUCER WATCH (GSW) and CITIZENS AGAINST UFO SECRECY (CAUS), filed suit against the CIA under the provisions of the Freedom of Information Act.

Researchers wishing to review the available material may obtain a researcher's permit from the National Archives and Record Service. The records are located in the Modern Military Branch. A catalogue of photographs, films and tape recordings of witnesses' interviews can be obtained by writing to the National Archives, Motion Picture and Sound Recording Branch, Room 20–E, Eighth and Pennsylvania N.W., Washington, D.C. 20408.

**NATIONAL ENQUIRER, THE,** weekly newspaper, established in 1952, with a circulation of over five million. It is available both at newsstands and by subscription. The range of subjects covered includes celebrities, romance, human interest, medical breakthroughs, adventure, the occult, horoscopes, diets, government waste, psychic predictions and UFO sightings. Although not a "UFO publication," the newspaper deals with the subject frequently and has a standing offer of one million dollars for "positive proof" that extraterrestrial spacecraft are visiting Earth. Additionally, *The National Enquirer* has established a Blue Ribbon Panel of UFO experts who review UFO sighting reports for cash rewards. Two regular members, engineer JAMES HARDER and psychologist LEO SPRINKLE, are joined by a changing cadre of UFOlogists.

Material is supplied by strangers, staffers and newspaper clippings. Freelance writers should query before submitting manuscripts. A scale of category payments and guidelines for freelance writers are available. The publisher purchases all rights.

The newspaper's Editor is Iain Calder. It is published by Generoso Pope, Jr., 600 S. East Coast Avenue, Lantana, Florida 33464.

## NATIONAL INVESTIGATIONS COMMITTEE ON AERIAL PHENOMENA (NICAP), 5012 Del Ray Avenue, Washington, D.C. 20014; telephone number: 301-654-8091.

The stated goals of this investigative organization are scientific investigation and research of reported unidentified flying objects, and encouragement of full reporting to the public by responsible authorities of all information which the government has accumulated. The group adheres to no specific theories regarding the identity of UFOs. Although beset with financial difficulties throughout its existence, NICAP has maintained a conservative and dignified reputation in the field, partially because of the credentials of the members of the board of governors. Over the years, these have included high-ranking military officers, former officials of the CENTRAL INTELLIGENCE AGENCY (CIA), politicians, businessmen, college professors and clergymen. In recent years, some UFOlogists have claimed that NICAP has been infiltrated by the CIA as part of a conspiracy to hinder UFO research and COVER UP UFO information.

This nonprofit organization was founded in 1956 by T. Townshend Brown, who served as its first director. Marine Corps Major DONALD KEYHOE assumed the Directorship from 1957 until 1969. He was succeeded by RICHARD HALL and others, until JOHN ACUFF took over as President in 1970. The present Board of Governors consists of JOSEPH BRYAN, JOHN FISHER, DEWEY FOURNET, BARRY GOLDWATER, JOSEPH HARTRANFT, DONALD KEYHOE, CHARLES LOMBARD, ROBERT RICHARDSON and EDWARD ROUSH. Seventy-five field investigators are located throughout the United States and overseas. Membership currently stands at about 2,600. In addition to a monthly newsletter, UFO INVESTIGATOR, NICAP has published several documents, including *The UFO Evidence* (1964); *UFOs: A New Look* (1969); and *Strange Effects from UFOs* (1969).

## NATIONAL INVESTIGATIONS COMMITTEE ON UFOs (NICUFO), Suite 207, 7970 Woodman Avenue, Van Nuys, California 91402; telephone number: 213-781-7704.

The purpose of this CONTACTEE organization is to investigate and to discover the truth concerning UFOs and associated phenomena. NICUFO claims to have proven that UFOs have existed as far back in recorded

history as 4,000 B.C. and that UFOs are of terrestrial as well as extraterrestrial origin. The group contends that those originating on Earth are secret devices made in the United States and the Soviet Union. It concedes that some UFOs represent natural phenomena and other misidentified objects.

This nonprofit organization was founded in 1967 by FRANK E. STRANGES, who serves as Director. The Board of Directors consists of Vice-Chairman Howard Moffitt, Secretary-Treasurer Denise F. Stranges, Engineer and Pilot Herbert Myers, Assistant Administrative Secretary Madeleine Udin, Financial Advisor Robert Price, Public Affairs Officer Robert Lemaire and Public Relations Officer for the Lecture Department, Robert Simmons. The National Advisory Board consists of James McNamara, Richard Tudor, Howard Strand, Merle S. Gould, Curtis McCall, Jr., CARL ANDERSON, DANIEL FRY, Albert Roy Davis, Donald Cooper, August C. Roberts, Howard Moffitt, William Caulfield, Ewing Brown and Jim Swift. Members of the International Advisory Board are Donald Emmerson in Canada, William Inlefeld in Puerto Rico, John E. Su in Hong Kong, John E. Lee in Macau, Leo Meller in Finland, Susanne Stebbing in England, Karl Wadenklee and Karl L. Veit in West Germany and Anton Szachnowski, an Anglo/Polish representative. The group has about 1,000 members. Annual membership brings each member an Official Identification Card identifying the member as an Investigator-at-Large of NICUFO, an Official Membership Certificate, a ten percent discount on books and tapes published by NICUFO, a twenty percent discount on conventions, seminars, lectures and other activities sponsored by NICUFO, and a subscription to the bimonthly *Confidential Newsletter*. The publication is edited by Stranges.

## NATIONAL UFO CONFERENCE (NUFOC), P.O. Box 163, Fort Lee, New Jersey 07024.

Founded in 1964 by Rick Hilberg and Allen Greenfield, NUFOC sponsors annual conventions in various cities around the United States. JAMES MOSELEY is Chairman. The eight members of the Permanent Organizing Committee are Rick Hilberg, Carol Hilberg, Robert Easley, Dale Rettig, Gene Steinberg, Charles Wilhelm, Allen Greenfield and Allen Manak,

## NATIONAL UNIDENTIFIED FLYING OBJECT RESEARCH (NUFOR), 4 Queen Square, Brighton BN1 3FD, Sussex, England; telephone number: 23010.

This investigative organization is dedicated to scientific research of all areas of UFOLOGY. The group holds that although there is no positive scientific evidence of the UFO phenomenon, its existence is unquestionable.

However, NUFOR has no beliefs about the identity and origin of UFOs.

This nonprofit organization was founded in 1974 by David Thomas Kay, who serves as Secretary/Organizer. He is supported by an Advisory Committee comprised of L. Bridger, who serves as Technical Adviser; D. Heard; N. Lewis, who serves as Assistant Secretary; and Trevor Poore. There are 500 members and 120 field investigators located throughout the south of England. NUFOR cooperates and shares information with about fifty other UFO organizations in the United Kingdom. The *NUFOR Newsletter* is published monthly and edited by Trevor Poore.

**NAZCA,** arid, elevated plain in southern Peru. Lines, trapezoids and animal forms are etched into the surface of the Nazca Plain. Some of the ruler-straight lines run for miles, traversing hills and precipices. The animal figures are drawn on such an enormous scale that their forms are discernible only from the air. Their outlines have been created by removing the small purplish brown rocks from the desert surface to reveal the ochre-colored soil beneath. The area's paucity of rain and natural erosion have left the lines intact over the centuries.

Author ERICH VON DÄNIKEN has postulated that the Nazca Lines represent an improvised airfield built by ANCIENT ASTRONAUTS. He suggests that after the extraterrestrials had left Earth, the Nazca people continued to expand and elaborate the etchings in order to entice the godlike beings back to Earth.

Von Däniken's detractors point out that if highly-advanced aliens had traversed the vast regions of space and set their craft down on an unmarked terrestrial plateau, they would have no need then to build an airfield. In fact, the surface of the Nazca Plain is not

The Lines of Nazca. *(Rapho/Photo Researchers)*

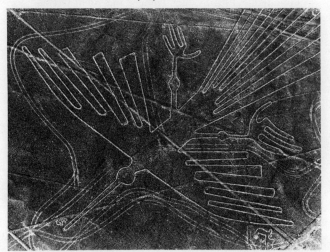

rigid enough to serve as a runway. Vehicles which run off the modern-day paths become stuck in the loose stones and sandy soil. In a television documentary entitled THE CASE OF THE ANCIENT ASTRONAUTS, written and produced by Graham Massey for the British Broadcasting Corporation's NOVA series, narrator Don Wescott draws attention to a misleading PHOTOGRAPH in von Däniken's book, *Chariots of the Gods?*. He points out that the markings which von Däniken compares to "the aircraft parking bays on a modern airport," are, in fact, part of the left leg of a huge condor which is not shown in its entirety in the photograph. Skeptics have contended that there is no mystery in the fact that the figures are meant to be viewed from the air. Many religious groups throughout history have placed their gods in the skies. With this in mind, it is quite possible that the Nazca people created the figures to be seen by the deities they believed in but had never seen. By analogy, Christian churches are shaped like a cross, discernible only from the air. Von Däniken has suggested that the Nazca Lines might have been built with guidance from airborne beings. However, small scale models have been found alongside some of the designs. It is probable, therefore, that the drawings were merely transferred from the models.

The most popular theory which counteracts von Däniken's hypothesis is propounded by German professor Maria Reiche. Since 1946, she has devoted her life to the study of the Nazca Lines. Reiche proposes that the markings represent an astronomical calendar, massive enough to remain unharmed by invading armies. Some of the lines point to where the sun sets at the summer and winter solstices—the harbingers of new seasons. In this drought-ridden region, the arrival of rain was an important event. Reiche observes that in the southern hemisphere the constellations of the Big Dipper, Leo and the Hunting Dogs resemble a monkey. A similar monkey appears among the animal figures on the Nazca Plain. A thin line connects the monkey to a broad line which points to the rising Big Dipper on December 21, the time when the rains brought relief and renewed life to the Nazca people. By making the monkey figure very large, Reiche speculates, they might have hoped to encourage their rain god to favor them with greater quantities of water.

Reiche's theories, although less exotic than von Däniken's, also have their detractors. Some researchers argue that because of the enormous number of lines and the multitude of astronomical bodies with which alignments can be made, her correlations are meaningless.

Bibliography: Von Däniken, Erich, *Return to the Stars* (New York: G. P. Putnam's Sons, 1971); Wilson, Clifford, *Gods in Chariots and Other Fantasies* (San Diego, California: Creation-Life Publishers, 1975); Morrison, Tony, with Gerald M. Hawkins, *Pathways to the Gods* (New York: Harper and Row, 1979).

**NAZI HYPOTHESIS**, theory proposing that UFOs are SECRET WEAPONS developed by Adolf Hitler and his lost battalion, supposedly headquartered in a tropical oasis in the Antarctic region. Proponents claim that international Antarctic expeditions in 1946 and 1947 were actually searches for Hitler, who was thought to be still alive. Current UFO sightings are explained as survey trips by Nazis in their flying saucers. The promoters of this theme are a group in Toronto known as SAMISDAT, a faction of the neo-Nazi Western Guard. Their advertisements in UFO magazines threaten that Nazis may one day take their revenge on the Allies with "UFO power." Some UFOLOGISTS have suggested that the group is merely using UFOs as a means of promoting Nazi propaganda.

**NEDERLANDS ONDERZOEK BUREAU VOOR UFOs (Werkgroep NOBOVO)**, Lange Akker 28, 9982 HL Uithuizermeeden (Gr.), Holland; telephone number: 05954-2901.

The purpose of this organization is to investigate UFO sightings in a scientific manner and to furnish information to the public. The only cases the group will investigate are those in which MULTIPLE WITNESSES sight UFOs from more than one point of observation, permitting triangulation. NOBOVO does not attach much value to the EXTRATERRESTRIAL HYPOTHESIS (ETH) nor to any other hypothesis. The group has concluded that "much rubbish" is published about UFOs.

This nonprofit organization was founded in 1965 by G. J. Kok and S. Sluis. Active members include W. B. v.d. Berg. J. R. Beuker, D. J. Bosga, A. Cramwinckel, R. Friso, H. H. Gosemeijer, G. J. Kok. W. A. Kuiper and G. P. Meijer. Advisors include W. deGraaff, J. F. Vrins, E. Westera, J. de Knegt and Rembert-Weijers. A network of field investigators is distributed throughout the country. The Dutch police force cooperates on an official basis by passing on to NOBOVO all UFO reports. In addition, Dutch amateur radio organizations cooperate with the group. *Tijdschrift voor UFOlogie* *(TvU)*, formerly known as *Vliegende Schotel Nieuws*, is published bimonthly. The newsletter has a circulation of 700.

**NEDERLANDS STUDIEKRING VOOR UFOLOGIE,** Borgerstraat 157, 1053 PH Amsterdam, Holland.

This CONTACTEE organization, formerly known as Plativolo, was founded in 1953 or 1954, and ceased its activities in 1959. A. F. van Wieringen was President.

The group published *UFO-GIDS* six times a year for circulation within Holland. For exchange purposes, the *International Paranormal Bulletin* was published irregularly. Publication of this bulletin was continued until 1978.

**NEFF, EARL, J.,** *see* **CLEVELAND UFOLOGY PROJECT**

**NEFF, WILBUR,** *see* **PORTAGE COUNTY, OHIO**

**NEGATIVE GRAVITY** *see* **GRAVITATION**

**NESTS** *see* **UFO NESTS**

**NETTLES, BONNIE LU TRUSDALE,** *see* **HUMAN INDIVIDUAL METAMORPHOSIS**

**NEUFO** *see* **NORTHEASTERN UFO ORGANIZATION**

**NEW AGE,** incoming era, also known as the Golden Age or the Aquarian Age, which began about 1960 and during which mankind is purportedly entering a new, improved state of spiritual development. The New Age movement consists of numerous independent groups whose members are known as New Agers. Although not unified in their concept of the New Age, most New Agers share a belief in Jesus Christ, reincarnation, astrology, parapsychology and the existence of ATLANTIS and other lost continents. In general, they are opposed to all present forms of government on Earth and believe that the New Age will bring a united world government and the abolishment of the monetary system which exists today. Many CONTACTEES, whose movement overlaps that of the New Age organizations, believe that the SPACE PEOPLE are visiting Earth to assist mankind in attaining spiritual enlightenment. They hold that Jesus Christ was merely one incarnation of a being whose predicted "Second Coming" will take the form of a mass UFO landing. This event will purportedly mark the official establishment of the New Age.

Bibliography: Nada-Yolanda, *Visitors from Other Planets* (Miami: Mark-Age MetaCenter, 1974).

**NEW AGE FOUNDATION (NAF),** Cedar Park, Ashford, Washington 98304; telephone number: 206-569-2594.

This organization is engaged in teaching and instruction in the fields of character building, psycho-cybernetics, survival experience, health and healing, and UFOLOGY. It holds that UFOs are representations of life forms from other worlds who utilize interdimensional travel to reach Earth from other PLANETS in our own and other solar systems. Their purpose, according to NAF, is to observe, communicate with and sometimes assist the evolving life on this and other planets. However, the group states that cosmic law requires non-interference with domestic planetary affairs. In 1978, NAF dedicated a fourteen-acre clearing near Washington's MOUNT RAINIER as a Spacecraft Protective Landing Area for the Advancement of Science and Humanities (SPLAASH). Official agencies have been asked to honor the zone's neutrality. The group hopes to encourage a landing. It believes that UFOnauts will know the area is neutral by monitoring Earth communications and by reading the thoughts of those who established the landing zone.

This nonprofit organization was founded in 1965 by WAYNE SULO AHO, who serves as President. The group was originally known as Washington Saucer Intelligence, which was founded in 1957 in Washington, D.C. Other staff members are Vice-President William Brafford, Second Vice-President Brian Phill and Coordinator Jeanette Tully. The group has approximately 150 members and seven affiliated charter groups. NAF holds annual conventions. It publishes the quarterly THE INTELLIGENTS' REPORT, and the semi-annual THE AQUARIAN DAWN.

## NEW ATLANTEAN JOURNAL, THE, quarterly

magazine, established in 1973, with a circulation of over 9,000. It is available both at newsstands and by subscription. The magazine publishes articles and reports on the unknown, the unexplained and the unexplored, including UFOs, YETI, ancient civilizations, pyramidology, rediscovery of ancient technology and science and prophecy relating to Earth changes.

Most of the magazine's material comes from readers throughout the world, who receive copies of the issues containing their articles as payment. The publishers pay for photographs which they consider unique. The magazine is edited by JOHN O'CONNELL and published by the NEW ATLANTEAN RESEARCH SOCIETY, 4280 68th Avenue North, Pinellas Park, Florida 33565.

## NEW ATLANTEAN RESEARCH SOCIETY,

4280 68th Avenue North, Pinellas Park, Florida 33565; telephone number: 813-527-2293.

The purpose of this investigative organization is to research the unexplained, the unexplored and the unknown. Its field of study covers all aspects of the paranormal and ancient civilizations, including UFOs, YETI, pyramidology, PSYCHOTRONICS, telekinesis and psychokinesis. The society believes that UFOs may be of extraterrestrial origin but that the mounting evidence

also seems to lend weight to the interdimensional concept.

The society was founded in 1973 by JOAN O'CONNELL and PATRICK O'CONNELL, who serves as President. The Board of Consultants consists of J. Manson Valentine, E. O. Wingo, Vincent Gaddis, Mary Levesque, Margaret Bennett, Arlen Andrews, Sr., BRINSLEY LE POER TRENCH, Robert Bennett, BRAD STEIGER, Tal Levesque, Michael Heleus, Buryl Payne, Ron Anjard, RILEY CRABB, GRAY BARKER, Betty Dickson and G. H. Williamson. Area Reporters are Marianna Marschke in Washington; Carolyn Redmond in California; Eula Lewis in Florida; Mary and Tal Levesque in New Mexico; Marion Nigl in New York; Ronald Kelly in Washington, D.C.; Tom Adams in Texas; Mary Robinson in New Jersey; Bob and Margaret Bennett in Texas; and Betty Dickson in Florida. The society sponsors scientific workshops on the objective investigation and analysis of UFO reports, sightings, landings and related paranormal effects. Training is provided by the group's qualified instructors on UFO investigative techniques. Access is provided, on a need-to-know basis, to the files and research materials of the society. One of the group's major activities is the publication of THE NEW ATLANTEAN JOURNAL, edited by Joan O'Connell.

## NEW ENGLAND UFO STUDY GROUP, 10

Peters Avenue, Marlborough, Massachusetts 01752.

Founded in 1957 by GEORGE FAWCETT, the group took its present name in 1964. The group holds regular meetings and publishes a newsletter.

## NEW HAMPSHIRE, location of one of the most

celebrated encounters in UFO history. The case involved Betty and Barney Hill, whose interracial marriage may have had some bearing upon the episode. Barney, a Black, worked for the United States Post Office, while Betty, a Caucasian, was a State of New Hampshire social worker. Both were active in the civil rights movement, as well as in social work. It was a second marriage for both, and Barney had two children by his previous marriage. At the time of the incident, Barney was thirty-nine years old and Betty was forty-one.

On the night of September 19, 1961, the Hills were driving toward their home in Portsmouth, New Hampshire, from Canada via U.S. Highway 3 through the White Mountains. Betty noticed a bright light which appeared to be moving erratically and flashing different colored lights. At times, it seemed to be spinning. They stopped a few times to look at it through binoculars. As the object approached, they discerned a large disk-shaped craft with windows around its rim. After stopping the car, Barney looked at the UFO through binoculars as it hovered silently, about fifty feet away from him. He could see at least six beings, wearing dark uniforms, watching him through the windows. All but one turned away to attend by a large control panel behind them. The object then continued its gradual descent. Two fins, each bearing a red light, were slowly extending from the right and left of the craft. Another extension was lowered from its base.

Barney became terrified by the eyes of the one crew member who continued to stare at him and who reminded him of a German Nazi. Convinced he was about to be captured, Barney ran back to the car, screaming. They drove off quickly. Soon they heard an irregular beeping sound coming from the trunk, and felt a tingling sensation and drowsiness. Another series of beeps aroused them and they discovered they had traveled thirty-five miles and could not recall what had happened in between. Their watches had stopped running.

The following day, Barney felt an unexplained soreness on the back of his neck and noticed that his shoes had become scuffed on the tops of the toes. Betty called her sister, Janet, since Janet and her family had seen a UFO four years before. Reportedly, Janet's neighbor, a physicist, suggested that the Hills test their car with a compass for radiation. It was then that Betty discovered round, shiny spots on the paint of the car's trunk. Apparently, the compass needle wavered when held near these spots. However, when Barney repeated the test, the needle remained steady. The test was of little significance, in any case, since radioactivity cannot be detected by a magnetic compass. Betty, however, became obsessed with the idea that they had been exposed to radioactivity. A report was filed with Pease Air Force Base but no description was given of the object when it was at its closest to the observers and no mention was made of windows or OCCUPANTS.

Ten days later, Betty began to have a series of vivid dreams in which she and Barney were taken aboard a flying saucer and medically examined. The dreams continued for five successive nights. She related these dreams to her friends and colleagues, and made a written record of all the details.

During an interview with civilian UFO investigators one month after the incident, Betty and Barney realized that the trip from Canada to Portsmouth had taken at least two hours longer than it should have. The investigators suggested that the Hills try to find out what had transpired during the missing time through HYPNOSIS.

Meanwhile, Barney had been suffering from ulcers, high blood pressure, exhaustion resulting from his long commute to work and stress due to his separation from his sons. In addition, a ring of warts had begun to develop in the area of his groin. From the summer of

1962 until the summer of 1963, Barney underwent psychiatric treatment. Little attention was paid to the UFO incident but eventually Barney asked his psychiatrist, Dr. Duncan Stephens, about the use of hypnotic regression to resolve the matter. Stephens arranged for him to see an eminent Boston psychiatrist, Dr. Benjamin Simon.

Betty accompanied Barney on his first visit to Dr. Simon in December 1963. It quickly became apparent to Simon that both Barney and Betty needed treatment. There followed a series of visits during which husband and wife independently underwent hypnotic regressions. Separately, they recounted a story of being taken aboard a spacecraft shortly after the first set of beeps. Barney had kept his eyes closed during most of the experience. They were able to communicate with the aliens telepathically and described them as humanoid, with large eyes that reached around to the side of the head, no nose, and a mouth that was a slit without lip muscles. The Hills were given medical examinations in separate rooms. At one point, Barney was aware of a circular instrument being placed around his groin. During Betty's exmination, a long needle was inserted in her navel. She was told it was a pregnancy test. Afterwards, she was shown a map of dots joined by lines which represented travel routes. Betty was told they would not remember the experience, but she was determined that she would. They were returned to their car, where their frightened dog was curled up in a ball under one of the seats. The craft increased in brilliance and resembled a glowing orange ball as it left.

Simon concluded that the Hills had undergone an imaginary experience caused by fear after an actual close UFO approach. Barney's hysteria while re-experiencing the incident under hypnosis left little doubt that he had

Betty Hill with star map and sculptured bust of UFO occupant.

indeed seen something and that it had been a very frightening experience. Simon suggests that long-standing racial tensions were one of the factors that played an important part in Barney's emotional condition. Many of the details recounted by Betty resembled typical symbolic characteristics of dreams, some of them sexual. Most of the details of Barney's alleged experience were described in Betty's account, but her account contained many details not included in Barney's. Since Betty had related her early dreams of the encounter many times in Barney's presence, it seemed that he might have acquired the story of the ABDUCTION exclusively from her. Following the hypnotherapy, the Hills' emotional tensions were relieved but not eliminated and, in February 1969, Barney died at age forty-six of a cerebral hemorrhage.

The Hill encounter has remained one of the most controversial cases on record. Subsequent reports of abductions seem to be patterned after the New Hampshire incident. However, there are many contradictory elements to the story. While under hypnosis, Barney said that the craft had rows of windows. Moments later, he described it as having a single row of windows. Betty, on the other hand, said she could see a double row of windows. Betty originally said that the crew's leader had spoken in English with a foreign accent. She later changed her story, saying that he communicated telepathically. While the leader seemed totally familiar with the mechanics of her dress zipper, he did not understand why Barney's teeth could be removed. When Betty explained that some older people need false teeth, he could not grasp the concept of age and time. Yet, moments later, he told her to "wait a minute."

With regard to the needle inserted in Betty's navel, there is a similar procedure, known as amniocentesis, in which fluid surrounding a fetus is withdrawn. However, this is not a test to establish pregnancy but rather a test to study amniotic fluid cells, usually for signs of chromosomal aberrations and sex-linked and metabolic disorders. Moreover, the procedure is generally limited to high risk cases because of the inherent danger of injury to the mother and the fetus. Some researchers have claimed that the procedure was not discovered until some years afterward and its use was therefore further evidence of the incident's reality. However, although amniocentesis was not widely used until the mid- to late-1960s, it was in the pioneering stage in the mid-1950s and a preliminary report detailing its clinical use was published as long ago as 1930 in the *American Journal of Roentgenology and Radiation Therapy*.

Some UFOLOGISTS who believe the Hill abduction to have been a real experience point out that something must have occurred to cause the Hills to arrive home more than two hours late. PHILIP KLASS suggests that after being frightened by the UFO, the Hills had turned onto an obscure side road. He states that since Barney feared capture, it was likely they would not have returned to the main road for a long time.

It has been suggested that Barney's warts were a psychosomatic symptom connected with the emotions experienced under hypnosis. However, the warts had first appeared in 1962, before his visits to Simon. In 1964, during the sessions, the warts became inflamed, suggesting that there might be some connection between them and the memories of the alleged abduction. However, it is possible that the warts may have been incorporated into the so-called memories in the same way that daily experiences are incorporated into nighttime dreams.

Under posthypnotic suggestion, Betty drew the star map she had supposedly seen aboard the alien craft. The tentative identification of the main star as ZETA RETICULI several years later led to much controversy. Some UFOlogists and astronomers have pointed out that there are at least three other constellations whose pattern matches that of Betty's map.

Whether or not the abduction part of the Hills' story was a subconscious fantasy, it is generally agreed that they did see a glowing UFO in the night sky. Skeptics argue that they probably saw a bright STAR or PLANET. Klass has suggested that they observed a PLASMA associated with the high-tension power line which runs alongside U.S. Highway 3. He points out that the appearance of spinning and the colors described by the Hills are characteristic of plasmas formed in the air. He also speculates that a glowing plasma might have a hypnotic effect on some observers, especially if seen at close range in darkness.

The incident received worldwide publicity. In 1975, the Hills' ordeal was dramatized in a nationwide television special called THE UFO INCIDENT.

Bibliography: Fuller, John G., *The Interrupted Journey* (New York: Dial Press, 1966); Klass, Philip J., *UFOs Identified* (New York: Random House, 1968).

## NEWHOUSE, DELBERT, *see* TREMONTON, UTAH

## NEWPORT NEWS, VIRGINIA,

location of a well-publicized UFO encounter on July 14, 1952. A Pan American Airways DC-4, flying at 8,000 feet, was approaching the Norfolk, Virginia, area en route to Miami at about 8:10 P.M. Captain William B. Nash and Third Officer William Fortenberry suddenly noticed a red brilliance in the sky, seemingly beyond and to the east of Newport News. The light quickly became distinguishable as six bright objects streaking toward the plane, at an altitude of about 2,000 feet, a mile below them. The six craft were fiery red. "Their shape was clearly outlined and evidently circular," Captain Nash later stressed. "The edges were well-defined, not phosphorescent or fuzzy in the least." The upper surfaces were glowing red-orange. Within seconds, they could see that the disks were holding a narrow-echelon formation, a slightly stepped-up line tilted to the right from the pilots' point of view, with the leader at the lowest point and each following object successively higher. The diameter of each disk was about one hundred feet. The lead object suddenly seemed to decelerate. The second and third objects wavered slightly and almost passed the leader. When the line of disks was almost directly beneath the airlines and slightly to the right front, their brightness diminished slightly and they flipped on edge in unison, the sides to the left of the plane going up and the glowing top surfaces facing right. In this position, the pilots were able to see that the UFOs were shaped rather like coins. Though the bottom surfaces did not become clearly visible, Nash and Fontenberry had the impression that they were unlit. The exposed edges, also unlit, appeared to be about fifteen feet thick, and the top surface seemed to be flat. While in this edgewise position, the last five slid over and past the leader so that the echelon was now in reverse order and still tilted. Then, flipping back into a horizontal position and resuming their former brightness, they darted off in a direction that formed a sharp angle with their first course, their sequence being as it was when the pilots had first spotted them.

Almost immediately, Nash and Fortenberry caught sight of two more identical but brighter craft as they darted out from under the airplane at the same altitude as the other six. As the two additional disks joined the formation, the lights of all eight blinked out, then came back on again. Still in line, the eight disks sped westward, north of Newport News. They climbed in a graceful arc above the altitude of the airlines and then blinked out one by one, but not in sequence. Nash and Fortenberry estimated the speed of the objects to be at least twelve thousand miles per hour.

The two men were interrogated at length by UNITED STATES AIR FORCE (USAF) investigators who informed them that the incident had been observed by seven other groups of observers, including a lieutenant commander and his wife.

Bibliography: Sachs, Margaret, with Ernest Jahn, *Celestial Passengers—UFOs and Space Travel* (New York: Penguin Books, 1977).

## NEWSCLIPPING SERVICES *see* AERIAL PHENOMENA CLIPPING AND INFORMATION CENTER (APCIC) and UFO NEWSCLIPPING SERVICE (UFONS)

**NEW ZEALAND.** A UFO WAVE occurred in New Zealand in 1960. The area's most famous incidents were the NEW ZEALAND SIGHTINGS of 1978/1979.

The country has several investigative organizations and its most prominent publication is the magazine, XENOLOG.

## NEW ZEALAND SCIENTIFIC APPROACH TO COSMIC UNDERSTANDING (NZSATCU or SATCU), 33 Dee Street, Timaru, New Zealand.

The purpose of this organization is to determine what UFOs are, why they are coming here, where they come from and, if they are coming to help mankind, how they can be helped in this endeavor. SATCU adheres to no one specific theory regarding the identity and origin of UFOs, although it now favors the PARALLEL UNIVERSE HYPOTHESIS over the EXTRATERRESTRIAL HYPOTHESIS. It belives UFOs may be a religious phenomenon whose purpose is to bring Earth's population back to a divine way of thinking. SATCU also considers the possibility that human beings might be owned by a superior force perceptible to us as UFOs.

This nonprofit organization was founded in 1954 by Fred and Phyllis Dickeson. Originally named the ADAMSKI CORRESPONDENT GROUP (after GEORGE ADAMSKI, whose claims the group no longer supports), its name was changed to the NEW ZEALAND SCIENTIFIC SPACE RESEARCH GROUP before being changed to its current name. The group has over 350 members. Nine voluntary investigators are located throughout New Zealand. Although SATCU formerly organized meetings throughout the country, it is now devoted exclusively to the publication of the quarterly magazine, XENOLOG, which is edited by Fred and Phyllis Dickeson.

## NEW ZEALAND SCIENTIFIC SPACE RESEARCH (NZSSR), organization founded in 1957 and now defunct. The Founders and Directors of the group were H. J. and B. M. Hinfelaar. A journal, called *Spaceview*, was published by the organization until 1974. Publication of the journal was continued by Victor Harris of Pakarunga, Auckland, until 1978. NZSSR held that the books of CONTACTEE GEORGE ADAMSKI revealed the truth about flying saucers. The group believed that great civilizations existed on this PLANET in ages past and that communication with extraterrestrial visitors has been going on for as long as Earth has been inhabited. This time, however, according to the group, mankind has developed a sufficiently advanced technology to enable him to join his fellow beings in space. But, NZSSR concluded, this step

cannot come until the majority, and not the minority, of Earth people have learned to practice the cosmic laws in their own lives and thereby graduate from the kindergarten of the solar system.

## NEW ZEALAND SCIENTIFIC SPACE RESEARCH GROUP, former name of NEW ZEALAND SCIENTIFIC APPROACH TO COSMIC UNDERSTANDING (NZSATCU OR SATCU).

## NEW ZEALAND SIGHTINGS—1978/1979. On New Year's Day, 1979, a RADAR/visual UFO sighting in New Zealand made headlines around the world. Some of the UFOs had been captured on film which became the focus point of an extensive investigation. Although worldwide news reports dealt primarily with the sightings which had occurred on the night of December 30/31, the incident was actually the culmination of a series of sightings.

A number of radar sightings had occurred about two weeks previously off the northeast coast of New Zealand's South Island. The first of the major radar/visual sightings, however, began on December 21. At about 12:30 A.M., air traffic controllers at Wellington Airport detected three unidentified targets on their radar screens. One object, estimated to be as large as a commercial airliner, had been tracked moving at high speed for sixty miles. Then it stopped and remained stationary. A New Zealand turboprop freighter, an Argosy, was in the vicinity. The pilot was asked by the controllers to take a look. At about 1:20 A.M., Captain Vern Powell radioed that he could see white lights similar to landing lights in the area. The lights appeared as targets on the airplane's weather radar. At about 3:30 A.M., Powell radioed that a bright red light was visible to the east of the freighter. Wellington controllers confirmed that their radar showed a target about twenty-three miles to the right of the plane. They watched the target as it tracked the aircraft for a distance of twelve miles. Shortly afterward, Powell reported that the object had changed from red to white with a red ring. The light was extremely bright and when it passed behind CLOUDS Powell could still see its glow. By this time, Wellington radar operators reported that they had five strong targets in the area. As he approached Christchurch, Powell radioed that his weather radar showed a target approaching the plane at high speed. It had traveled fifteen miles in five seconds. The blip disappeared from the screen. When Powell looked out, he saw a flashing white light off to the side of the airplane.

The sightings made front page headlines in Australia and New Zealand. Quentin Fogarty, a reporter for Australian Television Channel O, was vacationing in New Zealand at the time. He was asked by his Melbourne office to do a story on the incident. Fogarty hired a cameraman, David Crockett, whose wife, Ngaire Crockett, operated the recording equipment. The Crocketts were unknown to Fogarty before this time. Fogarty and the Crocketts interviewed and filmed the Wellington air traffic control radar operators and the pilot involved in the sightings.

At 10:15 P.M. on December 30, 1978, Fogarty and the Crocketts boarded an Argosy aircraft, piloted by Captain Bill Startup and copilot Robert Guard, for the purpose of filming a reconstruction of Powell's flight. The pilots were unknown to Fogarty and the Crocketts prior to the flight. They were flying south from Wellington with a full cargo of newspapers when the flight crew first noticed unusual lights in the direction of the Kaikoura peninsula. It was just after midnight. The flight crew contacted the Wellington radar controllers, who confirmed that they were picking up strong unidentified returns in that area. Fogarty and the Crocketts were alerted. During the next fifty minutes, until the airplane landed at Christchurch, those on board observed a spectacular and sometimes frightening UFO display. Because of the objects' apparent ability to appear and disappear at will, only a short segment of film footage was obtained. The Wellington radar operators reported that at times there were up to ten unknown radar targets and rarely were there fewer than two. At one point, one unidentified blip merged with that of the aircraft as if it were flying in formation with the Argosy. The passengers remembered with some trepidation the UFO-related DISAPPEARANCE of a pilot just over two months previously near MELBOURNE, AUSTRALIA.

The airplane landed at Christchurch at 1:00 A.M. After the newspapers had been unloaded, Fogarty and David Crockett boarded the aircraft again for the return flight. A reporter from Christchurch, Dennis Grant, who was a friend of Fogarty, took the place of Ngaire Crockett, who did not want to fly back through the area of the previous sightings. The airplane took off from Christchurch at 2:16 A.M. and climbed up through a low layer of clouds. As it broke through the clouds about three minutes after takeoff, those aboard saw a brilliant light ahead and to the right. Captain Startup, who compared the object to a featureless full moon, turned on the airplane's nose radar to the mapping mode. He picked up a strong target just over twenty miles away in the direction of the bright light. Later, the target approached within ten miles. The object remained in view for about twelve minutes and it was during this time that the cameraman took the now famous films with a 240 mm lens. He described the object as having a brightly lit base with what appeared to be a transparent dome. About thirty-five miles out of Christchurch, with the object still outside the window, Startup decided to turn toward it. He put the aircraft into a ninety-degree turn. The object, however, appeared to have moved to the right as the plane turned. The plane flew southeast for about a minute or more, during which time the UFO appeared to be at a lower altitude and appeared to move to the right of the aircraft. When Captain Startup turned to the left to resume his original flight path out of Christchurch, the object appeared ahead of him. He thinks the plane then flew over it. The bright object was not seen again. When the airplane was east of Kaikoura, Wellington air traffic controllers again reported targets around the aircraft. Several of these were observed by those on board. One brightly flashing light was filmed. The film shows a light which oscillates rapidly from very bright white or yellow-white to dim red-and-orange. The Argosy landed about 3:15 A.M. That same day, the Royal New Zealand Air Force put a Skyhawk jet fighter on standby alert to intercept any newly-sighted UFOs.

About a week after the sightings, the film was on its way to the United States to be analyzed. Channel O selected the NATIONAL INVESTIGATIONS COMMITTEE ON AERIAL PHENOMENA (NICAP) to perform the task. The project was assigned to physicist BRUCE MACCABEE. After initial tests had confirmed that something unusual had been captured on film, Maccabee visited both Australia and New Zealand to interview the principals in the case. On March 26, 1979, Maccabee's findings were released at a press conference in New York City. Maccabee stated that the film shot when the aircraft was ten-to-forty miles northeast of Christchurch shows a light that has various shapes, including almost round, almost triangular and bell-shaped. The bell-shaped image, obtained with a 240 mm lens, has a bright base and an upper portion which is less bright, in agreement with the cameraman's description of an object with an apparently transparent dome. Many of the images are overexposed, suggesting a very bright yellowish-white light. An estimate of the brightness of the source, if it were just over ten miles away from the plane, shows that it could have been as powerful as several hundred thousand candlepower, candlepower being a measure of the amount of visible light given off by a source of light. For comparison, a one hundred thousand watt incandescent bulb radiating in all directions would have about 200,000 candlepower. Maccabee also stated that the sizes of the images on the film suggest a source which, if it were just over ten miles away, would be about one hundred feet wide.

Maccabee and astronomer J. ALLEN HYNEK, after investigation and study, established that the UFOs were not VENUS or other PLANETS, STARS, METEORS, BALLOONS, other aircraft, ground lights, secret military maneuvers, fishing boats or a HOAX. They also discounted the possibility that the radar returns were ANGELS because the TEMPERATURE INVERSION was insufficient and too high and there had been little turbulence. In addition, states Maccabee, angels do not explain the dynamics of the targets. Maccabee and Hynek also reject the possibility of equipment malfunction because the radar needed no more than the normal maintenance at the time.

Other scientists joining Maccabee and Hynek in the opinion that the UFO film shows something very unusual are PLASMA physicist Peter Sturrock, optical physiologist Richard Haines, biophysicist Gilbert Levin and electronics specialist Neil Davis. Other scientists, most notably several government and industry radar specialists, who also endorsed this appraisal, requested that their names not be used in order to protect their sensitive professional positions.

**NEW ZEALAND UFO STUDIES CENTRE (NUSC)**, the UFO investigation division of the EARTH COLONIZATION RESEARCH ASSOCIATION (ECRA).

**NICAP** see **NATIONAL INVESTIGATIONS COMMITTEE ONAERIAL PHENOMENA**

**NICUFO** see **NATIONAL INVESTIGATION COMMITTEE ON UFOs**

**NL** see **NOCTURNAL LIGHT**

**NOCTURNAL LIGHT (NL)**, term coined by astronomer J. ALLEN HYNEK to denote an unidentified light seen at night which does not fit the pattern of lights from known sources. The general characteristics of nocturnal lights are brilliance of -2 to -3 stellar magnitude, floating, hovering, abrupt reversal of direction, zigzagging movements and sudden acceleration. Their color is often described as amber, orange or yellow, sometimes changing to blue or red. Changes in brightness are sometimes observed in association with speed and directional changes. When the lights disappear, many witnesses describe the effect as that of a light being switched off. Nocturnal lights are more frequently reported than daytime UFOs, referred to as DAYLIGHT DISKS.

Bibliography: Hynek, J. Allen, *The UFO Experience: A Scientific Inquiry* (Chicago: Henry Regnery Company, 1972).

**NORAD** see **NORTH AMERICAN AIR DEFENSE COMMAND**

**NORFOLK AND NATIONAL UFO INVES-**

TIGATION SOCIETY, copublisher of the UNEX-PLAINED PHENOMENA NEWS BULLETIN.

NORMAN, RUTH E. (b. August 18, 1900, Indianapolis, Indiana; address: P.O. Box 1042, El Cajon, California 92022; telephone number: 714-460-1972), CONTACTEE, Cofounder and President of the UNARIUS EDUCATIONAL FOUNDATION.

Norman claims that Earth is not her home PLANET but rather that she was incarnated here to lead Earth into membership in the Interstellar Confederation. She purports to be in mental communication with the leaders of fifty-nine other planets and with the souls of many famous Earth people. Her most frequent contacts, she reports, are with her soulmate, Nikola Tesla, previously incarnated as Leonardo da Vinci. Her late husband, Ernest Norman, claimed to have been Jesus in a previous incarnation. Norman is called the "Universal Seeress," "Archangel Uriel" and "Ioshanna" by her disciples, but to local nonbelievers she is known as "Spaceship Ruthie."

Ruth Norman.

A graduate of elementary school, Norman reportedly worked as a restauranteer and a real estate agent prior to becoming a contactee. She and her husband founded the Unarius Educational Foundation in 1956. Together they wrote and published numerous books presenting the purported communications of SPACE PEOPLE and spiritual beings. Ruth Norman opened the Center for the New World Teaching in El Cajon, California, in 1975. In 1977 she wrote, directed and starred in a ninety-minute motion picture, entitled *A Visit to the Underground Cities of Mars*.

NORSK UFO CENTER, Box 2119, 7001 Trondheim, Norway.

The purpose of this organization is to gain increased insight into the real substance of the UFO problem through the collection of data, investigation, release of information to the public and cooperation with other organizations and individuals involved in research and investigation.

This nonprofit organization was founded in 1972 by Kilbjørn Stenødegård, who serves as Director. The group has 200 members. Although the principal seat and central administration is located in Trondheim, NUFOC is a nationwide organization divided into "sections." Within each section are "groups" responsible for specialized tasks. These divisions are headed by Department Leaders, Section Leaders and Group Leaders. Representatives of NUFOC are divided into three categories, namely Reporters, Field Investigators and Advisors. In addition to specialized equipment available to Field Investigators, the organization has its own laboratory, as well as access to two other laboratories. Cooperation and exchange of information with other Scandinavian countries takes place automatically. International cooperation is maintained, particularly with the United States, England and France. English translations of Norwegian documents are sent to the major UFO organizations in these countries. NUFOC also contributes material to Norwegian and foreign newspapers, and organizes lectures and exhibitions. Two periodicals, UFO FORUM and RAPPORTNYTT, are published regularly.

NORTH AMERICAN AIR DEFENSE COM-MAND (NORAD), agency jointly operated by the United States and Canada. Its purpose is to keep track of all man-made objects orbiting Earth, to detect and identify unknown aircraft, and to detect and provide defense against enemy bombers and missiles. Twenty-four-hour-a-day observation is maintained utilizing RADAR, optical and radio equipment.

Since NORAD's installations are situated primarily in the coastal and border states looking outward toward the horizon, they do not give complete coverage of the airspace over the inland states.

NORAD registers 800 to 900 unknown radar returns on ballistic trajectories every day. The majority of these are due to auroral effects, while others may be caused by re-entering SATELLITES, electromagnetic noise pulses and METEORS. It is highly possible, however, that some of these unknown targets represent bona fide UFOs.

Bibliography: Hendry, Allan, *The UFO Handbook* (Garden City, N.Y.: Doubleday and Company, 1979).

## NORTHEASTERN UFO ORGANIZATION

**(NEUFO),** P.O. Box 233, North Tonawanda, New York 14120; telephone number: 716-694-0811.

The purpose of this organization is to engage in the search for "Universal Truth," to share a common interest in the science of UFOLOGY and to keep the public informed on the subject. The group holds that UFOs are the spacecraft of peaceful extraterrestrial beings.

This nonprofit organization was founded in 1975, although many of its members had frequently gathered informally for UFO discussions during the previous ten years. The administration is divided into the Executive Board, which is the governing body, and the elected positions held for one year by Active Members. Members of the Executive Board include Codirectors Leonard Kornacki, Sara Kornacki and Malcolm Williams; Public Relations Officer Thomas Grey; Coordinator of Internal Affairs Brian Berard; Chairman of the Board Robert Spurlin; Executive Secretary Les Washington; and Sergeant at Arms Ronald Kornacki. Elected positions include those of President, Vice-President and secretarial offices. In addition to holding various administrative positions, Active Members attend all monthly meetings and classes, investigate sightings and exercise their voting rights. Inactive Members do not take part in voting procedures and cannot hold administrative positions. NEUFO branches are located in Niagara Falls, Ontario, and Mississauga, Ontario. NEUFO exchanges correspondence with overseas organizations. Monthly meetings and lectures are open to the public. A monthly newsletter, *NEUFO News,* is available to members and is given out free-of-charge to the public during lectures. Public Relations Officer Tom Grey, headquartered in Mississauga, Canada, publishes and edits UFO UPDATE which is available both at newsstands and by subscription.

## NORTHERN LIGHTS *see* AURORAS

## NORTHERN OHIO UFO GROUP, 3403 West

119th Street, Cleveland, Ohio 44111; telephone number: 216-826-0225.

This investigative group is administered by Rick Hilberg. Public meetings are held monthly and a newsletter is also published monthly. The organization is a member of the UFO OHIO network.

## NORTHERN UFO NETWORK (NUFON), 23

Sunningdale Drive, Irlam, Greater Manchester M30 6NJ, England; telephone number: 061-775-4749.

NUFON is a freelance network open to any serious UFO investigator or local group. Most of the participating organizations have no set beliefs regarding the identity and origin of UFOs.

This nonprofit organization was founded in 1975 by an initial committee, consisting of JENNY RANDLES as Secretary, Peter Warrington as Treasurer and Trevor Whitaker, a longstanding official of the BRITISH UFO RESEARCH ASSOCIATION (BUFORA), as Chairman. The committee was discontinued as such when it found that the organization could function without an administrative bureaucracy. However, Randles, who acts as the focal point, is still referred to unofficially as the Secretary. Peter Warrington supervises financial affairs. Paul Whetnall transfers data to UFOCAT for the CENTER FOR UFO STUDIES (CUFOS). UFO reports are also channeled to the FLYING SAUCER REVIEW (FSR). Robert Morrell coordinates work at the Nottingham headquarters where files and a research library are housed. All the data is freely accessible to researchers. Overseas Liaison Officer Bryan Hartley maintains extensive flow of communications with over 100 organizations and independent researchers in over forty countries. NUFON serves as a liaison medium to about nineteen organizations and a number of independent researchers and investigators located throughout the entire area of the United Kingdom north of the West Midlands, including North and Mid Wales, Ireland and Scotland. Membership stands at about 450. In 1977, the liaison concept was expanded on a nationwide basis through the creation of the UFO INVESTIGATORS NETWORK (UFOIN), which, with Randles as unofficial general secretary, interacts to a great degree with NUFON. A liaison of about fifteen organizations in the south of Great Britain was set up in 1978 on the same basis as NUFON and is known as the SOUTHERN UFO NETWORK (SUFON). A monthly newsletter, NORTHERN UFO NEWS (NUFON), is edited by Randles.

## NORTHERN UFO NEWS, publication of THE NORTHERN UFO NETWORK (NUFON).

## NORTHERN UFO NEWS (NUFON), newsletter published by the DIRECT INVESTIGATION GROUP OF AERIAL PHENOMENA (DIGAP).

## NORTH HUDSON PARK, NEW JERSEY, location of a UFO encounter during January, 1975. Liquor store owner George O'Barski was driving through the park on his way home from work at about 2:00 A.M. when his car radio developed static. After a few moments, the radio went silent. Through the window, O'Barski heard a droning sound similar to that of a refrigerator motor. Looking up, he noticed a domed, disk-shaped object floating downward. About thirty-five feet in diameter and about seven feet high, the craft came to a stop about fifty feet away. Several illuminated vertical windows encircled the object. Spaced about one

foot apart, the windows were about one foot wide and four feet high. As the craft hovered or rested on unseen legs about four feet off the ground, a square illuminated opening appeared. A ladder dropped to the ground. About ten small creatures scrambled down to the ground. Approximately three-and-a-half feet tall, they resembled children wearing snowsuits. Their faces were hidden by round helmets. Each creature carried a small bag with a handle and a spoonlike shovel. They quickly scooped up samples of soil, which they placed in the bags. After a couple of minutes, they returned to their craft which took off at high speed and disappeared. O'Barski's radio functioned normally again.

After being publicized in newspapers and on television, the case was investigated by the MUTUAL UFO NETWORK (MUFON). The organization's investigators discovered that a doorman at the Stonehenge apartment complex overlooking the park had also observed a UFO on the night of O'Barski's encounter.

Bibliography: *The Village Voice* (New York: William Ryan, March 7, 1976)

**NORTH JERSEY UFO GROUP,** founded in 1954, the group is now defunct. It published thirteen issues of *UFO Newsletter,* edited by Lee R. Munsick. The group's general opinion was that UFOs were intelligently-controlled extraterrestrial vehicles. CONTACTEE claims were rejected.

**NOSTRA,** biweekly Portuguese newspaper published by NOSTRADAMUS.

**NOSTRADAMUS**—Editorial de Publicacoes, Lda., Rua Ernesto da Silva 30, 1500 Lisbon, Portugal; telephone number: 705649 or 703928.

Primarily a publishing house, this company publishes NOSTRA, a biweekly Portuguese newspaper dealing with numerous mysteries, including UFOs, parapsychology, the BERMUDA TRIANGLE, ancient mysteries, FIREBALLS, natural medicines, archaeology and astrology. Information is collected from newspapers and magazines all over the world. Nostradamus has three field investigators located in Lisbon who are available to travel to other parts of the country when necessary. The company coordinates research and investigative activities of other UFO organizations in Portugal. Of greatest interest to Nostradamus has been an ongoing case in which UFOs have been sighted regularly in a particular area of Portugal.

This company was founded in 1977. José Alberto Gomes Pereira is Director-President. Partners in the company are Humberto Guterres, António José Maya and Acácio Luís Faria.

**NOTICIAS OVNI,** publication of GRUPO A. A. OVNI.

**NOTIZIARIO INFORMATIVO INTERNO DEL CENTRO TORINESE RICERCHE UFO- LOGICHE,** publication of the CENTRO TORINESE RICERCHE UFOLOGICHE (CTRU).

**NOTIZIARIO UFO,** publication of the CENTRO UFOLOGICO NAZIONALE (CUN).

**NOTTINGHAM UFO INVESTIGATION SO- CIETY (NUFOIS),** 443 Meadow Lane, Nottingham NG2 3GB, England; telephone number: 0602-297575.

This organization is dedicated to the scientific investigation of UFOs. NUFOIS holds that all UFOs are probably explainable as natural phenomena or misidentified conventional objects. It believes, however, that there is a possibility that a few UFOs may be of extraterrestrial origin. The group is hostile to all speculation regarding paranormal and parapsychological HYPOTHESES.

This nonprofit organization was founded in 1970 as an amalgamation of several groups in the area. The staff consists of Chairman Robert W. Morrell, Secretary-Treasurer J. K. Cree, Membership Secretary Michael Crew, Technical Officer Stephen Hunter, Librarian Christopher Nelson and Sightings Coordinator John Mollow. There are between seventy and one hundred members. The group's operations include field investigation, analysis, information and data collection and development of investigative equipment. Field Investigators cover the Nottingham, Derbyshire and Leicestershire areas. Morrell is Editor of UFO RE- SEARCH REVIEW, which is published quarterly and covers all aspects of UFOLOGY.

**NUFOC** see **NATIONAL UFO CONFERENCE**

**NUFOIS** see **NOTTINGHAM UFO INVESTIGA- TION SOCIETY**

**NUFON** see **NORTHERN UFO NETWORK**

**NUFON (NORTHERN UFO NEWS),** newsletter published by the DIRECT INVESTIGATION GROUP ON AERIAL PHENOMENA (DIGAP).

**NUFOR** see **NATIONAL UNIDENTIFIED FLY- ING OBJECT RESEARCH**

**NUFOR NEWSLETTER,** publication of NATIONAL UNIDENTIFIED FLYING OBJECT RESEARCH (NUFOR).

**NUREMBERG, GERMANY,** location of a spectacular UFO sighting on April 14, 1561, depicted at the time
in a woodcut by Hans Glaser. In the early morning, the
sky was filled with cylindrical UFOs, from which there
emerged black, red, orange and blue-white spheres and
disks. The objects seemed to be fighting with each
other. In the lower right-hand corner of Glaser's woodcut are a number of smoking spheres which appear to
have crashed. The incident was interpreted by the
various observers as a supernatural or religious phenomenon.

Bibliography: Jung, Carl G., *Flying Saucers: A Modern Myth of Things Seen in the Sky* (New York:
Harcourt, Brace and Company, 1959).

**NUSC,** acronym for the New Zealand UFO Studies
Centre, the UFO investigation division of the EARTH
COLONIZATION RESEARCH ASSOCIATION (ECRA).

**NYHETSBLAD,** newsletter of the ARBETSGRUPPEN
FOR UFOLOGI (AFU).

**NZSATCU** *see* **NEW ZEALAND SCIENTIFIC
APPROACH TO COSMIC UNDERSTANDING
(NZSATCU OR SATCU).**

**NZ SCIENTIFIC APPROACH TO COSMIC**

Hans Glaser's woodcut showing UFOs seen at Nuremberg,
Germany, on April 14, 1561. *(Courtesy ICUFON)*

**UNDERSTANDING** *see* **NEW ZEALAND SCI-
ENTIFIC APPROACH TO COSMIC UNDER-
STANDING (NZSATCU OR SATCU)**

**NZSSR** *see* **NEW ZEALAND SCIENTIFIC
SPACE RESEARCH**

**OATES, WARREN,** actor who reportedly observed a UFO in the wilderness about twenty miles northeast of Palm Springs, California, on January 1, 1975. The object was also seen by musician Lee Clayton, Robert Mitchum's daughter Trina, writer Judy Jones and actor Ted Markland. Just before sunrise, the five friends saw the object traveling in a semi-circle across the cloudless, starlit night. They described it as an oval, metallic object flashing yellow, green and white lights. In the middle was one large orange light. Clayton, a former Navy jet pilot, watched the UFO through binoculars. He could distinguish a bell shape on top. He estimated the object to be at a distance of three to five miles away and at an altitude of 2,000 feet or less. The UFO stopped and hovered momentarily before moving off behind the mountains. Markland, a resident of the area, claims to have seen numerous UFOs on previous occasions. They are fairly consistent in appearance, he claims, appearing as colored pulsating lights that move swiftly and erratically across the sky.

**O'BARSKI, GEORGE,** *see* **NORTH HUDSON PARK, NEW JERSEY**

**OBERG, JAMES EDWARD** (b. November 7, 1944, New York, N.Y.; address: Route 2, Box 1813, Dickinson, Texas 77539), computer specialist and science popularizer.

Oberg's interest in the subject of UFOs began when he was about eleven years old. He has been reading UFO books since that time but his concurrent interest in science and logic led him to the conclusion that the standards of investigation and reporting of UFO incidents are very low. He states that published reports of sightings have very little in common with what actually occurs. He, himself, has observed unusual but identifia-

ble phenomena which other witnesses reported as UFOs. He fears that if some hitherto unknown phenomenon should manifest itself, it might not be recognized or it might be left in the hands of those investigators who have already lost their credibility. He is attempting to tighten the standards of investigation and reporting in order to avoid such an outcome, should the situation arise. His magazine articles attacking various UFOLOGISTS' claims have, according to Oberg, resulted in flurries of hate mail from both the United States and Canada. Some UFOlogists have suggested that Oberg is an Air Force spy acting under orders to discredit UFO researchers and to COVER UP secret government activities in the field. Oberg denies these charges, stating that all his activities in the UFO field are based on his own longstanding interest in the subject.

James Oberg. *(Photo by John Jurgenson)*

Oberg graduated *summa cum laude* from Ohio Wesleyan University with a major in mathematics. He was also elected to Phi Beta Kappa. He received his M.S. in Engineering Science from Northwestern University in 1970, and his M.S. in Computer Science from the University of New Mexico, in 1972.

Oberg did graduate work at Northwestern University from 1966 to 1969. As a First Lieutenant, he worked in Aero Laser Simulation in the Weapons Laboratory at Kirtland Air Force Base from 1970 to 1972. He was then promoted to Captain and worked as an Instructor at the Department of Defense Computer Institute at the Washington Navy Yard until 1975. Since 1975, he has worked as a Mission Control Computer Specialist at NASA's Johnson Space Center in Houston.

Oberg is Vice-Chairman of the UFO Subcommittee of the COMMITTEE FOR THE SCIENTIFIC INVESTIGATION OF CLAIMS OF THE PARANORMAL (CSICP). He is a UFO columnist of *OMNI* magazine, Associate Editor of *Space World* magazine and Contributing Editor of *Astronomy* magazine. He is a Fellow of CSICP and the British Interplanetary Society. He is a member of the L5 Society Board of Directors, the AMERICAN INSTITUTE OF AERONAUTICS AND ASTRONAUTICS (AIAA) and the Air Force Association.

Oberg received the National Space Club's Robert Goddard History Essay award in 1975 and 1977, and the AIAA Distinguished Lecturer award for 1977–78 and the CUTTY SARK Award in 1979 for a scientific paper on UFOLOGY.

Oberg is author of over 100 published articles on astronomy, space colonies and the Soviet space program. He has contributed to encyclopedia articles, and edited the Department of Defense publication, *Selected Computer Articles Manual,* in 1974 and 1975. He is coauthor of *Famous Spaceships* (Milwaukee, Wisconsin: Kalmbach Publishing Company, 1978); and author of *Terraforming* (Harrisburg, Pennsylvania: Stackpole Books, 1979).

**O'BRIEN REPORT,** document describing the proceedings, conclusions and recommendations of the UNITED STATES AIR FORCE (USAF) Scientific Advisory Board Ad Hoc Committee to Review PROJECT BLUE BOOK.

Increased concern about UFOs in 1965 led astronomer and Air Force consultant J. ALLEN HYNEK to propose that a panel of civilian scientists carefully review the UFO situation to establish whether or not a major problem really existed and to make recommendations about the program's future status within the Air Force. Consequently, on September 28, 1965, Major General E. B. LeBailly, Secretary of the Air Force Office of Information, wrote a memo to the Military Director of the Air Force's Scientific Advisory Board, requesting "that a working scientific panel composed of both physical and social scientists be organized to review Project Blue Book—its resources, methods, and findings—and to advise the Air Force as to any improvements that should be made in the program to carry out the Air Force's assigned responsibility."

As a result, the Ad Hoc Committee to Review Project Blue Book was formed, headed by physicist Brian O'Brien. On the panel were psychologist Launor F. Carter, psychologist Jesse Orlansky, electrical engineer Richard Porter, astronomer and space scientist CARL SAGAN and electrical engineer Willis H. Ware. All but Sagan were members of the Air Force Scientific Advisory Board. They met for only one day, February 3, 1966. The committee reviewed the ROBERTSON PANEL report of 1953 and was briefed by the then-head of Project Blue Book, Major HECTOR QUINTANILLA, and the staff of the Air Force's FOREIGN TECHNOLOGY DIVISION (a newly-formed division which took over UFO investigations). In March, the O'Brien group issued its report.

The committee concluded that the Air Force program dealing with UFO sightings had been well-organized, although the resources assigned to it had been quite limited. The report pointed out that "there is always the possibility that analysis of new sightings may provide some additions to scientific knowledge of value to the Air Force. Moreover, some of the case records which the committee looked at that were listed as 'identified' were sightings where the evidence collected was too meager or too indefinite to permit positive listing in the identified category. Because of this, the committee recommends that the present program be strengthened to provide opportunity for scientific investigation of selected sightings in more detail and depth than has been possible to date." To accomplish this, the committee's principal recommendation was that, "Contracts be negotiated with a few selected universities to provide scientific teams to investigate promptly and in depth certain selected sightings of UFOs. Each team should include at least one psychologist, preferably one interested in clinical psychology, and at least one physical scientist, preferably an astronomer or geophysicist familiar with atmospheric physics." The committee also suggested that Project Blue Book reports "should be given wide unsolicited circulation among prominent members of the Congress and other public persons as a further aid to public understanding of the scientific approach being taken by the Air Force in attacking the UFO problem."

The O'Brien Report resulted in the formation of the CONDON COMMITTEE, a team of scientific investigators and researchers at the University of Colorado, who conducted an eighteen-month Air Force/taxpayer-sponsored investigation and evaluation of UFOs.

Bibliography: Steiger, Brad (ed.), *Project Blue Book* (New York: Ballantine Books, 1976).

**OCALA, FLORIDA,** location of a RADAR/visual UFO sighting on May 14, 1978. Located in an isolated area of the Ocala Forest is the Pinecastle Electronic Warfare Range a Navy installation where military pilots are trained. At about 10:00 P.M., Duty Officer SK–1 Robert J. Clark received a telephone call from a woman in Silver Glen Springs. She reported seeing a bright light in the sky and wanted to know if the Navy was using flares at the time. Ten minutes later, Clark received another call from Rocky Morgan, a fishing guide from the Silver Glen Springs campgrounds. Morgan and eight other persons had observed an object approximately fifty-to-sixty feet in diameter with multicolored lights which passed over them at treetop level as they were driving on Highway 19. Clark contacted the base air controller, and together they went to the tower to check on the possibility that a commercial or military aircraft might have crashed or was experiencing mechanical difficulties. In addition, the Naval Air Station at Jacksonville was contacted to determine if any military or private aircraft were known to be in the area. The answer was negative.

While attempting to make visual contact, Clark notified external security and had them contact radar operator T.D.2 Timothy Collins. When Collins arrived at the tower, he was given a pair of binoculars, with which he observed a cluster of glowing lights that appeared to be moving from north to northwest, but he could make no identification. Although it was a quiet evening, he could hear no noise coming from the cluster of objects. He was asked to turn on the MSQ–102 tracking radar and to attempt to lock onto the targets. During the twenty minutes or so needed to warm up the radar, he searched the area with the periscopes and again sighted the object.

When the radar was fully operational, an object was detected approximately sixty miles to the north. Using the known bearing, range and elevation of an old Civil Defense tower located approximately three miles away, Collins locked the tracking antenna on the tower into automatic tracking. He then saw one stationary object and one other object moving slowly around the tower. The computer readout indicated that at the time the object was almost motionless in relation to ground velocity. Collins then switched to manual tracking and continued to search for other objects. He observed another object north of them, but was unable to lock onto it. Turning to the PPI (planned position indicator) radar, he then noticed a moving object northwest of the

range, three to five miles away and south from the general direction of the Civil Defense tower. As he locked onto the object, it accelerated rapidly, moving approximately five miles in one one-second sweep. After accelerating in a southerly direction, the object veered north in the direction of Pinecastle and decelerated as it approached the base. It then disappeared.

Science writer ROBERT SHEAFFER has conjectured that the Ocala UFO report of May 14, 1978, describes three different celestial bodies. He attributes the initial civilian visual sighting to VENUS, which was in its final stages of setting at about 10:00 P.M. The position of the object observed by the Pinecastle personnel, according to Sheaffer, matches that of Jupiter so well that it is difficult to avoid the conclusion that the object was indeed that brilliant PLANET. He states that the bouncing attributed to the UFO was probably the result of AUTOKINESIS, an effect frequently experienced by observers of celestial bodies. Sheaffer suggests that the second UFO seen by the Navy observers was the brilliant STAR Capella, which would have been at treetop level ten minutes after Jupiter's disappearance. Writer Allan Hendry argues that the Navy witnesses, who were shown Venus and Jupiter on subsequent nights, claimed to have seen those planets as well as the UFO on the night of May 14. Sheaffer states that since Venus had already set by the time the observations began at the Naval installation, their claim brought into question the reliability of their entire report. Hendry, however, points out that since there was uncertainty about the exact time the observations began, it was, in fact, possible for the Navy observers to have seen Venus. Moreover, Clark reported that the UFO was brighter than both planets. Hendry also points out that Capella was positioned twice as far to the north as the estimated position of the UFO and would already have been clearly visible before Jupiter set.

Sheaffer attempts to demonstrate that accounts of the sighting misrepresented the facts when describing the first radar lock-on. He claims that no unambiguous radar image of an airborne object was attained at that time. However, Collins later confirmed that, in addition to the image of the Civil Defense tower, there was a solid image of the size usually presented by a passing jetliner. The radarscope indicated that both images were at a range of about three miles. Hendry calculates the UFO to have been only 0.09 degrees above the tower, a position which could not be achieved by Venus or Jupiter. To explain the confusion about whether the radar had locked on to the UFO or the tower, Collins explained that it was not possible to determine whether the radar was locked on to the UFO or the tower.

Sheaffer questions why the radar operator was unable to lock on to the target while it was traveling at approximately 500 knots, a speed equal to that of military aircraft in the area. Hendry, however, points out that it was during the last couple of seconds when the UFO exceeded 500 knots that the radar operator could not achieve lock-on. Sheaffer suggests that since it had been a couple of hours since the Naval Air Station at Jacksonville had said there were no aircraft in the area, the final target might, in fact, have been an aircraft. Hendry, however, checked the Jackson Air Route Traffic Control Center's Track Analysis Program. The radar printout revealed that none of the airplanes which flew through the area during the sighting period could have been responsible for the rapid southbound trajectory observed.

In all, eight Naval personnel assigned to Pinecastle had observed the objects, either visually or electronically. Subsequently, additional telephone calls were received from civilian personnel about this sighting and other sightings occurring during the following weeks.

Bibliography: Jahn, Ernest T., "UFO Sighting at Pinecastle Electronic Warfare Range," *UFO Investigator* (Washington, D.C.: National Investigations Committee on Aerial Phenomena, September 1978); Hendry, Allan, "Navy Radar/Visual in Florida—Part 1," *International UFO Reporter* (Evanston, Illinois: Center for UFO Studies, June 1978); Hendry, Allan, "Navy Radar/Visual in Florida—Part 2," *International UFO Reporter* (Evanston, Illinois: Center for UFO Studies, July 1978); Sheaffer, Robert, "The Ocala Sighting—Did a UFO Penetrate Restricted Airspace?," *Second Look* (Washington, D.C.: Second Look, April 1979); Hendry, Allan, "A Second Look at the Ocala Sighting," *Second Look* (Washington, D.C.: Second Look, May 1979).

**OCCUPANTS.** The majority of reports by ABDUCTION victims describe UFO occupants as humanoid in appearance. Although height estimates vary from three to five feet, the average occupant is about four-and-a-half feet tall. His arms hang down to his knees, and he may have only three or four digits on each hand. His bald head is large with a pointed chin, wrap-around, almond-shaped eyes and a slit-like mouth. Although nostrils may be evident, there is usually no nose. Despite facetious references to LITTLE GREEN MEN, reports of green occupants are almost nonexistent. Occupants' skin is usually described as white or gray and sometimes scaly. Clothing is usually formfitting and uniform in color. The humanoid UFONAUT allegedly communicates telepathically and floats or glides instead of walking. Encounters involving this type of occupant allegedly occurred in NEW HAMPSHIRE, PASCAGOULA, MISSISSIPPI, and SOUTH ASHBURNHAM, MASSACHUSETTS.

Other types of occupants reported include small,

hairy, aggressive creatures with claws, such as those seen at KELLY-HOPKINSVILLE, KENTUCKY, and monsters such as that seen at FLATWOODS, WEST VIRGINIA. Occasionally, witnesses claim to have seen the legendary BIGFOOT during, just prior to or after a UFO sighting. This has led some UFOLOGISTS to speculate that bigfoot is a UFO occupant.

Some UFO reports describe entities that are apparently robots, such as in the alleged sightings at CISCO GROVE, CALIFORNIA, and FALKVILLE, ALABAMA.

Flying saucer occupants described by CONTACTEES are usually tall, blond and attractive. They are supposedly similar enough to humans, however, to walk among us unrecognized.

Bibliography: Bowen, Charles (ed.), *The Humanoids* (Chicago: Henry Regnery Company, 1974); Lorenzen, Coral and Jim, *Flying Saucer Occupants* (New York: New American Library, 1967).

**O'CONNELL, (COURTENAY) PATRICK** (b. November 27, 1942, Washington, D.C.; address: 4280 68th Avenue North, Pinellas Park, Florida 33565; telephone number: 813-527-2293), Cofounder and President of the NEW ATLANTEAN RESEARCH SOCIETY.

O'Connell has a B.S. in Engineering and has many years experience in the electronics and computer field. He has been researching UFOs since 1960. He and his wife, JOAN O'CONNELL, describe themselves as professional UFOLOGISTS. Together they have lectured and conducted workshops on UFOs and various aspects of parapsychology. They have also appeared on radio and television programs around the country.

**O'CONNELL, JOAN HELENE** (b. September 11, 1933; Montclair, New Jersey; address: 4280 68th Avenue North, Pinellas Park, Florida 33565; telephone number: 813-527-2293), author, Cofounder of the NEW ATLANTEAN RESEARCH SOCIETY and Editor of THE NEW ATLANTEAN JOURNAL.

O'Connell and her husband, PATRICK O'CONNELL, describe themselves as professional UFOLOGISTS. Together, they have lectured and conducted workshops on UFOs and various aspects of parapsychology. They have also appeared on radio and television programs around the country. O'Connell's articles have been published in several magazines.

**ODOR.** Witnesses rarely report sensing any specific odor in connection with a UFO encounter. In those rare cases, however, where some aroma is noted, it is usually compared to embalming fluid, brake liquid or sulphur. The latter has also been associated with alleged manifestations into our dimension of evil spirits.

ABDUCTION victims have occasionally reported a

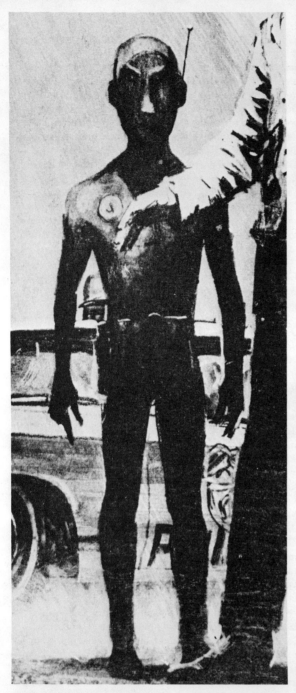

Composited by ICUFON
Art Department.(CVK)

*Above:* Small humanoid creature described by policeman Herbert Schirmer who was allegedly abducted in Ashland, Nebraska, on December 3, 1967. *(Courtesy ICUFON); Top right:* Drawing of an alien supposedly based on descriptions given by military witnesses of crashed flying saucers and their occupants. *(Courtesy ICUFON) Center right:* Photograph taken by fourteen-year-old Ronny Hill in Pamlico County, North Carolina, during the 1960s. The little "alien" has been identified as a model with an egg in the background. *(Courtesy ICUFON) Bottom right:* A scene from the motion picture *The Force Beyond* showing an artist's impression of the UFO occupants as seen by Barney Hill in New Hampshire in 1961. *(Courtesy Donn Davison)*

sweet odor sensed in the interior of alleged spaceships, as in the SOUTH ASHBURNHAM, MASSACHUSETTS, case.

**OFFICIAL UFO,** quarterly magazine, available at newsstands. It deals with all aspects of the UFO phenomenon. In 1978, the magazine lost some credibility in the eyes of UFOLOGISTS when it published as fact an untrue account of the destruction of an entire town in the Eastern United States by UFO OCCUPANTS.

The magazine is published by Myron Fass. The editorial offices are located at 257 Park Avenue South, New York, N.Y. 10010.

**OHIO SKY WATCHER, THE,** former quarterly magazine published by the OHIO UFO INVESTIGATORS' LEAGUE (OUFOIL). In 1979, the magazine merged with the PAGE RESEARCH LIBRARY NEWSLETTER and is now issued as UFO OHIO. *The Ohio Sky Watcher* had a circulation of two hundred-to-three hundred, and was edited by Robert A. Crocker.

**OHIO UFO INVESTIGATORS' LEAGUE (OUFOIL),** P.O. Box 436, Fairfield, Ohio 45014; telephone number: 513-867-0896.

The purpose of this organization is to gather and disseminate UFO information and to present this information to the public by means of official publications, meetings, and the news media. The group supports no one HYPOTHESIS regarding the identity and origin of UFOs because of the many different aspects involved in this phenomenon. However, OUFOIL's investigations have led it to believe that there may be an underground cavern system running through Ohio where strange creatures and UFOs could travel and escape from witnesses on the surface. The group's PARA-HOMINOID RESEARCH Division, headed by Ron Schaffner, has investigated local sightings of BIGFOOT, strange cats, large birds, lizard-like creatures and sabertooth tigers.

This nonprofit organization was founded in 1973 by Ex-Director Charles J. Wilhelm and Public Relations Director Geri Wilhelm. Other staff members include President James E. Miller, who also heads the Astronomy Division, Investigations Director Earl D. Jones and Secretary Mary Jane Focht. Qualified skindiver Bill Johns heads the Underwater Specialists Research Division, which investigates cases involving unidentified objects entering bodies of water such as rivers and lakes. There are fifty-two members. A network of twenty-seven officially-trained investigators covers half of Ohio as well as parts of Indiana and Kentucky. The group works in cooperation with the MUTUAL UFO NETWORK (MUFON) and the CENTER FOR UFO STUDIES (CUFOS). Achievement awards and the LEN STRINGFIELD Award are given to members for outstanding

accomplishments. Until 1979, Robert A. Crocker served as Editor of the quarterly magazine THE OHIO SKY WATCHER, which had a circulation of two hundred-to-three hundred. In 1979, the magazine merged with the PAGE RESEARCH LIBRARY NEWSLETTER, and is now issued as UFO OHIO, a publication representing several investigative organizations in Ohio. *UFO Ohio* is published by the UFO INFORMATION NETWORK (UFOIN).

**OHIO UFO REPORTER, THE,** defunct publication which was published and edited by BONITA ROMAN.

**OH-MAH** *see* **BIGFOOT**

**OINTS,** acronym for *other intelligences*, coined by IVAN SANDERSON to denote hypothetical beings existing alongside the human race but beyond our perception. Oints may be ETHEREANS or the pilots of UFOs explainable in terms of the PARALLEL UNIVERSE HYPOTHESIS.

Bibliography: Sanderson, Ivan T., *Invisible Residents* (New York: World Publishing Company, 1970).

**OLORON, FRANCE,** location of a classic UFO sighting which occurred toward the end of the 1952 European WAVE. On October 17, hundreds of people in and around Oloron observed a cloud of unusual shape in the clear blue sky. Above the cloud was a clearly-defined, narrow, white cylinder, tilted at a forty-five-degree angle and moving slowly toward the southwest. White smoke was emerging from its upper end. In front of the cylinder were about thirty objects resembling puffs of smoke. Through binoculars, these objects were distinguishable as red spheres, circled by yellow rings inclined at an angle in such a way that the bases of the spheres were almost completely hidden. The objects traveled in pairs following zigzag paths. When two moved close to each other, a white streak resembling an electric arc was formed. The objects left a trail of ANGELS' HAIR behind them, which drifted down in large quantities. Ten days later, the event reoccurred at GAILLAC, FRANCE.

Bibliography: Michel, Aimé, *The Truth About Flying Saucers* (New York: Criterion Books, 1956).

**OLSEN, THOMAS M.,** *see* **THE UFO INFORMATION RETRIEVAL CENTER**

**OLSON, EUGENE E.,** *see* **STEIGER, BRAD**

**OLSSON, ROBERT M.,** UNITED STATES AIR FORCE (USAF) lieutenant who served as acting Chief Officer of PROJECT BLUE BOOK during Edward Ruppelt's two-month tour of duty in the summer of 1953, and who headed the project from September 1953 to March 1954.

**OMNI,** monthly magazine, established in 1978, with a circulation of over 700,000. It is available at newsstands and by subscription. The magazine covers the latest developments in science and technology, paranormal phenomena, interviews with scientists and futurists, and science fiction.

The "UFO Update" columns are written by regular contributors. The Executive Editor is Frank Kendig. The magazine is published by Omni Publications International, 909 Third Avenue, New York, N.Y. 10022.

**ONIFE** *see* **ORGANIZACION NACIONAL IN-VESTIGADORA DE FENÓMENOS ES-PACIALES**

**OOPARTS,** acronym for *out of place artifacts,* term coined by IVAN SANDERSON to denote manufactured objects found in solid, undisturbed rock strata, just as fossilized animals and plants are found. Such objects are considered by some researchers as evidence of visitation to this PLANET by technologically-advanced extraterrestrials during ancient times. Reportedly, steel nails, gold threads, a metallic bell-shaped vessel, a gold chain and other unidentified artificial objects have been found in rock and coal beds millions and hundreds of millions of years old.

Bibliography: Sanderson, Ivan T., *Uninvited Visitors; A Biologist Looks at UFOs* (New York: Cowles Education Corporation, 1957).

**OPERATION DEEP FREEZE** *see* **ADMIRALTY BAY, ANTARCTICA**

**OPERATION LURE,** plan developed by DONALD KEYHOE to establish contact with UFONAUTS in order to exchange knowledge with them. The scheme required the construction of an isolated landing base with unusual structures and dummy flying saucers to arouse the curiosity of UFO pilots. Nearby buildings would contain educational exhibits. All enclosures would include glass roofs and walls to reassure the aliens that no humans were present. Hidden television cameras and microphones would relay all activities to underground observers located over a mile away. Keyhoe hoped that in this manner doctors, psychologists, anthropologists and linguists could learn about the UFONAUTS. After several visits, their trust could be gained, television communication initiated and a face-to-face encounter arranged.

Bibliography: Keyhoe, Donald E., *Aliens from Space* (Garden City, N.Y.: Doubleday and Company, 1973).

Artist Alex Tremulis's impression of extraterrestrial visitors communicating with humans through a translating machine. *(United Press International Photo)*

**OPERATION MAINBRACE,** military maneuvers conducted from September 13 to 25, 1952, in the vicinity of Denmark and Norway. The operation involved 80,000 men; 1,000 airplanes; and 200 ships from eight NATO countries and New Zealand. A WAVE of UFO sightings had begun in Europe during August. The first of those involving military personnel participating in Operation Mainbrace occurred on September 13. Danish Lieutenant Commander Schmidt Jensen and seven crew members aboard the destroyer *Willemoes* observed a bluish, glowing triangular UFO traveling at high speed. Four more outstanding sightings occurred on or around September 20. These involved shiny metallic spheres and rotating disk-shaped objects, which in some cases followed aircraft and took evasive action when pursued.

Bibliography: Hall, Richard H. (ed.), *The UFO Evidence* (Washington, D.C.: National Investigations Committee on Aerial Phenomena, 1964).

**OPERATION VERRUGOLI,** fifteen-day skywatch carried out in 1977 on Monte Verrugoli by a group of Italian researchers headed by Giovanni and Piero Mantero of the CENTRO INTERNAZIONALE RICERCHE E STUDI SUGLI UFO (CIRS UFO). The mountain, shaped like a truncated PYRAMID, is located near the town of La Spezia and reaches a height of about 465 feet above sea level. At its summit stand the antennas of several national broadcasting companies. The mountain is renowned for reports of strange phenomena.

During the skywatch a total of 108 NOCTURNAL LIGHTS

UFO photographed on August 9, 1978, during Operation Verrugoli. *(Courtesy G. and P. Mantero)*

were observed, eighty-two appearing as points of light, seven oblong in shape, seven spherical, one like a tilted plate, three discoid, one like a half-moon and seven other miscellaneous forms. Although the majority of the UFOs were yellow, some were reddish and others were blue. Occasionally, the unidentified lights seemed to increase in luminosity in response to signals made with a flashlight. During their presence, dogs in the neighborhood barked almost constantly. The objects disappeared when conventional aircraft appeared in the sky. Sounds of breaking tree branches were heard, unidentified voices were registered on a tape recorder, wristwatches malfunctioned and flattened areas of grass were found. On one of the last nights of the project, Giovanni Mantero claims to have observed a strange aerial being with a transparent face.

The operation began on August 3, 1977, and was terminated on August 18, 1977.

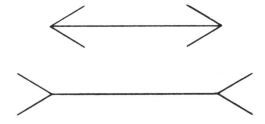

An optical illusion creates the impression that the bottom line is longer than the top line. Measurement proves that both lines are the same length.

**OPTICAL ILLUSION,** misidentification of an observed object which can be the result of its distance from the observer, lack of light, AUTOKINESIS, AUTOSTASIS, AFTERIMAGE and psychological preconceptions of the observer. Optical illusions have been given as the explanation for a number of UFO reports and often include the unusual visual effects created by METEOROLOGICAL PHENOMENA.

**ORGANIZACION NACIONAL INVESTIGADORA DE FENÓMENOS ESPACIALES (ONIFE),** Casilla de Correo 35, Sucursal 29(B), 1429 Buenos Aires, Argentina; telephone number: 781-0859.

This investigative organization is dedicated to the study of UFOs, parapsychology and archaeological mysteries. It holds that UFOs are extraterrestrial spaceships piloted by intelligent, humanoid beings.

ONIFE was founded in 1968 by Fabio Zerpa, who serves as President. Bettina Allen is Executive Director. The group has thirty-four scientific advisors and about forty members. Field investigators are located in South America, Spain and throughout the world. Contact is maintained with foreign UFO organizations. ONIFE maintains a library, offers courses and arranges lectures. It publishes the monthly magazine CUARTA DIMENSION, which is available both at newsstands and by subscription. It is edited by Ricardo Portal and has a circulation of 25,000.

**ORGONE ENERGY,** term invented in 1939 by the late WILHELM REICH to describe what he believed to be the universal life force that acts through the medium of magnetic current. He claimed that not only are all living creatures imbued and surrounded by an aura of energy, but that Earth itself is enveloped in orgone energy. He believed this energy to be the power souce of ETHEREAN craft and the animating energy of the atmospheric bioforms of ETHERIA.

Bibliography: Constable, Trevor James, *The Cosmic Pulse of Life* (Santa Ana, California: Merlin Press, 1976); Eden, Jerome, *Orgone Energy—The Answer to Atomic Suicide* (Hicksville, N.Y.: Exposition Press, 1972).

**ORGONOMY,** the science dealing with ORGONE ENERGY.

**ORTHOTENY,** term coined by author AIMÉ MICHEL to denote an alleged property of UFOs. Ortho- is a Greek prefix meaning "straight." In the UFO context, orthoteny refers to the straight lines which can be drawn to connect the locations of three or more UFO sightings during a twenty-four-hour period. Astronomer DONALD MENZEL contended that the number of such straight lines established by Michel are no greater than one would expect on the basis of chance and that, in any case, the criteria used to establish the locations of the sightings are too arbitrary.

Bibliography: Michel, Aimé, *Flying Saucers and the Straight Line Mystery* (New York: Criterion Books, 1958); Menzel, Donald H., "UFOs—The Modern Myth," in Sagan, Carl and Thornton Page (eds.), *UFOs—A Scientific Debate* (Ithaca, N.Y.: Cornell University Press, 1972).

**OTTO, JOHN** (b. July 15, 1914, Toronto, Canada; address: 2014 Burbank Boulevard, Burbank, California 91506; telephone number: 213-845-3928), UFO researcher and lecturer.

Otto has had many close encounters with UFOs and believes them to be extraterrestrial craft originating from many parts of the universe. He is best known in UFOLOGICAL circles for his attempts to communicate with flying saucer OCCUPANTS by sending audio messages using light beams as carriers, and by using ordinary radio communication. Tests have been carried out from 50,000 watt broadcasting stations, including KFI in Los Angeles, WOR in New York, and WGN in Chicago. During an experiment conducted by the latter station during 1954, extraterrestrial beings were asked to cut in on the WGN transmitter during a specified fifteen-second period. Although the station employees and listeners heard only silence, four members of the public, according to Otto, reported hearing some sound during the fifteen-second period. Of these, one had recorded something which resembled the sound of shortwave teletype code transmission. Otto obtained a copy of the recording, which was subsequently broadcast on several radio and television programs. The original recording, however, was handed over to a man named DeMelt E. Walker, who claimed to work for "National Security," worked out of a CENTRAL INTELLIGENCE AGENCY (CIA) office and was later identified as an Air Force officer. In his book, *Flying Saucers: An Analysis of the Air Force Project Blue Book Special Report No. 14* (White Plains, New York: Blue-Book Publishers, 1976), engineer LEON DAVIDSON describes his attempts to track down the tape analysis and Walker's true identity. After a series of communications with Walker, the CIA and the UNITED STATES AIR FORCE (USAF), Davidson was told that the tape and all pertinent information had been lost.

A high school graduate, Otto has had a varied career as a barnstorming pilot, traveler, adventurer, entrepreneur, aviation magazine reporter, gold miner, merchant mariner, Air Force reservist, businessman, PATENT development engineer and photographer. He has been active as a UFO investigator since 1947. He was a member of the Chicago Rocket Society and a Staff

John Otto.

Editor of its publication, *Journal of Space Flight*. In addition to lecturing on UFOs, Otto has appeared on nationwide radio and television networks and ran his own television show, *Let's Go Out of this World with John Otto,* on WBKB (ABC), Chicago (now known as WLS-TV, Chicago).

**OUTER SPACE CONNECTION, THE,** documentary (Sun Classic Pictures, 1975). Producer: Alan Landsburg; director: Fred Warshofsky; written by Fred Warshofsky; based on the book by Allan and Sally Landsburg; narrator: Rod Serling.

The film attempts to prove that man's origins lie with

A flying saucer shown in the documentary film *The Outer Space Connection. (Courtesy Sun Classic Pictures)*

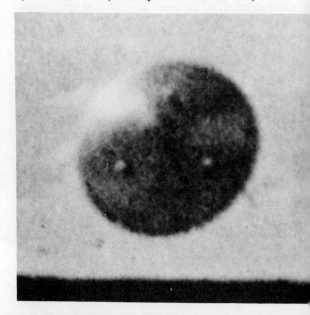

extraterrestrial beings who constructed a base in the Peruvian Andes thousands of years ago. The picture presents footage of UFOs and deals with the BERMUDA TRIANGLE, PYRAMID power, cloning experiments and artifacts allegedly left behind by space visitors. The prediction is made that these ancient visitors will return to Earth on December 24, 2011 A.D.

**OVERLORDS OF THE UFO,** documentary (Tower Films, 1977). Producer/writer: W. Gordon Allen.

This film promotes the theory that UFOs are interdimensional objects belonging to ETHEREAN overlords. UFO footage includes infrared movies taken by TREVOR JAMES CONSTABLE, which allegedly show "invisible critters" in the atmosphere. Several major UFO cases are recounted.

**OVNI,** abbreviation used by Spanish-speaking and French-speaking UFOLOGISTS to denote an "unidentified flying object." The equivalent of the English term "UFO," it stands for "*objetos voladores no identificados*" in Spanish and "*objets volants non identifies*" in French.

**OVNI,** publication of OVNIGRUPO 7.

**OVNI,** publication of UNION NACIONAL DE ESTUDIOS E INVESTIGACIONES CIENTIFICO COSMOLOGICAS (UN-EICC).

**OVNI,** monthly CONTACTEE newsletter established in 1977. *OVNI* is produced by contactee Luiz Rebouças Tôrres, who uses the nickname "OVNI" and claims he is an extraterrestrial being. According to Tôrres, UFOs are spacecraft—from other PLANETS and from inside Earth—whose OCCUPANTS are studying Earth and attempting to avert its complete destruction by nuclear warfare. Extraterrestrial beings, says Tôrres, are vegetarians, do not use money and are very peaceful. His newsletter contains information on alleged messages from extraterrestrials, parapsychology and youth-oriented cultural activities and events. Those wishing to contact other people in the field may have their name, address and photograph published in *OVNI* free-of-charge. All correspondence should be written in English, Portuguese or Spanish. The mailing address is A/C Book Center, Pca. Roosevelt 92, Loja-Centro, 01303 São Paulo, Brazil.

**OVNI DOCUMENTO,** quarterly magazine, established in 1978, with a distribution of 20,000. The magazine deals with UFOLOGY and related subjects in the social and physical fields. Since its purpose is to gather data, great stress is laid on reader participation. The magazine's parallel aim is to reveal the facts about UFOlogy, addressing itself to the more aware reader. Each issue contains an article on speculation and theory. Since great value is laid on illustrated case histories, one current case and one historical case are also included in each issue.

Articles are written by staff writers and freelance writers who are well-known in the field. IRENE GRANCHI is Editor. The magazine is published by Hunos, a publishing and motion picture production company. Its mailing address is Caixa Postal 363, Rio de Janeiro, RJ, Brazil.

**OVNIGRUPO 7,** Apartado 1985, 1006 Lisbon, Portugal; telephone number: 976455.

This investigative group aims to examine the subject of UFOLOGY in a scientific manner and to disseminate its findings. The organization was founded in 1977 by Fernando António Milhano Patinha. In addition to Patinha, staff members include J. Félix Gomes da Costa, Albino Luis Medeiros, Carlos Silva, Margarida Neves, Rui Gomes da Costa and António Agostinho dos Reis. There are about 200 members. Investigative teams are located throughout Portugal. Data is systematically analyzed, utilizing computer methods. The group publishes a quarterly magazine, OVNI, and an annual bulletin, *Eles nunca existiram . . . os OVNIs*.

Spanish representative: Manual Siurot, Bloque 3°, Seville, Spain.

**OWENS, TED** (b. February 10, 1920, Bedford, Indiana; address: 200 N.E. 76th Street, Vancouver, Washington 98665), psychic.

Known as the "PK (psychokinesis) Man" and the "UFO Prophet," Owens has earned a reputation as one of America's leading psychics. Some of his best-known feats have been the predictions of the shooting of George Wallace and former President Nixon's resignation from office. Owens attributes his alleged powers to UFO OCCUPANTS who, he claims, operated on his brain when he was a child. According to his account, the modification resulted in his being half-human and half-alien. However, it was not until a close encounter with a CIGAR-SHAPED UFO in 1965 that Owens became aware of his alleged ability to cause events to occur by the application of psychokinesis to nature's forces. He reportedly used this power to control weather, influence football games, heal the sick and create BLACKOUTS. Owens claims to be in two-way contact with saucer intelligences. It is in this manner, he states, that he can predict and arrange UFO sightings in specific areas during specific periods of time. One such sighting in 1973 was documented in an open letter by Max L.

Ted Owens.

Fogel, Director of Science and Education for Mensa, in which he concludes, ". . . an example of the type of occurrence predicted in Mr. Owens' letter to me, written in advance of the occurrence, did take place." Owens holds that flying saucer occupants are trying to save this PLANET by ending wars, killing, hatred, famine and unbalanced weather conditions. They are achieving this, he claims, by working through people on Earth. The beings themselves, Owens believes, are pure, invisible energy from another dimension. Top members of their group, according to the "PK Man," can construct a form with their intelligence and pour themselves into it.

Owens served in the United States Navy during World War II. After the war, he attended Duke University in North Carolina. Subsequently, he was engaged in fifty different occupations including lecturer, jazz drummer, magician, hypnotist, bodyguard, boxer, private investigator, office manager, fortune-teller, teacher of auto suggestion, instructor in knife throwing, jewelry designer, lifeguard, secretary, high-speed typist, bullwhip artist, judo expert, dance instructor, and rainmaker. He worked for two years with Professor J. B. Rhine at Duke University in various ESP experiments. His psychic work and research has been funded by private benefactors. In addition, Owens gives readings of past lives based on clients' portrait photographs, offers psychic counseling and teaches a system of developing a superior mind and increased psychic ability, a training method allegedly given to him by UFO occupants.

Owens has an IQ of 150 and is a member of Mensa, an international organization limited to members with high IQ test scores.

Owens's accomplishments have been documented in numerous books and magazines. He is author of *How to Contact Space People* (Clarksburg, West Virginia: Saucerian Press, 1968).

**OWLS.** A luminous fungus known as *Armillaria mellea*, which infests dead trees, has been known to stick to the feathers of owls while roosting in the daytime. Astronomer DONALD MENZEL has reported several cases occurring between 1866 and 1922 in which owls, glowing with the fungus, were seen in Norfolk, England. Witnesses, unaware of their identity, described the owls as bright lights resembling lanterns or lamps, which sometimes illuminated tree branches as they flew by. On one occasion, an owl was recognized by its call. In another case, the bird's identity was discovered after a gamekeeper shot at the mysterious light. The owl's body fell to the ground and continued to glow for several hours.

Bibliography: Menzel, Donald H., and Lyle G. Boyd, *The World of Flying Saucers* (Garden City, N.Y.: Doubleday and Company, 1963).

**PAGE, THORNTON LEIGH** (b. August 13, 1913, New Haven, Connecticut; address: 18639 Point Lookout Drive, Houston, Texas 77058), research astrophysicist.

Page believes that UFOs are not extraterrestrial visitors but thinks it is important to explain the five percent of UFO reports which remain unsolved. He was a member of the 1953 ROBERTSON PANEL and a participant in the 1969 symposium on unidentified flying objects sponsored by the AMERICAN ASSOCIATION FOR THE ADVANCEMENT OF SCIENCE (AAAS). Noting that the average layperson has a natural tendency to be intrigued by mysterious or unexpected appearances, he has suggested that teachers and scientists should take advantage of this interest to encourage the study of physical science as well as to correct public misconceptions about science.

Page received his B.S. from Yale University in 1934, and his Ph.D. from Oxford University, England, in 1938.

From 1938 to 1941, he was an Instructor and then an Assistant Professor at the University of Chicago. In 1941, he entered the United States Navy Reserves as a lieutenant (j.g.) and served for the duration of World War II, completing his tour of duty as a commander in 1948. From 1948 to 1968, he was Deputy Director of the Operations Research Office. In 1968, he assumed the position of Professor of Astronomy at Wesleyan University until 1970, when he began work as a Research Astrophysicist at the Naval Research Laboratory. In 1966, he was employed as a Research Astrophysicist at the NATIONAL AERONAUTICS AND SPACE ADMINISTRATION (NASA) Johnson Space Center, a position which he holds at the present time.

Page is a member of the Royal Astronomical Society, the International Astronomical Union, the AAAS, the American Astronomical Society, the American Astronautical Society, the Texas Academy of Sciences, the Cosmos Club and the Explorers' Club. He received an honorary Doctorate of Science from Cordoba University, Argentina, and a NASA medal for exceptional scientific achievement.

Page is coeditor of nine volumes of *Library of Astronomy* (New York: Macmillan Publishing Company, 1964, 1965, 1966, 1967, 1969, 1970, 1971, 1972, 1976); and, with Carl Sagan, of *UFOs—A Scientific Debate* (Ithaca, N.Y.: Cornell University Press, 1972). He has been a contributor to encyclopedias and textbooks and his articles appear regularly in scientific publications.

**PAGE RESEARCH LIBRARY** *see* **UFO INFORMATION NETWORK**

**PAGE RESEARCH LIBRARY NEWSLETTER,** irregularly published newsletter established in 1969 and reorganized as a bimonthly publication in 1977. In 1979, it merged with THE OHIO SKY WATCHER, and is now issued as UFO OHIO. *The Page Research Library Newsletter* had a circulation of approximately 1,500 and was available by subscription only. All aspects of UFOLOGY and FORTEAN research were covered. It was published by the UFO INFORMATION NETWORK (UFOIN) and edited by Dennis Pilichis.

**PALENQUE** *see* **MAYA**

**PALMER, RAYMOND ALFRED,** (b. August 1, 1910, Milwaukee, Wisconsin; d. August 15, 1977, Tallahassee, Florida), publisher, editor and writer.

Some writers have considered Palmer responsible for giving birth to the flying saucer "myth" in the late 1940s by publishing as fact sensational stories which were of questionable authenticity or which should have been presented as science fiction. Many considered him to have been an imaginative science fiction writer endowed with a flair for showmanship. A full year before the start of the MODERN ERA, in 1947, Palmer was promoting the idea of extraterrestrial visitation. In the July 1946 edition of *Amazing Stories*, he stated, "If you don't think space ships visit the earth regularly . . . then the files of CHARLES FORT and your editor's own files are something you should see. . . . And if you think responsible parties in world governments are ignorant of the fact of space ships visiting earth, you just don't think the way we do." In 1959, when UFOs had become a well-known phenomenon, he apparently dropped the EXTRATERRESTRIAL HYPOTHESIS (ETH) in favor of the HOLLOW EARTH HYPOTHESIS. However, he often presented his theories about flying saucers in the form of rhetorical questions, leaving in question the true nature of his beliefs. Those who have doubted Palmer's sincerity concerning the supposedly true stories he published over the years note the ambiguity of a statement he made to UFOlogist JAMES MOSELEY. In 1965, the latter asked him what he thought of flying saucers. Palmer replied, "What would you say if I told you the whole thing was a joke?"

Palmer attended the St. Anne's Business College. He wrote science fiction stories during his late teens and early twenties and, despite numerous rejections, he persevered until he achieved success as an author. In 1938, he became Managing Editor of *Amazing Stories* for the Ziff-Davis Publishing Company. He was also editor of their science fiction magazine, *Fantastic Adventures*. From 1944 to 1948, he astounded the readers of *Amazing Stories* with allegedly true accounts of an underground Atlantean civilization related by RICHARD SHAVER. In 1948, he moved on to the subject of flying saucers in his new magazine, FATE. The first issue dealt with Kenneth Arnold's UFO sighting over MOUNT RAINIER, WASHINGTON, and shortly afterward both Palmer and Arnold became involved in the MAURY ISLAND, WASHINGTON, case. In the early 1950s, Palmer started several other magazines, including SEARCH, *Mystic Universe* and *Other Worlds Science Stories*. *Fate* moved into the realm of mysticism and occultism (and later came under new ownership), while *Other Worlds* began to concentrate on flying saucers. After a brief suspension of publication due to a lull in business, *Other Worlds* was reinstated under a series of different names: *Other Worlds Science Stories*, *Flying Saucers from Other Worlds* and *Flying Saucers: the Magazine of Space Conquest*. In 1961, the magazine was changed to a pocket-size format and issued under the name *Flying Saucers*. Through the magazine, Palmer also advertised and sold items such as chili powder, itch preventer,

dandruff remover and hair color restorer. In 1977, *Flying Saucers* was incorporated into *Search*. In addition to his magazines, Palmer's company, Amherst Press, published a number of books on UFOs.

Palmer was a charter member of the Milwaukee Fictioneers and a member of the Lions Club. In 1962, he was an unsuccessful Republican nominee for lieutenant governor of Idaho.

Palmer was author of numerous articles and science fiction stories. He coauthored, with Kenneth Arnold, *The Coming of the Saucers* (Amherst, Wisconsin: Amherst Press, 1952); and, with Richard Shaver, *The Secret World* (Amherst, Wisconsin: Amherst Press, 1973).

**PAN** *see* **LEMURIA**

**PAN AMERICAN AIRWAYS** *see* **NEWPORT NEWS, VIRGINIA**

**PANCAKES** *see* **EAGLE RIVER, WISCONSIN**

**PANZANELLA, FRANK,** *see* **PORTAGE COUNTY, OHIO**

**PAPERO, ONILSON,** *see* **CATANDUVA, BRAZIL**

**PAPUA, NEW GUINEA** *see* **BOIANAI, PAPUA NEW GUINEA**

**PARAFYSISK STUDIESIRKEL** (Society for Paraphysical Research), c/o W. Simonsen, H. J. Kogstads vei 10, N–2040 Kløfta, Norway.

This society's primary purpose is to undertake studies and research on a critical basis within the fields of parapsychology, paraphysics and UFOlogy. The group considers that UFOs may be: 1. little-known or unknown phenomena or known natural phenomena seen under unusual conditions; 2. experiments of a technological nature carried out by one or more of Earth's nations; 3. some form of vehicle from a civilization other than our own; 4. phenomena of a parapsychological or paraphysical nature which is possibly related to ourselves in some manner; and 5. something which no one has conceived so far, and which may be outside the range and scope of human intelligence.

This nonprofit organization was founded in 1966 by Arne Olsson and Wilhelm S. Simonsen, and is a descendent of Norsk, UFO Studiesirkel founded in 1954 by Gunvald Weie. Board members include Trine Bjørnland, Vidar R. Gunhildrud, Jørn Wad Kristiansen, Tommy Pettersen and Wilhelm S. Simonsen. Field investigations are carried out within the southeastern area of Norway. Laboratory experiments are conducted.

The group holds weekly study courses on subjects such as the phenomenology of paranormal occurrences, relativity, instrument-aided research, epistemology and philosophy. The society has published a book, entitled *Basic Problems in the Study of Paranormal Phenomena*. Other works are in progress.

**PARA-HOMINOID RESEARCH,** division of the OHIO UFO INVESTIGATORS' LEAGUE (OUFOIL).

**PARALLEL SPACE-TIME CONTINUUM HYPOTHESIS** *see* **PARALLEL UNIVERSE HYPOTHESIS**

**PARALLEL UNIVERSE HYPOTHESIS.** The three-dimensional space in which we live is known as the universe. Although different from the three spatial dimensions of length, width and depth, time is referred to as *a* fourth dimension. Thus, the space-time continuum in which we live is four-dimensional. However, when scientists refer to *the* fourth dimension, they are speaking of a hypothetical spatial dimension. It has been conjectured that numerous spatial dimensions may exist beyond the three we know. In the field of UFOLOGY, proponents of the parallel universe hypothesis hold that UFOs originate from one or more universes which exist in the same space as ours but at a different vibrational frequency. Entities from such parallel universes would be visible to us only if they crossed over into our SPACE-TIME CONTINUUM.

Some UFOLOGISTS conjecture that extradimensional beings have been visiting us over the millenia, manifesting themselves in our dimension in forms compatible with the cultural beliefs of the existing civilization on Earth. Hence we have myths of Olympian gods, Nordic Valkyries, American Indian kachinas, European FAIRIES and space-age UFOs. The intent of such entities might be to guide our spiritual and technological progress or to entertain themselves by playing pranks on human beings. For example, the AIRSHIP WAVE of the 1890s may have been perpetrated by extradimensional beings as a joke to lead people astray or as a hint of future possibilities to spur mankind along the path of technological development.

The Christian religion promotes a belief in heaven, a nonphysical place where God and his angels reside and where the souls of good people go after death. Since heaven is a separate world beyond our physical senses, it might represent another dimension or space-time continuum. Some Christians speculate that UFOs might be God's ANGELS manifesting themselves in a form to which our culture can relate.

Some occultists hold that man was created in a higher spiritual dimension and over a long period of time

descended through various dimensions to the lower vibration of our physical universe. These and other states of existence can allegedly be revisited during out-of-body experiences or by astral travel.

Bibliography: Keel, John A., *Our Haunted Planet* (New York: Fawcett Publications, 1971); Vallee, Jacques, *Passport to Magonia* (Chicago: Henry Regnery Company, 1969).

**PARANORMAL AND PSYCHIC AUSTRALIAN,** quarterly magazine, established in 1976, with a circulation of 14,000. The magazine is available at newsstands. It is available by subscription to remote areas of Australia only. The range of subjects covered includes the Australian version of BIGFOOT, known as Yowie; the Yowie/UFO connection; analysis of UFO FLAP zones; and the paraphysical aspects of UFOLOGY. These subjects are dealt with from the Australian viewpoint.

Articles are contributed mainly by freelance writers and should range from 2,000 to 3,000 words in length. The publishers pay fifteen dollars per 1,000 words upon publication for first Australian serial rights. The magazine is published by Psychic Australian, P.O. Box 19, Spit Junction, 2088 New South Wales, Australia.

**PARANORMAL RESEARCH ORGANIZATION,** 219 Johnson Street W.W., Ashland, Kentucky 41101; telephone number: 606-324-6004.

This regional organization specializes in the investigation of reports of strange and unusual creatures. It works in cooperation with PARA-HOMINOID RESEARCH and is a member of the UFO OHIO network.

**PARASEARCH,** 554 Goresbrook Road, Dagenham, Essex RM9 4XD, England; telephone number: 01-593-4670.

Known as DPRG UFO Photo Archives (DUPA) until 1978, this small but active investigative group accepts the EXTRATERRESTRIAL HYPOTHESIS (ETH) and devotes particular attention to CE–III and CE–IV cases. Their stated goal is to further scientific investigation of UFOs, the occult and paraphysics for the better understanding of human beings.

Their UFO hotline is operational on a full-time basis and is utilized by the police, coastguards, the news media, universities and the public. Well-stocked archives contain a comprehensive data system on photographs and films of UFOs, OCCUPANTS and physical traces. Since 1975, Parasearch has been a rich source of visual materials for the news media, publishers and filmmakers in the United Kingdom.

This nonprofit organization was founded in 1974 by Barry M. King, who is Codirector with Andrew B.

Collins. Nicknamed the Starsky and Hutch of UFOLOGY, King and Collins share their fieldwork with eight other Parasearch investigators located throughout Great Britain. Their group forms part of the UFO INVESTIGATORS' NETWORK, and foreign representatives and contacts are spread around the world.

The organization's newsletter, PARASEARCH, is published sporadically, and information is also disseminated through lectures and slide shows.

**PARASELENAE,** unusual luminous images, also known as moondogs and mock moons, caused by refraction of moonlight within atmospheric ICE CRYSTALS. The phenomenon is explained in more detail under PARHELIA, its diurnal counterpart.

**PARAUFOLOGY,** the study of the UFO phenomenon based on the premise that either parapsychological processes are an inherent aspect of the phenomenon or that UFOs can be explained entirely as some form of psychic phenomenon.

**PARHELIA,** a variety of luminous patterns, also known as mock suns and sundogs, caused by refraction of sunlight within atmospheric ICE CRYSTALS. Similar images occurring in association with the MOON are known as mock moons, moon dogs and PARASELENAE.

Floating ice crystals may be present in a thin layer invisible to the observer or in a thick layer forming visible cirrus CLOUDS. The position of the crystals' axes affects the type of reflective image created. When the upper atmosphere is calm, allowing the crystals to lie flat, luminous mock suns appear twenty-two degrees on each side of the sun and at the same apparent altitude as the sun. Occasionally, this image spreads in a complete circle around the sun. Two such halos can occur simultaneously, one with a radius of about twenty-two degrees and the other with a radius of about forty-five degrees. The inner edges of the parhelia are usually reddish in color, while the outer edges are blue or violet. Luminous crosses can be formed under slightly turbulent atmospheric conditions when needle-shaped crystals are involved. The proximity of the cross to the observer corresponds to the proximity of the ice crystals. Under exceptional conditions, halos can be highlighted by four bright spots, one above, one below and one on each side. This pattern is traversed by a cross and crowned with an inverted arc. Although a fully developed parhelion of this type is rare, the late astronomer DONALD MENZEL believed this to be the inspiration for the controversial visions of EZEKIEL recounted in the Bible. Menzel believed sundogs could account for numerous modern-day UFO sightings. As does a rainbow, the sundog always remains at the same apparent distance from the observer. When the observer is traveling in an airplane, the image can appear to be tracking the craft. If the pilot then attempts to pursue the image, he is unable to close in, gaining the impression that the object is intentionally eluding him and therefore intelligently controlled. An example of sundog misidentification, according to Menzel, was the silvery disk observed in 1961 in SALT LAKE CITY, UTAH.

Bibliography: Menzel, Donald H., and Ernest H. Taves, *The UFO Enigma* (Garden City, N.Y.: Doubleday and Company, 1977).

**PARKER, CALVIN,** *see* **PASCAGOULA, MISSISSIPPI**

Two mock suns. *(The Bettmann Archive)*

**PARRY, MICHAEL VERDUN** (b. February 5, 1944, Pontpridd, United Kingdom; address: 21 Hargwyne Street, Stockwell, London SW9 9RQ, England; telephone number: 01-733-4814), Honorary President of the INTERPLANETARY SPACE TRAVEL RESEARCH ASSOCIATION (ISTRA)—UNITED KINGDOM.

Parry thinks it doubtful that UFOs are extraterrestrial craft since many natural phenomena and conventional objects provide explanations for UFO reports. He has seen several UFOs which were identified after careful investigation. He states that he would have been relieved to find that they were extraterrestrial vehicles, since this would have signified to him that mankind has a chance to improve his barbaric history and present-day insanity, and to achieve major advances to benefit the world rather than destroy it.

An import/export executive, Parry served six-and-a-half years in the Royal Air Force as a statistician, followed by a varied career as a professional broadcaster, disc jockey, writer and jack-of-all-trades. He became Honorary President of ISTRA-United Kingdom in 1969.

Parry is author of *Birth of a Movement* (London: Interplanetary Space Travel Research Association, 1969); *Teach Yourself UFOlogy* (London: Interplanetary Space Travel Research Association, 1970); and *A–Z UFOlogy* (London: Interplanetary Space Travel Research Association, 1971).

**PASCAGOULA, MISSISSIPPI**, location of one of the most publicized and publicly discussed UFO cases on record. On the evening of October 11, 1973, two shipyard workers, Charles Hickson and Calvin Parker,

were fishing off an abandoned pier on the Pascagoula River just outside the city of Pascagoula. Hearing a strange buzzing noise, the two men looked up to see a large, glowing, bluish-white, egg-shaped craft hovering nearby. Paralyzed with fear, the men watched as an opening suddenly appeared in the UFO and three five-foot-tall beings emerged. The OCCUPANTS floated toward Hickson and Parker. Their skin was gray and wrinkled. Pointed protrusions jutted out where noses and ears should be. Each creature had a small opening under its nose where a mouth should be. They had no necks. Their arms were exceptionally long, with hands resembling crab claws or mittens. Their straight, shapeless legs ended in round feet. Two of the UFONAUTS took hold of Hickson under the arms, while the other grabbed Parker, who had fainted. They were floated into the UFO, where Hickson was taken into a brilliantly-lit, circular room. There he was "LEVITATED" into a horizontal position while a free-floating object, resembling a huge eye, moved about his body as if giving him a physical examination. After about twenty minutes, both men were deposited on the riverbank and the UFO left. Parker regained consciousness.

Hickson and Parker called nearby Keesler Air Force Base but were referred to the sheriff. They then attempted to find a reporter at the local newspaper office but, the office being empty; they were again advised by a janitor to see the sheriff. This they did at about 10:30 P.M. At the sheriff's office, both men were left alone in a room with hidden sound-monitoring equipment. During this time, however, they said nothing which indicated a HOAX was involved. The sheriff later stated that something had happened to the two men because they were "scared to death and on the verge of a heart attack."

The following day Hickson and Parker were interrogated and medically examined at Keesler Air Force Base. The case was investigated by J. ALLEN HYNEK and University of California civil engineering professor JAMES HARDER, who serves as a consultant to the AERIAL PHENOMENA RESEARCH ORGANIZATION (APRO). The latter hypnotized Hickson but terminated the trance when Hickson appeared to be too frightened to continue. Hickson was interviewed by newspaper reporters and radio and television talk show hosts from around the country and overseas. Calvin Parker was subsequently hospitalized for a nervous breakdown.

Writer PHILIP KLASS has documented a number of discrepancies in the various accounts of the incident related by Hickson. On different occasions, Hickson specified several different size estimations for the UFO, ranging from eight feet to thirty feet. He first said that the encounter had occurred at 7:00 P.M., later changed the time to "between 8:00 P.M. and 9:00 P.M.," and still

Drawing of UFO occupant based on description by Charles Hickson.

later specified that it had happened "around 9:00." Just over a month after the incident, Hickson claimed to have suffered a severe eye injury during the ABDUCTION. This injury, he claimed, had persisted for three days, yet he made no mention of it to the Air Force doctors who had examined him at the time. Although Hickson usually described the UFOnauts as having no eyes, on one occasion, shortly after the encounter, he reported that they had slits for eyes. While being interviewed on the Dick Cavett Show, he stated that he had heard nothing resembling speech. However, later on during the same interview, Hickson reported that he had heard "some type of mumbling" from one of the creatures.

Klass notes that none of the passing motorists on nearby U.S. Highway 90 had seen the UFO. Furthermore, a bridge attendant, from whose post the abduction site was clearly visible, had seen nothing. In defense of his story, Hickson has claimed that high weeds, bushes and the bridge railings probably blocked the area from the view of passing motorists. As for the bridge attendant, Hickson reports that the attendant usually sat with his back to the abduction site.

Klass questions Hickson's reliability as a witness by pointing out that although Hickson's current employer had described him as a "good, steady worker," he had in fact been fired on November 20, 1972, by his previous employer for "conduct unbecoming a supervisor." Although company officials refused to discuss the details, journalist Joe Eszterhas reported that Hickson was borrowing money from subordinates and repaying them by attempting to arrange promotions. On July 6, 1973, Hickson had filed for bankruptcy.

Klass points out that a much-touted polygraph test passed by Hickson had been conducted by an inexperienced polygraphist who not only was not a member of the American Polygraph Association, but had never been certified by the school at which he had trained.

Charles Hickson points out the location where he says a UFO landed. (United Press International Photo)

Klass concludes that the Pascagoula sighting was a hoax. Author JOHN KEEL, on the other hand, believes that the two fishermen suffered "a rather routine HALLUCINATION."

Bibliography: Klass, Philip J., *UFOs Explained* (New York: Random House, 1974); Keel, John A., *The Mothman Prophecies* (New York: New American Library, 1976).

**PATENTS,** documents issued by the government granting inventors exclusive rights to produce, use, sell and profit from their inventions. The United States Patent Office has issued numerous patents for flying saucer-type aircraft. Archie L. Leggett was issued Patent 2,947,496 on August 2, 1960, for a rotating disk-shaped craft designed primarily as a rocket ship for interplanetary or SATELLITE travel, but also adaptable to jet propulsion within Earth's atmosphere. Constantin P. Lent, who was issued Patent 2,801,058 on July 30, 1957, stated in his application, "The flying saucer described in this invention is not a thing in the realm of phantasy [sic] but a very practical aircraft obeying approved aerodynamic principles." Intended for commercial and private, long distance and local flights carrying passengers or cargo, Lent's "Saucer-Shaped

Patented design for Archie Leggett's interplanetary craft.

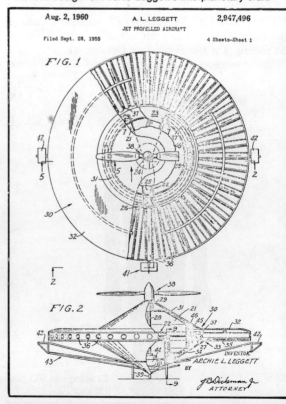

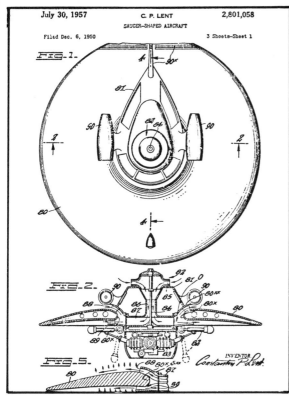

Patented design for Constantin Lent's flying saucer.

Patented design for Irwin Barr's rotating "Flying Machine."

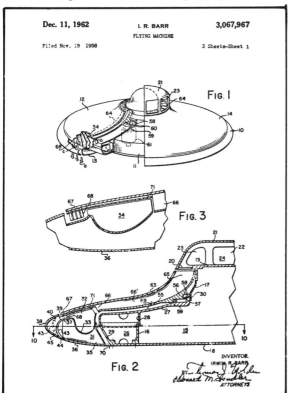

Aircraft" is designed to rise vertically instantaneously, move transversely, hover and travel at supersonic speeds. Another disk-shaped craft designed to "hover, travel at high speeds, and quickly turn and maneuver in azimuth heading" is Irwin R. Barr's "Flying Machine" which was awarded Patent 3,067,967 on December 11, 1962. Heinrich Fleissner's "Rotating Jet Aircraft With Lifting Disc Wing and Centrifuging Tanks," which was issued Patent 2,939,648 on June 7, 1960, "takes off from and lands vertically on any suitable ground or water surface and has the ability to remain in suspension at any point at any desired altitude regardless of weather conditions." Its inventor claims that, "Acute angle turning is made possible by the fact that all the turning devices are in proximity to the center of the aircraft and further, the center body is the only portion that is turned in that the wing, extending outwardly therefrom, is continuously rotating and is not affected by the turning of the central body."

Other disk-shaped aircraft include John C. Fischer's "Circular Aircraft," issued Patent 2,772,057 on November 27, 1956; Homer F. Streib's "Circular Wing Aircraft" and "Circular Wing Aircraft with Universally Tiltable Ducted Power Plant," issued Patent 2,876,964 and Patent 2,876,965 respectively on March 10, 1959;

Patented design for Heinrich Fleissner's disklike rotating flying device, which is capable of taking off and landing vertically on land or water and of executing acute angle turns.

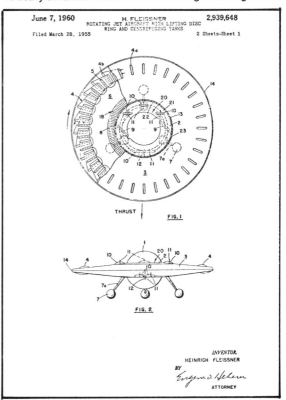

244

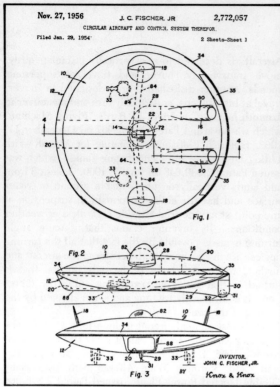

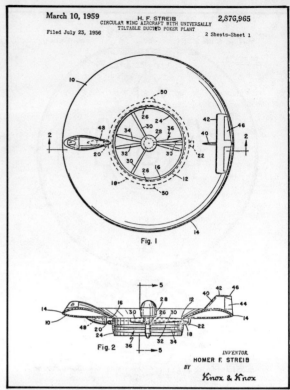

Patented design for John Fischer's rotating circular aircraft.

Patented design for Homer Streib's circular wing aircraft capable of vertical and lateral flight.

Patented design for Homer Streib's circular wing aircraft, with tiltable ducted power plant, capable of vertical and lateral flight.

Patented design for Nathan Price's "High Velocity High Altitude V.T.O.L. Aircraft."

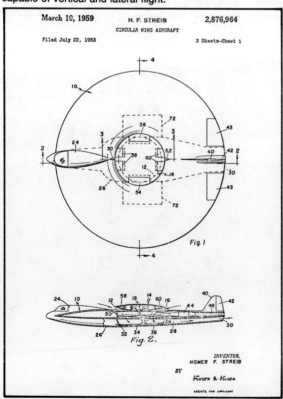

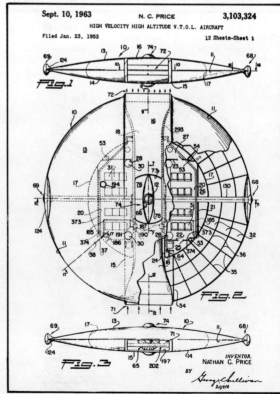

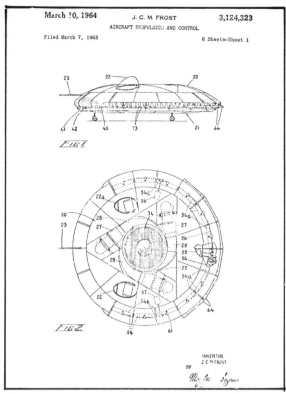

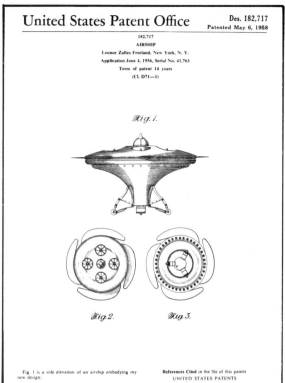

Patented design for J. C. M. Frost's circular aircraft.

Second of two patented designs by Leonor Zalles for a circular airship.

First of two patented designs by Leonor Zalles for a circular airship.

Patented design for Stefan Apostolescu Postelson's "Aero Space Ship."

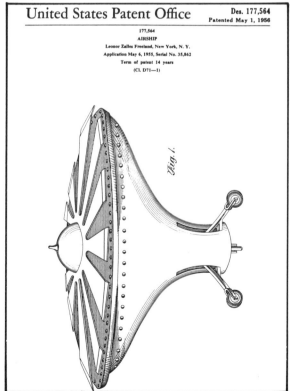

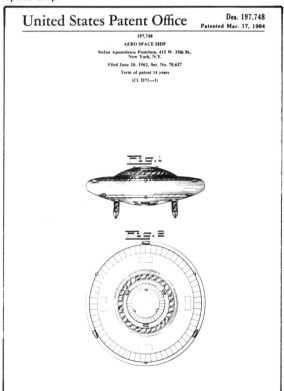

## United States Patent Office

Des. 200,183
Patented Jan. 26, 1965

200,183
AIRCRAFT
Donald Earl Ordway, Ithaca, N.Y., assignor to Therm,
Incorporated, Ithaca, N.Y., a corporation of New York
Filed Dec. 7, 1961, Ser. No. 67,830
Term of patent 14 years
(Cl. D71—1)

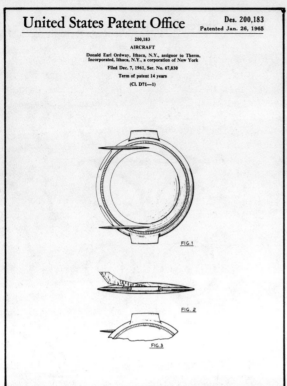

Patented design for Donald Ordway's circular aircraft.

Patented design for John Sherwood's "Vertical Lift Flying Machine."

## United States Patent Office

Des. 216,542
Patented Feb. 10, 1970

216,542
HOUSE
Matti J. Suuronen, Westend, Finland, assignor to Oy
Polykem AB, Helsinki, Finland, a firm of Finland
Filed Nov. 21, 1968, Ser. No. 14,587
Term of patent 14 years
Int. Cl. D25—04
U.S. Cl. D13—1

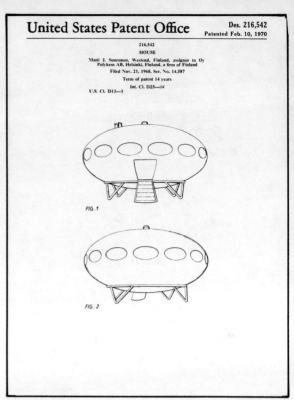

Patented design by Matti Suuronen for a house resembling a flying saucer.

Patented design by James Sides for a building resembling a flying saucer.

## United States Patent Office

Des. 213,529
Patented Mar. 11, 1969

213,529
VERTICAL LIFT FLYING MACHINE
John W. Sherwood, 806 Pine St., Atlantic, Iowa 50022,
and John W. Sherwood III, Rte. 3, Box 158, Guthrie
Center, Iowa 50115
Filed Apr. 3, 1967, Ser. No. 6,486
Term of patent 14 years
U.S. Cl. D71—1
Int. Cl. D12—07

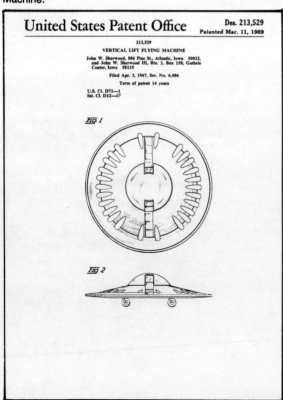

## United States Patent Office

Des. 218,291
Patented Aug. 11, 1970

218,291
BUILDING
James F. Sides, 9419 Covemeadow Drive,
Dallas, Tex. 75238
Filed Nov. 15, 1968, Ser. No. 14,496
Term of patent 14 years
Int. Cl. D25—04
U.S. Cl. D13—1

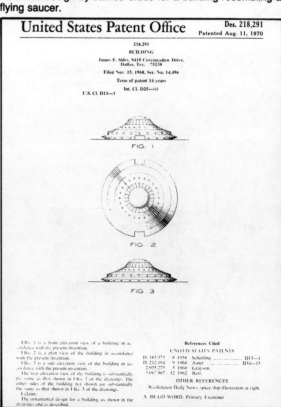

FIG. 1 is a front elevation view of a building in accordance with the present invention.
FIG. 2 is a plan view of the building in accordance
with the present invention.
FIG. 3 is a side elevation view of the building in accordance with the present invention.
The rear elevation view of the building is substantially
the same as that shown in FIG. 1 of the drawings. The
other sides of the building not shown are substantially
the same as that shown in FIG. 3 of the drawings.
I claim:
The ornamental design for a building, as shown in the
drawings and as described.

References Cited
UNITED STATES PATENTS
D. 183,375   8 1958   Schorling ............ D13—1
D. 212,194   9 1968   Asner ............ D34—15
2,935,275    5 1960   Grayson.
3,967,967   12 1962   Barr.
OTHER REFERENCES
Washington Daily News, space ship illustration at right.

A. HUGO WORD, Primary Examiner

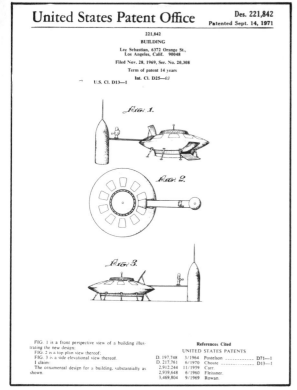

Patented design by Lee Sebastian for a building resembling a flying saucer.

Nathan C. Price's "High Velocity High Altitude V.T.O.L. Aircraft," issued Patent 3,103,324 on September 10, 1963; and J. C. M. Frost's circular aircraft, issued Patent 3,124,323 on March 10, 1964.

Patents for ornamental designs for circular aircraft include Leonor Zalles's Design Patent 177,564 and Design Patent 182,717, issued May 1, 1956, and May 6, 1958, respectively; Stefan Apostolescu Postelson's Design Patent 197,748, issued March 17, 1964; Donald Earl Ordway's Design Patent 200,183, issued January 26, 1965; John W. Sherwood's Design Patent 213,529, issued March 11, 1969; and PAUL S. MOLLER's Design Patent 238,938, issued February 24, 1976. The latter represents the basic design of experimental flying saucers being built by the DISCOJET CORPORATION of Davis, California.

Patents have also been issued by the U.S. Patent Office for buildings resembling flying saucers. These include Matti J. Suuronen's Design Patent 216,542, issued February 10, 1970; James E. Sides's Design Patent 218,291, issued August 11, 1970; and Lee Sebastian's Design Patent 221,842, issued September 14, 1971.

**PAUL, SAINT,** an Apostle who became the first great Christian missionary. Originally opposed to Jesus and his followers, Paul was converted to Christianity while on the road to Damascus. Not far from the city, a light flashed from the sky. Paul was knocked to the ground and allegedly heard Jesus speaking to him. He remained blinded by the flash for three days. Some UFOLOGISTS conjecture that Paul was, in fact, struck by a beam of light from a UFO. They compare his subsequent personality change to that undergone by some modern-day victims of close UFO encounters.

**PENNSYLVANIA AND NEW JERSEY TWO-STATE UFO STUDY GROUP,** organization founded in 1965 by GEORGE D. FAWCETT. It became defunct in 1969.

**PENTAGON OF DEATH** see **BERMUDA TRIANGLE**

**PERTH UFO RESEARCH GROUP,** P.O. Box 92, North Perth 6006, Australia; telephone number: 2716604.

The purpose of this investigative organization is to enlighten the public about all aspects of UFOs. Members adhere to independent beliefs and opinions regarding the identity and origin of UFOs.

This nonprofit organization was founded in 1955 by B. Perkins, Mr. and Mrs. C. Jones, R. McDonald, Marie Cook, Gordon Dellar and F. Nealon. Committee members include President and Treasurer E. Harper, Vice-President and Investigations Coordinator George A. Hume, Vice-President I. Hammett, Honorary Secretary K. Johnston and Correspondence Secretary L. Culshaw. There are approximately 150 members. Investigations are conducted by trained investigators. Reports are sent to AUSTRALIAN INTERNATIONAL UFO FLYING SAUCER RESEARCH for computerization and analysis. An up-to-date library is available to members. Guest speakers attend monthly meetings, which are open to visitors. The PERTH UFO RESEARCH GROUP NEWSLETTER is published monthly.

**PERTH UFO RESEARCH GROUP NEWSLETTER,** publication of PERTH UFO RESEARCH GROUP.

**PERU.** After BRAZIL, Argentina and Chile, Peru has recorded the fourth largest number of UFO sightings in Latin America. The AERIAL PHENOMENA RESEARCH ORGANIZATION (APRO) has a representative in Peru.

The country is famous for the lines of NAZCA, which some supporters of the ANCIENT ASTRONAUTS hypothesis believe to have been built as runways for extraterrestrial spacecraft.

**PERUVIAN INSTITUTE OF INTERPLAN-**

ETARY RELATIONS *see* INSTITUTO PERUANO DE RELACIONES INTERPLANETARIAS (IPRI)

PETROZAVODSK, SOVIET UNION *see* JELLYFISH UFO

PHENOMENA RESEARCH (WEST AUSTRALIA) P.O. Box 261, Bunbury, West Australia 6230.

The purpose of this investigative organization is to collect and research reports of strange phenomena and to share the findings with other interested parties. The group's principals hold that UFOs seem to originate both from earthly and interplanetary sources.

This nonprofit organization was founded in 1979 by DONALD FERGUSON and his wife, Jeanette Ferguson. Contact is maintained with several overseas organizations, including the BRITISH UFO RESEARCH ASSOCIATION (BUFORA); UFO CANADA and RES BUREAUX in Canada; ARBETSGRUPPEN FOR UFOLOGI (AFU) in Sweden; the SOCIETÉ VARIOSE D'ÉTUDE DES PHÉNOMÈNES SPATIAUX (SVEPS) in France; SKANDINAVISK UFO INFORMATION (SUFOI) in Denmark; and PROJECT STIGMA in the United States. A newsletter is published about three times a year.

PHÉNOMÈNES SPATIAUX, French-language magazine published by the GROUPEMENT D'ÉTUDE DE PHÉNOMÈNES AÉRIENS (GEPA).

PHOBOS *see* MARTIAN MOONS

PHOSPHENE, sensation of seeing bright images resulting from pressure on the eyeballs through closed eyelids or following adaptation of the eyes to a darkened environment. Phosphenes can produce images resembling any number of objects including flying saucers, CIGAR-SHAPED UFOs and moving lights.

Bibliography: Charroux, Robert, *The Mysterious Unknown* (London: Neville Spearman, 1972).

PHOTOGRAPHS. Still photographs of UFOs are extremely easy to fabricate. After analyzing over 700 pictures using computer enhancement techniques, GROUND SAUCER WATCH (GSW) identified ninety-five percent as HOAXES, photographic defects, MISIDENTIFIED conventional objects and natural phenomena. The processes utilized by GSW include the following: edge enhancement to reveal fine details not seen by the unaided eyes; color contouring to establish the density of the object and its surrounding area, reflectivity, the exact shape of the UFO, and the relationship of its true size to other objects in the photograph; a profiling cursor to reveal the object's real shape; and digital image enhancement to determine the object's distance. Although there is still controversy over some of the photographs GSW has labeled as bona fide, the organization's efforts have succeeded in rooting out many cases of mistaken identity and hoaxes, which otherwise would have continued to absorb the time and efforts of serious researchers.

Some of the well-known photographs which failed GSW's tests are those taken at ALBUQUERQUE, NEW MEXICO; CALGARY, ALBERTA; LUBBOCK, TEXAS; SAN JOSÉ DE VALDERAS, SPAIN and SANTA ANA, CALIFORNIA. Photographs and motion pictures identified by GSW as bona fide UFOs include those taken at GREAT FALLS, MONTANA; MCMINNVILLE, OREGON; ROUEN, FRANCE; TREMONTON, UTAH and TRINDADE ISLAND, BRAZIL. The much-publicized UFO filmed during the NEW ZEALAND SIGHTINGS of 1978/79 was analyzed by physicist BRUCE MACCABEE, who concluded that the object filmed did not represent any known phenomenon. His opinion was confirmed by a number of scientists.

A student who photographed the moon found this strange image on his negative. It was identified as a lens flare by the Intercontinental Galactic Spacecraft (UFO) Research and Analytic Network.

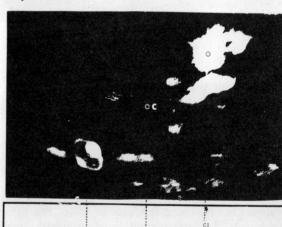

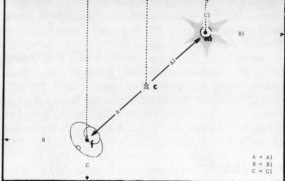

When photographing a UFO, witnesses should attempt to include reference points such as trees or mountains in the frame in order that analysts can make comparison studies. An image which appears on a photograph after processing, but which was not observed at the time the picture was taken, is usually attributable to a photographic defect. One of the most common of these is the lens flare, which occurs when the sun or some other light source is reflected within the lens structure. Original negatives should be made available to analysts, as they are vital for a complete and definitive study. Ultimately, however, many UFOLOGISTS feel that a UFO photograph is only as reliable as the person who photographed it.

A wide selection of UFO photographs is available from the following sources: ICUFON ARCHIVES, Apartment 46, 35–40 75th Street, Jackson Heights, New York 11372; GROUND SAUCER WATCH (GSW), 13238 N. 7th Drive, Phoenix, Arizona 85029; and PARASEARCH, 554 Goresbrook Road, Dagenham, Essex RM9, 4XD, England.

## PHYSICAL EFFECTS.

The most commonly reported physical effects accompanying UFO sightings are ELECTROMAGNETIC EFFECTS, PHYSIOLOGICAL EFFECTS and LANDING MARKS. In addition, witnesses have reported dried or carbonized tree branches, sticky deposits on the ground, discolored spots and bubbles in automobile paint, humming and buzzing SOUNDS and unusual ODORS. In rare cases, alleged DEBRIS from a UFO has been found. The most noted case of this type occurred in UBATUBA, BRAZIL.

Bibliography: Philips, Ted, *Physical Traces Associated with UFO Sightings: A Preliminary Catalogue* (Northfield, Illinois: Center for UFO Studies, 1975); Keyhoe, Donald E., and Gordon I. R. Lore (eds.), *Strange Effects from UFOs* (Washington, D.C.: National Investigations Committee on Aerial Phenomena, 1969).

## PHYSIOLOGICAL EFFECTS.

With few exceptions, the physiological effects experienced by witnesses in association with UFO sightings have been temporary and not severe. These effects include conjunctivitis, tingling sensations, numbness, paralysis, loss of consciousness, BURNS, rashes, peeling skin, nausea and a feeling of suffocation because of tremendous HEAT.

Writer PHILIP KLASS has suggested that those effects which resemble symptoms of ordinary sunburn could be due to exposure to ultraviolet radiation from PLASMAS which, he contends, are a probable source of many UFO reports. However, this explanation applies to only a limited number of UFO-related physiological effects. Furthermore, it is unlikely that it could account for such extreme effects as the overbearing heat experienced by two sentries at FORT ITAIPU, BRAZIL, and a pilot and his RADAR operator at WALESVILLE, NEW YORK.

**PIBAL,** acronym for *pilot bal*loon used to determine direction and speed of the wind. Pibals are one of the many types of BALLOONS that have been reported as UFOs.

Bibliography: Menzel, Donald H., and Lyle G. Boyd, *The World of Flying Saucers* (Garden City, N.Y.: Doubleday and Company, 1963).

**PIEDMONT, MISSOURI,** location of observations by more than 200 citizens of unidentified NOCTURNAL LIGHTS (NL) which blinked, flashed and moved erratically during February, March and April of 1973. In addition, several witnesses reported daytime sightings of metallic objects and one couple actually claimed to have seen a creature, resembling a man wearing a wet suit, walking down a highway. While a wide range of colors was associated with the UFOs, the most common were orange, red, green and white. The objects were generally round, sometimes described as having a dome on top and a band of portholes around the center. Three purported landing sites were found, and treetops at one site were described by investigators as having been broken off while the trees themselves were swirled in a counterclockwise direction. Some witnesses claimed to have seen UFOs entering and leaving the water of Clearwater Lake. On April 12, commercial pilot Kenneth Pingle pursued a circular light in his single-engined plane. The UFO, which was heading toward him, reversed its direction when Pingle came close. Several photographs were taken of unidentified lights.

The most publicized photograph, taken by high school photography teacher Maude Jefferis, was identified by astronomer J. ALLEN HYNEK and investigators of the INTERNATIONAL UFO BUREAU (IUFOB) as a lens flare. John H. Mullen, a scientist at the McDonnell Douglas Corporation's research laboratories in St. Louis, visited one of the alleged landing sites. There he found only the remnants of a large bonfire made of wood chips. IUFOB Director HAYDEN HEWES concluded that most of the UFOs were STARS whose appearance was distorted by excessive moisture in the air. Many sightings of glowing balls occurred near power lines and have been tentatively identified as PLASMA. Investigators have suggested that those objects which were not stars or plasma were probably high-flying aircraft reflecting light from the sun after it had sunk below the horizon. The consensus of the investigators was that the MIS-IDENTIFICATIONS of natural and conventional objects were caused by MASS HYSTERIA resulting from the nationwide news coverage given to the initial incidents.

Bibliography: Hewes, Hayden C., *Earthprobe* (Edmond, Oklahoma: International UFO Bureau, 1973).

## PILE D'ASSIETTES CLOUDS *see* CLOUDS

## PILICHIS, DENNIS, *see* UFO INFORMATION NETWORK (UFOIN), PAGE RESEARCH LIBRARY NEWSLETTER and UFO OHIO

## PINE, INA MARGARITE "MARGARET" (b. October 22, 1940, Bartlesville, Oklahoma; address: 506 Central Avenue, Mauldin, South Carolina 29662; telephone number: 803-963-8300), Founder and President of the GREENVILLE UFO STUDY GROUP.

Pine claims to have had psychic experiences but never to have seen a UFO. After twenty-two years of research, she thinks that information regarding the origin of UFOs is too varied to provide a single definite answer to the mystery. The biggest problem for UFOlogists, she believes, is not lack of information but rather a lack of time and money.

After graduating from high school, Pine attended the Bartlesville Business College in Oklahoma, and also took a Technical course in Psychology. As Founder and President of the Greenville UFO Study Group, she has set up a liaison between her organization and radio and television stations, newspapers, local Federal Aviation Administration control towers and independent sources of UFO sighting information. She is State Section Director of the MUTUAL UFO NETWORK (MUFON), Regional Director of the Georgia UFO BUREAU and an Investigator for the CENTER FOR UFO STUDIES (CUFOS). She is also President of the Quest Society, which organizes lectures on topics such as Kirlian photography, extrasensory perception, poltergeist phenomena, biofeedback, HYPNOSIS, PYRAMIDS and astrology. In addition, she works as a volunteer for the Republican Party. Pine lectures at local libraries, Sertoma Clubs, Mensa gatherings, civic clubs, Lions Clubs and radio talk shows. She has received two plaques of appreciation from the Sertoma Club.

## PIONEERS 10 AND 11, unmanned space probes launched from Earth in 1972 and 1973, respectively, on exploratory missions to Jupiter and Saturn and beyond. These first man-made objects to escape from the solar system into interstellar space each carry a pictorial plaque designed to show scientifically educated inhabitants of some other STAR system when each craft was launched, from where, and by what kind of beings. The design is etched into a six-inch-by-nine-inch gold-anodized aluminum plate attached to the spacecraft's antenna support struts in a position to help shield it

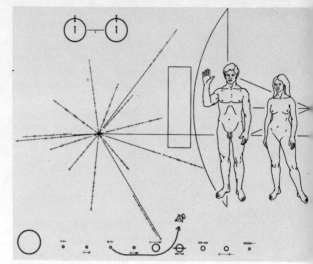

Message carried by Pioneer spacecraft to extraterrestrial beings. *(Courtesy NASA)*

from erosion by interstellar dust. The radiating lines at left represent the positions of fourteen PULSARS (cosmic sources of radio energy) arranged to indicate our Sun as the home star of the launching civilization. The "1-" symbols at the ends of the lines are binary numbers that represent the frequencies of these pulsars at the time of launch relative to that of the hydrogen atom shown at the upper left with a "1" unity symbol. The hydrogen atom is thus used as a "universal clock," and the regular decrease in the frequencies of the pulsars will enable another civilization to determine the time that has elapsed since the launch date. The hydrogen atom is also used as a "universal yardstick" for sizing the human figures and outline of the spacecraft shown on the right. The hydrogen wavelength of about eight inches multiplied by the binary number representing "8" shown next to the woman gives her height of sixty-four inches. The figures represent the type of creature that created Pioneer. The man's hand is raised in a gesture of good will. Across the bottom are the PLANETS, ranging outward from the Sun, with the spacecraft's trajectory arcing away from Earth, passing MARS, and swinging by Jupiter.

The plaque was designed by CARL SAGAN and Linda Salzman Sagan. Carl Sagan has compared this form of communiqué to that of a shipwrecked sailor placing a message in a bottle and casting it into the ocean.

## PIRI RE'IS MAP, a world chart drawn in 1513 by a Turkish admiral named Piri Re'is. The map was based on twenty different earlier charts, including a map used by CHRISTOPHER COLUMBUS, and Greek maps which dated back to the time of ALEXANDER THE GREAT. The Piri Re'is map was one of several found in the Topkapi Palace in Istanbul in 1929.

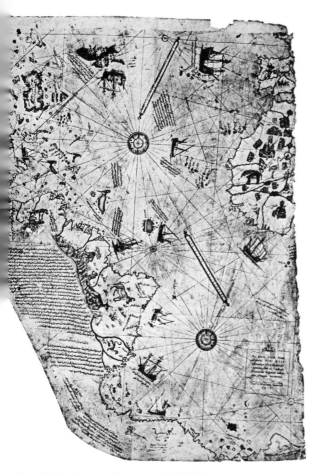

The Piri Re'is map. *(Courtesy ICUFON)*

In collaboration with the U.S. Navy Hydrographic Office and the Western Observatory of Boston, American cartographer Arlington H. Mallery carried out extensive studies and technical tests relating to the Piri Re'is map. The ancient map was considered remarkable because it depicts the coastlines of the Americas and Antarctica. The latter was not discovered until Captain Cook reached it in 1773, and some of its ice-covered mountain ranges shown on the Piri Re'is map were not discovered until echo soundings were conducted in 1952. However, there appeared to be something unusual about the map. Although it included a great deal of geographic data, much of it seemed to be misplaced. Mallery developed a grid system which brought the data into focus. He concluded that the map was based on an aerial survey of Earth from a position somewhere above Cairo. Supporters of the ANCIENT ASTRONAUTS theory hold that the original charts on which this map was based were drawn by the OCCUPANTS of an extraterrestrial spaceship.

Opponents of this theory argue that the map is extremely crude and that there is a total error of about five percent in the size of the land masses. Author

Clifford Wilson points out that the Amazon River is shown twice, almost a thousand miles of coastland is missing from the east side of South America, and Antarctica is shown as a landmass joined directly to South America.

Bibliography: Von Däniken, Erich, *Chariots of the Gods?* (New York: G. P. Putnam's Sons, 1970); Keyhoe, Donald E., *Aliens from Space* (Garden City, N.Y.: Doubleday and Company, 1973); Wilson, Clifford, *Crash Go the Chariots* (New York: Lancer Books, 1972); Thiering, Barry, and Edgar Castle (eds.), *Some Trust in Chariots* (New York: Popular Library, 1972).

**PITTS, BILL** (b. February 5, 1926, Fort Smith, Arkansas; address: 506 North 2nd Street, Fort Smith, Arkansas 72901; telephone number: 501-782-0373). Regional investigator for the NATIONAL INVESTIGATIONS COMMITTEE ON AERIAL PHENOMENA (NICAP), Field Investigator for the AERIAL PHENOMENA RESEARCH ORGANIZATION (APRO), State Director for the MUTUAL UFO NETWORK (MUFON) and Investigator for the CENTER FOR UFO STUDIES (CUFOS).

Pitts, who has been investigating UFO reports since 1949, believes that those UFOs which cannot be identified as HOAXES and MISIDENTIFICATIONS are metallic-like structured objects. In 1975, he organized America's first UFO Conference in Fort Smith, attended by representatives of the major UFO organizations and official representatives of government agencies, including the NORTH AMERICAN RADAR DEFENSE (NORAD), the UNITED STATES AIR FORCE (USAF) and the Federal Aviation Administration.

Pitts attended the University of Arkansas, Westark Community College and the University of Missouri. An industrial sales engineer, he is currently President of McKee-Pitts Industrials, Incorporated, in Fort Smith.

Pitts is International President of the International Brotherhood of Magicians, and President-elect of the

Bill Pitts making the opening speech at the Fort Smith conference in 1975. *(Courtesy Donn Davison)*

Fort Smith Exchange Club. He is a member of the National Occult Investigations Committee and the Society of American Magicians. He is the recipient of several awards and honors in Masonry and in magicians' organizations, including the Cross of Honor, the Order of DeMolay and the Order of Merlin.

Pitts lectures on UFOs throughout the United States and overseas. He is a Key Forum Speaker at the International Jaycees annual conventions. He is registered with the Arkansas State Police as official UFO investigator for the state of Arkansas.

Pitts's articles have been published in all international publications for magicians, as well as in UFO magazines and newsletters.

**PLANET,** celestial body which revolves around a sun. Earth is one of nine known planets revolving around a central STAR, known as the sun. The sun and its planets are known as a solar system. While the stars we see at night are incandescent bodies, the planets of our solar system glow from the reflected light of our sun. Planets, like stars, appear to rise in the east and set in the west because of the rotation of Earth on its axis. Although planets shine with a steadier light than stars, they are subject to the same atmospheric refraction and dispersion, particularly when rising and setting. Planets can appear to have unusual shapes, flash brilliantly with red, green and blue colors, and seem to move up and down, sideways, and back and forth. The impression of movement can also be created by AUTOKINESIS, changing density of thin CLOUD layers, and movement and directional changes of the vehicle in which the observer is traveling.

The bright planets most frequently reported as UFOs are VENUS, MARS, Jupiter and Saturn. Venus has so frequently been cited as an explanation for UFO reports that some skeptics refer to it as "the Queen of UFOs." At its brightest, it can even be seen in daylight.

**PLASMA,** a concentration of highly-electrified air which glows intensely in a spectrum of colors.

In addition to normal uncharged molecules, air always contains molecules of gases which have lost one or more electrons from their normal quota, leaving them with positive charges. Under normal conditions, these positively-charged particles, known as ions, are sparsely interspersed. However, under unusual conditions, the number of charged particles may be increased to form a small CLOUD of electrified particles, whose agitated motions generate a glow.

When this luminous effect occurs on or near power lines, it is known as corona discharge, a phenomenon similar to SAINT ELMO'S FIRE. Sometimes this ionized air detaches itself from the lines and moves about

19th-century French print depicting ball lightning.

independently of them. Spherical, flying plasmas are known as ball lightning, globe lightning or kugelblitz. Although ball lightning is usually associated with stormy weather, it has occasionally been seen during fair weather. It is a phenomenon so little understood that some scientists have denied its existence.

Ball lightning is usually described as a luminous sphere, ranging from a few inches to several feet in diameter. The balls hover, drift, glide and roll. Sometimes they enter buildings and seem to demonstrate curiosity as they move about furnishings and objects in an exploratory manner. They are usually red, orange, blue or white in color, and are sometimes accompanied by a hissing sound and a distinct ODOR. They exist for a time ranging from a few seconds to many minutes. Their evaporation occurs silently or explosively. Although some witnesses claim to have seen ball lightning pass through window panes and wire screens without leaving a mark, it has also been observed to cause damage by burning and melting. Contrary to the known laws that govern lightning, these mysterious balls sometimes ignore metallic and grounded conductors.

Writer PHILIP KLASS is the leading proponent of the theory that plasmas account for a large number of UFOs. He believes that an observer, seeing a cloud of illuminated particles moving through the air, might assume it to be some sort of flying machine. Conditioned to accept certain structural features as integral parts of aerial craft, the mind might distinguish dark areas as part of the structure, and lighter areas as windows. Many properties ascribed to UFOs are also attributable to plasmas. Not only are they good RADAR targets, but they can actually produce a stronger echo than a solid metal object. Low energy plasmas can sometimes be detected by radar without being seen visually. Sudden or gradual disappearance of plasma-

UFOs occurs when their energy is dissipated. Plasmas can change size and shape, and divide and merge just as UFOs are reported to do. Abrupt stops and sharp directional changes are easily accomplished by an essentially weightless and electrically-propelled plasma. The reddish-orange and bluish-white colors frequently reported by UFO witnesses are the characteristic colors of ionized nitrogen and oxygen, the principal constituents of air. Ultraviolet radiation generated by plasmas could cause sunburn and bloodshot eyes, PHYSIOLOGICAL EFFECTS often associated with UFOs. PHYSICAL EFFECTS characteristic of UFOs, such as radio and television interference, could be attributable to the agitated electrified particles which can serve both as generators of radio-frequency energy and as a screen to block other signals. An automobile battery might be short-circuited if the terminals were to be surrounded by plasma or if the plasma's proximity to the distributor were to change the shape of the spark sufficiently to cause engine failure. Although it is not understood how plasmas could penetrate metal structures such as the body of a car without dissipating their energy to the metal, there have been rare incidents in which ball lightning has been reported to have entered a metal aircraft without damage to either itself or the craft.

Klass suggests that a number of factors may have caused the increase in plasma-UFO sightings since World War II. In particular, he cites the worldwide expansion of high-tension power lines and the increased voltages at which they operate. Plasmas have been cited as the explanation for numerous UFO cases, including the World War II FOO FIGHTERS and the celebrated sightings at EXETER, NEW HAMPSHIRE; LEVELLAND, TEXAS and PIEDMONT, MISSOURI.

Opponents of the plasma theory claim that it is an invalid explanation for the majority of UFO sightings, since plasmas normally exist for only a few seconds near high-tension lines during severe thunderstorms. The majority of sightings, they claim, do not meet these criteria.

In a paper prepared for the HOUSE SCIENCE AND ASTRONAUTICS COMMITTEE HEARINGS in 1968, nuclear physicist STANTON FRIEDMAN stated that descriptions by UFO witnesses of bright glows, changes in the colors of glows associated with changes in speed, luminous boundary layers, and appearance on photographic film of regions not seen by the naked eye, do, in fact, indicate the presence of plasmas. However, he believed the plasmas were adjacent to vehicles, rather than ball lightning or corona discharge. Friedman testified that the development of lightweight, compact, high-field superconducting magnets had led to research on the potential benefits to be gained from placing a magnet within a high-speed vehicle to interact with a plasma surrounding the vehicle. Such an arrangement, he claimed, might be utilized to reduce vehicle heating, control aerodynamic drag, exert control forces on the vehicle, provide power for its operation, open a "magnetic" communications window and change the vehicle's radar profile. In addition, magnets might be used to provide shielding against space radiation. Thus, Friedman concluded, development of technology involving airborne vehicles and plasma might result in an entirely new electromagnetic approach to hypersonic flights which in many respects could duplicate UFO characteristics.

Bibliography: Klass, Philip J., *UFOs Identified* (New York: Random House, 1968); U.S. Congress, House Committee on Science and Astronautics, Symposium on Unidentified Flying Objects, Hearings, 90th Congress, 2nd Session, July 29, 1968 (Washington, D.C.: U.S. Government Printing Office, 1968).

**POHER, CLAUDE,** *see* **GROUPE D'ÉTUDES DES PHÉNOMÈNES AÉROSPATIAUX NON IDENTIFIÉS (GEPAN)**

**POLAND.** Flying saucers are known as "latajace talerze" in Poland. Both the MANCHESTER AERIAL PHENOMENA INVESTIGATION TEAM (MAPIT) and

UFO photographed at Muszyn, Poland, on December 22, 1958. *(Courtesy ICUFON)*

SKANDINAVISK UFO INFORMATION (SUFOI) have representatives there.

On December 22, 1958, Dr. Stanislaw Kowalezewski photographed a UFO through a window at Muszyn. The negative was examined by a number of specialists who found nothing suspicious about it.

A sensational incident allegedly occurred on February 21, 1959, at Gdynia. A UFO reportedly crashed into the harbor and a fragment was retrieved by some dock workers. A few days later, the injured OCCUPANT of the craft was found wandering in the area. He was taken to a local hospital, where he died when doctors tried to remove a band from his arm. His remains were purportedly shipped to the Soviet Union.

**POLICE.** A large proportion of UFO reports are made by policemen. This may be attributable to the fact that policemen are trained observers who spend many hours of the day and night on patrol. Some of the well-known sightings involving police witnesses are those which occurred at ALBANY, NEW YORK; FALKVILLE, ALABAMA; LEVELLAND, TEXAS; PORTAGE COUNTY, OHIO and RED BLUFF, CALIFORNIA.

**POLLS.** Numerous Gallup Polls since 1947 have demonstrated an increase in the number of people who believe UFOs are *real*. In this context, *real* denotes flying objects that are not identifiable as conventional aircraft, known astronomical phenomena, OPTICAL ILLUSIONS, HALLUCINATIONS or the products of imagination. In 1947, most of the ninety percent of the population aware of UFOs believed UFOs were not real and that we are alone in the universe. By 1978, fifty-seven percent of the ninety-five percent aware of UFOs believed them to be real, while only twenty-seven percent believed they could be explained in conventional terms. By 1966, thirty-four percent of the public believed in the existence of intelligent life elsewhere in the universe, and by 1978, this figure had risen to fifty-one percent. A 1971 Gallup Poll was taken of prominent politicians, businessmen, educators, scientists, doctors and other professionals in seventy-two nations. The results showed that fifty-three percent believed in the existence of extraterrestrial intelligence, while forty-seven percent ruled out the possibility.

UFOs have been observed by eleven percent of the adult population in the United States, a figure which represents about fifteen million people. This percentage is more than double the five percent who had observed UFOs in 1966. The 1974 Gallup Poll revealed that although sightings were not limited to any particular social stratum, there was a geographic disparity. Midwestern and Southern reports easily outnumbered those from the East and the Far West. However, in 1978,

George Gallup reported that younger people and those with college educations, as well as those living in the Far West, constituted the highest proportion of UFO witnesses and believers in their existence. People living in small towns and rural areas are more likely to report UFO sightings than are those living in metropolitan areas. This may be due, in part, to the fact that small town newspapers are more likely to publish such reports than are city newspapers.

In 1977, a private survey of astronomers revealed that although twenty-five percent favored scientific study of UFOs, only one quarter of one percent thought that UFOs warranted their personal attention.

**PORTAGE COUNTY, OHIO.** One of the most tragic cases in modern UFO history is the Portage County episode because it wreaked havoc in the life of one of the major witnesses.

On the night of April 16, 1966, Deputy Sheriff Dale F. Spaur and part-time Deputy Sheriff Wilbur Neff were on a road near Atwater Center in Ohio when a report of a UFO sighting came through on their police radio. Spaur and Neff listened with amusement as Robert Wilson, the radio operator on duty at the Ravenna police station, told them of a woman in Summit County, directly to the west of Portage County, who had observed a bright object, as big as a house, flying over her neighborhood. Joking about the subject, the deputies headed west on Route 224 on other business. Seeing an abandoned car parked on the south side of the road, they turned their vehicle around to approach the car from the rear. Cautiously, the two men exited their patrol car. Looking around to make sure no one was lurking in the nearby woods, Spaur caught sight of a bright object coming toward them. As its brightness increased and began to illuminate the area, Spaur told his unwitting partner to look over his shoulder. Neff turned. His face registered his shock. Dazzled by the UFO, both men looked down. The humming object stopped directly above them. It was no longer a joke. The frightened deputies jumped back into the patrol car. After a few moments, the object moved eastward. Embarrassed, Spaur contacted Wilson, whose first suggestion was, "Shoot it!" When they confirmed that the object was indeed as big as a house, they were ordered to follow it. A sensational high-speed chase ensued. Spaur and Neff pursued the UFO over a distance of seventy miles, at speeds sometimes reaching 105 miles per hour.

Police officer Wayne Huston of East Palestine, Ohio, about forty miles east of Ravenna, had been monitoring the radio communications. He waited by his car on Route 14 as the UFO flew over him at an altitude of about eight or nine hundred feet. He described its appearance as that of an ice cream cone with a flattened dome on top. As Spaur and Neff roared by, Huston fell in behind them. The object maintained a lead of about two-thirds of a mile.

Meanwhile, in nearby Conway, Pennsylvania, police officer Frank Panzanella was driving through the town when he saw a shining object in the sky. Stopping his car, he stepped out and studied the light. It was very bright, seemed to be about thirty feet in diameter and had the shape of a bisected football. Ten minutes later, Spaur, Neff and Huston pulled by his car. The four officers watched the UFO which was now flying at approximately one thousand feet above the ground. Suddenly, it stopped, shot up to a height of about 3,500 feet and stopped again. Then the object continued upwards at high speed until it disappeared.

The UNITED STATES AIR FORCE (USAF) investigation was conducted by Major HECTOR QUINTANILLA. His initial inquiry consisted of a two-and-a-half-minute telephone call to Spaur in which Quintanilla referred to the UFO as a MIRAGE. In a second telephone conversation between the two men, Quintanilla terminated the conversation after one-and-a-half minutes when Spaur refused to concur with his suggestion that the sighting had lasted only a few minutes. Based on these two brief exchanges, the Air Force's conclusion was that all four police officers had observed a SATELLITE, and then transferred their attention to VENUS. No satellite was visible over Ohio on that date. Venus and the UFO had been visible concurrently to the observers.

Congressional pressure forced Quintanilla to reopen the case. He traveled to Ravenna, where he conducted a taped interview with Spaur and Neff. The dialogue was unfriendly. The other two witnesses were not interviewed. The Air Force gave the incident an astronomical explanation against the advice of their astronomical consultant, J. ALLEN HYNEK.

Although little public attention had been given to Wayne Huston, the affair caused him considerable professional embarrassment. He resigned and moved to Seattle, where he found employment as a bus driver.

Dale Spaur was less fortunate. Having been singled out by the Air Force to be the victim of an interrogation conducted in a tactless and insulting manner, Spaur became the whipping boy of a humiliating publicity spree. He began to suffer acute depression. Two months later, he allegedly saw the object again. Haunted by nightmares, he turned in his badge and moved to a small town near Cleveland. His wife sued for divorce. Spaur found work as a painter. His new job provided him barely enough money to pay his meager rent and his child-support payments. Subsisting on a meager diet, Spaur's health deteriorated. The Air Force DE-

BUNKING program had mercilessly demonstrated its effectiveness.

Bibliography: Hynek, J. Allen, *The UFO Experience: A Scientific Inquiry* (Chicago: Henry Regnery Company, 1972).

**PORT OF THE MISSING** *see* **BERMUDA TRIANGLE**

**PPOANI** *see* **GRUPO PELOTENSE DE ESTUDOS E PESQUISAS DE PARAPSICOLOGIA, PSICOTRONICA E OBJECTOS AEREOS NAO IDENTIFICADOS**

UFO witness Elvis Presley.

**PRESLEY, ELVIS,** the world-famous singer of rock and roll who reportedly observed an unidentified light flying over the roof of his Bel Air mansion in California in 1966. Presley told the other two witnesses, Sonny West and Jerry Schilling, that he believed the UFO was a flying saucer driven by benevolent aliens who would one day make contact with Earth people.

Bibliography: Dunleavy, Steve, *Elvis, What Happened?* (New York: Ballantine Books, 1977).

**PRIVATE UFO INVESTIGATIONS (PUFOI),** Route 1, Hazleton, Iowa 50641; telephone number: 319-636-2620.

The purpose of this organization is to investigate and research UFOs in a serious, scientific manner, to inform the public about the true nature of the UFO problem, and to work with other responsible UFO groups in an effort to resolve the UFO mystery. The group holds that UFOs represent a real phenomenon involving some type of intelligent control whose identity is still unknown. The phenomenon, PUFOI contends, seems to be a part of a much broader mystery which at times seems to border on the occult. The organization thinks that the cases which are most apt to hold valuable information for the UFOLOGIST are the close encounter cases involving entities. These cases, however, sometimes prove to be deceiving as information given to witnesses does not always appear to be consistent.

This not-for-profit organization was founded in 1971 by Ralph C. DeGraw who serves as Director. Michael J. Buman is Assistant Director. There are approximately 100 members. Scientific Consultants are Donald G. Fingado and Robert E. Allen. The organization is represented by State Directors, State Section Directors, Field Directors, Foreign Sectional Directors and Foreign Correspondents. Foreign representatives include Brian G. Panter and Cliff A. Ball in England, Marek S. Iwaniec in Poland, DAVID A. HAISELL in Canada and Jean H. Sider in France. A quarterly newsletter, *The UFO Examiner*, has a circulation of over 300. DeGraw is Editor and Patrick N. Crowley is Staff Artist.

**PROBABILITY RATING,** assessment of the credibility of a UFO report. Factors which earn a report a high-probability rating include consistency in the report, consistency between reports from different witnesses, confirmation by MULTIPLE WITNESSES, witnesses' reputation for reliability, RADAR confirmation and PHYSICAL EVIDENCE.

**PROCEEDINGS,** publication of the MINISTRY OF UNIVERSAL WISDOM.

**PROJECT BLUE BOOK,** code name of the UNITED STATES AIR FORCE's investigative probe into the UFO phenomenon. It was the outcome of the upgrading of PROJECT GRUDGE from a project within a group to a separate organization in March 1952. The Blue Book chief, Captain EDWARD RUPPELT, had revitalized Project Grudge when he was placed in charge of the program six months previously. After the inception of Project Blue Book, his budget and manpower continued to increase as the number of UFO reports during 1952 climbed rapidly. He briefed Air Force officials of the Air Defense Command on the use of their radarscope cameras and contracted with the BATTELLE MEMORIAL INSTITUTE to conduct a statistical analysis of UFO characteristics. By the beginning of 1953, the AIR TECHNICAL INTELLIGENCE CENTER (ATIC) was over-

whelmed with UFO reports. The ROBERTSON PANEL, a committee of eminent scientists, was convened by the CENTRAL INTELLIGENCE AGENCY (CIA) to study the issue. The panel's report led the Air Force once more to change its position. The attitude now was that UFOs were not a threat to national security, but that UFO *reports* were. Project Blue Book's purpose became to lower public interest by means of a DEBUNKING effort. The Battelle statistical report (later released as SPECIAL REPORT NO. 14) was finally completed. It endorsed the Robertson Panel's conclusion that UFOs presented no threat to national security. Although the Robertson Panel had recommended that Project Blue Book be continued at the same level, the project's staff and budget began to shrink. By the time Ruppelt left the Air Force in August 1953, only he and two assistants remained. After Ruppelt's departure, the project was headed in turn by Captain CHARLES HARDIN, Captain GEORGE GREGORY, Lieutenant Colonel ROBERT FRIEND and Major HECTOR QUINTANILLA.

During the period from 1953 to 1966, Project Blue Book was engaged in a major public relations effort to debunk UFOs and to counteract interest raised by believers in the EXTRATERRESTRIAL HYPOTHESIS (ETH), in particular DONALD KEYHOE, Director of the NATIONAL INVESTIGATIONS COMMITTEE ON AERIAL PHENOMENA (NICAP). In 1955, the Air Force released *Special Report No. 14* to counteract charges that it was engaged in a COVER-UP. However, the report served only to increase public suspicion. While education of the public became Project Blue Book's primary concern, investigation was left to the private UFO organizations which began to flourish.

During the decade following the release of *Special Report No. 14*, one of Project Blue Book's primary concerns was that the UNITED STATES CONGRESS would call for hearings on its activities. To avoid this, whenever a congressman approached the Air Force on the matter, he was given a private briefing during which Air Force representatives convinced him that a hearing would merely serve to make the public think that UFOs were something to be concerned about. Two such briefings were given to the HOUSE OF REPRESENTATIVES SUBCOMMITTEE ON ATMOSPHERIC PHENOMENA in 1958 and the SMART COMMITTEE in 1960. Little change in Blue Book procedure resulted from these meetings.

In 1965, an increase in UFO reports and heightened public awareness led to the formation of the United States Air Force Scientific Advisory Board Ad Hoc Committee to review Project Blue Book. A panel of scientists headed by physicist Brian O'Brien met for one day (February 2, 1966) and issued its report, subsequently known as the O'BRIEN REPORT. The latter recommended strengthening Project Blue Book and negotiating with a few selected universities to provide scientific teams to investigate UFOs.

The O'Brien Report resulted in the formation of the CONDON COMMITTEE, a team of scientific investigators and researchers at the University of Colorado, who conducted an eighteen-month Air Force/taxpayer-sponsored investigation and evaluation of UFOs. The Colorado Project began operating in October 1966 and was completed in June 1968. Although there were many critics of the CONDON REPORT in the scientific community, the general public accepted the Condon conclusion that there was no value in continuing a study of the problem. The Air Force used this reasoning to cancel Project Blue Book in December 1969, and since then has had no official interest in the subject.

The termination of Air Force involvement brought about declassification of UFO records. However, researchers did not have access to the files. Only if a researcher knew of a specific case by name and date would the Air Force then pull that particular case file. In 1975, Project Blue Book records were transferred to the NATIONAL ARCHIVES in Washington, D.C. After confidential information had been censored, they became available to civilian researchers on July 12, 1976.

Bibliography: Smith, Marcia S., *The UFO Enigma* (Washington, D.C.: Library of Congress, Congressional Research Service, 1976); Flammonde, Paris, *UFO Exist!* (New York: G. P. Putnam's Sons, 1976).

## PROJECT CYCLOPS,

**PROJECT CYCLOPS,** system of multiple antennas designed to detect radio signals from extraterrestrial civilizations. Plans for the project were initiated in 1971. They called for a circular array of over fifteen hundred antennas, each larger in diameter than a football field, covering over twenty-five square miles. Each antenna would be connected to all the other antennas and to a central computer which would be used both to position the array properly and to assimilate the individual signals into a single one. Although this project would have allowed a realistic effort to eavesdrop on radio transmissions in outer space, its enormous size and cost made it somewhat impractical. It remained in the planning stage. Then, in 1976, the design of new equipment of unprecedented tunability and sensitivity presented a more feasible means of resuming the SEARCH FOR EXTRATERRESTRIAL INTELLIGENCE (SETI).

## PROJECT GRUDGE,

**PROJECT GRUDGE,** code name of the UNITED STATES AIR FORCE's investigative probe into the UFO phenomenon. It succeeded PROJECT SIGN, and, in turn, was succeeded by PROJECT BLUE BOOK. Like Project Sign, it was known publicly as PROJECT SAUCER.

Project Grudge came into existence on February 11,

Artist's contempt of the Cyclops system. *(Courtesy NASA)*

1949. Although most of the people involved believed UFOs were non-hostile and non-military in nature, the Air Force wanted to maintain the controlling hand in investigating UFO reports. Project Grudge shifted the focus of the Air Force's investigations from UFOs themselves to the people who reported them. A public relations campaign was launched to convince the public that UFOs did not represent anything unusual or extraordinary. As part of its DEBUNKING effort, the Air Force selectively granted permission to Sidney Shallet of the *Saturday Evening Post* to have access to their files for a two-part article on UFOs. They wanted to ensure that the article would expose UFOs as a waste of time. Although Shallet's article attempted to do just that, only days after the second part had been published, UFO sightings reached an all-time high. Project Grudge was deluged with reports. The Air Force believed that Shallet's article was responsible. To counteract the reaction, a press release was issued stating that UFOs were nothing but the products of MASS HYSTERIA and the MISIDENTIFICATION of natural phenomena. Project Grudge continued its attempts to prove that UFOs did not represent an unknown phenomenon. Astronomer J. ALLEN HYNEK was enlisted to aid in this program.

Only six months after its inception, in August 1949, Project Grudge issued its final report. Out of 244 cases, many had been given explanations which were somewhat speculative. Yet there still remained a residuum of twenty-three percent which were unidentified. The Grudge report commented that, "There are sufficient psychological explanations for the reports of unidentified flying objects to provide plausible explanations for reports not otherwise explainable." The implication was that any UFOs which could not be identified must be psychologically motivated. The report concluded that the investigation of UFOs should be reduced in scope so that only those reports "clearly indicating realistic technical applications" would be submitted to the AIR TECHNICAL INTELLIGENCE CENTER (ATIC). It did, however, suggest that the Psychological Warfare Division be informed of the study results since mass hysteria could ensue if the enemy simultaneously placed a series of aerial objects over the United States and started rumors that they were alien craft. The report recommended that the investigation and study of UFO reports be downgraded. Believing that the very existence of a special investigative body lent credence to the belief in UFOs, the Air Force issued a press release on December 27, 1949, announcing the termination of Project Grudge. However, the organization continued to operate on a subdued level for over two more years and its data remained classified.

In September 1951, Captain EDWARD RUPPELT was placed in charge of Project Grudge. More open-minded than his predecessors, he revitalized the program by reorganizing the data files, making standardized reporting forms available and formally appointing Hynek as chief scientific consultant to Project Grudge under Air Force contract. By 1952, Grudge had become a well-organized effort but its work was hampered by insufficient funds. Six months after Ruppelt had begun his reorganization of the same project, the Air Force upgraded Grudge from a project within a group to a separate organization. Its code name was changed to Project Blue Book in March 1952.

Bibliography: Jacobs, David Michael, *The UFO Controversy in America* (Bloomington, Indiana: Indiana University Press, 1975); Steiger, Brad (ed.), *Project Blue Book* (New York: Ballantine Books, 1976).

## PROJECT MAGNET *see* CANADA

PROJECT OZMA, earliest effort in the SEARCH FOR EXTRATERRESTRIAL INTELLIGENCE (SETI), named after the Princess of OZ, a place far away, difficult to reach, and populated by exotic beings. Directed by FRANK DRAKE, the project began on April 8, 1960. Using the 1,420 Mc frequency and a narrow bandwidth of 100 cycles, the radio telescopes at the National Radio Astronomy Observatory at Green Bank, West Virginia, were aimed at Tau Ceti and Epsilon Eridani. These two STARS were chosen because they both lie within eleven light years of Earth and because their resemblance to our own sun in age and type makes it possible that they have planetary systems not unlike our own. When the receiver was focused on Epsilon Eridani, within a couple of minutes a very strong signal was detected. There was great excitement in the control room. However, the mysterious pulse was later attributed by government officials to an Earth-based signal related to a secret military experiment. Project Ozma was terminated after three months. Although not successful, it was not a failure, for it had focused on only two stars out of billions for a total observing time of 150 hours.

Some UFOLOGISTS have been suspicious of the official explanation for the signals received. They question the claim by the observatory's Director, Otto Struve, that the search for intelligent messages from other PLANETS was a waste of time. This statement was a complete contrast to his initial enthusiasm for the project. Suspicion was further increased when, shortly afterward, Drake, Struve and a number of other scientists produced the GREEN BANK FORMULA, an equation assessing the probable number of extant technical civilizations on planets within our galaxy. For these reasons, some UFOlogists believe that Drake's team did, in fact, tune in on an extraterrestrial civilization.

Bibliography: Sullivan, Walter, *We Are Not Alone* (New York: McGraw Hill, 1964); Drake, Frank R., "A Reminiscence of Project Ozma," *Cosmic Search* (Delaware, Ohio: Cosmic-Quest, January 1979).

PROJECT SAUCER, name by which the first two UNITED STATES AIR FORCE (USAF) UFO investigations, PROJECT SIGN (1947 to 1949) and PROJECT GRUDGE (1949 to 1951), were known to the public.

PROJECT SIGN, code name of the first UNITED STATES AIR FORCE (USAF) investigative probe into the UFO phenomenon. It was known publicly as PROJECT SAUCER. Project Sign was implemented on January 22, 1948, under the jurisdiction of the Intelligence Division of the Air Force's Air Material Command at Wright Field, Ohio (now Wright-Patterson Air Force Base). This division was later renamed the AIR TECHNICAL INTELLIGENCE CENTER (ATIC). Its function was to "collect, collate, evaluate and distribute to interested government agencies and contractors all information concerning sightings and phenomena in the atmosphere which can be construed to be of concern to the national security." Although there were a variety of opinions regarding the identity of UFOs, those who thought they were extraterrestrial spaceships held the reins of power at Project Sign during its early months in 1948. After the Chiles/Whitted Sighting near MONTGOMERY, ALABAMA, in July 1948, they issued an ESTIMATE OF THE SITUATION. Classified Top Secret, the report concluded that UFOs were extraterrestrial vehicles. The estimate received considerable attention until it reached Chief of Staff General Hoyt S. Vandenberg, who rejected it on the grounds that it lacked proof. Some months later, the report was declassified and incinerated. Its rejection led to a change in policy at Project Sign and those who believed UFOs were conventional objects took charge. Claiming that the classified name "Sign" had been compromised, the Air Force changed its name to PROJECT GRUDGE on February 11, 1949. A final report issued by Project Sign expressed the conflicting opinions of the staff in its conclusion, which states that: "no definite and conclusive evidence is yet available that would prove or disprove the existence of these unidentified objects as real aircraft of unknown or unconventional configuration. It is unlikely that positive proof of their existence will be obtained without examination of the remains of crashed objects. Proof of non-existence is equally impossible to obtain unless a reasonable and convincing explanation is determined for each incident." However, the change of policy was evident in the report's recommendation that: "Future activity on this project should be carried on at the minimum level necessary to record, summarize and evaluate the data received on future reports and to complete the specialized investigations now in progress. When and if a sufficient number of incidents are solved to indicate that these sightings do not represent a threat to the security of the nation, the assignment of special project status to the activity could be terminated. Future investigations of reports would then be handled on a routine basis like any other intelligence work."

Bibliography: Steiger, Brad (ed.), *Project Blue Book* (New York: Ballantine Books, 1976); Jacobs, David Michael, *The UFO Controversy in America* (Bloomington, Indiana: Indiana University Press, 1975).

## PROJECT STARLIGHT INTERNATIONAL (PSI), P.O. Box 5310, Austin, Texas 78763; telephone number: 512-458-2031.

The purpose of this organization is to document scientifically and irrefutably the existence of UFOs. Research is conducted on field trips and at the Laboratory for Instrumented UFO Research on a 400-acre site northwest of Austin. In two laboratory buildings and on surrounding hillsides, the facility houses the most modern instruments available to detect and record UFO activity. Technical equipment includes RADAR, a laser system, magnetometers, a gravimeter, microcomputer, ambient and parabolic microphones, an eight-channel sensor-activated chart recorder, video equipment, motion picture cameras and 33 mm still cameras. In the event of UFO activity, Operation ARGUS (Automated Ring-up on Geolocated UFO Sightings) goes into effect. The ARGUS computer automatically telephones all volunteers located within the computed visibility radius of the UFO. When a volunteer answers, a recording announces, "This is an Operation ARGUS alert. Please do as you are instructed." Volunteers then attempt to locate the UFO visually, make notes and take photo-

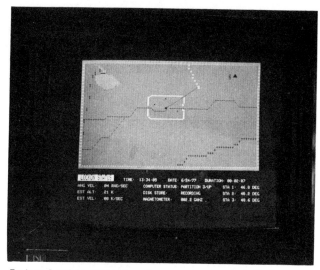

Project Starlight International's computer terminal displays data in simulated UFO tracking program. *(Courtesy PSI)*

graphs. Meanwhile, at Operation ARGUS headquarters, data acquired from the instruments is fed in binary format into the computer. It immediately calculates and displays, in both video and typed form, the horizontal distance, altitude and size of an object. The path of the UFO appears on a video display superimposed over an image of the area beneath it. Additionally, a three-dimensional video model of the magnetic field around a UFO can be displayed, showing each component in a different color. If required, a modulatable Liconix 605M helium neon laser can transmit voice, code or television signals. Any modulated light response which a UFO might make to the laser signals can be displayed as sound or as a television image.

PSI takes no stand on the origin of UFOs, but believes that some appear to represent an advanced technology, possibly involved in surveillance. Cases involving PSI staff members, wherein instruments have recorded UFO data, are undergoing in-depth analysis. In 1974, PSI obtained the first UFO light pulsation measurement by photographic means. In 1977, the first instrumented recordings were obtained of UFO PLASMA emissions, shock wave emissions and propagation, magnetic field-effect Faraday-rotation rings, and instrumented data providing precise UFO size determinations. In 1978, PSI obtained the first two known magnetometer recordings of UFO magnetic effects, the first documented UFO sound effect recording, the first gravimeter recording of possible gravitylike effects of UFOs, and the first photographically recorded UFO light spectrum.

This nonprofit organization, a research division of the ASSOCIATION FOR THE UNDERSTANDING OF MAN (AUM), was founded in 1964 by RAY STANFORD, who is Managing Director. The group is financed by the tax-deductible contributions of persons who believe instrumented UFO tracking and monitoring to be a worthwhile endeavor. PSI is not a membership organization.

**PROJECT STIGMA,** P.O. Box 1094, Paris, Texas 75460.

The primary objective of this organization is to investigate reports of ANIMAL MUTILATIONS. The group considers unidentified helicopters which, along with UFOs, have been reported at or near mutilation sites, to be a pertinent aspect of this phenomenon. Although Project Stigma admits that there *seems* to be evidence to support the hypothesis linking animal mutilations to UFO activity, it also considers the possibilities that the incidents may be attributable to terrestrial cults, secret societies or governmental experimentation.

This nonprofit organization was founded in 1977 by Thomas R. Adams, who serves as Director. It is not a membership organization. Information is collected through an informal network of investigators and researchers, including news media representatives, official investigative agencies and private individuals. A few of the project's contributors and investigators are located in foreign countries. The organization is engaged in obtaining information regarding mutilations and their investigations from Federal agencies under the Freedom of Information Act. The organization owns a four-wheel-drive vehicle, which serves as a mobile investigative unit. A newsletter, *Stigmata*, reports on various aspects of the ongoing investigation into the nature and extent of animal mutilations. It is published irregularly and has a circulation of about 300. Thomas Adams is Editor.

**PROJECT SUM (SOLVING UFO MYSTERIES) UFO RESEARCH,** 21 Prince Charles Drive, St. Catherines, Ontario, Canada L2N 3Y4; telephone number: 416-934-9756.

The three major purposes of this investigative organization are: 1. To be a place where persons across North America can report their UFO experiences without the fear of unwanted publicity or ridicule and to pursue a serious study of these reports; 2. To be a source of reliable information and data; and 3. To seriously study the phenomenon of unidentified flying objects, using a scientific approach. The group has concluded that there does appear to be some form of intelligence behind the UFO phenomenon, although it remains open-minded as to whether that intelligence is terrestrial or extraterrestrial. Project SUM's statistical studies have revealed, among other facts, that a large percentage of UFO sightings occur around the western tip of Lake Ontario, lending some support, albeit inconclusive, to a theory proposed by a number of researchers that the lake holds an underwater UFO base.

This nonprofit organization was founded in 1974 by Kenneth J. Kroeker, who serves as Director. Staff members consist of Vice-Director Brian Woodrow; Clint Thorne, who is in charge of Physical Traces Study; J. Fegan, who is in charge of Organizational Study; Patrick Diplock and Rob Kroeker, who are in charge of the Astronomy Department; Public Relations Officer J. Starbuck; Assistant Researchers Bill MacMillan and Rodney Stone; and Technical Researcher Doug Delonge. Field Investigators include Joe DeVincentis in Hamilton, Ontario; Arnold Hudson in Purple Springs, Alberta; and Howard Kaufman in Burbank, California. The Consultant Panel includes M. J. Moll (Psychology); David Moll (Statistics); Paul R. Sanberg (Psychology); C. Kaner (Psychology); R. De A'Morelli (Parapsychology); B. A. Kroeker (Photography and Videography); Michael Strange (Photography); D. W. Delong (Technology); Phyllis M. Kroeker (Journalism); DAVID A. HAISELL (Agrology); and Marcello Truzzi (Sociology). Newspapers and radio stations in southern Ontario are involved in the group's cooperative reporting network. Project SUM is organized into departments in order to facilitate specialized study and research. The four major divisions are Internal and External Affairs, Publications, Investigations and Research. These in turn are divided into various other departments for further specialization. Following investigations, cases which remain unidentified are coded through Project SUM's UFO Classification Code System (CCS). The system codes almost every possible characteristic of UFO sightings. Statistics, research and investigative efforts, as well as news from around the world, are reported in UFO INFORMER, a quarterly publication edited by Kenneth Kroeker and reaching a readership of almost 500.

In 1978, Project SUM established the first CANADIAN UFO REPORT EXCHANGE NETWORK (CUFOREN), composed of UFO groups and researchers who exchange UFO reports as they are received.

**PROJECT TO RESEARCH OBJECTS, THEORIES, EXTRATERRESTRIAL AND UNUSUAL SIGHTINGS (PROTEUS),** 274 Second Street, Elizabeth, New Jersey 07206; telephone number: 201-352-6761

The purposes of this investigative organization are to stimulate interest in UFOLOGY, to provide a forum for discussion and debate, to investigate local sightings, to exchange information, and to obtain insight into extraterrestrial realities. The group holds that UFOs are technologically-advanced vehicles from distant planetary systems which have bases under our oceans and on the moons in our solar system. PROTEUS believes that UFOs are engaged in scientific research and commerce on a galactic level and that most sightings represent accidental meetings, although some represent local spacefaring races' attempts to reach mankind.

This nonprofit organization was founded in 1979 by KENNETH W. BEHRENDT, who serves as Director, and DIANE M. HICKS, who serves as Assistant Director. There are fewer than one hundred members. They investigate sightings throughout northern and central New Jersey, participate in skywatches and psychic experiments and interact with other organizations. *The PROTEUS Journal* is published irregularly.

**PROJECT TWINKLE,** classified study of GREEN FIREBALLS coordinated by the UNITED STATES AIR FORCE's Cambridge Research Laboratory and directed by Dr. Lincoln La Paz, head of the University of New Mexico's Institute of Meteoritics and a world-renowned authority on astronomy. The project was initiated in September 1949. Its primary goal was to establish three cinetheodolite stations in New Mexico to photograph and record the altitude, size, speed and spectrum of the luminous UFOs. However, only one camera was made available and it never found anything to photograph. The green fireballs, ubiquitous during 1948 and 1949, had vanished from the skies. Project Twinkle was cancelled. On December 27, 1951, the project's final report was issued, declaring the undertaking a failure.

Bibliography: Menzel, Donald H., and Lyle G. Boyd, *The World of Flying Saucers* (Garden City, N.Y.: Doubleday and Company, 1963).

**PROJECT UFO,** television series (Mark VII Limited/ NBC, 1978). Executive Producer: Jack Webb; producers: WILLIAM COLEMAN and Don Widener.

Each episode of this series presented a dramatization of actual cases reported in the files of the UNITED STATES AIR FORCE's PROJECT BLUE BOOK. The leading actors played two Air Force officers who investigated sightings. The series gave a factual representation of Air Force procedure. The shows were highlighted by special effects.

**PROJECT UNUFUO,** a proposal drafted at the 1977 First International UFO Conference in Acapulco, Mexico, urging the UNITED NATIONS to sponsor UFO research.

**PROJECT VISIT (VEHICLE INTERNAL SYSTEMS INVESTIGATIVE TEAM),** P.O. Box 877, Friendswood, Texas 77546.

The purpose of this research organization is to evaluate engineering, medical and physiological data obtained by abductees while restrained aboard UFOs. Since many UFO witnesses describe irregular motions and hovering characteristics, the group thinks that the

"F" in UFO may be inappropriate. It therefore refers to such objects as USVs or Unidentified Space Vehicles. It is Project Visit's hope that through the review of a number of abduction cases, carried out with the cooperation of psychologist R. LEO SPRINKLE, characteristic USV systems will be identified. The organization has determined that there are distinct correlations between numerous ABDUCTION cases. However, it believes that much information which should be acquired during an investigation is not being sought by the investigators.

This nonprofit organization was founded in 1976 by John Schuessler, who serves as President; Gravill Pennington, who serves as Vice-President; Alan Holt, who serves as Secretary; and Dave Kissinger, who serves as Treasurer. Consultants, most of whom possess doctorates, serve in an advisory capacity. The group has nine members. Membership in VISIT is by invitation of one of the Directors or Officers of the corporation. Although not a popular membership organization, VISIT's objective is to interchange information with the general public, educational institutions, government agencies, doctors, scientists, responsible UFO organizations, the news media and other specialized experts. The interchange is accomplished through letters; semimonthly public meetings; articles in scientific journals, magazines and newspapers; participation in symposia, television and radio presentations; and other similar activities.

**PROTEUS** *see* **PROJECT TO RESEARCH OBJECTS, THEORIES, EXTRATERRESTRIAL AND UNUSUAL SIGHTINGS**

**PROTEUS,** publication of the UNIDENTIFIED FLYING OBJECTS STUDIES, INVESTIGATION SERVICE (UFOSIS).

**PSI** *see* **PROJECT STARLIGHT INTERNATIONAL**

**PSYCHOLOGICAL AND PSYCHIATRIC EXPLANATIONS.** The most noted psychologist and psychiatrist to deal with the UFO question was the late CARL JUNG, who speculated that UFO reports result from the human being's need to believe in the existence of a higher power. Author PHILIP KLASS describes the belief in extraterrestrial visitation as "a fairy story that is tailored to the adult mentality." Although some UFO reports can be attributed to ambulatory schizophrenia, HALLUCINATIONS, HYPNOPOMPIC and hypnagogic imagery, the ISAKOWER PHENOMENON, HYSTERICAL CONTAGION, MASS HYSTERIA and perhaps the FREUDIAN HYPOTHESIS, these conditions do not explain all the UFO sightings. In many cases, however, it is the simple desire to believe in extraterrestrial spaceships that has led witnesses to misperceive and misinterpret natural and conventional aerial objects.

An unusual type of psychosis, known as *folie à deux*, may explain a UFO experience shared by two people. This mental condition is one in which the dominant partner in an intimate relationship transfers his or her delusions to the submissive, emotionally dependent partner. This shared psychosis usually affects a husband and wife, a parent and child, or two siblings.

UFO witnesses are rarely subjected to any kind of psychiatric evaluation to establish their credibility. An examination of a UFO witness conducted by neuro-psychiatrist Sydney Walker III, and presented at the 1968 HOUSE SCIENCE AND ASTRONAUTICS COMMITTEE HEARINGS by scientist ROBERT BAKER, demonstrates the value of such studies. The case involved a thirty-seven-year-old bank official who reported a UFO sighting to the police. Walker noted that, "Without the benefit of the results of this medical evaluation, one would probably be inclined to view [the witness] as a highly creditable observer" because of "his respectable bank position . . . his general demeanor . . . his seeming good health and . . . the nature and quality of his report of the 'light' observed event to the police." Walker's findings revealed that the subject had, in fact, undergone the first major hallucinatory experience of his life. While in a drowsy state, he had perceived some kind of stimulus in the sky which was transformed into a symbolic representation of his underlying character pathology and his unconscious desires, which involved a belly dancer's disklike nipple coverlets. The subject's resistance to the experience was reduced by depression, visual distortion due to eye disease, and the adverse effects of drug-related and liver-related toxins on his central nervous system. These conditions were apparent only after extensive neuro-ophthalmic, neurologic and psychiatric examination.

Another psychological aspect to be considered in UFOLOGY applies to UFOLOGISTS themselves. It deals again with belief systems. Sociologist Robert Hall has pointed out that organizations of people become committed to defending their positions. Thus, many UFOLOGISTS, although believing themselves to be unbiased about the identity of UFOs, find themselves attempting to prove that UFOs are an exotic phenomenon in order to justify the time and effort they have expended on the subject. This social psychological problem, of course, can likewise condition the thinking of those who believe the study and investigation of UFOs to have no value.

Bibliography: U.S. Congress, House, Committee on Science and Astronautics, Symposium on Unidentified Flying Objects, Hearings, 90th Congress, 2nd Session, July 29, 1968 (Washington, D.C.: U.S. Government Printing Office, 1968); Grinspoon, Lester, and Alan D. Persky, "Psychiatry and UFO Reports," in Sagan, Carl, and Thornton Page (eds.), *UFOs—A Scientific Debate* (Ithaca, N.Y.: Cornell University Press, 1972).

**PSYCHOTRONIC TECHNOLOGY,** the applied science of MIND CONTROL through the use of physical devices. UFOLOGIST JACQUES VALLEE has proposed that the UFO phenomenon may be an enormous deception, the result of systematic manipulation of the human consciousness, perhaps brought about by groups on Earth for the purpose of social and political change.

Bibliography: Vallee, Jacques, *Messengers of Deception* (Berkeley, California: And/Or Press, 1979).

**PUCKETT, JACK E.,** *see* **FLORIDA**

**PUFOI** *see* **PRIVATE UFO INVESTIGATIONS**

**PULSAR,** celestial object which emits radio pulses at regular intervals and is thought to be a rapidly spinning neutron STAR.

During the summer of 1967, British astronomer S. Jocelyn Bell Burnell spotted a curious set of markings on the paper graph of her radio telescope. When these markings reappeared at intervals, it became apparent that somewhere in outer space someone or something was broadcasting a signal. Because of the fleeting suspicion that these highly-rhythmic radio pulses might be coming from distant civilizations, they were initially nicknamed LGM, for "LITTLE GREEN MEN." Long investigation, however, revealed the existence of pulsating stars, which were named pulsars for short.

To date, more than 100 pulsars have been discovered. Since each one emits a different identifiable signal, it has been suggested that they might serve as "landmarks" to facilitate intergalactic navigation.

Bibliography: Burnell, S. Jocelyn Bell, "Little Green Men, White Dwarfs or Pulsars?" *Cosmic Search* (Delaware, Ohio: Cosmic-Quest January 1979).

**PURSUIT,** publication of the SOCIETY FOR THE INVESTIGATION OF THE UNEXPLAINED (SITU).

**PYRAMID,** a large structure with a square base and four triangular sides meeting in a point at the top. The pyramids of Egypt are the oldest of the Seven Wonders of the World. The most famous of these monuments are located along a fifty-mile stretch of the Nile Valley. The best-known are the three pyramids at Giza, which include one of the largest structures ever erected. It was built by the Pharaoh Khufu (whose Greek name was Cheops) and is often referred to as the Great Pyramid. Some proponents of the ANCIENT ASTRONAUTS hy-

A scene from the motion picture *The Outer Space Connection* showing the three pyramids at Giza. *(Courtesy Sun Classic Pictures)*

pothesis contend that the Great Pyramid was built by extraterrestrials who moved the enormous blocks of stone by means of LEVITATION. Hidden chambers supposedly contain information which will be revealed to the human race at an appropriate point in time. Supporters of this theory also claim that one of the visitors' spaceships is buried near the structure. CONTACTEE REINHOLD SCHMIDT purports to have been taken in a flying saucer to Egypt where SPACE PEOPLE took him on guided tour of the secret recesses of the Great Pyramid. Among other things, he was allegedly shown an historical document, written in modern-day English, furnishing the details of Earth's past, present and future. Schmidt claimed that those records showed the end of the present "Earth cycle" to be due in 1998.

Author ERICH VON DÄNIKEN has speculated that extraterrestrials did not actually build the Great Pyramid themselves, but provided the ancient Egyptians with the necessary knowledge and tools. He disputes the claims of scholars and archaeologists that wooden rollers and ropes were used to transport the blocks of stone to the building site. The Egyptians, he asserts, had no rope or wood. However, not only do these items appear in ancient Egyptian illustrations, but samples of both have been found near the pyramids.

Von Däniken questions the ability of the Egyptians to have leveled the ground on which the Great Pyramid was built. In a television documentary entitled THE CASE OF THE ANCIENT ASTRONAUTS, written and produced by Graham Massey for the British Broadcasting Corporation's NOVA series, a simple leveling method is proposed as one possibly used by the ancient builders. After flooding the area with water, holes could be drilled to a fixed depth below the level water surface. After the water had been drained away, the rock could be cut away to the depth of the bases of the drilled holes, thus forming a level surface.

Von Däniken asserts that the stone blocks were joined together to a thousandth-of-an-inch, a feat beyond the capability of the ancient Egyptians. Authors DONALD MENZEL and Ernest Taves refute this claim. They point out that the average thickness of the joints is about two-hundredths-of-an-inch, an accuracy that was within the capability of the Egyptians. Again with regard to measurements, von Däniken asks if it is by chance that the ratio of the pyramid's height to its sides involves the figure *pi*. The latter, which represents the ratio of

the circumference of a circle to the diameter, was unknown to the Egyptians. Because of *pi*'s relationship to the circle, Menzel and Taves have conjectured that a round drum might have been used as a measuring device in the construction of the pyramids. By rolling the drum along the ground and using its circumference to measure the sides, while using its diameter to measure height, the Egyptians could have unwittingly incorporated *pi* into the dimensions of the pyramid. Von Däniken asks if it is also by chance that the height of the Great Pyramid multiplied by one billion gives the approximate distance to the sun. The pyramid's original height of 481.4 feet, multiplied by one billion, equals 91,170,000 miles. This figure is 1,830,000 miles below the average distance of 93,000,000 miles between Earth and the sun. Von Däniken's detractors have remarked that such a discrepancy is not what one would expect from advanced space travelers.

Von Däniken argues that no architect today could build a copy of the Great Pyramid. He adds that under the best conditions it would have taken human workers, unaided by extraterrestrial technology, about 664 years to complete the task. However, the archaeological evidence indicates that the Great Pyramid and several other pyramids were all built within one century using the available terrestrial resources. The chronological study of Egyptian funerary edifices shows a development from simple tombs to the true pyramids, indicating that the Great Pyramid was the culmination of two centuries of experience in pyramid building.

The striking similarity of the Egyptian pyramids to those built by the MAYANS in Central America has led some researchers to conclude that the pyramids are the cultural vestiges of the lost continent of ATLANTIS, which may have been located in the Atlantic Ocean between Egypt and Central America. Some proponents of the HOLLOW EARTH HYPOTHESIS conjecture that the pyramids were built by antedeluvian Atlanteans to protect passageways to the PLANET's interior. Many occultists profess that all pyramid-shaped objects, including the Egyptian and Mayan pyramids, have some kind of cosmic power which preserves and energizes organisms within their confines. Moreover, the pyramid shape is said to have a beneficial effect on inanimate objects such as razor blades which can supposedly be kept sharp by "pyramid power."

Bibliography: Von Däniken, Erich, *Chariots of the Gods?* (New York: G. P. Putnam's Sons, 1970); Menzel, Donald H., and Ernest H. Taves, *The UFO Enigma* (Garden City, N.Y.: Doubleday and Company, 1977); Thiering, Barry, and Edgar Castle (eds.), *Some Trust in Chariots* (New York: Popular Library, 1972); Mendelssohn, Kurt, *The Riddle of the Pyramids* (New York: Praeger, 1974).

**QUARTERLY REPORT,** publication of Suomen UFOtutkijat Ry.

**QUASAR,** also known as quasi-stellar radio source, quasi-stellar source or quasi-stellar object, any of a number of STARlike objects that emit immense quantities of light or of powerful radio waves, or both, and that appear to exist at a great distance from Earth.

**QUEST,** publication of UFO International (UFOI).

**QUETZALCOATL,** a major deity of ancient Mexico whose MAYAN counterpart was the god Kulkulcan. He was the god of learning, of writing and of books. Quetzalcoatl's symbol was a feathered serpent which some supporters of the ANCIENT ASTRONAUTS hypothesis consider to be reminiscent of a spaceship. Modern-day writers have suggested that he originated from VENUS, the PLANET with which he was identified in ancient myths. According to one version of his departure from Central America, he went down to the Atlantic Ocean, where he flung himself on a funeral pyre and ascended from the flames to Venus.

Bibliography: Drake, W. Raymond, *Gods and Spacemen throughout History* (Chicago: Henry Regnery Company, 1975).

**QUINTANILLA, HECTOR,** United States Air Force (USAF) major who headed Project Blue Book from August 1963 until its termination in 1969.

**RADAR,** acronym for *r*adio *d*etecting *a*nd *r*anging, an electronic device which determines the presence and location of an object by measuring the time it takes the echo of a radio pulse to return from the object to the emitting antenna, and by establishing the direction from which the echo returns. The sweep hand on the radarscope keeps pace with the rotation of the radar antenna as it scans the sky. The radar return is registered as a spot of light on the radarscope and is referred to as a "blip" or a "target." The object's speed is determined by the distance it moves on the scope from one sweep of the scanning beam to the next.

Skeptics place little value on radar observations of UFOs. Unidentified blips are usually referred to as "ANGELS," "GHOSTS," "phantoms" or "uncorrelated targets (UCTs)." They may be attributable to numerous natural causes such as equipment malfunction, unusual weather conditions, PLASMAS, flocks of BIRDS and swarms of INSECTS.

Anomalous propagation can occur when TEMPERATURE INVERSIONS or layers of humidity in the atmosphere deflect radar beams toward ground objects, such as buildings or cars. The returning beam is reflected back toward the atmospheric layer from which it then bounces back to the original source. Radar operators, unaware of the deflections, may assume that the blip on the radarscope represents an aerial object. Changes within the atmospheric layers may cause the blip to disappear or may cause the beam to pick up another ground object at a different location. A radar operator, seeing a blip appear at one spot on one sweep, and at another spot on the following sweep, may assume that it represents the same object. This would lead to the incorrect conclusion that the first object seen had traveled the distance between the two positions within the period of the sweep.

Despite the fallibilities of radar, it is considered as supplementary evidence by most UFOLOGISTS, particularly in cases where the location, speed and movement of a visually observed UFO are matched exactly by the blip on the radarscope.

Some of the best-known radar/visual UFO cases occurred at ALBANY, NEW YORK; BENTWATERS AND LAKENHEATH, ENGLAND; NEW ZEALAND (1978/79); OCALA, FLORIDA and WASHINGTON, D.C. (1952).

Bibliography: Menzel, Donald H. and Lyle G. Boyd, *The World of Flying Saucers* (Garden City, N.Y.: Doubleday and Company, 1963); Klass, Philip J., *UFOs Identified* (New York: Random House, 1968).

**RADIESTHESIA,** the alleged ability of human beings to detect low electromagnetic fields through the use of such items as pendulums and dowsing rods. Although not directly connected with UFOLOGY, it is a technique pursued by some members of CONTACTEE and NEW AGE groups.

**RADIO AND TELEVISION INTERFERENCE,** one of the ELECTROMAGNETIC EFFECTS associated with UFO sightings. Skeptics have pointed out that electromagnetic interference can be instigated by conventional and natural causes, such as aircraft and METEORS, objects which also give rise to reports of visually-observed UFOs. The interference usually involves static or complete loss of transmission.

A much-publicized case involving an overriding broadcast signal occurred on November 26, 1977, in the United Kingdom. At 5:12 P.M., an authoritative voice interrupted a news bulletin being read by Ivor Mills on Southern I.T.V. The speaker announced himself as, "Gramaha, the representative of the Asta Galactic Command." During the five-and-a-half minutes that he spoke, he warned mankind against the use of nuclear energy and cautioned that, "You have but a short time to live together in peace and good will." Hundreds of thousands of viewers heard the broadcast in locations as distant as Winchester, Andover, Newbury, Reading, London, Southampton and Oxford. Although the authorities pronounced the incident a HOAX, some UFOLOGISTS have questioned this explanation. They contend that because at least five different transmitters were "taken over" simultaneously and because engineers were powerless to cut off the broadcast, normal electricity was not being used. Furthermore, the cost of such an operation would have been enormous. Those who believe the voice was nonhuman hold that the broadcast was achieved with occult power.

**RADIOASTRONOMY,** branch of astronomy which deals with long wave radio radiation from heavenly bodies. It is utilized in the SEARCH FOR EXTRATERRESTRIAL INTELLIGENCE (SETI).

**RADIONICS,** the science of radiation detection utilized by some parapsychologists to study and allegedly to manipulate little-known radiation patterns in and around us. Combined with appropriate equipment, this method purportedly enables the parapsychologist to analyze and discover information about an item, such as a UFO photograph, that is unattainable by conventional means.

**RADIOSONDE,** an instrument attached to a small BALLOON which takes soundings in the upper atmosphere and sends back information on atmospheric conditions by radio.

**RAINBOW ARCK RESEARCH CENTER,** Route 9, Box 12–A, Midwest City, Oklahoma 73130; telephone number: 405-737-3037.

The purpose of this organization is to investigate and research FORTEAN events and PanUFOlogy. The latter term is used to denote the entire spectrum of UFO experiences, based on the concept that every UFO is a reality whether that reality is imaginary in a sick or deluded mind, or whether it leaves PHYSICAL EVIDENCE of its reality.

This nonprofit organization was founded in 1977 by Larry H. Stephens. There are about sixty members. The group participates in the collection of information through newspaper clippings, library sources and exchange with other groups and individuals, creative theoretical thinking sessions, and lectures. The group's publication, *The PanUFOlogy Twelves,* explores the idea of panUFOlogy and the practical, philosophical and theoretical aspects of UFOLOGY.

**RANDLES, JENNIFER "JENNY" CHRISTINE** (b. October 30, 1951, Bacup, England; address: 23 Sunningdale Drive, Irlam, Greater Manchester M30 6NJ, England), journalist and full-time UFOLOGIST.

Randles holds that the small percentage of UFOs which are not misidentified known phenomena may be phenomena of a psychological/psychic nature which achieve transient physical reality in the presence of sensitive witnesses. She also considers the possibility that UFOs are transdimensional objects.

Randles received Advanced Level General Certificates of Education in Chemistry, Mathematics and Physics. She did Post Advanced Level studies in Geography and Geology, and received City and Guilds Certificates with distinctions in Audio-Visual Technology and Education.

During 1972, Randles was employed as an office worker in an insurance company. From 1972 to 1974, she was a teacher at a Cheshire Middle School. From 1977 to 1978, she worked as an Audio-Visual Technician in a college of education, servicing teachers. From 1975 to 1977, she served as Research Coordinator on the council of the BRITISH UFO RESEARCH ASSOCIATION (BUFORA). Since 1978 she has worked as a full-time UFOlogist. She is Secretary of the NORTHERN UFO NETWORK (NUFON) and the UFO INVESTIGATORS' NETWORK (UFOIN). She is involved in procuring reports on high strangeness cases in the United Kingdom and subediting, as well as administrative and secretarial activities, for the FLYING SAUCER REVIEW (FSR). As a freelance journalist, she also works for radio and television.

Randles is coauthor, with Peter Warrington, of *UFOs: A British Viewpoint* (London: Robert Hale, 1979).

**RAPPORTNYTT,** publication of NORSK UFO CENTER.

**RB-47** *see* **SOUTH CENTRAL UNITED STATES**

**REAL, LUIZ DO ROSÁRIO** (b. August 26, 1923, Herval-Sul, Brazil; address: Rua Marcilio Dias 1566, 96.100 Pelotas, Rio Grande do Sul, Brazil; telephone number: 0532-228514), Founder and President of the SOCIEDADE PELOTENSE DE INVESTIGACAO E PESQUISA DE DISCOS VOADORES (SPIPDV).

Real believes that UFOs are spacecraft piloted by highly-evolved beings from PLANETS in our own solar system and other solar systems of our galaxy. In 1938, he and three other witnesses observed a metallic, disk-shaped object, about sixty-five feet in diameter, hovering in a clear sky at an altitude of about 3,300 feet. After about two minutes, the UFO rose upward until it disappeared from view. Real has no doubt that what he observed was an extraterrestrial spacecraft.

Real served in the Brazilian Expeditionary Forces, and worked for twenty-five years as a civil servant in the Ministry of Agriculture. He began researching UFOs in 1954, and founded SPIPDV in 1972. He has been a UFO columnist for the Brazilian newspaper, *Diario Popular*, since 1969.

Real is a member of the Associacao dos Ex-Combatentes da FEB, the Associacao dos Servidores Civis do Estado and the Clube Brilhante. He received military medals for his service in the Brazilian Expeditionary Forces during World War II.

**RÉALITÉ OU FICTION,** publication of the GROUPE PRIVÉ UFOLOGIQUE NANCÉIEN (GPUN).

**RED BLUFF, CALIFORNIA,** location of a UFO sighting lasting two hours and fifteen minutes during a six-day concentration of sightings in northern California between August 13 and 18, 1960, which included at least fourteen police officers among the numerous witnesses.

Ten minutes before midnight on August 13, State Highway Patrolmen Charles A. Carson and Stanley Scott were searching for a speeding motorcyclist when they saw an enormous craft dropping out of the cloudless night sky. They stopped abruptly and leaped from the patrol car to get a better view of what they were sure was going to be an airplane crash. The silent object was 100-to-200 feet off the ground when suddenly it reversed its direction at high speed and gained an altitude of approximately 500 feet. There, it stopped. By now, the object was clearly visible to both men. It was shaped somewhat like a football, about 150 feet long and forty feet high, and was surrounded by a white glow. Red lights glowed from each end and at times about five white lights became visible between them. As the two officers watched, the UFO performed fantastic aerial maneuvers, sometimes remaining motionless, sometimes changing or reversing direction while moving at incredibly high speeds. The patrolmen radioed the Tehama County Sheriff's Office, requesting that the local RADAR base be contacted. Radar operators confirmed that an unknown target was visible on their radar screens at the same location as the UFO. Each time Scott and Carson attempted to approach the object, it retreated. When it came toward the patrol car, there was radio interference. The object was sweeping the ground and sky with a beam of red light. When Scott turned the red light on the patrol car toward the UFO, it immediately moved away. Eventually, it began moving slowly in an easterly direction and the patrolmen followed at a respectful distance. As they reached the Vina Plains Fire Station, they saw a similar object approaching from the south. It moved near the first UFO and both stopped, remaining in that position for some time, occasionally emitting the beam of red light. Finally, both objects disappeared below the eastern horizon.

The UFO was also seen clearly by two deputy sheriffs, the night jailer and several prisoners who had been marched out onto the roof of the jail to witness the event.

UNITED STATES AIR FORCE (USAF) investigators attributed the sightings to a number of STARS and PLANETS refracted by multiple TEMPERATURE INVERSIONS. However, none of the heavenly bodies cited would have set in the east, where the UFOs disappeared. Furthermore, the astronomical explanation did not account for the beam of red light, the radio interference associated with the close approach of the object and the radar confirmation.

Bibliography: Sachs, Margaret, and Ernest Jahn, *Celestial Passengers—UFOs and Space Travel* (New York: Penguin Books, 1977).

**REES, DAVID LESLIE** (b. May 18, 1954, Sale, England; address: 92 Hillcrest Road, Offerton, Stockport, Cheshire SK2 5SE, England; telephone number: 061-483-4210), Cofounder and Secretary of the MANCHESTER AERIAL PHENOMENA INVESTIGATION TEAM (MAPIT).

Interested in UFOs since the age of eleven, Rees says he has no idea what the identity of UFOs might be. He cofounded MAPIT in 1973 and has been its Secretary and Editor of its bimonthly magazine, *Skywatch*, since that time. His articles have been published in various magazines. In addition, he writes a regular news column for NORTHERN UFO NEWS (NUFON) and is an overseas correspondent and English Director for the UFO BUREAU of Georgia in the United States.

David Rees.

**REICH, WILHELM (1897–1957),** Austrian doctor, psychoanalyst, sexologist and writer. Although he was one of Sigmund Freud's favored pupils, the latter refused to analyze him in 1927. After becoming a communist, Reich tried to reconcile Marxism and Freudianism, but finally broke with both. He moved to Scandinavia where, in 1939, he "discovered" what he believed to be the "universal life force." This energy, which he named "ORGONE ENERGY" and which he claimed glowed with a bluish light, was the ordinary electric potential possessed by bodies. Reich went to the United States to set up an institute and it was at this stage in his life that, according to biographers, he became seriously insane and developed persecutory symptoms.

On May 12, 1954, Reich reportedly observed two flying saucers above his laboratory at Rangeley, Maine. Believing that their illumination might derive from an encompassing field of orgone energy, he fired on the UFOs with his "cloudbuster," a device he had invented for liquidating CLOUDS. Reportedly, the UFO began to fade away. Reich's conviction that the UFOs were extraterrestrial spacecraft set him on the path to investigating the means by which orgone energy might be used for an earthborn space program.

Reich also believed that orgone energy had healing powers. When he attempted to market his "orgone accumulater," the Food and Drug Administration (FDA) had him arrested. He refused to go to court and was put in prison, where he died of a long-standing heart condition.

A cloudbuster. *(Courtesy ICUFON/Jerome Eden)*

His writings and teachings are promoted by CONTACTEE TREVOR JAMES CONSTABLE and writer JEROME EDEN.

**REMOTELY PILOTED VEHICLE (RPV)** *see* **SECRET WEAPON HYPOTHESIS**

**REPEATER,** term used to describe a person who claims to see UFOs frequently. Although reports by repeaters are often regarded with skepticism by investigators, there are several reasons why an individual may be the witness to more than one bona fide UFO sighting. Some persons, because of a natural interest in the heavens, or a tendency to always look upward instead of downward, or having an occupation which involves observing the skies, spend more time watching the sky than the average person and therefore have a greater chance of observing unusual aerial objects. Other repeaters may merely reside in or habituate an area where unusual aerial phenomena manifest themselves frequently.

**RES BUREAUX,** Box 1598, Kingston, Ontario, Canada K7L 5C8; telephone number: 613-542-7277.

The Res Bureaux was established for the investigation of FORTEAN matters. Its sole proprietor, a Canadian researcher whose legal name is X, thinks that UFOs have not been adequately explained either by scientists or by UFOLOGISTS. He believes that while the majority of UFOs can be explained as misidentified objects, HOAXES and natural phenomena, there are some which fit none of these categories. X spent four years searching for Canada's equivalent to the PROJECT BLUE BOOK files. Known as the Project Second Story files, their existence was denied by government officials. After X had located them, they were made available in 1978. However, as in the case of the Project Blue Book files, much pertinent information had been deleted.

X founded the Res Bureaux in 1974. It is not a membership organization. Information is collected from newspapers, libraries and correspondents located in Canada, the United States and thirteen other countries. Two publications are available through the Res Bureaux: a newsletter, RES BUREAUX BULLETIN, and a review, CHAOS: THE REVIEW OF THE DAMNED. Both publications are edited by X.

**RES BUREAUX BULLETIN,** publication of RES BUREAUX.

**RESEARCH BALLOONS** *see* **BALLOONS**

**RICHARDSON, ROBERT C.,** retired United States Air Force Brigadier General who serves on the

Board of Governors of the NATIONAL INVESTIGATIONS COMMITTEE ON AERIAL PHENOMENA (NICAP). Richardson states, "While I hold no great belief in the possibility that there is, or ever has been, any extraterrestrial origin associated with the so-called UFO sightings and reports, I am very much interested in early identification of new scientific facts or technologies, whether initiated by us or by others."

**RIGAU, NOEL,** *see* **CENTRO DE ESTUDIO OBJETOS VOLADORES NO IDENTIFICADOS (CEOVNI)**

**RIGBERG, JAMES S.,** *see* **FLYING SAUCER BOOKSTORE**

**RIVERS, L. MENDEL,** *see* **HOUSE ARMED SERVICES COMMITTEE HEARINGS**

**ROBERT LOFTIN MEMORIAL AWARD,** UFOLOGIST-of-the-year award given out by the NATIONAL UFO CONFERENCE (NUFOC) and named after the late Robert Loftin, UFO author and a founding member of NUFOC. Recipients include JOHN KEEL (1967), John J. Robinson (1969), Allen Manak (1970), GRAY BARKER (1971), Allen Greenfield (1972), JAMES MOSELEY (1973), Yonah Ibn Aharon (1974), Rick Hilberg (1976), Robert Easley (1977) and Charles Wilhelm (1978). The award is not given annually, and hence there were no recipients in 1968, 1975 and 1979.

**ROBERTSON PANEL,** group of eminent scientists convened by the CENTRAL INTELLIGENCE AGENCY (CIA) in 1953 to study UFO reports and to determine whether these phenomena constituted any threat to the security of the United States.

The panel was chaired by mathematician and physicist H. P. Robertson, who was Director of the Weapons System Evaluation Group in the Office of the Secretary of Defense and a CIA classified employee. The other members were physicist and Nobel Prize-winner Luis W. Alvarez; geophysicist and radar specialist Lloyd V. Berkner, who was one of the directors of the Brookhaven National Laboratories; physicist Samuel Goudsmit, who was on the staff of Brookhaven National Laboratories; and astronomer and astrophysicist THORNTON PAGE, who was Deputy Director of the Johns Hopkins Operations Research Office. In addition to the five panel members, other participants included astronomer J. ALLEN HYNEK, who was a consultant to the UNITED STATES AIR FORCE (USAF); army ordnance test station director Frederick C. Durant, who served as reporter for the panel; and Commanding General of the AIR TECHNICAL INTELLIGENCE CENTER (ATIC), William

M. Garland. The three CIA representatives present were Assistant Director of the Office of Scientific Intelligence (OSI) H. Marshall Chadwell, Deputy Assistant Director of the OSI Ralph L. Clark, and CIA agent Philip G. Strong. Also present were Air Force officers EDWARD RUPPELT and DEWEY FOURNET, and Navy Photo Interpretation Laboratory representatives R. S. Neasham and Harry Woo.

There has been some confusion about the dates on which the panel convened. Several sources report that it opened on January 12. The group's final report, dated January 16, gives the opening and closing dates as January 14 and 18. Over a period of twelve hours during the first three days, the panel examined selected cases from PROJECT BLUE BOOK files and saw the TREMONTON, UTAH, and GREAT FALLS, MONTANA, movies. On the fourth day, it discussed tentative conclusions and recommendations, and commissioned Robertson to draft the final report. On the final day, the panel members corrected and altered the draft.

The panel concluded that there was no evidence of a direct physical threat to national security and that the "continued emphasis on the reporting of these phenomena, in these parlous times, result in a threat to the orderly functioning of the protective organs of the body politic." They therefore recommended: "a. That the national security agencies take immediate steps to strip the Unidentified Flying Objects of the special status they have been given and the aura of mystery they have unfortunately acquired,"; and "b. That the national security agencies institute policies on intelligence, training and public education designed to prepare the material defenses and the morale of the country to recognize most promptly and to react most effectively to true indications of hostile intent or action." To accomplish these ends, the panel proposed a public education program to train people to identify correctly-known objects, as well as a DEBUNKING effort to lower public interest. The members were, they said, impressed by the lack of sound data in the majority of case histories, as well as by the "lack of speedy follow-up due primarily to the modest size and limited facilities of the ATIC section concerned." In sum, they suggested that the Air Force investigative project be continued at its present level, only with a change in emphasis from attempting to determine the nature of UFOs to convincing the public that nothing unusual was occurring in the skies.

Hynek, who was not officially a member of the panel, was not asked to sign the final report. He later stated that he would not have done so in any case. He considered it unreasonable that the panel could come to a conclusion about UFOs in four days, when he himself had spent more than four years in the field.

Not until five years later, on April 9, 1958, did the Air

Force make public a sanitized version of the panel's report. More than sixteen years passed before the CIA finally declassified the report and made copies available in December 1974.

Bibliography: Flammonde, Paris, *UFO Exist!* (New York: G. P. Putnam's Sons, 1976); Jacobs, David Michael, *The UFO Controversy in America* (Bloomington, Indiana: Indiana University Press, 1975).

## ROBIOU, SEBASTIAN, *see* CENTRO DE ESTUDIO OBJETOS VOLADORES NO IDENTIFICADOS (CEOVNI)

## ROBOZERO, SOVIET UNION, location of one of Russia's most famous UFO sightings. On August 15, 1666, shortly before midday, worshippers at the church in the village of Robozero heard a loud crashing sound in the sky. The members of the congregation rushed outside. There they saw a ball of fire descending from the clear, sunny sky. It was about 130 feet in diameter. Two fiery beams, also about 130 feet in length, projected from the front of the object. Passing over the church, the UFO disappeared over the lake and moved off in a southwesterly direction. After it had traveled almost one-third of a mile, it vanished again. However, it soon reappeared, this time traveling westward. It remained visible over Robozero for about an hour-and-a-half. Fishermen on the lake about a mile away were badly burned by the HEAT of the UFO. The lake itself, which was illuminated to a depth of thirty feet, seemed to be covered with rust under the glow. The fish in the lake fled to the banks.

Although it has been hypothesized that the huge fiery object over Robozero was a meteorite or ball lightning, UFOLOGISTS have pointed out several reasons why these explanations are inapplicable. One of their primary arguments is that the slow speed and long duration of the phenomenon are inconsistent with the known characteristics of meteorites and ball lightning. The fact that the object was sighted only by the inhabitants of Robozero makes it unlikely that it was a COMET, since a comet would have been visible over a far greater area.

Bibliography: Hobana, Ion, and Julien Weverbergh, *UFOs from Behind the Iron Curtain* (New York: Bantam Books, 1972).

## ROERICH, NIKOLAY, Russian artist and archeologist who observed a UFO at about 9:30 A.M. on August 5, 1927. During an expedition through the wilds of Mongolia, Roerich and six other members of his party saw a large oval object moving from north to south. As it crossed their camp, it changed direction from south to southwest. Before it disappeared from view, the surprised men had time to look through their binoculars. They were able to discern a distinct oval object with a shiny surface which reflected the sun on one side. Roerich's travel diary describes the event as "something remarkable!"

Bibliography: Roerich, Nikolay, *Altai-Himalya: A Travel Diary* (New York: Frederick A. Stokes Company, 1929).

## ROGERS PARK, ILLINOIS, location of a UFO photographed by Walter McCann in 1897 during the AIRSHIP WAVE. Reportedly, numerous other witnesses saw an airship in the vicinity. The *Chicago Times-Herald* printed a pen-and-ink etching of the PHOTOGRAPH, accompanied by an analysis stating that chemical tests revealed the print had not been tampered with. The *New York Herald* also endorsed the photograph's authenticity. Nevertheless, on the same day the *Chicago Tribune* declared the photograph a fake, pointing out that it was perspectively impossible to have included such a wide field within the scope of the lens. Moreover, the picture showed a man taking a photograph of the airship. The newspaper queried the fact that the photographer seemed to have captured himself and his camera in the photograph. However, the possibility remains that another photographer was at the scene. Reportedly, two photographs had been taken and the one published by the *Chicago Times-Herald* did not show the photographer.

Bibliography: Jacobs, David Michael, *The UFO Controversy in America* (Bloomington, Indiana: Indiana University Press, 1975).

## ROMAN, BONITA (b. November 7, 1939, Aurora, Indiana; address: 4256 Springboro Road, Lebanon, Ohio 45036; telephone number: 513-932-6515), Founder and Director of the UFO INFORMATION CENTER (UFOIC).

Roman claims to have had a number of psychic experiences since her early childhood and to have sighted UFOs on many occasions since 1962.

Roman received a diploma from the North American Institute of Police Science, and diplomas from the American Police Academy in Private Security and Private Investigation. She is a member of the American Police Reserves Association.

Roman has been investigating and researching UFOs since 1962. She is a past member of the NATIONAL INVESTIGATIONS COMMITTEE ON AERIAL PHENOMENA (NICAP), the AERIAL PHENOMENA RESEARCH ORGANIZATION (APRO) and the MUTUAL UFO NETWORK (MUFON). She was formerly the publisher and editor of FLYING SAUCER BULLETIN, which pioneered the promotion of UFO detection instruments, and THE OHIO

UFO REPORTER, which specialized in local investigative reporting, as well as providing national and international news. Both publications are now defunct. She founded UFOIC in 1968. She discontinued the group in 1975, but re-established it in 1977.

## ROME, ITALY,

location of a UFO sighting involving thousands of witnesses on September 17, 1954. The object appeared over the city at about 6:30 P.M. and was tracked on RADAR as it performed complicated maneuvers, stopping abruptly then achieving speeds up to 175 miles per hour almost instantaneously. A little over an hour later, the UFO ascended and disappeared toward the northwest. The incident was publicized in newspapers all over Europe during the following days.

The following month, on October 28, another UFO was seen over Rome by dozens of witnesses, including United States Ambassador CLARE BOOTH LUCE.

Bibliography: Vallee, Jacques and Janine, *Challenge to Science—The UFO Enigma* (Chicago: Henry Regnery Company, 1966).

## ROSEN, ARTHUR F., *see* the MARYLAND CENTER FOR INVESTIGATION OF UNCONVENTIONAL PHENOMENA (MARCEN)

## ROSICRUCIANS *see* SECRET SOCIETIES

## ROUEN, FRANCE,

location at which a French military pilot photographed a UFO in 1954. The picture closely resembles the famous UFO photographs taken at MCMINNVILLE, OREGON, four years previously. In July, 1957, the French photograph was published by *RAF Flying Review,* which described it as "one of the few [photographs] which seem authentic."

UFO photographed by French military pilot over Rouen, France, in 1954. *(Courtesy Ground Saucer Watch)*

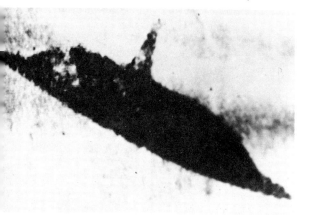

## ROUND ROBIN,

former name of the JOURNAL OF BORDERLAND RESEARCH, newsletter of the BORDERLAND SCIENCES RESEARCH FOUNDATION.

## ROUSH, J. EDWARD,

former U.S. Congressman who, in 1968, chaired the HOUSE SCIENCE AND ASTRONAUTICS COMMITTEE HEARINGS on UFOs. He is a member of the Board of Governors of the NATIONAL INVESTIGATIONS COMMITTEE ON AERIAL PHENOMENA (NICAP).

## RPV,

acronym for REMOTELY PILOTED VEHICLE.

## RUECKERT, CARLA L.

(b. July 16, 1943, Lake Forest, Illinois; address: P.O. Box 5195, Louisville, Kentucky 40205), CONTACTEE.

Rueckert is a partner of L/L RESEARCH and has experimented in contacting extraterrestrial entities since 1962.

Rueckert received her B.A. in English Literature, and her M.A. in Library Service. She was employed as a teacher and a librarian until 1970, when she became a researcher and writer for L/L Research.

Rueckert is coauthor, with DONALD ELKINS, of *Secrets of the UFO* (Louisville, Kentucky: L/L Company, 1977).

## RUHL, RICHARD HANS

(b. February 26, 1931, Brooklyn, New York; address: 649 Central Avenue, Massapequa, Long Island, N.Y. 11758; telephone number: 516-798-1930), commercial artist and field investigator for the AERIAL PHENOMENA RESEARCH ORGANIZATION (APRO).

Ruhl has sighted UFOs on four occasions. In 1966, he and his wife observed a brilliant, chromelike ellipsoid object which remained in view for several hours and was apparently in geosynchronous orbit. In 1972, 1974 and 1977, he observed a number of NOCTURNAL LIGHTS, some of which maneuvered erratically.

Ruhl thinks it likely that some UFOs represent sophisticated weaponry, possibly of Soviet origin. He also considers it possible that UFOs are physical manifestations of some godly or satanic force which presages the end of the world. He believes that in order to deal with the subject scientifically, all explanations should be examined with an open mind, however ridiculous some theories might seem.

Ruhl graduated from the High School of Industrial Art (now the High School of Art and Design) in New York in 1950, majoring in Magazine Illustration. From 1953 to 1957, he attended Evening Art School at the Pratt Institute in Brooklyn, New York, where he majored in Advertising Art and Design. He studied Photo

Retouching for one year at Hunter College and also attended the School of Visual Arts in New York.

From 1950 to 1968, Ruhl worked as a commercial artist for several art studios, advertising agencies and a magazine publisher. Since 1968, he has worked as a freelance photo retouching specialist for advertising agencies and studios. In 1979, he founded and became President of Galaxy Four Productions, a company which produces video-taped educational materials.

Ruhl has won several awards for photography and was the recipient of the CLIO Award for Retouching in Media Promotion/Entertainment for WNEW Radio, New York.

Ruhl has served as a consultant and panelist on numerous radio programs dealing with UFOs. He lectures at libraries and colleges on Long Island. He is a consultant to OMNI Magazine's UFO UPDATE column and has written several magazine articles.

**RUH VE MADDE,** publication of the SPACE PHE-NOMENA RESEARCH GROUP.

**RUMANIA.** Flying saucers are referred to as "farfurii zburatoare" in Rumania. A UFO organization was established in 1971. It consists of scientists, university professors, engineers and students and publishes a newsletter. Both the AERIAL PHENOMENA RESEARCH ORGANIZATION (APRO) and the MUTUAL UFO NET-WORK (MUFON) have representatives there.

One of the best-known cases in Rumania involved technician Emil Barnea, who photographed an alleged UFO at CLUJ in 1968.

**RUPPELT, EDWARD J.,** UNITED STATES AIR FORCE (USAF) Captain who was placed in charge of PROJECT GRUDGE in 1951. When the program was upgraded to PROJECT BLUE BOOK, he was retained as project director until 1953. He was responsible for reorganizing the program and for improving the Air Force's investigative procedures.

In 1956, Ruppelt authored *The Report on Unidentified Flying Objects* (Garden City, N.Y.: Doubleday and Company). In 1959, he revised the book and added three chapters in which he reversed his previously open-minded approach and stated that UFOs were definitely not extraterrestrial spaceships. Some UFOLOGISTS believe this action was the result of pressure from official quarters. Others believe it was the result of a reaction to the wild claims of CONTACTEES.

Ruppelt died in 1960 of a heart attack.

**RUSSIA** *see* **SOVIET UNION**

**RV,** acronym for *radar/visual* and used in connection with UFO sightings which are confirmed both visually and by RADAR.

**SAF-OI** *see* **SECRETARY OF THE AIR FORCE, OFFICE OF INFORMATION**

**SAGAN, CARL** (b. November 9, 1934, New York, N.Y.), astrophysicist.

Although Sagan rejects the evidence supplied by author ERICH VON DÄNIKEN to support the ANCIENT ASTRONAUTS hypothesis, he accepts the possibility that we may have been visited by extraterrestrials in the distant past or that we might be visited in the distant future. He thinks it very unlikely that UFOs represent extraterrestrial travelers and believes that interest in the subject may be at least partly due to unfulfilled religious needs. He rejects the EXTRATERRESTRIAL HYPOTHESIS (ETH) as an explanation for contemporary UFO reports, primarily on mathematical grounds. Based on an estimate of the number of PLANETS worth visiting and the number of extant technical civilizations at least as advanced as ours, he calculates that each civilization would have to make 10,000 launches per year in order for Earth to be visited just once a year. Sagan contends that the most feasible way to resolve the question of extraterrestrial intelligence is through the utilization of radio astronomy to search space for intelligent radio communications, a field in which he has been highly active.

Sagan received his B.A. and B.S., an M.S. in Physics and his Ph.D. in Astronomy and Astrophysics, all from the University of Chicago, in 1954, 1955, 1956 and 1960, respectively.

Sagan was a Miller research fellow in astronomy at the University of California, Berkeley, from 1960 to 1962; a lecturer and later Assistant Professor of Astronomy at Harvard University from 1962 to 1968; an astrophysicist at the Astrophysical Observatory of the Smithsonian Institution in Cambridge, Massachusetts, from 1962 to 1968; an Associate Professor at Cornell University from 1968 to 1970; and Professor of Astronomy and Space Sciences, beginning in 1970. He is currently David Duncan Professor of Astronomy and Space Sciences, Director of the Laboratory for Planetary Studies and Associate Director of the Center for Radiophysics and Space Research.

Sagan's additional professional activities have included positions as Visiting Assistant Professor of Genetics at Stanford University Medical School from 1962 to 1963; Condon Lecturer at the University of Oregon and Oregon State University from 1967 to 1968; Vanuxem Lecturer at Princeton University in 1973; Jacob Bronowsky Lecturer at the University of Toronto in 1975; Anson Clark Memorial Lecturer at the University of Texas at Dallas in 1976; and Christmas Lecturer at the Royal Institution, London, in 1977.

Sagan was a member of the Committee to Review PROJECT BLUE BOOK. He has worked as an Experimenter on the Mariner Mission to VENUS, the Mariner and Viking Missions to MARS and the Mariner Mission to Jupiter and Saturn. He is a lecturer and consultant to the Astronaut Training Program of the NATIONAL AERONAUTICS AND SPACE ADMINISTRATION (NASA) and a consultant to the NATIONAL ACADEMY OF SCIENCES (NAS).

Sagan is a member of the International Astronomical Union (member of the organizing committee of the Commission on the Physical Study of Planets), the International Council of Scientific Unions (member of the executive council of the committee on space research and cochairman of the working group on MOON and planets), the American Astronomical Society, the American Physical Society, the American Geophysical Union, the Astronomical Society of the Pacific, the Genetics Society of America, the Society for the Study of Evolution and Sigma Xi. He is a Fellow of the AMERICAN ASSOCIATION FOR THE ADVANCEMENT OF SCIENCE (AAAS), the American Astronautical Society and the British Interplanetary Society, and Associate Fellow of the American Institute of Aeronautics and Astronautics.

Sagan was the recipient of a National Science Foundation post-doctoral fellowship in 1960; an Alfred P. Sloan Foundation research fellowship at Harvard University from 1963 to 1967; the Smith Prize from Harvard University in 1964; the Apollo Achievement Award from NASA in 1970; a Medal for Exceptional Scientific Achievement in 1972; the Prix Galabert (International Astronautics Prize) in 1973; the Klumpke-Roberts Prize from the Astronomical Society of the Pacific in 1974; the John W. Campbell, Jr., Memorial Award in 1974; the Golden Plate Award from the American Academy of Achievement in 1975; the Joseph Priestley Award from Dickinson College in 1975; a D.Sc. from Rensselaer Polytechnic University in 1975, from Denison University in 1976, and Clarkson College in 1977; and a D.H.L. from Skidmore College in 1976.

Sagan is author of radio and television scripts and a regular contributor to numerous scientific journals, newspapers and popular magazines. He has also been a contributor to numerous books and encyclopedias. He is author of *Planetary Exploration: The Condon Lectures* (Eugene, Oregon: University of Oregon Press, 1970); *The Cosmic Connection: An Extraterrestrial Perspective* (Garden City, N.Y.: Doubleday and Company, 1973); *Other Worlds* (New York: Bantam Books, 1975); *The Dragons of Eden: A Speculative Essay on the Origin of Human Intelligence* (New York: Random House, 1977); *The Murmurs of Earth* (New York: Random House, 1977); *The Backbone of Night: An Introduction to the Natural Sciences* (W.H. Freeman, 1978); *Viking and Mars* (New York: Random House, 1978); and *Broca's Brain* (New York: Random House, 1979). Sagan coauthored, with W. W. Kellogg, *The Atmosphere of Mars and Venus* (National Academy of Sciences, 1961); with I. S. Shklovskii, *Intelligent Life in the Universe* (San Francisco: Holden-Day, 1963); with Jonathan Leonard, *Planets* (New York: Time-Life, 1966); with R. Littauer and others, *The Air War in Indochina* (Ithaca, N.Y.: Center for International Studies, Cornell University, 1971); with Ray Bradbury, Arthur C. Clarke, Bruce Murray and Walter Sullivan, *Mars and the Mind of Man* (New York: Harper and Row, 1973); and, with R. Berendzen, A. Montagu, P. Morrison, K. Stendhal, and G. Wald, *Life Beyond Earth and the Mind of Man* (Washington, D.C.: U.S. Government Printing Office, 1973). Sagan was Editor of the following books: with T. Owen and H. J. Smith, *Planetary Atmospheres* (D. Reidel, 1971); with K. Y. Kondratyev and M. Rycroft,

*Space Research XI*, two volumes (Akademie Verlag, 1971); with Thornton Page, *UFOs: A Scientific Debate* (Ithaca, N.Y.: Cornell University Press, 1972); and *Communication with Extraterrestrial Intelligence* (Cambridge, Massachusetts: M.I.T. Press, 1973).

**SAGA'S UFO REPORT** *see* **UFO REPORT**

**SAIGON, VIETNAM,** location of a UFO sighting by a member of the U.S. 524th Military Intelligence Detachment at about 2:20 A.M. on April 17, 1967. The witness's report stated: "... I observed five large, illuminated oval-shaped objects, traveling in close formation and at a very high rate of speed across the sky. At that time, I was on the roof of the Saigon Field Office of the 524th MI Detachment. . . . I first saw these objects near the horizon to my left and watched them cover the entire field of my vision in what I believe to be less than five seconds. During that period of time, the objects traveled from where I first saw them, near the horizon to my left, passed almost directly over me at what seemed to be a very great height, and then moved out of sight behind a CLOUD formation at the horizon to my right. The sky was partly cloudy but, at the time of the sighting, the area of the sky over which they traveled was very clear, with the exception of a few small patches of scattered clouds, which they seemed to be above. As the objects passed over these clouds, they were obscured from my vision until they emerged on the other side. I also observed that, as they passed between my line of sight and a star, they covered the STAR and blocked out its light until they had passed. This indicated to me that the objects were not transparent. It was apparent that they were not any form of conventional aircraft due to their size, shape, rate of speed and the fact that they made no noise audible to me. Prior to the sighting of these objects, I had been observing various conventional aircraft, both propeller- and jet-powered, and there is no question in my mind that they were a great deal larger than any craft I have ever seen in the sky. They were also traveling at a rate of speed which I would estimate to be at least five times greater than any jet-powered aircraft I have ever seen. They were too distant and traveling too fast for a detailed description to be possible. I was only able to see that they were definitely oval in shape and glowed a steady white. They seemed to be in a vertical attitude, rather than horizontal, in relation to the Earth, and their formation slowly fluctuated as they passed. Approximately five minutes after they passed out of sight, several jet-powered aircraft, which seemed to be at high altitude and traveling very fast, came from my far right and to my back as I faced the same direction as when I had seen the ovals. They proceeded to the area where I had lost sight of the objects and, upon reaching that point, they turned to their right and pursued the same course as the objects I had previously sighted. These aircraft were not in a formed pattern, but were scattered. I have never held any opinion concerning unidentified flying objects. Neither have I ever seen any, previously. However, I believe that these objects were space craft of some kind. I am convinced that they were not reflections, conventional aircraft, meteorites or PLANETS."

The report was forwarded to PROJECT BLUE BOOK, but no evaluation was made.

**SAINT ELMO'S FIRE,** flamelike electrical discharge that appears during stormy weather on the tips of pointed objects such as ship's masts, steeples, trees, mountain peaks, and the propellers and wings of aircraft. It is usually accompanied by a crackling or fizzling noise. Saint Elmo's fire is a corruption of Sant' Ermo, the Italian name for Saint Erasmus, patron saint of the Mediterranean. Sailors aboard old sailing ships believed the fiery lights on their masts signified the presence of the saint.

Some UFOLOGISTS have cited Saint Elmo's fire as the explanation for the famous FOO FIGHTERS of World War II. Other UFOs have also been attributed to a similar phenomenon occurring on the pointed surfaces of INSECTS flying in large swarms. PLASMA occurring as a corona discharge on power lines, another effect similar to Saint Elmo's fire, has also been cited as a cause for UFO reports.

Woodcut showing Saint Elmo's fire on a ship's mast. *(The Bettmann Archive)*

**ST. GEORGE, MINNESOTA,** location of a UFO sighting on October 21, 1965. Arthur Strauch, Deputy Sheriff of Sibley County, Minnesota, was driving home from a hunting trip in the company of his wife, Katherine, their son Gary, aged sixteen, and Donald and Ann Crewe of Gaylord, Minnesota. At about 6:10 P.M., they saw a stationary light in the sky to the northwest. They stopped the car to get a better look.

Strauch looked at the object through his binoculars. It was a large disk with a silvery-gray dome, about fifty feet in diameter and five feet high. Near the top of the dome were four small windows which emitted a yellow light. The area below the windows glowed with a bluish light. The outer ring between the blue light and the rim was rotating counterclockwise, casting off a halo of light that changed from orange to white with an overall tinge of blue and green. The rim itself was bright orange and did not rotate. An indentation was visible on one side of the UFO.

Using a Kodak Instamatic 804 with Ektachrome-X color film, Strauch took three photographs, then changed the roll of film and took one more photograph.

After the object had been in view for about ten minutes, it suddenly accelerated. With a high-pitched whine, it shot almost directly over the witnesses and disappeared in the distance.

The roll of film containing the first three photographs was accidentally thrown away in the mistaken belief that it was a defective roll of unexposed film. However, the second roll of film produced a photograph of an object with a reddish-orange rim and a white core. Many of the details observed visually by Strauch and his companions were not captured on the photograph. Writer PHILIP J. KLASS has concluded that the photograph shows a PLASMA. An analysis by GROUND SAUCER WATCH (GSW), utilizing computer image enhancement methods, however, revealed that the object in the photograph was a solid, disk-shaped UFO which was at a great distance from the camera. No evidence of any supporting device, such as a wire, could be found.

Bibliography: Klass, Philip J, *UFOs Identified* (New York: Random House, 1968).

**SAINT PAUL** *see* **PAUL, SAINT**

**SALEM, MASSACHUSETTS,** location of a UFO sighting by Coast Guard seaman Shell Alpert on July 16, 1952. Alpert happened to glance through a window and see four brilliant, egg-shaped objects traversing the sky. He grabbed a camera and managed to snap a picture before the UFOs disappeared from view.

Astronomer DONALD MENZEL reported that UNITED STATES AIR FORCE (USAF) experiments reproduced the

UFOs photographed at Salem, Massachusetts, on July 16, 1952. *(Courtesy Donn Davison)*

same effect as that shown in the Salem photograph by photographing floodlights reflected on window glass.

Bibliography: Maney, Charles A., and Richard Hall, *The Challenge of Unidentified Flying Objects* (Washington, D.C.: the authors, 1961); Menzel, Donald H., and Lyle G. Boyd, *The World of Flying Saucers* (Garden City, N.Y.: Doubleday and Company, 1963).

**SALISBURY, FRANK B.** (b. August 3, 1926, Provo, Utah; address: Plant Science Department, Utah State University UMC 48, Logan, Utah 84322), professor of plant physiology and writer.

While a graduate student, Salisbury published an article for *Science* about the possibility of life on MARS. The correspondence generated by the article led to his interest in UFOs. He has lectured on the subject in universities and other institutions in many states, Canada and Europe. Although he admits one cannot prove the small percentage of unexplained UFOs are not extraterrestrial craft, he now strongly doubts that they are.

Frank Salisbury.

Salisbury received his B.S. in Botany, and his M.A. in Botany and Biochemistry from the University of Utah in 1951 and 1952, respectively. He received his Ph.D. in Plant Physiology and Geochemistry from the California Institute of Technology in 1955.

Salisbury served in the United States Army Air Force in 1945. From 1946 until 1949, he was a Church of Jesus Christ of Latter-Day Saints missionary in German-speaking Switzerland. From 1949 to 1950, he was a photographer at the Boyart Studio and, since 1950, has worked part time as a commercial and portrait photographer. He was Assistant Professor of Botany at Pomona College from 1954 to 1955, and Assistant Professor of Plant Physiology at Colorado State University from 1955 to 1961. From 1960 to 1962, he was on the Board of Trustees of the Colorado State University Research Foundation. He was Professor of Plant Physiology and Head of Plant Science at Utah State University from 1966 to 1970. From 1973 to 1974, he was Technical Representative in Plant Physiology to the U.S. Atomic Energy Commission in Germantown, Maryland. He became Professor of Plant Physiology in 1966 and Professor of Botany in 1968 at Utah State University, positions which he holds at the present time.

Salisbury is a Fellow of the AMERICAN ASSOCIATION FOR THE ADVANCEMENT OF SCIENCE (AAAS), and a member of the American Society of Plant Physiologists; the American Institute of Biological Sciences (AIBS); the Botanical Society of America; the Ecological Society of America; the Utah Academy of Arts, Letters, Science; the Western Society of Naturalists; the NATIONAL INVESTIGATIONS COMMITTEE ON AERIAL PHENOMENA (NICAP), and the AERIAL PHENOMENA RESEARCH ORGANIZATION (APRO). He is a former member of the Board of Directors of NICAP and a former consultant to APRO. He served as a consultant to the NATIONAL AERONAUTICS AND SPACE ADMINISTRATION (NASA), and on two NASA-AIBS sponsored committees, one on biological experiments in an orbiting laboratory, and one, as chairman, on possible uses of the Lunar Receiving Laboratory for research on extreme environments. He presently serves on a NASA-AIBS Space Biology Panel to evaluate research proposals.

Salisbury has published over one hundred technical papers and popular articles on a variety of topics, including the subject of unidentified flying objects. He is author of *The Flowering Process* (Oxford: Pergamon Press, 1963); *Truth by Reason and by Revelation* (Salt Lake City: Deseret Book Company, 1965); *The Biology of Flowering* (New York: Natural History Press, 1971); *The Utah UFO Display: A Biologist's Report* (Old Greenwich, Connecticut: Devin Adair Company, 1974); and *The Creation* (Salt Lake City: Deseret Book Company, 1976). He coauthored, with R. V. Parke, *Vascular*

*Plants: Form and Function* (Belmont, California: Wadsworth, 1970); with W. A. Jensen, *Botany: An Ecological Approach* (Belmont, California: Wadsworth, 1972); and, with C. Ross, *Plant Physiology, Second Edition* (Belmont, California: Wadsworth, 1978).

**SALT LAKE CITY, UTAH,** location of a UFO sighting by private pilot Waldo J. Harris, a real estate broker, at noon on October 2, 1961. As he prepared to take off from Utah Central Airport in a Mooney Mark 20A, Harris noticed a bright spot in the sky, which he assumed to be a turning aircraft reflecting in the sun. After he was airborne, he noticed that the light had not moved. He changed his course, proceeding toward the spot for a closer look. He found himself at the UFO's altitude when he was just over 6,000 feet. As he drew nearer, he could see that the object had no wings nor tail nor any other exterior control surfaces protruding from what appeared to be the fuselage. It seemed to be hovering, with a slight rocking motion. As it rocked away from Harris, he could distinguish its disk shape. The object seemed to be about fifty-to-fifty-five feet in diameter and eight-to-ten feet thick at the center. Its surface was like sandblasted aluminum. When Harris was within an estimated two miles of the object, it rose abruptly to about 1,000 feet above him. It then took off to the southeast. It was soon an estimated ten miles or more away. Harris continued his attempt to close in. The object hovered again, with the same rocking motion. Then it began rising and moving westward at high speed. In a few seconds, it passed out of sight.

In the meantime, about eight witnesses on the ground at the airport had been taking turns viewing the UFO through binoculars. As Harris returned to the airport, the ground observers alerted him that they had the object in sight again. He turned and saw it in the distance for about a second or two before it vanished. The ground observers reported that it had shot straight up as it finally left. All the witnesses confirmed that the object had wobbled while hovering. One noted that when Harris's plane was merely a speck in the sky, the disk was clearly visible to the naked eye. Physicist JAMES MCDONALD suggested that this might indicate the object's size to have been substantially larger than Harris's estimated fifty feet.

The official UNITED STATES AIR FORCE (USAF) explanation for the sighting was that the witnesses had misidentified VENUS. However, the object's appearance in front of a mountain ruled out that possibility. The Air Force later accepted the proposal by astronomer DONALD MENZEL that the UFO was a sundog. Although McDonald claimed that the UFO's elevation did not conform to that of a sundog, Menzel claimed that the object was precisely where one would expect to see that

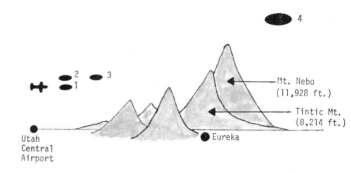

Diagram showing the consecutive positions of the UFO observed at Salt Lake City, Utah, on October 2, 1961.

portion of the PARHELIA, in the area of the lower tangential arc. Although the witnesses reported cloud-free skies and the Weather Bureau logs showed completely clear skies and forty miles visibility, Menzel reports that one witness observed a very slight haze over the mountains, a condition favorable to the manifestation of parhelia. According to McDonald, all witnesses agreed that the object was at first low on the horizon in front of a distant mountain, and that it suddenly took off at high speed in a steep climb. Menzel, on the other hand, states that the ground observers observed no movement whatsoever, but rather saw the object vanish at intervals, only to reappear seconds later in a different place. Menzel conjectures that the pilot thought the object was moving only because he was in a moving plane, changing his position relative to the UFO.

Bibliography: Hall, Richard H. (ed.), *The UFO Evidence* (Washington, D.C.: National Investigations Committee on Aerial Phenomena, 1964); Menzel, Donald H., and Lyle G. Boyd, *The World of Flying Saucers* (Garden City, N.Y.: Doubleday and Company, 1963); U.S. Congress, House, Committee on Science and Astronautics, Symposium on Unidentified Flying Objects, Hearings, 90th Congress, 2nd Session, July 29, 1968 (Washington, D.C.: U.S. Government Printing Office, 1968).

**SAMISDAT,** 206 Carlton Street, Toronto, Ontario, Canada M5A 2L1. This UFO organization and publishing company is a faction of the neo-Nazi Western Guard. Its members promote the NAZI HYPOTHESIS and publish a number of books on the subject.

**SANDERSON, IVAN TERENCE** (b. January 30, 1911, Edinburgh, Scotland; d. February 19, 1973, Knowlton Township, N.J.), zoologist, author, radio and television personality.

Sanderson witnessed UFOs on four occasions. The first sighting occurred during World War II, while he was engaged in counterespionage duties in the Caribbean. While sailing off the coast of Nicaragua, he and his boat's captain saw a bright green-and-blue sphere which approached the observers until it was the apparent size of a plate. It then exploded silently in a blinding flash of light. In 1958, Sanderson and his wife observed a DAYLIGHT DISK (DD) flashing on and off and flipping about over the Delaware Water Gap. In 1965, Sanderson and his assistant saw a solid, flashing bright-red object which split into two pieces, each half moving off in a different direction. Before disappearing in the distance, one of the twin objects performed rapid angular turns, changing to white as it did so. In 1966, Sanderson and four friends watched an oval UFO as it traversed the night sky during a twenty-two-minute period.

Sanderson considered that the possibilities relating to the origin and identity of UFOs are probably infinite. He believed that, "it is at least *possible* that our PLANET has been visited throughout geologic time by life forms, and even intelligent ones," and that there are "four basic possibilities as to the nature of what is landing on our planet: first, life forms indigenous to our solar system; second, controlled constructions made within our solar system, either on other solid bodies or in space; third, living entities not indigenous to our little bit of the universe; and fourth, constructions coming to us from outside that 'bit,' either in space or time." He speculated that some UFOs could be robots while others could be "manned." But, he stated, "if manned, their OCCUPANTS must be either animated machines, artificial 'animals,' or natural living entities." He sug-

Ivan Sanderson. *(Photo by Richard Harpster)*

gested that the creators of UFOs have mastered a procedure such as instant transference (ITF) or TELEPORTATION to achieve interstellar travel. The theory that he particularly favored was that some UFOs could be projections from another SPACE-TIME CONTINUUM. He noted that UFOs "throughout the ages are reported to have appeared in just those forms that were at least partly understandable to those to whom they appeared." Sanderson conjectured, "Might it not be that at least some . . . are so far ahead of our present status that they have completely lost control of themselves and just plain given up *thinking,* just as we appear to have given up *instinct* in favor of thinking when we stumbled on technology? . . . That they are for the most part overcivilized and quite mad is, in my opinion, an open-ended question but quite probable."

Sanderson attended private schools from 1916 to 1923. He attended Eton College from 1924 to 1927. He received M.A.s with Honors in Zoology, Geology and Botany from Cambridge University in 1932. He did postgraduate studies at Cambridge University and the University of London from 1933 to 1934.

As a child, Sanderson traveled extensively with his parents. Between 1924 and 1927, he visited Europe and North Africa biannually, collecting animals. From 1927 to 1929, he traveled around the world alone, collecting animals for the British Museum from Egypt, India, Ceylon, Malaya, the Indonesian Islands, New Guinea, Indochina, China, Japan, Tahiti and the South Pacific, Hawaii and the United States. Between 1929 to 1932, he went on three trips to collect animals in the East Mediterranean area and North Africa. He also engaged in research at Marine Biological Laboratories and at sea off the coast of Devon, England. From 1932 to 1933, he was the leader of the Percy Sladen Expedition to the Cameroon, West Africa, on behalf of the British Museum, the Royal Society of London, Cambridge University, University College in London, and other institutions. Between 1933 and 1935, he was engaged in research at London University and went on a collecting trip to the High Atlas, Morocco. Between 1936 and 1937, he was invited by the Trinidadian government to investigate Human Rabies carried by bats and went on collecting trips to the West Indies and Haiti. In 1938, he was the leader of a scientific expedition to Surinam. In 1939 and 1940, he went on an expedition to Jamaica, the British Honduras and Mexico. He conducted a faunal survey and the preparation of Game Laws for British Honduras and did a botanical survey of the country. In Mexico, he did specialized collecting for the British Museum and the Chicago Natural History Museum. From 1940 to 1941, he worked in Naval Intelligence and, from 1945 to 1947, he worked in the field of Information and Overseas Press Analysis for the British

Government Services in New York. In 1947, Sanderson became a resident of the United States and began his radio and television career. He lectured and wrote about natural sciences. He started importing rare animals and founded a private zoo, which was destroyed by floods in 1955. In 1958, he retired from television and continued his original research, news reporting and writing. In 1959, he made a 60,000-mile trip around the North American continent to examine its Phytogeography and basic biotic ecology. From 1961 to 1965, he was Senior Trade Editor and Special Science Editor of Chilton Books in Philadelphia. In 1965, he founded the SOCIETY FOR THE INVESTIGATION OF THE UNEXPLAINED (SITU) and, during the following two years, worked as a freelance writer and editor. From 1968 to 1970, he was a staff member of *Argosy* magazine and, during this period, continued writing, editing and news reporting. He also established a promotion and public relations organization. He was a Trustee and Administrative Director of SITU until the time of his death in 1973.

Sanderson wrote numerous articles for magazines. He was the author of *Animal Treasure* (New York: Viking Press, 1937); *Animals Nobody Knows* (New York: Viking Press, 1938); *Caribbean Treasure* (New York: Viking Press, 1939); *Living Treasure* (New York: Viking Press, 1940); *Mystery Schooner* (New York: Viking Press, 1941); *Animal Tales* (New York: Alfred A. Knopf, 1948); *How to Know the North American Mammals* (Boston: Little, Brown and Company, 1950); *The Silver Mink* (Boston: Little, Brown and Company, 1952); *John and Juan in the Jungle* (New York: Dodd, Mead and Company, 1953); *Living Mammals of the World* (New York: Hanover House, 1955); *The Status Quo* (New York: Merlin Press, 1956); *Follow the Whale* (Boston: Little, Brown and Company, 1956); *The Monkey Kingdom* (New York: Hanover House, 1957); *Abominable Snowmen* (Radnor, Pennsylvania: Chilton Book Company, 1961); *The Continent We Live On* (New York: Random House, 1961); *The Dynasty of Abu* (New York: Alfred A. Knopf, 1962); *Book of Great Jungles* (New York: Julian Messner, 1965); *This Treasured Land* (New York: G. P. Putnam's Sons, 1966); *Uninvited Visitors: A Biologist Looks at UFOs* (New York: Cowles Education Corporation, 1967); *Things* (New York: Pyramid Publications, 1967); *Abominable Snowmen*, abridged edition (New York: Pyramid Publications, 1968); *More "Things"* (New York: Pyramid Publications, 1969); *Invisible Residents* (New York: World Publishing Company, 1970); and *Investigating the Unexplained* (Englewood Cliffs, N.J.: Prentice-Hall, 1972).

## SAN JOSÉ DE VALDERAS, SPAIN, suburb of

Madrid where a UFO was sighted by MULTIPLE WITNESSES on June 1, 1967. The object appeared at

Flying saucer allegedly photographed at San José de Valderas, Spain, on June 1, 1967. *(Courtesy ICUFON)*

sundown and maneuvered over the area for about twelve minutes, flying so low that it almost grazed the treetops. About forty feet in diameter, it resembled a rounded soup dish inverted over a flat-based pie pan. On the underside was a large insignia resembling the astronomical sign for Uranus—a capital "H" with a vertical line through the center. The object flew off along the Extremadura Highway, where it was seen by numerous other witnesses, who described it as a ball of fire. It landed near a restaurant called La Ponderosa in the suburb of Santa Monica. Witnesses reported that it lowered three landing legs prior to setting down on the ground.

Later examination of the landing site revealed three rectangular indentations which formed an equilateral triangle. At the center of the triangle, the grass was burned and metallic powder was found. Small metal

The San José de Valderas flying saucer tilted to reveal the insignia on its base. *(Courtesy ICUFON)*

rods, about five inches long, were picked up by several people. According to a young boy, when he broke one open with a pair of pliers, liquid poured out and evaporated. Inside the tube were two green strips engraved with the same symbol seen on the underside of the UFO. The tube and the green strips were analyzed by INTA, the Spanish Institute for Space Research. The tube was made of nickel of an extremely high degree of purity. The green strips were identified as polyvinyl fluoride, a type of plastic not yet available commercially. At that time, it was manufactured exclusively by the American firm of Dupont de Nemours for the NATIONAL AERONAUTICS AND SPACE ADMINISTRATION (NASA), who used it as a protective facing for rockets and SATELLITES.

Two sets of photographs were produced by two alleged witnesses to the incident. The first set was supplied by an anonymous telephone caller, who left them at a photographic laboratory to be collected by a Madrid newspaper. The second set was supplied by a man who identified himself over the telephone as Antonio Pardo but who refused to meet with investigators. Neither man was ever located.

The mysterious insignia seen on the San José de Valderas UFO was already familiar to a number of people in Spain prior to June 1, 1967. Since 1965, and earlier according to some reports, several individuals, including professional people and UFO researchers, had been receiving letters from people claiming to be extraterrestrials living on Earth. The crossed-H insignia, which also appeared on these letters, is allegedly the symbol of the government of their home planet UMMO, in the solar system of Wolf 424. The Spanish contacts continue to receive telephone calls and correspondence from the alleged Ummites, most of these communications being scientific and philosophical in nature.

Analysis of the photographs, conducted by GROUND SAUCER WATCH (GSW), revealed that the alleged UFO is a model hanging on a thread. Some researchers consider the UMMO case to be part of a worldwide deception conducted by a group of humans engaged in a conspiracy to bring about social change on Earth through the use of MIND CONTROL.

Bibliography: Ribera, Antonio, "The San José de Valderas Photographs," *Flying Saucer Review* (Maidstone, Kent, England: Flying Saucer Review Publications, September-October, 1969); Vallee, Jacques, *The Invisible College* (New York: E. P. Dutton, 1975).

**SANTA ANA, CALIFORNIA,** location of an alleged UFO sighting by highway traffic engineer Rex Heflin on August 3, 1965. According to the witness, his two-way radio was cut off just before noon as he was driving near the Santa Ana Freeway. Moments later, he saw an unusual craft flying over the road just ahead of him. He stopped his vehicle and snapped three Polaroid pictures of the strange object, which was shaped like a straw hat. He estimated it to be about 30 feet in diameter and approximately 750 feet away, at an altitude of about 150 feet. The UFO moved off into the haze leaving a ring of black smoke, which Heflin also photographed. The highway engineer did not report the sighting but showed his PHOTOGRAPHS to coworkers at the end of the day. Over the following six weeks, numerous copies were made of the photographs and circulated among the community of Santa Ana. Finally, they were brought to the attention of the Santa Ana *Register,* which published them on September 20, 1965. The next day, the story and the photographs were picked up by United Press International. On September 23, a UNITED STATES AIR FORCE (USAF) investigator interviewed Heflin. The latter reported that just the previous day he had handed over the original Polaroid prints to an investigator in civilian clothes from the NORTH AMERICAN AIR DEFENSE COMMAND (NORAD). Heflin had not, however, checked the man's credentials nor obtained a receipt for the pictures. NORAD officials denied that anyone from their organization had contacted Heflin. The original photographs have never been located.

Two years later, during the CONDON COMMITTEE's investigation of the case, Heflin was reportedly visited again by investigators whose identity was suspect. Dressed in Air Force uniforms, the visitors allegedly questioned him about the photographs and asked him if he knew anything about the BERMUDA TRIANGLE. Parked outside Heflin's house was a car with some kind

Object photographed by Rex Heflin at Santa Ana, California, on August 3, 1965. *(Courtesy ICUFON)*

of marking on the front door. A strange violet light glowed inside the vehicle. A figure was seated in the back. Heflin believed the conversation was being recorded, as he could hear popping sounds on his radio, which he had left on during the interview. Although the traffic engineer made a careful note of the visitors' names, civilian UFO investigators were unable to trace them.

Air Force photo analysts concluded that the object in the photograph was actually less than two feet in diameter and only about fifteen-to-twenty feet above the ground. The photographs were labeled a HOAX by PROJECT BLUE BOOK chief HECTOR QUINTANILLA. The Condon Committee, however, reached a different conclusion. Project Coordinator ROBERT LOW, after interviewing Heflin at the scene of the incident, declared the photographs to be among the ". . . top four or five examples of photographic evidence of the existence of UFOs." The case is listed in the CONDON REPORT as unidentified. Finally, computer analysis conducted by GROUND SAUCER WATCH (GSW) established that the picture was a hoax.

Bibliography: Condon, Edward U. (ed.), *Scientific Study of Unidentified Flying Objects* (New York: Bantam Books, 1969).

## SANTANA, WILLIAM, *see* CENTRO DE ESTUDIO OBJETOS VOLADORES NO IDENTIFICADOS

**SAPIENZA, ROBERT** (b. October 2, 1947, Rome, Italy; address: 256 Frenette, Rosemere, Quebec, Canada J7A 2Z2; telephone number: 514-621-1743), Codirector of UFO CANADA.

Although Sapienza has observed UFOs on two occasions, once in the company of several other aviation employees, he ascribes to no particular theory regarding the identity of UFOs.

Sapienza received a high school Honors Diploma in Arts and Sciences, and subsequently attended university for two years. Since 1965, he has been employed by a European commercial airline company, working as an Office Clerk from 1965 to 1969, as a Ticket Agent from 1969 to 1971, as an Operations Agent from 1971 to 1972, and as a Flight Operations Officer since 1972. He has been Codirector of UFO Canada since its inception in 1977. He has written articles on UFOs for various newspapers, magazines and newsletters.

**SARAJEVO, YUGOSLAVIA,** location of a UFO sighting involving hundreds of thousands of witnesses on October 18, 1968. The conical object appeared shortly after 5:00 P.M., traveling from the northwest toward the southeast. The brilliantly luminous UFO was originally bright blue, changing first to a whitish-blue and then to a reddish color. When it reached a point just south of Sarajevo and to the northeast of the town of Mostar, the object changed direction toward the east. It remained in view between one-and-a-half and two hours.

Members of the local Akademski Astronomsko-Astronautiki Klub took several photographs of the object. The organization formed a group to study the incident. Six months later, it issued a report which established that the UFO had been almost sixteen miles above Sarajevo, moving at an average speed of almost twenty miles per hour and guided by stratospheric air streams, rather than by self-propulsion. The group concluded that the object was a stratosphere BALLOON of unknown origin, possibly involved in military reconnaissance.

Bibliography: Hobana, Ion, and Julien Weverbergh, *UFOs from Behind the Iron Curtain* (New York: Bantam Books, 1975).

**SARGASSO SEA,** an elliptical, calm tract in the North Atlantic Ocean within the BERMUDA TRIANGLE. Lying between the parallels twenty degrees and thirty-five degrees north, and thirty degrees and seventy degrees west, it is strewn with free-floating seaweed of the genus *Sargassum.*

Many early navigators were intimidated by the unfounded myths that ships throughout the ages had become entangled in the weed, never to escape. The Sargasso Sea was said to be an enormous graveyard

The Sargasso Sea. *(Courtesy The New York Public Library Picture Collection)*

littered with hundreds of decaying ghost ships. Tales of sea monsters and dangerous octopi added to the horror.

As part of the Bermuda Triangle, the area shares a reputation as a danger zone for modern ships. However, stories from the nineteenth century and the beginning of the twentieth century provide a chilling variation on the usual theme. The ships involved in these reports did not disappear. Their crews and passengers, however, vanished mysteriously. Although the empty MARIE CELESTE was discovered north of the Sargasso Sea, her story is the most frequently quoted example of the area's unknown power.

Some UFOLOGISTS hypothesize that the passengers and crews of the abandoned ships were victims of extraterrestrial pirates. Studies have been carried out to find a connection between the *Sargassum* seaweed and the DISAPPEARANCES of craft in the area, but none has been found.

Bibliography: Berlitz, Charles, *The Bermuda Triangle* (Garden City, N.Y.: Doubleday and Company, 1974); Kusche, Lawrence D., *The Bermuda Triangle Mystery—Solved* (New York: Harper and Row, 1975).

**SASQUATCH,** American Indian name for BIGFOOT.

**SATCU** *see* **NEW ZEALAND SCIENTIFIC APPROACH TO COSMIC UNDERSTANDING (NZSATCU or SATCU)**

**SATELLITE OBJECT,** also known as a scoutship, small UFO which emerges from and re-enters a larger UFO, usually referred to as a MOTHER SHIP. Satellite objects are usually disk-shaped, while the mother ship is cigar-shaped. Exponents of the EXTRATERRESTRIAL HYPOTHESIS (ETH) suggest that mother ships are interstellar craft, while satellite objects are designed for flight within the planetary atmosphere.

Classic UFO cases involving satellite objects were those of OLORON and GAILLAC in France in 1952 and TEHERAN, IRAN, in 1976.

**SATELLITES.** Since 1957, artificial satellites have added another source of misidentified objects to the collection of UFO reports. To the naked eye, a bright satellite in an elliptical orbit may appear as a faint STAR moving rapidly, sometimes with an apparent zigzag motion, which is attributable to AUTOSTASIS. Since the movement of all satellites is precisely known, such sightings can be rapidly identified by checking with the North American Air Defense Command Space Detection Tracking System or the Smithsonian Institution at Cambridge, Massachusetts.

**SATURNO,** publication of the GRUPO DE ESTUDOS E PESQUISAS ULTRATERRENOS "MARCUS DE ORION" (GEPU).

**SAUCEDO, PEDRO,** *see* **LEVELLAND, TEXAS**

**SAUCER AND UNEXPLAINED CELESTIAL EVENTS RESEARCH SOCIETY (SAUCERS),** investigative organization which was dedicated to finding the solution to the flying saucer mystery. The group was founded in 1954 by JAMES MOSELEY and had a peak of about 8,000 members in 1967. GRAY BARKER was Executive Officer. Moseley edited the organization's publication, *Saucer News*. The group concluded that the UFO mystery may actually be impossible to solve in our era.

Although the group ceased functioning for a time, it has been reinstated by Barker, who claims a current membership of about 6,000. The group's current official publication is *Gray Barker's Newsletter*, which was established in 1977 and is edited by Barker.

**SAUCERIAN,** the OCCUPANT of a flying saucer.

**SAUCERIAN BULLETIN,** defunct magazine published by GRAY BARKER.

**SAUCER NEWS,** defunct magazine published by GRAY BARKER.

**SAUCERIAN PRESS,** Box 2228, Clarksburg, West Virginia 26301; telephone number: 304-269-2719.

This company publishes and distributes UFO books. Manager GRAY BARKER publishes *Gray Barker's Newsletter*, which also offers a service of procuring books and materials on the subject of UFOs, including out-of-print items and reprints of rare works.

**SAUCERITE,** derogatory or humorous term applied to someone who has an extreme enthusiasm for the subject of flying saucers.

**SAUCEROLOGY,** the study of flying saucers, a discipline which is considered less scientific than that described as "UFOLOGY."

**SAUCERS** *see* **SAUCER AND UNEXPLAINED CELESTIAL EVENTS RESEARCH SOCIETY**

**SAUCERS, SPACE AND SCIENCE** *see* **S. S. & S. PUBLICATIONS**

**SAUCER "XYZ,"** a non-scheduled newsletter published and edited by JAMES MOSELEY, P.O. Box 163, Fort Lee, N.J. 07024. "XYZ" represents the last part of the publication's name, which changes from issue to issue, and which runs in sequences of rhyming words. The purpose of the publication is to show, in an interesting and humorous way, the foibles of the UFO hard core, including both the believers and the skeptics. Moseley describes his sources of information as dreams, "trips" and intuition, as well as the usual sources, such as letters and newsclippings. The publication also serves as a forum in which those interested in the UFO phenomenon exchange views, information, humor, accusations and insults. It is available free-of-charge to deserving, interested people. Moseley feels that all issues should be put in a time capsule for twenty-first-century sociologists, Martian invaders or whomever.

**SAUL** *see* **PAUL, SAINT**

**SAUNDERS, DAVID,** *see* **CONDON COMMITTEE**

**SBEDV** *see* **SOCIEDADE BRASILIERA DE ESTUDOS SOBRE DISCOS VOADORES**

**SBI** *see* **SCIENTIFIC BUREAU OF INVESTIGATION**

**SBI REPORT, THE,** publication of the SCIENTIFIC BUREAU OF INVESTIGATION (SBI).

**SCANDINAVIA.** Although the term "MODERN ERA" in UFOlogy denotes the period dating from 1947 until the present, Scandinavia experienced its first widespread UFO activity in 1946 when there was a WAVE of sightings of GHOST ROCKETS. In 1952, NATO's OPERATION MAINBRACE, conducted in the vicinity of Denmark and Norway, was highlighted by several UFO sightings. In 1954, the famous SCANDINAVIAN ECLIPSE FILM provided one of the earliest pieces of photographic evidence of UFOs. SPITSBERGEN, NORWAY, became a center of interest in UFO circles in the mid-1950s when unconfirmed reports were published that a flying saucer had crashed there in 1952.

UFO investigation and research today is carried out by various regional and national organizations in Norway, Sweden and Denmark.

**SCANDINAVIAN ECLIPSE FILM,** ten seconds of 16 mm color film showing two shiny white rotating disks. The UFOs were observed for about thirty seconds by fifty people aboard three planes flying near Lifjell, Denmark. The witnesses included scientists and newsmen who were on an expedition to observe and film a total eclipse of the sun during 1954. The film was shown

Alleged UFO photographed by M. Lauersen at Viborg, Denmark, on November 17, 1974. *(Courtesy ICUFON/Hans C. Petersen)*

on American television on December 26 of that year, and a copy is stored in the Motion Picture Department of the Library of Congress.

**SCANDINAVIAN UFO INFORMATION** *see* **SKANDINAVISK UFO INFORMATION (SUFOI)**

**SCHIRRA, WALTER,** *see* **MERCURY 8**

**SCHMIDT, REINHOLD O.,** CONTACTEE and grain buyer from California who claimed to have encountered his first flying saucer near Kearney, Nebraska, in 1955. He supposedly accompanied the OCCUPANTS on trips to outer space and to the Arctic Circle through the waters under the North Pole. Later, he raised funds from investors to develop a cancer cure and a free energy source utilizing terrestrial minerals located for him by the SPACE PEOPLE. Eventually, the investors sued him for fraud and he was given a prison sentence. Schmidt related his alleged experiences with the Space People in a book entitled *Edge of Tomorrow—The Reinhold O. Schmidt Story* (California, the author, 1963).

**SCHMITT, HARRISON,** ASTRONAUT who believes that "spacecraft from other solar systems may have visited Earth." He points out that "one hundred years from now, we may even be visiting other solar systems." Therefore, he surmises, "it is not reasonable to say that visits in our own (solar system) are impossible." However, he concludes that "so far there appears to have been no definitive communication from them or proof of their visits."

In May 1979, Schmitt held a conference in ALBUQUERQUE, NEW MEXICO on the situation regard-

Astronaut Harrison Schmitt. *(Courtesy NASA)*

Luis Schönherr.

ing ANIMAL MUTILATIONS. It was attended by nationwide law enforcement officials and independent private investigators.

**SCHÖNHERR, LUIS** (b. June 12, 1927, Innsbruck, Austria), systems analyst in electronic data processing, UFO researcher and writer.

Schönherr studies the UFO phenomenon from as many different angles as possible and finds it difficult to make definitive statements on the subject. He suggests that since the UFO phenomenon consists of a physical as well as a psychical component, each of them equally pronounced, it might represent a sort of "missing link" between physical and psychical events. He believes there is an indication that the ultimate cause for this phenomenon must be sought in higher dimensions, beyond that four-dimensional pattern of elementary particles which physically represent the space-time matrix. Schönherr states that if the UFO phenomenon should involve a nonhuman intelligence whose activities are relevant to mankind, in order to interact and communicate with it actively, instead of remaining as passive observers, we must first understand the technology by which it interacts with us and our environment. He points out that, on the other hand, the UFO phenomenon may be shaped by human intelligence, created in a manner similar to the way in which an image is created by a mirror or transponder. He compares our perception of such a process to the confusion experienced by a kitten which, seeing its reflection in a mirror, finds that there is no other cat behind the mirror.

Schönherr is employed as a systems analyst in electronic data processing. His first interest in the UFO

phenomenon began during the French WAVE in 1954. At that time, he began to collect reports from the news media. During 1969 and 1970, he developed and compiled CODAP, a catalogue of more than 3,000 UFO incidents. From 1971 to 1975, he exchanged data with, and contributed to, UFOCAT in the United States. He is presently working on the formal problems of the description and documentation of UFO events.

Schönherr has written more than seventy popular articles on various scientific and technical subjects which have been published in Austrian and German newspapers and periodicals. His theoretical studies and analyses of the UFO phenomenon have been published in a series of articles in the FLYING SAUCER REVIEW (FSR). Other articles by Schönherr on UFOs have appeared in English-language and German-language magazines.

**SCHOOL OF THOUGHT,** P.O. Box 257, June Lake, California 93529; telephone number: 714-648-7405.

The purpose of this CONTACTEE organization is to receive guidance from advanced people in the cosmos and to prepare to be "lifted" by them "into the cosmos." The group holds that UFOs originate from many galaxies in many universes and multiple dimensions, and they are here to prepare people for "life in the universe" when our world is no longer habitable. First to be taken, according to the group, will be those who have been trained by the cosmic entities. They will be followed by astronomers, ministers and theologists, who will be followed by the "good people" on Earth. Purportedly, "the Cosmic Sons" deliver information to the School of Thought three times a week via "cosmic telephone."

This nonprofit organization was founded in 1960 by Hope Troxell, who serves as President and Director. Nathaniel Faust and John Stow serve as Vice-Presidents. Grace Bancroft is Treasurer. The group has twenty local members and fifty correspondents. The organization corresponds with interested parties, organizations and contactees in Australia, New Zealand, England, Canada, Sweden, Italy and North Africa. Services available to members include classes, which are allegedly delivered from the "cosmos" while craft are visible overhead. Two hundred books and eight hundred tape recordings of material allegedly received from cosmic entities, together with literature on UFOs, contactees, astronomy, geology, archeology and spiritual philosophy comprise the School of Thought's Library of the New Essenes of INYO. The organization's quarterly magazine, *Cosmic Frontiers*, is no longer published.

## SCHUESSLER, JOHN, *see* PROJECT VISIT (VEHICLE INTERNAL SYSTEMS INVESTIGATIVE TEAM)

## SCHWARZ, BERTHOLD ERIC (b. October 20, 1924, Jersey City, N.J.; address: 74 South Mountain Avenue, Montclair, New Jersey), psychiatrist, overseas consultant to the FLYING SAUCER REVIEW (FSR) and member of the Scientific Board of the CENTER FOR UFO STUDIES (CUFOS).

For the past twenty years, Schwarz has studied telepathy and investigated the accomplishments of physics. He has applied these psychiatric-parapsychological studies and techniques to UFOLOGY, where his interests are focused on the element of reality, psychopathology and induced psychophysiology in reference to close UFO sightings, landings and OCCUPANTS.

Schwarz received his B.A. from Dartmouth College, and his Diploma in Medicine from the Dartmouth Medical School in 1945. He graduated from the New York University College of Medicine in 1950, and interned at Mary Hitchcock Memorial Hospital in Hanover, New Hampshire, in 1951. He received an M.S. in Psychiatry from the Mayo Graduate School of Medicine in 1957.

From 1951 to 1955, Schwarz was a Fellow in Psychiatry at the Mayo Foundation. The Fellowship included, in addition to the basic studies required by the American Board of Psychiatry and Neurology, experience as first assistant offering consulting service to all Sections of the Mayo Clinic, the psychosomatic and closed divisions of St. Mary's Hospital, child psychiatry and neurological services, and management of the consulting service for the downtown hospitals. He has done depth electrographic and clinical research on LSD and mescaline and clinical electroencephalography at the Medical Sciences Building in the Section of Physiology. Other studies included neurophysiological studies on animals and humans, psychoanalytic investigations on the Mayo Clinic schizophrenia, delinquency and perversion projects, as well as didactic and personal psychoanalysis. Since 1955, he has been in private practice in Montclair, New Jersey. He is a Consultant to the Brain Wave Laboratory at Essex County Hospital Center, and Assistant Medical Director of the National Institute for Rehabilitation Engineering.

Schwarz is a Fellow of the American Psychiatric Association, the AMERICAN ASSOCIATION FOR THE ADVANCEMENT OF SCIENCE (AAAS) and the Academy of Medicine of New Jersey. He is a member of the American Medical Association, the American Electroencephalographic Society and the Editorial Staff of the *Journal* of the American Society of Psychosomatic Dentistry and Medicine. He is a Diplomat of the American Board of Psychiatry and Neurology.

Schwarz has written more than eighty-five reports, including numerous UFO articles which have been published in both medical publications and UFO magazines. He is author of *Psychic-Dynamics* (New York: Pageant Press, 1965), *The Jacques Romano Story* (New York: University Books, 1968), and *Parent-Child Telepathy* (New York: Garrett Publications, 1971). He is coauthor, with B. A. Ruggieri, M.D., of *Parent-Child Tensions* (Philadelphia: J. B. Lippincott Company, 1958), and *You CAN Raise Decent Children* (New Rochelle, New York: Arlington House, 1971).

Berthold Schwarz.

## SCIENTIFIC ADVISORY BOARD AD HOC COMMITTEE TO REVIEW PROJECT BLUE BOOK see O'BRIEN REPORT

## SCIENTIFIC BUREAU OF INVESTIGATION

(SBI), 23 Mac Arthur Avenue, Staten Island, N.Y. 10312; telephone number: 212-356-6696/201-254-1224.

This investigative organization is dedicated to the solution of the UFO enigma. The SBI believes that this goal is achievable by employing the following techniques: 1. maintenance of a network of investigators across the world who conduct prompt, professional investigations; 2. use of the volunteered services of a consulting panel comprised of experts in the fields of science, astronomy, medicine, and engineering; and 3. maintenance at high level of membership morale and loyalty by showing the organization's appreciation in the form of promotions, compensation for expenses, availability of equipment and material necessary for investigating, use of modern techniques and computers, issuance of professional identification cards and badges to investigators, open-mindedness about all HYPOTHESES presented by witnesses and members and cooperation with all local, city, state, federal, military and civilian agencies. The SBI holds that many older UFO organizations have come to a dead-end in their efforts to solve the mystery because of animosity among themselves, reluctance to improvise new procedures and innovations, and narrow-minded adherence to favorite theories.

This nonprofit organization was founded in 1979 by several researchers from other UFO organizations. Its staff consists of International Directors Peter Mazzola and Jim Fillow, Director of Research Marvin Weinstein, Public Relations Officer Joan Studer, Secretary-Treasurer Elaine Mazzola, Recording Secretary Margaret Fillow, Office Manager Dorothy Soultanokis and Legal Advisor Edward J. Ramp. The group has 1,200 members and investigators, 108 consultants in the various scientific fields and thirty-five representatives in foreign countries. Some of the consultants are members of the UNITED STATES AIR FORCE (USAF), the Department of Defense, the NATIONAL AERONAUTICS AND SPACE ADMINISTRATION (NASA) and the Civil Defense. Forty-two percent of the organization's members are U.S. law enforcement officers. The SBI has a photographic analysis office for microscopic analysis and has access to a laboratory for soil, metallurgy and liquid analysis. It publishes a monthly newsletter called *The SBI Report*.

## SCOTT, BRIAN (b. October 12, 1943, Philadelphia, Pennsylvania; address: Suite 6B, 17901 East Chapman Avenue, Orange, California 92669; telephone number: 714-538-8537), CONTACTEE.

According to Scott his "strange saga" began at age sixteen when he encountered a beeping ball of orange light. Two months later, he fell into a trance and tattooed a spider on his right arm. One month later, he fell into another trance and this time tattooed a jaguar on his left arm.

In 1971, he was allegedly beamed aboard a UFO. Inside the craft, he met up with an old friend who had the misfortune to find himself in the same predicament. They waited in a mist-filled room until a nearby door "dissolved." Four seven-foot-tall humanoid beings entered. They were heavily built, their thick wrinkled skin covered with patches of hair. Enormous ears ran down the entire length of their faces. An extra layer of hide covered their lower torsos, thighs and knees. The odor of their breath reminded Scott of "dirty socks."

Both men were subjected to physical examinations. Before the two were returned to the ground, one of the entities telepathically injected information into Scott's mind. Although he had no memory of the incident at the time, his brain allegedly functioned faster than usual from that time onward.

Between 1971 and 1976, Scott was reportedly abducted five more times, on two occasions by a different group of aliens who were hostile to the first group. During this period, he continued to be plagued by the beeping ball of orange light, and to be subject to bouts of automatic writing. During HYPNOSIS sessions conducted by clinical hypnotist William McCall and English professor ALVIN LAWSON, Scott recalled his alleged ABDUCTIONS. At times, while in hypnotic trances, his voice changed as if other personalities were speaking through him. His case was investigated by researchers from the AERIAL PHENOMENA RESEARCH ORGANIZATION (APRO), the MUTUAL UFO NETWORK (MUFON), U.C.L.A. and other organizations.

In 1976, during his final abduction, his memory of all previous abductions was supposedly restored. The meaning of the contacts was made clear to Scott and he was given instructions by his extraterrestrial contacts to receive telepathic transmissions on specific dates from a lunar SATELLITE. Shortly afterward, he visited the ancient ruins of Tiahuanaco in Bolivia. There he allegedly found a replica of his tattooed spider on a statue of the god Tici Viracocha. (The spider is also similar, he says, to one of the symbols on the NAZCA Plain in Peru.) At Tiahuanaco, Scott reportedly experienced a "quantum evolution of mind." On a second visit to South America in June 1977, he supposedly underwent the second phase of his "transformation," his personality being replaced by Voltar, an entity from Epsilon Eridani. Scott claims to be possessed by the extraterrestrial to this day. However, since Voltar cannot present himself publicly, Scott's personality is allowed to exist during the transpiration of daily affairs.

In 1978, Scott founded the CONGRESS FOR INTERPLANETARY TECHNOLOGY AND EDUCATION (CITE). He is currently engaged in the execution of the assignments allegedly given him by the SPACE PEOPLE. They are as follows: to write the Space People's history; to design solar-powered PYRAMIDS to be built in Bolivia, Egypt, England and the United States; to create a technology by which machines respond to mental commands; to bury time capsules; and to create a technology of "quantum displacement physics" for space travel.

Scott's early career is, by his own admission, not very impressive. After being expelled from four high schools, he joined the Merchant Marines as a cook for two years. Subsequently, he served time in prison in three states for fraud. In 1973, however, while working as a punch press operator, he began studying Mechanical Drafting at night school. Allegedly, his drafting abilities excelled under the influence of his UFO-engendered mental invigoration. He was hired by Burrough's Corporation in Mission Viejo, California. In early 1977, he was promoted from draftsman to Design Engineer and also began to work as a freelance agent for various companies in the electronics-aerospace field.

During the hypnotic regressions conducted by Lawson and McCall, the two researchers were finally persuaded to discontinue their work with Scott because of what they referred to as "a succession of HOAXlike activities." With regard to the various voices supposedly channelled through Scott by other personalities, Lawson and McCall were not convinced that they originated from anywhere but Scott himself. "However," says Lawson, "his case remains most intriguing in some ways, and it is our feeling at this point that initially some 'real' UFO event may well have happened to Brian. His claims other than the CE–I and possibly CE–III events, however, we cannot vouch for."

## SCOTT, STANLEY, see RED BLUFF, CALIFORNIA

## SCOUTSHIP see SATELLITE OBJECT

**SEARCH,** quarterly magazine established in 1954. It is available at newsstands and by subscription. It incorporates the former magazine, FLYING SAUCERS. The publication deals with all factual and occult mysteries, including UFOs.

*Search* is one of the many magazines started by the late RAY PALMER. Material is contributed free-of-charge by readers. Marjorie Palmer is Editor. The magazine is published by Palmer Publications, Route 2, Box 36, Amherst, Wisconsin 54406.

**SEARCH FOR EXTRATERRESTRIAL INTELLIGENCE (SETI),** current name of the U.S. program to intercept signals from extraterrestrial civilizations through the use of RADIO ASTRONOMY.

Our initiation of radio communication only sixty years ago may have been preceded by thousands if not millions of years by extraterrestrial intelligences on other PLANETS. Their mastery of the technique and ability to transmit signals over great distances probably far surpasses our progress in the field. PROJECT OZMA, the first attempt to detect radio signals from other worlds, was carried out in 1960. It failed. Since then, several other attempts, in which the different investigators chose different targets, have met with equal failure. However, the odds for success were very slight. The number of STARS that have been investigated is less than .1 percent of the number that would have to be examined if there were to be a reasonable statistical chance of finding one extraterrestrial civilization.

In 1971, the NATIONAL AERONAUTICS AND SPACE ADMINISTRATION (NASA) initiated plans for PROJECT CYCLOPS, a system whose design called for a circular array of over fifteen hundred antennas, each larger in diameter than a football field, covering over twenty-five square miles. Although this project would have allowed a more realistic effort to eavesdrop on radio transmissions in outer space, its enormous size and cost made it somewhat impractical. It remained in the planning stage.

In 1976, scientists and engineers at the Caltech Jet Propulsion Laboratory (JPL) in Pasadena, California, designed new equipment of unprecedented tunability and sensitivity. Utilizing existing antennas at the Deep Space Network in Goldstone, California, this equipment can survey the entire sky. In a joint effort planned by JPL and NASA's Ames Research Center, JPL will perform an all-sky survey while Ames will conduct a targeted study of selected stars within one thousand light years of Earth.

Meanwhile, mankind has been unintentionally sending messages out into space for the past fifty years or so in the form of commercial radio and television waves. The first of those signals are now fifty light years distant and may already have been picked up by other civilizations. In 1974, Earth sent its first deliberate announcement from the Arecibo Observatory in Puerto Rico. The message, composed by astronomers FRANK DRAKE and CARL SAGAN, is a coded signal describing our numerical system, the chemistry of life on Earth, the advancement of man's structure, growth and brain, population figures, the position of our planet in the solar system, and information about the transmitting telescope. Although the chances are excellent that intelligent beings will intercept this communication since it will reach all three hundred thousand stars of a group called Messier 13 in the Great Cluster of Hercules, Messier 13's distance of 24,000 light years means that it will be at least forty-eight thousand years before mankind can receive an answer.

The first messages to be sent by unmanned space probes are aboard PIONEERS 10 AND 11, in the form of plaques engraved with pictorial scientific language. The Voyager spacecrafts, launched in 1977, bear a message from Earth in the form of golden records that will play greetings in sixty languages. Sagan has compared this form of communiqué to a message placed in a bottle and cast into the ocean by a shipwrecked sailor.

The consequence of contact with extraterrestrial civilizations could be beneficial or detrimental to Earth. By announcing our existence to the Universe we might be exposing ourselves to the threat of military invasion. Alternatively, an alien civilization might exploit our relative ignorance and subvert us with seemingly beneficient broadcasts. A 1960 report, prepared for NASA, pointed out that, "Anthropological files contain many examples of societies, sure of their place in the universe, which have disintegrated when they have had to associate with previously unfamiliar societies espousing different ideas and different life ways." On the other hand, the acquisition of greater understanding in the fields of medicine, technology, ecology, culture and even spiritual development could bring about a highly rewarding stage of evolution on the planet Earth.

Bibliography: Edelson, Edward, *Who Goes There?* (Garden City, N.Y.: Doubleday and Company, 1979).

**SECOND LOOK,** monthly magazine, established in 1978, with a circulation of 15,000. It is available by subscription and at a few bookstores. The magazine brings to the layperson new theories by scientists and investigative journalists concerning the possibility and nature of extraterrestrial intelligence, including new aspects of the ANCIENT ASTRONAUTS thesis, astronomical anomalies, alleged UFO sightings and encounters, and the broader philosophical implications of the existence or absence of extraterrestrial life.

About eighty-five percent of the material is written by freelance writers, including Isaac Asimov, Ronald Bracewell, Ray Bradbury, Bevan French, Sir Fred Hoyle, J. ALLEN HYNEK, Robert Anton Wilson and JACQUES VALLEE. Prospective contributors should query first and should present resumés and previously published articles. Self-addressed, stamped envelopes should accompany submissions. Articles should range from 400 to 3,000 words in length. Payment up to fifteen cents per word is made upon publication for first serial and anthology rights. The magazine pays for photographs. Robert K. G. Temple and Randall T. Fitzgerald are the Senior Editors.

William Bonner is the Publisher. Offices are located at 10 East Street S.E., Washington, D.C. 20003.

**SECRECY** *see* **COVER-UP**

**SECRETARY OF THE AIR FORCE, OFFICE OF INFORMATION (SAF-OI),** official channel for the release to the news media of all information gathered by the UNITED STATES AIR FORCE (USAF) regarding UFOs during its official investigation program.

**SECRET SOCIETIES,** secret fraternal orders, such as the Freemasons and the Rosicrucians, who claim to possess esoteric knowledge handed down from ancient times. It is rumored that some of the teachings of these societies originate from extraterrestrial sources.

Bibliography: Bergier, Jacques, *Extraterrestrial Visitations from Prehistoric Times to the Present* (Chicago: Henry Regnery Company, 1973).

**SECRETS OF THE GODS** *see* **THE FORCE BEYOND**

**SECRET WEAPON HYPOTHESIS,** theory that secret devices being tested by earthly governments are misinterpreted as extraterrestrial machines. Based on the sightings of the MODERN ERA, beginning in 1947, most UFOLOGISTS believe it is unlikely that any government, if it had devices with the alleged capabilities of UFOs, would continue to sponsor the construction of conventional military aircraft whose capabilities are primitive in comparison. It is also questionable that such devices could be kept secret for over thirty years. Although the Manhattan Project (the program activated by the United States War Department in June 1942 to create a bomb utilizing the nuclear fission process) was kept secret during its operation, astronomer J. ALLEN HYNEK expresses doubt that the secrecy could have been maintained for more than a few years. Moreover, the vast number of people necessary for an operation having the proportions of the worldwide UFO phenomenon, would further diminish the chances of maintaining secrecy.

However, author Robert Temple has pointed out the existence of an aerodynamic technology of a secret nature possessed by all the major powers and which could explain a number of UFO sightings, particularly those occurring near military installations. Although the public knows little about them, remotely piloted vehicles (RPVs) are used as military spycraft and fly constantly through our skies. These devices can perform right angle turns, sudden descents and ascents, and other maneuvers often attributed to UFOs. Although designed for RADAR invisibility, their giant wingspans sometimes reflect light from certain angles. Temple suggests that the technology might be adapted to carry human beings by restricting the RPV's maneuverability.

The overriding argument against the secret weapon hypothesis, however, is that UFO reports date back more than 2,500 years to such celebrated sightings as those of EZEKIEL and THUTMOSE III. If these ancient UFOs represent the same phenomenon reported today, it is hardly likely that they could be explained as misidentified man-made craft.

Bibliography: Temple, Robert K. G., "UFOs as Government Spycraft," *Second Look* (Washington, D.C.: Second Look, November, 1978).

## SEEDING HYPOTHESIS *see* EARTH COLONIZATION HYPOTHESIS

**SEISMIC HYPOTHESIS,** theory that some UFOs, particularly those reported just prior to earthquakes, are an electrical phenomenon directly related to seismic activity. Seismic pressure on rock crystals can create electric fields through a process known as piezoelectricity. The resultant electric field can ionize the area causing the air to glow.

VESTIGIA, a New Jersey-based investigative organization, has tentatively concluded that seismic pressure on quartz-bearing rock explains the regular reports of flying saucers flying over the Wanaque Reservoir in northern Passaic County, New Jersey. The reservoir is located near the Ramapo Fault, where several mild tremors have been reported during recent years.

Bibliography: Finkelstein, D., and J. Powell, "Earthquake Lightning," *Nature* (No. 228, 1970); Derr, J. S., "Earthquake Lights: A Review of Observations and Present Theories," *Bulletin of the Seismological Society of America* (No. 63, 1973).

## SEPIB *see* SOUTH EAST PARANORMAL INFORMATION BUREAU

**SETI,** acronym for the SEARCH FOR EXTRATERRESTRIAL INTELLIGENCE.

**SEXUAL ENCOUNTERS.** Alleged victims of UFO ABDUCTIONS occasionally claim to have had sexual relations with the occupants of extraterrestrial spaceships. Such an incident is referred to by some writers as a CLOSE ENCOUNTER OF THE FOURTH KIND (CE–IV), although others use the term to denote only an abduction in which no sexual activity has occurred. The most famous case in which a human being was allegedly coerced into performing sexual intercourse with a UFO OCCUPANT was that of a Brazilian farmer, ANTONIO

VILLAS-BOAS. South African CONTACTEE ELIZABETH KLARER claims to have given birth on another PLANET to a son fathered by a resident of that planet.

Mating between earthlings and extraterrestrials is a theme encountered in the arguments of supporters of the ANCIENT ASTRONAUTS hypothesis. Many of them believe that the human race was actually the result of the interbreeding of extraterrestrials and some advanced species of animal on Earth, such as BIGFOOT. Their allegations are based on various religious records which tell of gods taking human women as their wives and producing demigods as offspring. One of the most often quoted verses in this context is in Chapter 6 of the Book of Genesis, wherein it is stated, ". . . the sons of God saw the daughters of men that they were fair and they took them wives of all which they chose."

## SHAMBALLA *see* HOLLOW EARTH HYPOTHESIS

**SHAPES.** The majority of UFO reports describe disks or cigar-shaped objects. The former come in a variety of shapes, including coinlike, flat-bottomed, domed and convex on top and bottom. Other UFO shapes are described as resembling spheres, cylinders, hats, footballs, eggs, cones, rockets, torpedos, bells, rods, barrels, pears, doughnuts, wheels, spindles, crosses, crescents, triangles, lozenges, squares, diamonds, teardrops and the PLANET Saturn. (See chart on page 372.)

**SHATNER, WILLIAM,** actor and star of the television series and motion picture *Star Trek*, who reportedly saw a UFO in California's Mojave Desert. Shatner was on a motorcycle trip with four friends when he stopped to have a drink of water. After his companions had gone out of view, he discovered that his bike would not start. He tried to repair the machine but was unsuccessful. In the scorching 130-degree heat, he soon used up his supply of water. He tried to push his motorcycle but, unsure of the way and exhausted, he finally collapsed. It was then that a shiny, streamlined craft passed eerily over him. Something inside him told him to walk in a certain direction. Believing that he might be receiving telepathic messages from some intelligence connected with the UFO, he pushed his stalled bike along, following the silent voice. Finally, he found a road which led him to a gas station and help. He was apparently convinced that the UFO had saved his life.

**SHAVER, RICHARD SHARPE,** welding machine operator from Pennsylvania who in 1944 claimed to have heard voices which helped him remember an alleged former life in the legendary lost continent of LEMURIA.

According to Shaver, the lost continents of ATLANTIS, Lemuria and MU had been populated in the distant past by beings from another PLANET. These extraterrestrials finally fled from Earth when poisonous radiation from the sun caused them to age and die. However, some of them supposedly stayed behind and created an underground civilization. Their descendants allegedly live on today, occasionally interfering in the lives of Earth's surface inhabitants. Those who bring harm to human beings are known as dero (deranged or detrimental robots). Those who attempt to protect mankind from the evil dero are known as tero (terrestrial or integrative robots).

Shaver's stories, sometimes referred to as the Great Shaver Mystery or the Great Shaver Hoax, were published as non-fiction in the science fiction magazine *Amazing Stories* from 1944 to 1948. Managing Editor RAY PALMER rewrote and expanded most of the material. Although many readers protested the presentation of these stories as fact, thousands of new readers were attracted to the magazine and began to report their own alleged memories of past lives.

The Shaver stories are the source of many beliefs concerning the HOLLOW EARTH HYPOTHESIS, and Palmer stated that, "Flying saucers are a part of the Shaver Mystery—integrally so."

Bibliography: Palmer, Ray (ed.), *The Hidden World, No. A–1* (Amherst, Wisconsin: Palmer Publications, 1961).

**SHEAFFER, ROBERT M.** (b. May 21, 1949, Chicago, Illinois), Computer Systems Analyst and Vice-Chairman of the UFO Subcommittee of the COMMITTEE FOR THE SCIENTIFIC INVESTIGATION OF CLAIMS OF THE PARANORMAL (CSICP).

Robert M. Sheaffer.

Sheaffer claims that there is no evidence that UFOs represent a phenomenon unknown to science. He believes that, since psychologists' tests reveal the human sensory apparatus to be extremely error-prone and imprecise, there would undoubtedly be reports of strange phenomena even if no unknown phenomena were present in our skies. As one who has spent many hours looking at the night sky, Sheaffer has seen many objects that those less familiar with astronomy might mistake for UFOs. Over the years, he has seen brilliant METEORS, sundogs and moon dogs, a peculiar auroral phenomena resulting in "flying disks," unusual-looking Earth SATELLITES, brilliant PLANETS, high-altitude BALLOONS after sunset, and even an ICE-CRYSTAL-refracted image of the planet Jupiter. After investigating many reports of alleged UFOs which turned out to be ordinary celestial phenomena, he came to realize that since common phenomena can give rise to many UFO reports, unusual phenomena can, when subjected to similar misreporting, result in even more seemingly inexplicable UFO reports. Sheaffer states that, given the manner in which well-known UFO proponents have repeatedly endorsed cases that turned out to be HOAXES or MISINTERPRETATIONS, little confidence should be placed in the results of their allegedly scientific investigations. He concludes that if UFOs were some nonimaginary phenomenon, after thirty years of sightings there would have been at least one UFO that did not slip away before the evidence became too convincing.

Sheaffer received his B.A. from Northwestern University in 1971, with a major in Mathematics and a minor in Astronomy. He received his Master's Degree in Education from Northwestern University in 1972.

Sheaffer was a teacher of mathematics at public schools from 1971 to 1973 and, since 1973, has been a Minicomputer Systems Programmer/Analyst in the Washington, D.C., area.

Sheaffer's articles on UFOs, extraterrestrial life and other scientific subjects have appeared in numerous scientific publications and UFO magazines.

**SHOOTING STARS** *see* **METEORS**

**SI,** acronym for saucer intelligences or space intelligences, which refers to the OCCUPANTS of flying saucers.

**SIBERIAN METEOR** *see* **TUNGUSKA REGION, SOVIET UNION**

**SIDIP** *see* **DETECTOR SIDIP (SOCIETÉ INTERNATIONALE DE DEVELOPPEMENT DES IDÉES POUR LE PROGRÉS)**

**SIMONTON, JOE,** *see* **EAGLE RIVER, WISCONSIN**

**SIRAGUSA, EUGENIO,** Italian CONTACTEE and founder of the group CENTRO STUDI FRATELLANZA COSMICA (Study Center of the Cosmic Brotherhood).

**SIRIUS,** binary star in the constellation Canis Major. Only about 8.6 light years from Earth, it includes brilliant Sirius A., also known as the Dog Star, and Sirius B, invisible to the naked eye. Although the existence of Sirius B was not suspected until 1844 and not telescopically confirmed until 1862, anthropologist Robert Temple contends that artifacts of the Dogon tribe in Mali reveal accurate knowledge of the movements of both stars. He suggests that beings from the planetary system of Sirius B visited Africa thousands of years ago, leaving behind them evidence of their technological superiority in the form of religious relics. Ancient illustrations of fish-tailed gods may be an indication that the Siriusians were amphibious creatures resembling a combination of human being and dolphin.

Bibliography: Temple, Robert K. G., *The Sirius Mystery* (New York: St. Martin's Press, 1976).

**SITGREAVES NATIONAL FOREST, ARIZONA,** location of an alleged UFO ABDUCTION of a young woodcutter in 1975.

On November 5, seven young men, ranging in age from seventeen to twenty-eight, were thinning out scrub in the Sitgreaves National Forest, 156 miles northwest of Phoenix. The team was headed by Michael Rogers and consisted of Travis Walton, Ken Peterson, Alan Dalis, Steven Pierce, John Goulette and Dwayne Smith. At about 6:00 P.M. they stopped working and left for home in Rogers's truck. They had gone only about 100 yards when they noticed a strange glow behind some trees. As they came around a bend in the logging road, a clearing came into view. Hovering about fifteen feet above the ground was a UFO. The object was about fifteen-to-twenty feet in diameter and about eight feet high, with a dome on top. It glowed with a milky-yellow color. Rogers put his foot on the brake. Before the truck had come to a complete stop, Walton jumped out and walked quickly into the clearing. As he stood there looking up at the smooth base of the UFO, a beeping sound could be heard. Suddenly, the object began to rumble. As the noise increased, the UFO began to spin on its vertical axis. Alarmed, Walton took cover behind a log. As the others shouted at him to get back to the truck, he started to stand. Suddenly, a beam of greenish-blue light shot out of the base of the object. It struck Walton in the head and chest. A bright flash surrounded his body. He shot straight up into the air, his body stiffened, his head knocked back and his arms and legs outflung. He was hurtled backward and fell to the ground several feet away. Terrified, his companions sped off in the truck. About a quarter-mile down the bumpy road, they stopped. While they were trying to decide what to do, a flash of light shot up above the trees and disappeared into the black sky. The woodcutters returned to the clearing but could find no sign of Walton or the UFO. Finally, they went to the local sheriff's office to report the incident. A search was conducted and, when nothing was found, Walton's mother was informed of her son's disappearance. A full-scale search was carried out over the following two days but no trace of Walton was found nor was there any evidence that a craft had landed.

On November 11, Walton called his sister's home from a telephone booth in the nearby town of Heber. His voice was weak. He asked his brother-in-law, Grant Neff, to come and get him. Neff and Walton's brother, Duane, found Walton slumped on the floor of the booth in a confused mental state. He was twelve miles from the place where he had disappeared five days previously.

Walton related that, after being knocked unconscious by the beam of light from the UFO, he had awakened in a low-ceilinged room. The air was hot and damp. Three entities, about five feet tall with large, bald, domed heads, were watching him. Although the creatures' mouths, noses and ears were small, their brown, staring eyes were enormous. Hysterical, Walton tried to attack them. The entities left the room, turning to the right as they exited the doorway. Walton went to the door. He saw a corridor which curved around to the right and left. He turned and ran in panic. He passed a door but kept going. When he reached a second door which was open, he decided to go in. He found himself in a round room with an apparently transparent wall which showed the STARS. In the center of the room was a chair with buttons and a lever on the armrests. Walton pressed some buttons, then moved the lever. The stars, visible through the wall, began to move. Walton turned and saw a human being standing in the doorway. The man wore a helmet. He led Walton out of the craft into a large enclosure where the air was fresher and where several other disk-shaped objects were parked. Walton followed the man into another craft where he saw three other human beings. An object resembling an oxygen mask was placed over his face. He passed out.

When Walton regained consciousness, he was lying back on the road. A disk-shaped craft was rising up into the sky directly above him. HEAT from the object engulfed him. He could see the doors in its base closing. When the object had disappeared, he walked to the nearest telephone booth to call his sister's home.

The case was one of the most controversial of the 1970s. Writer PHILIP J. KLASS has uncovered a great deal of information to support his theory that the incident was a HOAX perpetrated by all the members of the woodcutting crew. On November 10, a polygraph test was administered to the six other woodcutters while Walton was still missing. The fact that five of the six men appeared to be telling the truth has been presented as corroboration of their story. However, three of the four questions asked were designed to determine whether or not Walton had been the victim of foul play on the part of his companions. The sixth man, Allan Dalis, was the only one whose results were inconclusive. An accused burglar, who was convicted and jailed for armed robbery several months later, Dalis was probably uncooperative out of fear that his criminal activities might be revealed during the examination. The last question, asking the men if they were telling the truth about having seen a UFO, had been posed at the request of the local sheriff. The polygraph examiner, Cy E. Gilson, stated, "That one question does not make it a valid test as far as verifying the UFO incident."

On February 7, 1976, Walton took a polygraph test administered by George J. Pfeiffer, an employee of Tom Ezell Associates of Phoenix. The fact that Walton passed the test was much publicized. Klass, however, questions the procedures employed and the reliability of the examiner. Pfeiffer, who had only two years' experience in polygraph work, wrote in his report that Walton had "dictated" the questions to be asked. Writer Jerome Clark has pointed out that Walton was dissatisfied with the first set of questions that had been prepared because it did not cover certain accusations which had been made against him. Pfeiffer later stated that Walton "suggested" rather than "dictated" the questions he wanted to be asked. Pfeiffer's employer said that it was perfectly proper for the sponsor of a test, which in this case was the AERIAL PHENOMENA RESEARCH ORGANIZATION (APRO), to indicate the areas which should be explored. Later, however, he wrote to Klass that, "Because of the dictation of the questions to be asked, this test should be invalidated." In defense of Pfeiffer's qualifications, Clark points out that Ezell had originally planned to conduct the examination himself. However, the day before, he had asked APRO Director JAMES LORENZEN if it would be all right if his associate, Pfeiffer, gave the test. "He's as qualified as I am," Ezell had assured Lorenzen. His disagreement with Pfeiffer's results, however, was revealed when he wrote in a letter to Klass, "The reactions on the charts, to my way of interpretation, could not be readable. You would not be able to say if he (Walton) is telling the truth or if he's lying."

One of the most damaging pieces of evidence against

Walton's claims came to light when Klass discovered that Walton had been given a previous polygraph test on November 15, 1975. The arrangements for the examination were made by Lorenzen, and paid for by THE NATIONAL ENQUIRER. The examination was administered by John J. McCarthy, the most experienced polygraph examiner in the state of Arizona and a graduate of the U.S. Army Fort Gordon School, widely regarded as the best polygraph school in the United States, if not the world. McCarthy concluded that Walton had been "attempting to perpetrate a UFO hoax, and that he has not been on any spacecraft." His report also stated that Walton had attempted unsuccessfully to distort his respiration pattern in an effort to deceive the examiner. *The National Enquirer* instructed McCarthy not to reveal that he had examined Walton, and the follow-up report on the case published in APRO's newsletter made no mention of the test. When these facts were later made public by Klass, Lorenzen claimed that the test was invalid because Walton was still anxious due to his recent ordeal.

A great deal of suspicion was aroused by the fact that Walton's mother, Mary Walton Kellett, showed no surprise or distress upon hearing of her son's mysterious DISAPPEARANCE. When questioned about this later, however, she claimed that she never shows emotion.

Investigators became further discouraged and confused by conflicting reports that the entire Walton family had a prior interest in UFOs. According to Town Marshal Sanford Flake, the Walton family talked about them all the time. He reported that Walton's mother had told him she frequently watched them while sitting on her porch. It was also reported that before the incident occurred, Walton had called a radio talk show, volunteering to be a guest. The show's host called him a "kook." After the alleged abduction, Walton again called the talk show and said, "Who's a kook now?" However, author Bill Barry claims that Deputy Sheriff Ken Coplan, who was identified as the source of this story, subsequently denied ever having recounted such an incident. Clark asserts that the Walton family's interest in UFOs was no greater than that of any other American and had arisen from the fact that Walton's brother, Duane, had seen a disk-shaped object in 1964. Although the press reported that after the 1964 sighting Duane and Travis had made a pact in the event of future sightings, Clark says that this was an inaccurate claim. According to Clark, Travis had once jestingly suggested to Duane, "If one of those things ever grabs you, make sure they come back and get me." Clark stresses that the Waltons were not interested enough in UFOs to read any books or magazines on the subject and were not even aware of the existence of UFO research organizations.

Klass questions Walton's credibility as a witness. On May 5, 1971, Walton and Charles Rogers, younger brother of the head of the woodcutting crew, pleaded guilty to first-degree burglary and forgery charges. They had stolen bank payroll checks and cashed them under a forged signature. Walton and Rogers agreed to repay the funds and were placed on two years' probation.

In a paper, entitled "Would Mike Rogers Resort to Falsehoods to Deceive the U.S. Government?," Klass has presented his theory that Rogers engineered the incident to establish a legal basis for terminating his money-losing contract with the U.S. Forest Service to thin out 1,277 acres of National Forest Land. Rogers had been given an extension by the Forest Service when it became apparent that he could not complete the work by the original deadline. However, he was penalized one dollar per acre for all work performed after the original deadline and ten percent of the payment was being withheld until completion of the entire job. His new deadline was November 10, 1975. In October, it was already obvious that the second deadline could not be met. In a letter to Forest Service Contracting Officer Maurice Marchbanks on October 20, 1975, Rogers stated, "I cannot honestly say whether or not we will finish on time. However, we are working every day. . . ." In fact, Rogers had been secretly moonlighting on other better-paying jobs. He had spent only three days of the month on the Forest Service job. If he requested another extension, Rogers could expect another pay cut. Furthermore, with winter at hand, the work could not be completed until the following spring, delaying payment still longer. Clark argues that since Rogers was working concurrently on three other jobs for which he was being paid, he was not in financial trouble. However, Rogers later admitted to Klass that he had to use food stamps in December 1975. Coincidentally, on the night that he had written to the Forest Service Contracting Officer, NBC Television had broadcast THE UFO INCIDENT, a dramatization of the alleged UFO abduction of Betty and Barney Hill in NEW HAMPSHIRE. It is possible that Rogers or Walton saw or heard of this program which might have sparked the idea of perpetrating a hoax in order to solve Rogers's problem. The alleged abduction of Walton allowed Rogers to terminate his contract on the basis that his crew was afraid to return to the site. Thus, he was entitled to collect the withheld funds and pay his crew.

Author Barry has argued that the consistency of the accounts related by the individual crew members is too great to suggest fraud. It was not a tightly knit group, he claims, and one of the men, Dwayne Smith, had joined the team only three days prior to the incident. Furthermore, when Dalis was later convicted and jailed for armed robbery, he confessed to "everything he had ever done in his life but stuck absolutely to his UFO story." Klass finds no mystery in this. He suggests that Rogers might have offered his crew members a share in the withheld funds when they were paid off, as well as in any other income that might be forthcoming from the publicizing of the UFO story. Since Sheriff Marlin Gillespie subsequently threatened prosecution of those involved if a hoax were proved, the woodcutters risk a jail term if they now deny their story.

Bibliography: "Walton Abduction Cover-Up Revealed," UFO Investigator (Washington, D.C.: National Investigations Committee on Aerial Phenomena, June 1976); Clark, Jerome, "Saucer Central U.S.A," UFO Report (Brooklyn, N.Y.: Gambi Productions, March 1977); Barry, Bill, Ultimate Encounter (New York: Pocket Books, 1978); Walton, Travis, The Walton Experience (New York: Berkley Publishing Corporation, 1978).

**SITU** *see* **SOCIETY FOR THE INVESTIGATION OF THE UNEXPLAINED**

**SKANDINAVISK UFO INFORMATION (SUFOI),** Postbox 6, DK 2820 Gentofte, Denmark; telephone number: 02-57 07 36.

The purpose of this organization is to research and investigate the UFO phenomenon and to disseminate information to the public via publications, lectures and articles. The group remains open-minded about the identity and origin of UFOs. It has handled about 6,000 cases during its existence and notes that the number of reports seems to be increasing year by year.

This nonprofit organization was founded in 1957 by Captain H. C. Petersen and other officers of the Danish Air Force. Flemming Ahrenkiel has been President since 1974. Board Members include Iver O. Kjems, Xavier P. Madsen, Henrik Pedersen, Carsten H. Pedersen and Jens H. Glintborg. The group has approximately 3,000 members. About twenty-two trained field investigators are located throughout Denmark. Foreign representatives include Steve Hatzopoulos in Greece, G. Wielunski in Poland, Levent Ural in Turkey, V. I. Sanarov in the Soviet Union, Hansjürgen Köhler in West Germany, Ernst Berger in Austria, Jorge Sanchez Gonzales in Mexico and Kiril Terziev in Yugoslavia. Additionally, SUFOI exchanges publications and information with organizations all over the world. The group has an Alarm Section, which consists of a network of reporters who can be reached by telephone twenty-four hours a day. All SUFOI literature, including books and booklets, is published in Danish. *UFO-NYT*, a bimonthly magazine, contains UFO-related articles, as well as articles about space and astronomy. SUFOI NEWSLETTER, published in English three or four times a year, deals primarily with Scandinavian sightings and SUFOI's investigative work.

**SKUFOD,** brand name of a UFO DETECTOR sold by Skywatch UFO Detectors, 102 Nelson Road, Chingford E4 9AS, England.

**SKYHOOK BALLOON,** giant BALLOON made of partially transparent plastic. The first Skyhook balloon was launched on September 25, 1947, from St. Cloud, Minnesota. The balloon had been developed to enable scientists to collect information about the atmosphere, the winds in the stratosphere and the incidence of cosmic rays at altitudes above the ceiling of then-existing aircraft. The various forms assumed by Skyhook balloons have been described as teardrop-shaped, pear-shaped, conical and circular. During the daytime, they reflect sunlight, sometimes producing a rainbow of colors. A hundred feet or more in diameter, Skyhook balloons in the late 1940s were sometimes visible at distances of fifty or sixty miles as they shifted from one wind stream to another, adopting each stream's direction and speed. High-altitude jet wind streams sometimes carried the balloons along at speeds as high as 150 miles per hour.

A program was initiated by the CENTRAL INTELLIGENCE AGENCY (CIA) to utilize Skyhook balloons for military reconnaissance. Balloons carrying reconnaissance cameras could be launched from Europe. After they had been carried by winds over the Soviet Union, the cameras could be released over Japan by radio commands. After parachuting to the ground, the cameras would be recovered. The obviously secret nature of this operation meant that a very small number of people was aware of the existence of the Skyhook balloons. When the Office of Naval Research eventually released the facts about the Skyhook program in 1950, numerous UFO reports were attributed to the giant balloons. The most famous of such cases occurred at GODMAN AIR FORCE BASE, KENTUCKY, in 1948. Captain Thomas Mantell was killed while pursuing a UFO, later identified as a probable Skyhook balloon.

Bibliography: Klass, Philip J., *UFOs Explained* (New York: Random House, 1974); Menzel, Donald H., and Lyle G. Boyd, *The World of Flying Saucers* (Garden City, N.Y.: Doubleday and Company, 1963).

**SKYLOOK,** former name of the MUFON UFO JOURNAL, newsletter of the MUTUAL UFO NETWORK (MUFON).

**SKY QUAKES** *see* **AIR QUAKES**

40-story tall Skyhook balloon. *(U.S. Navy/United Press International Photo)*

**SKYSCAN GROUP PROJECT,** 59 Rydal Close, Warndon, Worcester, England.

Since 1975 this regional organization has published the annual *Skyscan Magazine*, which contains articles by members on local sightings and general aspects of UFOLOGY. It has a circulation of 100, and is available directly from the organization. Keith Knight is Editor.

**SKY SHIP,** flying saucer-shaped aircraft being developed in the United Kingdom to carry cargoes up to 400 tons over distances up to 1,000 miles at a speed of about 100 miles per hour. The craft's shape is intended

Sky Ship. *(United Press International Photo)*

to minimize the effect of ground winds and to allow for a better distribution of load. Sky Ship uses vectored thrust from its fan jets for docking maneuvers. Its low operating costs are intended to make it a suitable form of transport for Third World development projects.

**SKYWATCH,** organized surveillance of the sky conducted by members of a UFO organization, usually at night.

**SKYWATCH,** publication of the MANCHESTER AERIAL PHENOMENA INVESTIGATION TEAM (MAPIT).

**SKY WATCH INTERNATIONAL,** coordinated effort by numerous European UFO organizations to survey skies from different locations on specific, predetermined dates.

**SMART COMMITTEE,** group consisting of Spencer Beresford, Richard Haines and Frank Hammil, who were staff members of the House Science and Astronautics Committee, and headed by Robert Smart, a staff member of the House Armed Services Committee. In 1960, both committees had called for a briefing by the UNITED STATES AIR FORCE (USAF) on the UFO project. In addition to Smart's group, the meeting was attended by representatives of the CENTRAL INTELLIGENCE AGENCY (CIA), Air Force officers and astronomer J. ALLEN HYNEK.

Noting that the investigative ability of Air Force bases was limited to routine cases, the committee recommended that financing should be provided by the Office of the Secretary of the Air Force to give PROJECT BLUE BOOK the personnel, the mobility and the capability to investigate cases indicating high intelligence or scientific potential, as well as those generating an unusual amount of public interest. In addition, Smart requested that summaries of all significant cases be forwarded to his office. None of the recommendations or Smart's request was implemented.

Bibliography: Hynek, J. Allen, *The UFO Experience: A Scientific Inquiry* (Chicago: Henry Regnery Company, 1972).

**SMIT, BENNIE,** *see* **FORT BEAUFORT, S. AFRICA**

**SMITH, WARREN,** *see* **CALGARY, ALBERTA**

**SNEIDER, ROBERT R.,** UNITED STATES AIR FORCE (USAF) captain who headed the Air Force UFO project, initially as PROJECT SIGN and subsequently as PROJECT GRUDGE, from November 1948 until March 1951.

**SNIPPY,** three-year-old Appaloosa saddle pony whose much publicized death made him the most famous victim of the mysterious ANIMAL MUTILATIONS of the 1960s and 1970s. His body was found in Alamosa County, Colorado, on September 15, 1967, after he had been missing for two days. He had been skinned, leaving bleached bones exposed around the skull and shoulders. An incision around the neck was so smooth it appeared to have been made with a surgeon's scalpel. The vital organs were gone and no blood remained in the carcass or on the ground. A medicinal ODOR pervaded the site. Fifteen circular impressions resembling exhaust marks were spread over an area of approximately five thousand square yards and some bushes had been flattened. No footprints were found in the vicinity of the body. Snippy's own tracks stopped one hundred feet from where he lay dead. When Mrs. Lewis, the horse's owner, punctured a piece of horse-flesh encased in some skin found near the body, a green viscous substance oozed out into her hand, which burned until she washed it. An ongoing rash of UFO sightings in the area, plus subsequent mutilations in Pennsylvania, launched Snippy's name into the headlines. Sightseers and investigators poured into Alamosa County during the following weeks. Representatives were sent by the CONDON COMMITTEE, the NATIONAL INVESTIGATIONS COMMITTEE ON AERIAL PHENOMENA (NICAP) and the AERIAL PHENOMENA RESEARCH ORGANIZATION (APRO). Autopsies, sample gathering and examination of the site resulted in a confusion of conflicting reports and multiple explanations of the case. Two bullets were later found in Snippy's body, which might have laid the case to rest had not four more horses and four cows succumbed to the phantom slaughterers.

Various groups attributed Snippy's death to carnivorous flying saucer OCCUPANTS, practical jokers and a good samaritan, who may have slit the animal's throat to save him from a slow death caused by an infection. There was enough reported evidence to lend some

Forestry aide Duane Martin tests Snippy's body for radiation. Mrs. Berle Lewis, the horse's owner, points to the exposed bones while local teacher Leona Wellington looks on. *(United Press International Photo)*

credence to any one of these hypotheses. Snippy remains a tourist attraction today in Alamosa where his skeleton is on display in a pottery shop.

Bibliography: Saunders, David, and R. Roger Harkins, *UFOs? Yes!* (New York: New American Library, 1968).

**SOBEPS** *see* **SOCIÉTÉ BELGE D'ÉTUDE DES PHÉNOMÈNES SPATIAUX**

**SOCIEDADE BRASILIERA DE ESTUDOS SOBRE DISCOS VOADORES (SBEDV),** Caixa Postal No. 16.017, Correio do Largo do Machado, Rio de Janeiro, Brazil.

The purpose of this investigative organization is to explain the UFO phenomenon and to study the behavior of UFO OCCUPANTS, particularly in relation to their contacts with human beings.

SBEDV's staff consists of President Walter Karl Buhler, Vice-President Guilherme Pereira, Treasurers Wilson Teixeira and Amanda Alves Pinto, and Assistant Treasurers Otto Erwin Gluck, Almiro Barauna and Francisco Sá Borges. The group conducts field investigations and collects and analyzes information from other UFO publications. It publishes the biannual BOLETIM SBEDV, which contains reports of landings and ABDUCTIONS. English summaries are included. The group exchanges information with other UFO organizations.

**SOCIEDADE PELOTENSE DE INVESTIGACAO E PESQUISA DE DISCOS VOADORES (SPIPDV),** Rua Marcilio Dias 1566, 96.1000 Pelotas, Rio Grande do Sul, Brazil; telephone number: 228514.

The purposes of this investigative organization are to investigate local sightings, to research worldwide UFO reports in order to establish UFO characteristics and patterns, to exchange information with other groups, to disseminate its findings to the public and to maintain a library and archives. The group holds that UFOs are spaceships piloted by highly-evolved beings from PLANETS in our own solar system and from other solar systems within our galaxy. Although it does not claim to know the aims of the extraterrestrials, SPIPDV holds that some UFO crews are benevolent, while others are hostile. It is particularly interested in cases where UFO OCCUPANTS have allegedly been seen collecting samples of plants, minerals, animals and even human beings. The group speculates that the purpose of these activities might be to populate another planet or to prepare for adaptation to living on Earth at a future time. The case which SPIPDV considers its most important to date is that of the 1978 ABDUCTION of a student named José Inacio Alvaro, who was allegedly forced to have sexual intercourse with a blond, humanoid woman.

SPIPDV was founded in 1972 by LUIZ DO ROSÁRIO REAL, who serves as President. Other staff members include Vice-President Moacyr Barbosa de Leon, Secretary Wilson da Silva Stone, Treasurer Antonio Joaquim de Moraes and Financial Advisors Rafael Alves Caldela, Indú Ferrari and Domingos Bachilli. The group has twenty members. Its four field investigators are located in Pelotas and neighboring towns. Information is released through the Brasilian newspaper *Diario Popular*, and through the group's own publication, *Boletim SPIPDV*.

**SOCIÉTÉ BELGE D'ÉTUDE DES PHÉNOMÈNES SPATIAUX (SOBEPS),** Avenue Paul Janson 74, B–1070 Brussels, Belgium; telephone number: 02-524 28 48.

The purpose of this investigative organization is to observe and study spacial phenomena and related problems such as UFOs, and to disseminate collected data to the public. The group is engaged in the statistical analysis of UFOs and the study of the sound of a UFO recorded on a magnetophone. While it gives consideration to numerous HYPOTHESES, SOBEPS takes no position regarding the identity and origin of UFOs.

This nonprofit organization was founded in 1971. Its staff consists of Chairman and Editor Michel Bougard, Director and Publisher Lucien Clerebaut, and Assistant Editors Alice Ashton and Jean-Luc Vertongen. Fifty field investigators are located throughout Belgium and data is studied by a staff of scientists. Information is released through conferences, debates and a bimonthly review entitled INFORESPACE.

**SOCIÉTÉ INTERNATIONALE DE DÉVELOPPEMENT DES IDÉES POUR LE PROGRES** *see* DETECTOR SIDIP

**SOCIÉTÉ PARISIENNE D'ÉTUDE DES PHENOMENES SPATIAUX ET ÉTRANGES (SPEPSE),** Domaine de Montval 5, allée Sisley, 78160 Marly le Roi, France; telephone number 958.98.09.

This organization stresses that its structure is based on analytic thought and debate about the UFO phenomenon, rather than on field investigation. The main goals of SPEPSE are to prove the reality or nonreality of UFOs and other strange phenomena, to discover their origin and to research their scientific, technical, social, psychological and spiritual implications. SPEPSE's other purposes are to research bona fide reports of strange phenomena, to study, analyze and collectively reflect on such reports, to publicize all relevant information and the latest findings regarding the subject, and to organize conferences, debates and public expositions. The group has no beliefs regarding the identity, origin and purpose of UFOs, since it is involved only in researching and studying the subject.

This nonprofit organization was founded in 1978 by Raymond Bonnaventure, who serves as Secretary. Michel Monnerie is President, and Pascal Montreuil is Treasurer. There are thirty members. The group collects data on every significant sighting reported in the publications of other organizations and from national and international sources. Members are assigned to teams specializing in various aspects of research. These divisions include the DETECTUFO group (which runs an automatic control station for the detection of UFOs), the ASTRO UFO group (which serves as a source of astronomical information and organizes skywatches), the FICHUFO group (which maintains a card-index file on unusual phenomena), a documentation group (which collects, classifies and organizes information on UFOLOGY and associated phenomena and on technical and scientific research), a thematic research group (which conducts analytic research, research based on previous studies, and a sociopsychological study of the contact phenomenon which is code-named Project MAGONIA) and an investigative group (which incorporates Project MARINUFO, a study of bona fide reports of marine sightings). Information files and a library are available to members. SPEPSE publishes *UFOlogie Contact,* a quarterly newsletter providing general worldwide information on UFO policy, news of current and upcoming events and some articles. It also publishes *UFOlogie Contact Special,* which is issued not more than three times a year and deals with specialized research.

SPEPSE is a member of the COMITÉ EUROPÉEN DE COORDINATION DE LA RECHERCHE UFOLOGIQUE (CECRU).

**SOCIÉTÉ VAROISE D'ÉTUDE DES PHÉNOMÈNES SPATIAUX (SVEPS),** 6 rue Paulin-Guérin, 83000 Toulon, France; telephone number: 1694-927928.

This investigative organization publishes a quarterly magazine, *Approche*. The group is a member of the COMITÉ EUROPÉEN DE COORDINATION DE LA RECHERCHE UFOLOGIQUE (CECRU).

**SOCIÉTÉ VAUCLUSIENNE D'ÉTUDE DES PHÉNOMÈNES SPATIAUX (SOVEPS),** c/o Christian Langlume, "Les Confines," Entrée No. 4, 84270 Vedene, France; telephone number: 32 22 11.

The purpose of this investigative organization is to study unexplained and aerial phenomena, which SOVEPS believes might bring us evidence of an extraordinary intellectual, technical and social advancement.

This organization was founded in 1976 by Roger Tralongo, who serves as President; Christian Langlume, who serves as General Secretary; and P. Lescop. Additional staff members include Vice-Presidents Bernadette Langlume, Mrs. Philippon and Mrs. Etienne; Administrative Secretary Christiane Coste; and Treasurer Marie Claude Rami. Investigations are carried out in Vaucluse and in the bordering French departments. The organization conducts research, study groups, expositions and conferences, as well as exchanging information with other organizations. A quarterly magazine, *Approche,* is published in association with the SOCIÉTÉ VAROISE D'ÉTUDE DES PHÉNOMÈNES SPATIAUX (SVEPS).

**SOCIETY FOR THE INVESTIGATION OF THE UNEXPLAINED (SITU),** Box 265, Little Silver, New Jersey 07739; telephone number: 201-842-5229.

SITU exists for the purpose of collecting data on the unexplained, for promoting proper investigation of both individual reports and general subjects and for reporting significant data to its members. The range of subjects dealt with includes BIGFOOT; living frogs and toads found entombed in rock; metal chains of unknown origin embedded in rock; manufactured objects found in chunks of coal; creatures living at great depths within the Earth; "bottomless" stairs going deep underground; giant, red-haired mummies; sea monsters; giant-spoked, phosphorescent, submarine "lightwheels"; phantom ships; strange DISAPPEARANCES at sea; bottomless lakes; polywater; migration and homing instincts; ATLANTIS; UFOs; MEN IN BLACK; NAZCA; Stonehenge; LEY LINES; the PIRI RE'IS MAP; Noah's Ark; FAFROTSKIES; ball lightning; TEKTITES; time travel; the fourth dimension; extrasensory perception; psychokineses; dowsing; biomagnetics; biorhythms; TELEPATHY; TELEPORTATION; the hollow Earth hypothesis; reincarnation; black holes; ghosts and poltergeists.

This nonprofit organization was founded by the late IVAN SANDERSON. Staff members include President Robert C. Warth, Vice-President R. Martin Wolf, Treasurer Steven N. Mayne, Secretary Albena Zwerver, Greg Arend and Susan Malone. The Scientific Advisory Board consists of George A. Agogino (Archaeology), Carl H. Delacato (Mentalogy), J. ALLEN HYNEK (Astronomy), George C. Kennedy (Geomorphology and Geophysics), Martin Kruskal (Mathematics), Samuel B. McDowell (General Biology), Vladimir Markotic (Ethnosciology and Ethnology), Kirtley F. Mather (Geology), John R. Napier (Physical Anthropology), Michael A. Persinger (Psychology), FRANK B. SALISBURY (phytochemistry), BERTHOLD ERIC SCHWARZ (Mental Science), Roger W. Westcoff (Cultural Anthropology and Linguistics), A. Joseph Wraight (Geography and Oceanography) and Robert K. Zuck (Botany). The group has approximately 1,500 members and several field investigators. Bob Rickard, Editor of FORTEAN TIMES, is SITU's foreign representative in the United Kingdom. A reference library and files are available to members. The society publishes a quarterly journal, called PURSUIT.

## SOCIETY OF METAPHYSICIANS, Archers' Court, Stonestile Lane, The Ridge, Hastings, Sussex, England; telephone number: 0424-751 577.

The purpose of this organization is to establish a neometaphysical system that encompasses all aspects of human development. The group holds that UFOs originate on other PLANETS, other solar systems or from other dimensions and are piloted by beings who utilize extradimensional sciences. The Archers' Court Research Group, an associate group of the society, has tested flying saucer PHOTOGRAPHS with an aura biometer. This device, according to the group, can be used as a spectograph, can verify the authenticity of paintings and signatures, can be used as a diagnostic instrument and can ascertain the "energy content" of any object. The organization claims that tests using the biometer show that some of the objects in the famous GEORGE ADAMSKI photographs are spacecraft whose propulsion system may in some intimate manner be interconnected with the life of the crew. The society is concerned with the development of dimensional sciences in order to establish communication at a level which qualifies mankind for inclusion in the worlds of higher dimensions.

This nonprofit organization was founded in 1944 by Royal Air Force scientists. Its ten-person staff includes Founder-President John J. Williamson, Director of Research Alan J. Mayne and General Secretary A. Ross. The society has 2,000 active members and 60,000 contact members. Approximately 200 field investigators are located throughout the world, including Iron Curtain countries. The society produces and distributes books and tape cassettes, organizes conferences and lectures, coordinates research activities, provides correspondence courses and local courses and offers free advisory service to members. Book, tape cassette and equipment lists are published regularly. METAPHYSICAL DIGEST is published annually. The society's newsletter is published about four times a year.

Nigerian headquarters: 54 Adeyi Avenue, Bodija, Ibadan, Nigeria.

## SOCORRO, NEW MEXICO, location of one of the classic sightings of modern UFO history. At approximately 5:45 P.M. on April 24, 1964, Deputy Marshal Lonnie Zamora was chasing a speeding motorist on the outskirts of town. Suddenly, his attention was diverted by a roar and a descending blue and orange flame in the sky about 4,000 feet to the southwest. Abandoning his chase, he turned off onto a rough road leading to the area. After repeated attempts to drive up a steep incline, Zamora finally reached the top. About 800 feet away, he could see an egg-shaped object, shiny-white like aluminum, sitting in a shallow gully. At first glance, Zamora thought the object was a crashed car standing on end. Then, he noticed two people in white coveralls beside the object. They were small, leading Zamora to think they were either small adults or large children. One of the figures seemed startled as it apparently caught sight of the watching police officer. Zamora continued down the road to get closer to the object. As he passed behind a ridge, his view of the craft was temporarily blocked. He stopped at a point about 100 feet from the object. The white-clad figures were no longer visible. As he stepped out of his car and started walking toward the object, he could see that it was standing on two legs. On its side was a strange red insignia, about two feet high. Suddenly, there was a load roar. Thinking the object was about to explode, Zamora ran to take cover behind the car. The craft began to rise slowly, emitting a light-blue and orange flame. Still alarmed, Zamora continued to run until he was about 200 feet away from the site. When the roar stopped, he turned to watch, now without his glasses, which he had dropped by the car. At the height of about ten feet, the object began to move slowly in a southwesterly direction. Then it rose higher and took off, disappearing in the distance. Zamora was joined by Sergeant Sam Chavez. They examined the site where

Sketch of craft and its insignia seen by Lonnie Zamora at Socorro, New Mexico, on April 24, 1964.

they found burned brush and four depressions in the ground.

The case was investigated by numerous civilian UFO organizations and journalists, as well as by the UNITED STATES AIR FORCE (USAF) and an agent of the FEDERAL BUREAU OF INVESTIGATION (FBI), who happened to be in Chavez's office at the time. The four depressions in the ground were considered by many investigators to have been made by landing pads. Opel Grinder, a local gas station attendant, reported that an unidentified motorist had mentioned seeing a strange craft headed toward a mesa. After the object had dropped out of view, the motorist saw a police car headed toward the area. A newspaper story about two men from Iowa, Paul Kies and Larry Kratzer, who had supposedly seen the Socorro UFO, was followed up in 1978 by PRIVATE UFO INVESTIGATIONS (PUFOI). Kies and Kratzer were interviewed, and, while their accounts of the incident suggested that one of them might have been the motorist referred to by Grinder, there were many discrepancies between the two men's reports, as well as between their accounts and Zamora's. The PUFOI investigators suggest that these discrepancies might be attributable to the fourteen-year time lapse, during which time it is not unusual for a person to forget or sometimes add details while attempting to recall an experience.

J. ALLEN HYNEK, investigating in his official capacity as consultant to the Air Force, told the news media it was one of the soundest, best-substantiated reports. He warned Major HECTOR QUINTANILLA, current head of PROJECT BLUE BOOK, that UFO organizations would consider it the best-authenticated landing case on record, and would use it as leverage to try to obtain a long-sought Congressional investigation of the UFO situation. Quintanilla contacted the NATIONAL AERONAUTICS AND SPACE ADMINISTRATION (NASA), the Jet Propulsion Laboratory (JPL) and fifteen industrial firms to find out if they were conducting any experiments with lunar landing models. The reply in each case was negative. The Air Force found no explanation for the case. It is the only landing, trace and OCCUPANT case listed as "unidentified" in Blue Book files.

Author and computer scientist JACQUES VALLEE has pointed out that the insignia described by Zamora is the

same as a medieval Arabic sign for VENUS. Engineer LEON DAVIDSON, on the other hand, has used the insignia to make a case for his theory that the Socorro UFO was a man-made craft. He has demonstrated that by rotating and moving the lines of the insignia, the initials "CIA" and "AD" can be formed. The latter, in Davidson's opinion, represented the initials of Allen Dulles, head of the CENTRAL INTELLIGENCE AGENCY (CIA) at the time of the sighting. Davidson states that although it might seem incredible that the CIA would paint its own initials on a saucer HOAX, "Dulles had enough 'chutzpah' to order such a stunt." Alternatively, he suggests that a rival agency such as the Defense Intelligence Agency (DIA), in concert with the FBI, staged the event as part of an effort to downgrade the CIA's public image. The speeding motorist, Davidson conjectures, was a decoy to lead Zamora to the landing site.

Writer PHILIP KLASS, who originally proposed that Zamora had seen a PLASMA, now believes the case to be a hoax. He has pointed out numerous changes made by Zamora in his repeated retelling of the incident. Klass questions the fact that Zamora's drawing of the craft at a distance of 800 feet shows a *vertical* egg-shaped object standing on two legs, while his drawing of the craft at a distance of 100 feet shows a *horizontal* egg-shaped object standing on two legs. After visiting the site, Klass claimed that from the position of the alleged pad prints, Zamora would have been able to see at least three legs, if not all four. Moreover, he points out, the locations of the indentations indicate a craft whose landing gear is completely lacking in symmetry. The prints themselves were different from one another and could easily be reproduced with a shovel or by the removal of a rock from the sandy soil. Another discrepancy in the report concerns the arrival of Chavez. While Zamora claimed to have inspected the alleged landing site while awaiting Chavez, the latter claimed that Zamora had been so shaken by the event that he had asked Chavez to lead the way down into the gully. Klass also points out that pictures of the site taken by Chavez show charring on only one mesquite bush and a clump of grass, while other bushes, grass and small twigs remain unaffected by the alleged blast of flame. He also expresses surprise that not only did commuters on the nearby highway fail to see the UFO, but Mr. and Mrs. Phillips, the occupants of a nearby house, had seen and heard nothing. Their home was located only 1,000 feet from the site. Their windows and French doors had been open at the time. Yet Zamora, supposedly, had heard the initial roar of the object above the noise of his automobile engine at a distance of 4,000 feet. Klass concludes that the incident was a hoax, perpetrated with the aim of bringing tourist dollars to the town. The purported landing site lay conveniently between the two major highways leading into Socorro. It was on property owned by Mayor Holm Bursum, who was Zamora's boss and the town banker. Within one year of the alleged sighting, the road to the location, connecting it with both major highways, had been improved. However, posters directing tourists to the site were never erected as had originally been planned in 1965 by the Chamber of Commerce.

Thirty-one hours after Zamora's sighting, Orlando Gallego claims to have seen an identical UFO land at La Madera, New Mexico. Police officers who examined the alleged landing site reported evidence of burning and four depressions on the ground. Gallegos and his family denied any knowledge of the Socorro incident.

Bibliography: Klass, Philip J., *UFOs Explained* (New York: Random House, 1974); Davidson, Leon, leaflet entitled *The CIA and the Saucer* (White Plains, N.Y.: Blue-Book Publishers, 1977); Keyhoe, Donald E., and Gordon I. R. Lore (eds.), *Strange Effects from UFOs* (Washington, D.C.: National Investigations Committee on Aerial Phenomena, 1969).

**SODOM AND GOMORRAH,** neighboring cities which, according to the Bible, were burned to the ground by God because of the wickedness of their inhabitants. A man named Lot, warned in advance by two ANGELS, was able to escape. However, his wife, disobeying the angels' instructions not to look at the destruction, was turned into a pillar of salt. Supporters of the ANCIENT ASTRONAUTS hypothesis believe that extraterrestrials destroyed Sodom and Gomorrah with an atomic bomb. Lot's wife, reluctant to leave, lingered too far behind the fleeing party and was reduced to a pile of white ashes by the nuclear blast.

Bibliography: Von Däniken, Erich, *Chariots of the Gods?* (New York: G. P. Putnam's Sons, 1970).

**SOMMER, ELKE,** German-born actress and film star who reportedly saw a UFO in November 1977. While standing in her backyard one evening at about 10:30, she saw a glowing reddish-orange sphere floating by some trees about 150 feet away. The object was about twenty feet in diameter. After hovering for a few moments at a height of about one hundred feet, the UFO began to move toward her very slowly. Then it began to descend at a thirty-degree angle until it was twenty-five-to-fifty feet off the ground. Sommer ran indoors to fetch her husband, but by the time they returned the object had vanished.

**SONIC BOOM,** explosive sound caused by the shock wave generated by an aircraft or other object flying faster than the speed of sound. In cases where no sonic booms have been reported in association with UFOs accelerating beyond the speed of sound, it is probable that the booms created are heard by people miles away rather than by witnesses directly below the object. AIR QUAKES caused by sonic booms in 1977 and 1978 on the East Coast of the United States are attributed to UFOs by some UFOLOGISTS

Lot flees the destruction of Sodom. *(Culver Pictures)*

Bibliography: Vallee, Jacques and Janine, *Challenge to Science—The UFO Enigma* (Chicago: Henry Regnery Company, 1966).

**SORATOBU ENBAN KENKYU,** publication of the MODERN SPACE FLIGHT ASSOCIATION (MSFA).

**SOUND.** Most witnesses do not report any sounds connected with UFOs. In most cases where a sound is heard, it is described as a hum or a buzz. On rare occasions, witnesses have described hearing crackling, thunderous or swishing sounds or a series of sharp explosive noises. SONIC BOOMS are rarely reported in association with UFO sightings. However, AIR QUAKES caused by sonic booms in 1977 and 1978 on the east coast of the United States were attributed to UFOs by some UFOlogists.

It has been conjectured that ANIMAL REACTIONS to UFOs are induced by ultrasonic waves imperceptible to the human auditory system.

**SOURCEBOOK PROJECT,** P.O. Box 107, Glen Arm, Maryland 21057.

This publishing and mail order bookselling project is run by William R. Corliss. His Handbooks and Source-books are volumes containing collections of accounts of strange phenomena and discoveries over the past 200 years. Material is reprinted from periodicals, such as *American Naturalist, Journal of Geophysical Research, Journal of Psychology, Meteorological Magazine, Monthly Weather Review, Nature, New Scientist, Science, Scientific American, Weather* and *Zoologist.*

In addition, Corliss sells books by popular authors dealing with UFOs, ATLANTIS, BIGFOOT, parapsychology and other occult subjects.

**SOUTH AMERICA.** This part of the world accounts for more UFO reports than any other area. The majority of Latin American sightings occur in BRAZIL, followed by Argentina, Chile, PERU, Venezuela and Uruguay. A large proportion of these sightings involve landings and OCCUPANTS. The general public tends toward a fairly casual acceptance of the EXTRATERRESTRIAL HYPOTHESIS (ETH).

**SOUTH ASHBURNHAM, MASSACHUSETTS,** location of the alleged ABDUCTION of Betty Andreasson by UFO entities on January 25, 1967.

Andreasson was at home with her family in the evening, when a power failure occurred. A glowing light was visible through the windows. Moments later, the house lights came on again. Andreasson's family seemed to be frozen, as if in suspended animation. She, however, was unaffected and watched as four creatures entered the house, passing right through the closed wooden door. The entities were about three-and-a-half to four feet tall. Their heads were pear-shaped, large on top with narrow chins. They had holes for noses and scarlike slits for mouths. Their large, almond-shaped eyes slanted around to the sides of their heads. Each sleeve of their dark blue, skintight uniforms bore a symbol resembling a bird with outstretched wings. The leader, who identified himself as Quazgaa, began to converse telepathically with Andreasson. He gave her a thin, blue book in exchange for a Bible.

Andreasson was then taken outside to an oval craft. Once aboard, she was submitted to a frightening and painful physical examination. Afterwards, she was placed on a chair where air hoses were attached to her nose and mouth. A glasslike cover was placed over both her and the chair in such a way that she was enclosed in an airtight compartment. It was then filled with fluid. She sat for a while, experiencing pleasant, pulsing vibrations. Then the liquid was drained from the enclosure.

Andreasson had apparently been brought to an alien realm. The entities led her through a dark tunnel to a place where the atmosphere and everything in it were colored red. Creatures resembling lemurs were climbing all over square, cementlike buildings. Andreasson was frightened of the animals, which had eyes on stems where their heads should have been. Soon, she and her companions arrived in an area where everything was green. The succession of strange sights culminated in the appearance of a bird, about fifteen feet tall, standing in front of a brilliant source of light. Andreasson was overcome by HEAT. When the discomfort subsided, the bird had vanished and in its place was a fire. The flames shrank into a pile of ashes from which there emerged a large, fat worm. Then Andreasson heard a voice speaking to her. Believing the voice to be that of God, she was overcome with joy. She was told she had been chosen for a mission which would be revealed to her at a later time.

Andreasson was returned to her home, where the members of her family remained frozen like statues. She went to bed and fell asleep while one of the entities watched over her. When she awakened the following morning, her family was up and going about its normal business.

Later investigations revealed that Andreasson's father and her eldest daughter, Becky, were apparently conscious during part of the time that the aliens were purportedly in their house. Their recollections confirmed Andreasson's story. The major details of her alleged experience—many of them extremely bizarre—were recalled under regressive HYPNOSIS. During these sessions, it sometimes seemed that the UFO entities themselves were channeling messages directly through Andreasson.

It was also revealed that Andreasson had supposedly been abducted by aliens on a previous occasion and had sighted strange beings several times in the interim. The blue book given to her by the creatures had disappeared shortly after the incident.

Andreasson's alleged experience shared many characteristics with other well-known abduction cases. However, RAYMOND FOWLER, who participated in the investigation, claims that some of the details of her story match those of several unpublished cases, leading him to surmise that Andreasson did not adopt her story, either intentionally or subconsciously, from the UFO literature. The experience is marked by strong religious overtones, which seem to tie in with Andreasson's Christian beliefs. The vision of the gigantic bird was an enactment of the ancient legend of the Phoenix, an early Christian symbol of resurrection. Fowler speculates that this might have been a programmed vision created by the aliens. They might have been attempting to gain her confidence by associating themselves with the God in whom she believes. Other theories Fowler contemplates are that UFO OCCUPANTS are God's ANGELS or that they are extraterrestrials undertaking genuine missionary work.

A tragic incident occurred in 1977, reportedly as an aftermath of the case. While Andreasson was talking on the telephone with another alleged UFO abduction victim, alien voices reportedly interrupted the conversation. Although their language was unintelligible, Andreasson sensed anger and a threat of some imminent disaster. That night two of her sons were killed in a car crash.

Bibliography: Fowler, Raymond E., *The Andreasson Affair* (Englewood Cliffs, N.J.: Prentice-Hall, 1979).

**SOUTH BERWICK, MAINE,** residence of Frances Swann, who claims to have been in contact with SPACE PEOPLE for the past twenty years. During the middle of 1959, two Navy intelligence officers went to South Berwick to meet Swann at the request of retired Admiral H. B. Knowles, who lived in the town. Swann demonstrated a phenomenon known as automatic writing to the two officers, claiming that the words she wrote were transmitted by UFO OCCUPANTS. The messages stated that the sender was a being named Affa from Uranus. Reportedly, Swann was able to answer questions posed by the intelligence officers that were beyond her education and technical knowledge.

In Washington, D.C., on July 6, 1959, one of the two Navy officers, just back from Maine, went into a trance while in the company of the other naval intelligence officer (allegedly Robert Nisham, a Navy photo analyst

assigned to the CENTRAL INTELLIGENCE AGENCY [CIA] at the time) and CIA officer Arthur Lundahl. Reportedly, he, too, received messages from Affa through automatic writing. Affa was supposedly one of a four-man extraterrestrial patrol team of the "OEEV" (Universal Association of PLANETS) assigned to Project "EU" or "Euenza" (Earth). When asked if his craft could be seen as proof of his existence, Affa told the three men to go to the window. Allegedly, they saw a flying saucer fly by. According to some accounts of this incident, a check with Washington Center RADAR revealed that the radar return was blocked in the sector indicated by the officers.

UNITED STATES AIR FORCE (USAF) Major ROBERT FRIEND, acting chief of PROJECT BLUE BOOK, was asked to come to Washington to evaluate the situation. The experiment was repeated in Friend's presence on July 9, 1959. The naval intelligence officer lapsed into a trance and began to respond to questions by using automatic writing. When Affa was asked to arrange a fly-by, the reply was, "The time is not right."

When Friend returned to Wright-Patterson Air Force Base, he prepared a memorandum on the case for his commanding general, who stated that he would personally take charge of further evaluation.

Although Friend has substantiated the preceding information, Lundahl has denied that a flying saucer was seen on July 6, 1959, or that the naval officer went into a trance during Friend's presence on July 9, 1959. He confirms only that the naval officer demonstrated automatic writing which he claimed to have learned from Swann. Today, Swann continues to receive alleged messages from Space People on an almost daily basis. However, she no longer uses the automatic writing method, but merely allows the messages to enter her mind. Reportedly, she has maintained her involvement with U.S. intelligence, an involvement which she has allegedly been told to keep secret.

Bibliography: Emmeneger, Robert, *UFOs, Past, Present and Future* (New York: Ballantine Books, 1974); Gourley, Jay, "The Day Naval Intelligence Established 'Contact,'" *Second Look* (Washington, D.C.: Second Look, May 1979).

**SOUTH CENTRAL UNITED STATES,** location of a classic RADAR/visual UFO sighting on July 17, 1957. An Air Force RB–47, equipped with Electronic Countermeasures (ECM) gear and carrying six officers, was followed by a UFO for over 700 miles as it flew from Mississippi, through Louisiana and Texas and into Oklahoma. The intense light was seen visually, was tracked by ground radar and was detected by the onboard ECM monitoring equipment. In several instances, the UFO's sudden appearances and

DISAPPEARANCES were observed by all three at once. The object trailed about ten miles behind the RB–47 for some time, then moved rapidly to a position in front of the aircraft. The pilot headed toward the light but, as he approached, it disappeared. As the pilot turned to resume his course, the target appeared below the RB–47. He put the plane into a dive in an attempt to intercept the object, but again it disappeared. Low on fuel, the RB–47 returned to its home base.

Unable to find the Air Force records on the case, the CONDON COMMITTEE based its evaluation on witnesses' testimony given ten years after the incident. The CONDON REPORT lists the case as "unidentified." After atmospheric physicist JAMES MCDONALD had located the original records, the AMERICAN INSTITUTE OF AERO-NAUTICS AND ASTRONAUTICS (AIAA) selected his report on the case for publication as one that demonstrated a truly anomalous phenomenon. Writer PHILIP KLASS, however, concluded that the various observations were not interrelated and could be attributed to ground radar returns, relay malfunctions and MISIDENTIFICATIONS of a METEOR, conventional craft and astronomical objects. His analysis of the case was later accepted as a plausible explanation by the pilot and radar operator of the RB–47.

Bibliography: McDonald, James E., "Science in Default: Twenty-two Years of Inadequate UFO Investigations," in Sagan, Carl, and Thornton Page (eds.), *UFOs—A Scientific Debate* (Ithaca, N.Y.: Cornell University Press, 1972); Klass, Philip J., *UFOs Explained* (New York: Random House, 1974).

## SOUTH EAST PARANORMAL INFORMATION BUREAU (SEPIB), 1539 Kenwood Avenue South West, Winter Haven, Florida 33880; telephone number: 813-299-5228.

The principal objectives of this investigative organization are: 1. to provide a place where people wishing to report experiences involving paranormal phenomena may do so without fear of ridicule or unnecessary publicity; 2. to serve as an information service for those who are interested in paranormal phenomena; 3. to establish a library on paranormal phenomena; and 4. to establish a museum on paranormal phenomena. The group has no official opinion regarding the identity of UFOs. The sightings it has studied reveal no scientific evidence to support the possibility of extraterrestrial visitation.

This nonprofit organization was founded in 1975 by L. West Perrine, who serves as Director; and Larry W. Daniel, who serves as Copresident. Earl Parker, Roger Phillips and Dan William are Officers of the Board. SEPIB's twenty-six Active Members serve as Field Investigators within the central Florida area.

## SOUTHERN LIGHTS *see* AURORAS

## SOUTHERN UFO NETWORK (SUFON), 23 Sunningdale Drive, Irlam, Greater Manchester M30 6NJ, England; telephone number: 061-4749.

This freelance network of about fifteen organizations in southern Britain was set up in 1978 on the same lines as the NORTHERN UFO NETWORK (NUFON), with which it coordinates closely.

## SOVEPS *see* SOCIÉTÉ VAUCLUSIENNE D'É-TUDE DES PHÉNOMÈNES SPATIAUX

## SOVIET UNION. Flying saucers are known as "Letaiushkie tarelki" in Russian. UFO reports began in 1946, and there were WAVES in 1949 and 1966. There

*May 26, 1976, Kirovsk, USSR:* A disk-shaped craft with a transparent dome on its top. The craft type shows similarity to the Rex Hefflin craft over California, Emil Barnea's photograph over Cluj, Rumania, and Elisabeth Klarer's photo over Natal, Union of South Africa. *(ICUFON/Jyri Lina)*

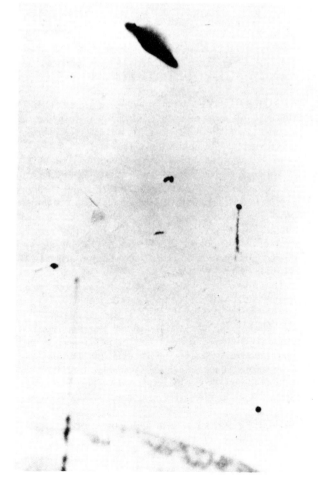

are no UFO investigative organizations in the Soviet Union as there are in other countries but foreign groups such as the MANCHESTER AERIAL PHENOMENA INVESTIGATION TEAM (MAPIT) and SKANDINAVISK UFO INFORMATION (SUFOI) have representatives there. Russian authorities have never conducted any programs such as PROJECT BLUE BOOK, nor do they give the subject any support. However, in 1967, an official meeting was held by the All-Union Cosmonautics Committee to discuss the subject. The meeting was chaired by Air Force Major General Porfiri Stolyarov. FELIX ZIGEL, the Soviet Union's best-known UFO researcher, was vice-president of the committee meeting.

An early UFO sighting occurred in ROBOZERO. An unidentified object which crashed and exploded in the TUNGUSKA REGION in Siberia in 1908 has been the subject of debate for many years among scientists and UFOLOGISTS alike. In 1977, a well-publicized sighting of a jellyfish UFO occurred at Petrozavodsk.

**SPACE BROTHERS,** term used by CONTACTEES to denote flying saucer OCCUPANTS and inhabitants of other PLANETS. They are more often referred to as the SPACE PEOPLE.

**SPACECRAFT PROTECTIVE LANDING AREA FOR THE ADVANCEMENT OF SCIENCE AND THE HUMANITIES (SPLAASH)** *see* NEW AGE FOUNDATION (NAF)

**SPACE DIGEST,** annual review established in 1977. It is available to members of the INTERPLANETARY SPACE TRAVEL RESEARCH ASSOCIATION—UNITED KINGDOM (ISTRA) only. The publication serves as a yearly review of ISTRA activities and the spacial scene in general.

Although *Space Digest* relies heavily on ISTRA resources, special reports showing future trends are accepted from freelance writers. Self-addressed, stamped envelopes should be sent with submissions. Articles should range in length from 250 to 1,000 words. Payment of one pound per 100 words for the purchase of all rights is made upon acceptance. The publishers pay for photographs.

The review is published by ISTRA, 21 Hargwyne Street, Stockwell, London SW9 9RQ, England.

**SPACELINK,** quarterly magazine last published in 1971. Its contents included UFO reports, space books, book reviews, reference information, photographs and illustrations. Back issues are available from its publisher, Lionel Beer, 15 Freshwater Court, Crawford Street, London W1H 1HS, England.

**SPACE PEOPLE,** term used by CONTACTEES to

denote flying saucer OCCUPANTS and inhabitants of other PLANETS. They are also referred to as the SPACE BROTHERS.

**SPACE PHENOMENA RESEARCH GROUP,** P.O. Box 1157, Istanbul, Turkey.

The aim of this organization is to undertake a serious investigation of the UFO phenomenon in Turkey and other parts of the world. The group holds that UFOs are extraterrestrial spacecraft visiting Earth to help the evolution of mankind. It has concluded that by synthesizing and evaluating the knowledge gained from material sources, UFOs and life beyond Earth could be understood more clearly. The organization claims that although it has not received any reports of UFO sightings, SPACE PEOPLE do, in fact, visit Turkey. One of the most important discoveries made by this group is the alleged close relationship between "spiritology" and UFOLOGY.

This nonprofit organization, in conjunction with the Metaphysic Research Society of Turkey, was founded in 1950 by Bedri Ruhselman. It is headed by Selman Gerceksever, Can Sümer and Mehmet Ali Usta. There are fifty members. The group corresponds with well-known UFO and parapsychological organizations in other countries. It has published Turkish-language books on UFOs and maintains a collection of books, photographs and slides. Public conferences are held weekly. A journal, called RUH VE MADDE, and a bulletin, called EVRENDE ZEKI HAYAT, are published monthly and deal with spiritualism, new discoveries, parapsychology, the evolution of man, UFOlogy and intelligent life in the universe.

**SPACE-TIME CONTINUUM,** a level of existence consisting of spatial dimensions and time.

UFO photographed in Spain by Gunter Fansky-Wildemann on November 23, 1966. The witness claimed that it was rotating but scientists explained the object as a cloud. *(Courtesy ICUFON/A. Baguhn)*

**SPAIN.** The Spanish word for UFO is "OVNI," which stands for "objeto volador no identificado" (unidentified flying object). Flying saucers are referred to as "platillos voladores."

The country has a large number of UFO organizations, and the magazine STENDEK is well-known internationally. Spain's best-known UFOLOGISTS are VICENTE-JUAN BALLESTER-OLMOS and author Antonio Ribera.

One of Spain's most famous UFO cases was a sighting at SAN JOSÉ DE VALDERAS in 1967, which initiated subsequent claims that the UFO originated from the PLANET UMMO. Photographs allegedly taken at the time of the sighting were later proven to be HOAXES.

**SPARKS, BRAD C.,** *see* **CITIZENS AGAINST UFO SECRECY (CAUS)**

**SPATIAL DISORIENTATION,** the inability to assess body position, motion and altitude in relation to the environment. Airplane pilots deprived of visual references may sometimes become confused by very gradual changes or abrupt changes in motion, which can create false sensations of ascending, descending and turning. In addition, visual MISINTERPRETATIONS can result in the identification of ground lights as STARS and moving objects. The phenomenon can be counteracted by thorough training in the recognition of its effects and through the use of instrumentation.

Bibliography: *Encyclopedia Britannica* (1976 edition, Volume IX, page 404).

**SPAULDING, WILLIAM H.** (b. November 26, 1941, Cleveland, Ohio), aerospace engineer and West-

William Spaulding.

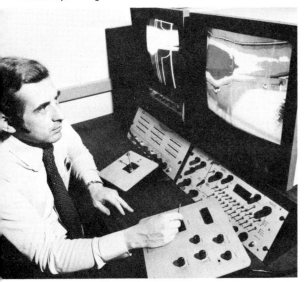

ern Division Director of GROUND SAUCER WATCH (GSW).

Spaulding, who supports the EXTRATERRESTRIAL HYPOTHESIS (ETH), became actively involved in UFOLOGY in 1958. In 1975, with the assistance of some aerospace associates, he developed the computerized UFO photographic evaluation system utilized by GSW to distinguish HOAXES and misidentified conventional objects from bona fide UFOs.

Since 1962, Spaulding has been employed at AiResearch Manufacturing Company, the world's largest builder and designer of gas turbine engines and specialized aerospace components. He is currently Senior Quality Assurance Engineer and Supervisor of the Nondestructive Testing Department. He is a member of the American Society for Nondestructive Testing, from which he has received NDT Level III certification. He is on the editorial committee of *Metal Progress* magazine.

In addition to holding the directorship of GSW, Spaulding is the Arizona State Director of the MUTUAL UFO NETWORK (MUFON). He teaches scientific UFOlogy classes for the city of Phoenix, and has written numerous technical and UFO-related papers, which have been published in aerospace and UFO magazines, respectively.

**SPECIAL REPORT NO. 14,** updated version of the BATTELLE MEMORIAL INSTITUTE report which was distributed by the UNITED STATES AIR FORCE'S PROJECT BLUE BOOK to authorized departments and individuals in 1954 and released to the public in 1955, allegedly to counteract charges of a COVER-UP made by DONALD KEYHOE in his then-newly published book, *The Flying Saucer Conspiracy*. The researchers' assignment had been to determine if anything in the air represented technological developments not known to this country, and to build a model of a flying saucer from the data. With regard to statistical studies of UFO characteristics, the report stated that, "Scientifically evaluated and arranged, the data as a whole did not show any marked patterns or trends. The inaccuracies inherent in this type of data, in addition to the incompleteness of a large proportion of the reports, may have obscured any patterns or trends that otherwise would have been evident. This absence of indicative relationships necessitated an exhaustive study of selected facets of the data in order to draw any valid conclusions." *Special Report No. 14* concluded that ". . . the probability that any of the unknowns considered in this study are 'flying saucers' is concluded to be extremely small, since the most complete and reliable reports from the present data, when isolated and studied, conclusively failed to reveal even a rough model, and since the data as a whole failed to reveal any marked patterns or trends. Therefore, on the basis of this evaluation of the information, it is considered to be highly improbable that any of the reports of unidentified aerial objects examined in this study represent observations of technical developments outside the range of present-day scientific knowledge."

Bibliography: Davidson, Leon, *Flying Saucers: An Analysis of the Air Force Project Blue Book Special Report No. 14* (White Plains, New York: Blue-Book Publishers, 1976).

**SPEED.** There have been reports which estimated the speed of UFOs to be as high as 45,480 miles per hour. A considerable number of reports have shown that when a nocturnal UFO accelerates, its luminosity may increase and its colors change toward the red end of the spectrum. Conversely, deceleration can be accompanied by diminished luminosity and color change toward the violet end of the spectrum. Some observers have noted instant acceleration as opposed to gradual acceleration. Others have reported the sudden DISAPPEARANCE of a moving nocturnal light, which has given them the impression of a light being switched off. Some UFOLOGISTS have speculated that this phenomenon may indicate instant transference or TELEPORTATION of the UFO. Those who consider the PARALLEL UNIVERSE HYPOTHESIS as a possibility, theorize that sudden disappearance may indicate the moment of the UFO's return to its original universe.

In cases where a misidentified astronomical phenomenon or object, such as a PARHELION or VENUS, is involved, the false impression is that the object is moving at a specific speed at which the witness is traveling. Another type of misidentified flying object, that of a reflection of light on CLOUD cover, may be seen to move at incredible speeds. In the case of a spotlight which swivels on an axis, the illuminated spot it creates on a cloud will skim across the sky at a tremendous speed.

**SPEED OF LIGHT,** velocity at which visible light travels in a vacuum and which, according to the laws of physics, cannot be exceeded. Light reaches its highest speed of about 186,000 miles per second in a vacuum. This limitation has reduced the plausibility of the EXTRATERRESTRIAL HYPOTHESIS (ETH), for it establishes unreasonably long travel periods between solar systems. The hypothetical TACHYON, although it demonstrates the possibility of the existence of particles which always travel beyond the speed of light, does not solve the problem of crossing the speed of light boundary to achieve shorter or instantaneous interstellar journeys.

**SPENCE, ROBERT F.**, UNITED STATES AIR FORCE

(USAF) major who served as the Pentagon UFO spokesman during 1957.

**SPEPSE** *see* **SOCIETÉ PARISIENNE D'ÉTUDE DES PHÉNOMÈNES SPATIAUX ET ÉTRANGES**

**SPIPDV** *see* **SOCIEDADE PELOTENSE DE INVESTIGACAO E PESQUISA DE DISCOS VOADORES**

**SPITSBERGEN, NORWAY,** location of one of the most popular legends about CRASHED FLYING SAUCERS. Spitsbergen is made up of five large islands and numerous small islands set within the remote archipelago of Svalbard, 580 miles north of Tromsø, northern Norway. Svalbard has no indigenous inhabitants. The number of settlers rose from about 1,500 during the 1950s to approximately 3,000 in the 1970s.

For a number of years, the main source for the Spitsbergen story was an alleged report in the September 5, 1955, issue of the West German newspaper, *Stuttgartar Tageblatt*. The article claims that a board of enquiry of the Norwegian General Staff was planning to publish a report on the examination of remains of a UFO that crashed near Spitsbergen in early 1952. Chairman of the Board Colonel Gernod Darnbyl was said to have announced that publication was being delayed until certain sensational facts were discussed with British and American experts. It was declared that previous information indicating the UFO's Russian origin was incorrect. The materials used in the disk's construction were completely unknown. It had been established that the craft had not been built by any country on Earth. The article went on to describe the repeated UFO sightings by Second Lieutenants Bobs and Tyllensen, who had been assigned as special observers in the Arctic area following the Spitsbergen event.

The CONDON COMMITTEE, in an attempt to check the validity of this report, contacted the Norwegian Defense Research establishment and was informed that the only fragments retrieved from Spitsbergen had been identified as conventional space hardware. Presumably, such fragments were not the origin of the 1952 story, since the first man-made SATELLITE, Sputnik I, was not launched until 1957. Apparently, there was some official interest during 1952, for the Condon Committee located an American Air Intelligence Information Report dated September 12 of that year which announced that the Norwegian government had no knowledge of a crashed flying saucer in Spitsbergen. The committee attributed the story's origin to a July 9, 1952, edition of another West German newspaper, *Berliner Volksblatt*, which reported that a disk-shaped object, made of unknown metal, and having a diameter of one hundred feet, had crashed in Spitsbergen. Russian symbols on the instrument panel had led to the conclusion that the craft had been built in the Soviet Union. The Condon Committee deduced that the Spitsbergen story was unfounded.

A third account was soon brought forth as evidence. An article in the June 28, 1952, issue of yet another West German newspaper, *Saarbrucken Zeitung,* gave details of the alleged discovery of the disk by Norwegian jet fighters. Experiencing radio interference in the vicinity of the crash site, the pilots had circled until they spotted the remains of a 125-foot disk encircled by a ring of forty-six exhaust jets on its outer rim. Air Force officials dismantled the craft and removed it to Narvik, where experts were waiting to carry out an examination.

Although rumors continue to circle about the alleged Spitsbergen crash, no conclusive evidence has been presented to support the story.

## SPLAASH *see* NEW AGE FOUNDATION

**SPRINGHEEL JACK,** legendary character whose name refers to his ability to spring to great heights from a standing jump. A tall, thin and powerful creature, Springheel Jack was extremely agile. His facial features were distinguished by a prominent nose and cropped or pointed ears. His bony fingers resembled claws. Under a long, flowing cloak, he wore closely-fitting garments of some glittering material resembling oilskin or metal mesh. His headgear consisted of a tall, metallic helmet.

Between November 1837 and February 1838, inhabitants of a London suburb were terrorized by Springheel Jack as he prowled dark alleyways and appeared unexpectedly on people's doorsteps. Two women, who had the misfortune to come face-to-face with Springheel Jack, were knocked unconscious when he sprayed a fiery blue gas at them from a lamp attached to his chest. Horse patrols were mobilized at night to capture the mysterious man but he was always able to leap beyond the reach of his pursuers.

Springheel Jack reappeared in 1877 in Aldershot, Hampshire, England. Two sentries fired at him as he flew over their heads. He retaliated by shooting blue fire at them from his lamp. The sentries were stunned. Springheel Jack had vanished.

Although he has never been observed in conjunction with a UFO, some UFOLOGISTS, who embrace the PARALLEL UNIVERSE HYPOTHESIS, consider Springheel Jack as a possible denizen from the world from which UFOs might emanate. In this respect and in some aspects of his appearance he has been associated with the twentieth-century MOTHMAN.

Bibliography: Vallee, Jacques, *Passport to Magonia* (Chicago: Henry Regnery Company, 1969).

**SPRINKLE, R. (RONALD) LEO** (b. August 30, 1930, Rocky Ford, Colorado; address: Division of Counseling and Testing, University of Wyoming, Box 3708, Laramie, Wyoming 82071; telephone number: 303-766-2187), counseling psychologist and specialist in UFO/psychic phenomena.

Sprinkle was a scoffer of UFO reports until 1950, when he and a fellow student at the University of Colorado observed a UFO. He became a skeptic until 1956, when he and his wife observed a brilliant, red nocturnal light near Boulder, Colorado. The light repeatedly moved and hovered. At one point, they noticed that it had descended between them and the Rocky Mountain foothills, eliminating any possibility that it was a PLANET. Sprinkle became a believer in the EXTRATERRESTRIAL HYPOTHESIS (ETH). Since that time he has sighted several NOCTURNAL LIGHTS during UFO investigations. It is his opinion that humans are being conditioned to accept the UFO experience as an indication that we are not alone and to remind us that we are responsible for the safety and stability of Earth. This process is called cosmic consciousness conditioning.

Sprinkle received his B.A. and M.P.S. from the University of Colorado in 1952 and 1956, respectively, and his Ph.D. from the University of Missouri in 1961. At the University of North Dakota, he was Assistant Professor of Psychology from 1961 to 1964, Assistant Director of the Counseling Center from 1962 to 1963, and Director of the Counseling Center from 1963 to 1964. In 1964, he joined the faculty of the University of Wyoming as Associate Professor of Guidance Education until 1965, Counselor and Assistant Professor of Psychology from 1965 to 1967, Counselor and Associate Professor of Psychology from 1967 to 1970, Director of

R. Leo Sprinkle.

Counseling and Testing and Associate Professor of Psychology from 1970 to 1977, and Director of Counseling and Testing and Professor of Counseling Services from 1977 until the present.

Sprinkle is a lifetime member of the AMERICAN ASSOCIATION FOR THE ADVANCEMENT OF SCIENCE (AAAS); the American Personnel and Guidance Association, a clinical member of the American Association of Marriage and Family Counselors; and a member of the American Association of Sex Educators, Counselors, and Therapists; the American Association of University Professors; the American Psychological Association; the American Society of Clinical Hypnosis; the American Society of Psychical Research; the International Society of Hypnosis; the National Register of Health Service Providers in Psychology; the Parapsychological Association; the Rocky Mountain Psychological Association; the Wyoming Personnel and Guidance Association; and the Wyoming Psychological Association.

Sprinkle has conducted surveys of UFO witnesses to establish personality profiles. He has interviewed approximately fifty UFO witnesses under HYPNOSIS. He utilized hypnotic time regression procedures in an attempt to gain more information about the UFO incidents, as well as to reduce anxiety and tension associated with the experiences. From more than twenty-five of these witnesses, he obtained information on ABDUCTIONS which supposedly occurred within amnesic or loss-of-time periods during the UFO encounters.

Sprinkle is a consultant to the AERIAL PHENOMENA RESEARCH ORGANIZATION (APRO) and the UFO panel of THE NATIONAL ENQUIRER. He was a consultant to the CONDON COMMITTEE in 1968 and, since that time, has acted as consultant to local and national television productions and the *Playboy Magazine* UFO panel. He has written numerous articles that have been published in magazines and as contributing chapters to books on UFO research. He has presented papers at conventions and symposiums, including the 1968 HOUSE SCIENCE AND ASTRONAUTICS COMMITTEE HEARINGS on UFOs.

## SPW *see* STUDIEGROEP PROGRESSIEVE WETENSCHAPPEN

**S.S. & S. PUBLICATIONS,** 17 Shetland Street, Willowdale, Ontario, Canada M2M 1X5.

From 1959 to 1973, this company published *Saucers, Space and Science,* a quarterly magazine that featured Canadian UFO reports and had a circulation of 800. Publisher and Editor GENE DUPLANTIER now runs the company primarily as a mail order service supplying UFO booklets and magazines published by S.S. & S. Publications, books, audio cassette tapes and records.

## STACK OF PLATES CLOUDS *see* CLOUDS

**STANFORD, RAY DENE** (b. June 21, 1938, Robstown, Texas; address: P.O. Box 5310, Austin, Texas 78763; telephone number: 512-458-2031), Founder and Managing Director of PROJECT STARLIGHT INTERNATIONAL (PSI) and State Section Director for the MUTUAL UFO NETWORK (MUFON).

Stanford's interest in UFOs was kindled by personal sightings that date back to 1954. His most awesome encounter, prior to his PSI activities, occurred one night in 1956. Together with three friends, he observed a blue-white oblate spheroid, about thirty-five-to-forty feet in diameter. The UFO circled the witnesses, landed at a distance of about 180 feet, then took off, leaving a glowing trail behind it. The object later passed only three-to-ten-feet over the observers' heads. All four of them remained paralyzed while the UFO was within a range of approximately ninety feet. The monitoring of UFO hard data became of extreme importance to Stanford, and he decided to discontinue his research on rocket engineering. He has no beliefs regarding their origin, but holds that some UFOs give evidence of a highly-advanced technology.

A high school graduate, Stanford has an extensive background of private study in physics, art history and

Ray Stanford with UFO tracking equipment. *(Courtesy PSI)*

psychic phenomena. Although he reportedly has demonstrated highly-developed psychic abilities, he considers them irrelevant to his pursuit of hard-data research. He founded PSI in 1964 but it did not have sufficient funding for an extensive array of UFO-monitoring instruments until it was taken under the financial wing of the ASSOCIATION FOR THE UNDERSTANDING OF MAN (AUM), of which Stanford was a founder in 1971. In 1973, he began planning and acquiring basic instrument systems for PSI. Since then, he and his associates have measured and recorded the effects of UFOs on several occasions.

Stanford received first-place award for research in the physical sciences from the Texas Junior Academy of Science in 1955 for research in the multi-stage principle of rocketry.

Stanford is Editor-in-Chief of PSI's newsletter. He is author of *Socorro "Saucer" in a Pentagon Pantry* (Austin, Texas: Blueapple Books, 1976); and a modified and expanded version, *Socorro Saucer* (London: Fontana, 1978).

**STAR,** a sun, which may or may not have a planetary system. The distance between stars is so vast that, despite their motion, their position in relationship to each other and to Earth appears to remain unchanged over the years. Since Earth rotates on its axis from west to east as it moves around the sun, the stars appear to rise in the east and set in the west. Although bright stars and PLANETS account for numerous UFO reports, their consistent positions in the sky usually permit rapid identification by knowledgeable investigators. Earth's atmosphere causes light rays from stars and reflected sunlight from planets to be refracted and appear to twinkle. Since the lower, dense areas of the atmosphere increase this effect, refraction and dispersion of light is exaggerated when stars and planets are rising and setting. Stars and planets may appear to have unusual SHAPES and to flash brilliantly with red, green and blue colors. In addition, stars and planets may seem to move up and down, sideways, and back and forth. The impression of movement can also be created by AUTOKINESIS, changing density of thin CLOUD layers and movement and directional changes of the vehicle in which an observer is traveling.

The sixteen brightest stars visible from the Northern Hemisphere are SIRIUS, Vega, Capella, Arcturus, Rigel, Procyon, Altair, Beltelgeuse, Aldebaran, Pollux, Spica, Antares, Fomalhaut, Deneb, Regulus and Castor. Many of these, especially Sirius, Capella and Arcturus, are often reported as UFOs.

**STAR OF BETHLEHEM,** celestial body, described in the Gospel According to St. Matthew, which led

The three sages contemplate the Star of Bethlehem. *(The Bettmann Archive)*

three sages from the East to the birthplace of Jesus Christ in Bethlehem. Christian theologians consider the phenomenon as a miracle performed by God. Modern astronomers have explained the celestial objects as any one of a number of natural events including planetary conjunctions, COMETS, novae and supernovae. Some UFOlogists believe that the star of Bethlehem was a gigantic spaceship which flew in front of the wise men and hovered over the birthplace of the young child. Some believe, moreover, that Jesus Christ himself was the son of an extraterrestrial ASTRONAUT.

Bibliography: Le Poer Trench, Brinsley, *The Sky People* (Hackensack, New Jersey: Wehman Brothers, 1961).

**STAR PEOPLE,** human beings who claim to have memories of having come to this PLANET from somewhere else or who have supposedly experienced interaction with paranormal entities since childhood. The term was coined by writer BRAD STEIGER. James Beal, a former NASA engineer, refers to such people as "the Helpers" because of their alleged mission to serve as guides in mankind's future evolution.

According to Steiger, profiles of Star People contain some or all of the following elements: unusual blood type, lower body temperature, low blood pressure, extra vertebrae and lower back problems, unusually sharp hearing, light-sensitive eyes, chronic sinusitis, natural abilities with art, music, mathematics, healing and acting, artwork or dreams which involve a multi-moon planetary environment, and an attraction for children and animals. In addition, Steiger states that a

Star Person may have been an unexpected child, thrive on little sleep, appear hypersensitive to electricity and electromagnetic force fields, seem to have been "reborn" in cycles such as those occurring from 1934 to 1938, 1944 to 1948 and 1954 to 1958, have felt that his or her mother and father were substitute parents, complain of a feeling of having little time to complete life goals, feel that his or her real ancestors originate from another world or another dimension, have had unseen companions during childhood, experience buzzing or clicking noises in the ears prior to or during psychic events, have had an unusual experience around the age of five involving a white light or a visitation from entities bringing information and comfort, have maintained contact with nonhuman intelligence, and do his or her best work at night.

The VENUS RESEARCH organization, which supports Steiger's theory about Star People, is dedicated to helping such people prepare for the NEW AGE.

Bibliography: Steiger, Brad, *Gods of Aquarius: UFOs and the Transformation of Man* (New York: Harcourt, Brace and Jovanovich, 1976).

## STATUS INCONSISTENCY THEORY. D. I. Warren, in the November 6, 1970, edition of *Science*, proposed the theory that UFO reports are more likely to be made by people whose economic status is inconsistent with their intellectual capacity and education. Thus, well-trained, intelligent people holding low economic and social status would constitute a large proportion of UFO witnesses. UFOLOGISTS have found little evidence to support the status inconsistency theory.

## STEBBING BOOK SERVICE, 41 Terminus Drive, Belthinge, Herne Bay, Kent, England. This outfit sells books on UFOs and astronomy, and is run by British UFOLOGIST Susanne Stebbing.

## STEIGER, BRAD (b. February 19, 1936, Fort Dode, Iowa; address: P.O. Box 4902, Scottsdale, Arizona 85258; telephone number: 602-996-5557), writer and lecturer.

A childhood observation of an elfin creature put Steiger on the road to investigating poltergeist disturbances, UFOs and haunted houses. Since then he has encountered UFOs, ghosts and séance manifestations. He has heard unidentifiable sounds including ethereal music and disembodied voices. Although he does not rule out the EXTRATERRESTRIAL HYPOTHESIS (ETH), he leans toward the theory that UFOs may be our neighbors existing in another SPACE-TIME CONTINUUM. He believes that, through the ages, UFO intelligences have been provoking mankind into higher spirals of intellectual and technological maturity and guiding men and women toward ever-expanding mental and spiritual awareness. He believes it is an integral part of the UFO phenomenon to lead us to a clearer understanding of our role in the cosmic scheme and to direct us to a level of awareness whereby we might more readily attain a state of oneness and self-sufficiency. Steiger holds that one of the ways in which they achieve these goals is by showing us that the impossible can be accomplished and that the rules of physics are made to be broken. He suggests that their maneuvers might be demonstrating the possibility of dematerialization, invisibility and rematerialization. Thus, he concludes, they might be showing us that the best way to deal with space travel over great distances is not to travel through space but to avoid it altogether. Steiger is convinced that there is a subtle kind of symbiotic relationship which exists between mankind and the UFO intelligences. He thinks that in some way, which we have yet to determine, they need us as much as we need them. He also suggests that, in some instances, objects which have been described as spaceships may have been the actual form of the intelligence, rather than vehicles transporting OCCUPANTS.

Brad Steiger is the pseudonym for Eugene E. Olson. He received his B.A. in 1957 from Luther College in Decorah, Iowa, and attended the University of Iowa in 1963. He was a high school English teacher in Clinton, Iowa, from 1957 to 1963, and a teacher of literature and creative writing at Luther College from 1963 to 1967. From 1970 to 1974, he was President of Other Dimensions, Incorporated, in Decorah.

Steiger was a recipient of the Genie award for Metaphysical Writer of the Year in 1974, was awarded

Brad Steiger.

the Dani Award in Philadelphia for services to humanity, and received initiation into the Seneca Indian Medicine Lodge.

Steiger is coscriptwriter of *Unknown Powers,* winner of the Film Advisory Board's Award for Excellence for 1978. His short stories and articles have been published in magazines and anthologies. He is author of almost seventy books in the metaphysical, paranormal and inspiration fields. These include: *Strange Guests* (New York: Ace Books, 1966); *The Unknown* (New York: Popular Library, 1966); *ESP: Your Sixth Sense* (New York: Award Books, 1966); coauthored, with Chaw Mank, *Valentino* (New York: Macfadden, 1966); *Strangers from the Skies* (New York: Award Books, 1966); coauthored, with Joan Whritenour, *Flying Saucers Are Hostile* (New York: Award Books, 1967); *The Mass Murderer* (New York: Award Books, 1967); *The Enigma of Reincarnation* (New York: Ace Books, 1967); *Real Ghosts, Restless Spirits and Haunted Minds* (New York: Award Books, 1968); coauthored, with John Pendragon, *Pendragon: A Clairvoyant's Power of Prophecy* (New York: Award Books, 1968); (editor only), Pendragon, John, *The Occult World of John Pendragon* (New York: Ace Books, 1968); *Voices from Beyond* (New York: Award Books, 1968); coauthored, with Joan Whritenour, *New UFO Breakthrough* (New York: Award Books, 1968); *In My Soul I Am Free* (New York: Lancer Books, 1968); coauthored, with Joan Whritenour, *The Allende Letters* (New York: Award Books, 1968); *Sex and the Supernatural* (New York: Lancer Books, 1968); *The Mind Travelers* (New York: Award Books, 1968), coauthored, with Pendragon, *Cupid and the Stars* (New York: Ace Books, 1969); coauthored, with Ron Warmoth, *Tarot* (New York: Award Books, 1969); *Sex and Satanism* (New York: Ace Books, 1969); *Judy Garland* (New York: Ace Books, 1969); coauthored, with Dorothy Spence Lauer, *How to Use ESP: The Hidden Powers of Your Mind* (New York: Lancer Books, 1969); *The Weird, the Wild, and the Wicked* (New York: Pyramid Publications, 1969); coauthored, with Loring G. Williams, *Other Lives* (Hawthorn, 1969); coauthored, with Warren Smith, *What the Seers Predict in 1971* (New York: Lancer Books, 1970); coauthored, with William Howard, *Handwriting Analysis* (New York: Ace Books, 1970); *Know the Future Today: The Amazing Prophecies of Irene Hughes* (Paperback Library, 1970); *Aquarian Revelations* (New York: Dell Publishing Company, 1971); coauthored, with Williams, *Minds through Space and Time* (New York: Award Books, 1971); *Secrets of Kuhuna Magic* (New York: Award Books, 1971); *Haunted Lovers* (New York: Dell Publishing Company, 1971); *The Psychic Feats of Olof Jonsson* (Englewood Cliffs, N.J.: Prentice-Hall, 1971); *Strange Encounters with Ghosts* (New York: Popular Library, 1972); *Irene Hughes on Psychic Safari* (New York: Paperback Library, 1972); *Revelation: The Divine Fire* (Englewood Cliffs, N.J.: Prentice-Hall, 1973); *Atlantis Rising* (New York: Dell Publishing Company, 1973); *Mysteries of Time and Space* (Englewood Cliffs, N.J.: Prentice-Hall, 1974); *Medicine Power: The American Indian's Revival of His Spiritual Heritage and Its Relevance for Modern Man* (Garden City, N.Y.: Doubleday and Company, 1974); *Medicine Talk: A Guide to Walking in Balance and Surviving on the Earth Mother* (Garden City, N.Y.: Doubleday and Company, 1975); *Words from the Source* (Englewood Cliffs, N.J.: Prentice-Hall, 1975); edited, with John W. White, *Other Worlds, Other Universes: Playing the Reality Game* (Garden City, N.Y.: Doubleday and Company, 1975); *A Roadmap of Time: How the Maxwell/Wheeler Energy Cycles Predict the History of the Next Twenty-Five Years* (Englewood Cliffs, N.J.: Prentice-Hall, 1975); edited, with Hayden Hewes, *UFO Missionaries Extraordinary* (New York: Pocket Books, 1976); *Psychic City—Chicago: Doorway to Another Dimension* (Garden City, N.Y.: Doubleday and Company, 1976); *Gods of Aquarius: UFOs and the Transformation of Man* (New York: Harcourt, Brace, Jovanovich, 1976); edited *Project Blue Book* (New York: Ballantine Books, 1976); *Alien Meetings* (New York: Ace Books, 1978); *You Will Live Again* (New York: Dell Publishing Company, 1978); *Worlds Before Our Own* (New York: Berkley Publishing Company, 1978); *The Hypnotist* (New York: Dell Publishing Company, 1979).

**STENDEK,** publication of the Centro de Estudios Interplanetarios, (CEI)

**STEVENS, WENDELLE C.** (b. January 18, 1923; Round Prairie, Minnesota; telephone number: 602-296-6753), retired Air Force pilot, military logistics officer and UFO investigator.

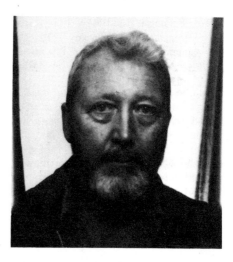

Wendelle Stevens.

During his twenty years as a UFO investigator, Stevens has acquired over 3,000 PHOTOGRAPHS of UFOs, purportedly the largest private collection in existence. He believes that many UFOs are real physical craft, while others are less physical in nature. They originate, he holds, from a large number of extraterrestrial sources and are here to observe mankind.

During his military career, Stevens attended Military Pilot Training School, Military Flight Test School, Squadron Officers School and Command and Staff School. He entered the U.S. Army in 1941, transferring to the Air Corps in 1942 as a mechanic. Subsequently, he became a fighter pilot and a test pilot. He served in the Pacific Theater, Alaska and South America. He retired from the Air Force in 1963, and worked for Hamilton Aircraft until 1972.

Stevens is a member of the Aircraft Owners and Pilots Association.

## STONE DISKS *see* CHINESE DISKS

## STORY, RONALD DEAN (b. February 12, 1946, Joplin, Missouri; address: 4739 East Waverly Street, Tucson, Arizona 85712; telephone number: 602-327-5035), science writer.

Story thinks that UFOs represent a wide variety of different phenomena, some natural, some man-made, and some, perhaps, of extraterrestrial origin. Although he is open to many possibilities, he has not, as yet, found evidence that is totally convincing, which establishes that UFOs have an exotic or supernatural origin.

Story received his B.A. with honors in Philosophy from the University of Arizona in 1970. He was on the Dean's Honor List in 1968, and received University Scholarship Honors in 1969.

Story served as an Interior Communications Electrician in the U.S. Navy from 1965 to 1967, and is a Vietnam veteran. He was a Manager-trainee and Assistant Manager of retail stores from 1970 to 1972, and a Buyer for the Tucson Gas and Electric Company from 1972 to 1978. He began part-time writing in 1973, and became a full-time writer in February 1978.

Story is a member of the AERIAL PHENOMENA RESEARCH ORGANIZATION (APRO) and the ANCIENT ASTRONAUT SOCIETY.

Story is author of *The Space-Gods Revealed: A Close Look at the Theories of Erich von Däniken* (New York: Harper and Row); and *Visitors from Beyond?* (London: New English Library, 1979).

## STRANGENESS RATING. This term was established by astronomer J. ALLEN HYNEK to qualify the strangeness of a UFO report. Used precisely, it can represent the number of details that make an individual case difficult to understand. For example, an unidentified NOCTURAL LIGHT which moves across the sky would have a low strangeness rating because the only aspect that requires explanation would be its movement. On the other hand, a report of a spinning disk-shaped object that performed right angle turns, landed on a road causing car engines to stall and then took off again leaving marks on the ground, would receive a high strangeness rating because it contains several independently strange elements.

Bibliography: Hynek, J. Allen, *The UFO Experience: A Scientific Inquiry* (Chicago: Henry Regnery Company, 1972).

## STRANGES, FRANK E. (b. October 6, 1927, Brooklyn, New York), CONTACTEE, Founder and Director of the NATIONAL INVESTIGATIONS COMMITTEE ON UFOs (NICUFO).

Stranges's interest in investigating UFOs began when one of his college roommates, a Marine flyer, mentioned strange sightings experienced while on a combat mission in the Pacific. Since 1956, Stranges, himself, has sighted saucer-shaped and egg-shaped UFOs on four different occasions in Florida, Mexico, Finland and Los Angeles. He believes that UFOs are craft, many of them from places other than this PLANET.

Stranges received his doctorates in Theology from Florida State University in 1961, in Divinity from Williams College in 1962, in Psychology from Florida State University in 1963, in Philosophy from Florida State University in 1964, in Humanities from Florida State University in 1966, and in Criminology from the National Institute of Criminology, Washing-

Frank Stranges.

ton, in 1966. He also received his Th.B. from Florida State University in 1964. He did further studies at the Graduate Theological Seminaries in Macau and Hong Kong, and at the Society of St. Luke the Physician in London, England.

Stranges's main profession has been as International President of the International Evangelism Crusades. According to Stranges, he worked as an undercover agent for a number of Secret Service Agencies from 1949 to 1970 in Minneapolis, Boston and California. He was an Accredited Diplomat of the American Academy of Professional Arts and served on its Advisory Board. He worked as a columnist for *Hollywood Citizen News,* and as a feature writer for *New Age World* and *Cosmos.* He founded NICUFO in 1967, and has been its Director since that time. He has lectured on UFOs throughout the United States and in England, Sweden, Finland, France, Germany, Canada, Korea and Mexico. He has been a guest on several radio and television programs.

Stranges is a Board Member and Scientific Advisor of the World University and an Honorary Attorney General of the State of Louisiana. He is a member of the United Science Federation in Florida, the Washington Association of Social Psychology, the California State Marshall's Association and the Los Angeles Mayor's Advisory Council.

Stranges is Editor of NICUFO's *Confidential Newsletter,* and is author of *Flying Saucerama* (New York: Vantage Press, 1959); *Stranger at the Pentagon* (New York: Vantage Press, 1977); and *My Friend from Beyond Earth* (Kitchener, Ontario: Galaxy Press, 1972).

## STRAUCH, ARTHUR, *see* ST. GEORGE, MINNESOTA

## STRINGFIELD, LEONARD H. (b. December 17, 1920, Cincinnati, Ohio; address: 4412 Grove Avenue, Cincinnati, Ohio 45227; telephone number: 513-271-4248), writer, Field Investigator for the CENTER FOR UFO STUDIES (CUFOS), Director of Public Relations and State Section Director for the MUTUAL UFO NETWORK (MUFON) and Investigator for GROUND SAUCER WATCH (GSW).

Stringfield's interest in UFOs was sparked during World War II, while serving in the Intelligence Service of the 5th Air Force in the Southwest Pacific Theatre. On August 28, 1945, he was one of twelve passengers aboard a C–46 flying to Iwo Jima en route to Tokyo when three teardrop-shaped, glowing objects approached the aircraft and flew parallel to it. Suddenly, the airplane's left engine stalled. No sooner had the pilot warned his passengers that they might have to bail out than the UFOs retreated into a CLOUD bank and

disappeared. The engine revved up and the aircraft continued on its course. A subsequent check of the airplane found nothing wrong with it.

Stringfield is employed as Director of Public Relations and Marketing Services of DuBois Chemicals, a Division of Chemed Corporation, headquartered in DuBois Tower in Cincinnati.

From 1953 to 1957, Stringfield was Director of CIVILIAN RESEARCH, INTERPLANETARY FLYING OBJECTS (CRIFO), and was Publisher and Editor of its monthly newsletter, *Orbit*. During this period he worked on a cooperative basis with the UNITED STATES AIR FORCE (USAF), screening and passing on UFO reports as he received them. He was assigned the code number Fox Trot Kilo 3–0 Blue, to be used when telephoning reports to the Air Defense Command in Columbus, Ohio. Although the Air Force's public pronouncements on UFOs were negative, their expressed concern with the data being given them by Stringfield led him to conclude that important information was being concealed. During the late 1950s, Stringfield served as President of the Cincinnati UFO Society, whose members were mainly professional people. From 1957 to 1970, he was Public Relations Officer, Advisor and Field Investigator for the NATIONAL INVESTIGATIONS COMMITTEE ON AERIAL PHENOMENA (NICAP). From 1967 to 1969, he worked as Early Warning Coordinator for the CONDON COMMITTEE. During 1969, he conducted a course in UFOlogy at Mariemont High School. During 1977 and 1978, he served as Advisor to the nation of GRENADA in its efforts to establish a UFO research agency within the framework of the UNITED NATIONS. In 1978, he presented a sixty-three-page paper entitled

Leonard Stringfield.

*Retrievals of the Third Kind*, subtitled *A Case Study of Alleged UFOs and Occupants in Military Custody*, at the ninth annual MUFON Symposium held in Dayton, Ohio. The paper includes eighteen abstracts revealing data from military informants concerning alleged recovery and storage of crashed alien craft and the recovery and medical study of deceased alien humanoids. In addition to his active positions with CUFOS, MUFON and GSW, Stringfield also serves on the Board of Directors of MUFON, and is a Consultant to the OHIO UFO INVESTIGATORS' LEAGUE (OUFOIL).

Stringfield is author of *Inside Saucer Post, 3–0 Blue* (Cincinnati, Ohio: the author, 1957) and *Situation Red: The UFO Siege* (Garden City, N.Y.: Doubleday and Company, 1977).

## STUDIEGROEP PROGRESSIEVE WETEN-SCHAPPEN (SPW), Jasmijnstraat 67, B–9000 Gent, Belgium.

The aims of this investigative organization are: 1. to establish a catalogue of Belgian sightings; 2. to explain as many UFO reports as possible; 3. to conduct analyses and statistical studies when possible; and 4. to publish the organization's findings, particularly with respect to Belgian cases. The group holds that some UFOs seem to represent an intelligent phenomenon which may be some sort of unknown pure energy form.

This nonprofit organization was founded in 1971 by JACQUES BONABOT, who is Director of its sister organization, GROUPEMENT POUR L'ETUDE DES SCIENCES D'AVANT-GARDE (GESAG). Cedric Heyndrickx is head of SPW's sighting department and field investigators. There are about 170 members. Approximately thirty field investigators are located throughout the Flemish-speaking part of Belgium. Through GESAG, all cases are filed with UFOCAT at the CENTER FOR UFO STUDIES (CUFOS). The group maintains contact with many investigators and organizations around the world. Rudy De Groote is Director and Editor of the Dutch-language publication UFO INFO, which is published quarterly and includes a French and English summary at the end of each issue.

## SUBMARINE HYPOTHESIS, theory that UFOs are the craft of an underwater civilization on Earth. Such entities might have evolved on this PLANET or might have migrated to bases under Earth's oceans from another planet. Many UFO reports describe objects entering and emerging from bodies of water. An unidentified object or light seen below the ocean's surface is referred to as an UNIDENTIFIED SUBMARINE OBJECT (USO).

Bibliography: Sanderson, Ivan T., *Invisible Residents* (New York: World Publishing Company, 1970).

## SUBMOON see SUBSUN

## SUBSUN. An observer in an airplane or on a mountaintop can occasionally perceive beneath him a brilliant reflection of the sun on stratus CLOUD layers consisting of millions of tiny ICE CRYSTALS. The subsun, as this phenomenon is named, is usually diffused and can have the elliptical shape commonly attributed to UFOs. It appears to move in unison with the observer and disappears when a point is reached where the layer of ice crystals no longer exists. A subsun can develop its own PARHELIA in the form of subsundogs and halos. The same effect created by the reflection of the moon is known as a submoon.

In order to identify a UFO as a subsun or a submoon, it would be necessary to verify that the light observed lay between the witness and the sun itself. In addition, temperature and humidity conditions should be checked to establish whether or not they were suitable for the formation of ice crystals.

Bibliography: Menzel, Donald H., and Ernest H. Taves, *The UFO Enigma* (Garden City, N.Y.: Doubleday and Company, 1977).

## SUFOI see SKANDINAVISK UFO INFORMATION

## SUFOI NEWSLETTER, publication of SKANDINAVISK UFO INFORMATION (SUFOI).

## SUFON see SOUTHERN UFO NETWORK

## SUMER. ERICH VON DÄNIKEN conjectures that this southern area of ancient Babylon was inhabited almost 500,000 years ago by semi-savage people who were visited by benevolent extraterrestrial ASTRONAUTS. He bases his speculation on the sudden arrival in Sumer of advanced astronomy, culture and technology. Moreover, according to old cuneiform inscriptions, the ten original kings of Sumer ruled for the duration of 456,000 years and, following the flood, the reign of the next twenty-three kings spanned a period of 24,510 years. Däniken suggests that these kings were extraterrestrials who laid the foundations of civilization and then returned to their own PLANET. Every one hundred terrestrial years, they returned to monitor the results of their efforts. The theory of relativity establishes that if these astronauts traveled just under the SPEED OF LIGHT they would have aged very little between their departing and returning flights, thus explaining the extraordinarily long reign of each king. As conclusive evidence of extraterrestrial intervention, Däniken claims that pictures drawn by the Sumerians show STARS circled by planets of different sizes. Since the Sumerians did not

have the equipment we have today to make such observations, the information must have been given to them by someone else.

Bibliography: Von Däniken, Erich, *Chariots of the Gods?* (New York: G. P. Putnam's Sons, 1970).

**SUNDOGS** *see* **PARHELIA**

**SUOMEN UFOTUTKIJAT RY,** also known as UFO Research of Finland, 17950 Kylämä, Finland; telephone number: 919-5885.

The purposes of this investigative organization are to study the UFO phenomenon, to gather and disseminate UFO data and to educate members.

This nonprofit organization was founded in 1973. Ilkka Serra is Chairman. Noted Finnish UFOlogist and author Tapani Kuningas is Vice-Chairman. Other board members include Arja Kuningas, Kari Kuure, Kalevi Pusa, Urpo Häyrinen, Lasse Ahonen, Olavi Kiviniemi and Antti Piha. The group has approximately fifty members. Fifteen field investigators are located throughout Finland. The group organizes summer conferences, sells and lends investigative apparatus and maintains contact with the scientific community. In addition to the QUARTERLY REPORT, special reports about the most significant cases are published from time to time. Translations are mailed all over the world.

**SUPERSPACE** *see* **HYPERSPACE**

**SURVEILLANCE HYPOTHESIS,** theory that UFOs are extraterrestrial spacecraft engaged in the surveillance of Earth for any one of several reasons.

Extraterrestrials might be monitoring our nuclear activities and the progress of our space program in order to step in, should the need arise, and prevent us from committing any acts that would endanger other communities in space.

Proponents of the INVASION HYPOTHESIS believe that UFOs are engaged in military reconnaissance in preparation for the destruction of our civilization or the colonization of our planet. Supporters of the MIGRATION HYPOTHESIS hold that such reconnaissance might be conducted with a view to eventual coexistence on peaceful terms.

Surveillance by aliens might be part of a scientific project. Some advocates of the EARTH COLONIZATION HYPOTHESIS suggest that the entire human race might be guinea pigs in some kind of experiment being conducted by a cosmic power. If this were the case, our masters would need to monitor our progress and their presence, although not understood, would undoubtedly be apparent to us in some way.

**SUTTON FAMILY** *see* **KELLY-HOPKINS-VILLE, KENTUCKY**

**SVALBARD, NORWAY,** *see* **SPITSBERGEN, NORWAY**

Will-o'-the-wisp seen in Lincolnshire, England, in 1811. *(The Bettmann Archive)*

**SVEPS** *see* **SOCIETÉ VAROISE D'ÉTUDES DES PHÉNOMÈNES SPATIAUX**

**SWAMP GAS,** methane, carbon dioxide, nitrogen and phosphine generated by decaying vegetable matter in marshy areas. When ignited, the first three of these combustible gases produce faint flames not more than five inches long and two inches wide. They usually remain on the ground or float about four inches above it. Wind can carry them for a few feet before they are extinguished. Phosphine, on the other hand, does not burn with a hot flame but is luminescent.

Several names have been given to marsh gas or swamp gas over the centuries. These include will-o'-the-wisp, jack-o'-lantern, friar's lanthorn and foxfire. The ancient Romans called it "ignis fatuus," or foolish fire, because nighttime travelers were lured off the roads by it into swamps, thinking it came from dwellings. It is considered an ominous sign in most popular myths. Russian superstition holds that swamp gases are the spirits of stillborn children who drift between heaven and hell. A similar legend purports that they are the souls rejected by hell who carry their own coals on their wanderings.

Swamp gas became a household word in the United States in 1966. Following a rash of sightings involving about one hundred witnesses in Michigan, astronomer J. ALLEN HYNEK was sent by the UNITED STATES AIR FORCE (USAF) to investigate. The area was swarming with reporters. After interviewing witnesses, Hynek called a press conference. Later, he claimed that the Air Force had ordered him to issue a public statement explaining the sightings. PROJECT BLUE BOOK chief, HECTOR QUINTANILLA, on the other hand, claimed that Hynek requested permission to hold the conference. Because of public reaction to Hynek's misquoted statements, neither one wanted to be held responsible. Hynek indicated swamp gas as the possible explanation for the DEXTER and HILLSDALE sightings, since they had occurred over marshland and involved very faint lights. The press pounced on this theory and presented it as Hynek's definitive explanation for all of the Michigan sightings. The swamp gas solution became a national joke and the subject of hundreds of cartoons in magazines and newspapers. To the dismay of its residents, Michigan became known as the Swamp Gas State.

Bibliography: Jacobs, David Michael, *The UFO Controversy in America* (Bloomington, Indiana: Indiana University Press, 1975).

**SWANN, FRANCES,** *see* **SOUTH BERWICK, MAINE**

**SWEDISH ROCKETS** *see* **GHOST ROCKETS**

**SWIFT, JONATHAN,** greatest satirist in the English language and author of the world famous *Gulliver's Travels*. First published in 1726, the story leads its hero to the flying island of LAPUTA, where astronomers have discovered two SATELLITES revolving around the PLANET MARS. Similarities between the description of the flying island and certain attributes of flying saucers led some researchers to connect Swift with the UFO phenomenon. His awareness of the MARTIAN MOONS, prior to their discovery in 1877 by Asaph Hall, further encourages their belief in the theory that he had access to arcane knowledge. Some actually claim that Swift was a Martian. The renowned Dr. Johnson described his complexion as muddy, while others referred to it as olive-colored, bronze or brown. As further demonstration of his alien appearance, he has been described as wall-eyed. Proponents of this theory assert that, because of his extraterrestrial origin, Swift was a misfit in eighteenth century society and was probably insane when he died in 1745.

Bibliography: Drake, W. Raymond, *Gods and Spacemen throughout History* (Chicago: Henry Regnery Company, 1975).

**SWITZERLAND.** There are several UFO organizations in Switzerland, of which one of the best-known is the GROUPEMENT UFOLOGIQUE BULLOIS (GUB). The country's best-known researcher is author ERICH VON DÄNIKEN.

**TACHYON,** term derived from a Greek word meaning "swift" used to describe a hypothetical particle which always travels faster than the SPEED OF LIGHT. According to Einstein's theory of relativity, an object which always travels above the speed of light and never travels at or below 186,282 miles per second does not cross the speed of light boundary, and therefore does not violate the laws of physics.

In our universe, a motionless object has zero energy, which increases as the speed of the object increases. It achieves infinite energy at the speed of light. Conversely, in a universe of tachyons, an object with infinite energy moves slightly faster than the speed of light and, as the energy diminishes, the object accelerates until it achieves infinite speed with zero energy.

Detection of such a universe would be extremely difficult since even the slowest tachyon would leave an imperceptible trace of light that exists for an infinitesimal fraction of a second. If tachyons exist, then objects within their universe could cross the interstellar reaches within extremely short periods of time. However, if UFOs are travelers from a tachyon universe, the theory does not account for the manifestation of such objects within our universe.

Bibliography: Feinberg, Gerald, "Particles that Go Faster than Light," *Scientific American* (New York: Scientific American, Inc., February 1970).

**TACKER, LAWRENCE J.,** UNITED STATES AIR FORCE (USAF) lieutenant colonel who was the Pentagon UFO spokesman from 1958 to March 1961.

**TACOMA, WASHINGTON,** *see* **MAURY ISLAND, WASHINGTON**

**TAKANASHI, JUN-ICHI** (b. April 1, 1923, Osaka, Japan; address: 2–7–12 Yuuhigaoka, Toyonaka City, Osaka 560, Japan; telephone number: 06-852-7746), businessman, author, lecturer, Founder and Chairman of the MODERN SPACE FLIGHT ASSOCIATION (MSFA).

Takanashi believes UFOs are interplanetary spacecraft containing intelligent beings from other solar systems. But, he also believes some UFO phenomena are of psychic origin. Takanashi thinks there is too much confusion in the UFO research field due to poor analysis and sifting of the data. He is willing to exchange data and opinions with serious UFO investigators throughout the world and is convinced that this enormous riddle can be solved only by the close cooperation of all UFO investigators throughout the world.

Takanashi graduated from Kansei Gakuin University in 1945. He was a teacher of science and English in five junior high schools from 1947 to 1955. He served in the Export Department of several companies as Export

Jun-Ichi Takanashi.

Manager from 1958 to 1970. In 1971, he founded and is now operating Crystal Sphinx International, an export and import company.

Takanashi founded MSFA in 1956. He is Special Representative for Japan for the AERIAL PHENOMENA RESEARCH ORGANIZATION (APRO), and Japan Director for the MUTUAL UFO NETWORK (MUFON).

Takanashi is author of *Sinrei No Hiko O Hirakite* (Tokyo: Light Shobou, 1956); *Sekai No Yojigen Gensho I, II, III* (Tokyo: Tairiku Shobou, 1971–1972); *Soratobu Enban Jitsuzai No Shoko* (Tokyo: Kobunsha, 1973); *Soratobu Enban No Choryo* (Tokyo: Kobunsha, 1973); *Soratubo Enban Sawagi No Hottan* (Tokyo: Kobunsha, 1974); *UFO Nippon Shinryaku* (Tokyo: Suponichi Shuppan, 1976); *Sekai No UFO Shashin-Shu* (Tokyo: Kobunsha, 1976).

**TAORMINA, SICILY.** A famous but obviously fraudulent UFO PHOTOGRAPH was taken in 1954 in Taormina, Sicily. Three men stand at the railing of a bridge, shading their eyes as they stare at some distant spot. A fourth man appears to be running to join them. Two images, resembling inverted teapot lids, cavort in the sky above them. Reports claim that thousands of people watched the flying teapot lids, which did not leave the scene until chased away by an Italian Air Force jet.

None of the men in the photograph has his head tilted at the correct angle to observe the objects overhead. Instead, all seem to be looking straight ahead at a hill in the background. The most blatant discrepancy is to be found in the lighting. While the obviously brilliant sunshine falling on the scene casts distinctively dark

Fake UFOs photographed at Taormina, Sicily, in 1954. *(Courtesy ICUFON)*

shadows on the men and their surroundings, the UFOs show only faintly shadowed areas. An even more careless error shows that while one UFO is shaded on the left, the other is shaded on the right.

Bibliography: Cohen, Daniel, *Myths of the Space Age* (New York: Dodd, Mead and Company, 1967).

**TARGET,** term used, especially by the military, to refer to a luminous image on a RADARscope, also known as a blip.

**TARHEEL UFO STUDY GROUP,** P.O. Box 412, Rural Hall, North Carolina 27045; telephone number: 919-969-1280.

The purpose of this organization is to investigate and evaluate UFO reports in North Carolina and southwestern Virginia and to educate the public about UFOs and related subjects. The group holds that UFOs are made by a civilization with a technology superior to that of mankind.

This nonprofit organization was founded in 1973 by Richard C. Austin and GEORGE D. FAWCETT. Its staff consists of President Nolie L. Bell, Vice-President and Public Relations Officer C. Ray Rhein, Secretary-Treasurer Gayle C. McBride and Group Advisor George D. Fawcett. The group has thirty members. Field investigators participate in a comprehensive training program before being permitted to interrogate witnesses. Liaison is maintained between the group and local law enforcement agencies, the news media and other UFO organizations. The organization conducts field trips, monthly meetings and lectures. *Tarheel UFO Study Group* is published monthly, and deals with local UFO events, significant UFO experiences in other parts of the world, astronomy, physics and other related subjects.

**TASMANIAN UNIDENTIFIED FLYING OBJECTS INVESTIGATION CENTRE (TUFOIC),** G.P.O. Box 1310N, Hobart 7001, Tasmania.

The purpose of this investigative organization is to collect and examine information on the UFO phenomenon, especially in Tasmania, and to inform the public of its findings. Investigations are conducted in a scientific manner and the group is open minded regarding the identity of UFOs.

This nonprofit organization was founded in 1965 by Robert Burge. Its staff consists of President Neil Russell-Green, Investigations Coordinator Keith Roberts and Secretary Steven Brooks. The centre's committee is composed of Paul Jackson, G. Marshall, C. Mortimer, J. Pauley and D. Harris. There are approximately fifty members. Field investigators are located in Hobart, Huon Valley, Maydena in Derwent Valley and Northern Tasmania. The centre maintains contact with about thirty-five organizations and private individuals in twelve overseas countries. Services provided by TUFOIC include a book, magazine and tape cassette library, an annual publication entitled UFO TASMANIA, and two newsletters, published in May and September, dealing with Tasmanian sightings and information of local interest. The centre has a complete record of Tasmanian sightings from 1948 to the present.

**TASSILI FRESCOES,** ancient rock paintings discovered in the nineteenth century in a mountainous region of the Algerian Sahara. Author ERICH VON DÄNIKEN contends that some of the drawings represent people floating in space with round helmets and antennae on their heads. According to von Däniken, the Tassili sphere, discovered by Frenchman Henri Lhote on the underside of a semi-circular rock, shows a spaceship with an open hatch and a protruding television antenna.

A more conventional explanation for the markings on the heads of the human figures is that they are decorative or religious masks. Archaeologists have been unable to definitely date the rock paintings. Since scholars have not succeeded in deciphering the hieroglyphs on the rocks, the significance of the paintings remains a mystery.

Bibliography: Von Däniken, Erich, *Gods from Outer Space* (New York: G. P. Putnam's Sons, 1971).

One of the strange beings depicted in the Tassili Frescoes. *(Courtesy ICUFON)*

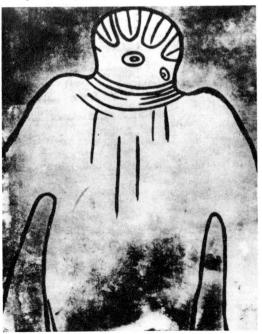

**TAU CETI,** one of two stars targeted in PROJECT OZMA, a 1961 search for intelligent radio signals from space. It is 11.9 light years from Earth and considered to be a potential source of EXTRATERRESTRIAL LIFE.

**TAURANGA UFO INVESTIGATION GROUP,** 38 Brookfield Terrace, Outmoetai, Tauranga, New Zealand; telephone number: 66-088.

The purpose of this organization is to investigate and research all aspects of the UFO phenomenon and to assist others in understanding the situation. The group believes that UFOs are extraterrestrial and extradimensional craft which now use local bases on Earth, possibly under the oceans. Their basic purpose, according to the group, is to keep an eye on mankind and to serve as guides without direct interference. The organization also believes that some of the UFOs reported since 1955 are of American origin.

This nonprofit organization was founded in 1954 by H. L. Cooke. Harvey Cooke is President. Board Members are Norman Decke, Peter Eccles, Derek Kendall, Gary Vogt, Mrs. Card and Mrs. Ewan. There are approximately 100 local members. Local sightings are covered by field investigators. The group cooperates with other groups in New Zealand, as well as groups in the United States and Canada. Information is disseminated to the public through lectures to schools, service clubs and youth groups, newspaper articles, conventions and seminars. A library is available to members and meetings are held once a month. The organization has no publication but supports and supplies information to New Zealand's quarterly magazine, XENOLOG.

**TEHERAN, IRAN,** location of a bizarre UFO encounter involving two Iranian Air Force F–4 Phantom jets in 1976. In a confidential report from the United States military attaché in Iran to the Pentagon, it was reported that at about 12:30 A.M. on September 19, anxious citizens in the Shemiran area of Teheran began calling Iranian Air Force headquarters to report a strange object in the sky. The UFO was flashing intensely brilliant strobe lights, arranged in a rectangular pattern and alternating blue, green, red and orange in color. Controllers at Mehrabad airport reported the object's altitude to be approximately 5,000 feet.

At 1:30 A.M., an F–4 was scrambled from Shahrokhi Air Force Base. When the interceptor approached within a range of just under thirty miles, all instrumentation and communications were lost. The confidential communiqué stated, "When the F–4 turned away from the object and apparently was no longer a threat to it, the aircraft regained all instrumentation and communications." At 1:40 A.M., a second F–4 was launched. As the backseater RADAR operator tracked the object, he compared the size of the return to that of a 707 tanker. As the second F–4 pursued it southwards, the UFO maintained a distance of almost thirty miles. Suddenly, another bright object, estimated to be one-half to one-third the apparent size of the MOON, came out of the original object. The second UFO sped toward the jet. The pilot attempted to fire an AIM–9 missile but at that moment his weapons control panel went off and he lost all communications. As the jet dove out of the way, the UFO circled behind it, then returned to the MOTHER SHIP. Moments later, another object emerged from the opposite side of the mother ship and descended at high speed. It came to rest gently on the ground, casting a bright light over a one-and-a-half mile area. The F–4 pilot descended to a lower altitude and continued to observe the UFO. The object ascended again, rejoining the mother ship which then departed. As the F–4 came in to land at the airport, the pilot and radar operator noticed overhead yet another cylindrical UFO with steady lights on each end and a flashing light in the middle. Tower controllers saw it as it passed over the jet.

After daybreak, the F–4 crew flew over the UFO landing site in a helicopter. No traces were observed, although a strange beeper signal was picked up west of the location. The occupants of a house in the area reported that they had heard a loud noise and seen a bright illumination similar to lightning. The UNITED STATES AIR FORCE (USAF) has asserted that it made no follow-up investigation.

Bibliography: Declassified communiqué from United States Embassy in Teheran to U.S. Secretary of State on October 1, 1976, available from the Freedom of Information Office, Department of State, Washington, D.C.

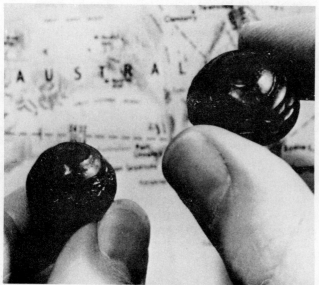

**TEKTITES,** small glassy objects found in areas of the East Indies, Australia, North America, central Europe and Eastern Africa, and whose origin is unknown. Tektites range in size from that of a pinhead to that of a man's head and, in weight, from fractions of an ounce to nearly a pound. Some of their shapes resemble splash forms such as teardrops, spheroids, buttons, cylinders, dumbbells, disks and rods, while others display totally irregular shapes. In reflected light, tektites appear dark, but thin edges and sections transmit light and reveal colors ranging from yellow to bottle green and from olive brown to dark brown to black.

Tektites are composed largely of silica (up to eighty percent), which gives them their characteristic glassy appearance. They also contain small quantities of oxides such as aluminum, iron, magnesium, calcium, sodium and potassium. They bear no geological or mineralogical affinity to any rock chemistry on Earth. The oldest tektites found are about forty-five million years old, the youngest only a few thousand. They are found widely strewn in large groups as if some giant hand had reached down out of the sky and sprinkled them over the land.

Among early theories of their origin was the belief that tektites could be the fragments of a lost, shattered PLANET of the solar system. Today, it is generally agreed that they are the result of an impact somewhere on Earth or on the MOON, since many specimens contain nickel-iron spherules of definite meteoric origin. However, there is still much debate as to which of these celestial bodies is the true source.

Russian physicist Modest Agrest has hypothesized that tektites might be the remains of nuclear detonations or experiments conducted by extraterrestrial visitors in ancient times.

Bibliography: Sachs, Margaret, with Ernest Jahn, *Celestial Passengers—UFOs and Space Travel* (New York: Penguin Books, 1977).

**TELEPATHY,** alleged transference of thought between two or more people by some means other than the normal sensory channels. Both CONTACTEES and ABDUCTION victims claim to communicate with flying saucer OCCUPANTS by means of telepathy.

**TELEPORTATION,** term coined by CHARLES FORT to denote the hypothetical ability of instantaneous movement of physical matter from one place to another, irrespective of distance or intervening matter. The term means, literally, "far-carrying." Author IVAN T. SANDERSON coined the synonymous term "instant transference" and its acronym "ITF."

An often quoted case of teleportation is that of a

A button-shaped tektite (right) is compared with a synthetic tektite shaped by Earth atmospheric entry conditions simulated in a high speed wind tunnel. *(Courtesy NASA)*

Spanish guard, Gil Perez, who, on October 25, 1593, had allegedly been on duty at the governor's palace in Manila in the Philippines, when he suddenly found himself in Mexico. His story was not believed. As proof, he reported that the governor of the Philippines had been assassinated the night before. Two months later a ship arrived from the Philippines bringing news of the governor's death and seemingly confirming Perez's claims. A more recent case of alleged teleportation was that of Argentinian attorney GERARDO VIDAL, who reportedly was teleported from Argentina to Mexico in 1968.

Alleged incidents such as these are considered by some UFOLOGISTS to be the work of flying saucer OCCUPANTS. The apparent ability of UFOs to appear and disappear instantaneously has led some to the conclusion that they are, in fact, capable of teleportation. It is hypothesized that this could be achieved either by moving through a hypothetical fourth dimension, known as HYPERSPACE, or by achieving the SPEED OF LIGHT and causing time to stop. If teleportation is indeed possible, it would diminish the arguments against the EXTRATERRESTRIAL HYPOTHESIS (ETH), which are based on the implausibility of interstellar travel.

## TELEVISION INTERFERENCE see RADIO AND TELEVISION INTERFERENCE

## TEMPERATURE INVERSION.

Under normal conditions, air gets colder as altitude increases. However, this situation is sometimes reversed. If the ground cools off extremely rapidly during the night, it imparts its coldness to the layer of air immediately above. Since the air above that layer is warmer, a temperature inversion has been created. When such a condition exists, light rays passing through the air are bent, causing images to appear distorted and/or displaced. When there are several layers of alternating hot and cold air, the effects are compounded and exaggerated. A STAR or a PLANET seen through a multiple temperature inversion may appear to have unusual SHAPES, to flash different colors and to move about erratically in the sky. A star, planet or the sun, while below the horizon, may project one or more images of itself that are visible above the horizon.

Temperature inversions can have similar effects on radio waves, causing false RADAR images known as ANGELS, GHOSTS or phantoms. A series of angels may actually represent reflections of several different ground objects as opposed to a single object in the sky. Since inversion layers move and change, on one sweep the radarscope may show the return of one ground object and, on the next sweep, another object miles away from

the first. An inexperienced radar operator might be misled into believing that, during the second sweep, he was observing the first object after it had traveled the distance between the two spots. In the case of radio waves, large inversions are not required to produce the false images resulting from refraction. Humidity in the atmosphere can also cause radar rays to bend earthward, picking up ground objects. Numerous radar sightings of UFOs have been attributed to temperature inversion. Some investigators have attributed the 1952 WASHINGTON, D.C., sightings to this phenomenon, although the case remains highly-controversial today.

Bibliography: Menzel, Donald H., and Lyle G. Boyd, *The World of Flying Saucers* (Garden City, N.Y.: Doubleday and Company, 1963).

## TEXAS SCIENTIFIC RESEARCH CENTER FOR UFO STUDIES,

1002 Edmonds Lane, Lewisville, Texas 75067. Waco branch: 1924 Pine Street, Waco, Texas 76708.

Formerly known as the Texas UFO Study Group, this investigative organization deals primarily with the study and analysis of physical traces left by UFOs. Research is carried out by a staff of technicians and at various university laboratories.

This nonprofit organization, with 150 members, was founded in 1976 by TOMMY ROY BLANN, who is the current Research Director. The board members are President Earl R. Snow, Vice-President James W. Tomlinson, Deputy Director Neil Fread, Associate Directors Christian P. Lambright, John M. Kinard and Charles Martin, Corporate Secretary Yvonne Snow, Secretary Dana L. Perry, Corporate Treasurer Linda Kay Blann and Public Relations Director Sheila Fread.

## TEXAS UFO STUDY GROUP see TEXAS SCIENTIFIC RESEARCH CENTER FOR UFO STUDIES

## THANT, U,

Secretary General of the UNITED NATIONS from 1962 to 1971. In a column entitled "UFOs High Among Thant's Worries," in the June 27, 1967, edition of *The Washington Post*, Drew Pearson and Jack Anderson reported that Thant had confided to friends that he considered UFOs the most important problem facing the United Nations, next to the war in Vietnam. Thant later denied the story.

## THOUGHT FORM HYPOTHESIS,

theory that UFOs are psychic projections originating from the mind of the observer. It has been conjectured that such projections might manifest themselves in a manner visible also to other persons in the company of the projecting observer.

**THUTMOSE III,** renowned Egyptian king of the 18th dynasty whose annals refer to a spectacular UFO sighting. The papyrus, dating back to circa 1504–1450 B.C., was found among the papers of the late Professor Alberto Tulli, former Director of the Egyptian Museum at the Vatican. The papyrus, badly damaged with many gaps in the hieroglyphics, was translated by Prince Boris de Rachewiltz. The first UFO was described as "a circle of fire coming in the sky . . . it had no head. From its mouth came a breath that stank. One rod long was its body and a rod wide, and it was noiseless." The report continues, "Now, after some days had gone by, behold, these things became more numerous in the skies than ever. They shone more than the brightness of the Sun and extended to the limits of the four supports of the heavens. . . . Dominating in the sky was the station of these fire-circles. The army of the Pharaoh looked on with him in their midst. It was after supper. Thereupon, these fire-circles ascended higher in the sky towards the south. Fishes and winged animals or BIRDS fell down from the sky."

This UFO sighting is considered to be one of the earliest on record.

Bibliography: Wilkins, Harold, *Flying Saucers Uncensored* (New York: Citadel Press, 1955).

**THY KINGDOM COME,** semireligious magazine established in 1957 and published by the LOS ANGELES INTERPLANETARY STUDY GROUPS. It was replaced by AFSCA WORLD REPORT in 1959 when the Los Angeles Interplanetary Study Groups evolved into the AMALGAMATED FLYING SAUCER CLUBS OF AMERICA (AFSCA).

**TIME TRAVEL HYPOTHESIS,** theory that UFOs are craft carrying visitors from future generations.

**TOKARZ, HARRY,** *see* **CANADIAN UFO RESEARCH NETWORK**

**TOMBAUGH, CLYDE W.,** American astronomer who in 1930 at the age of twenty-four discovered the *planet* Pluto, and who later witnessed UFOs on several occasions.

His most publicized sighting occurred on August 20, 1949. In the company of his wife and mother-in-law, Tombaugh observed a geometrically arranged group of six-to-eight rectangles of light, windowlike in appearance and yellowish-green in color, which moved from northwest to southeast over Las Cruces, New Mexico. In *The World of Flying Saucers* (Garden City, N.Y.: Doubleday and Company, 1963), DONALD MENZEL and Lyle G. Boyd quote Tombaugh as saying, ". . . the faintness of the object, together with the

Formation of luminous rectangles seen traversing the night sky by Clyde Tombaugh.

manner of fading in intensity as it traveled away from zenith towards the southeastern horizon, is quite suggestive of a reflection from an optical boundary or surface of slight contrast in refractive index, as in an inversion layer." However, in a letter to RICHARD HALL, dated September 10, 1957, and published in *The UFO Evidence* (Washington, D.C.: National Investigations Committee on Aerial Phenomena, 1964), Tombaugh stated, "I doubt that the phenomenon was any terrestrial reflection. . . ." He concluded the letter by saying, "I was so unprepared for such a strange sight that I was really petrified with astonishment." In an interview published in the August 1975 issue of *Science Digest,* Tombaugh notes that he was working at the White Sands Missile Range at the time of the sighting and knew that "we didn't have anything that could do that." He reported it to the FBI with the request that it not be made public. However, the story leaked out and Tombaugh was deluged with crank letters. When he later observed two other strange phenomena, he did not report them in order to protect his professional reputation. As to what he might have seen, Tombaugh states, "It is still a very open question."

**TOMIKAWA, PETER MASAHIRO** (b. March 30, 1942, Nara, Japan), Asian representative of the INTERCONTINENTAL GALACTIC SPACECRAFT (UFO) RESEARCH AND ANALYTIC NETWORK (ICUFON).

Tomikawa has no firm conviction about the identity and origin of UFOs but believes that they are probably amphibious flying vehicles from other PLANETS which may be monitoring mankind. He emphasizes the need for all UFO researchers to unite their efforts to establish

Peter Tomikawa.

an international UFO research and information exchange organization within the UNITED NATIONS to cope with the worldwide phenomenon.

Tomikawa received his B.A. in 1965 from Waseda University in Tokyo, and an M.A. in International Management in 1976 from the American Graduate School of International Management in Glendale, Arizona. From 1965 to 1971, he was employed by a Japanese chemical firm in Tokyo and, since 1972, has been employed by a Japanese chemical firm in New York.

Tomikawa investigates UFO sightings and writes articles for magazines.

**TORME, MEL,** singer who reportedly observed a UFO over New York City in August 1963. While walking his dog at 2:00 one morning, Torme saw a pinpoint of red light in the night sky. As the object moved overhead, he was able to distinguish a saucer-shaped craft behind the red glow. He estimated its altitude to be about 5,000 feet. Suddenly, the UFO darted off in a southerly direction only to come to an abrupt stop within a fraction of a second. It began to perform figures of eights and loops. Torme, who has a pilot's license, had never seen anything maneuver at high speed. The object's sharp turns defied the laws of aerodynamics. After about five minutes, the object took off and disappeared. Torme believes that what he saw was probably a craft from another world.

**TÔRRES, LUIZ REBOUCAS,** *see* **OVNI**

**TRANSMOGRIFICATION,** term sometimes used in UFOLOGY to denote the transformation of objects and intelligent entities from another dimension into a form recognizable by and visible to human beings.

**TRAVOLTA, JOHN,** movie star who reportedly saw a UFO while at his family's home in Englewood, New Jersey. According to a popular version of the story, after the object had shot a beam of light at him, Travolta found himself sitting alone in a small, dark room. A voice told him of several events that would occur to him in the future. He saw no entities, nor did he remember how he returned to his backyard. Although this report has appeared in several publications as a factual account, Travolta denies that it ever took place.

**TREMONTON, UTAH,** location of a UFO sighting by Naval Chief Warrant Officer Delbert C. Newhouse, his wife and two children on July 2, 1952. At about 11:10 A.M. they were driving on a highway near Tremonton when they saw a group of about twelve objects milling about in the sky in a rough formation and heading in a westerly direction. Newhouse happened to have a Bell and Howell 16 mm. movie camera in the trunk of his car. An experienced photographer, he had logged more than a thousand hours on aerial photograph missions, and twenty-two hundred hours as chief photographer. Using a three-inch telescopic lens, he shot about forty feet of color film of the objects before they disappeared. He described them as flat and circular like "two pie pans, one inverted on top of the other." Although he guessed that the objects were huge and traveling at very high altitude at supersonic speeds, he was unable to estimate accurately their speed, size, altitude or distance because of the absence of reference points in the sky.

UFOs filmed by Delbert Newhouse near Tremonton, Utah, on July 2, 1952. *(Courtesy Ground Saucer Watch)*

The film was studied by the UNITED STATES AIR FORCE's PROJECT BLUE BOOK staff, which concluded that the group of objects was probably a flock of BIRDS. Meanwhile, the Naval Photographic Interpretation Laboratory was conducting a frame-by-frame evaluation. After studying the film for a total of 1,000 hours, Naval analysts concluded that the objects were neither birds, BALLOONS, nor aircraft, and were self-luminous. They determined that they were unknown objects under intelligent control. The ROBERTSON PANEL, however, rejected the results of this anaylsis and concluded that the sighting could be explained as a flock of ducks or other birds reflecting the strong desert sunlight. However, in his report of a photogrammetric analysis of the Tremonton film, scientist ROBERT M. L. BAKER stated that, "The motion of the objects is not exactly what one would expect from a flock of soaring birds (not the slightest indication of a decrease in brightness due to periodic turning with the wind or flapping)." The CONDON REPORT, which presented evidence both for and against the bird hypothesis, concluded that the objects were, in fact, birds.

Newhouse claimed that when the film was returned to him after completion of the Air Force evaluation, several frames of the movie were missing. These frames had shown a single UFO moving away over the horizon and hence provided some ranging information.

In 1976, the Trementon film was subjected to computer image processing by GROUND SAUCER WATCH (GSW). Their analysis determined that the objects were disks, about fifty feet in diameter and thicker at the center than at the periphery. The UFOs were calculated to be about five-to-seven miles from the observer, traveling in a tight formation in controlled flight.

Bibliography: Condon, Edward U. (ed.), *Scientific Study of Unidentified Flying Objects* (New York: Bantam Books, 1969); Spaulding, William H., "Modern Image Processing Revisits the Great Falls, Montana and Tremonton, Utah Movies," *1977 MUFON UFO Symposium Proceedings* (Seguin, Texas: Mutual UFO Network, 1977).

## TRENT, PAUL, *see* McMINNVILLE, OREGON

## TRIANGLE OF DEATH *see* BERMUDA TRIANGLE

## TRIANGLE OF TRAGEDY *see* BERMUDA TRIANGLE

## TRI-COUNTY UFO STUDY GROUP (North East Ohio Region), P.O. Box 2, Sebring, Ohio 44672; telephone number: 216-938-9167.

The purpose of this organization is to investigate sightings in northeastern Ohio and relay its reports to other groups, the news media and the general public at monthly meetings, which are open to the public. The group also aims to educate the public about UFOLOGY. Its motto is, "Ridicule without investigation is the crown of ignorance upon the head of a fool." The organization holds that UFOs are spacecraft from other worlds, engaged in exploration and desirous of sharing their knowledge with us.

This nonprofit organization was founded in 1975 by James Rastetter, who serves as Chairman. Other staff members include Cochairman Paul J. L. Rozich, Group Coordinator James Carnes and Membership Chairperson Ruth Christiforis. There are ninety members. Field investigators are located throughout the Tri-County area. Guest speakers attend meetings. Members have access to a lending library and participate in skywatches. The organization is part of the UFO OHIO network and its work is represented in UFO OHIO, published by the UFO INFORMATION NETWORK (UFOIN).

## TRINDADE ISLAND, BRAZIL, location of an alleged UFO sighting which resulted in one of the most famous and most controversial series of photographs.

The Brazilian Navy training ship *Almirante Saldanha*, converted into a floating laboratory to carry out research for the International Geophysical Year (IGY), was preparing to leave Trindade Island on its return trip to Rio de Janeiro on January 16, 1958. On board was a civilian group of submarine explorers, including professional marine photographer Almiro Barauna, retired Brazilian Air Force officer Captain José Teobaldo Viegas, and the leader of the group, Amilar Vieira. The popular version of the incident relates that, at about noon, Viegas and Vieira spotted a UFO. Viegas shouted, "Flying saucer!" Barauna immediately attempted to photograph the object. Many of the one hundred officers and crewmen on deck, attracted by the commotion, looked up to see the glowing, flattened sphere, its center encircled by a large ring or platform. In the excitement, Barauna was jostled by people rushing to get a better look at the UFO. However, he managed to take six shots of the craft as it maneuvered back and forth by a nearby mountain peak. Within about twenty seconds, the object took off at an incredible speed, disappearing in the distance. Barauna developed the film in a dark room on board. Four of the six exposures showed the strange object, which was identified by the other witnesses as the object they had seen in the sky.

When Barauna reached Rio de Janeiro, he made prints and turned them over, together with the negatives, to the Brazilian Navy. They were analyzed by both the Navy Photo Reconnaissance Laboratory and

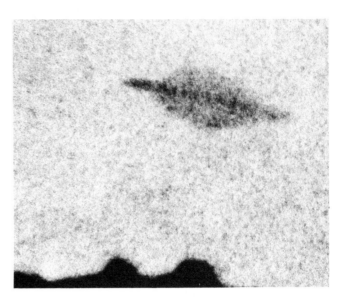

UFO photographed near Trindade Island, Brazil, on January 16, 1958. *(Courtesy ICUFON/A. Barauna)*

An enlarged close-up of the Trindade Island UFO. *(Courtesy ICUFON)*

the Cruzeiro do Sul Aerophotogrammetric Service, both of which agreed the photographs were authentic. For several weeks, the incident was kept secret. However, when the prints were taken to the President of Brazil, he released them to the public. They were published in Brazilian newspapers on February 21, 1958, five weeks after they had been taken. On February 25, United Press reported that the Brazilian Navy Ministry vouched for the Trindade photographs. The report also stated, "Navy Minister Admiral Antonio Alves Camara said, after meeting with President Juscelino Kubitschek in the summer Presidential Palace at Petropolis, that he also vouched personally for the authenticity of the pictures." When the pictures were televised in the United States, Air Force UFO investigators declared them to be fakes.

The late astronomer and author DONALD MENZEL believed that the Trindade Island photographs were almost certainly a HOAX. He points out that, although UFOs had been reported in the area frequently prior to January 16, 1958, the sightings had occurred after the initiation of daily weather BALLOON launches. According to Menzel and cowriter Lyle G. Boyd, when the ship finally docked a few weeks after the incident, interviews by news reporters revealed that none of the officers or crew members had actually seen the UFO. The ship's captain, although listed as a witness, was not on deck at the time of the sighting. Author FRANK SALISBURY, however, claims that newspaper accounts and UFO investigators' reports confirm that "virtually all the sailors witnessed the object." Although the United Press International reported the Brazilian Navy's endorsement of the photographs, Menzel and Boyd quote a Naval Ministry unofficial spokesman, who stated, "The

Navy has no connection with the case, and its only connection with the occurrence was the fact that the photographer was aboard the school ship, and came back with the ship to Rio." In a newspaper interview, another unofficial Navy spokesman declared, "No officer or sailor from the N.E. *Almirante Saldanha* witnessed the event."

Menzel and Boyd strengthened their case by revealing that Barauna had a prior interest in UFOs. Shortly before the alleged Trindade sighting, Barauna had published an intentionally humorous magazine article, entitled "A Flying Saucer Hunted Me at Home." The article was accompanied by admittedly fake photographs. Barauna had developed the Trindade photographs unobserved by anyone except his friend, Viegas. Menzel and Boyd question how anyone could confirm that the object shown on the negative was the same as the UFO allegedly seen in the sky. Because of the small size of the negative, the UFO would have appeared merely as a tiny blur about one-sixteenth-of-an-inch in length and no thicker than a pencil line. No prints had been made from the negative until Barauna went ashore several weeks later. Furthermore, despite the claim of Barauna and his two associates that the UFO was glowing brightly, the photographs show an object which does not give any impression of luminosity. Menzel suggests that, prior to boarding the ship, Barauna shot a series of pictures of a model flying saucer against a black background. He then reloaded his camera with the same film and shot a second series of pictures from the *Almirante Saldanha*. When the film was developed, the flying saucer appeared to be hovering in the sky.

Despite Menzel's and Boyd's arguments, many UFOLOGISTS continue to believe that the Trindade

Island photographs present strong evidence of the reality of the UFO phenomenon. After conducting computer image • enhancement testing, GROUND SAUCER WATCH (GSW) has pronounced the photographs to be bona fide.

Bibliography: Menzel, Donald H., and Lyle G. Boyd, *The World of Flying Saucers* (Garden City, N.Y.: Doubleday and Company, 1953); Hall, Richard H. (ed.), *The UFO Evidence* (Washington, D.C.: National Investigations Committee on Aerial Phenomena, 1964).

**TROXELL, HOPE,** *see* **SCHOOL OF THOUGHT**

**TRUE FLYING SAUCERS AND UFOs QUARTERLY,** magazine established in 1976. It is available both at newsstands and by subscription. All aspects of UFOLOGY and paranormal phenomena are covered.

Articles are written by freelance and staff writers. Tom McArdell is Editor. The magazine is published by Histrionics Publishing Company, 21 West 26th Street, New York, New York 10010.

**TRUMAN, HARRY S.,** thirty-third president of the United States, who stated at a press conference on April 4, 1950, "I can assure you that flying saucers, given that they exist, are not constructed by any power on Earth."

**TUFOIC** *see* **TASMANIAN UNIDENTIFIED FLYING OBJECTS INVESTIGATION CENTRE**

**TUNGUSKA REGION, RUSSIA.** Nearly forty years before the United States detonated the first atomic bomb, an unidentified flying object exploded over Siberia, releasing energy equivalent to that of a twenty-megaton hydrogen bomb. The source of that explosion remains a matter of debate and conjecture for scientists and UFOLOGISTS alike.

In the early dawn of June 30, 1908, travelers in the Gobi Desert saw an enormous object traversing the sky over China. At about 7:00 A.M., inhabitants of the sparsely-populated Tunguska forest caught sight of the fiery cylindrical body as it soared through the sky, leaving behind it a trail of multicolored smoke. With a roar, the object plunged toward the ground. Suddenly, it exploded. Simultaneously, a blinding flash of light illuminated the sky. A fierce wave of HEAT shot across the countryside. Nomadic villages were annihilated. The ground heaved, flinging helpless people into the air. Boatmen hundreds of miles away were hurled into the river. Those who were not injured or unconscious watched with horror and disbelief as a huge pillar of smoke rose into the air and spread out into the shape of

a mushroom. A blanket of ashes covered the devastated land. Directly below the location of the airborne explosion, charred trees stood upright. Around them, extending to a forty-mile radius, trees were flattened with their peaks directed away from the epicenter. All over the world the effects of the explosion were registered on seismographs and barographs. That night, in Siberia and throughout Europe, brilliant sunsets were highlighted by massive silver clouds tinged with a yellow-green light, which sometimes changed to a red or orange or rosy hue. At midnight, people were able to read their newspapers without the aid of artificial light. These unusual conditions prevailed during the following nights but with diminishing intensity.

Twenty years passed before the first team of scientists set out for the remote area. They had expected to find evidence of a meteoritic impact. What they found did not concur with their knowledge of the burgeoning science of meteoritics but, for lack of better explanation, the phenomenon was classified as the Tunguska meteorite.

Another twenty years passed before Alexander Kazantsev, Russian scientist and author, having observed the effects of the nuclear devastation at Hiroshima, saw the similarities between the two blasts. He presented his speculation in the form of a science fiction story, entitled, "Guest from the Cosmos." He noted that the flattened trees of the Tunguska region, the mushroom CLOUD and the subsequent illuminated nights were now established characteristics of a nuclear explosion. To test his theory, a new expedition set out for the blast site. The team found an abnormally high degree of radiation in samples of trees, plants, ash and soil. Tiny globules of extraterrestrial matter were embedded in the soil. These particles contained small amounts of metals including copper and germanium, materials used in the construction of electrical and technical equipment. An unusually accelerated growth of plants and trees was evident in the region, yet another known aftereffect of nuclear explosions. Surviving witnesses revealed that a strange black rain had fallen over Siberia on the day of the mysterious explosion, just as it had in Hiroshima almost forty years later. During the weeks that followed the disaster, local reindeer had fallen victim to an unknown disease which produced scabs on their bodies resembling the radiation blisters found on cattle exposed to the radiation debris of the ALAMAGORDO experimental atom bomb. Based on witnesses' reports and ballistic wave evidence, it was established that the UFO had changed course at least once, possibly twice, during the last stage of its doomed journey. The general consensus of the study team was that on June 30, 1908, an atomic-powered device weighing over fifty thousand tons exploded over the Tunguska forest at an altitude of

The site of the 1908 explosion in Siberia. (*Courtesy Donn Davison*)

Hiroshima in 1945 after the atom bomb was dropped. (*Courtesy Donn Davison*)

just over three miles. Kazantsev believes that device to have been an extraterrestrial spacecraft which was attempting to land when its engines exploded.

Further research has been carried out to support Kazantsev's theory. Aerial mapping of the boundaries of the destroyed area showed an asymmetrical elliptical shape which led Russian scientists A. V. Zolotov and FELIX ZIGEL to conclude that the explosive material responsible for the blast was enclosed in a container made of another nonexplosive material. Calculations on the object's trajectory revealed its speed of entry into the atmosphere to be lower than that of natural astronomical bodies. Moreover, it was estimated that as the UFO neared the ground, it decelerated to a velocity comparable to that of a high altitude reconnaissance aircraft. Some UFOlogists today believe that an extraterrestrial crew, realizing they were bound for disaster, deliberately changed their ship's course in order to avoid endangering a heavily populated region of our PLANET. Of the many tales told of CRASHED FLYING SAUCERS, the story of the Tunguska explosion is the only one which has provided extensive evidence. Whether that evidence proves the theory of visitation by extraterrestrial intelligences is still disputed.

More conservative theorists propose that the UFO could have been a friable stony meteorite or a COMET. Zigel points out that it is not feasible for a comet to change its course. Furthermore, a comet would have been clearly visible long before it impacted Earth.

A less conservative hypothesis suggests that a small quantity of ANTIMATTER may have leaked into our world from another dimension. The collision of negative and positive atoms could have resulted in a devastating explosion.

A recent theory proposes that a hypothetical mini-BLACK HOLE passed through Earth in 1908. Some reject this explanation on the basis that an encounter with a mini-black hole, if such a thing exists, would have blown up the entire planet.

Whether or not the explanation lies in one of the aforementioned theories or one yet to be formulated, mankind was fortunate in 1908, for the explosion did not kill one human being.

Bibliography: Baxter, John, and Thomas Atkins, *The Fire Came By* (Garden City, N.Y.: Doubleday and Company, 1976); Sachs, Margaret, with Ernest Jahn, *Celestial Passengers—UFOs and Space Travel* (New York: Penguin Books, 1977).

**20th CENTURY UFO BUREAU,** 756 Haddon Avenue, Collingswood, New Jersey 08108; telephone number: 609-858-0700.

Based on the belief that the public has the right to know, this organization's goal is to secure hard core data on UFOs and present it to the public. The group claims to have obtained hard evidence relating to CRASHED FLYING SAUCERS from several highly reliable contacts, some within government circles and others formerly within government circles. It holds that while some UFOs represent ANGELS and a very small percentage represent satanic beings, the majority are piloted by extraterrestrial humanoids who are superior to human beings on Earth.

The Bureau was founded in 1973 by Carl McIntire, Director of the *20th Century Reformation Hour* broadcast, headquartered in Collingswood. UFO researcher and investigator Robert D. Barry has been full-time Director of the Bureau since its inception. The organization presents annual week-long conferences at the Christian Admiral Hotel in Cape May, New Jersey, during the summer and at the Gateway to the Stars Motel Auditorium in Cape Canaveral, Florida, during the winter. Barry has lectured at numerous Churches, educational institutions and civic organizations, including the NATIONAL ACADEMY OF SCIENCES (NAS) in Washington, D.C., the University of Pennsylvania, the University of Delaware, the Salem Community College in Penns Grove, New Jersey, and the International Management Club in Lancaster, Pennsylvania.

**TWILIGHT ZONE FUNZINE,** bimonthly publication, established in 1979, with a circulation of about 100. The range of subjects covered includes all aspects of UFOLOGY, science fiction stories, the motion pictures *Star Wars* and CLOSE ENCOUNTERS OF THE THIRD KIND, BIGFOOT and poetry.

Material is obtained from staff writers, freelance writers, readers and newspaper clippings. Articles should range in length from half-a-page to one page. Self-addressed, stamped envelopes should accompany submissions. The amount of payment for articles and photographs is established by mutual agreement and is made upon acceptance. Writers retain all rights to their own material. *Twilight Zone Funzine* is edited by Linda M. Burton and Publisher Janice M. Croy. The mailing address is: Suite 206, 137 S. Pennsylvania, Denver, Colorado 80209.

**TWO, THE,** *see* **HUMAN INDIVIDUAL META-MORPHOSIS**

**2001: A SPACE ODYSSEY,** motion picture (MGM, 1968). Producer/director: Stanley Kubrick; associate producer; Victor Lyndon; screenplay by Stanley Kubrick and Arthur C. Clarke, based on the story "The Sentinel" by Arthur C. Clarke. Cast: Keir Dullea, Gary Lockwood, Douglas Rain, William Sylvester, Leonard Rossiter, Robert Beatty, Frank Miller, Penny Brahms, Edwina Carroll, Daniel Richter, Margaret Tyzack, Jean Sullivan and Alan Gifford.

This visually spectacular film deals with the interference of unseen extraterrestrial intelligences in the evolution of mankind. The picture opens with apelike creatures changing to aggressive, thinking beings after encountering a mysterious monolith. Then, in the year 2001, ASTRONAUTS discover a similar monolith on the MOON. A beam of sunlight is reflected from the monolith toward Jupiter. The United States launches a mission to the PLANET. The spacecraft's computer, HAL, attempts to take over, killing all the crew members but one before it is put out of commission. The surviving astronaut, continuing his journey, finds a third monolith on one of Jupiter's moons. An invisible alien force takes control of him, supplying him with a home and food for the remainder of his life. At his death, a fetus appears, signifying the beginning of a new stage of human evolution.

**UAO,** acronym for *u*nidentified *a*erial *o*bject or *u*nidentified *a*quatic *o*bject.

**UBATUBA, BRAZIL,** coastal town where three fishermen saw a flying disk plunging towards the ocean on September 10, 1957. Just as it seemed about to enter the water, the object turned sharply upward and exploded into thousands of fiery fragments. The fishermen were able to retrieve some metallic DEBRIS which had fallen near the beach. They sent samples with an anonymous letter to a Rio de Janeiro newspaper. UFO investigator OLAVO FONTES acquired three of the small fragments and had one of them analyzed at the Mineral Production Laboratory of the Brazilian Agricultural Ministry. After chemical analysis, it was announced that the metal was magnesium of a higher purity than attainable in purification methods known to mankind. It seemed that, after many documented tales of CRASHED FLYING SAUCERS, physical evidence had finally been produced.

Subsequent tests in the United States revealed that, although the samples were indeed very pure, magnesium of a higher purity was being produced by the Dow Chemical Company. However, at the time, the Brazilians did not have a sample of magnesium from the U.S. Bureau of Standards that equaled or surpassed the purity of the Ubatuba fragments.

Nevertheless, the major impurities detected in the Ubatuba samples were considered unusual. They consisted of about five hundred parts per million of strontium, about five hundred parts per million of zinc and smaller amounts of barium, manganese and chromium. The high percentage of strontium once more cast doubt on the terrestrial origin of the metal. However, the CONDON COMMITTEE discovered that, since 1940, experiments had been conducted with magnesium using samples containing from 0.1 percent to forty percent strontium. The committee's conclusion was that, in 1957, the technology existed to produce magnesium of the type reportedly found in Ubatuba.

Authors David Saunders and Roger Harkins argue that the most significant aspect of the Ubatuba fragments concerns the absence of certain elements. They claim that if the metal were a terrestrial alloy, it might contain aluminum or copper or both. There was no aluminum and only a trace of copper. In addition, they point out, there was no calcium in the fragments. Had someone performed the extremely difficult task of removing the calcium, he or she would almost certainly have had to use a quartz vessel which would have contaminated the magnesium with a minute quantity of silicon. Yet analysis revealed no silicon. Utilizing the best techniques known to purify magnesium at that time would have required repeated sublimation of the metal under a very high vacuum. The mercury-vapor pump that could create the necessary vacuum would have resulted in mercury contamination. No mercury was found in the samples.

Engineer James Harder has described the magnesium as having a close-packed hexagonal crystalline structure. Since hexagonal crystals have only one slip plane, they tend to be brittle but very strong. The strength of this alloy may be relevant in the context of spacecraft construction.

Walter Walker and Robert Johnson, metallurgists and consultants to the AERIAL PHENOMENA RESEARCH ORGANIZATION (APRO), have found that the metal was solidified in such a way that the grain runs in a single direction. Their claim that no studies in directional graining were carried out before 1957 lends support to the validity of the fishermen's claims.

It remains a debated issue whether or not the

techniques existed in 1957 to produce magnesium identical in every way to the Ubatuba fragments. However, if the Brazilian fisherman's story is fabricated, they succeeded in executing the most sophisticated and perplexing UFO HOAX to date.

Bibliography: Lorenzen, Coral E., *The Great Flying Saucer Hoax* (New York: William Fredericks Press, 1962); Saunders, David, and R. Roger Harkins, *UFOs? Yes!* (New York: New American Library, 1968).

**UCHOA, ALFREDO MOACYR DE MEN-DONCA** (b. April 21, 1906, Muricy, Brazil; address: SOS 104, Ble., Apt° 305, Brasilia, Brazil; telephone number: 2242157), President of the CENTRO NACIONAL DE ESTUDOS UFOLOGICOS (CENEU).

Uchoa believes that UFOs are spacecraft from many different PLANETS both within and beyond our solar system. Uchoa has had several close sightings of solid, metal structures, usually disk-shaped.

A civil engineer and a professor, Uchoa served in the Brazilian army from 1932 to 1963, achieving the rank of General. He was the recipient of several military and educational medals.

Uchoa is author of three books dealing with UFOs and parapsychology and published in Brazil.

**UCT** see **UNCORRELATED TARGET**

**UFO** see **UNIDENTIFIED FLYING OBJECT**

**UFO-ASPEKT,** regular publication of the Danish UFO organization, FRIT UFO STUDIUM (FUFOS).

**UFOB,** original abbreviation for unidentified flying object used by the UNITED STATES AIR FORCE (USAF). Pronounced *youfob*, it was replaced by the abbreviation UFO.

**UFO BUREAU (NATIONAL UFO COMMUNI-CATION NETWORK),** 118 Main Street, Camilla, Georgia 31730; telephone number: 912-336-5615.

The purpose of this organization is to research, investigate and analyze the UFO phenomenon. The group holds that UFOs are powered, metal spacecraft from outer space which are here to watch us and learn all they can about us. The group also believes that ANIMAL MUTILATIONS are connected with UFOs and notes that, in its own investigations of such cases, it has encountered reports of BIGFOOT and UFOs sighted in the same areas during the same periods.

This nonprofit organization was founded in 1966 by radio newsman Billy J. Rachels, who serves as Director. Rachels is also a representative of the INTERNATIONAL UFO BUREAU (IUFOB) and the MUTUAL UFO NET-

WORK (MUFON). DAVID REES, of the MANCHESTER AERIAL PHENOMENA INVESTIGATION TEAM (MAPIT), serves as foreign correspondent and English Director. Other foreign representatives include Harold Hokanson in Canada and Bryan M. Hartley in England. Mike Williford is Associate Director. The group has thirty members in the United States, Canada and the United Kingdom. U.S. field investigators cover fourteen states in the western, central and eastern regions. Investigators are also located in England and Canada. The monthly *NUFOCN News Release* is edited by Howard H. Barker.

**UFO CANADA,** P.O. Box 145, Chomeday, Lavel, Quebec, Canada H7W 4K2; telephone number: 514-621-1260.

UFO Canada was established with the intention of creating a central clearing house for Canadian UFO reports and research. Its main purpose is to investigate, research and computer-store such reports. Another of the organization's goals is to establish a cooperative effort with the Canadian news media to strip the UFO of its dramatic and sensationalist aura. Open-minded about the identity of UFOs, the organization believes the UFO should be treated as a phenomenon to be studied, and not as a horror story or melodrama.

This nonprofit organization was founded in 1977 by Howard Gontovnick, who runs it, together with ROBERT SAPIENZA. It is not a membership organization. Contact is maintained with researchers and organizations throughout Canada, as well as in the United States, England, France, Norway, Finland, Sweden, Germany, Russia, Japan, Hong Kong and Belgium. Interested individuals and organizations are offered a library service which enables them to obtain suggested reading lists, private research documents and past government documents. An audio-visual presentation of general and scientific interest is available upon written request. UFO Canada publishes periodic research papers and catalogues pertaining to various aspects of UFO research. UFO CANADA, a journal of Canadian UFO/IFO studies, is published monthly.

UFO Canada is a member of the CANADIAN UFO REPORT EXCHANGE NETWORK (CUFOREN).

**UFO CANADA,** publication of UFO CANADA.

**UFOCAT,** computerized catalogue of UFO reports and related information. UFOCAT was created in the early 1970s by David Saunders of the CENTER FOR UFO STUDIES (CUFOS). Information is contributed by various UFO organizations around the world. The heterogeneous nature of the material and the questionable validity of individual entries create unavoidable weaknesses in the search for overall patterns. Of particular interest to Saunders are the dates and geographical distribution of sightings. The catalogue has grown at a rate averaging 10,000 entries per year and is considered the most comprehensive collection of UFO data.

**UFOCENTRE ALPHA TORQUAY,** 15A Market Street, Torquay, Devon, England; telephone number: 27833.

The purpose of this local organization is to investigate and discuss the UFO phenomenon. Press and Public Relations Officer Robert Wyse has observed UFOs on five occasions since 1953. The most recent sighting occurred in 1977 when, together with seven other members of the organization participating in a sky watch, he saw a huge, silent, rotating UFO with numerous flashing white lights. The object was also reported by nineteen independent witnesses located between Minehead and Torquay. The opinion of the principals of the organization is that UFOs are of extraterrestrial origin.

This nonprofit group was founded in 1977 by Robert John Wyse, who serves as President. Olive Wyse is Vice-President and Robert Wyse, Sr., is Press and Public Relations Officer. There are twenty members. The centre organizes sky watching weekends and coordinates the exchange of books between members. A newsletter, ENCOUNTERS, is published quarterly and deals with local and interesting sightings.

**UFOCUS RESEARCH,** c/o. James R. Harris, Route 4, Lisa Lane, Mt. Carmel, Illinois 62863; telephone number: 618-262-5581.

The purpose of this organization is to research historical accounts of FORTEAN phenomena. UFOCUS has no specific set of beliefs regarding the identity and origin of UFOs. One of the most important cases investigated by the group was that of a landing case near Reader, West Virginia, which was witnessed by three women in a car. When UFOCUS investigators did a follow-up in June, 1978, to their initial investigation, they were not able to find any traces of the witnesses, and townspeople with whom they talked could provide no information to confirm that the women had ever existed.

UFOCUS was founded in 1977 by James R. Harris, who serves as Director of Research, and Carl Wilfong. The group has ten active members. Membership is closed to the public. Although UFOCUS carries out much of its work at libraries, sightings in Illinois are investigated and field trips are made to FLAP areas, such as Southeastern Missouri and West Virginia. One of the organization's main activities is the producing of its newsletter, *UFOCUS*, which is mainly editorial, often satirical in content, and has maintained a policy of being highly critical of the UFOLOGICAL establishment. The newsletter is published irregularly, and anyone may subscribe. Harris is Editor, and Wilfong is Assistant Editor. Jeff N. Haugh is Consultant and Editor-at-Large.

**UFODOM,** term generally used in a satirical manner to refer to the field of UFOLOGY and the experts in that field.

**UFO FORUM,** publication of NORSK UFO CENTER.

**UFOI** *see* **UFO INTERNATIONAL**

**UFOIC** *see* **UFO INFORMATION CENTER**

**UFO IDENTIFICATION BUREAU AND SCIENCE MUSEUM (UFO/IB),** P.O. Box 9454, Winter Haven, Florida 33880; telephone number: 813-299-6111.

The purpose of this organization is to investigate UFOs, serve as a clearing house for information on UFO sightings and to establish a UFO museum in the Winter Haven area. Although opinions regarding the identity of UFOs vary among members, President James E. Lear believes UFOs may be spacecraft piloted by extraterrestrial beings and that a large percentage of them may not be friendly. He compares the danger we face by not being prepared for extraterrestrial hostility to that of the aerial attack on Pearl Harbor in 1941. Lear suggests that anyone who wants to see a UFO should get up every morning at four o'clock and watch the skies. He guarantees that this will result in at least one UFO sighting within a five-year period.

This nonprofit organization was founded in 1976 by Lear. Staff members include Director and Photographer Gary Hauft, Engineer Oliver Fielder, Pilot Ron Lear, Psysiologist Rick Abramson, Teacher Gary Edwards and Tony Leugot. Seven field investigators are located throughout Florida. Membership stands at approximately 150. Upon joining the organization, members receive a small, lightweight, loaded Recordflex camera, carrying strap, and return-mailer carton. All cameras are sealed and have recorded serial numbers. If a UFO is photographed, the camera is mailed to the organization which arranges for the film to be processed by an independent company. Prints are sent to the photographer. UFO/IB retains the negative and may negotiate for the purchase or lease of the PHOTOGRAPH.

**UFOIL** *see* **UFO INVESTIGATORS' LEAGUE**

**UFOIN** *see* **UFO INFORMATION NETWORK**

**UFOIN** *see* **UFO INVESTIGATORS' NETWORK**

**UFO INCIDENT, THE,** motion picture (NBC Television, 1975). Producers: Richard Colla and Joe L. Cramer; director: Richard Colla; teleplay by S. Lee Pogostin and Hesper Anderson, based on the book *The Interrupted Journey* by John G. Fuller. Cast: James Earl Jones, Estelle Parsons, Barnard Hughes, Beeson Carroll, Dick O'Neill and Terrence O'Connor.

This movie is a dramatization of the Betty and Barney Hill case, dealing with their sighting of a UFO in NEW HAMPSHIRE and the subsequent hypnotic regressions and psychiatric treatment they underwent.

Estelle Parsons and James Earl Jones in the motion picture *The UFO Incident. (Courtesy Universal Television)*

**UFO INFO,** publication of STUDIEGROEP PROGRESSIEVE WETENSCHAPPEN (SPW).

**UFO INFO EXCHANGE LIBRARY,** 49 The Down, Trowbridge, Wiltshire, England; telephone number: 61918.

The purpose of this nationwide investigative organization is to assist serious UFO researchers in every way possible and to assist the public with their queries on the subject. The group considers the identity and origin of UFOs as unknown.

This nonprofit organization was founded in 1975 by Barry C. Golding, who serves as President, Douglas Chaundy and John Rousten. Staff members include Douglas Chaundy, Michael Timmis, Terry Chivers and Jenny Chaundy. The organization's patrons are the Earl of Clancarty (BRINSLEY LE POER TRENCH), Baron Nugent and Lady Lethbridge. There are over 1,000 members. The group's 250 field investigators work as individuals or in teams of approximately six to eight members. Each team or individual covers an area of an approximately 100-mile radius. The organization works in cooperation with organizations and individuals in West Germany, France, Sweden, Ireland and New Zealand. All material obtained by the group is filed by subject and is available to members. A magazine, *UFO INFO Exchange Library,* is published quarterly and edited by Golding.

**UFO-INFORMATION,** publication of UFO-SVERIGE.

**UFO INFORMATION CENTER (UFOIC),** 4256 Springboro Road, Lebanon, Ohio 45036; telephone number: 513-932-6515.

The purpose of this organization is to conduct investigative studies of UFO sighting reports and related information submitted to UFOIC by the general public. The group makes a concerted effort to separate fact from fiction. UFOIC specializes in the study of close encounters and other unexplainable phenomena. The cases it believes to be of most importance are the many cases involving persons who have experienced both UFO and psychic manifestations on a repeated basis.

This nonprofit organization was founded in 1968 by BONITA ROMAN, who serves as Director. She discontinued the group in 1975 but re-established it in 1977. UFOIC is not a membership group. An investigative network functions independently of public UFO groups and consists of individuals who prefer to contribute information or investigative assistance on a confidential basis.

**UFO INFORMATION NETWORK (UFOIN)** and **PAGE RESEARCH LIBRARY (PRL),** P.O. Box 5012, Rome, Ohio 44085.

The purpose of these sister organizations, founded in 1969 by owner-operator Dennis Pilichis, is to document, organize and distribute data on UFOLOGY and other FORTEAN topics. The group conducts first-hand investigations as well as collecting information from newsclipping services and through massive exchange programs with organizations and individuals around the world. The latest worldwide UFO news and events were formerly disseminated to approximately 1,500 subscribers through the PAGE RESEARCH LIBRARY NEWSLETTER. In 1979, the newsletter merged with THE OHIO SKY WATCHER, and is now issued as UFO OHIO. It represents several investigative organizations in Ohio. New subscribers receive *The Visual UFO Book and Publication Catalogue,* which lists a vast selection of rare, old and new books and magazines for sale by UFOIN. The group maintains a cooperative research library and publishes its own research booklets.

## UFO INFORMATION RETRIEVAL CENTER,
P.O. Box 57, Riderwood, Maryland 21139; telephone numbers: 301-435-0705 and 301-825-3011.

The purpose of this organization is to collect, analyze, publish and disseminate international information on reports of UFOs. It holds that UFOs are probably of extraterrestrial origin but that the possibility of visitation by future terrestrial archaeologists should not be ruled out.

This nonprofit organization was founded in 1966 by Thomas M. Olson, who serves as Director; Louis L. Olsen, who serves as Treasurer; and Irene M. Olsen, who serves as Secretary. It is not a membership organization. Investigations are conducted only in the case of local sightings. The organization compiles statistics, conducts research programs and maintains a library. Information is obtained from the publications of investigative organizations and the UNITED STATES AIR FORCE (USAF). The center responds to reasonable requests for statistics and information at cost. The organization publishes *The Reference for Outstanding UFO Sighting Reports,* a volume which is updated at infrequent intervals and which contains a worldwide selection of exclusively hard-core UFO cases.

## UFO INFORMATIONS, newsletter of the ASSOCIATION DES AMIS DE MARC THIROUIN (AAMT).

## UFO INFORMER, publication of PROJECT SUM (SOLVING UFO MYSTERIES) UFO RESEARCH

## UFO INSIGHT, publication of FEDERATION UFO RESEARCH (FUFOR).

## UFO INTERNATIONAL, newsletter published by the AMALGAMATED FLYING SAUCER CLUBS OF AMERICA (AFSCA) from 1962 to 1965, replacing AFSCA WORLD REPORT and in turn replaced by FLYING SAUCERS INTERNATIONAL.

## UFO INTERNATIONAL (UFOI), 63 Malvern Drive, North Common, Warmley, Bristol, Avon, England.

The purpose of this organization is to investigate and research UFOs, to organize the data, to promote public interest and scientific study and to cooperate with other individuals and organizations. UFOI is noncommittal regarding the identity and origin of UFOs, believing that there could be more than one solution. The group

holds that greater cooperation between international organizations might facilitate solving the UFO mystery.

This nonprofit organization was founded in 1977 by Terry R. Hooper, who serves as Director; John R. Casey, who serves as Deputy Director; Peter H. Tate, who serves as Chairman; and John Cooper. This is not a public membership organization. Rather, the forty members are researchers and investigators located throughout the world. Data is sent to members upon request. UFOI publishes a bimonthly magazine, QUEST, which is edited by Allan Parsons.

## UFO INVESTIGATOR, publication of the NATIONAL INVESTIGATIONS COMMITTEE ON AERIAL PHENOMENA (NICAP).

## UFO INVESTIGATORS' LEAGUE (UFOIL),
Suite 1306, 303 Fifth Avenue, New York, New York 10016; telephone number: 212-685-4080.

The purpose of this informal group is to promote an exchange of information and a free flow of data between people of all walks of life. UFOIL aims to fill the gap left by more conservative organizations which, it holds, do not allow constructive thinking and debate among their members.

UFOIL was founded in 1978 by TIMOTHY GREEN BECKLEY. Members receive a subscription to the bimonthly tabloid UFO REVIEW, published by the UFO NEWS SERVICE, as well as to the *UFO Spotters' Newsletter,* which allegedly contains top-secret information on previously unpublished incidents. Other membership benefits include a personalized membership card which entitles the bearer to investigate UFO sightings as a UFOIL representative, a UFO investigator's certificate and a UFO investigators' field manual.

## UFO INVESTIGATORS' NETWORK (UFOIN),
23 Sunningdale Drive, Irlam, Greater Manchester M30 6NJ, England; telephone number: 061-775-4749.

UFOIN is a freelance network of the United Kingdom's most active and experienced organizations and independent investigators. Entrance is on a selective basis, in as much as prospective members must prove their ability to conduct comprehensive, in-depth investigations. UFOIN deals only in high strangeness cases and insures that members work on such cases as part of an informal team, thus avoiding overlap of investigative activities.

UFOIN was formed in 1977 as an expanded nationwide version of the successful concept established by the regional NORTHERN UFO NETWORK (NUFON). Although UFOIN has no official staff and no existence as an independent organization, it is administered by NUFON's JENNY RANDLES, Peter Warrington, Bryan

Hartley, Paul Whetnall and Robert Morell, who perform for it the same functions they perform for NUFON, including the transfer of data to UFOCAT, the channeling of information to the FLYING SAUCER REVIEW (FSR), the organization and housing of files and a library at the Nottingham headquarters and the maintenance of communications with foreign organizations and individuals. FSR provides UFOIN with a small fund to cover extraneous investigative costs.

**UFOJA** *see* **UFOs OVER JERSEY ASSOCIATION**

**UFOLOGICAL,** of or according to UFOLOGY.

**UFOLOGIE BULLETIN,** former publication of the defunct French organization CERCLE INTERNATIONAL DES JEUNES UFOLOGUES (CIJU).

**UFOLOGIST,** a person versed in UFOLOGY.

**UFOLOGY,** the study of the UFO phenomenon.

**UFOLOGY BULLETIN,** defunct monthly bulletin which was published for two years in Ventura, California.

**UFOLORE,** the traditions and facts relating to UFOs.

**UFOMANIA,** excessive and persistent tendency to apply the UFO label to any aerial phenomenon without making any effort to find a conventional explanation.

**UFOMANIAC,** a person who has UFOMANIA. The term is sometimes used in a derogatory manner to refer to all UFO witnesses and UFOLOGISTS.

A 30-foot UFO nest found in Tully, Queensland, Australia, on January 26, 1966, following the sighting of a spinning UFO. *(Courtesy ICUFON/UFOIC)*

**UFO-NACHRICHTEN,** publication of DEUTSCHE UFO/IFO-STUDIENGESELLSCHAFT (DUIST).

**UFONAUT,** a UFO OCCUPANT.

**UFO NESTS,** circular LANDING MARKS found in swampy vegetation. The term was created in 1965 to describe traces allegedly left by UFOs in Australian swamplands.

**UFO NEWS BULLETIN,** newsletter of the BRITISH FLYING SAUCER BUREAU.

**UFO NEWSCLIPPING SERVICE (UFONS),** Box 220, Route 1, Plumerville, Arizona 72127.

Initiated in 1969, this newsclipping service supplies international coverage of UFO reports and FORTEAN events. All foreign-language clippings are translated into English. A minimum number of twenty legal size, photo offset pages is sent monthly to subscribers by first-class mail in the United States, Canada and Mexico, and by airmail to other countries. All subscriptions must be for a minimum time period of three months. LUCIUS FARISH has been UFONS' editor since 1977.

**UFO NEWSLETTER** *see* **UFO RESEARCH (UFOR)—NEW SOUTH WALES (NSW)**

**UFO NEWS SERVICE,** Suite 1306, 303 Fifth Avenue, New York, New York 10016; telephone number: 212-685-4080.

This company, headed by TIMOTHY GREEN BECKLEY, publishes the bimonthly tabloid UFO REVIEW and UFO books, as well as distributing audio cassette tapes on UFOs.

**UFONOTAS,** publication of the CENTRO DE ESTUDOS UFOLOGICOS (CEU).

**UFONS** *see* **UFO NEWSCLIPPING SERVICE**

**UFO OHIO,** magazine and investigative network established in 1979 as the result of a merger of the PAGE RESEARCH LIBRARY NEWSLETTER and THE OHIO SKY WATCHER. It represents several organizations in Ohio, including the UFO INFORMATION NETWORK (UFOIN), the OHIO UFO INVESTIGATORS' LEAGUE (OUFOIL) and the TRI-COUNTY UFO STUDY GROUP.

Dennis Pilichis is Editor-in-Chief. The magazine is published by UFOIN, P.O. Box 5012, Rome, Ohio 44085.

**UFO PHENOMENA, INTERNATIONAL ANNUAL REVIEW (UPIAR),** academic journal devoted to the scientific study of UFO phenomena, published by Editecs Publishing House, in conjunction with the Comitato Nazionale Indipendente per lo Studio dei Fenomeni Aerei Anomali (CNIFAA). The main goal of *UFO Phenomena* is to provide, each year, an up-to-date summary of the most significant advances achieved in the field of scientific UFO study. The journal publishes original papers concerned with the physical aspects of UFO phenomena, the gathering and processing of data, Close Encounters of the Third Kind (CE–III), the psychological and perceptive aspects of UFOlogy and the epistemology of UFO research.

The journal's staff includes physicist Roberto Farabone, who serves as Editor-in-Chief; biochemist Francesco Izzo, who serves as Managing Editor; and author and publisher Renzo Cabassi, who serves as Managing Publisher. The Advisory Board consists of Richard F. Haines, J. Allen Hynek, Jean Claude Ribes, Frank B. Salisbury, Berthold E. Schwarz and Ronald M. Westrum. The Editorial Board consists of Kenneth V. Anderson, Vicente-Juan Ballester-Olmos, Fred H. Beckman, Ernst Berger, Jack M. Bostrack, Micahel L. Broyles, Fabrizio Cerquetti, Maurice G. de San, Geoffrey G. Doel, P. M. H. Edwards, Ivor Grattan-Guinness, Miguel Guasp, Rodolfo Guzzi, Terry A. Hartman, Harold I. Heaton, Bruce S. Maccabee, Terry L. Maple, Gianluigi Parmeggiani, Claude Rifat, Jacques Scornaux, Willy Smith, R. Leo Sprinkle and David F. Webb.

The journal publishes contributions written in English, and occasionally in French. Anyone may submit papers, which are then submitted to the appropriate members of the Advisory and Editorial Boards for acceptance. Authors should send two copies of their manuscripts, typed and single-spaced on white paper, to Editecs Publishing House, Casella Postale 190, 40100 Bologna, Italy. The original, which will be published by a direct photographic reproduction process, must be very clear. All illustrations should be in the desired final size. Contributions should be classified by authors as one of the following: review articles, original papers (patterns and hypotheses), case histories, book reviews or letters to the editor. The first page of each paper should carry the title (main title underlined), the authors' names and the name of the department, institute or association in which the research work was done. Original papers must be divided into chapters in the following order: a summary of 200 to 300 words, an introduction, material and methods, results, discussion and references. Review articles and case histories may be divided into chapters at the authors' discretion. A list of five to fifteen key words for indexing purposes must be given by the authors, after the summary. Papers in French should also have a full English summary, with

an English translation of the title. Contributors are requested not to use technical terms or jargon. There is no payment for contributions. The publisher acquires the sole copyright for all languages and countries.

**UFO PHENOMENA NEWS BULLETIN,** former name of the Unexplained Phenomena News Bulletin.

**UFO/PSI STUDY GROUP,** c.o. Kent Yngve Johansson, Kljutbanegatan 23 An.b., 723 39 Västerås, Sweden; telephone number: 021-132661.

The purpose of this investigative organization, which agrees with the conclusions introduced by John A. Keel and Jacques Vallee, is to study the correlations between psychic phenomena and UFO manifestations.

This nonprofit organization was founded in 1977 by Kent Yngve Johansson, who serves as President. It is not a membership group and consists of active co-workers only. Field investigations are carried out in Sweden and abroad. The group also conducts experiments in the field of psychic phenomena.

**UFO QUEBEC,** P.O. Box 53, Dollard-des-Ormeaux, Quebec, Canada H9G 2H5.

This organization, founded in 1975, represents an association of university professors, scientists and researchers who were previously involved in UFOlogy on an individual basis. *UFO Quebec* is also the name of its French-language quarterly magazine, which has a circulation of 1,200 and is available by subscription and at some newsstands. The editors are Norbert Spehner, Marc Leduc, W. Hoville, Philippe Blaquiere and Claude MacDuff.

**UFOR (FNQ)** *see* **UFO RESEARCH (UFOR)—FAR NORTH QUEENSLAND (FNQ)**

**UFOR (NSW)** *see* **UFO RESEARCH (UFOR)—NEW SOUTH WALES (NSW)**

**UFOR (NT)** *see* **UFO RESEARCH (UFOR)—NORTHERN TERRITORY (NT)**

**UFOR (QLD)** *see* **UFO RESEARCH (UFOR)—QUEENSLAND (QLD)**

**UFOR (SA)** *see* **UFO RESEARCH (UFOR)—SOUTH AUSTRALIA (SA)**

**UFOR (WA)** *see* **UFO RESEARCH (UFOR)—WESTERN AUSTRALIA (WA)**

**UFO REPORT,** magazine established in 1969 with a

circulation of 150,000. It is published nine times yearly, with an Annual edition. It is available both at newsstands and by subscription. The range of subjects covered includes UFOs, latest discoveries in space science, psychic phenomena, ancient mysteries, the occult, the BERMUDA TRIANGLE and BIGFOOT.

Material is obtained from a worldwide network of regular contributing writers, freelance writers, news wire leads and investigative pieces, which the magazine develops. It is preferable that freelance writers query prior to submitting articles, which should range in length from 1,000 to 6,000 words. Stamped, self-addressed envelopes should accompany submissions. Payment of 200 to 450 dollars is made upon acceptance for first North American rights. The publishers prefer that a writer telephone collect rather than submit a manuscript without knowing their needs at the time. Thomas Steers is the Managing Editor. The magazine is published by Gambi Publications, a Division of Web Offset Industries, Limited, 333 Johnson Avenue, Brooklyn, New York 11206.

## UFO REPORT CENTER OF ORANGE COUNTY, c/o Alvin H. Lawson, English Department, California State University at Long Beach, Long Beach, California 90840; telephone number: 714-897-4UFO.

This twenty-four-hour hotline has been run by English professor ALVIN LAWSON since 1975. Police and UNITED STATES AIR FORCE (USAF) agencies cooperate in referring sighting reports to the number. There are on the average about two calls a day, most of which are requests for information. However, during the first three years of its operation, the center has received reports of about three dozen sightings which have defied explanation even after investigation.

## UFO RESEARCH ASSOCIATES, 3122 North Beachwood Drive, Los Angeles, California 90068; telephone number: 213-463-5219.

This investigative organization publishes the UFO RESEARCH NEWSLETTER, and is run by Gordon I. R. Lore.

## UFO RESEARCH (UFOR)—FAR NORTH QUEENSLAND (FNQ), P.O. Box 1585, Cairns, Queensland 4780, Australia; telephone number: 070-531919.

The prime objective of this organization is to investigate UFO sightings in Far North Queensland and to evaluate all reports received. UFOR (FNQ) is not interested in proving or disproving any particular theories or beliefs relating to UFOs. However, a majority of its members favor the EXTRATERRESTRIAL HYPOTHESIS (ETH) or the PARALLEL UNIVERSE HYPOTHESIS.

This nonprofit organization was founded in 1977 by Di Van-Wijk. Committee members include Coordinator Daryl Knowles, Liaison Officer Holly Goriss, Assistant Liaison Officer E. R. Wells and Treasurer Russell Boundy. There are approximately thirty members. Sighting reports are investigated by field investigators. Assistance is given by the Department of Civil Aviation of the Department of Transport, the police, the Royal Australian Air Force, the Meteorology Department and local news media. Reports of objects which remain unidentified are sent to the Australian UFO Computer File at the CENTRE FOR UFO STUDIES—AUSTRALIAN CO-ORDINATION SECTION (ACOS). Public meetings are held monthly. The UFO RESEARCH (FNQ) NEWSLETTER is published quarterly.

## UFO RESEARCH INSTITUTE (UFORI), P.O. Box 502, Union City, California 94587; telephone number: 415-471-0160.

The purpose of this organization is to make available to the public scientific materials on UFOs which are difficult to obtain. It also supplies information about other good sources of UFO related materials.

The institute was founded in 1970 by nuclear physicist and lecturer STANTON FRIEDMAN, who runs its operation. He offers free book lists on radio and television programs. Mail orders are filled from those mailings and from book lists left at lectures by Friedman. Although UFORI is not an investigative organization, Friedman does investigate cases occasionally. The institute's erstwhile newsletter, UFO Review, is no longer published.

## UFO RESEARCH (FNQ) NEWSLETTER, publication of UFO RESEARCH (UFOR)—FAR NORTH QUEENSLAND (FNQ).

## UFO RESEARCH NEWSLETTER, established in 1971 and published monthly or bimonthly. It is available by subscription only. The range of subjects covered includes UFO OCCUPANTS, ABDUCTIONS, electromagnetic effects, ANIMAL REACTIONS, PHYSIOLOGICAL EFFECTS, scientific research and book reviews.

Material is supplied by staff writers and field investigators. Gordon I. R. Lore is Editor. The newsletter is published by UFO Research Associates, 3122 North Beachwood Drive, Los Angeles, California 90068.

## UFO RESEARCH (UFOR)—NEW SOUTH WALES (NSW), P.O. Box 6, Lane Cove, New South Wales 2066, Australia.

This investigative organization publishes UFO Newsletter four to six times a year and organizes public meetings. It is a participating member of the CENTRE

FOR UFO STUDIES—AUSTRALIAN CO-ORDINATION SECTION (ACOS)

## UFO RESEARCH (UFOR)—NORTHERN TERRITORY (NT), 44 Carpentier Crescent, Wagaman, Darwin, Northern Territory, Australia.

The purpose of this organization is to investigate and study UFOs and to enlighten others about the subject. UFOR (NT) considers that UFOs are possibly piloted by extraterrestrial or extradimensional beings engaged in SURVEILLANCE of our technical development and our capacity for nuclear warfare.

This nonprofit, nonreligious organization was founded in 1978 by Clifford John Palmer, who serves as President and Correspondence Secretary. John Roberts is Treasurer. There are five members, all of whom participate as field investigators in the Darwin area. The group also exchanges newsclippings and sighting reports from other groups around the world.

## UFO RESEARCH OF FINLAND see SUOMEN UFOTUTKIJAT RY

## UFO RESEARCH (UFOR)—QUEENSLAND (QLD), P.O. Box 111, North Quay, Queensland 4000, Australia.

This investigative organization is a participating member of the CENTRE FOR UFO STUDIES—AUSTRALIA CO-ORDINATION SECTION (ACOS).

## UFO RESEARCH REVIEW, publication of the NOTTINGHAM UFO INVESTIGATION SOCIETY (NUFOIS).

## UFO RESEARCH (UFOR)—SOUTH AUSTRALIA (SA), 2A Castle Avenue, Prospect, South Australia; telephone number: 08.445435.

The purpose of this organization is to investigate the nature of the UFO phenomenon. UFOR (SA) holds that there is presently not enough firm data on which to base a definitive conclusion regarding the identity, origin and purpose of UFOs. It believes that a large number of OCCUPANT reports can probably be explained as hypnagogic and HYPNOPOMPIC images.

This nonprofit organization was founded in 1968 by V. Godic, who serves as Liaison Officer. H. Aspinall is the Coordinator and T. Mills is Treasurer. There are 130 members. Ten field investigators are scattered throughout the state of South Australia. The group is a participating member of the CENTRE FOR UFO STUDIES—AUSTRALIAN CO-ORDINATION SECTION (ACOS). UFOR (SA) publishes a bimonthly newsletter, as well as papers and articles of interest to the UFO researcher.

## UFO RESEARCH (UFOR)—WESTERN AUS-

TRALIA (WA), 84 Acton Avenue, Rivervale, Western Australia 6103; telephone number: 09-277 3803.

The purpose of this organization is to investigate and obtain scientific data on UFO sightings throughout Western Australia for inclusion in the Australian computer file run by the CENTRE FOR UFO STUDIES—AUSTRALIAN CO-ORDINATION SECTION (ACOS). No final conclusions regarding the identity, origin and purpose of UFOs have been reached by the group which holds that more scientific research is required before a definite decision can be made.

This organization was founded in 1975 by Jeff Bell and Steven Briggs. Membership is limited to persons who approach the subject on a serious, scientific level. Report forms are sent to all UFO witnesses in Western Australia. Qualified field investigators, located throughout the state, are on immediate call to interview witnesses if more details are required or if physical traces are involved. Scientific advisors are available, and UFOR (WA) maintains close contact with all sectors of the news media.

## UFO REVIEW, bimonthly newspaper established in 1978 with a circulation of over 40,000. It is available by subscription and is in limited distribution at newsstands. The range of subjects covered includes CLOSE ENCOUNTERS OF THE THIRD KIND (CE–III), analysis of UFO photographs, personal experiences described by readers, MEN IN BLACK (MIB), space kidnappings, mysterious creatures and interviews with experts in the field.

Fifty percent of the tabloid's material is written by staff writers and fifty percent by freelance writers. The newspaper does not rehash old sightings or use newsclippings. Articles range in length from 750 to 3,000 words. Submissions should be accompanied by self-addressed, stamped envelopes. Payment up to one hundred dollars is made upon publication. There is a payment of five dollars for each photograph published. TIMOTHY GREEN BECKLEY is Editor. Subscription to the tabloid is one of the benefits received by members of Beckley's organization, the UFO INVESTIGATOR'S LEAGUE (UFOIL). *UFO Review* is published by UFO NEWS SERVICE, 303 Fifth Avenue, Suite 1306, New York, New York 10016.

## UFORI see UFO RESEARCH INSTITUTE

## UFORIA, term generally used in a satirical manner to denote a mood of increased enthusiasm regarding the subject of UFOs. Increased public interest in the phenomenon during FLAPS is sometimes referred to as mass UFOria.

## UFORIAN, term generally used in a satirical manner

to denote a person having an exaggerated enthusiasm for the subject of UFOs.

**UFOs ARE REAL,** motion picture (Group I Films, 1980). Producer: Brandon Chase; director: Ed Hunt; consultant: STANTON FRIEDMAN; written by Ed Hunt and Stanton Friedman.

This documentary deals with well-known sightings and interviews with personalities in the field, including high government officials, military officials and ranking members of the scientific community.

**UFOSIS** *see* **UNIDENTIFIED FLYING OBJECTS STUDIES, INVESTIGATION SERVICE**

**UFOs OVER JERSEY ASSOCIATION (UFOJA),** Hautes Murailles, Samares Lane, St. Clement, Jersey, Channel Islands, United Kingdom; telephone number: 53229.

The purpose of this investigative organization is to keep Jersey residents informed about UFO activity around the world and to keep the world informed about UFO activity over Jersey. UFOJA holds that UFOs originate from other dimensions and that they are here to study Earth's strategic areas.

This nonprofit organization was founded in 1976 by A. Chilvers and Dean Preston, who serves as Chairman. Author Michael Hervey is Honorary President. Robert Fielding is Secretary. There are fifty members. The group has four field investigators in Jersey, as well as overseas investigators. Members participate in sky-watches. The UFOJA newsletter, UNIDENTIFIED ENCOUNTERS, is published twice a year and deals mainly with CLOSE ENCOUNTERS OF THE THIRD KIND (CE–III).

**UFO-SVERIGE (UFO-SWEDEN),** P.O. Box 16, S-596 00 Skänninge, Sweden; telephone number: 0142-440 30.

The aims of this organization are: 1. to investigate UFO reports; 2. to inform the general public about the reality of the UFO phenomenon; and 3. to stimulate research into ufology and other fields that might be related to the UFO phenomenon. The organization holds that some UFOs are controlled by intelligent forces but are not made or controlled by human beings.

This nonprofit organization was founded in 1970 by UFO-Motala, a UFO group located in Motala and formed in 1968. UFO-Sverige is an association of twenty UFO groups in different parts of Sweden. A Central Group, elected or re-elected at annual meetings, manages the organization. The Secretary's office is located in Skänninge, about twenty kilometers from Motala. The organization has about 2,500 members. Approximately 110 field investigators are located throughout the country, with a heavy concentration in central Sweden. The group organizes exhibitions and annual meetings held in different cities each year. The meetings include lectures and film shows for the public and are well-covered by the news media. A bimonthly magazine, UFO-INFORMATION, deals with UFO reports from all over the world but particularly from Sweden, articles on UFOLOGY and related subjects and book reviews.

**UFO TASMANIA,** publication of the TASMANIAN UNIDENTIFIED FLYING OBJECTS INVESTIGATION CENTRE (TUFOIC).

**UFO UPDATE,** magazine established in 1977 and published nine times a year. It is available both at newsstands and by subscription. The magazine deals with all aspects of the UFO phenomenon and carries a large number of reports on UFOs sighted in Ontario.

The magazine is published and edited by Tom Grey, in association with the NORTHEASTERN UFO ORGANIZATION (NEUFO). The publication's address is 573 North Service Road, 402 Mississauga, Ontario, Canada L5A 1B6.

**UFO UPDATE,** quarterly magazine established in 1975, with a circulation of 210,000. It is available at newsstands. All areas of UFOLOGY are covered, and articles are well supplemented with PHOTOGRAPHS and artists' renderings.

Articles are written by staff writers and freelance writers. Additional material is obtained from newspaper clippings, United Press International and investigators. Guidelines for writers are supplied upon receipt of a self-addressed, stamped envelope. Articles between 2,000 and 3,000 words in length should be submitted with a self-addressed, stamped envelope and payment is made upon publication at a rate of three cents per word for the acquisition of all rights. There is no payment for photographs.

Harry Belil is the Editor and Publisher. His publishing company, BRM Publications, Inc., is located at 303 West 42nd Street, New York, New York 10036.

**ULTRATERRESTRIAL HYPOTHESIS** *see* **PARALLEL UNIVERSE HYPOTHESIS**

**UMMITE,** inhabitant of the alleged PLANET UMMO, which supposedly orbits the STAR Wolf 424.

**UMMO,** PLANET which supposedly orbits the star Wolf 424. Reportedly, inhabitants of Ummo domiciled on Earth have been contacting various individuals in Spain since 1965. These contacts, who include professional people and UFO researchers, receive telephone calls

Insignia which allegedly represents a planet called Ummo.

and letters from the so-called UMMITES, imparting philosophical and scientific information. Some of the material indicates that they have made their existence known to persons in Canada, France, Austria and Yugoslavia.

The communications from the so-called Ummites have also revealed a great deal about life on the alleged planet UMMO. Letters and documents claim that the Ummites are an older, more advanced civilization than ours. Although similar in appearance to earthlings, most adults on Ummo must use TELEPATHY because their vocal cords become sclerosed between the ages of fourteen and sixteen. Those who are able to telephone human contacts are exceptions to the case. Ummo is governed by four leaders selected by psychophysiological evaluation. Money is obsolete because production of consumer goods exceeds demand. The Ummites believe in a Creator or God and the existence of the soul. Although cosmic morality forbids social interference on other planets, the alleged Ummites claim that there is little risk their modest attempts at communication will result in any change on Earth because of the skepticism with which they are met.

Written communications, which are mailed by the so-called Ummites from various parts of the world, bear a stamped insignia resembling the astronomical symbol for Uranus, a capital H with a vertical line through the center. This symbol was allegedly seen on UFOs sighted at Aluche, Spain, on February 6, 1966, and SAN JOSÉ DE VALDERAS, SPAIN, on June 1, 1967. PHOTOGRAPHS purporting to show the UFO seen in the latter sighting were exposed as HOAXES.

Author JACQUES VALLEE has proposed that the Ummo affair might be part of a secret military intelligence project. He makes this suggestion because of the proximity of the sightings to a military technical school and airfield, and the discovery near San José de Valderas, after the 1967 sighting of tubes containing polyvinyl fluoride, a material whose use was restricted at the time to aeronautical and military applications. He also considers the possibility that the Ummo case might be part of a worldwide deception conducted by a group of humans engaged in a conspiracy to bring about social change on Earth by means of MIND CONTROL.

Bibliography: Vallee, Jacques, *The Invisible College* (New York: E. P. Dutton, 1975); Ribera, Antonio, and Rafael Farriols, *Un Caso Perfecto* (Barcelona: Pomaire, 1969).

## UNARIUS EDUCATIONAL FOUNDATION,

P.O. Box 1042, El Cajon, California 92022; telephone number: 714-447-4170.

The stated goal of this CONTACTEE organization is to teach man and to help him to move forward in his evolution. Unarius is an acronym for *Universal Articulate Interdimensional Understanding of Science*, supposedly the key to lifting students into higher mental states. UFOs, according to the organization, are spaceships manned by friendly beings who wish to acquaint us with their craft in order to convince us that they mean no harm. RUTH NORMAN, Director of Unarius, claims to be in mental contact with fifty-nine planetary leaders who directed her to buy sixty-seven acres of land to serve as a landing site for spaceships. Norman predicts that the ships will land sequentially at this site, one on top of the other, forming a thirty-three-story city. Unarius has wagered several thousand dollars with Ladbroke Investors, a London betting agency, that

The arrival of flying saucers on Earth as foreseen by the Unarius Educational Foundation. *(Painting by Ruth Norman)*

the craft would arrive by specific dates during the past few years. Although the predicted landings did not occur, the group has continued to place more bets. According to Unarius, the SPACE BROTHERS are waiting for Earth to accept an invitation to join the interstellar Confederation, at which time Earth will be unified under the leadership of Norman. The group professes that when Martians came to our planet 65,000 years ago to teach spacecraft building, mankind retaliated by attacking MARS. Norman and a group member have described psychic visits to subterranean cities on Mars. However, they explain, Earth's attack was not the reason the Martians went underground. Allegedly, when Martian astronomers saw a "great nova" headed for their PLANET, the populace moved underground to avoid destruction. Using miniature models, Unarius has made a ninety-minute motion picture, entitled *A Visit to the Underground Cities of Mars*.

This nonprofit organization was founded in 1956 by the late Ernest L. Norman and Ruth Norman, who serves as President. Board Members are Dorothy Ellerman, Vaughn Spaegel, Thomas Miller, David Osborne, Daniel Smith, Helen Moore, Leila Landass, Christine Veazy and Wayne Strong. There are 275 members. The group has published more than forty books, many of which purport to contain direct communications from the souls of hundreds of famous people such as Aristotle, Moses, Shakespeare, Beethoven, Leonardo da Vinci, Sigmund Freud, Karl Marx, Albert Einstein, Kung Fu, John F. Kennedy and Gary Cooper. Courses are given weekly, dealing with the understanding of higher consciousness and the presence of other people in other worlds. A magazine, *Unarius Light,* is published quarterly.

**UNCORRELATED TARGET (UCT),** an unidentified RADAR blip.

**UNDERSTANDING,** bimonthly magazine, established in 1956, with a circulation of 400 to 500. It is available by subscription only. The range of subjects covered includes articles on political trends today, poetry, UFO reports, details of government investigations of sightings, conclusions reached about the validity of sightings and government investigations, general interest articles, book reviews and reports on the organization and its conventions.

Material is derived from staff writers, freelance writ-

A model of a Martian city constructed by students of the Unarius Educational Foundation and based on alleged eyewitness descriptions by Ruth Norman.

ers and newspaper clippings. Freelance writers should query first and send self-addressed, stamped envelopes with submissions. First rights only are purchased and payment is made at a rate of one-cent-per-word upon publication. Articles should range in length from 800 to 1,000 words. PHOTOGRAPHS are not used unless submitted by staff members. Editor DANIEL FRY recommends that writers avoid articles of the personal confession type and reports of "far-out" phenomena.

The magazine is the official publication of Fry's CONTACTEE organization, UNDERSTANDING. The editorial office is located at 1606 Mountain View Drive, Alamogordo, New Mexico 88310.

**UNDERSTANDING,** Star Route, Box 588 F. Tonopah, Arizona 85354; telephone number: 602-386-3832.

The stated purpose of this CONTACTEE organization is to bring about peace on this PLANET through cooperation with others and to learn cooperation through understanding. The group has concluded that the group of SPACE PEOPLE who supposedly sent an emissary to Earth, with the help of DANIEL FRY, are vitally interested in the well-being and the continuation of the human race.

This nonprofit organization was founded in 1956 by Daniel Fry, who is now President Emeritus. The staff consists of President Lloyd G. Sellman, Executive Vice-President Lee Yates, First Vice-President Jeffrey Perry, Second Vice-President Tahahlita B. Wiese, National Membership Chairman Marie Jean Cullen and Recording and Corresponding Secretary Rita Sellman. The organization has individual units located in various parts of the United States and overseas. The national Directors are Benjamin T. Cullen in Spring Valley, California; John William Boushka in New York City; Robert Reid in Coleharbor, North Dakota; Wilma E. Thompson in Tonopah, Arizona; Hetty Miller in Phoenix, Arizona; Tahahlita B. Wiese in Merlin, Oregon; Clarence R. Gahlbeck in Lawndale, California; Daniel Fry in Alamogordo, New Mexico; Gerry Bringle in Bagdad, Arizona; and Virginia Perry in Woodlands, California. The following are overseas representatives: Per Axel. Atterbom, Box 206, 434–01 Kungsbacka, Sweden; Herbert D. Clark, 885 Keith Road, West Vancouver, British Columbia, Canada V7V 3N3; and Timothy Good, 20 Morley Court, The Avenue, Beckenham, Kent, England. The group has between 200 and 350 members.

The organization carries out field investigations of UFO sightings, collects information from newspapers and organizes lectures. Services available to members include space at headquarters at nominal rates, nonprofit admission prices to seminars and conventions, and a library of rare and out-of-print books on UFOs.

The organization's magazine, UNDERSTANDING, is published bimonthly and edited by Daniel Fry.

**UNDERSUN** *see* **SUBSUN**

**UNEICC** *see* **UNION NACIONAL DE ESTUDIOS E INVESTIGACIONES CIENTIFICO COSMOLOGICAS**

**UNEXPLAINED PHENOMENA INVESTIGATION BUREAU (UPIB),** 74 Cudliss Street, Eaton, West Australia 6232 or 8 Doolan Street, Bunbury, West Australia.

Primarily a social group, this nonprofit organization was founded in 1974 by Steve Pavlovich, Ron Jennings and Phil Harden. It has about seven members, who meet once a month. During the first few years of its existence, UPIB recorded a number of sightings and a newsletter was published by two of its members, Jeanette and DONALD FERGUSON, who left the group in 1978 to form their own organization.

UPIB is a participating organization in the network headed by the CENTRE FOR UFO STUDIES—AUSTRALIAN CO-ORDINATION SECTION (ACOS).

**UNEXPLAINED PHENOMENA NEWS BULLETIN,** bimonthly publication available by subscription only. It was established in 1977 as the KENT UFO NEWS BULLETIN. Its name was changed to the UFO PHENOMENA NEWS BULLETIN in the same year and to its current name in 1978. The bulletin deals with all unexplained mysteries, including ghosts and monsters. The main topic, UFOLOGY, is covered in all its aspects.

Material is contributed by staff and freelance writers. Subjects are treated in a sober, non-sensational manner. Articles should range from 200 to 5,000 words. There is no payment for contributions, and all rights remain with the author.

The bulletin is published by Editor D. J. Parry and the Norfolk and National UFO Investigation Society, 132 Ramnoth Road, Wisbech, Cambridgeshire PE13 2JD, England.

**UNIDENTIFIED AQUATIC OBJECT (UAO)** *see* **UNIDENTIFIED SUBMARINE OBJECT (USO)**

**UNIDENTIFIED ENCOUNTERS,** publication of the UFOs OVER JERSEY ASSOCIATION (UFOJA).

**UNIDENTIFIED FALLING OBJECTS** *see* **FAFROTSKIES, ANGELS' HAIR and DEVILS' JELLY**

An Idaho license plate. *(Courtesy Donn Davison)*

**UNIDENTIFIED FLYING OBJECT (UFO),** term coined by UNITED STATES AIR FORCE (USAF) Captain EDWARD RUPPELT to replace the earlier term, "flying saucer." Although the letters "UFO" are usually pronounced individually, they are occasionally pronounced as one word, *"you-foe."* Many UFOLOGISTS use the term to describe only those objects which remain unidentified after investigation and which they therefore consider to represent a single, consistent unknown phenomenon. Objects reported as UFOs which are subsequently identified are known as IDENTIFIED FLYING OBJECTS (IFOs).

Some ufologists prefer the term ANOMALISTIC OBSERVATIONAL PHENOMENA (AOP) since not all UFOs are unidentified, flying, or substantive objects.

**UNIDENTIFIED FLYING OBJECTS (UFO),** docudrama (United Artists, 1956). Producer: Clarence Greene; associate producer: Fernando Carrere; screenplay by Francis Martin.

This semi-documentary dramatization of the U.S. government's investigations of UFOs centers on the experiences of ALBERT M. CHOP, former UNITED STATES AIR FORCE (USAF) public relations official, who handled UFO information in the Pentagon. Chop is portrayed by Tom Towers, Aviation Editor of the *Los Angeles Examiner*. The footage includes the UFO films taken in GREAT FALLS, MONTANA, and TREMONTON, UTAH.

Official reaction to the picture was expressed in the Air Defense Command order to the 4674th Ground Observer Squadron, dated May 17, 1957, stating, "Disapprove requests for GOC Display in connection with commercial film pertaining to the controversial subject of flying saucers. Use of Display would involve the risk that Air Force could be considered as endorsing subject matter and authenticity of the filmed version of flying saucers."

**UNIDENTIFIED FLYING OBJECTS STUDIES, INVESTIGATION SERVICE (UFOSIS),** 71 Wentworth Way, Harborne, Birmingham B32 2UX, England; telephone number: 021-427-6914.

The purpose of this investigative organization is to promote unbiased interest in UFOs, to provide information on all aspects of the UFO phenomenon, and to collect data and reports relative to UFOs for scientific investigation.

This nonprofit organization was founded in 1975 by Geoffrey Westwood, Margaret Westwood, Ted Horton and M. Pritchard. It was reorganized in 1978. The staff includes Chairman Geoffrey Westwood, Secretary Margaret Westwood, Investigations Coordinator Ted Horton and Treasurer Sheila Pritchard. There are about sixty members. Over fifteen field investigators cover the counties of Worcestershire, Warwickshire and Staffordshire. UFOSIS works in liaison with other large UFO organizations. The quarterly publication, PROTEUS, is edited by E. Westley and A. Millard.

Canadian Regional Consultant: C. Rutkowski, Suite 16, Cockburn Street North, Winnipeg R3M 2N9, Manitoba, Canada.

**UNIDENTIFIED FLYING OBJECT SURVEILLANCE AND COLLECTION OF ALIEN NEWS (UFOSCAN),** organization founded and run by KENNETH BEHRENDT prior to the formation of PROJECT TO RESEARCH OBJECTS, THEORIES, EXTRATERRESTRIALS AND UNUSUAL SIGHTINGS (PROTEUS).

**UNIDENTIFIED SUBMARINE OBJECT (USO),** term used to describe an unidentified object seen below the ocean surface or an amphibious UFO. Ship logs contain numerous reports of unusual lights seen on or beneath the ocean surface, particularly during the latter half of the last century and the first half of this century. In some instances, the objects were seen entering or emerging from the water. One of the most common descriptions is that of a revolving luminous wheel with spokes of light radiating from its center. The wheels sometimes measured hundreds of yards in diameter. Supporters of the SUBMARINE HYPOTHESIS conjecture that these lights are emitted by the vehicles of an advanced submarine civilization or by UFOs which utilize underwater bases. It has also been suggested that UFOs, even if of extraterrestrial origin, might contain water, rather than air or some other gas.

Proponents of the ANCIENT ASTRONAUTS hypothesis believe that the earliest reference to a USO is found in the Biblical story of JONAH. The whale which allegedly

An amphibious flying object. *(Culver Pictures)*

swallowed him might have been a cigar-shaped USO, resembling a modern-day submarine in appearance.

Marine biologists point out that many glowing lights in the ocean can be attributed to phosphorescent plant and animal life. The tropical seas carry dense blankets of single-celled luminous planktonic organisms which glow when stimulated mechanically, as by the movement of waves. Some flash brightly. The single-cell *Cypridina Noctiluca,* when distributed by a beam of light, responds by ejecting a luminous cloud in the water. Luminous crustaceans, especially copepods, are widely distributed throughout the world. Some live on the surface, while others live in the ocean depths. Other organisms which create large patches of light in the sea are jellyfish and other coelenterates and ctenophores.

The study of marine phosphorescence has not provided the answer to all reports of USOs, particularly those where objects have been seen entering and emerging from the water. The question of their identity remains an open one.

Bibliography: Sanderson, Ivan T., *Invisible Residents* (New York: World Publishing Company, 1970).

## UNION NACIONAL DE ESTUDIOS E INVESTIGACIONES CIENTIFICO COSMOLOGICAS (UNEICC),

% Fray Rosendo Salvado 2, 7°B, Santiago de Compostela, La Coruna, Spain; telephone number: 981-59 04 23.

The main purpose of this investigative organization is to help explain the UFO phenomenon and to inform the public of its activities. The group has no collective opinion regarding the identity and origin of UFOs, although it considers the possibilities that they are extraterrestrial spaceships, Soviet and American secret craft engaged in espionage and military maneuvers, or extradimensional craft. UNEICC also studies FORTEAN phenomena.

This nonprofit organization was founded in 1971 by FERNANDO CERDÁ GUARDIA, following the dissolution of ERIDANI, one of Spain's most prestigious groups. Until 1979, UNEICC was headquartered in Madrid. The governing board consists of Jorge Lozano, Alfredo Llecha, Eugenio Crespo and Constantino Rábade. The group currently has about thirty-five members. Field investigations are carried out, primarily in the province of Galicia. Information is exchanged with other organizations. UNEICC publishes a quarterly bulletin, OVNI.

**UNITED KINGDOM.** The first series of UFO sightings in the United Kingdom occurred in 1909, when mysterious airships appeared in the skies. Today, there are more reported sightings per square mile in Britain than there are in the United States. However, the government has never established any official group to study UFOs. The Ministry of Defence maintains that, "Reports which are received from various sources, such as members of the public and the police, are examined by various staff members within the Ministry of Defence solely to see if they contain any defence implications. Once it is clear there are no defence implications, we do

Mystery airship seen over Peterborough, England, on March 23, 1909. *(Courtesy ICUFON)*

not pursue our research further." Since researchers and investigators who ask to see Ministry of Defence UFO files are told that the papers must remain confidential, there have been rumors of a COVER-UP. However, since the files contain correspondence from people whose identities cannot be divulged, the files have to remain closed under the rules laid down in the Public Record Acts, which preclude disclosure until thirty years from the date of each particular item of correspondence. Since the earliest reports the Ministry of Defence holds are dated 1962, none will be available until 1992.

In 1979, the HOUSE OF LORDS conducted a UFO debate initiated by the well-known British UFOlogist BRINSLEY LE POER TRENCH (the Earl of Clancarty). His proposal for the establishment of a governmental study of UFOs was rejected by the government.

The best-known of the United Kingdom's many UFO organizations are the BRITISH UFO RESEARCH ASSOCIATION (BUFORA) and CONTACT INTERNATIONAL. In 1977, many of Britain's organizations and independent UFOlogists formed a cooperative liaison known as the UFO INVESTIGATORS' NETWORK (UFOIN) to coordinate investigative and research efforts and to exchange information.

Britain's major UFO magazine, FLYING SAUCER REVIEW (FSR), has worldwide distribution and is considered by most UFOlogists to be one of the best publications in the field.

One of the many cases which has found considerable attention with foreign UFOlogists was that involving the RADAR/visual sightings at BENTWATERS AND LAKENHEATH in 1956.

One of the most famous UFO films originating from England was that taken by Jean Oldfield through a plane window in 1966. The object photographed is

Object photographed through plane window by Jean Oldfield in 1966. *(Courtesy ICUFON/Oldfield)*

torpedo-shaped, with ventral and dorsal fins. A BBC cameraman later duplicated the image, which was determined to be the tip of the aircraft's tail optically detached and reflectively doubled by the curvature of the thick windowpane. Further support of this explanation is given by viewing the original film. The image can be seen to grow longer and shorter as the viewing angle changes.

**UNITED NATIONS.** During 1966, COLMAN VONKEVICZKY, Director of the INTERCONTINENTAL GALACTIC SPACECRAFT (UFO) RESEARCH AND ANALYTIC NETWORK (ICUFON), made the first attempt to interest then-Secretary General of the United Nations U THANT in a U.N.-sponsored study of UFOs. Although Thant was quoted as saying that he considered UFOs the most important problem facing the U.N., next to the war in Vietnam, he later denied having made the statement.

On July 14, 1978, Sir ERIC GAIRY, Prime Minister of GRENADA, met with U.N. Secretary General Kurt Waldheim to discuss the subject of U.N. support for UFO studies. The meeting was also attended by astronomer J. ALLEN HYNEK, writer JACQUES VALLEE, former ASTRONAUT GORDON COOPER, French scientist CLAUDE POHER, psychologist DAVID SAUNDERS, writer LEONARD STRINGFIELD, film producer Lee Spiegel and Morton Gleisner of the Special Political Committee. Waldheim recommended that the group attempt to organize an international committee "which would then make specific recommendations to the Special Political Committee regarding the seriousness of UFOs."

On November 27, 1978, Gairy brought his delegation back to the United Nations to address the General Assembly's Special Political Committee. On this occasion, his delegation consisted of Grenada's Minister of Education Wellington Friday, Hynek, Vallee, Spiegel and nuclear physicist STANTON FRIEDMAN. Gairy proposed that the U.N., in consultation with the appropriate specialized agencies, "initiate, conduct and coordinate research into the nature and origin of unidentified flying objects and related phenomena." Spiegel made an audio/visual presentation, highlighted by the personal appearance of Lawrence Coyne, the principal witness in a much-publicized UFO sighting near MANSFIELD, OHIO, in 1973. Speeches were also made by Hynek, Vallee and Friedman.

On December 8, 1978, the Special Political Committee adopted a compromise resolution which read as follows: "The General Assembly invites interested member States to take appropriate steps to coordinate on a national level scientific research and investigation into extraterrestrial life, including unidentified flying objects, and to inform the Secretary-General of the observations, research and evaluation of such activities.

Meeting at the United Nations on July 14, 1978, to discuss the need for U.N. support for UFO studies. *Left to right:* Gordon Cooper, Jacques Vallee, Claude Poher, J. Allen Hynek, Prime Minister of Grenada Sir Eric Gairy, U.N. Secretary General Kurt Waldheim, Morton Gleisner, Lee Speigel, Leonard Stringfield (head only) and David Saunders. *(United Nations/Photo by Saw Lwin)*

"The General Assembly requests the Secretary-General to transmit the statements of the delegation of Grenada and the relevant documentation to the Committee on the Peaceful Uses of Outer Space, so that they may consider them at their 1979 meeting.

"The Committee on the Peaceful Uses of Outer Space will permit Grenada, upon its request, to present their views to the Committee at its next session. The Committee's deliberation will be included in its report which will be considered by the General Assembly at its 34th session."

In 1979, Gairy was ousted from his position as Prime Minister of Grenada. However, efforts to enlist international governmental sponsorship of a UFO study are being continued by VonKeviczky who, in 1980, launched a project to establish a World Authority for Spatial Affairs (WASA).

**UNITED STATES AIR FORCE (USAF).** A major fear caused by UFO reports in the late 1940s was that they might be new aircraft or secret weapons developed by an unfriendly nation. Thus, in July 1947, following sightings by pilots and other reputable observers, the Air Force began investigating UFO reports seriously. On January 22, 1948, PROJECT SIGN was established at Wright-Patterson Air Force Base in Ohio to "collect, collate, evaluate and distribute to interested government agencies and contractors all information concerning sightings and phenomena in the atmosphere which can be construed to be of concern to the national

security." Project members issued an ESTIMATE OF THE SITUATION, in which they concluded that UFOs were craft from other worlds. It was rejected, however, by then-Chief of Staff General Hoyt S. Vandenberg, on the grounds that it lacked supportive evidence. This led to a policy change, and with it a change of name. PROJECT GRUDGE was established on February 11, 1949. Reports were now evaluated on the premise that UFOs could not exist. Captain EDWARD RUPPELT took charge of Grudge in 1951, and revitalized the program through extensive reorganization and an increase in budget and staff. In 1952, a boom year for UFO reports, the Air Force upgraded Grudge from a project to a separate organization, named PROJECT BLUE BOOK. Ruppelt contracted with a private research organization, the BATTELLE MEMORIAL INSTITUTE, to conduct a statistical analysis of UFO characteristics. By the beginning of 1953, the project was overwhelmed with reports. In January, the CENTRAL INTELLIGENCE AGENCY (CIA) formed the ROBERTSON PANEL, a group of eminent scientists, to study the issue. The panel concluded that there was no evidence of a "direct physical threat to national security," and that the "continued emphasis on the reporting of these phenomena, in these parlous times, result in a threat to the orderly functioning of the protective organs of the body politic." As a result, Blue Book became primarily concerned with DEBUNKING UFOs. Its staff and budget began to shrink. The Battelle Memorial Institute's study was completed in 1953 (later released as SPECIAL REPORT NO. 14). Although the

Institute had been commissioned to carry out a statistical study, not explain the unidentified reports or solve the UFO problem, it nevertheless corroborated the Robertson Panel's position that UFOs presented no threat to national security.

The Air Force became involved in an enduring and sometimes clumsy public relations effort to convince the public that UFOs were nothing to be concerned about. To counteract attacks by retired Marine Corps Major DONALD KEYHOE and the NATIONAL INVESTIGATIONS COMMITTEE ON AERIAL PHENOMENA (NICAP), it released *Special Report No. 14* in 1955. However, the report served only to increase public suspicion that the Air Force was involved in a COVER-UP, possibly under orders from the CIA.

During the late 1950s, the Air Force managed to stave off hearings on their activities by giving individual briefings to individual members of the UNITED STATES CONGRESS, who broached the subject. In each case, the congressman was convinced by the Air Force that a hearing would only make the public think that UFOs were something to be concerned about. Two of these briefings were given to the Subcommittee On Atmospheric Phenomena in 1958, and the SMART COMMITTEE in 1960. Although the latter group recommended some improvements in the Air Force's program, Blue Book continued as before. By 1963, Congressional interest had dropped considerably, and this lull continued through 1964. In 1965, public interest in UFOs was renewed. On February 6, 1966, the Ad Hoc Committee to Review Project Blue Book met and issued a report, known as the O'BRIEN REPORT. Despite its approval of the Air Force's handling of the UFO investigation, the report recommended that the program be strengthened to provide "opportunity for scientific investigation of selected sightings in more detail and depth than had been possible to date."

In October 1966, the University of Colorado's CONDON COMMITTEE was formed. This Air Force/taxpayer-sponsored team of scientific investigators and researchers was supposed to be an impartial group. However, shortly after the project's inception, doubts began to arise about the committee's attitude, particularly that of its head, physicist EDWARD U. CONDON. Dissension within the group further compromised its credibility. By the time the study was completed in 1968, a shadow of suspicion had fallen over the final report. To strengthen his position, Condon submitted the report to the NATIONAL ACADEMY OF SCIENCES (NAS), which gave the report its stamp of approval. The main conclusion of the CONDON REPORT, as stated by Condon in his summary, was that "nothing has come from the study of UFOs in the past twenty-one years that has added to scientific knowledge. Careful consid-

eration of the record as it is available to us leads us to conclude that further extensive study of UFOs probably cannot be justified in the expectation that science will be advanced thereby." Many critics in the scientific community pointed out that Condon's summary was merely a reflection of his personal opinions and actually contradicted the conclusions reached by the authors of the various chapters. However, the public accepted the Condon conclusion that there was no value in continuing a study of the problem. The Air Force used this reasoning to cancel Project Blue Book in December 1969 and, since then, has had no official interest in the subject.

Between 1948 and 1969, the Air Force had received 12,618 UFO reports. Its final conclusion was that although 701 remained unidentified, they were not enemy weapons or extraterrestrial craft, but only natural or conventional objects that could not be identified due to insufficient information.

During its twenty-one years of existence, the Air Force UFO project was directed by the following Chief Officers: Captain ROBERT R. SNEIDER (November 1948–March 1951); Lieutenant JERRY CUMMINGS (March 1951–September 1951); Captain EDWARD J. RUPPELT (September 1951-September 1953); Lieutenant ROBERT M. OLSSON (September 1953–March 1954); Captain CHARLES A. HARDIN (March 1954–April 1956); Captain GEORGE T. GREGORY (April 1956–October 1958); Major ROBERT J. FRIEND (October 1958–August 1963); and Lieutenant Colonel HECTOR QUINTANILLA (August 1963–December 1969). Pentagon spokesmen for the UFO project were: ALBERT M. CHOP (April 1952–March 1953); various officers (March 1953–1954); Captain ROBERT WHITE (1955); Major ROBERT F. SPENCE (1957); Lieutenant Colonel LAWRENCE J. TACKER (1958–March 1961), Major WILLIAM T. COLEMAN (April 1961–January 1962), Major CARL R. HART (February 1962–summer 1963) and Major MASTON JACKS (summer 1963–December 1969).

Speculation continues today about the true role of the Air Force in the UFO field. UFOLOGISTS ask why the Air Force, if it considered UFOs nothing more than MISIDENTIFICATIONS and HOAXES, continued to investigate them for twenty-one years. Some explanations given for sightings were so poorly substantiated that they had to be retracted later when exposed by civilian investigators. The issue was further clouded by the ridiculing of witnesses, many of whom were sincere and reputable people. Astronomer and consultant to the Air Force J. ALLEN HYNEK has commented that, "Blue Book files are replete with cases labeled 'Insufficient Information,' whereas in many cases the proper label should have been, 'Insufficient Follow-up.'" In many cases, *possible* and *probable* explanations qualified a report to be categorized as "Identified." Hynek points out that UFO cases were not investigated in the same thorough manner that the FEDERAL BUREAU OF INVESTIGATION (FBI) investigates kidnapping, narcotics and bank robbery cases. Blue Book had too small a staff to permit extensive investigations and the low-ranking officers involved did not have the leverage to initiate the type of investigations needed. Bearing all this in mind, numerous researchers have considered the possibility that the Air Force project was a front for a real investigation being carried out by another agency, such as the CIA. Engineer LEON DAVIDSON has proposed that the Air Force investigation was intentionally understaffed and its denials purposely absurd. He believes their project to have been part of a CIA plan to trick the Russians into believing that the United States had secret devices. The purpose of such a deception would have been to waste the Russians' time and effort on designing defenses against nonexistent objects.

The records of Project Blue Book were transferred to the NATIONAL ARCHIVES in 1975. After confidential information had been censored, they became available to civilian researchers on July 12, 1976.

In October and November of 1975, a series of UFO sightings by military personnel occurred over several Air Force bases in the United States and a Canadian Forces station in Ontario. According to a confidential CINC-NORAD communication dated November 11, 1975, a copy of which was obtained by GROUND SAUCER WATCH (GSW), Air Guard helicopters, Strategic Air Command (SAC) helicopters and NORTH AMERICAN RADAR DEFENSE (NORAD) F–106s were scrambled but failed to produce positive identifications. In a priority message sent from the SAC headquarters at Offutt Air Force Base to numerous Air Force bases during the same month, the Air Force revealed its continuation of the policy of denying Air Force interest in the subject. The communication stated, "In recent weeks there have been various reports of unidentified flying objects, including some sightings in the vicinity of SAC installations. . . . News media queries concerning such unidentified overflights are properly the concern of the Air Defense Command, and queries should be referred to CINC-NORAD/OI. . . . Media queries received by bases which concern solely SAC matters should be taken and answers prepared for coordination with NAF or CINSSAC/OI. . . . Interviews with base personnel may be requested as an outgrowth of these incidents. The following policy guidance applies to interviews. Interviews will be with the consent of the interviewee. Remarks should be confined to personal experiences and care should be taken to avoid speculation or to imply Air Force interest beyond security of the installation."

Bibliography: Ruppelt, Edward J., *The Report on Unidentified Flying Objects* (Garden City, N.Y.: Doubleday and Company, 1956); Hall, Richard H. (ed.), *The UFO Evidence* (Washington, D.C.: National Investigations Committee on Aerial Phenomena, 1964); Hynek, J. Allen, *The UFO Experience: A Scientific Inquiry* (Chicago: Henry Regnery Company, 1972); Jacobs, David Michael, *The UFO Controversy in America* (Bloomington, Indiana: Indiana University Press, 1975).

## UNITED STATES AIR FORCE SCIENTIFIC ADVISORY BOARD AD HOC COMMITTEE TO REVIEW PROJECT BLUE BOOK see O'BRIEN REPORT

**UNITED STATES CONGRESS.** Soon after its formation in late 1956, the NATIONAL INVESTIGATIONS COMMITTEE ON AERIAL PHENOMENA (NICAP) began to press for Congressional hearings as a step toward bringing scientific attention to UFOs. As NICAP began to publish information on the subject, sending occasional reports to Congress, interest grew among congressmen. Besieged by requests for information from their constituents, many members of Congress experienced some professional embarrassment because of their lack of knowledge of the matter.

During the late 1950s and early 1960s, the effort to prevent Congressional hearings became a primary concern of the UNITED STATES AIR FORCE'S PROJECT BLUE BOOK. The Air Force feared that hearings might imply the UFO phenomenon was something to be concerned about and cause a panic which would be a threat to the national interest. Additionally, the Air Force did not want to open itself up to criticism of its UFO investigation and the possibility that it would be forced to declassify its files. To avert this outcome, whenever a congressman approached the Air Force on this matter, he was given an individual briefing and convinced that a hearing would merely lead the public to believe UFOs were something to be concerned about. One of these briefings was given to the HOUSE OF REPRESENTATIVES SUBCOMMITTEE ON ATMOSPHERIC PHENOMENA on August 8, 1958. At the end of the session, the subcommittee Chairman, Congressman John McCormack, declared that he was satisfied with the Air Force's handling of the UFO investigation and no formal hearings would be necessary.

However, controversy over the subject continued and in 1960 a briefing was given to the SMART COMMITTEE, a group representing the House Science and Astronautics Committee and the House Armed Services Committee. The committee recommended that financing be provided to give Project Blue Book the personnel, the mobility and the capability to investigate cases indicating high intelligence or scientific potential, as well as those generating an unusual amount of public interest. However, the recommendations were not implemented.

By 1963, Congressional interest had dropped considerably. This lull continued through 1964. However, 1965 brought renewed activity and interest in the UFO field. In 1966, GERALD R. FORD, who was then House Republican minority leader, requested that Congressional hearings be held to assess the Air Force's involvement in UFOs. The HOUSE ARMED SERVICES COMMITTEE HEARINGS were held on April 5, 1966. Only three people were invited to testify. Although the committee expressed confidence in the Air Force's handling of the UFO investigation, it also gave its approval to the recommendation of the recent O'BRIEN REPORT that contracts be negotiated with universities to provide scientific investigative teams. This led to the establishment of the CONDON COMMITTEE, an Air Force/taxpayer-sponsored study conducted at the University of Colorado.

Continuing controversy and public dissatisfaction with the Air Force's program resulted in the HOUSE SCIENCE AND ASTRONAUTICS COMMITTEE HEARINGS, which were held on July 29, 1968. On this occasion, testimony was presented by a number of scientists, the majority of whom favored continued and increased investigation and study of UFOs. Since the purpose of the hearings was to serve as a forum, not to resolve the UFO situation, the symposium did not lead to the establishment of any new programs or any change in Air Force policy.

Bibliography: Jacobs, David Michael, *The UFO Controversy in America* (Bloomington, Indiana: Indiana University Press, 1975).

## UNITED STATES GOVERNMENT. Officially, all UFO investigations on behalf of the United States government were carried out from 1948 to 1969 under the auspices of the UNITED STATES AIR FORCE (USAF). However, during that time, reports were also gathered by the FEDERAL BUREAU OF INVESTIGATION (FBI) and the CENTRAL INTELLIGENCE AGENCY (CIA). Some UFOLOGISTS believe the much criticized Air Force program was, in fact, a front for a real investigation being carried out by the CIA. While the Air Force program was in progress, the UNITED STATES CONGRESS held hearings on the subject in 1966 and 1968.

When JIMMY CARTER campaigned for the presidency, he promised that, if elected, he would release to the public all official data on UFOs. His interest was spurred by a personal UFO sighting in 1969. However, at the time of his election, declassification of the Air Force's PROJECT BLUE BOOK files was already under-

way. Carter's science adviser, Dr. Frank Press, charged with answering UFO-related mail, was deluged with letters claiming that additional secret files existed and demanding their release. Government agencies denied having files on UFOs. Overwhelmed by the volume of mail, Press asked Dr. Robert Frosch, Director of the NATIONAL AERONAUTICS AND SPACE ADMINISTRATION (NASA), if his organization would take over the task. In addition, he asked if NASA would consider convening a panel to decide whether or not a new investigation was warranted. After several months, NASA determined that further investigation was not warranted. Frosch, however, offered to make NASA laboratories available for analysis of any physical evidence of UFOs.

Carter's subsequent silence on the subject has led to considerable speculation among UFOlogists. Victor Marchetti, former Executive Assistant to the Deputy Director of the CIA, states that if Carter's UFO sighting had been explained to him as a natural or conventional event, or the testing of a secret weapon, there is no reason why Carter should not admit this publicly. If, on the other hand, Marchetti proposes, what Carter saw was a UFO, then his behavior might indicate that he is conceding to pressure from international powers to participate in a COVER-UP.

## UNIVERSAL BROTHERHOOD, P.O. Box 21, Balingup 6253, West Australia; telephone number: 097-641062.

The purpose of this NEW AGE organization is to demonstrate that humanity has a divine nature and an inherent ability to communicate and cooperate with God. It aims to show that humanity is capable of achieving the acme of civilization and the enjoyment of greater health, happiness, peace, virtue and true culture. The group holds that UFOs are terrestrial and extraterrestrial spacecraft. While it believes that some extraterrestrial UFOs are here out of scientific curiosity and for the express purpose of utilizing our PLANET for their own material gain, it holds that the majority of flying saucer OCCUPANTS are here to assist in the evolutionary changes now occurring on Earth. They are allegedly attempting to influence humanity through telepathic suggestion to expand its consciousness into a greater awareness of its responsibility to life on Earth and its role within the Universe. According to the organization, these extraterrestrial beings are charged with the responsibility of preventing the planet from being destroyed by nuclear war. In the event of any major cataclysm which would threaten life on the planet, they are prepared to evacuate a percentage of Earth's population which has proven itself capable of managing the affairs of this planet in accordance with

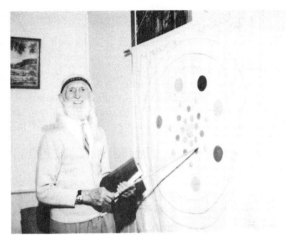

Fred Robinson, Founder of the Universal Brotherhood.

the spiritual principles which maintain the harmony and stability of the Universe.

In 1963, Fred and Mary Robinson founded a New Age information center known as Shalam at Armadale in West Australia. Nine years later, as the result of a series of lecture tours undertaken by Fred, a small group of people converged on Shalam with the intent of living communally and exploring the New Age consciousness more deeply. Hence, in 1972, the Universal Brotherhood was founded as a nonprofit corporation. Mary Robinson serves as Principal. Other staff members include Vice-Principal Stephen Carthew, Director Samuel Purves, Secretary Rosemary Gilmore and Treasurer David Fosdick. The group has sixty members. The organization serves as a demonstration and information center dealing with the subjects of health, healing, organic agriculture, human relationships, fraternal democracy, spiritual science, UFO phenomena, Christ consciousness and world transformation. The brotherhood contacts and cooperates with other individuals and groups who share its goals. It also encourages people to visit the center and participate in its work.

## UNIVERSAL INDUSTRIAL CHURCH OF THE NEW WORLD COMFORTER, 345 West Clay Street, Stockton, California 95206; telephone number: 209-465-1422.

The purpose of this CONTACTEE organization, which embraces a system called Uni-Communism, is to bring absolute freedom and security to this PLANET and to grant to each individual abundant food, clothing, shelter, recreation, care, transportation and utilities. The group holds that the purpose of UFOs is to bring about peace, freedom and an end to usury. Jesus, according to

this church, was a Venusian contactee who had a space command backing him.

This nonprofit organization was founded in 1947 by Allen-Michael. Its staff includes Bill Hannaford, Dian Michael, Michael Bobier, Allen-Michael, Del Parry, Michael Parry and Kathy Hannaford. There are seventy-five members. The group claims that it maintains telepathic contact with UFO OCCUPANTS and that some of its members have had close encounters. It states that it takes into its metaphysical church all kinds of people who have had UFO experiences and who can no longer function in society as it is. Publications and other services are available free-of-charge.

## UNIVERSARIUN FOUNDATION, 3620 S.E. 84th Avenue, Portland, Oregon 97266; telephone number: 503-775-2140.

This CONTACTEE organization is dedicated to the dissemination of physical, mental and spiritual knowledge relating to the past, present and future of Earth. The objectives of the organization are to gather as much of this information and knowledge as is possible. This is done primarily, according to the group, through communication with highly-evolved beings from other PLANETS in our solar system and beyond, and with ascended masters and teachers domiciled primarily in the etheric realms of Earth's skies. These beings are purportedly in charge of, or vitally interested in the illumination and emancipation of our planet from its fear, chaos and confusion. The group claims its principal mentors are Master "H," Nikola Tesla, Lord Michael, Kuthumi, and Sananda. The organization holds that UFOs originate from outer space and the inner Earth and that their purpose is to repair some of the damage inflicted on the planet by some of its lunatics and eventually to evacuate the "Sons of God" and others on the arrival of "D Day" on Earth.

This nonprofit organization was founded in 1962 by ZELRUN KARSLEIGH, LeRoy Roberts and A. H. Albrecht. The five Board Members are President Harry Talbert, Secretary-Treasurer Karsleigh, Margaret Petty, Chuck Cole and Marian L. Hill. The group has 420 members. One affiliate is located in Syracuse, New York, and two affiliates are located in Phoenix, Arizona. A large library consisting of 1,500 volumes of metaphysical, UFO, scientific and religious books is available to members. Biweekly morning meetings and weekly evening meetings are held throughout the year, except during August. Additionally, the group schedules occasional meetings with well-known speakers on such subjects as UFOs, extrasensory perception, reincarnation, karma, New Age philosophy, life after death and spiritual education. A sixty-page magazine, *The Voice of Unarius,* is published monthly and contains alleged messages from the ascended masters and the SPACE PEOPLE. Karsleigh is the Editor.

## UNIVERSITY OF COLORADO *see* CONDON COMMITTEE

## UPIAR *see* UFO PHENOMENA, INTERNATIONAL ANNUAL REVIEW

## UPIB *see* UNEXPLAINED PHENOMENA INVESTIGATION BUREAU

## U.P. (UNIDENTIFIED PHENOMENA) INVESTIGATIONS RESEARCH, P.O. Box 455, Streetsville, Mississauga, Ontario, Canada L5M 2B9; telephone number: 416-826-6073.

The purpose of this investigative organization is to investigate, research, document and lecture on the subject of unidentified phenomena. It holds that the UFO mystery probably represents a combination of many different unknown phenomena.

This nonmembership organization was founded in 1977 by DAVID HAISELL and Paula Haisell, who serve as Codirectors. The group has three field investigators, two located in Southern Ontario and one located in British Columbia. Consultants include Eugene Duret (Meteorology), Michael Gudz (Photo Analysis), Allen Kozlov (Parapsychology), John McCarrick (Soil Analysis) and Dwight Whalen (FORTEAN Phenomena). Ralph DeGraw of PRIVATE UFO INVESTIGATIONS (PUFOI) in the United States is the group's foreign correspondent. David Haisell is Editor of *Journal UFO (JUFO)*, which is published quarterly.

UROS, Habrouckstraat 1, 3841 Kerniel, Belgium; telephone number: 012-742306.

This investigative organization is dedicated to the scientific examination of all phenomena which fall outside the bounds of conventional science. It holds that the subjects of astronomy, space travel, archaeology, parapsychology and ufology are all interconnected. UROS believes that UFOs are extraterrestrial spacecraft engaged in a study of our PLANET and its various life forms.

This nonprofit organization was founded in 1972 by Pieter Borms and Ghyslain Struys, who serve as Codirectors with Frans Borms. The Board Members are Marc Broux and Raymond Knaepen. There are approximately 100 members. The group has one field investigator who investigates sightings throughout Belgium. UROS has an information center, a library and two telescopes. It organizes slide shows, debates and lectures. A newsletter, *Uros,* is published bimonthly.

## USAF *see* UNITED STATES AIR FORCE

## USO *see* UNIDENTIFIED SUBMARINE OBJECT

USV, acronym for *u*nidentified *s*pace *v*ehicle.

UT, acronym for *u*l*t*raterrestrial, an extradimensional being.

## UTAH FILM *see* TREMONTON, UTAH

**VALENTICH, FREDERICK,** *see* **MELBOURNE, AUSTRALIA**

**VALLEE, JACQUES F.** (b. September 24, 1939, Pontoise, France), scientist and writer.

Originally a skeptic about UFO reports, Vallee became seriously interested in the subject in 1961 when he and several other French astronomers tracked and tape-recorded the coordinates of a UFO. They planned to calculate the object's exact path but the astronomer in charge decided to erase the tape rather than risk bringing ridicule to the observatory. In the following years, Vallee devoted his spare time to analyzing and compiling a computerized catalogue of UFO data. His books have earned him the reputation of being one of the most original thinkers in the field. He has explored the relationship of the UFO mystery to human folklore. He believes that UFOs represent a force that has been utilizing mass manipulation to influence the human race over the centuries. He holds that CONTACTEES are part of the scheme which is bringing into being an expectation of extraterrestrial contact and thus a belief in

Jacques Vallee speaking on the subject of UFOs before the General Assembly of the United Nations on November 27, 1978. *(United Nations/Photo by Y. Nagata)*

imminent salvation from a higher power. The aim of the unknown manipulators, he conjectures, may be to achieve social changes on Earth.

Vallee received his B.S. in Mathematics from the Sorbonne in 1959, his M.S. in Astrophysics from Lille University in 1961 and his Ph.D. in Computer Science from Northwestern University in 1967.

Vallee was a research scientist for the French Committee for Space Studies in Paris from 1961 to 1962, a research engineer for the French branch of the Thompson-Houston Company in 1962, a research associate at the University of Texas and McDonald Observatory from 1962 to 1963, a Texas computer consultant on the MARS MAP Project from 1962 to 1965 and a mathematical analyst for the Northwestern University Technological Institute from 1963 to 1967. Subsequently, he was associated with several research institutions, including Stanford University, where he served as Manager of Information Systems. He now runs his own computer company in Northern California. He is a member of the Editorial Board of *Telecommunications Policy*.

Vallee is a member of the American Mathematical Society and *Alpha Pi Mu*.

Vallee was the model for the character "Lacombe" in the film CLOSE ENCOUNTERS OF THE THIRD KIND. In 1975, he was a speaker at a United Nations meeting on the proposed establishment of an agency or a department to conduct and coordinate research into UFOs and related phenomena.

Vallee has published numerous articles in scientific and popular journals. His first two books in French were science fiction novels, the first of which was awarded the Jules Verne prize in 1961. He is author of *Anatomy of a Phenomenon: Unidentified Objects in Space—A Scientific Appraisal* (Chicago: Henry Regnery Company, 1965); with Janine Vallee, *Challenge to Science—The UFO Enigma* (Chicago: Henry Regnery Company, 1966); *Passport to Magonia* (Chicago: Henry Regnery Company, 1969); with J. Allen Hynek, *The Edge of Reality* (Chicago: Henry Regnery Company, 1975); *The Invisible College* (New York: E. P. Dutton, 1975); *Messengers of Deception* (Berkeley, California: And/Or Press, 1979).

**VAN TASSELL, GEORGE** (b. 1910, Jefferson, Ohio; d. February 9, 1978, Santa Ana, California), CONTACTEE and Founder and Director of the MINISTRY OF UNIVERSAL WISDOM.

Van Tassell spent the last twenty-five years of his life building the "Integraton," a four-story high, dome-shaped machine whose purpose was to rejuvenate the old and prevent the aging of the young. The designs for the machine were allegedly dictated to Van Tassell by the SPACE PEOPLE, with whom he supposedly main-

tained constant contact. He reportedly spent two hundred thousand dollars on the project but never completed it. During the last years of his life, he claimed that it would eventually work when the Space People came to calibrate it for him. After Van Tassell's death, the Integraton was purchased by the Christology Church, P.O. Box 4648, San Diego, California 92104.

Van Tassell entered the field of aviation in Ohio in 1927 and three years later moved to California, where he was employed by the Douglas Aircraft Corporation until 1941. From 1941 to 1943, he was the personal flight instructor for Howard Hughes in the testing of his experimental aircraft. He worked as a flight safety inspector for Lockheed Aircraft Corporation from 1943 until 1947, when he assumed a flight test inspection position with Constellation aircraft. Then, in 1947, he started operation of the Giant Rock Airport near Yucca Valley, California, and remained the owner of it until the early 1970s.

Van Tassell founded the Ministry of Universal Wisdom in 1953, and was its Director until the time of his death. He was Editor of its newsletter, PROCEEDINGS. He initiated and organized the annual GIANT ROCK CONVENTION. He was a guest on numerous radio and television shows, and lectured in the United States and Canada. He was author of *I Rode a Flying Saucer* (Los Angeles: New Age Publishing Company, 1952); and *The Council of Seven Lights* (Los Angeles: De Vorss and Company, 1958).

**VEHICLE INTERNAL SYSTEMS INVESTIGATIVE TEAM** *see* **PROJECT VISIT**

**VEIT, KARL L.**, *see* **UFO/IFO—STUDIENGESELLSCHAFT (DUIST)**

**VENTLA-VERLAG,** German publishing company owned by Karl L. Veit, President of the DEUTSCHE UFO/IFO-STUDIENGESELLSCHAFT (DUIST). German-language UFO and CONTACTEE books may be ordered directly from the company at Postfach 130 185, 6200 Wiesbaden 13, West Germany.

**VENUS,** the second PLANET from the sun and the closest planet to Earth. Centuries ago, those who viewed the skies either as a profession or as a navigational guide, were, by necessity, better at visual observation than the average person is today. Even so, Venus was a mystery to them. They failed to associate Venus in the night sky with Venus in the morning sky. The bright evening light was known as Hesperus and the morning object was known as Phosphorus. During this century, Venus has been cited as the source of thousands of UFO sightings. Aside from the sun and MOON, there is no

Venus photographed at a distance of 40,920 miles by the Pioneer Venus Orbiter on March 3, 1979. *(Courtesy NASA)*

brighter object in the sky. Since it never moves more than forty-five degrees from the sun, it is most often visible near sunrise or sunset. An object seen close to the horizon is separated from the observer by more air than an object located directly overhead in space. Thus, when Venus appears low in the sky, its light is twisted and bent as the beam passes through the air toward an observer. Under various atmospheric conditions it has been seen to bounce, spin, twinkle and fracture into many points of light. In addition, the varying densities of the air bend the light, as does a prism, splitting the white light into various colors of the rainbow. Thus, movement and color changes can create a spectacular visual effect.

When at its greatest brilliance, Venus can be seen in the daytime sky. A pilot, deprived of visual references, might be surprised to see the small, white disk, apparently racing along in the sky with his aircraft.

Observations of FOO FIGHTERS over the Pacific Ocean during World War II were attributed to the planet Venus by American intelligence officers. ROBERT SHEAFFER also attributed the UFO sighting reported by JIMMY CARTER in 1973 to Venus.

Several CONTACTEES have claimed contact with flying saucer OCCUPANTS from Venus. Contactee JOHN LANGDOM WATTS is one of several who claim to have actually visited the planet. He described his alleged experiences in a book, entitled *The Reason for Life—and Now—Visit Venus* (Post Orange, Florida: Dixie Venus Books, 1975). Reports that surface temperatures on Venus exceed 900 degrees Fahrenheit have not discouraged contactees. GABRIEL GREEN argues that the SPACE PEOPLE themselves are responsible for feeding this

allegedly misleading information into the communications systems of Russian space probes. CALVIN GIRVIN, on the other hand, retorts, "Why should the Soviet gadget which reported unbearable temperatures on Venus be so reliable? After all, it might have landed in somebody's barbecue pit."

Bibliography: Menzel, Donald H., and Lyle G. Boyd, *The World of Flying Saucers* (Garden City, N.Y.: Doubleday and Company, 1963).

**VENUS RESEARCH,** also known as Venus Venous Research, P.O. Box 6, San Lorenzo, California 94580; telephone number: 415-586-2548.

The stated purpose of this organization is to prepare mankind, particularly persons with Rh negative blood, for the Aquarian Age. Venus Research holds that RH negative blood is the blood of the gods and that earthlings who have such blood are the products of genetic engineering. Such persons have been described as STAR PEOPLE by writer BRAD STEIGER. Codirector Bonnie Marie Royce asserts that UFOs are here to awaken the consciousness of those who have the blood of the gods and to guide mankind out of the chaos created by lust, greed and nuclear waste.

This nonprofit organization was founded in 1975 by Bonnie Marie Royce and Mabel Ola Royce, who serve as Codirectors. Venus Research publishes a newsletter, called *ICHOR*.

**VENUS VENOUS RESEARCH** *see* **VENUS RESEARCH**

**VERONICA** (Vérification et Études des Rapports sur les OVNI pour Nimes et la Contrée Avoisinante), 1 rue Vauban, 30000 Nimes, France.

The purpose of this investigative organization is to collect evidence, conduct investigations, disseminate information to the public, study the phenomenon and to detect its manifestations with electronic equipment. The group believes that UFOs represent one or more extraterrestrial civilizations predominantly from our own galaxy. VERONICA holds that they are probably here to study us and to guide us in our research and along the road to peace.

This nonprofit organization was founded in 1974 by C. Gouiran. The group's officers include President Robert Lascols, Vice-President Gerard Jarretie, Secretary Chrisiane Monzoniz, Assistant Secretary Christine Abric, Treasurer André Martinez and Assistant Secretary/Assistant Treasurer Maryline Maimi. An administrative council consists of Henri Asencio, Christophe Danan, Eric Monzoniz, Denis Virgile, Albert Romanos, Daniel Vidal and Mr. Trepel. The group has about 110 members. It has foreign representatives in the Persian

Gulf, Australia and Brazil. Individual commissions deal with the various activities of the organization.

VERONICA is a member of the COMITÉ EUROPÉEN DE COORDINATION DE LA RECHERCHE UFOLOGIQUE (CECRU).

**VESTIGIA,** RD2 Brookwood Road, Stanhope, New Jersey 07874; telephone number: 201-347-3638.

The purpose of this organization is to investigate and research tangible unexplained phenomena in a scientific manner. As a scientific organization, Vestigia does not have an official point of view regarding the identity and origin of UFOs. After intensive investigation, the group has concluded that flying saucers seen and photographed over the Wanaque Reservoir and ghostly lights seen over railroad tracks in Long Valley are caused by the illumination of air molecules in a piezoelectrically-generated energy field, which is itself due to seismic pressures on quartz-bearing granite.

This nonprofit organization was founded in 1976 by Robert E. Jones, who serves as President. Vice-Presidents are Walter Puzia, Katherine Krogstad, Walter Hnot, Arthur Steinberger and Stanley Zebroski. Manfred Saul is Treasurer. There are about 160 members, half of whom actively participate as field investigators and researchers. The organization is divided into Biological, Earth Sciences, Aerial Phenomena and Parapsychological Investigative Teams. There are also four consultant committees and several service groups. Library files are maintained and the *Vestigia Newsletter* is published quarterly.

**VICTORIAN FLYING SAUCER SOCIETY,** former name of the VICTORIAN UFO RESEARCH SOCIETY (VUFORS).

**VICTORIAN UFO RESEARCH SOCIETY (VUFORS),** P.O. Box 43, Moorabbin, Victoria 3189, Australia.

The purpose of this organization is to investigate UFOs and to disseminate its findings to the general public. The society espouses no beliefs or opinions regarding the nature and origin of UFOs. However, after examination of the available evidence accumulated over thirty years, it holds that, beyond doubt, phenomena occur which have no known explanation and which constitute a scientific problem demanding close scrutiny.

This nonprofit organization was founded in 1957 by Peter Norris. Prior to 1967, it was known as the VICTORIAN FLYING SAUCER SOCIETY. Staff members include President Judith Magee, Vice-President Paul Norman, Secretary John Bell and Treasurer Clive Yates. There are about 500 members in Australia and throughout the world. Field investigators are Paul Norman, John Thompson, Patrick Gildea, Judith Magee, Charles Osborne, Les Bristol, Rodney Morrow, Ian Scott, Douglas Memomery and John Bell. Information is exchanged with a global network of scientific and research organizations. VUFORS participate in the computer filing of UFO reports by the CENTRE FOR UFO STUDIES—AUSTRALIAN CO-ORDINATION SECTION (ACOS). Close cooperation is received from the news media and from several anonymous scientists. Members lecture to various civic groups, schools and churches. The society's library is available to all Australian members. The society's former publication, AUSTRALIAN FLYING SAUCER REVIEW, has been discontinued. The *Australian UFO Bulletin* is published quarterly and deals with major Australian UFO reports and investigations and significant overseas information. The publication maintains a conservative, scientific approach to UFOLOGY and does not promote any particular theory on the origin of UFOs. L. Bristol is Editor.

**VIDAL, GERARDO,** Buenos Aires attorney who, with his wife, was an alleged victim of a classic case of TELEPORTATION. In May 1968, the Vidals were driving between Chascomus and Maipu in Argentina when they encountered a dense fog. They lost consciousness and awakened almost two days later to find themselves on a dirt road outside Mexico City, almost 4,500 miles away. Their Peugeot 403 appeared to have been subjected to some tremendous HEAT force and there was no longer any paint on it.

Some researchers have speculated that the Vidals and their car were kidnapped by flying saucer OCCUPANTS for some unknown purpose, after which they were deposited near Mexico City.

Bibliography: Le Poer Trench, Brinsley, *Operation Earth* (London: Neville Spearman, 1969).

**VIEWPOINT AQUARIUS,** monthly magazine, established in 1971. It is available by subscription only. The range of subjects covered includes flying saucers, contacts with space visitors, occult law, yoga and meditation. The editors describe their publication as factual, serious, enthusiastic and not afraid to venture beyond earthling science.

All material is contributed voluntarily, since *Viewpoint Aquarius* is a nonprofit organization. The Editors are Rex Dutta and Jean Coulsting. The magazine's mailing address is: % Fish Tanks, Ltd., 49 Blandford Street, London W1 3AF, England.

**VIGILANCE,** publication of DETECTOR SIDIP (SO-CIÉTÉ INTERNATIONALE DE DÉVELOPPEMENT DES IDÉES POUR LE PROGRÉS).

# VILJO, EKSO, *see* IMJARVI, FINLAND

**VILLA, PAUL,** resident of Los Lunas, New Mexico, who has taken numerous PHOTOGRAPHS of alleged UFOs, including the well-known ALBUQUERQUE, NEW MEXICO, photograph. Analyses of numerous Villa photographs have revealed them to be fakes. Villa, who describes himself as "far from being an intellectual giant, or a self-proclaimed UFO expert," sends his UFO photographs and "literature," free of charge, to "prime ministers, presidents, governors, mayors and plain ordinary folks" in order that they may use them to help "prisoners, orphans, the sick, the poor and the elderly." He predicts that one day he will produce photographs that will prove beyond any doubt what UFOs are and who he, himself, is. UFOs, he states, are only "a small part of God's huge armies that will soon invade PLANET Earth and redeem humanity from their [sic] present immoral fallen condition." According to Villa, UFO OCCUPANTS live among us, helping us to prepare for "the Great day when we shall meet our maker."

**VILLAS-BOAS, ANTONIO.** The most celebrated case of a SEXUAL ENCOUNTER with a UFOnaut occurred in 1957 near the town of São Francisco de Salles in the state of Minas Gerais near the border of the state of São Paulo in Brazil. On October 5, a twenty-three-year-old farmer named Antonio Villas-Boas observed a brilliant beam of white light shining down from the sky outside his bedroom window. Nine days later, he was ploughing a field at night with a tractor when a brilliant light appeared again. Villas-Boas chased the light from one end of the field to the other about twenty times before stopping in exhaustion. He stood and watched the light as it sent out sparkling rays in all directions. Then, as if it had been turned off, the light disappeared. Villas-Boas's brother was also a witness to both of these sightings.

The following night, October 15, Villas-Boas was alone in the field when a red light appeared, growing larger as it approached him. Before long, the object, shaped like a large elongated egg, had landed on three metal legs close to Villas-Boas. A rotating cupola on top of the craft changed from red to green as it decelerated. Three spikes protruded from the front of the object, illuminated by the red phosophorescence of a front headlight. Small purple lights surrounded the craft. Villas-Boas tried to flee but his tractor stalled. Three males and a female, all suited from head to toe in concealing, tightly fitting gray garments, dragged the struggling farmer into the parked machine.

After conversing between themselves in strange growls and grunts, the UFOnauts forcibly undressed Villas-Boas and smeared a clear, viscous substance over his body. Although he later assumed this to be an aphrodisiac, investigators concluded that it might have been a disinfectant or deodorizer. Villas-Boas was then escorted to a small room furnished with a couch. Tubes were applied to either side of his chin and blood was extracted. He was then left alone. After a while he began to notice a strange ODOR. Looking around the room, he noticed tiny metal pipes in the walls which were discharging thin puffs of gray smoke. Finding it difficult to breathe and sickened by the odor, Villas-Boas vomited in one corner of the room.

A long time passed before the door opened again. In walked a beautiful, naked woman. Blonde and blue-eyed, she had high cheekbones, extremely thin lips and a wide face that narrowed to a point at the chin. When the woman made her purpose clear, Villas-Boas forgot his fear and responded with enthusiasm. After performing sexual intercourse twice, the woman lost interest in Villas-Boas. Later, he expressed his indignation at being used as a stallion to improve someone else's stock. Moreover, he complained that the woman's grunting had almost spoiled an otherwise pleasurable experience, for it had given him the impression of lying with an animal. Before the woman left, she smiled at Villas-Boas, patted her stomach and pointed to the STARS as if implying that she would soon bear their child on another PLANET.

After unsuccessfully attempting to steal a souvenir, Villas-Boas was taken on a tour of the exterior of the craft and then dismissed. The craft began to ascend, its lights brightening and its landing legs withdrawing into its base. At about 114 feet above the ground, the object again increased its brightness, began to rotate at a tremendous speed, and vanished into the distance with an incredible burst of speed. Villas-Boas discovered that he had spent four hours and fifteen minutes aboard the craft. During the weeks that followed, he suffered unusual lesions on his hands, forearms and legs. These wounds became purple as they healed and left scars.

This case was investigated by the late OLAVO FONTES, who seemed to afford it a fairly high degree of credibility. He based his positive reaction on the fact that Villas-Boas appeared to be honest and was in a state of excellent mental health. However, Fontes himself pointed out that the report was so heavily embellished with fantastic details that Villas-Boas either had a remarkably good visual memory or was a very clever liar. Other investigators have pointed out that the specific details of what occurred at the moment of the craft's landing have been described differently by Villas-Boas on two different occasions. This case has been given more serious consideration by some researchers than other similar reports, a fact that may be due to the credentials and reputation of the investigator rather than the case itself.

Bibliography: Lorenzen, Coral and Jim, *Flying Saucer Occupants* (New York: New American Library, 1967).

## VILLELA, RUBENS, J., *see* ADMIRALTY BAY, ANTARCTICA

**VIMANAS.** The two great epic poems of India, the Mahabharata and the Ramayana were written between 1,700 and 2,400 years ago based on events that supposedly occurred more than 3,000 years ago. Both works mention flying vehicles called vimanas which could maneuver in any direction and could travel over vast distances. Vimanas were said to ride on a ray and to cause a loud noise.

In the eighth book of the Mahabharata is an account of a projectile being dropped on a city from a mighty vimana. The description of a rising CLOUD of white hot smoke that reduced the city to ashes is reminiscent of the detonation of a modern-day hydrogen bomb.

Bibliography: Von Däniken, Erich, *Chariots of the Gods?* (New York: G. P. Putnam's Sons, 1970).

**VISIONS,** annual magazine, established in 1970, with a circulation of 500. It is available by subscription only. According to its Editor, CONTACTEE Colin Cameron, the magazine consists of messages from God, a spaceman called David and Colin himself. According to the

Artist's concept of a vimana published by Italy's *Domenica del Corriere* on December 9, 1962. *(Courtesy ICUFON)*

alleged messages published in the magazine, good spacemen are ANGELS who have infiltrated our society and work alongside us. DERO and the MEN IN BLACK (MIB) are evil spacemen who are led by the Devil. Supposedly, Jesus, who has been appointed Master of this galaxy by God, has chosen Earth to be his headquarters after the second coming, due to occur before the end of the millenium. At that time, says Cameron, spaceships, two centimeters apart, will dot our sky and teleport the righteous to safety. Earth, he contends, will then be melted down to PLASMA and reformed. Once the new society is established, according to this magazine, New Agers will become ambassadors for Jesus throughout space.

The magazine is published by Jesiam Productions, 5 Tennyson Street, Kew 3101, Melbourne, Victoria, Australia.

## VISIT *see* PROJECT VISIT (VEHICLE INTERNAL SYSTEMS INVESTIGATIVE TEAM)

**VON DÄNIKEN, ERICH** (b. April 14, 1935, Zofingen, Switzerland; address: Bonstetten, Switzerland; telephone number: 065-231113), author.

Von Däniken is responsible for popularizing the theory that Earth was visited thousands of years ago by advanced extraterrestrial beings who seemed like gods to the primitive humans living at the time. He speculates that these ANCIENT ASTRONAUTS imparted knowledge and skills to Earth's inhabitants and fertilized selected Earthwomen to create a new stage in human evolution. Von Däniken finds his evidence to support these theories in ancient legends, the Bible, and archeological structures and artifacts. Although his detractors criticize his unscholarly approach, his books on the subject have sold millions of copies worldwide.

Von Däniken graduated from the St. Michel College in Friburg, Switzerland. He initially pursued a career as a hotelier. His early articles on ancient astronauts were published in several newspapers between 1959 and 1968. After the publication of his first book, *Chariots of the Gods?*, he began a series of lecture tours at universities around the world. CHARIOTS OF THE GODS? was also the title of a documentary film based on his first two books. It was later adapted into a television special, entitled IN SEARCH OF ANCIENT ASTRONAUTS.

Von Däniken is author of *Chariots of the Gods?* (New York: G. P. Putnam's Sons, 1970); *Gods from Outer Space,* originally published as *Return to the Stars* (New York: G. P. Putnam's Sons, 1971); *The Gold of the Gods* (New York: G. P. Putnam's Sons, 1973); *In Search of Ancient Gods* (New York: G. P. Putnam's Sons, 1973); *Miracles of the Gods* (New York: Delacorte Press, 1975); and *Von Däniken's Proof,* originally published as

Erich von Däniken.

*Däniken According to the Evidence*. New York: Bantam Books, 1977.)

## VonKEVICZKY, COLMAN S. (b. August 21, 1909, Hungary; address: Apartment 4G, 35–40 75th Street, Jackson Heights, N.Y. 11372; telephone number: 212-672-7948), Founder and Director of the INTERCONTINENTAL GALACTIC SPACECRAFT (UFO) RESEARCH AND ANALYTIC NETWORK (ICUFON).

VonKeviczky holds that UFOs represent an intergalactic task force which will destroy Earth unless the world's leaders put an end to their hostile actions against UFOs. He believes that UFOs are responsible for the kidnapping of MIAs in Vietnam and that they are conducting a continuing surveillance of secret military installations throughout the world. He considers the threat of the intergalactic forces to be the most serious problem facing the world, and has officially called for a UNITED NATIONS committee to investigate and study UFOs on an international basis. He has also suggested that the U.N. establish a zone where UFOs may land safely and peacefully communicate with mankind. His arguments and evidence are presented in a one-hundred-page *Memorandum to the United Nations General Assembly,* authored and published by VonKeviczky in 1978.

VonKeviczky received his M.M.S.E. (Master of Military Science and Engineering) from the Royal Hungarian Maria Ludovika Military University in Budapest in 1932.

VonKeviczky served in the former Royal Hungarian Armed Forces from 1927 to 1945 and achieved the rank of Major. He was Chief of the Military Audio-Visual Education Department of the Royal Hungarian General Staff from 1932 to 1945. From 1946 to 1952, he was a motion picture director and public relations officer for the United States Government Administration in Heidelberg and Munich, Germany. Subsequently, he moved to the United States where, from 1954 to 1964, he was owner of Highlight Motion Picture and Photographic Enterprises and Editor-in-Chief of *Hungarian Illustrated*. From 1964 to 1966, he was a film and photo technician at the U.N. Secretariat's Office of Public Information in New York City. In 1966, he founded ICUFON and has been its Director since that time. He currently maintains private archives of UFO PHOTOGRAPHS.

VonKeviczky is a member of the AMERICAN INSTITUTE OF AERONAUTICS AND ASTRONAUTICS (AIAA), a Knight of the Order of St. John of Jerusalem and an honorary member of several UFO organizations. He was awarded the Hungarian military order Signum Laudis.

VonKeviczky has lectured widely on UFOs, and his articles have been published in several international UFO publications.

## VON LUDWIGER, ILLO BRAND (b. July 20, 1937), Stettin, Poland; address: 8152 Feldkirchen-Westerham, Gerhart-Hauptmann-Str. 5, West Germany), Director of the German-speaking section of the MUTUAL UFO NETWORK (MUFON)—Central European Section (CES).

In the summer of 1945, in Stendal, near Berlin, von Ludwiger saw a black plate, whose diameter was one-eighth that of the MOON, flying against the wind below the CLOUDS. His theoretical studies of the UFO phenomenon have led him to the conclusion that UFOs are physical expressions of a strange intelligence. Based on studies showing that gravitational waves move at velocities greater than the SPEED OF LIGHT, von Ludwiger suggests that further studies in this area might reveal a method of moving an object from one point of space, via a route outside the physical SPACE-TIME CONTINUUM, to

Colman VonKeviczky.

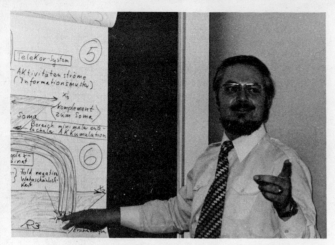

Illo Brand von Ludwiger lecturing at a MUFON-CES conference in Germany.

another point by transforming electromagnetic radiations. Some UFOs, he holds, are explainable only in terms of phantom projections which have the appearance of solid physical objects and which have been sent from one physical space through the fifth and sixth dimensions to another physical space.

After receiving his high school degree, von Ludwiger received his pre-diploma degree from the University of Erlangen-Nuernberg in 1964. He is employed as a Systems Analyst by the Messerschmidt-Bolkow-Blohm Corporation in Munich-Ottobrunn. He worked on the European Launcher Project ELDO in Australia in 1966. Subsequently, he worked on the German satellite project AZUR, in the field of automation of civil flight control and collision avoidance. Since 1973, he has been Project Manager of news transportation systems.

Von Ludwiger is a member of the DGRR (German Society for Rocket Technology and Space Science) and the Curatorium of the German Institute for Force Field Physics and General Cosmology in Northeim.

As Director of MUFON-CES, von Ludwiger has coauthored and edited MUFON-CES conference reports since 1975.

**VORTICES.** Ivan T. Sanderson maintained that there exists on Earth a network of twelve vortices of electromagnetic aberrations which play some role in the disappearance of ships and airplanes. Five of the vortices are located in the northern hemisphere, five in the southern hemisphere and one at each pole. The areas are lozenge shaped and those in the northern and southern hemisphere lie between latitudes thirty degrees and forty degrees north and south of the equator. The most famous of Sanderson's vile vortices are the Bermuda Triangle and the Devil's Sea. (See map on page 382.)

Bibliography: Sanderson, Ivan T., *Invisible Residents* (New York: World Publishing Company, 1970).

**VUFORS** *see* **VICTORIAN UFO RESEARCH SOCIETY**

**VULCAN,** hypothetical planet said to exist between Mercury and the sun. Eighteenth and nineteenth century astronomical reports of opaque bodies passing in front of the sun led to the belief that an unidentified planet might exist within our solar system. Some saucerologists claim that such a planet lies in the same orbit as Earth on the opposite side of the sun. The theme was developed in the 1969 motion picture, *Journey to the Far Side of the Sun.*

Vulcan is sometimes referred to as Clarion or Maldek, names more often applied to a hypothetical planet whose remnants supposedly constitute the asteroid belt.

Bibliography: Vallee, Jacques and Janine, *Challenge to Science—The UFO Enigma* (Chicago: Henry Regnery Company, 1966).

**WAGERS.** The most publicized wager made with regard to UFOs is writer PHILIP KLASS's "ten thousand dollar offer." Parties who wish to enter into a signed agreement with Klass must pay him 100 dollars each year up to a maximum of one thousand dollars or until adequate evidence is supplied proving that extraterrestrial visitation has occurred during this century. Within thirty days of the provision of such proof, Klass will pay ten thousand dollars to each signatory of the agreement. He will accept as proof any crashed spacecraft or other evidence which the U.S. NATIONAL ACADEMY OF SCIENCES (NAS) announces to be affirmation of visitation by extraterrestrial intelligences, or the appearance before the National Assembly of the UNITED NATIONS or on a national television program of an extraterrestrial visitor born on another PLANET. Klass's obligations to pay ten thousand dollars remain in force until the death of either one of the two parties in the agreement. Fewer than a dozen UFOlogists have signed an agreement with Klass, and only one has kept up his annual payments. In addition, Klass has offered to buy back all copies of his book, *UFOs Explained,* if any evidence of extraterrestrial visitors is found that meets the conditions specified in his ten thousand dollar offer.

In 1956, U.S. Air Force Colonel JOSEPH BRYAN asked Lloyds of London what odds they would give him on a one hundred dollar bet that the existence of UFOs would be proved by 1965, and on another one hundred dollars that we would establish communication with them. Lloyds would not accept the wager.

The UNARIUS EDUCATIONAL FOUNDATION, a CONTACTEE organization, has wagered several thousand dollars with a London betting agency, Ladbroke Investors, that extraterrestrial spaceships will arrive on Earth. Although landings have not occurred on any of the dates predicted so far, Unarius continues to place more bets with the agency.

**WALESVILLE, NEW YORK,** site of a tragic UFO-related disaster. Shortly before noon on July 1, 1954, an unidentified RADAR target was tracked over New York state by controllers at Griffiss Air Force Base. A F–94 Starfire jet was scrambled and the pilot headed towards the object guided by his radar operator. As he broke through the CLOUDS, he spotted a gleaming, disk-shaped apparatus. He began to close in but almost immediately an unbearable, suffocating HEAT filled the craft. Overcome by the high temperature and unable to operate the airplane, the pilot and radar observer bailed out. As they parachuted to safety, the two men watched the jet as it hurtled toward Walesville. Smashing into a building, it burst into flames and careened into a car. A man, his wife and their two children were killed. Five other people were injured. Soon after the pilot had landed on the outskirts of town, a reporter arrived on the scene. The half-dazed pilot told him of the sudden heat. Before he could finish his story, a UNITED STATES AIR FORCE (USAF) car pulled up and whisked off the pilot and the radar observer.

The following day, a PHOTOGRAPH appeared in *The New York Times,* showing the gruesome scene of destruction. Bitterness was expressed by those who thought the pilots should not have abandoned their aircraft over a populated area. When the Walesville reporter's story of the strange heat was published, the Air Force denied it and blamed engine failure for the accident. Interviews with the pilot and radar operator were prohibited and the official report was classified secret.

Extreme heat has been felt on several occasions by witnesses in the proximity of a UFO and it has been suggested that in the Walesville case it was used as a defensive weapon to prevent the F–94 from closing in.

Bibliography: Keyhoe, Donald E., *Aliens from Space* (Garden City, N.Y.: Doubleday and Company, 1973); Hynek, J. Allen, and Jacques Vallee, *The Edge of Reality* (Chicago: Henry Regnery Company, 1975).

**WALSTON RAY,** stage and screen actor who, in the early 1960s reportedly observed a UFO hovering over his home in Beverly Hills, California. The object was at an altitude of about 3,000 or 4,000 feet and resembled a bathtub in shape and size. Its surface was like aluminum. Walston watched the UFO until it suddenly shot away and out of view.

**WALTER, TRAVIS,** *see* **SITGREAVES NATIONAL FOREST, ARIZONA**

**WALTER, WERNER ERWIN** (b. August 11, 1957, Mannheim, West Germany; address: 6800 Mannheim-31, Eisenacher Weg 16, West Germany; telephone number: 0621/701370), Cofounder of CENTRALES ERFURSCHUNGS-NETZ AUSSERGEWOHNLICHER PHENOMENE (CENAP) and UFO investigator.

Walter became interested in UFOs after he sighted a mysterious dark object outlined in red in 1973 in Mannheim-Vogelstang in West Germany. He believes, however, that the majority of UFOs are unidentified man-made objects and natural phenomena. He remains open minded about the identity, origin and purpose of the remaining percentage which have no conventional explanation. He holds that UFOLOGY is hampered by the large number of publicity seeking groups and individuals who do not approach the subject in a serious manner. He believes that the lack of progress made over the past thirty years can be solved by a strong cooperation between UFO organizations around the world.

A trade school graduate, Walter works as a radio and television retailer. He is a member of the anti-atom and anti-war movements. Since cofounding CENAP in 1973, he has worked as a UFO field investigator and researcher.

**WAR OF THE WORLDS, THE,** motion picture (Paramount, 1953). Producer: George Pal; director: Byron Haskin; screenplay by Barre Lyndon, based on the novel by H. G. Wells. Cast: Gene Barry, Ann Robinson, Les Tremayne, Bob Cornthwaite, Sandro Giglio, Lewis Martin, Ann Codee, Walter Sande, Houseley Stevenson, Jr., Paul Frees, Vernon Rich, Bill Phipps, Paul Birch, Jack Kruschen, Robert Rockwell and Sir Cedric Hardwicke.

The traditional English setting of the story has been changed to California in this film. The story begins when an extraterrestrial spacecraft lands in a small town. A crowd gathers around to watch. A priest approaches with a message of peace but is struck dead by a death ray. The Martian monsters emerge. Immune to every man-made weapon, they rampage across the world, killing and destroying as they go. As the last human survivors await their end in a church, the noise of the invaders stops. Their systems have succumbed to terrestrial germs.

**WAR OF THE WORLDS, THE,** Orson Welles's radio adaption of H. G. Wells's novel by the same name. The radio play was aired on Halloween in 1938, at a time when anxiety was high over the threat of war, for Hitler had recently invaded Austria, and the Japanese were marching on China. The drama was presented as a series of realistic news bulletins and interviews. Hundreds of thousands of listeners who tuned in after the introductory disclaimer were startled to hear the details of an apparent invasion of New Jersey by monsters from MARS. Panic ensued. Impromptu shotgun brigades were formed. Many residents of New Jersey fled their homes and headed for the hills. Reportedly, there were some suicides. Telephone lines and several highways were blocked for hours before the MASS HYSTERIA subsided.

Some UFOLOGISTS mention this incident as a demonstration of the need for further study and education in the field of UFOLOGY. They contend that if UFOs should prove to represent an extraterrestrial threat, it would be advantageous to be prepared. Authors DONALD MENZEL and Ernest Taves, on the other hand, have cited this episode as an indication of the gullibility of a large portion of the population, implying that such widespread credulousness is also partially responsible for the continuing belief in flying saucers.

Bibliography: Cantril, H. *The Invasion from Mars* (Princeton: Princeton University Press, 1940); Menzel, Donald H., and Ernest H. Taves, *The UFO Enigma* (Garden City, N.Y.: Doubleday and Company, 1977).

**WARRINGTON, PETER,** *see* **MANCHESTER UFO RESEARCH ASSOCIATION (MUFORA), NORTHERN UFO NETWORK (NUFON)** and **UFO INVESTIGATORS NETWORK (UFOIN)**

**WASHINGTON, D.C. (1952).** During the 1952 WAVE the most famous series of RADAR/visual sightings occurred over Washington, D.C. The sensational events made headlines around the country.

Between 11:40 P.M. and 5:00 A.M. on the night of July 19–20, two radarscopes at Washington National Airport picked up eight unidentified targets which were violating the restricted air corridors above the White House

*Above:* Photograph allegedly depicting UFOs seen over Washington, D.C., on July 19/20, 1952. *(Courtesy ICUFON/ DUIST);* Analysis by the Intercontinental Galactic Spacecraft (UFO) Research and Analytic Network showing how the rows of lamps in the lower half of the photograph created lens flares in the upper half of the photograph. The presence of a Christmas tree and scaffolding reveals that the photograph was actually taken in 1965.

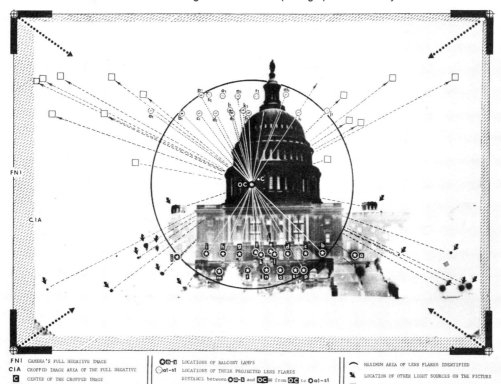

and the Capitol. Sauntering along at 100 to 300 miles per hour, the objects would suddenly accelerate to fantastically high speeds. Numerous airline crews were also reporting strange lights that moved up, down and sideways. These erratic maneuvers corresponded with those observed on the radar screens. An intercept flight had been recommended by Chief Radar Controller Harry Barnes but the squadron responsible for defending the capital had been secretly moved from nearby Bolling Air Force Base because of repair work being carried out on the runways. The jet fighters were temporarily stationed in Wilmington, Delaware. Reportedly, the interceptors had already been scrambled to investigate similar visual/radar UFO sightings over New Jersey. Whether for this reason or because they were not scrambled immediately from distant Wilmington, the interceptors did not reach Washington until about 3:30 A.M. As they had done earlier in New Jersey, the UFOs disappeared upon the arrival of the jets, only to reappear after their departure. Radar controllers at Andrews Air Force Base also tracked the unidentified targets and at one point made visual contact with a huge, fiery orange sphere hovering above them.

One week later, on the night of July 26–27, a repeat performance began at 9:00 P.M. Between six and twelve UFOs were tracked on radar at various times. At about 2:00 A.M., two UNITED STATES AIR FORCE (USAF) interceptors were scrambled. Although the UFOs had been present for several hours, they disappeared just as the two airplanes appeared on the radar screens. After about ten minutes, the aircraft were sent back to Wilmington. At the exact moment they disappeared from the radarscopes, the UFOs reappeared. At 3:00 A.M., another intercept flight was airborne at Wilmington. About twenty minutes later, the Air Force jets appeared once more on the radar screens. This time the UFOs remained visible. Finally, one of the interceptors, piloted by Lieutenant William Patterson, made visual contact with the unidentified objects. Patterson described them as tremendous blue-white lights. As he approached a cluster of UFOs, they formed a ring around him. The frightened pilot asked what he should do. There was a stunned silence in the radar control room. After a tense moment, the UFOs withdrew and left the scene. At approximately 3:45 A.M., the interceptors departed for Wilmington. The unidentified targets were tracked on radar until dawn.

Under pressure from the news media, the Air Force convened a press conference on July 29. Major General John Samford, Chief of Air Force Intelligence, explained that the unknown targets observed over Washington were the result of TEMPERATURE INVERSIONS. As official Air Force spokesman for the UFO project, ALBERT CHOP personally participated in the radar

observations and communications with the interceptor flights on July 26–27. Chop later revealed that the temperature inversion over Washington on that particular night was insufficient to cause such radar anomalies. Chief Radar Controller Barnes confirmed that many of the blips were strong and bright, not diffuse, shapeless blobs such as one gets from ground returns under anomalous propagation. Chop says that at the time this information was not released to the press, who seemed satisfied with General Samford's explanation. PROJECT BLUE BOOK classified the sighting as "unknown."

Bibliography: Sachs, Margaret, with Ernest Jahn, *Celestial Passengers—UFOs and Space Travel* (New York: Penguin Books, 1977); Ruppelt, Edward J., *Report on Unidentified Flying Objects* (Garden City, N.Y.: Doubleday and Company, 1956).

**WASHINGTON, D.C. (1964–1965).** In December 1964 and January 1965, a FLAP occurred in Washington and the neighboring countryside.

Sometime during late December three unidentified targets were tracked on RADAR traveling at an estimated speed of 4,800 miles per hour. Weeks later, the Air Force announced that faulty equipment had caused the blips to appear on the radar screens.

One of the most remarkable sightings occurred on December 21. Horace Burns of Grottoes, Virginia, was traveling on U.S. Highway 250 between Staunton and Waynesboro when he saw a huge cone-shaped object gliding across the road in front of him. His car stalled. The craft landed in a nearby meadow. Six concentric rings encircled the object, which was crested with a dome and emitted a bluish glow. After a few moments, the craft took off and disappeared. Independent tests by college professor Ernest Gehman and two DuPont engineers revealed a concentration of radiation at the landing site which spread over an area corresponding to the estimated size of the UFO. The Air Force investigated the case more than three weeks later. By that time, however, the meadow had been trampled by sightseers and scourged by rain and snow. The official explanation for the sighting was that Burns had seen a MIRAGE. However, less than a month later, a similar object was seen by two motorists driving in opposite directions on U.S. Highway 60 near Williamsburg.

The sighting which caused the most controversy during the two-month flap occurred on January 11. Six Army Signal Corps engineers watched strange spots in the sky from their office windows in the Munitions Building in downtown Washington. The disks zigzagged across the sky toward the Capitol. Suddenly, two delta-wing jets appeared on the scene. As the jets raced toward them, the UFOs took off at high speed leaving the jets far behind them. When news reporters tried to follow up on the story, they were told by the Defense Department and by military officials that the incident had never happened.

Bibliography: Steiger, Brad (ed.), *Project Blue Book* (New York: Ballantine Books, 1976).

**WASHINGTON SAUCER INTELLIGENCE,** organization founded by WAYNE SULO AHO in 1957 and superseded by the NEW AGE FOUNDATION (NAF) in 1965.

**WATTS, JOHN LANGDON** (b. October 19, 1910, Columbia, South Carolina; address: 148 Reef Road, South Daytona, Florida 32019), CONTACTEE.

Watts holds that there are nine PLANETS in our solar system, one of them permanently hidden behind the sun, and 200 in the seven known solar systems which have life forms identical to our own. He claims that the majority of outer SPACE PEOPLE with whom he communicates come from VENUS and belong to a Federation of Planets. Their intent, he says, is to try to assist Earth through a cataclysm due to occur around the year two thousand. According to Watts, the Venusians, who are 2,500 years ahead of mankind, keep in superb physical shape with organic foods and exercise, especially swimming. In fact, he asserts, their larger spaceships have swimming pools. Watts claims to have visited a domed city on Venus as the guest of an extraterrestrial woman named Mara. In his books, he has described at some length cosmetic formulas and vegetarian menus which he allegedly acquired while enjoying Mara's hospitality.

Watts studied Mechanical Engineering for three years at Clarkson College of Technology in Potsdam, New York. He was employed as a Technical Field Engineer by Agfa Ansco Camera and by Eastman Camera Works in Rochester, New York. During World War II, he served in the U.S. Army in the European Theater. Following the war, he became Owner and President of the Dixie Venus Corporation, a plastics company. Now semi-retired, he is making and experimenting with PYRAMIDS allegedly designed by outer space people.

Watts is a member of the Space Science Christianity Research Foundation.

During the 1960s, according to Watts, the CENTRAL INTELLIGENCE AGENCY (CIA) prevented him from publishing a book entitled *Hello Venus*. This and another book, *Religious Philosophies of the Planets*, were eventually combined into an expanded book, entitled *The Reason for Life—and Now—Visit Venus* (Post Orange, Florida: Dixie Venus Books, 1975).

**WAVE,** term denoting a period of several weeks or months during which multiple nationwide or worldwide UFO sightings occur. It is distinguished from a FLAP which denotes a highly-publicized concentration of UFO sightings within a small geographical area or a short time period.

The first major series of sightings was the AIRSHIP WAVE which began in the United States in 1896 and ended the following year. A similar wave occurred in England in 1909. During World War II, pilots encountered numerous UFOs, known as FOO FIGHTERS, in both the Pacific and Atlantic theaters of war. In 1946, the GHOST ROCKET sightings began in Scandinavia, and the following year brought the first U.S. wave of the MODERN ERA. Since then, numerous waves have occurred in different parts of the world. The most outstanding of these were the 1952 wave in the United States and Europe, and the 1954 wave which began in France and spread throughout Europe and to other parts of the world. The latter series, which involved numerous reports of landings and OCCUPANTS in France, may have been the largest UFO wave ever. In 1973 and 1974, another major wave occurred in the United States and France. (See map on page 375.)

Bibliography: Hall, Richard H. (ed.), *The UFO Evidence* (Washington, D.C.: National Investigations Committee on Aerial Phenomena, 1964); Vallee, Jacques and Janine, *Challenge to Science—The UFO Enigma* (Chicago: Henry Regnery Company, 1966); Emenegger, Robert, *UFOs, Past Present and Future* (New York: Ballantine Books, 1974).

**WEATHER BALLOONS** *see* **BALLOONS**

**WEBER-RICHTER, FRANK,** *see* **MEKIS, KARL**

**WEGNER, WILLY,** *see* **DANSK UFO CENTER**

**WEIGHTLESSNESS,** a feeling experienced by some witnesses in the vicinity of UFOs. Occasionally livestock, apparently victims of the same effect, have been seen grouped closely together in an orderly pattern like iron filings around a magnet. Sometimes the animals have stood on tiptoe, their heads held high, as if suspended by some invisible force.

The absence of a number of animals after a UFO's departure has led UFOLOGISTS to suppose that they may have been ABDUCTED by means of LEVITATION.

Bibliography: Le Poer Trench, Brinsley, *Mysterious Visitors—The UFO Story* (New York: Stein and Day, 1973).

**WELLES, ORSON,** *see* **WAR OF THE WORLDS, THE**

**WERKGROEP NOBOVO** *see* **NEDERLANDS ONDERZOEK BUREAU VOOR UFOs**

**WEST, ALAN** (b. July 16, 1947, Kingston, United Kingdom; address: Radio Hallam, P.O. Box 194, Hartshead, Sheffield S1 1GP, England), broadcaster and writer.

West believes that ninety-eight percent of reported UFOs are MISIDENTIFICATIONS. Of the remaining two percent, he believes that less than one percent are unidentifiable by current standards.

A former Director of the Great Britain UFO REGISTRY, West has worked as a broadcaster and writer, mainly in the field of radio. He is currently employed by Radio Hallam in Sheffield.

West is author of *World of the Unknown: All About UFOs* (London: Osborne, 1977); and *Close Encounters: The Strange Truth About UFOs* (London: Arrow Books, 1978).

**WHITE, ROBERT,** UNITED STATES AIR FORCE (USAF) captain who served as the Pentagon UFO spokesman during 1955.

**WHITE SANDS, NEW MEXICO,** location of numerous UFO sightings, of which the most famous occurred on April 24, 1949, and November 3, 1957. The area is of strategic interest because it is the home of the U.S. government proving ground where atomic research projects are tested.

The earlier incident occurred at 10:20 A.M. Engineer Charles B. Moore and four enlisted personnel from the White Sands Proving Ground Navy Unit were preparing a site for the launching of a SKYHOOK BALLOON. J. Gordon Vaeth was present as the Navy representative in charge of the ground handling and BALLOON phases of the operation. A small weather balloon had been released to establish wind patterns. Suddenly, a second object was observed moving eastward through the sky. Elliptical in shape, it was two-and-a-half times as long as it was wide. The gleaming white UFO was pale yellow at the lower tail end. Although Moore was able to capture the object through a theodolite, its rapid speed prevented him from focusing sharply on it. The object was visible for about one minute before disappearing in a steep climb. A test of wind conditions by a second balloon, released fifteen minutes after the UFO sighting, confirmed that the object could not have been a balloon.

The 1957 sighting occurred only a few hours after a series of sensational encounters involving an elliptical UFO in and around LEVELLAND, TEXAS. Two military policemen, Corporal Glenn H. Toy and Private First-Class James Wilbanks, were patrolling the White Sands

Proving Grounds in a jeep, at about 3:00 A.M. on November 3, when they observed a brilliant reddish-orange egg-shaped UFO. The object descended to a point about fifty yards above a bunker and then vanished. A few minutes later, the light blinked on again. Once more it began to descend, this time on a slant, and once more disappeared. The UFO did not reappear and a search party was unable to find any trace of it. The two witnesses estimated it to have been between seventy-five and 100 yards in diameter. Toy later commented that "It looked like a completely-controlled landing."

Later, at about 8:00 P.M. in the evening of November 3, another two-man jeep patrol observed a UFO above the same bunker. The witnesses, Specialist Third-Class Forest R. Oakes and Specialist Third-Class Barlow, estimated that the brilliant light was between 200 and 300 feet long. As the UFO ascended slowly at a forty-five-degree angle, its light pulsated on and off. After stopping and starting several times, the object finally diminished in size to a point of light resembling a star and then disappeared.

Authors DONALD MENZEL and Lyle G. Boyd speculated that the early morning sighting on November 3, 1957, was a MISIDENTIFICATION of the MOON whose appearance might have been distorted by moving CLOUDS. They concluded that the 8:00 p.m. sighting was a misidentification of the PLANET VENUS, which was almost at maximum brilliance at the time and very conspicuous in the western sky.

Bibliography: Vaeth, J. Gordon, *200 miles Up—The Conquest of the Upper Air* (New York: Ronald Press Company, 1951); Hall, Richard H. (ed.), *The UFO Evidence* (Washington, D.C.: National Investigations Committee on Aerial Phenomena, 1964); Menzel, Donald H., and Lyle G. Boyd, *The World of Flying Saucers* (Garden City, N.Y.: Doubleday and Company, 1963).

**WHITE WATER,** term used to describe the ocean surface in the BERMUDA TRIANGLE when both the sea and the sky assume a milky appearance, blending in such a way that the horizon is undistinguishable. The phenomenon has been associated with the mysterious DISAPPEARANCES alleged to occur in the area.

**WHITTED, JOHN B.,** *see* **MONTGOMERY, ALABAMA**

**WILL-O'-THE-WISP** *see* **SWAMP GAS**

**WILSON,** name of a UFOnaut encountered in several different towns in Texas during the AIRSHIP WAVE of 1896 to 1897.

The first incident occurred in Beaumont on April 19, 1897. J. B. Ligon, a local agent for the Magnolia brewery, and his son, Charles, found four men standing beside a large object in a field. One of the men asked Ligon for two buckets of water. Another, identifying himself as Wilson, explained that they were on a return trip in their flying machine to a small town in Iowa where the airship and four similar craft had been made. He told Ligon that electricity powered the propellers and wings.

The following day, Sheriff H. W. Baylor of Uvalde discovered three men standing by an airship in his backyard. One of the men gave his name as Wilson and told the sheriff that he wanted to see an old acquaintance, C. C. Akers, the former sheriff of Zavalia County. Baylor replied that Akers had moved to Eagle Pass but that he visited him quite frequently. Wilson asked to be remembered to Akers. After collecting some water, the men boarded their craft and flew away. A letter signed by C. C. Akers appeared in the *Galveston Daily News* one week later, confirming that Akers had known a wealthy inventor named Wilson who worked in the field of aerial navigation.

In Kountze on April 23, two men reported meeting airship OCCUPANTS named Wilson and Jackson. Two other airship encounters on April 22 and April 30 apparently involved the same craft, although the name Wilson was not specifically mentioned.

Reports of this kind naturally misled many people into believing that great advances had been made in the art of mechanical flight. It is in retrospect that the mystery deepens. Primitive airships of this type had been developed in Europe but, at the time of the FLAP,

no large powered craft of this type existed in the United States. Nothing has been heard of Wilson and his five airships since April 30, 1897.

Bibliography: Jacobs, David Michael, *The UFO Controversy in America* (Bloomington, Indiana: Indiana University Press, 1975).

## WINGS OVER THE WORLD (WOW).

In his prophetic *Things to Come*, H. G. Wells describes a ravaged, war-torn Earth, on which the surviving scientists and thinkers join forces in an organization called Wings over the World or WOW. They fly around the PLANET as they go about the arduous task of restoring civilization to the degenerate and brutalized people.

Writer JOHN KEEL has suggested that such an organization is not of the future but of the past. He hypothesizes that members of WOW may have been helping man along the road of technological evolution since ancient times. The many artifacts, which some UFOLOGISTS claim to be evidence of ANCIENT ASTRONAUTS, may instead be evidence of intervention by WOW. According to this theory, the members of WOW still watch over us and occasionally are seen as they travel in their craft which we call UFOs.

Bibliography: Keel, John, *Our Haunted Planet* (New York: Fawcett Publications, 1971).

## WISCONSIN PANCAKES *see* EAGLE RIVER, WISCONSIN

## WOW *see* WINGS OVER THE WORLD

**X,** legal name of the Founder and Sole Proprietor of the RES BUREAUX.

**XENOCHEMISTRY,** term used by astronomer DONALD MENZEL to denote the analysis of substances which are determined to originate from other PLANETS.

**XENOLOG,** quarterly magazine, established in 1954, with a circulation of approximately 500. It is available by subscription only. The magazine serves as a forum on UFOLOGY and related matters for New Zealanders and overseas contacts. It deals with sightings in New Zealand, interesting overseas reports and all aspects of international ufology.

The Editors are Fred and Phyllis Dickeson. The magazine is published by NEW ZEALAND SCIENTIFIC APPROACH TO COSMIC UNDERSTANDING (NZSATCU OR SATCU), 33 Dee Street, Timarus, New Zealand.

**X–15,** high-altitude aircraft built in 1955 for a research program under the joint sponsorship of the UNITED STATES AIR FORCE (USAF), the Navy and the NATIONAL AERONAUTICS AND SPACE ADMINISTRATION (NASA). Reportedly, during a flight piloted by Joe Walter on April 30, 1962, a PHOTOGRAPH was taken by a mounted camera of half-a-dozen disk-shaped or cylindrical objects. On July 17 of the same year, Major Robert M. White achieved a high-altitude record when he flew the X–15 to 314,750 feet. White was startled by the sight of a gray-white object which flew alongside him for about five seconds, then darted above and behind the plane. "There are things out there," he yelled to ground controllers over the radio. A UFO, believed to be that spotted by White, was captured on film by a movie camera mounted in the lower tail of the aircraft. The film shows an object, of undetermined size and gray-white in color, tumbling above and behind the X–15 as it climbed through 270,000 feet. NASA officials believe the object may have been ICE CRYSTALS flaking off the frosty surface of the research aircraft.

Bibliography: Hall, Richard H. (ed.), *The UFO Evidence* (Washington, D.C.: National Investigations Committee on Aerial Phenomena, 1964).

**YE ANCIENT AND SECRET ORDER FOR QUIET BIRDMEN,** 1900 Euclid Avenue, Cleveland, Ohio 44115. An organization of aircraft pilots whose 126 groups meet monthly in 126 cities throughout the United States. The organization states that pilots do not report UFOs because of the excessive number of forms they are required to complete in such cases. The Quiet Birdmen believe that false information about UFOs is being promoted for the personal gain of those involved.

**YETI,** legendary Tibetan creature similar to the American BIGFOOT.

**YOUNG, JOHN,** *see* **GEMINI 10**

**YOWIE,** legendary Australian creature similar to the American BIGFOOT.

**YUCCA VALLEY UFO CLUB,** P.O. Box 39, Yucca Valley, California 92284; telephone number: 714-365-1141.

The stated purposes of this CONTACTEE organization are: 1) to help to educate the public about the nature and purpose of flying saucers, the SPACE PEOPLE and their advanced way of life; 2) to make the club a meaningful instrument of the NEW AGE; 3) to bring to the community prominent speakers in the flying saucer-New Age movement; and 4) to play an active role in helping to bring about a positive transformation of all things in keeping with the divine plan for the evolution and upliftment of the nation, the planet, and all mankind.

President, Vice-President, Secretary-Treasurer and the Board of Directors of this nonprofit club are elected annually. A Board of Advisors is appointed by the Board of Directors and consists of up to thirteen prominent members of the community or the UFO field whose guidance is solicited from time to time. Meetings are held monthly. Past guest speakers have included GABRIEL GREEN, BRIAN SCOTT, DANIEL FRY and Barbara Beaver.

**YUGOSLAVIA.** Flying saucers are referred to as "leteci tanjiri" in Yugoslavia. Although there are no national UFO organizations, there are some independent researchers who serve as Yugoslav representatives for foreign groups, such as the AERIAL PHENOMENA RESEARCH ORGANIZATION (APRO), the MUTUAL UFO NETWORK (MUFON) and SKANDINAVISK UFO INFORMATION (SUFOI). An astronomical academy undertook the investigation of a MULTIPLE WITNESS sighting at SARAJEVO in 1968. The group concluded that the object was a stratosphere BALLOON.

Yugoslavia experienced UFO WAVES in 1954, 1967, 1969 and 1971.

**ZACATECAS, MEXICO,** location where Mexican astronomer José Bonilla, Director of the Zacatecas Astronomical Observatory, sighted UFOs in 1883. During August 12 and 13, Bonilla and his assistant observed over 400 cigar-shaped, disk-shaped and spindle-shaped objects moving in groups across the face of the sun. He photographed the UFOs, which appeared to be solid.

Bibliography: Fort, Charles, *The Book of the Damned* (New York: Boni and Liveright, 1919).

Photograph taken by astronomer José Bonilla showing a UFO in front of the sun. *(Courtesy ICUFON)*

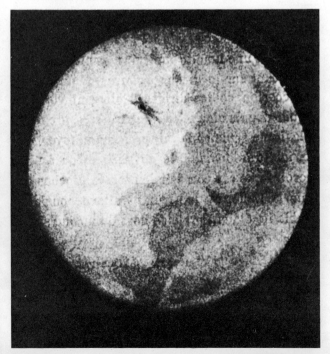

Cover of French astronomer Camille Flamarion's magazine *L'Astronomie* in which Bonilla's photograph was first published in 1886. *(Courtesy ICUFON)*

## ZAMORA, LONNIE, *see* SOCORRO, NEW MEXICO

**ZETA RETICULI,** two fifth-magnitude STARS which are prime candidates for the search for extraterrestrial life and which have been tentatively identified as the home base of extraterrestrials allegedly encountered by Betty and Barney Hill in NEW HAMPSHIRE in 1961. Zeta 1 and Zeta 2 are located in the southern constellation Reticulum, which is invisible to observers north of Mexico City's latitude. In galactic terms, they are close neighbors of Earth, being only thirty-seven light years away. According to current theories of planetary formation, each star should have an entourage of PLANETS similar to that of our solar system. However, there is, as yet, no way to determine if any of the probable planets of either star is similar to Earth.

In 1964, under posthypnotic suggestion, Betty Hill drew a two-dimensional duplicate of a three-dimensional map she had allegedly seen aboard an alien spacecraft in 1961. The stars were represented by dots and circles, some of which were joined by curved lines. The ship's leader reportedly told Betty that the heavy lines represented trade routes, the solid lines less-frequently traveled routes and the broken lines represented expeditions. Although there were many stars on the map, Betty was able to specifically recall only the prominent ones linked by lines and a distinctive triangular formation on the left. She tried to show the size and depth of the stars by the relative size of the circles she drew.

Between 1968 and 1973, Marjorie Fish, an Ohio schoolteacher, amateur astronomer and member of Mensa, constructed several three-dimensional models of the stars in the vicinity of our sun in an attempt to detect a pattern similar to that of the Hill pattern. Following the publication of new data in the 1969 edition of the Gliese *Catalog of Nearby Stars,* Fish found a configuration which was a close match. According to the position of the connecting lines, Zeta 1 and Zeta 2 Reticuli form the starting point of the trade routes and the sun is at the end of one of the supposedly regular trade routes. Using a computer program that can duplicate the appearance of star fields from various viewpoints in space, independent tests carried out by Walter Mitchell, Professor of Astronomy at Ohio State University in Columbus, and Mark Steggert, of the Space Research Coordination Center at the University of Pittsburgh, confirmed the star pattern obtained by Fish with only minor variations.

Skeptics have pointed out that two other patterns have been identified as resembling the Hill map. In 1965, Betty Hill observed a similarity between her map and a map of the constellation Pegasus. Charles Atterberg, an employee of an aeronautical communications company in Illinois, found a pattern of stars similar to the Hill sketch in which Epsilon Eridani and Epsilon Indi appeared to form the home base. However, in the construction of her map, Fish had enforced several restrictions, in particular that all the stars be solar-type stars with the probability of having planets and that the apparent travel routes represent a logical pattern with regard to the three-dimensional distances involved. Neither Betty Hill's interpretation of Pegasus nor Atterberg's map met the criteria.

Astronomers CARL SAGAN and Steven Soter assert that by removing the connecting lines from the Hill map and from Mitchell's computer map, little similarity remains. Authors Ernest Taves and DONALD MENZEL were able to duplicate a pattern similar to the Hill map

*Top:* Star map allegedly seen aboard a UFO by Betty Hill; *Bottom:* Marjorie Fish's interpretation of the Hill map showing Zeta Reticuli as the ufonaut's home base.

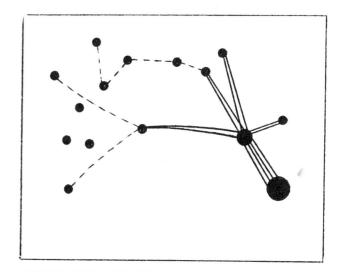

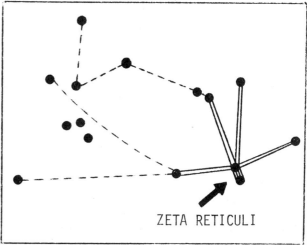

ZETA RETICULI

from a randomly distributed pattern of forty-seven points, the approximate number of stars from which the computer map was selected. Since they succeeded in their very first attempt, they claim that any randomly distributed assemblage of forty-seven points could supply fifteen that matched the Hill drawing or any other random pattern. This, they purport, invalidates the map as substantiation of the reality of the Hill encounter.

Further study and measurement of the stars in the Zeta Reticuli map may change their relative positions. This may result in a distortion of the configuration beyond the limits of coincidence, ending speculation on the matter. On the other hand, the change might provide a perfect match between the maps, failing to resolve the controversy definitively but keeping alive the possibility that Earth has been visited by aliens from Zeta Reticuli.

Bibliography: Dickinson, Terence, "The Zeta Reticuli Incident," *Astronomy* (December 1974, Vol. 2, No. 12); and follow-up commentaries in the July, August and September 1975 issues of *Astronomy;* Menzel, Donald H., and Ernest H. Taves, *The UFO Enigma* (Garden City, N.Y.: Doubleday and Company, 1977).

**ZETETIC SCHOLAR,** journal established in 1978, with a circulation of approximately 300. It is published three times per year and is available by subscription only. The *Zetetic Scholar* is an attempt to enhance communication between critics and proponents of claims of the paranormal. It is concerned not only with adjudication of such claims but also with the sociology and psychology of the disputes themselves.

The nucleus of the journal's network of researchers consists of a panel of Consulting Editors, which includes Theodore X. Barber, Milbourne Christopher, Harry Collins, Richard de Mille, Persi Diaconis, Martin Ebon, Christopher Evans, Robert Galbreath, Michel Gauquelin, C. E. M. Hansel, Bernard Heuvelmans, Ellic Howe, Ray Hyman, J. ALLEN HYNEK, David M. Jacobs, Joseph G. Jorgensen, Seymour H. Mauskopf, Edward J. Moody, Robert L. Morris, William Nagler, John Palmer, William F. Powers, Charles T. Tart, Roy Wallis, James Webb, and Ron Westrum. The journal is edited and published by Marcello Truzzi, Department of Sociology, Eastern Michigan University, Ypsilanti, Michigan 48197.

**ZIGEL, FELIX,** Professor of Higher Mathematics and Astronomy at the Moscow Aviation Institute and a leading proponent of UFOs in the Soviet Union.

**ZIGGURATS,** terraced PYRAMIDS built between 2,200

Drawing of the restored ziggurat at Ur. *(The Bettmann Archive)*

and 500 B.C. in the major cities of ancient Mesopotamia. Averaging about 170 feet square at their rectangular bases, the ziggurats were built with bricks and had no internal chambers. Although some were designed with ramps and staircases, almost half of the known ziggurats still standing today have no apparent means of ascent. Some, like the Hanging Gardens of Babylon, were superbly landscaped with luxuriant shrubs and trees. None of today's ziggurats still stands at its original height. The best-preserved is at Ur, and the largest at Choga Zambil in Elam. While conventional archaeologists refer to these mysterious, man-made mountains as temples, some UFOLOGISTS have suggested that they may have been launching pads for ANCIENT ASTRONAUTS.

**ZOND 4,** Russian space probe launched into orbit on March 2, 1968, which may have been the source of numerous UFO reports the following evening from Indiana, Kentucky, Massachusetts, New York, Ohio, Pennsylvania, Tennessee, Virginia and West Virginia.

Some witnesses claimed to have seen a cigar-shaped craft with lighted windows while others reported three luminous objects flying in formation. Numerous witnesses asserted that the objects were flying between treetop level and 1,500 feet. Some reports described directional changes performed by the UFOs. A science teacher in Ohio, who observed the objects through binoculars, compared them to "inverted saucers." She claimed that her dog reacted with fear and that she herself experienced an unusual drowsiness.

The official UNITED STATES AIR FORCE (USAF) explanation, accepted at the time by all investigators, was that DEBRIS from Zond 4 had re-entered the atmosphere and disintegrated. In 1974, writer PHILIP KLASS cited NORTH AMERICAN RADAR DEFENSE (NORAD) as showing in its records that the re-entry of one of Zond 4's booster rockets had coincided with the time of the sightings. Consequently, the Zond 4 episode is frequently quoted as an example of witnesses' inaccuracy in describing what they have seen when they are suddenly exposed to a brief and unexpected event. Klass concludes that claims of drowsiness on the part of a witness and fear experienced by an animal could be ascribed to the suggestibility of a witness who was already familiar with the alleged attributes of UFOs.

In 1976, Marcia S. Smith, Science and Technology Analyst of the Science Policy Research Division at the Library of Congress, checked NORAD, Space Detection and Tracking Systems (SPADATS), Radio Astronomy Explorer Satellite (RAE) and Goddard Satellite Situation reports for that date and found that no such re-

entry had been recorded. According to those sources, the first debris from Zond 4 came down on March 5, two days after the sightings. PROJECT BLUE BOOK files show several inconsistencies regarding the episode. Two Air Force memos, one stating the sightings were caused by Zond 4 debris, the other saying they were not, were both dated March 4, 1968. A letter to a private citizen from Major HECTOR QUINTANILLA, dated April 19, 1968, states that the Space Detection Center at Colorado Springs, aware that a piece of SATELLITE debris was re-entering the atmosphere, was especially vigilant at the time. They determined that the target impact point (TIP) was in either northern Pennsylvania or southern New York.

As a result of the discrepancies found by Smith, Klass contacted NORAD. In a letter to him, dated January 28, 1976, NORAD stated that part of Zond 4 did decay that night, but the TIP system was not tracking the object and they did not notice it. This directly contradicts Quintanilla's letter of April 19, 1968. They claimed that when they discovered a decrease in the number of objects associated with Zond 4 debris in orbit, they recorded its decay as occurring on March 7, 1968, the last day it could have come down. NORAD stated that they could not understand the conflicting reports in Blue Book's files, but that they were quite certain that it was part of Zond 4 that caused the sightings on March 3, 1968.

JAMES OBERG of NASA's Johnson Space Center calculated Zond 4's ground trace for the night of March 3, 1968, and concluded that the probe was indeed passing over the sighting areas at the time of the reports. Brad Sparks, Cofounder and Board Member of CITIZENS AGAINST UFO SECRECY (CAUS), disputes this conclusion. His analysis indicates that the probe was over the Azores at the time.

Smith questions the fact that the Air Force did not send search teams to recover the decayed material. She points out that when Kosmos 316 impacted over the southwestern United States the following year, three or four states were combed for debris. In a report prepared for the Library of Congress, Smith states that the incident does not have a definite solution. It could have been a Zond 4 fragment, she adds, but NORAD records were of little help on this point. She concludes that the number of discrepancies in the Air Force records "brings into question their thoroughness in investigating other UFO reports."

Bibliography: Smith, Marcia S., *The UFO Enigma* (Washington, D.C.: Library of Congress, Congressional Research Service, 1976); Klass, Philip J., *UFOs Explained* (New York: Random House, 1974).

# supplements

Commonly reported UFO shapes. *(Courtesy ICUFON/NICAP)*

| UFO SHAPE | BOTTOM VIEW | BOTTOM ANGLE | SIDE VIEW |
|---|---|---|---|
| **1. FLAT DISC**<br>A. 10-54 Cox<br>7-2-52 Newhouse<br>B. 7-9-47 Johnson<br>7-14-52 Nash | ⬭ | A  B<br>oval | A  B<br>*lens-shaped*  "coin-like" |
| **2. DOMED DISC**<br>A. 9-21-58 Fitzgerald<br>4-24-62 Gasslein<br>B. 5-11-50 Trent<br>8-7-52 Janson | ⬭ | A  B<br>*hat-shaped* | A  B<br>*World War I helmet* |
| **3. SATURN DISC** (Double dome)<br>A. 10-4-54 Salandin<br>1-16-58 Trindade<br>10-2-61 Harris<br>B. 8-20-56 Moore | A ◯<br>B ⬭<br>elliptical or *winged oval* | "diamond-shaped" | *Saturn-shaped* |
| **4. HEMISPHERICAL DISC**<br>9-24-59 Redmond<br>1-21-61 Pulliam<br>2-7-61 Nalley | ⬭ | *parachute* | *mushroom* *half moon* |
| **5. FLATTENED SPHERE**<br>10-1-48 Gorman<br>4-27-50 Adickes<br>10-9-51 C.A.A. | ◯ | ⬭ | ⬭  sometimes with peak |
| **6. SPHERICAL** (Circular from all angles)<br>3-45 Dolarof<br>1-20-52 Baller<br>10-12-61 Edwards | A ◯<br>metallic-appearing ball | ball of glowing light  B | |
| **7. ELLIPTICAL**<br>12-20-58 Arboreen<br>11-2-57 Levelland<br>8-13-60 Carson | *football* *egg-shaped* | ⬭ | ⬭ |
| **8. TRIANGULAR**<br>5-7-56 G.O.C.<br>5-22-60 Majorca | ◁ | ◁ | *tear-drop* |
| **9. CYLINDRICAL** (Rocket-like)<br>8-1-46 Puckett<br>7-24-48 Chiles | "cigar-shaped" | **10. LIGHT SOURCE ONLY**<br>"star-like" or "planet-like" | |

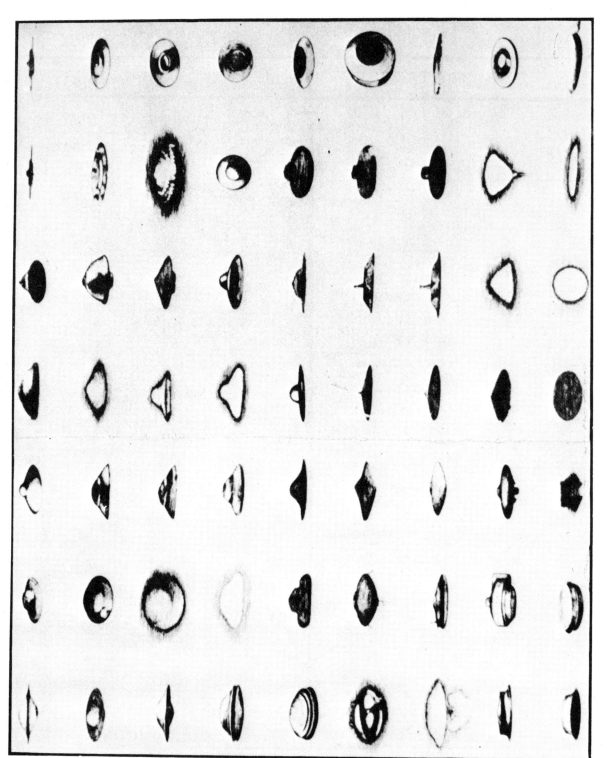

A selection of UFOs (some of which are proven hoaxes). *(Courtesy ICUFON)*

UFO formations and maneuvers. *(Courtesy ICUFON/ACOM)*

| UFO FORMATIONS | UFO MANEUVERS |
|----------------|---------------|

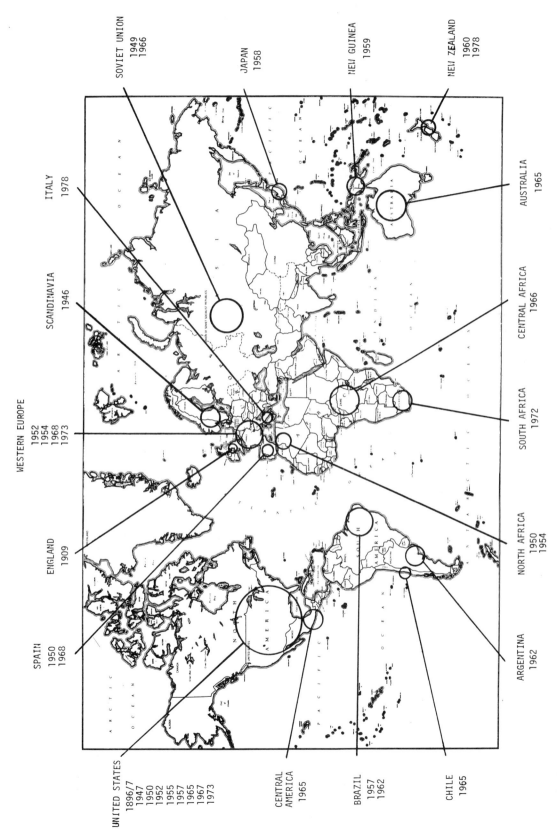

SOVIET UNION
1949
1966

JAPAN
1958

NEW GUINEA
1959

NEW ZEALAND
1960
1978

ITALY
1978

SCANDINAVIA
1946

WESTERN EUROPE

1952
1954
1968
1973

AUSTRALIA
1965

CENTRAL AFRICA
1966

SOUTH AFRICA
1972

NORTH AFRICA
1950
1954

SPAIN
1950
1968

ENGLAND
1909

UNITED STATES
1896/7
1947
1950
1952
1955
1957
1965
1967
1973

CENTRAL
AMERICA
1965

BRAZIL
1957
1962

CHILE
1965

ARGENTINA
1962

**Major UFO waves**

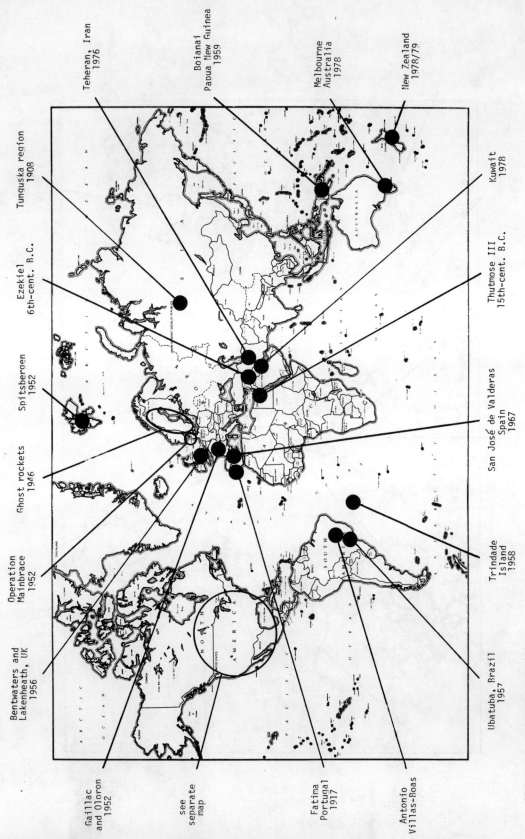

Teheran, Iran
1976

Bojanai
Papua New Guinea
1959

Melbourne
Australia
1978

New Zealand
1978/79

Tunguska region
1908

Kuwait
1978

Ezekiel
6th-cent. B.C.

Thutmose III
15th-cent. B.C.

Spitsbergen
1952

San José de Valderas
Spain
1967

Ghost rockets
1946

Operation
Mainbrace
1952

Trindade
Island
1958

Bentwaters and
Lakenheath, UK
1956

Ubatuba, Brazil
1957

Gaillac
and Oloron
1952

see
separate
map

Fatima
Portugal
1917

Antonio
Villas-Boas

**Major UFO events overseas.**

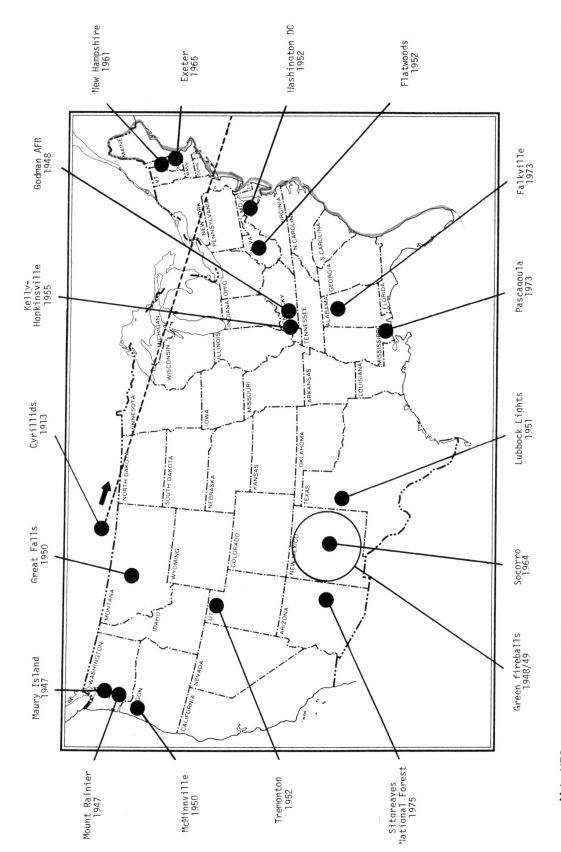

New Hampshire
1961

Exeter
1965

Washington DC
1952

Flatwoods
1952

Godman AFB
1948

Falkville
1973

Kelly-
Hopkinsville
1955

Pascagoula
1973

Cyrillids
1913

Lubbock Lights
1951

Great Falls
1950

Socorro
1964

Maury Island
1947

Green fireballs
1948/49

Mount Rainier
1947

McMinnville
1950

Tremonton
1952

Sitgreaves
National Forest
1975

**Major UFO events in the United States.**

HAMMOND'
SUPERIOR MAP OF
# EUROPE
AND THE NEAR EAST
Copyright by C.S. HAMMOND & CO., N.Y.

SCALE OF MILES

SCALE OF KILOMETRES

National Capitals............................★
Administrative Centers......................●
International Boundaries...................
Internal Boundaries.......................
Canals....................................

# MID-EAST CRISIS
# GALACTIC (U.F.O.)
# SURVEILLANCE
# 1970-79

INTERCONTINENTAL GALACTIC SPACECRAFT(U.F.O.)RESEARCH AND ANALYTIC
NETWORK (35-50 75th street, Jackson Heights, N.Y., 11372,U.S.A.)

ROUTE OF MILITARY

ROUTE OF MILITARY CARG

KEY:

◯  STRATEGICAL and NAVAL KEY POINTS

⋀  FORCE IN FORMATION  R E D reported bet. 1970 - 1972

●  1 - 3 CRAFTS  BLACK reported bet. 1973 - 1979

Registered reports: crafts in flight, landings, dis-
embarked crew members, (humanoids)

Average Locations: military and air force bases,air-
ports, ports, industrial districts,
capitals.

⋀  NAVAL ROUTES TO THE MIDDLE EAST.

A,B,C. FLIGHT CHANNELS (ESTIMATED) based on the crafts general flight direction and terri-
torial distribution.

# FLIGHT CHANNEL A

# FLIGHT C

Map prepared by the Intercontinental Galactic Spacecraft (UFO) Research and Analytic Network (ICUFON). It shows the locations of UFO sightings in Europe between 1970 and 1979 and the alleged flight channels of "intergalactic surveillance forces." ICUFON supports the invasion hypothesis and holds that the presence of UFOs around the Mediterranean and in Europe is associated with the political situation in the Middle East. *(Courtesy ICUFON)*

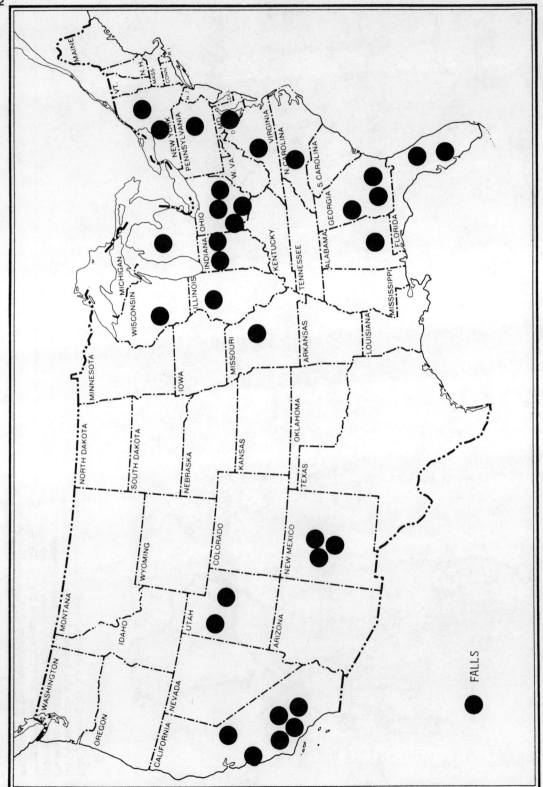

The locations of major falls of angels' hair in the United States.

FALLS

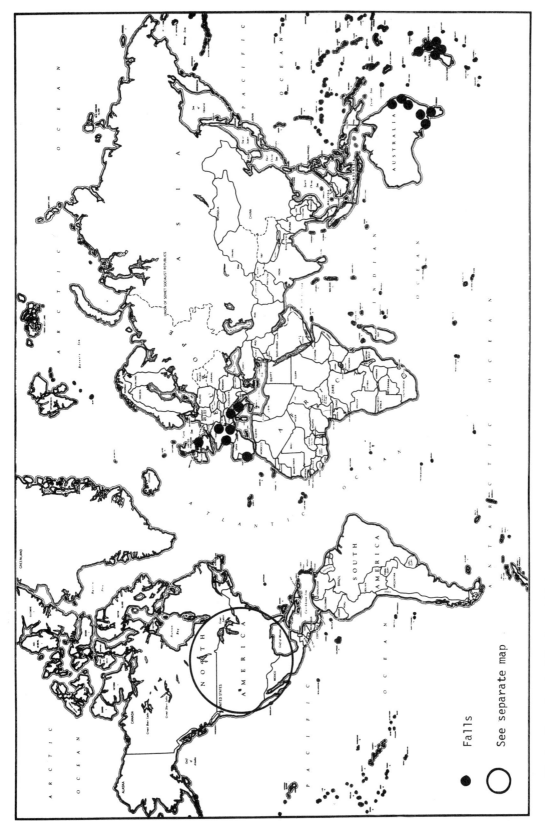

Falls

See separate map

The locations of major falls of angels' hair overseas.

384

Areas of alleged magnetic deviation, named "vile vortices" by Ivan Sanderson. Two vortices not shown on this map are at the poles. In the upper row, the second and fifth circles from the left represent the Bermuda Triangle and the Devil's Sea, respectively.

# ufo organizations and contactee groups

## UNITED STATES

### Arizona

**AERIAL PHENOMENA RESEARCH ORGANIZATION (APRO)**
3910 Kleindale Road
Tucson, Arizona 85712

**GROUND SAUCER WATCH (GSW)**
13238 N. 7th Drive
Phoenix, Arixona 85029

**UNDERSTANDING**
Star Route, Box 588 F
Tonopah, Arizona 85354

### California

**AETHERIUS SOCIETY**
6202 Afton Place
Hollywood, California 90028

**AMALGAMATED FLYING SAUCER CLUBS OF AMERICA (AFSCA)**
P.O. Box 39
Yucca Valley, California 92284

**BORDERLAND SCIENCES RESEARCH FOUNDATION (BSRF)**
P.O. Box 548
Vista, California 92083

**CONGRESS FOR INTERPLANETARY TECHNOLOGY AND EDUCATION (CITE)**
Suite 6B, 17901 E. Chapman Avenue
Orange, California 92669

**GEORGE ADAMSKI FOUNDATION**
314 Lado de Loma Drive
Vista, California 92083

**INTERPLANETARY THINK-IN**
Suite D, 257 Van Buren
Monterey, California 93940

**NATIONAL INVESTIGATIONS COMMITTEE ON UFOs (NICUFO)**
Suite 207
7970 Woodman Avenue
Van Nuys, California 91402

**SCHOOL OF THOUGHT**
P.O. Box 257
June Lake, California 93529

**UFO REPORT CENTER OF ORANGE COUNTY**
c/o Alvin H. Lawson
English Department
California State University at Long Beach
Long Beach, California 90840

**UFO RESEARCH ASSOCIATES**
3122 North Beachwood Drive
Los Angeles, California 90068

**UFO RESEARCH INSTITUTE (UFORI)**
P.O. Box 502
Union City, California 94587

**UNARIUS EDUCATIONAL FOUNDATION**
P.O. Box 1042
El Cajon, California 92022

**UNIVERSAL INDUSTRIAL CHURCH OF THE NEW WORLD COMFORTER**
345 West Clay Street
Stockton, California 95206

**VENUS RESEARCH**
P.O. Box 6
San Lorenzo, California 94580

**YUCCA VALLEY UFO CLUB**
P.O. Box 39
Yucca Valley, California 92284

### Colorado

**DENVER EXTRATERRESTRIAL RESEARCH GROUP (DERG)**
330 East 10th Avenue, Apt. 902
Denver, Colorado 80203

### District of Columbia

**COMMITTEE FOR THE SCIENTIFIC INVESTIGATION OF CLAIMS OF THE PARANORMAL (CSICP)—UFO SUBCOMMITTEE**
c/o Philip J. Klass
560 "N" Street S.W.
Washington, D.C. 20024

**NATIONAL INVESTIGATIONS COMMITTEE ON AERIAL PHENOMENA (NICAP)**
5012 Del Ray Avenue
Washington, D.C. 20014

### Florida

**MARK-AGE**
327 N.E. 20 Terrace
Miami, Florida 33137

NEW ATLANTEAN RESEARCH
SOCIETY
4280 68th Avenue North
Pinellas Park, Florida 33565

SOUTH EAST PARANORMAL
INFORMATION BUREAU (SEPIB)
1539 Kenwood Avenue South West
Winter Haven, Florida 33880

UFO IDENTIFICATION BUREAU
AND SCIENCE MUSEUM
(UFO/IB)
P.O. Box 9454
Winter Haven, Florida 33880

## Georgia

UFO BUREAU (NATIONAL UFO
COMMUNICATION NETWORK)
118 Main Street
Camilla, Georgia 31730

## Illinois

ANCIENT ASTRONAUT SOCIETY
1921 St. John's Avenue
Highland Park, Illinois 60068

CENTER FOR UFO STUDIES
(CUFOS)
1609 Sherman Avenue
Evanston, Illinois 66201

UFOCUS Research
c/o James R. Harris
Route 4, Lisa Lane
Mt. Carmel, Illinois 62863

## Indiana

FROGSTEIN'S FLYING SAUCER
MUSEUM
2140 North Pennsylvania Street
Indianapolis, Indiana 46202

INTERNATIONAL UFO REGISTRY
(IUFOR)
P.O. Box 3073
Munster, Indiana 46321

## Iowa

PRIVATE UFO INVESTIGATIONS
(PUFOI)
Route 1
Hazleton, Iowa 50641

## Kentucky

L/L RESEARCH
P.O. Box 5195
Louisville, Kentucky 40205

PARANORMAL RESEARCH
ORGANIZATION
219 Johnson Street
Ashland, Kentucky 41101

## Maryland

FLYING SAUCER INFORMATION
CENTER
7803 Ruanne Court
Pasadena, Maryland 21122

INTERNATIONAL FORTEAN
ORGANIZATION (INFO)
7317 Baltimore Avenue
College Park, Maryland 20740

MARYLAND CENTER FOR
INVESTIGATION OF
UNCONVENTIONAL
PHENOMENA (MARCEN)
Box 218
Kensington, Maryland 20795

UFO INFORMATION RETRIEVAL
CENTER
P.O. Box 57
Riderwood, Maryland 21139

## Massachusetts

NEW ENGLAND UFO STUDY GROUP
10 Peters Avenue
Malborough, Massachusetts 01752

## Missouri

INTERNATIONAL SOCIETY FOR
A COMPLETE EARTH (HOLLOW
EARTH SOCIETY)
c/o Tawani W. Shoush
RR 1, Box 63
Houston, Missouri 65483

## New Jersey

CELESTIAL INTERPRETORS OF
NAPPA (CION)
552 Estate Road
Maple Shade, New Jersey 08052

NATIONAL AERIAL AND PSYCHIC
PHENOMENA ASSOCIATION (NAPPA)
552 Estate Road
Maple Shade, New Jersey 08052

NATIONAL UFO CONFERENCE (NUFC
P.O. Box 163
Fort Lee, New Jersey 07024

PROJECT TO RESEARCH OBJECTS,
THEORIES, EXTRATERRESTRIALS
AND UNUSUAL SIGHTINGS (PROTEUS
274 Second Street
Elizabeth, New Jersey 07206

SOCIETY FOR THE
INVESTIGATION OF THE
UNEXPLAINED (SITU)
Box 265
Little Silver, New Jersey 07739

20TH CENTURY UFO BUREAU
756 Haddon Avenue
Collingswood, New Jersey 08108

VESTIGIA
RD2 Brookwood Road
Stanhope, New Jersey 07874

## New York

FLYING SAUCER NEWS CLUBS
OF AMERICA (FSNCA)
359 West 45th Street
New York, N.Y. 10036

INTERCONTINENTAL GALACTIC
SPACECRAFT (UFO) RESEARCH
AND ANALYTIC NETWORK
(ICUFON)
Apartment 4G, 35-40 75th Street
Jackson Heights, N.Y. 11372

NORTHEASTERN UFO
ORGANIZATION (NEUFO)
P.O. Box 233
North Tonawanda, N.Y. 14120

SCIENTIFIC BUREAU OF
INVESTIGATION (SBI)
23 Mac Arthur Avenue
Staten Island, N.Y. 10312

UFO INVESTIGATORS' LEAGUE
(UFOIL)
Suite 1306, 303 Fifth Avenue
New York, N.Y. 10016

## North Carolina

CAROLINA UFO NETWORK
315 Cedarwood Lane
Matthews, North Carolina 28105

TARHEEL UFO STUDY GROUP
P.O. Box 412
Rural Hall, North Carolina 27045

## Ohio

AERIAL PHENOMENON
CLIPPING AND INFORMATION
CENTER (APCIC)
P.O. Box 9073
Cleveland, Ohio 44137

CLEVELAND UFOLOGY
PROJECT
11309 Pleasant Valley
Parma, Ohio 44130

CLEVELAND UFO SOCIETY
537 Juneway Drive
Bay Village, Ohio 44140

FLYING SAUCER
INVESTIGATING COMMITTEE
748 Alameda Avenue
Cuyahoga Falls, Ohio 44221

NORTHERN OHIO UFO GROUP
3403 West 119th Street
Cleveland, Ohio 44111

OHIO UFO INVESTIGATORS'
LEAGUE (OUFOIL)
P.O. Box 436
Fairfield, Ohio 45014

TRI-COUNTY UFO STUDY GROUP
(NORTH EAST OHIO REGION)
P.O. Box 2
Sebring, Ohio 44672

UFO INFORMATION CENTER
(UFOIC)
4256 Springboro Road
Lebanon, Ohio 45036

UFO INFORMATION NETWORK
(UFOIN) and PAGE RESEARCH
LIBRARY (PRL)
P.O. Box 5012
Rome, Ohio 44085

YE ANCIENT AND SECRET
ORDER FOR QUIET BIRDMEN
1900 Euclid Avenue
Cleveland, Ohio 44115

## Oklahoma

INTERNATIONAL UFO
BUREAU (IUFOB)
P.O. Box 441
Edmond, Oklahoma 73034

RAINBOW ARCK RESEARCH
CENTRE
Route 9, Box 12–A
Midwest City, Oklahoma 73130

## Oregon

UNIVERSARIUN FOUNDATION
3620 S.E. 84th Avenue
Portland, Oregon 97266

## Pennsylvania

DEL VAL UFO
948 Almshouse Road
Ivyland, Pennsylvania 19874

## South Carolina

GREENVILLE UFO STUDY
GROUP
506 Central Avenue
Mauldin, South Carolina 29662

## Texas

ASSOCIATION FOR THE
UNDERSTANDING OF MAN (AUM)
P.O. Box 5310
Austin, Texas 78763

MUTUAL UFO NETWORK
(MUFON)
103 Oldtowne Road
Seguin, Texas 78155

PROJECT STARLIGHT
INTERNATIONAL (PSI)
P.O. Box 5310
Austin, Texas 78763

PROJECT STIGMA
P.O. Box 1094
Paris, Texas 75460

PROJECT VISIT (VEHICLE
INTERNAL SYSTEMS
INVESTIGATIVE TEAM)
P.O. Box 877
Friendswood, Texas 77546

TEXAS SCIENTIFIC RESEARCH
CENTER FOR UFO STUDIES
1002 Edmonds Land
Lewisville, Texas 75067

## Washington

NEW AGE FOUNDATION (NAF)
Cedar Park
Ashford, Washington 98304

# FOREIGN

## Argentina

CENTRO DE ESTUDIOS DE
FENÓMENOS AEREOS
INUSUALES (CEFAI)
Casilla de Correo No. 9
Suc. 26 (1426)
Buenos Aires

CENTRO DE INVESTIGACION
SOBRE FENÓMENOS DE
INTELIGENCIA
EXTRATERRESTRE (CIFEX)
Casilla de Correo 4046
1000 Buenos Aires

FEDERACION PANAMERICANA
DE ESTUDIOS CIENTIFICO-
FILOSOFICO DE VIDA
EXTRATERRESTRE
Juncal 2061–1–13
Buenos Aires

ORGANIZATION NACIONAL
INVESTIGATORA DE
FENÓMENOS ESPECIALES
(ONIFE)
Casilla de Correo 35
Sucursal 29 (B)
1429 Buenos Aires

## Australia

AUSTRALIAN INTERNATIONAL
UFO FLYING SAUCER
RESEARCH
Box 2004 G.P.O.
Adelaide, South Australia 5023

CENTRE FOR UFO STUDIES—
AUSTRALIAN CO-ORDINATION
SECTION (ACOS)
P.O. Box 546
Gosford, New South Wales 2250

PERTH UFO RESEARCH GROUP
P.O. Box 92
North Perth 6006

PHENOMENA RESEARCH (WEST AUSTRALIA)
P.O. Box 261
Bunbury, West Australia 6230

UFO RESEARCH (UFOR)—FAR NORTH QUEENSLAND (FNQ)
P.O. Box 1585
Cairns, Queensland 4870

UFO RESEARCH (UFOR)—NEW SOUTH WALES (NSW)
P.O. Box 6
Lane Cove, New South Wales 2066

UFO RESEARCH (UFOR)—NORTHERN TERRITORY (NT)
44 Carpentier Crescent
Wagaman, Darwin,
Northern Territory

UFO RESEARCH (UFOR)—QUEENSLAND (QLD)
P.O. Box 111
North Quay, Queensland 4000

UFO RESEARCH (UFOR)—SOUTH AUSTRALIA (SA)
2A Castle Avenue
Prospect, South Australia

UFO RESEARCH (UFOR)—WESTERN AUSTRALIA (WA)
84 Acton Avenue
Riverdale, Western Australia 6103

UNEXPLAINED PHENOMENA INVESTIGATION BUREAU (UPIB)
74 Cudliss Street
Eaton, Western Australia
or
8 Doolan Street
Bunbury, Western Australia

UNIVERSAL BROTHERHOOD
P.O. Box 21
Balingup, Western Australia 6253

VICTORIAN UFO RESEARCH SOCIETY (VUFORS)
P.O. Box 43
Moorabbin, Victoria 3189

## Belgium

CENTRE INTERNATIONAL D'UFOLOGIE (CIU)
80 rue de la Haie
1301 Bierge

DETECTOR SIDIP (SOCIÉTÉ INTERNATIONALE DE DÉVELOPPEMENT DES IDÉES POUR LE PROGRÈS)
Résidence Amboise, Domaine de

Mont St. Alban
Boulevard Emile Bockstael 431
1020 Brussels

GROUPEMENT POUR L'ÉTUDE DES SCIENCES D'AVANTE-GARDE (GESAG)
Leopold I laan 141
B-8000 Bruges

SOCIÉTÉ BELGE D'ÉTUDE DES PHÉNOMÈNES SPATIAUX (SOBEPS)
Avenue Paul Janson 74
B–1070 Brussels

STUDIEGROEP PREGRESSIEVE WETENSCHAPPEN (SPW)
Jasmijnstraat 67
B–9000 Gent

UROS
Habrouckstraat 1
3841 Kerniel

## Brazil

CENTRO DE ESTUDOS UFOLOGICOS (CEU)
Caixa Postal 689
CEP 60,000, Fortaleza, Ceara

CENTRO DE INVESTIGACAO CIVIL DOS OBJECTOS AEROS NAO IDENTIFICADOS (CICOANI)
Caixa Postal 1675
Belo Horizonte, M.G.

CENTRO NACIONAL DE ESTUDOS UFOLOGICOS (CENEU)
SQS, 104 Ble., Apto. 305
Brasilia

GRUPO AGARTHA DE PESQUISAS (GAP)
Caixa Postal No. 8414
Curitiba Paraná, C.E.P. 80.000

GRUPO DE ESTUDOS E PESQUISAS ULTRATERRENOS "MARCUS DE ORION"
Caixa Postal No. 83
83.100 Sao Jose do Rio Preto, S.P.

GRUPO DE PESQUISAS AEROESPACIAIS ZENITH (G-PAZ)
Caixa Postal No. 4108
Agencia Alameda
40.000 Salvador, Bahia

GRUPO PELOTENSE DE ESTUDOS E PESQUISAS DE PARAPSICOLOGIA, PSICOTRONICA E OBJECTOS

AEREOS NAO IDENTIFICADO (PPOANI)
Rua Benjamin Constant 1548
Caixa Postal 289
Pelotas—RS. 96.100

IRMANDADE COSMICA CRUZ DO SUL—GRUPO DE PESQUISA E DIVULGACAO SOBRE NAVEXOLOGIA
Caixa Postal 72
94.000 Gravatay
Rio Grande do Sul

SOCIEDADE BRASILIERA DE ESTUDOS SOBRE DISCOS VOADORES (SBEDV)
Caixa Postal No. 16.017
Correio do Largo do Machado, Rio de Janeiro

SOCIEDADE PELOTENSE DE INVESTIGACAO E PESQUISA DE DISCOS VOADORES (SPIPDV)
Rua Marcilio Dias 1566
96.100 Pelotas
Rio Grande do Sul

## Canada

CAMBRIDGE UFO RESEARCH GROUP
362 Kitchener Road
Cambridge, Ontario N3H 1A6

CANADIAN UFO RESEARCH NETWORK (CUFORN)
P.O. Box 15, Station A
Willowdale, Ontario M2N 5S7

EDMONTON UFO SOCIETY
8008 129A Avenue
Edmonton, Alberta T5C 1XZ

FLYING SAUCER—HOLLOW EARTH SOCIETY
27 Kingsmount Park Road
Toronto, Ontario M4L 3L2

PROJECT SUM (SOLVING UFO MYSTERIES) UFO RESEARCH
21 Prince Charles Drive
St. Catharines, Ontario, L2N 3Y4

RES BUREAUX
Box 1598
Kingston, Ontario, K7L 5C8

SAMISDAT
206 Carlton Street
Toronto, Ontario, M5A 2L1

UFO CANADA
P.O. Box 145
Chomeday, Laval, Quebec,
H7W 4K2

UFO QUEBEC
P.O. Box 53
Dollard-des-Ormeaux
Quebec, H9G 2H5

U.P. (UNIDENTIFIED
PHENOMENA) INVESTIGATIONS
RESEARCH
P.O. Box 455
Streetsville, Mississauga
Ontario L5M 2B9

## Colombia

FRATERNIDAD UNIVERSAL
VIAJEROS DEL ESPACIO (FUVE)
Apartado Aereo 4485
Cali

## Denmark

DANSK UFO CENTER
P.O. Box 7938
DK–9210 Aalborg SØ

FRIT UFO STUDIUM (FUFOS)
Haraldsgade 41
DK 2200 Copenhagen N

SKANDINAVISK UFO
INFORMATION (SUFOI)
Postbox 6
DK 2820 Gentofte

## Finland

SUOMEN UFOTUTKIJAT RY
(UFO Research of Finland)
17950 Kylämä

## France

AMATEURS D'INSOLITE, LES
Boîte Postale 186
71007 Macon

ASSOCIATION DE RECHERCHE
SUR LES PHÉNOMÈNES
INEXPLIQUÉS (ARPI)
13 rue Fortune Jourdan
13003 Marseille

ASSOCIATION DES AMIS DE
MARC THIROUIN (AAMT)
29 rue Berthelot
26000 Valence

ASSOCIATION D'ÉTUDE SUR
SOUCOUPES VOLANTES (AESV)
40 rue Mignet
13100 Aix en Provence

ASSOCIATION DIJONNAISE DE
RECHERCHES UFOLOGIQUES
ET PARAPSYCHOLOGIQUES
(ADRUP)
11 Le Breiul Orgeux
21490 Ruffey-les-Echirey

ASSOCATION POUR LA
DÉTECTION ET L'ÉTUDE DES
PHÉNOMÈNES SPATIAUX (ADEPS)
12 Avenue de Maréchal Joffre
06160 Juan les Pins

CENTRE D'ÉTUDES ET DE
RECHERCHES DES
PHÉNOMÈNES INEXPLIQUÉS
(CERPI)
51 rue Saint Pallais
17100 Saintes

CERCLE DE RECHERCHE
UFOLOGIQUE NIÇOIS (CRUN)
420 Avenue de Pessicart
06100 Nice

CERCLE D'ÉTUDE DES
MYSTÉRIEUX OBJECTS
CÉLESTES ET DES PHÉNOMÈNES
INCONNUS (CEMOCPI)
19 rue Massenet
42270 St. Priest en Jarez

CERCLE DUNQERQUOIS DE
RECHERCHES UFOLOGIQUES
(CDRU)
57 rue de Normandie Coudekerque
Branche 59 210

CERCLE FRANÇAIS DE
RECHERCHES UFOLOGIQUES
(CFRU)
Boîte Postale 1
57601 Forbach-Cédex

COMITÉ SAVOYARD D'ÉTUDES
ET DE RECHERCHES
UFOLOGIQUES (CSERU)
266 Quai Charles Ravet
73000 Chambery

E.P.I. GROUPE 03100 SECTION
FRANÇAISE DE QUEZACOLOGIE
13 rue Beaumarchais
03100 Montlucon

FRONT UFOLOGIE NOUVELLE
Boîte Postale 41
94202 Ivry Principal Cédex

GROUPE D'ÉTUDE DES OBJETS
SPATIAUX (GEOS)
St. Denis-les-Rebais
77510 Rebais

GROUPE D'ÉTUDES DES
PHÉNOMÈNES AÉROSPATIAUX
NON IDENTIFIÉS (GEPAN)
Centre Spatial de Toulouse
18 Avenue Edouard Belin
31055 Toulouse

GROUPE D'ÉTUDES DU
PHÉNOMÈNE OVNI (GEPO)
École Publique
Rue des Écoles
42470 Saint Symphorien de Lay

GROUPE D'ÉTUDES NORMAND
DES PHÉNOMÈNES INCONNUS
(GENPI)
18 rue Vauquelin
14300 Caen

GROUPE 5255
20 rue de la Maladière
52000 Chaumont

GROUPEMENT DE RECHERCHE
ET D'ÉTUDE DU PHÉNOMÈNE
OVNI (GREPO)
Maison de Jeunes et d'Education
Permanente
avenue Pablo Picasso
84700 Sorgues

GROUPEMENT DE
RECHERCHES ET
D'INFORMATIONS PHOCÉEN
SUR LES MYSTÉRIEUX OBJETS
CÉLESTES (GRIPHOM)
Boîte Postale 74
13368 Marseille Cédex 4

GROUPEMENT D'ÉTUDE DE
PHÉNOMÈNES AÉRIENS (GEPA)
69 rue de la Tombe-Issoire
75014 Paris

GROUPEMENT D'ÉTUDE
RÉGIONAL DES OVNI (GERO)
Boîte Postale 1263
25005 Besançon Cédex

GROUPEMENT D'ÉTUDES ET DE
RECHERCHES UFOLOGIQUES
(GERU)
21 rue Duguesclin
59100 Roubaix

GROUPEMENT LANGEADOIS DE
RECHERCHES UFOLOGIQUES
(GLRU)
c/o Gilbert Peyret
Résidence le Poitou
Bat. F., Vals près le Puy
43000 Le Puy

GROUPEMENT NORDISTE
D'ÉTUDES DES OVNI (GNEOVNI)
Route de Béthune
62136 Lestrem

GROUPE PALMOS
1 rue Parlier
34000 Montpellier

GROUPE PHOBOS
64 Bd. St. Michel
91150 Etampes

GROUPE PRIVÉ UFOLOGIQUE
NANCÉIEN (GPUN)
15 rue Guilbert de Pixérécourt
54000 Nancy

GROUPE TROYEN DE
RECHERCHE SUR LES OVNI
(GTR/OVNI)
2 rue Louis Ulbach
10000 Troyes

INSTITUT MONDIAL DES
SCIENCES AVANCÉES (IMSA)
Imp. Les Platanes No. 04
La Beaucaire, 83200 Toulon

SOCIÉTÉ PARISIENNE D'ÉTUDE
DES PHÉNOMÈNES SPATIAUX
ET ÉTRANGES (SPEPSE)
Domaine de Montval 6
allée Sisley
78160 Marly le Roi

SOCÍETÉ VAROISE D'ÉTUDE
DES PHÉNOMÈNES SPATIAUX
(SVEPS)
6 rue Paulin-Guérin
83000 Toulon

SOCÍETÉ VAUCLUSIENNE
D'ÉTUDE DES PHÉNOMÈNES
SPATIAUX (SOVEPS)
c/o Christian Langlume
"Les Confines," Entrée No. 4
84270 Vedène

VERONICA (VÉRIFICATION ET
ÉTUDES DES RAPPORTS SUR
LES OVNI POUR NÎMES ET LA
CONTRÉE AVOISINANTE)
1 rue Vauban
30000 Nîmes

## Germany

CENTRALES ERFURSCHUNGS-
BETZ AUSSERGEWOHNLICHER
PHENOMENE (CENAP)
D-6800 Mannheim-31
Eisenacher Weg 16, West Germany

DEUTSCHE UFO/IFO-
STUDIENGESELLSCHAFT
(DUIST)
Postfach 130 185
6200 Wiesbaden 13, West Germany

## Holland

NEDERLANDS ONDERZOEK
BUREAU VOOR UFO'S
(WERKGROEP NOBOVO)
Lange Akker 28
9982 HK Uithuizermeeden (Gr.)

## Indonesia

INDONESIAN UFO REGISTRY
P.O. Box 908, Chalan Piao
Saipan, Mariana Islands CM 96950

## Italy

CENTRO INTERNAZIONALE
RICERCHE E STUDI SUGLI UFO
(CIRS UFO)
Via G. Ratto 41/9
16157 Genoa

CENTRO STUDI E RICHERCHE
CTA 102
Sky Residence
Corso Francia 222
10093 Collegno

CENTRO TORINESE RICERCHE
UFOLOGICHE (CTRU)
Via Avigliana 38
10138 Turin

CENTRO UFOLOGICO
NAZIONALE (CUN)
Via Vignola 3
20136 Milan

COMITATO NAZIONALE
INDEPENDENTE PER LO
STUDIO DEI FENOMENI AEREI
ANOMALI (CNIFAA)
Via Rizzoli 4, sc. B
40125 Bologna

## Japan

JAPAN FLYING SAUCER
ASSOCIATION (JFSA)
2–10–18 Higashi-Gotanda
Shingawa-ku, Tokyo

JAPAN SPACE PHENOMENA
SOCIETY (JSPS)
5–2 Kamiyama-cho
Shibuya-ku, Tokyo

JAPAN SPACE UNIDENTIFIED
FLYING OBJECT SOCIETY
Kaguchi-ura, Takanabe-cho
Koyo-gun, Miyazaki Prefecture

JAPAN UFO RESEARCH
ASSOCIATION (JUFORA)
142–161 Ioroi Kande-cho
Tarumi-ku, Kobe

MODERN SPACE FLIGHT
ASSOCIATION (MSFA)
C.P.O. Box 910
Osaka

## Luxemburg

COMMISSION
LUXEMBOURGEOISE D'ÉTUDES
UFOLOGIQUES (CLEU)
Boîte Postale 9
Belvaux

## New Zealand

EARTH COLONIZATION
RESEARCH ASSOCIATION (ECRA)
39 Callender Terrace
Paraparaumu

NEW ZEALAND SCIENTIFIC
APPROACH TO COSMIC
UNDERSTANDING (NZSATCU OR
SATCU)
33 Dee Street
Timaru

TAURANGA UFO
INVESTIGATION GROUP
38 Brookfield Terrace
Otumoetai, Tauranga

## Norway

NORSK UFO CENTER
Box 2119
7001 Trondheim

PARAFYSISK STUDIESIRKEL
(Society for Paraphysical Research)
c/o W. Simonsen; H.J. Kogstads vei
10
N–2040 Kløfta

## Peru

INSTITUTO PERUANO DE
RELACIONES
INTERPLANETARIAS (IPRI)
Jr. Junin 402
Barranco, Lima 4

## Portugal

CENTRO DE ESTUDOS
ASTRONOMICOS E DE
FENÓMENOS INSOLITOS
(CEAFI)
Rua de Sa da Bandeira 331–3°, salas
31 e 32
4000 Porto

OVNIGRUPO 7
Apartado 1985
1006 Lisbon

## Puerto Rico

CENTRO DE ESTUDIO OBJETOS
VOLADORES NO
IDENTIFICADOS (CEOVNI)
Box 1626
San Juan 00903

## South Africa

INTERSTELLAR RESEARCH
GROUP
3 Cottage Place
420 Rifle Range Road
Towerby, Johannesburg 2190

## Spain

CENTRO DE ESTUDIOS
INTERPLANETARIOS (CEI)
Apartado de Correos 282
Barcelona

GRUPO A. A. OVNI
c/o Martin F. Villaran
5-bajo C
Portugalete (Vizcaya)

UNION NACIONAL DE ESTUDIOS
E INVESTIGACIONES CIENTIFICO
COSMOLOGICAS (UNEICC)
c/o Fray Rosendo Salvado 2
7°B Santiago de Compostela
La Coruna

## Sweden

ARBETSGRUPPEN FOR UFOLOGI
(AFU)
Box 5046, S-151 05
Södertalje 5

INTERNATIONAL URD
FOUNDATION
Box 454
S–101, 26 Stockholm

UFO/PSI STUDY GROUP
c/o Kent Yngve Johansson
Kljutbanegatan 23 An.b.
723 39 Västerås

UFO SVERIGE (UFO-SWEDEN)
P.O. Box 16
S–596 00 Skänninge

## Switzerland

GROUPEMENT UFOLOGIQUE
BULLOIS (GUB)
La Casa
1635 La Tour-de-Treme

## Tasmania

TASMANIAN UNIDENTIFIED
FLYING OBJECTS
INVESTIGATION CENTRE
(TUFOIC)
G.P.O. Box 1310N
Hobart 7001

## Turkey

SPACE PHENOMENA RESEARCH
GROUP
P.O. Box 1157
Istanbul

## United Kingdom

AETHERIUS SOCIETY
757 Fulham Road
London SW6 5UU

BORDERLINE SCIENCE
INVESTIGATION GROUP
3 Dunwich Way, Oulton Road
Lowestoft, Suffolk NR32 4R2

BRITISH FLYING SAUCER
BUREAU (BFSB)
71 Chedworth Road
Horfield, Bristol B27 9RX

BRITISH UFO RESEARCH
ASSOCIATION (BUFORA)
95 Taunton Road
London SW12 8PA

BRITISH UFO SOCIETY
47 Belsize Square
London NW3

CHRYSIS
48 Brittania Place
Dormanstown, Cleveland

CONTACT INTERNATIONAL
5/15 Kew Gardens Road
Richmond, Surrey

DIRECT INVESTIGATION GROUP
ON AERIAL PHENOMENA
(DIGAP)
24 Bent Fold Road
Unsworth, Bury BL9 8NG

ESSEX UFO STUDY GROUP
(EUFOSG)
16 Raydons Road
Dagenham, Essex

FEDERATION UFO RESEARCH
(FUFOR)
2 Acer Avenue
Crewe, Cheshire

INTERPLANETARY SPACE
TRAVEL RESEARCH
ASSOCIATION—UNITED
KINGDOM (ISTRA)
21 Hargwyne Street
Stockwell, London SW9 9RQ

IRISH UFO RESEARCH CENTRE
(IUFORC)
205 Dunluce Avenue
Belfast BT9 17AX, Northern Ireland

MANCHESTER AERIAL
PHENOMENA INVESTIGATION
TEAM (MAPIT)
92 Hillcrest Road
Offerton, Stockport, Cheshire
SK2 5SE

MANCHESTER UFO RESEARCH
ASSOCIATION (MUFORA)
597 Mauldeth Road West
Chorton, Manchester M21 2SH

NATIONAL UNIDENTIFIED
FLYING OBJECT RESEARCH
(NUFOR)
4 Queen Square
Brighton, BN1 3FD, Sussex

NORTHERN UFO NETWORK
(NUFON)
23 Sunningdale Drive
Irlam, Greater Manchester M30 6NJ

NOTTINGHAM UFO
INVESTIGATION SOCIETY
(NUFOIS)
443 Meadow Lane
Nottingham NG2 3GB

PARASEARCH
554 Goresbrook Road
Dagenham, Essex RM9 4XD

SKYSCAN GROUP PROJECT
59 Rydal Close
Warndon, Worcester

SOCIETY OF METAPHYSICIANS
Archers' Court
Stonestile Lane, The Ridge
Hastings, Sussex

SOUTHERN UFO NETWORK
(SUFON)
23 Sunningdale Drive
Irlam, Greater Manchester M30 6NJ

UFO CENTRE ALPHA TORQUAY
15A Market Street
Torquay, Devon

UFO INFO EXCHANGE LIBRARY
49 The Down
Trowbridge,
Wiltshire

UFO INTERNATIONAL (UFOI)
63 Malvern Drive
North Common, Warmley
Bristol, Avon

UFO INVESTIGATORS'
NETWORK (UFOIN)
23 Sunningdale Drive
Irlam, Greater Manchester M30 6NJ

UFO'S OVER JERSEY
ASSOCIATION (UFOJA)
Hautes Murailles, Samares Lane
St. Clement, Jersey, Channel Islands

UNIDENTIFIED FLYING OBJECTS
STUDIES, INVESTIGATION SERVICE
(UFOSIS)
71 Wentworth Way
Harborne, Birmingham B32 2UX

# publications dealing with ufos and related subjects

## UNITED STATES

**AETHERIUS SOCIETY
NEWSLETTER**
Aetherius Society
6202 Afton Place
Hollywood, California 90028

**AETHERIUS SOCIETY SPIRITUAL
HEALING BULLETIN**
Aetherius Society
6202 Afton Place
Hollywood, California 90028

**ANCIENT SKIES**
Ancient Astronaut Society
1921 St. John's Avenue
Highland Park, Illinois 60068

**APRO BULLETIN**
Aerial Phenomena Research
Organization
3910 E. Kleindale Road
Tucson, Arizona 85712

**THE AQUARIAN DAWN**
New Age Foundation
Cedar Park
Ashford, Washington 98304

**BELIEVE IT**
Maryland Center for Investigation of
Unconventional Phenomena
Box 218
Kensington, Maryland 20795

**BEYOND REALITY MAGAZINE**
BRM Publications, Inc.
303 West 42nd Street
New York, N.Y. 10036

**CAUSE AND EFFECT
NEWSLETTER**
Denver Extraterrestrial Research Group
330 East 10th Avenue, Apartment 902
Denver, Colorado 80203

**CONFIDENTIAL NEWSLETTER**
National Investigations Committee on
UFOs
Suite 207
7970 Woodman Avenue
Van Nuys, California 91402

**COSMIC BULLETIN**
George Adamski Foundation
314 Lado de Loma Drive
Vista, California 92083

**DEL VAL UFO NEWSLETTER**
Del Val UFO
948 Almshouse Road
Ivyland, Pennsylvania 18974

**EDEN BULLETIN**
Eden Press
Box 34
Careywood, Idaho 83809

**ENERGY HOTLINE**
Energy Unlimited
3562 Moore Street
Los Angeles, California 90066

**EXPLORING OTHER
DIMENSIONS**
David Graham Associates
Box 401
Decorah, Iowa 52101

**FATE**
Clark Publishing Company
500 Hyacinth Place
Highland Park, Illinois 60035

**FLYING SAUCER NEWS**
Flying Saucer News Clubs of America
359 West 45th Street
New York, N.Y. 10036

**FLYING SAUCERS INTERNATIONAL**
Amalgamated Flying Saucer Clubs of
America
P.O. Box 39
Yucca Valley, California 92284

**FROGSTEIN PAPERS**
Frogstein's Flying Saucer Museum
2140 North Pennsylvania Street
Indianapolis, Indiana 46202

**GRAY BARKER'S NEWSLETTER**
Saucerian Press
Box 2228
Clarksburg, West Virginia 26301

**GSW BULLETIN**
Ground Saucer Watch
13238 N. 7th Drive
Phoenix, Arizona 85029

**THE HEFLEY PSYCHIC REPORT**
U.S. Research, Incorporated
P.O. Box 7242
Burbank, California 91505

**ICHOR**
Venus Research
P.O. Box 6
San Lorenzo, California 94580

**IDEAL'S UFO MAGAZINE**
Ideal Publishing Corporation
2 Park Avenue
New York, N.Y. 10016

**INFO JOURNAL**
International Fortean Organization
7317 Baltimore Avenue
College Park, Maryland 20740

**THE INTELLIGENTS' REPORT**
New Age Foundation
Cedar Park, Ashford, Washington 98304

INTERNATIONAL UFO
REPORTER
Center for UFO Studies
1609 Sherman Avenue
Evanston, Illinois 66201

JOURNAL OF BORDERLAND
RESEARCH
Borderland Sciences Research
Foundation
P.O. Box 548
Vista, California 92083

MAIN
Mark-Age
327 N.E. 20 Terrace
Miami, Florida 33137

MUFON UFO JOURNAL
Mutual UFO Network
103 Oldtowne Road
Seguin, Texas 78155

THE MUNDO MONITOR
Flying Saucer Information Center
7803 Ruanne Court
Pasadena, Maryland 21122

THE NATIONAL ENQUIRER
600 S. East Coast Avenue
Lantana, Florida 33464

NEUFO NEWS
Northeastern UFO Organization
P.O. Box 233
North Tonawanda, New York 14120

THE NEW ATLANTEAN JOURNAL
New Atlantean Research Society
4280 68th Avenue North
Pinellas Park, Florida 33565

NUFOCN NEWS RELEASE
UFO Bureau (National UFO
Communication Network)
118 Main Street
Camilla, Georgia 31730

OFFICIAL UFO
Myron Fass
257 Park Avenue South
New York, N.Y. 10010

OMNI
Omni Publications International
909 Third Avenue
New York, N.Y. 10022

THE PANUFOLOGY TWELVES
Rainbow Arck Research Center
Route 9, Box 12–A
Midwest City, Oklahoma 73130

PURSUIT
Society for the Investigation of the
Unexplained
Box 265
Little Silver, New Jersey 07739

THE PROTEUS JOURNAL
Project to Research Objects,
Theories, Extraterrestrial and
Unusual Sightings
274 Second Street
Elizabeth, New Jersey 07206

SAUCER "XYZ"
James Moseley
P.O. Box 163
Fort Lee, New Jersey 07024

THE SBI REPORT
Scientific Bureau of Investigation
23 Mac Arthur Avenue
Staten Island, N.Y. 10312

SEARCH
Palmer Publications
Route 2, Box 36
Amherst, Wisconsin 54406

SECOND LOOK
William Bonner
10 East Street S.E.
Washington, D.C. 20003

THE SKEPTICAL INQUIRER
Committee for the Scientific
Investigation of Claims of the
Paranormal
560 "N" Street S.W.
Washington, D.C. 20024

STIGMATA
Project Stigma
P.O. Box 1094
Paris, Texas 75460

TARHEEL UFO STUDY GROUP
NEWS
Tarheel UFO Study Group
P.O. Box 412
Rural Hall, North Carolina 27045

TRUE FLYING SAUCER'S AND
UFOs QUARTERLY
Histrionics Publishing Company
21 West 26th Street
New York, N.Y. 10010

TWILIGHT ZONE FUNZINE
Janice M. Croy
Suite 206, 137 S. Pennsylvania
Denver, Colorado

UFOCUS
UFOCUS Research
c/o James R. Harris
Route 4, Lisa Lane
Mt. Carmel, Illinois 62863

THE UFO EXAMINER
Private UFO Investigations
Route 1
Hazelton, Iowa 50641

UFO INVESTIGATOR
National Investigations Committee on
Aerial Phenomena
5012 Del Ray Avenue
Washington, D.C. 20014

UFO OHIO
UFO Information Network
P.O. Box 5012
Rome, Ohio 44085

UFO REPORT
Gambi Publications
333 Johnson Avenue
Brooklyn, N.Y. 11206

UFO RESEARCH NEWSLETTER
UFO Research Associates
3122 North Beachwood Drive
Los Angeles, California 90068

UFO REVIEW
UFO News Service
Suite 1306, 303 Fifth Avenue
New York, N.Y. 10016

UFO SPACE NEWSCLIPPING
JOURNAL
P.O. Box 45673
Dallas, Texas 75245

UFO SPOTTERS' NEWSLETTER
UFO Investigators' League
Suite 1306, 303 Fifth Avenue
New York, N.Y. 10016

UFO UPDATE
BRM Publications, Inc.
303 West 42nd Street
New York, N.Y. 10036

UNARIUS LIGHT
Unarius Educational Foundation
P.O. Box 1042
El Cajon, California 92022

UNDERSTANDING
1606 Mountain View Drive
Alamogordo, New Mexico 88310

VESTIGIA NEWSLETTER
Vestigia
RD2 Brookwood Road
Stanhope, New Jersey 07874

THE VOICE OF UNIVERSARIUS
Universarium Foundation
3620 S.E. 84th Avenue
Portland, Oregon 97266

ZETETIC SCHOLAR
Marcello Truzzi
Department of Sociology
Eastern Michigan University
Ypsilanti, Michigan 48197

# FOREIGN

## Argentina

**CEFAI-BOLETIN**
Centro de Estudios de Fenómenos
Aereos Inusuales
Casilla de Correo No. 9
Suc. 26 (1426), Buenos Aires

**CIFEX BULLETIN**
Centro de Investigacion Sobre
Fenómenos de Inteligencia
Extraterrestre
Casilla de Correo 4046
1000 Buenos Aires

**CUARTA DIMENSION**
Organizacion Nacional Investigadora
de Fenómenos Especiales
Casilla de Correo 35
Sucursal 29(B), 1429 Buenos Aires

## Australia

**ACOS BULLETIN**
Centre for UFO Studies—Australian
Co-Ordination Section
P.O. Box 546
Gosford, New South Wales 2250

**AUSTRALIAN INTERNATIONAL
FLYING SAUCER RESEARCH
MAGAZINE**
Box 2004, G.P.O.
Adelaide, South Australia 5023

**AUSTRALIAN UFO REVIEW**
Victorian UFO Research Society
P.O. Box 43
Moorabbin, Victoria 3189

**PARANORMAL AND PSYCHIC
AUSTRALIAN**
Psychic Australian
P.O. Box 19
Spit Junction, 2088 New South Wales

**PERTH UFO RESEARCH GROUP
NEWSLETTER**
Perth UFO Research Group
P.O. Box 92
North Perth 6066

**UFO NEWSLETTER**
UFO Research—New South Wales
P.O. Box 6
Lane Cove, New South Wales 2066

**UFO RESEARCH (FNQ)
NEWSLETTER**
UFO Research—Far North
Queensland
P.O. Box 1585
Cairns, Queensland 4870

**VISIONS**
Jesiam Productions
5 Tennyson Street, Kew 3101
Melbourne, Victoria

## Brazil

**BOLETIM INFORMATIVO**
Irmandade Cosmica Cruz do Sul—
Grupo de Pesquisa e Divulgacio
Sobre Navexologia
Caixa Postal 72, 94.000 Gravatay
Rio Grande do Sul

**BOLETIM INFORMATIVO G-PAZ**
Grupo de Pesquisas Aerospacials
Zenith
Caixa Postal No. 4108
Agencia Alameda
40.000 Salvador, Bahia

**BOLETIM SBEDV**
Sociedade Brasiliera de Estudos
Sobre Discos Voadores
Caixa Postal No. 16.017
Correio do Largo do Machado
Rio de Janeiro

**BOLETIM SPIPDV**
Sociedade Pelotense de Investigacao
e Pesquisa de Discos Voadores
Rua Marcilio Dias 1566
96.1000 Pelotas
Rio Grande do Sul

**DELTA**
Grupo Pelotense de Estudos e
Pesquisas de Parapsicologia,
Psicotronica e Objectos Aereos Nao
Identificados
Rua Benjamin Constant 1548
Caixa Postal 289
Pelotas—RS. 96.100

**OVNI**
Luiz Rebouças Tôrres
A/C Book Center
Pca. Roosevelt 92
Loja-Centro
01303 São Paulo

**OVNI DOCUMENTO**
Hunos
Caixa Postal 363
Rio de Janeiro, RJ

**SATURNO**
Grupo de Estudos e Pesquisas
Ultraterrenos "Marcus de Orion"
Caixa Postal No. 83
83.100 São José do Rio Presto, S.P.

**UFONOTAS**
Centro de Estudos UFOlogicos
Caixa Postal 689, CEP 60,000
Fortaleza, Ceara

## Belgium

**BULLETIN DU GESAG—UFO
INFO**
Groupement pour l'Étude des
Sciences d'Avant-Garde
Leopold I laan 141
B–800 Bruges

**INFORESPACE**
Société Belge d'Étude des
Phénomènes Spatiaux
Avenue Paul Janson 74
B–1070 Brussels

**UFO-INFO**
Studiegroep Progressieve
Wetenschappen
Jasmijnstraat 67
B–9000 Gent

**UROS**
Uros
Habrouckstraat 1
3841 Kerniel

**VIGILANCE**
Detector SIDIP
Résidence Ambrose, Domaine de
Mont St. Alban
Boulevard Emile Bockstael 431
1020 Brussels

## Canada

**CAMBRIDGE UFO RESEARCH
GROUP NEWSLETTER**
Cambridge UFO Research Group
362 Kitchener Road
Cambridge, Ontario N3H 1A6

**CANADIAN UFO REPORT**
P.O. Box 758
Duncan, British Columbia V9L 3Y1

**CHAOS: THE REVIEW OF THE
DAMNED**
Res Bureaux
Box 1598, Kingston
Ontario K7L 5C8

**RES BUREAUX BULLETIN**
Res Bureaux
Box 1598, Kingston
Ontario K7L 5C8

**UFO CANADA**
UFO Canada
P.O. Box 145
Chomeday, Laval
Quebec H7W 4K2

**JOURNAL UFO (JUFO)**
U.P. (Unidentified Phenomena)
Investigations Research
P.O. Box 455
Streetsville, Mississauga
Ontario L5M 2B9

**UFO INFORMER**
Project SUM (Solving UFO
Mysteries) UFO Research
21 Prince Charles Drive
St. Catharines, Ontario L2N 3Y4

**UFOLK**
Gene Duplantier
S.S.&S. Publications
17 Shetland Street
Willowdale, Ontario M2M 1X5

**UFO UPDATE**
Tom Grey
573 North Service Road
402 Mississauga
Ontario L5A 1B6

**UFO QUEBEC**
UFO Quebec
P.O. Box 53
Dollard-des-Ormeaux
Quebec H9G 2H5

## Colombia

**CONTACTO SIDERAL**
Fraternidad Universal Viajeros del
Espacio
Apartado 4485
Cali

## Denmark

**UFO-ASPEKT**
Frit UFO Studium
Haraldsgade 41
DK 2200 Copenhagen

**UFO-NYT and SUFOI
NEWSLETTER**
Skandinavisk UFO Information
Postbox 6
DK 2820 Gentofte

**UFORALIA—TIDSSKRIFT FOR
UFO-LITTERATUR**
Danks UFO Center
P.O. Box 7938
DK-9210 Aalborg SØ

## Finland

**QUARTERLY REPORT**
Suomen UFOtutkijat Ry
(UFO Research of Finland)
17950 Kylämä

## France

**AESV**
Association d'Étude sur les
Soucoupes Volantes
40 rue Mignet
13100 Aix en Provence

**APPROCHE**
Société Vauclusienne d'Étude des
Phénomènes Spatiaux
c/o Christian Langlume
"Les Confines," Entrée No. 4
84270 Vedène
and/or
Société Varoise d'Étude des
Phénomènes Spatiaux
6 rue Paulin-Guerin
83000 Toulon

**CERPI**
Centre d'Études et de Recherches de
Phénomènes Inexpliqués
51 rue Saint Pallais
17100 Saintes

**ENTRE NOUS**
Groupe Troyen de Recherche sur les
OVNI
2 rue Louis Ulbach
1000 Troyes

**GEPO INFORMATIONS**
Groupe d'Étude du Phénomène
OVNI
École Publique
rue des Ecoles
42470 Saint Symphorien de Lay

**INFO OVNI**
E.P.I. Groupe 03100 Section
Française de Quezacologie
13 rue Beaumarchais
03100 Montlucon

**KRUPTOS**
Boîte Postale No. 114
65643 Caluire Cédex

**L'AUTRE MONDE**
23 rue Clauzel
75009 Paris

**LE PHÉNOMÈNE OVNI**
Comité Savoyard d'Études et de
Recherches UFOlogiques
266 Quai Charles Ravat
73000 Chambery

**LES EXTRATERRESTRES**
Groupe d'Études des Objets Spatiaux
St. Denis-les-Rebais
77510 Rebais

**LIMITES**
Groupement d'Étude Régional des
OVNI
B.P. 1263
25005 Besancon Cédex

**LUMIÈRES DANS LA NUIT**
(LDLN)
R. Veillith
"Les Pins"
43400 Le Chambron sur Lignon

**OVNI-INFO 34**
Groupe Palmos
1 rue Parlier
34000 Montpellier

**OVNI 43**
Groupement Langeadois de
Recherches UFOlogiques
c/o Gilbert Peyret
Résidence le Poitou
Bât. F., Vals près le Puy
43000 Le Puy

**PHÉNOMÈNES SPATIAUX**
Groupement d'Étude des
Phénomènes Aépariens
69 rue de la Tombe-Issoire
Paris 75014

**RÉALITÉ OU FICTION**
Groupe Privé UFOlogique Nancéien
15 rue Guilbert de Pixérécourt
54000 Nancy

**RECHERCHES UFOLOGIQUES**
Groupement Nordiste d'Études des
OVNI
Route de Béthune
62136 Lestrem

**UFO INFORMATIONS**
Association des Amis de Marc
Thirouin
29 rue Berthelot
2600 Valence

**UFOLOGIA**
Cercle Français de Recherches
UFOlogiques
Boîtes Postale 1
57601 Forbach-Cédex

UFOLOGIE CONTACT and
UFOLOGIE CONTACT SPECIAL
Société Parisienne d'Étude des
Phénomènes Spatiaux et Étranges
Domaine de Montval 6
allée Sisley
78160 Marly le Roi

VAUCLUSE UFOLOGIE
Groupement de Recherche et
d'Étude du Phénomène OVNI
Maison de Jeunes et d'Education
Permanente
avenue Pablo Picasso
84700 Sorgues

## Germany

CENAP REPORT
Centrales Erfurschungs-Netz
Aussergewohnlicher Phenomene
D–6800 Mannheim-31
Eisenacher Weg 16, West Germany

KONTAKT-BERICHTE
Postfach 200 432
D–40000 Düsseldorf 1, West
Germany

UFO-NACHRICHTEN
Deutsche UFO/IFO-
Studiengesellschaft
Postfach 130 185
6200 Wiesbaden 13, West Germany

## Holland

TIJDSCHRIFT VOOR UFOLOGIE
(TvU)
Nederlands Onderzoek Bureau voor
UFOs
(Werkgroep NOBOVO)
Lange Akker 28
9982 HL Uithuizermeeden (Gr.)

## Italy

CLYPEUS
Centro Studi Clypeologici
Casella Postale 604
10100 Torino

GIORNALE DEI MISTERI
Corrado Tedeschi Editore
Via Massaia 98
50134 Florence

GLI ARCANI
Armenia Editore s.r.l.
Viale Ca Granda 2
20162 Milan

NOTIZIARIO INFORMATIVO
INTERNO DEL CENTRO TORINESE
RICERCHE UFOLOGICHE
Centro Torinese Ricerche
UFOlogiche
Via Avagliana 38
10138 Turin

NOTIZIARIO UFO
Centro UFOlogico Nazionale
Via Vignola 3
20136 Milan

SELEZIONE UFO
Centro Internazionale Richerche e
Studi Sugli UFO
Via G. Ratto 41/9
16157 Genoa

UFO PHENOMENA,
INTERNATIONAL ANNUAL
REVIEW
Editecs Publishing House
Casella Postale 190
40100 Bologna

## Japan

JSPS's UFO INFORMATION
Japan Space Phenomena Society
5–2 Kamiyama-cho
Shibuya-ku, Tokyo

JUFORA
Japan UFO Research Association
142–161 Ioroi Kande-cho
Tarumi-ku, Kobe

MSFA UFO REPORT
Modern Space Flight Association
C.P.O. Box 910
Osaka

SORATOBU ENBAN KENYLA
Modern Space Flight Assocation
C.P.O. Box 910
Osaka

UFO
Japan Space Unidentified Flying
Object Society
Kaguchi-ura, Takanabe-cho
Koyu-gun, Miyazaki Prefecture

UNIDENTIFIED FLYING
OBJECTS—INFORMATION AND
STUDIES
Japan Space Phenomena Society
5–2 Kamiyama-cho
Shibuya-ku, Tokyo

## Luxembourg

LES CHRONICLES DE LA CLEU
Commission Luxembourgeoise
d'Études UFOlogiques
Boîte Postale 9
Belvaux

## Mexico

CONTACTOS EXTRATERRESTRES
Editorial Posada
José Maria Rico No. 204
Mexico 12, D.F.

## New Zealand

EARTH COLONIZATION REPORT
Earth Colonization Research Association
39 Callender Terrace
Paraparamu

XENOLOG
New Zealand Scientific Approach to
Cosmic Understanding
33 Dee Street
Timarus

## Peru

MAS ALLA
Instituto Peruano de Relaciones
Interplanetarias
Jr. Jutin 402
Barranco, Lima 4

## Norway

UFO FORUM and RAPPORTNYTT
Norsk UFO Center
Box 2119
7001 Trondheim

## Portugal

INSOLITO
Centro de Estudos Astronomicos e de
Fenómenos Insolitos
Rua de Sa da Bandeira 33–3°
Salas 31 e 32, 4000 Porto

NOSTRA
Nostradamus-Editorial de
Publicacoes, Lda.
Rua Ernesto da Silva 30
1500 Lisbon

OVNI
Ovnigrupo 7
Apartado 1985
1006 Lisbon

## Puerto Rico

CEOVNI BULLETIN
Centro de Estudio Objetos Voladores
No Identificados
Box 1626
San Juan, Puerto Rico 00903

## Spain

MUNDO DESCONOCIDO
Pje. José Llovera 5
Barcelona 21

NOTICAS OVNI
Grupo A.A. OVNI
c/o Martin F. Villaran
5-bajo C
Portugalete (Vizcaya)

OVNI
Union Nacional de Estudios e
Investigaciones Cientifico
Cosmologicas
c/o Fray Rosendo Salvado 2
7°B1 Santiago de Compostela
La Coruna

STENDEK
Centro de Estudios Interplanetarios
Apartado de Correos 282
Barcelona

## Sweden

NYHETSBLAD
Arbetsgrupen for UFOlogi
Box 5046
S–151 05 Södertalje

UFO-INFORMATION
UFO-Sverige
P.O. Box 16
S–59600 Skänninge

## Switzerland

GUB BULLETIN
Groupement UFOlogique Bullois
La Casa
1635 La Tour-de-Treme

## Tasmania

UFO TASMANIA
Tasmanian Unidentified Flying
Objects Investigation Centre
G.P.O. Box 1310N
Hobart 7001

## Turkey

EVRENDE ZEKI HAYAT
Space Phenomena Research Group
P.O. Box 1157
Istanbul

RUH VE MADDE
Space Phenomena Research Group
P.O. Box 1157
Istanbul

## United Kingdom

AD ASTRA
Rowlot, Ltd.
22 Offerton Road
London S.W.4

ALPHA
Pendulum Publishing Company, Ltd.
20 Regent Street
Fleet, Hants GU13 9NR

AWARENESS
Contact International
5/15 Kew Gardens Road
Richmond, Surrey

BUFORA JOURNAL
British UFO Research Association
95 Taunton Road
London SE12 8PA

CHRYSIS 79
Chrysis
48 Brittania Place
Dormanstown, Cleveland

COSMOLOGY NEWSLINK
CNK Press
37 The Close
Dunmow, Essex CM6 1EW

EARTHLINK
Essex UFO Study Group
16 Raydons Road
Dagenham, Essex

ENCOUNTERS
UFO Centre Alpha Torquay
15A Market Street
Torquay, Devon

FLYING SAUCER REVIEW
FSR Publications, Limited
West Malling
Maidstone, Kent

FORESIGHT
Foresight Organization
29 Beaufort Avenue
Hodge Hill, Birmingham B34 6AD

FORTEAN TIMES
R. J. M. Rickard
c/o FT-DTWAGE
9–12 St. Annes Court
London W1

INTERPLANETARY NEWS
Interplanetary Space Travel Research
Association—United Kingdom
21 Hargwyne Street
Stockwell, London SW9 9RQ

IRISH UFO NEWS
Irish UFO Research Centre
205 Dunluce Avenue
Belfast BT9 7AX, Northern Ireland

ISTRA JOURNAL
Interplanetary Space Travel Research
Association—United Kingdom
21 Hargwyne Street
Stockwell, London SW9 9RQ

LANTERN
Borderline Science Investigation
Group
3 Dunwich Way, Oulton Broad
Lowestaft, Suffolk NR32 4R2

THE LEY MAGAZINE—THE
MAGAZINE OF EARTH
MYSTERIES
Paul Devereux
P.O. Box 152
London N. 10

LINK
Manchester UFO Research
Association
597 Mauldeth Road West
Chorton, Manchester M21 2SH

METAPHYSICAL DIGEST
Society of Metaphysicians
Archers' Court
Stonestile Lane, The Ridge
Hastings, Sussex

METEMPIRICAL UFO BULLETIN
(MUFOB)
11 Beverly Road
New Malden, Surrey KT3 4AW

NORTHERN UFO NEWS (NUFON)
Northern UFO Network
23 Sunningdale Drive
Irlam, Greater Manchester M30 6NJ

NUFON (NORTHERN UFO NEWS)
Direct Investigation Group on Aerial
Phenomena
24 Bent Fold Drive
Unsworth, Bury BL9 8NG

NUFOR NEWSLETTER
National Unidentified Flying Object
Research
4 Queen Square
Brighton BN1 3FD, Sussex

PARASEARCH
Parasearch
554 Goresbrook Road
Dagenham, Essex RM9 4XD

PROTEUS
Unidentified Flying Objects Studies,
Investigation Service
71 Wentworth Way
Harborne, Birmingham B32 2UX

QUEST
UFO International
63 Malvern Drive
North Common, Warmsley
Bristol, Avon

SKYSCAN MAGAZINE
Skyscan Group Project
59 Rydal Close
Warndon

SKYWATCH
Manchester Aerial Phenomena
Investigation Team
92 Hillcrest Road
Offerton, Stockport
Cheshire SK2 5SE

SPACE DIGEST
Interplanetary Space Travel Research
Association—United Kingdom
21 Hargwyne Street
Stockwell, London SW9 9RQ

UFO INFO EXCHANGE LIBRARY
UFO Info Exchange Library
49 The Down
Trowbridge, Wiltshire

UFO INSIGHT
Federation UFO Research
2 Acer Avenue
Crewe, Cheshire

UFO NEWS BULLETIN
British Flying Saucer Bureau
71 Chedworth Road
Horfield, Bristol B27 9RX

UFO RESEARCH REVIEW
Nottingham UFO Investigation
Society
443 Meadow Lane
Nottingham NG2 3GB

UNEXPLAINED PHENOMENA
NEWS BULLETIN
D. J. Parry and Norfolk and National
UFO Investigation Society
132 Ramnoth Road
Wisbech, Cambridgeshire PE13 2JD

UNIDENTIFIED ENCOUNTERS
UFOs Over Jersey Association
Haute Murailles, Samares Lane
St. Clement, Jersey, Channel Islands

VIEWPOINT AQUARIUS
c/o Fish Tanks, Ltd.
49 Blandford Street
London W1 3AF

# newsclipping services photo archives booksellers

**NEWSCLIPPING SERVICES**

AERIAL PHENOMENA CLIPPING
AND INFORMATION CENTER
(APCIC)
P.O. Box 9073
Cleveland, Ohio 44137

UFO NEWSCLIPPING SERVICE
(UFONS)
Box 220, Route 1
Plumerville, Arizona 72127

**PHOTO ARCHIVES**

GROUND SAUCER WATCH (GSW)
13238 N. Seventh Drive
Phoenix, Arizona 85029

ICUFON ARCHIVES
Apartment 4G
35–40 75th Street
Jackson Heights, N.Y. 11372
U.S.A.

PARASEARCH
554 Goresbrook Road
Dagenham, Essex RM9 4XD
England

**BOOKSELLERS**

FLYING SAUCER BOOKSTORE
359 West 45th Street
New York, N.Y. 10036, U.S.A.

GLOBAL COMMUNICATIONS
303 Fifth Avenue, Suite 1306
New York, N.Y. 10016, U.S.A.

HEALTH RESEARCH
P.O. Box 70
Mokelumne Hill, California 95245,
U.S.A.

SAUCERIAN PRESS
Box 2228
Clarksburg, West Virginia 26301,
U.S.A.

SOURCEBOOK PROJECT
P.O. Box 107
Glen Arm, Maryland 21057, U.S.A.

S. S. & S. PUBLICATIONS
17 Shetland Street
Willowdale, Ontario
Canada M2M 1X5

STEBBING BOOK SERVICE
41 Terminus Drive
Belthinge
Herne Bay, Kent
England

UFO INFORMATION NETWORK
(UFOIN)
P.O. Box 5012
Rome, Ohio 44085, U.S.A.

VENTLA-VERLAG
Postfach 130 185
6200 Wiesbaden 13
West Germany

# bibliography— ufos and related subjects

Adamski, George, *Inside the Spaceships* (London, New York: Abelard-Schuman, 1955). Also published in paperback as *Inside the Flying Saucers* (New York: Warner Paperback Library, 1967; 1974).

——*Flying Saucers Farewell* (London, New York: Abelard-Schuman, 1961). Also published in paperback as *Behind the Flying Saucer Mystery* (New York: Warner Paperback Library, 1967; 1974).

Adler, Bill (ed.), *Letters to the Air Force on UFOs* (New York: Dell Publishing Company, 1967).

——(ed.), *Flying Saucers Have Arrived!* (New York: World Publishing Company, 1970).

Allen, Gordon, *Space-Craft From Beyond Three Dimensions* (New York: Exposition Press, 1959)

Allingham, Cedric, *Flying Saucers From Mars* (New York: British Book Centre, 1955).

Anderson, Carl Arthur, *Two Nights to Remember* (Los Angeles: New Age Publishing Company, 1956).

Angelucci, Orfeo, *The Secret of the Saucers* (Amherst/Wisconsin: Amherst Press, 1955).

——*Son of the Sun* (Los Angeles: De Vorss and Company, 1959).

Arnold, Kenneth, and Ray Palmer, *The Coming of the Saucers* (Amherst, Wisconsin: Amherst Press, 1952).

Ashtar, *In Days to Come* (Los Angeles: New Age Publishing Company, 1955).

Babcock, Edward J., and Timothy G. Beckley, *UFOs Around the World* (New York: Global Communications, 1978).

Baker, Robert M. L., *Investigations of Anomalistic Observational Phenomena* (El Segundo, California: the author, 1968).

Ballester-Olmos, Vicente-Juan, *A Catalogue of 200 Type-I UFO Events in Spain and Portugal* (Evanston, Illinois: Center for UFO Studies, 1976).

Bardens, Dennis, *Mysterious Worlds* (New York: Cowles Book Company, 1970).

Barker, Gray, *They Knew Too Much About Flying Saucers* (New York: University Books, 1956).

——*The Strange Case of Morris K. Jessup* (Clarksburg, West Virginia: Saucerian Press, 1963).

——*Gray Barker's Book of Saucers* (Clarksburg, West Virginia: Saucerian Press, 1965).

——*Gray Barker's Book of Adamski* (Clarksburg, West Virginia: Saucerian Press, 1967).

——*The Book of Spaceships in Their Relationship with Earth* (Los Angeles: DeVorss and Company, 1967).

——*The Silver Bridge* (Clarksburg, West Virginia: Saucerian Press, 1970).

——*Gray Barker at Giant Rock* (Clarksburg, West Virginia: Saucerian Press, 1974).

Barry, Bill, *Ultimate Encounter* (New York: Pocket Books, 1978).

Barton, Michael X., *Flying Saucer Revelations* (Los Angeles: Futura Press, 1957).

——*Venusian Secret Science* (Los Angeles: Futura Press, 1958).

——*D-Day Seers Speak* (Los Angeles: Futura Press, 1959).

——*Secrets of Higher Contact* (Los Angeles: Futura Press, 1959).

——*Venusian Health Magic* (Los Angeles: Futura Press, 1959).

——*Rainbow City and the Inner Earth People* (Los Angeles: Futura Press, 1960).

——*The Spacemasters Speak* (Los Angeles: Futura Press, 1960).

——*We Want You* (Los Angeles: Futura Press, 1960).

——*Your Part in the Great Plan* (Los Angeles: Futura Press, 1960).

——*Release Your Cosmic Power* (Los Angeles: Futura Press, 1961).

Baxter, John, and Thomas Atkins, *The Fire Came By* (Garden City, N.Y.: Doubleday and Company, 1976).

Beckley, Timothy Green, *Inside the Saucers* (New Brunswick, N.J.: Interplanetary News Service, 1962).

——*The Shaver Mystery and the Inner Earth Mystery* (Clarksburg, West Virginia: Saucerian Press, 1967).

——*UFOs Around the World* (New York: Global Communications, 1968).

——*The Book of Space Brothers* (Clarksburg, West Virginia: Science Research Publishing, 1969).

——*People of the Planet Clarion* (Clarksburg, West Virginia: Saucerian Press, 1970).

——*Men in Black—The Aliens Among Us* (New York: Global Communications, 1978).

Beer, Lionel, *An Introduction to Flying Saucers* (London: the author, 1964).

Beere, D. Chessman, *USP—A Physics for Flying Saucers: An Interpretation from Memory of a Communication from Atos Xetrov, Visitor* (Del Mar, California: USP Press, 1973).

Bender, Albert K., *Flying Saucers and the Three Men* (Clarksburg, West Virginia: Saucerian Press, 1962).

Berendzen, R., A. Montagu, P. Morrison, C. Sagan, K. Stendhal and G. Wald, *Life Beyond Earth and the Mind of Man* (Washington, D.C.: U.S. Government Printing Office, 1973).

Bergier, Jacques, *Extraterrestrial Visitations from Prehistoric Times to the Present* (Chicago: Henry Regnery Company, 1973).

Bergier, Jacques, and the Editors of INFO, *Extraterrestrial Intervention—The Evidence* (Chicago: Henry Regnery Company, 1974).

Bergrun, Norman R., *Tomorrow's Technology Today* (Campbell, California: Academy Press, 1972).

Berlitz, Charles, *The Mystery of Atlantis* (New York: Grosset and Dunlap, 1969).

———*Mysteries from Forgotten Worlds* (Garden City, N.Y.: Doubleday and Company, 1972).

———*The Bermuda Triangle* (Garden City, N.Y.: Doubleday and Company, 1974).

Bernard, Raymond, *The Hollow Earth* (Mokelumne Hill, California: Health Research, 1963).

———*Flying Saucers from the Earth's Interior* (Mokelumne Hill, California: Health Research, 1967).

Berry, Adrian, *The Next Ten Thousand Years* (New York: New American Library, 1975).

Bethurum, Truman, *Aboard a Flying Saucer* (Los Angeles: De Vorss and Company, 1954).

Binder, Otto O., *Flying Saucers Are Watching Us* (New York: Larchmont Books, 1968).

Bloecher, Ted, *Report on the UFO Wave of 1947* (Washington, D.C.: the author, 1967).

Blum, Ralph, with Judy Blum, *Beyond Earth—Man's Contact with UFOs* (New York: Bantam Books, 1974).

Blumrich, Josef F., *The Spaceships of Ezekiel* (New York: Bantam Books, 1974).

Bourdages, Joseph O., *Humanity and UFOs* (San Francisco: Anthelion Press, 1976).

Bowen, Charles (ed.), *The Humanoids* (Chicago: Henry Regnery Company, 1974).

Bradbury, Ray, Arthur C. Clarke, Bruce Murray, Carl Sagan and Walter Sullivan, *MARS and the Mind of Man* (New York: Harper and Row, 1973).

Brasington, Virginia F., *Flying Saucers in the Bible* (Clarksburg, West Virginia: Saucerian Press, 1963).

Bray, Arthur, *Science, the Public, and the UFO: A Philosophical Study* (Ottawa, Canada: Bray Book Service, 1967).

Briazack, Norman J., and Simon Mennick, *The UFO Guidebook* (Secaucus, N.J.: Citadel Press, 1978).

Buckle, Eileen, and Oliver Norman, *The Scoriton Mystery* (London: Neville Spearman, 1967).

Bull, F. Malcolm, *UFO Handbook* (London: British UFO Research Association, 1964).

Burt, Eugene H., *UFOs and Diamagnetism: Correlations of UFO and Scientific Observations* (New York: Exposition Press, 1970).

Byrne, Peter, *The Search For Bigfoot—Monster, Myth or Man?* (Washington, D.C.: Acropolis Books, 1975).

Cade, C. Maxwell, and Delphine Davis, *The Taming of the Thunderbolts* (London: Abelard-Schuman, 1969).

Calder, Nigel, *Spaceships of the Mind* (New York: Viking Press, 1978).

Campione, Michael J., *Reality of UFOs—Their Danger, Their Hope* (Cinnaminson, N.J.: the author, 1965).

———*UFOs—20th Century's Greatest Mystery* (Cinnaminson, N.J.: the author, 1968).

———*Anti-"Black" Magic* (Cinnaminson, N.J.: the author, 1973).

Cantril, H., *The Invasion from Mars* (Princeton, N.J.: Princeton University Press, 1940).

Carman, Oneal, *God Is Alive and Well* (New York: Exposition Press, 1976).

Cathie, Bruce, *Harmonic 33* (Wellington, New Zealand: A.H. and A. W. Reed, 1968).

———*Harmonic 288, the Pulse of the Universe* (Wellington, New Zealand: A. H. and A. W. Reed, 1977).

Cathie, Bruce, and Peter N. Temm, *Harmonic 695: The UFO and Anti-Gravity* (Wellington, New Zealand: A. H. and A. W. Reed, 1971).

———*UFOs and Anti-Gravity* (Harrisburg, Pennsylvania: Stackpole Books, 1977).

Catoe, Lynn E. (ed.), *UFOs and Related Subjects: An Annotated Bibliography* (Detroit: Gale Research, 1978).

Chambers, Howard V., *UFOs* (Los Angeles: Sherbourne Press, 1967).

———*UFOs for the Millions* (New York: Grosset, 1967).

Chapman, Robert, *UFO—Flying Saucers Over Britain* (England: Mayflower Books, 1969).

Charroux, Robert, *One Hundred Thousand Years of Man's Unknown History* (New York: Berkley Publishing Corporation, 1971).

———*The Mysterious Unknown* (London: Neville Spearman, 1972).

———*Forgotten Worlds* (New York: Walker and Company, 1973).

———*The Gods Unknown* (New York: Berkley Publishing Corporation, 1974).

———*Legacy of the Gods* (New York: Berkley Publishing Corporation, 1974).

———*Masters of the World* (New York: Berkley Publishing Corporation, 1974).

Chartrand, Robert L., and William F. Brown, *Facts About Unidentified Objects* (Washington, D.C.: Library of Congress, Legislative Reference Service, 1966).

Chase, Frank Martin, *Document 96* (Clarksburg, West Virginia: Saucerian Press, 1968).

Chatelain, Maurice, *Our Ancestors Came From Outer Space* (Garden City, N.Y.: Doubleday and Company, 1977).

Churchward, James, *The Children of Mu* (New York: Ives Washburn, 1931).

———*The Lost Continent of Mu* (New York: Ives Washburn, 1931).

Claflin-Chalton, Sandra, and Gordon J. MacDonald, *Sound and Light Phenomena—A Study of Historical and Modern Occurrences* (McLean, Virginia: Mitre Corporation, 1978).

Clark, Adrian V., *Cosmic Mysteries of the Universe* (West Nyack, N.Y.: Parker Publishing Company, 1968).

Clark, Jerome, and Loren Coleman, *The Unidentified: Notes*

*Toward Solving the UFO Mystery* (New York: Warner Paperback LIbrary, 1975).

Clarke, Arthur C., *Profiles of the Future* (New York: Harper and Row, 1963).

Cohen, Daniel, *Myths of the Space Age* (New York: Dodd, Mead and Company, 1967).

Collins, Jim, *Unidentified Flying Objects* (Milwaukee, Wisconsin: Raintree Publishers, 1977).

Condon, Edward U. (ed.), *Scientific Study of Unidentified Flying Objects* (New York: E.P. Dutton, 1969).

Constable, Trevor James, *They Live in the Sky* (Los Angeles: New Age Publishing Company, 1958).

——*The Cosmic Pulse of Life* (Santa Ana, California: Merlin Press, 1976).

——*Sky Creatures—Living UFOs* (New York: Pocket Book Library, 1978).

Cowles and UPI, *Flying Saucers: Twenty-One Years of UFOs* (New York: Cowles Education Corporation, 1967).

Cox, Donald W., *America's Explorers of Space, Including a Special Report on UFOs* (Maplewood, N.J.: Hammond, 1967).

Cramp, Leonard G., *Space, Gravity and the Flying Saucer* (New York: The British Book Center, 1955).

——*Piece for a Jigsaw* (Cowes, Isle of Wight, England: Somerton Publishing Company, 1966).

David, Jay, *The Flying Saucer Reader* (New York: New American Library, 1967).

——*Flying Saucers Have Arrived* (New York: World Publishing Company, 1970).

Davidson, Leon, *Flying Saucers: An Analysis of the Air Force Project Blue Book Special Report No. 14* (White Plains, N.Y.: Blue-Book Publishers, 1976).

Dean, John W., *Flying Saucers and the Scriptures* (New York: Vantage Press, 1964).

——*Flying Saucers Closeup* (Clarksburg, West Virginia: Gray Barker, 1969).

DeHerrera, John Andrew, *Etherean Invasion* (Los Alamitos, California: Hwong Publishing Company, 1978).

Dickhoff, Robert Ernst, *Agharta* (Boston: Bruce Humphries, 1951).

——*Homecoming of Martians* (Ghaziabad, India: Barti Association Publications, 1958).

Dione, R. L., *God Drives a Flying Saucer* (New York: Exposition Press, 1969).

Downing, Barry, *The Bible and Flying Saucers* (Philadelphia: J. B. Lippincott Company, 1967).

Drake, W. Raymond, *Gods or Spacemen?* (Amherst, Wisconsin: Amherst Press, 1964).

——*Gods and Spacemen in the Ancient East* (London: Neville Spearman, 1973).

——*Gods and Spacemen in the Ancient West* (New York: New American Library, 1974).

——*Gods and Spacemen of the Ancient Past* (New York: New American Library, 1974).

——*Gods and Spacemen throughout History* (Chicago: Henry Regnery Company, 1975).

Duplantier, Gene, *UFOLK* (Toronto: S.S.&S. Publications, 1978).

Dutta, Rex, *Flying Saucer Viewpoint* (London: Pelham Books, 1970).

——*Flying Saucer Message* (London: Pelham Books, 1972).

Earley, George W., *Unidentified Flying Objects: An Historical Perspective* (Bloomfield, Connecticut: the author, 1967).

——*Encounters With Aliens* (Los Angeles: Sherbourne Press, 1968).

Edelson, Edward, *Who Goes There?* (Garden City, N.Y.: Doubleday and Company, 1979).

Eden, Jerome, *Orgone Energy—The Answer to Atomic Suicide* (New York: Exposition Press, 1972).

——*Planet in Trouble—The UFO Assault on Earth* (New York: Exposition Press, 1973).

——*View from Earth: Talks to Students of Orgonomy* (Hicksville, N.Y.: Exposition Press, 1976).

Edwards, Frank, *My First Ten Million Sponsors* (New York: Ballantine Books, 1956).

——*Strangest of All* (Secaucus, N.J.: Citadel Press, 1956).

——*Stranger Than Science* (New York: Lyle Stuart, 1959).

——*Strange World* (New York: Lyle Stuart, 1964).

——*Flying Saucers—Serious Business* (New York: Lyle Stuart, 1966).

——*Flying Saucers Here and Now* (New York: Lyle Stuart, 1967).

Elkins, Don, and Carla Rueckert, *Secrets of the UFO* (Louisville, Kentucky: L/L Company, 1977).

Emenegger, Robert, *UFOs, Past, Present and Future* (New York: Ballantine Books, 1974).

Emerson, Willis George, *The Smoky God* (New York: Fieldcrest Publishing Company, 1964).

Erskine, Allen L., *Why Are They Watching Us?* (New York: Tower Books, 1967).

Farris, Joseph, *UFO Ho Ho* (New York: Popular Library, 1968).

Fawcett, George D., *Quarter Century Studies of UFOs in Florida, North Carolina and Tennessee* (Mount Airy, North Carolina: Pioneer Printing Company, 1975).

Festinger, Leon, Henry Riecken and Stanley Shackter, *When Prophecy Fails* (New York: Harper and Row, 1964).

Flammonde, Paris, *The Age of Flying Saucers* (New York: Hawthorn, 1971).

——*UFO Exist!* (New York: G. P. Putnam's Sons, 1976).

Flindt, Max, and Otto Binder, *Mankind: Child of the Stars* (New York: Fawcett Publications, 1974).

Foley, Bernice W., *Spaceships of the Ancients* (New York: Viking Press, 1978).

Ford, Brian J., *The Earth Watchers* (London: Leslie Frewin, 1973).

Fort, Charles, *The Book of the Damned* (New York: Boni and Liveright, 1919).

——*New Lands* (New York: Boni and Liveright, 1923).

——*Lo!* (New York: Claude H. Kendall, 1931).

——*Wild Talents* (New York: Claude H. Kendall, 1932).

Fowler, Raymond E., *UFOs—Interplanetary Visitors* (New York: Exposition Press, 1974).

——*The Andreasson Affair* (Englewood Cliffs, N.J.: Prentice-Hall, 1979).

Friedrich, George, *UFO or God?* (New York: Carlton Press, 1975).

Fry, Daniel W., *The White Sands Incident* (Los Angeles: New Age Publishing Company, 1954).

——*Alan's Message to Men of Earth* (Los Angeles: New Age Publishing Company, 1955).

——*Steps to the Stars* (Lakemont, Georgia: C.S.A. Publishing Company, 1956).

——*Atoms, Galaxies and Understanding* (El Monte, California: C.S.A. Publishing Company, 1960).

——*The Curve of Development* (Lakemont, California: C.S.A. Publishing Company, 1965).

————*The White Sands Incident* (Louisville, Kentucky: Best Books, 1966). This volume combines *The White Sands Incident* and *A-lan's Message to Man*.

Fuller, John G., *Incident at Exeter* (New York: G. P. Putnam's Sons, 1966).

————*The Interrupted Journey* (New York: Dial Press, 1966).

————(ed.), *Aliens in the Skies (The Scientific Rebuttal to the Condon Committee Report)* (New York: G. P. Putnam's Sons, 1969).

Gaddis, Vincent H., *Invisible Horizons* (Philadelphia: Chilton Company, 1965).

————*Mysterious Fires and Lights* (New York: David McKay Company, 1967).

Gardner, Marshall, *Journey to the Interior of the Earth* (Aurora, Illinois: the author, 1913).

Gardner, Martin, *In the Name of Science* (New York: G. P. Putnam's Sons, 1952).

Gatti, Art, *UFO: Encounters of a Fourth Kind* (New York: Zebra, 1978).

Geller, Uri, *Uri Geller: My Story* (New York: Praeger, 1975).

Gelman, Rita, and Marcia Seligson, *UFO Encounters* (Englewood Cliffs, N.J.: Scholastic Book Service, 1978).

Gibbons, Gavin, *They Rode in Spaceships* (London: Neville Spearman, 1957).

————*The Coming of the Spaceships* (New York: Citadel Press, 1958).

————*On Board the Flying Saucers* (New York: Warner Paperback Library, 1967).

Girvan, Ian Waveney, *Flying Saucers and Common Sense* (New York: Citadel Press, 1956).

Girvin, Calvin C., *The Great Accident* (Los Angeles: the author, 1957).

————*A Vital Message* (Los Angeles: the author, 1958).

————*The Night Has a Thousand Saucers* (El Monte, California: Understanding Publishing Company, 1958).

Glemser, Kurt, *UFOs: Menace from the Skies* (Kitchener, Ontario: Galaxy Press, 1972).

Goodwin, Harold, *The Science Book of Space Travel* (New York: Franklin Watts, 1954).

Grant, Robert, *UFOs Uncensored* (Hollywood, California: Facts Uncensored Publishing Company, 1966).

Green, Gabriel, and Warren Smith, *Let's Face the Facts About Flying Saucers* (New York: Popular Library, 1967).

Greenbank, Anthony, *Creatures from Outer Space* (New York and Evanston: Harper and Row, 1967).

Greenfield, Irvine A., *The UFO Report* (New York: Lancer Books, 1967).

Guieu, Jimmy, *Flying Saucers Come from Another World* (London: Hutchinson, 1956).

Gurney, Gene and Clare, *Unidentified Flying Objects* (London: Abelard-Schuman, 1970).

Haisell, David A., *The Missing Seven Hours* (Markham, Ontario: PaperJacks, 1978).

Hall, Richard H. (ed.), *The UFO Evidence* (Washington, D.C.: National Investigations Committee on Aerial Phenomena, 1964).

Hansen, L. Taylor, *He Walked the Americas* (Amherst, Wisconsin: Amherst Press, 1963).

Hauck, Dennis William, *The UFO Manual* (Munster, Indiana: International UFO Registry, 1976).

Heard, Gerald, *Is Another World Watching? The Riddle of the Flying Saucers* (New York: Bantam Books, 1953).

Hendry, Allan, *The UFO Handbook* (Garden City, N.Y.: Doubleday and Company, 1979).

Hervey, Michael, *UFOs over the Southern Hemisphere* (London: Robert Hale, 1975).

————*UFOs: The American Scene* (New York: St. Martin's Press, 1976).

Hewes, Hayden, *The Truth about Flying Saucers* (Edmond, Oklahoma: International UFO Bureau Press, 1966).

————*The Aliens* (Edmond, Oklahoma: International UFO Bureau Press, 1970).

————*The Intruders* (Edmond, Oklahoma: International UFO Bureau Press, 1970).

————*Earthprobe* (Edmond, Oklahoma: International UFO Bureau Press, 1973).

Hobana, Ion, and Julien Weverbergh, *UFOs from Behind the Iron Curtain* (New York: Bantam Books, 1975).

Hoffman, John, *What In Hell Is Going On?—The Coming of the Lord* (Los Angeles: the author, 1972).

Holiday, F. W., *Creatures from the Inner Sphere* (New York: Popular Library, 1974).

Howard, Dana, *Up Rainbow Hill* (Los Angeles: Llewellyn Publications, 1959).

Hubbard, Harold W., *Visitors from Lanulos: As Related by Woodrow W. Derenberger to the Author* (New York: Vantage Press, 1971).

Hudson, Jan, *Those Sexy Saucer People* (Canterbury, New Hampshire: Greenleaf Classics, 1967).

Hunter, Don, with René Dahinden, *Sasquatch* (New York: New American Library, 1975).

Hutin, Serge, *Alien Races and Fantastic Civilizations* (New York: Berkley Publishing Corporation, 1975).

Hynek, J. Allen, *The UFO Experience: A Scientific Inquiry* (Chicago: Henry Regnery Company, 1972).

————*The Hynek UFO Report* (New York: Dell Publishing Company, 1977).

Hynek, J. Allen, and Jacques Vallee, *The Edge of Reality* (Chicago: Henry Regnery Company, 1975).

Jacobs, David Michael, *The UFO Controversy in America* (Bloomington, Indiana: Indiana University Press, 1975).

Jessup, Morris, K., *The Case for the UFO* (New York: Citadel Press, 1955).

————*The UFO and the Bible* (New York: Citadel Press, 1956).

————*The UFO Annual* (New York: Citadel Press, 1956).

————*The Expanding Case for the UFO* (New York: Citadel Press, 1967).

Jung, Carl G., *Flying Saucers: A Modern Myth of Things Seen in the Sky* (New York: Harcourt, Brace and Company, 1959).

Keel, John A., *Why UFOs?* (New York: Manor Books, 1970).

————*Strange Creatures from Time and Space* (New York: Fawcett Publications, 1970).

————*UFOs: Operation Trojan Horse* (New York: G. P. Putnam's Sons, 1970).

————*Our Haunted Planet* (New York: Fawcett Publications, 1971).

————*The Mothman Prophecies* (New York: New American Library, 1976).

Kent, Malcolm, *The Terror Above Us* (New York: Tower Publications, 1967).

Kettlecamp, Larry, *Investigating UFOs* (New York: William Morrow, 1971).

Keyhoe, Donald E., *Flying Saucers Are Real* (New Yorl Fawcett Publications, 1950).

———*Flying Saucers from Outer Space* (New York: Henry Holt, 1953).

———*The Flying Saucer Conspiracy* (New York: Henry Holt, 1955).

———*Flying Saucers: Top Secret* (New York: G. P. Putnam's Sons, 1960).

———*Aliens from Space* (Garden City, N.Y.: Doubleday and Company, 1973).

Keyhoe, Donald E., and Gordon I.R. Lore (eds.), *Strange Effects from UFOs* (Washington, D.C.: National Investigations Committee on Aerial Phenomena, 1969).

Klass, Philip J., *UFOs Identified* (New York: Random House, 1968).

———*Secret Sentries in Space* (New York: Random House, 1971).

———*UFOs Explained* (New York: Random House, 1974).

Knaggs, Oliver, *Let the People Know* (Capetown, South Africa: Howard Timmins, 1966).

Knight, David C., *Those Mysterious UFOs: The Story of Unidentified Flying Objects* (New York: Parents Magazine Press, 1975).

Kolosimo, Peter, *Not of This World* (London: Souvenir Press, 1970).

Kraspedon, Dino, *My Contact with Flying Saucers* (New York: Citadel Press, 1959).

Kusche, Lawrence D., *The Bermuda Triangle Mystery—Solved* (New York: Harper and Row, 1975).

Landsburg, Alan and Sally, *In Search of Ancient Mysteries* (New York: Bantam Books, 1974).

Lang, Daniel, *From Hiroshima to the Moon* (New York: Simon and Schuster, 1959).

Layne, Meade, *The Coming of the Guardians* (Vista, California: Borderland Sciences Research Associates Foundation, 1964).

Lee, Gloria, *The Going and the Glory* (Auckland, New Zealand: Heralds of the New Age, 1966).

Leonard, George H., *Somebody Else Is on the Moon* (New York: David McKay Company, 1978).

Leonard, R. C., *Flying Saucers, Ancient Writings and the Bible* (New York: Exposition Press, 1969).

Le Poer Trench, Brinsley, *Flying Saucer Review's World Round-up of UFO Sightings and Events* (New York: Citadel Press, 1958).

———*Men Among Mankind* (London: Neville Spearman, 1962; and published as *Temple of the Stars* by Ballantine Books, New York, 1974).

———*Forgotten Heritage* (London: Neville Spearman, 1964).

———*The Flying Saucer Story* (London: Neville Spearman, 1966).

———*Operation Earth* (London: Neville Spearman, 1969).

———*The Eternal Subject* (London: Souvenir Press, 1973; and published as *Mysterious Visitors: The UFO Story* by Stein & Day, New York, 1973).

———*Secret of the Ages: UFOs from Inside the Earth* (London: Souvenir Press, 1974).

Leslie, Desmond, and George Adamski, *Flying Saucers Have Landed* (New York: British Book Center, 1953).

Lethbridge, T. C., *The Legends of the Sons of God* (London: Routledge and Kegan Paul, 1972).

Levitt, Zola, and John Weldon, *UFOs What on Earth Is Happening* (Montreal, Canada: Harvest House, 1975).

Ley, Willy, *For Your Information: On Earth and in the Sky* (Garden City, N.Y.: Doubleday and Company, 1967).

Lindsay, Gordon, *The Riddle of the Flying Saucers* (Dallas, Texas: The Voice of Healing Publishing Company, 1966).

Liss, Howard, *Unidentified Flying Objects* (New York: Hawthorn, 1968).

Loftin, Robert, *Spookville's Ghost Lights* (Tulsa, Oklahoma: the author, 1967).

———*Identified Flying Saucers* (New York: David McKay Company, 1968).

Lore, Gordon I. R., and Harold H. Deneault, *Mysteries of the Skies: UFOs in Perspective* (Englewood Cliffs, N.J.: Prentice-Hall, 1968).

Lorenzen, Coral E., *The Great Flying Saucer Hoax* (New York: William Fredericks Press, 1962).

———*Flying Saucers—The Startling Evidence of the Invasion from Outer Space* (New York: New American Library, 1970).

———*Shadow of the Unknown* (New York: New American Library, 1970).

Lorenzen, Coral and Jim, *Flying Saucer Occupants* (New York: New American Library, 1967).

———*UFOs over the Americas* (New York: New American Library, 1968).

———*UFOs—The Whole Story* (New York: New American Library, 1969).

———*Encounters with UFO Occupants* (New York: Berkley Publishing Corporation, 1976).

———*Abducted: Close Encounters of a Fourth Kind* (New York: Berkley Publishing Corporation, 1977).

Lunan, Duncan, *Mysterious Signals from Outer Space* (New York: Bantam Books, 1974).

Lusar, Rudolph, *German Weapons and Secret Weapons of World War II and Their Development* (New York: Philosophical Library, 1959).

Magor, John, *Our UFO Visitors* (Victoria, British Columbia: Hancock House, 1977).

Manas, John, *Flying Saucers and Spacemen* (New York: Pythagorean Society, 1962).

Maney, Charles A., and Richard Hall, *The Challenge of Unidentified Flying Objects* (Washington, D.C.: the authors, 1961).

Martin, Dan, *Seven Hours Aboard a Space Ship* (Detroit, Michigan: the author, 1959).

McCampbell, James M., *UFOlogy: New Insights from Science and Common Sense* (Millbrae, California: Celestial Arts, 1976).

McWane, Glen, and David Graham, *The New UFO Sightings* (New York: Warner Paperback Library, 1974).

Mendelssohn, Kurt, *The Riddle of the Pyramids* (New York: Praeger, 1974).

Menger, Howard, *From Outer Space to You* (Clarksburg, West Virginia: Saucerian Press, 1959).

Menzel, Donald H., *Flying Saucers* (Cambridge, Massachusetts: Harvard University Press, 1953).

Menzel, Donald H., and Lyle G. Boyd, *The World of Flying Saucers* (Garden City, N.Y.: Doubleday and Company, 1963).

Menzel, Donald H., and Ernest H. Taves, *The UFO Enigma* (Garden City, N.Y.: Doubleday and Company, 1977).

Michael, Cecil, *Roundtrip to Hell in a Flying Saucer* (New York: Vantage Press, 1955).

Michel, Aimé, *The Truth About Flying Saucers* (New York: Criterion Books, 1956).

———*Flying Saucers and the Straight Line Mystery* (New York: Criterion Books, 1958).

Michell, John, *The Flying Saucer Vision* (London: Sidgwick and Jackson, 1967).

———*The View Over Atlantis* (New York: Ballantine Books, 1969).

———*Secrets of the Stones* (New York: Penguin Books, 1977).

Miller, Max B., *Flying Saucers—Fact or Fiction* (Los Angeles: Trend Books, 1957).

Mimnaert, M., *The Nature of Light and Color in the Open Air* (New York: Dover Publications, 1954).

Misraki, Paul, *Les Extraterrestres* (Paris: Plon, 1962).

Mitchell, Helen and Betty, *We Met the Space People* (Clarksburg, West Virginia: Saucerian Press, 1967).

Mooney, James W., *Colony: Earth* (New York: Stein and Day, 1974).

Morrison, Philip, John Billingham and John Wolfe (eds.), *The Search For Extraterrestrial Intelligence (SETI)* (Washington, D.C.: NASA/U.S. Government Printing Office, 1977).

Morrison, Tony, with Gerald M. Hawkins, *Pathways to the Gods* (New York: Harper and Row, 1979).

Moseley, James E., *Jim Moseley's Book of Saucer News* (Clarksburg, West Virginia: Saucerian Press, 1967).

———*The Wright Field Story* (Clarksburg, West Virginia: Saucerian Press, 1971).

Moyer, Ernest P., *Day of Celestial Visitation* (Hicksville, N.Y.: Exposition Press, 1975).

Mundo, Laura, *Flying Saucers and the Father's Plan* (Clarksburg, West Virginia: Saucerian Press, 1956).

———*Pied Piper from Outer Space* (Los Angeles: Planetary Space Center Working Committee, 1964).

Nada-Yolanda, *Visitors from Other Planets* (Miami: Mark-Age MetaCenter, 1974).

National Investigations Committee on Aerial Phenomena, *UFOs: A New Look* (Washington, D.C.: National Investigations Committee on Aerial Phenomena, 1969).

Nebel, Long John, *Way Out World* (Englewood Cliffs, N.J.: Prentice-Hall, 1961).

New Dimensions Foundation, *Worlds Beyond* (Berkeley, California: And/Or Press, 1978).

Newman, Bernard, *The Flying Saucer* (New York: Macmillan Publishing Company, 1950).

Noorbergen, Rene, *The Soul Hustlers: An Exposé of the Hoax of Astrology, the UFO Mystery That Will Not Die and What the Psychics Don't Tell You* (Grand Rapids, Michigan: Zondervan, 1976).

Norkin, Israel, *Saucer Diary* (New York: Pageant, 1957).

Norman, Eric, *Gods and Devils from Outer Space* (New York: Lancer Books, 1970).

———*Gods, Demons and Space Chariots* (New York: Lancer Books, 1973).

Olsen, Thomas, M., *The Reference for Outstanding UFO Reports* (Riderwood, Maryland: UFO Information Retrieval Center, 1967).

Ostrander, Sheila, and Lynn Schroeder, *Psychic Discoveries Behind the Iron Curtain* (Englewood Cliffs, N.J.: Prentice-Hall, Inc., 1971).

Owens, Ted, *How to Contact Space People* (Clarksburg, West Virginia: Saucerian Press, 1968).

Palmer, Ray (ed.), *The Hidden World, No. A–1* (Amherst, Wisconsin: Palmer Publications, 1961).

Parry, Michael V., *Birth of a Movement* (London: Interplanetary Space Travel Research Association, 1969).

———*Teach Yourself UFOlogy* (London: Interplanetary Space Travel Research Association, 1970).

———*A–Z UFOlogy* (London: Interplanetary Space Travel Research Association, 1971).

Pelley, W. D., *Star Guests* (Noblesville, Indiana: Soulcraft Press, 1950).

Peters, Ted, *UFOs—God's Chariots? Flying Saucers in Politics, Science and Religion* (Atlanta, Georgia: John Knox Press, 1977).

Philips, Ted, *Physical Traces Associated with UFO Sightings: A Preliminary Catalog* (Northfield, Illinois: Center for UFO Studies, 1975).

Phillip, Brother, *Secret of the Andes* (Clarksburg, West Virginia, Saucerian Press, 1961).

Phylos, *A Dweller on Two Planets* (Alhambra, California: Borden Publishing Company, 1952).

Priest, Christopher, *The Space Machine* (New York: Harper and Row, 1977).

Prytz, John M., *UFOlogy and the UFO: An Anthology of Selected Papers on UFOs, Exobiology and Astronomy* (Kitchener, Ontario: Galaxy Press, 1970).

Puharich, Andrija, *Uri—A Journal of the Mystery of Uri Geller* (Garden City, N.Y.: Doubleday and Company, 1974).

Rampa, T. Lobsang, *My Visit to Venus* (Clarksburg, West Virginia: Saucerian Press, 1966).

Reeve, Bryant and Helen, *Flying Saucer Pilgrimage* (Amherst, Wisconsin: Amherst Press, 1957).

Rehn, K. Gosta, *UFOs Here and Now* (London: Abelard-Schuman, 1974).

Rich, E., *Flying Scared* (New York: Stein and Day, 1971).

Rovin, Jeff, *UFO Movie Quiz Book* (New York: New American Library, 1978).

Ruppelt, Edward J., *The Report on Unidentified Flying Objects* (Garden City, N.Y.: Doubleday and Company, 1956; revised edition, 1959).

Ryan, Peter, and Ludek Pesek, *UFOs and Other Worlds* (New York: Penguin Books, 1975).

Sable, Martin H., *UFO Guide* (Beverly Hills, California: Rainbow Press, 1967).

Sachs, Margaret, with Ernest Jahn, *Celestial Passengers—UFOs and Space Travel* (New York: Penguin Books, 1977).

Sagan, Carl, *The Cosmic Connection: An Extraterrestrial Perspective* (Garden City, N.Y.: Anchor Press, 1973).

———*Other Worlds* (New York: Bantam Books, 1975).

Sagan, Carl, *Viking and Mars* (New York: Random House, 1978).

———(ed.) *Communication with Extraterrestrial Intelligence* (Cambridge, Massachusetts: M.I.T. Press, 1973).

Sagan, Carl, and Thornton Page (eds.), *UFOs—A Scientific Debate* (Ithaca, N.Y.: Cornell University Press, 1972).

Salisbury, Frank B., *The Utah UFO Display: A Biologist's Report* (Old Greenwich, Connecticut: Devin-Adair Company, 1974).

Sanderson, Ivan T., *Abominable Snowmen* (Radnor, Pennsylvania: Chilton Book Company, 1961).

———*Uninvited Visitors: A Biologist Looks at UFOs* (New York: Cowles Education Corporation, 1967).

———*Invisible Residents* (New York: World Publishing Company, 1970).

———*Investigating the Unexplained* (Englewood Cliffs, N.J.: Prentice-Hall, 1972).

Santesson, Hans Stefan, *Flying Saucers in Fact and Fiction* (New York: Lancer Books, 1968).

Saunders, David, and R. Roger Harkins, *UFOs? Yes!* (New York: New American Library, 1968).

Schmidt, Reinhold O., *Edge of Tomorrow—The Reinhold O. Schmidt Story* (California, the author, 1963).

Science and Mechanics Editors, *Official Guide to UFOs* (New York: Ace Books, 1970).

Scully, Frank, *Behind the Flying Saucers* (New York: Henry Holt and Company, 1950).

Segraves, Kelly L., *Sons of God Return* (New York: Pyramid Books, 1975).

———*Great Flying Saucer Myth* (San Diego, California: Beta Books, 1977).

Sendy, Jean, *The Coming of the Gods* (New York: Berkley Publishing Corporation, 1970).

———*Those Gods Who Made Heaven and Earth* (New York: Berkley Publishing Corporation, 1972).

———*The Moon: Outpost of the Gods* (New York: Berkley Publishing Corporation, 1975).

Shaver, Richard, and Ray Palmer, *The Secret World* (Amherst, Wisconsin: Amherst Press, 1973).

Shklovski, I. S., and Carl Sagan, *Intelligent Life in the Universe* (San Francisco: Holden-Day, 1966).

Shuttlewood, Arthur, *Warminster Mystery* (London: Neville Spearman, 1967).

———*Warnings from Flying Friends* (Warminster, England: Portway, 1968).

———*UFOs—Key to a New Age* (New York: Regency Press, 1971).

Smith, Marcia S., *Extraterrestrial Intelligence and Unidentified Flying Objects: A Selected, Annotated Bibliography* (Washington, D.C.: Library of Congress, Congressional Research Service, 1976).

———*The UFO Enigma* (Washington, D.C.: Library of Congress, Congressional Research Service, 1976).

Soule, Gardner, *UFOs and IFOs: A Factual Report on F ing Saucers* (New York: G. P. Putnam's Sons, 1967).

Spence, Louis, *An Encyclopedia of Occultism* (New Hyde Park, N.Y.: University Books, 1960).

Spencer, John Wallace, *Limbo of the Lost* (New York: Bantam Books, 1973).

———*No Earthly Explanation* (Springfield, Massachusetts: Phillips Publishing Company, 1974).

Stanford, Ray, *Socorro "Saucer" in a Pentagon Pantry* (Austin, Texas: Blueapple Books, 1976). Revised and expanded edition published as *Socorro Saucer* (London: Fontana, 1978).

Stanton, Jerome L., *Flying Saucers: Hoax or Reality?* (New York: Belmont Books, 1966).

Stanway, R. H., and A. R. Pace, *Flying Saucers* (Stoke-on-Trent, England: New Chapel Observatory, 1968).

Steiger, Brad, *Strangers from the Skies* (New York: Award Books, 1966).

———*Strange Guests* (New York: Ace Books, 1966).

———*The Unknown* (New York: Popular Library, 1966).

———*Atlantis Rising* (New York: Dell Publishing Company, 1973).

———*Mysteries of Time and Space* (Englewood Cliffs, N.J.: Prentice-Hall, 1974).

———*Gods of Aquarius: UFOs and the Transformation of Man* (New York and London: Harcourt, Brace, Jovanovich, 1976).

———(ed.), *Project Blue Book* (New York: Ballantine Books, 1976).

———*Alien Meetings* (New York: Ace Books, 1978).

Steiger, Brad, and Hayden Hewes (eds.), *UFO Missionaries Extraordinary* (New York: Pocket Books, 1976).

Steiger, Brad, and John W. White (eds.), *Other Worlds, Other Universes: Playing the Reality Game* (Garden City, N.Y.: Doubleday and Company, 1975).

Steiger, Brad, and Joan Whritenour, *New UFO Breakthrough* (New York: Award Books, 1968).

———*The Allende Letters* (New York: Award Books, 1968).

Stemman, Roy, *Visitors From Outer Space* (Garden City, N.Y.: Doubleday and Company, 1976).

Stonely, Jack, with A. T. Lawton, *Is Anyone Out There?* (New York: Warner Paperback Library, 1974).

Story, Ronald, *The Space Gods Revealed: A Close Look at the Theories of Erich von Däniken* (New York: Harper and Row, 1976).

———*Visitors from Beyond?* (London: New English Library, 1979).

Stranges, Frank E., *Flying Saucerama* (New York: Vantage Press, 1959).

———*My Friend from Beyond Earth* (Kitchener, Ontario: Galaxy Press, 1972).

———*The Stranger at the Pentagon* (New York: Vantage Press, 1977).

Strentz, Herbert J., *A Survey of Press Coverage of Unidentified Flying Objects, 1947–1973* (Evanston, Illinois: Ph.D. Thesis, Journalism Department, Northwestern University, 1970).

Stringfield, Leonard H., *Inside Saucer Post, 3–0 Blue* (Cincinnati, Ohio: the author, 1957).

———*Situation Red: The UFO Siege* (Garden City, N.Y.: Doubleday and Company, 1977).

Stuart, John, *UFO Warning* (Clarksburg, West Virginia: Saucerian Press, 1963).

Sullivan, Walter, *We Are Not Alone* (New York: McGraw-Hill, 1964).

Sumner, F. W., *The Coming Golden Age* (Los Angeles: New Age Publishing Company, 1957).

Tacker, Lawrence J., *Flying Saucers and the U.S. Air Force* (Princeton, N.J.: D. Van Nostrand Company, 1960).

Temple, Robert K. G., *The Sirius Mystery* (New York: St. Martin's Press, 1976).

Thiering, Barry, and Edgar Castle (eds.), *Some Trust in Chariots* (New York: Popular Library, 1972).

Thomas, Paul, *Flying Saucers through the Ages* (Hackensack, N.J.: Wehman Brothers, 1965).

Tomas, Andrew, *We Are Not the First* (New York: G. P. Putnam's Sons, 1971).

Troxell, Hope, *The Wisdom of the Universe* (Pasadena, California: Jensen Printing, 1963).

———*From Matter to Light* (Pasadena, California: Jensen Printing, 1968).

———*The Mohada Teachings* (Pasadena, California: Jensen Printing, 1969).

———*The Mystery of the Spirit of Truth* (Bishop, California: Chatfaut Press, 1974).

———*The Winged Life of Cosmos: Testimony of Sister Hope* (Bishop, California: Chatfaut Press, 1974).

Twitchell, Cleve, *The UFO Saga* (Lakemont, Georgia: CSA Press, 1966).

Tyler, Steven, *Are the Invaders Coming?* (New York: Tower Publications, 1968).

Unger, George, *Flying Saucers—Physical and Spiritual Aspects* (East Grinstead, England: New Knowledge Books, 1971).

U.S. Congress, House, Committee on Armed Services, Unidentified Flying Objects, Hearings, 89th Congress, 2nd Session, April 5, 1966 (Washington, D.C.: U.S. Government Printing Office, 1966).

U.S. Congress, House, Committee on Science and Astronautics, Symposium on Unidentified Flying Objects, Hearings, 90th Congress, 2nd Session, July 29, 1968 (Washington, D.C.: U.S. Government Printing Office, 1968).

Vaeth, J. Gordon, *200 Miles Up—The Conquest of the Upper Air* (New York: Ronald Press Company, 1951).

Vallee, Jacques, *Anatomy of a Phenomenon: Unidentified Objects in Space—A Scientific Appraisal* (Chicago: Henry Regnery Company, 1965).

———*Passport to Magonia* (Chicago: Henry Regnery Company, 1969).

———*The Invisible College* (New York: E. P. Dutton, 1975).

———*Messengers of Deception* (Berkeley, California: And/Or Press, 1979).

Vallee, Jacques and Janine, *Challenge to Science—The UFO Enigma* (Chicago: Henry Regnery Company, 1966).

Van Tassel, George W., *I Rode a Flying Saucer* (Los Angeles: New Age Publishing Company, 1952).

———*The Council of Seven Lights* (Los Angeles: De Vorss and Company, 1958).

Von Däniken, Erich, *Chariots of the Gods?* (New York: G. P. Putnam's Sons, 1970).

———*Gods from Outer Space,* originally published as *Return to the Stars* (New York: G. P. Putnam's Sons, 1971).

———*The Gold of the Gods* (New York: G. P. Putnam's Sons, 1973).

———*In Search of Ancient Gods* (New York: G. P. Putnam's Sons, 1973).

———*Däniken According to the Evidence* (London: Souvenir press, 1977).

Vesco, Renato, *Intercept—But Don't Shoot: The True Story of the Flying Saucers* (New York: Grove Press, 1971).

Von Kericzky, Colman S., *Memorandum to the United Nations General Assembly* (New York: the author, 1978).

Walsh, Martin, *Stranger than Fiction* (New York: Scholastic Book Service, 1973).

Walton, Travis, *The Walton Experience* (New York: Berkley Publishing Corporation, 1978).

Warrington, Peter, and Jenny Randles, *UFOs: A British Viewpoint* (London: Robert Hale, 1979).

Watts, John Langdon, *The Reason for Life—and Now—Visit Venus* (Port Orange, Florida: Dixie Venus Books, 1975)

West, Alan, *World of the Unknown: All about UFOs* (London: Osborne, 1977).

———*Close Encounters: The Strange Truth About UFOs* (London: Arrow Books, 1978).

White, Dale, *Is Something Up There?* (New York: Scholastic Book Service, 1969).

Wilkins, Harold T., *Flying Saucers on the Attack* (New York: Citadel Press, 1954).

———*Flying Saucers on the Moon* (London: Peter Owen, 1954).

———*Flying Saucers Uncensored* (New York: Citadel Press, 1955).

———*Strange Mysteries of Time and Space* (New York: Citadel press, 1959).

Willcox, P. J., *The UFO Question: Not Yet Answered* (Roslyn Heights, N.Y.: Libra, 1976).

Williamson, George Hunt, *Other Tongues—Other Flesh* (Amherst, Wisconsin: Amherst Press, 1958).

———*Secret Places of the Lion* (Amherst, Wisconsin: Amherst Press, 1958).

———*Road in the Sky* (London: Neville Spearman, 1959).

Williamson, George Hunt, and John McCoy, *UFOs Confidential* (Corpus Christi, Texas: Essene Press, 1958).

Wilson, Clifford, *Crash Go the Chariots* (New York: Lancer Books, 1972).

———*UFOs and Their Mission Impossible* (New York: New American Library, 1974).

———*Gods in Chariots and Other Fantasies* (San Diego, California: Creation-Life, 1975).

Winer, Richard, *The Devil's Triangle* (New York: Bantam books, 1974).

Wright, T. M., *The Intelligent Man's Guide to Flying Saucers* (South Brunswick: Barnes, 1968).

Young, Mort, *UFO Top Secret* (New York: Simon and Schuster, 1967).